# PERSPECTIVES FOR THE
# UNIFICATION AND HARMONISATION
# OF FAMILY LAW IN EUROPE

# PERSPECTIVES FOR THE UNIFICATION AND HARMONISATION OF FAMILY LAW IN EUROPE

Edited by

KATHARINA BOELE-WOELKI

Intersentia
Antwerp – Oxford – New York

*Distribution for the UK:*
Hart Publishing
Salter's Boat Yard
Folly Bridge
Abingdon Road
Oxford OX1 4LB
UK
Tel: + 44 1865 24 55 33
Fax: + 44 1865 79 48 82

*Distribution for North America:*
Transnational Publishers
410 Saw Mill River Road
Ardsley
New York 10502-2615
USA
Tel: + 1 914 693 5100
Fax: + 1 914 693 4430

*Distribution for Switzerland and Germany:*
Schulthess Verlag
Zwingliplatz 2
CH-8022 Zürich
Switzerland
Tel: + 41 1 251 93 36
Fax: + 41 1 261 63 94

*Distribution for other countries:*
Intersentia Publishers
Churchilllaan 108
2900 Schoten
Belgium
Tel: + 32 3 680 15 50
Fax: + 32 3 658 71 21

Perspectives for the Unification and Harmonisation of Family Law in Europe
Katharina Boele-Woelki (ed.)

© 2003 Intersentia
Antwerp – Oxford – New York
http://www.intersentia.com

ISBN 90-5095-287-9
D/2003/7849/36
NUR 822 and 828

# PREFACE

For the first time in European legal history, a truly international conference devoted to the perspectives for the unification and harmonisation of family law in Europe took place in Utrecht from 11th – 14th of December 2002. The contributions to this conference, which was organised under the auspices of the Commission on European Family Law (CEFL), are compiled in this book. The main objective of the CEFL, founded in September 2001, is to study the feasibility of and to initiate practical steps towards the harmonisation of family law in Europe. The Conference was aimed to provide a strong and very necessary impetus in European countries to seriously consider the problems and possible solutions for reshaping national family law in accordance with the needs and purposes of the emerging "European citizenship". It enabled family and comparative lawyers to extensively discuss the arguments for and against the Europeanisation of family law. The final written contributions are witness to the incredibly high level scientific standard in all respects of the contributions at the Conference. It is with great pride and gratefulness to be able to look back at the success of the conference and to be the editor of its proceedings.

In November 2002 at a conference in Amsterdam I listened to a presentation that was delivered by a young law professor. He spoke about the idea of *ius commune* and the harmonisation of private law in general by taking a great deal of aspects into account while he focused on the economic parts of private law. In answer to my question as to whether we should not include family law in the overall process of the harmonisation of private law he answered – and it did not come as a surprise to me – that this field of law is definitely culturally defined and that the opportunities for any harmonization are very limited. I doubted whether this is actually the case and asked him why he holds this view. He replied spontaneously. "You can read it in Zweigert/Kötz's book on comparative law." This argument is – notwithstanding the uncontested authority of the cited book – no longer convincing. The numerous gathering of more than 140 family and comparative law specialists in Utrecht representing 27 mostly European jurisdictions clearly demonstrated that in the field of family law in Europe major changes have taken place.

In March 2001 we, Masha Antokolskaia, Bente Braat, Marianne Hofman, Mieke Scheffer, Ian Sumner and myself, began with the organisation of the Utrecht conference. For me personally it was a challenging endeavour.

Yet the whole team was totally devoted to the idea of making the conference a pleasant and successful event. However, without the financial support of many institutions and organisations the conference and the following publication would not have been possible. I am greatly indebted to Utrecht University and its Law Faculty, the Royal Dutch Academy of Science (KNAW), the Netherlands Congress Bureau, The Dutch Association of Comparative Law, the Ius Commune Research School, the publishing house Intersentia, the Dutch Ministry of Justice and the European Commission. The advantages of our successful application to the High-Level Scientific Conference Programme of the European Commission were twofold. First, family law has been placed on the European research agenda and second, persons under the age of 35 years, were able to attend the conference free of charge. Nearly 60 participants fell under this category. This is to be considered a great achievement, which would not have been attained without the European Commission's stimulating grant for the conference. In addition, thirteen young researchers delivered papers which together with the contributions of many already very well-known specialists in the field of (international) family and comparative law are published in this book.

Finally, is the unification and harmonisation of (international) family law in Europe necessary? Is it feasible, desirable and possible? Reading the different contributions to this book may certainly inspire those who would like to find the right answers to these questions.

Katharina Boele-Woelki

Utrecht, 15 May 2003

# LIST OF AUTHORS

*Dr. Masha Antokolskaia*
Senior Research Fellow at the Molengraaff Institute for Private Law, University of Utrecht

*Ms. Miglena Baldjieva*
Senior Expert at the State Agency for Child Protection, Sofia

*Prof. Dr. Katharina Boele-Woelki*
Professor of Private International Law, Comparative Law and Family Law at the Molengraaff Institute for Private Law, University of Utrecht; Chair of the Commission on European Family Law

*Mr. Matteo Bonini-Baraldi*
LL.M. (University of British Columbia); Ph.D. candidate at Università di Bologna

*Dr. David Bradley*
Reader in Law, Law Department, London School of Economics and Political Science

*Dr. Janeen M. Carruthers*
Lecturer, School of Law, University of Glasgow

*Prof. Dr. Nina Dethloff*
Professor of Civil Law, Private International Law, Comparative Law and European Private Law, Rheinische Friedrich-Wilhelms-Universität, Bonn

*Ms. Monica Ekström*
Administrator at the "Judicial Cooperation Civil Matters" unit at the European Commission's Directorate-General Justice and Home Affairs

*Dr. Aristides N. Hatzis*
Lecturer of Philosophy of Law and Theory of Institutions, University of Athens

*Dr. Sandrine Henneron*
Professor at EDHEC, Business School and member of the LERADP, University of Lille II

*Prof. Dr. Ewoud Hondius*
Professor of Private Law at the Molengraaff Institute for Private Law, University of Utrecht

*Prof. Dr. Maarit Jänterä-Jareborg*
Professor of Private International Law and International Procedural Law, University of Uppsala

*Ms. Christina G. Jeppesen De Boer*
Ph.D. researcher at the Molengraaff Institute for Private Law, University of Utrecht

*Ms. Suzana Kraljić*
Lecturer in Law, University of Maribor

*Prof. Dr. Andrzej Mączyński*
Jagiellonian University in Cracow, Chair of Private International Law

*Ms. Rosa Martíns*
Assistant Lecturer and Researcher at the Family Law Centre of the Faculty of Law of Coimbra

*Prof. Dr. Dieter Martiny*
Professor of Civil Law, Private International Law and Comparative Law, Europa-Universität Viadrina, Frankfurt/Oder

*Prof. Nancy G. Maxwell*
Professor of Law, Washburn University School of Law, Topeka, Kansas

*Dr. Peter McEleavy*
Lecturer in Law, University of Aberdeen

*Dr. Clare McGlynn*
Reader in Law, University of Durham

*Prof. Dr. Marie-Thérèse Meulders-Klein*
Emeritus Professor at the Catholic University of Louvain, Past President of the International Society of Family Law

*Prof. Dr. Esin Örücü*
Professor of Comparative Law, University of Glasgow and Erasmus University Rotterdam

Intersentia

*Prof. Dr. Walter Pintens*
Professor of Law, Catholic University of Leuven,
University of Saarbrücken

*Dr. Elena Rodríguez Pineau*
Lecturer in Private International Law, University of Madrid

*Prof. Dr. Ingeborg Schwenzer*
Professor of Civil Law, University of Basel

*Dr. Helen Stalford*
Lecturer in Law, The Liverpool Law School, Liverpool University

*Ms. Yvette Tan*
Lecturer and doctoral candidate, School of Law, University of Manchester

*Mr. Mário Tenreiro*
Head of the "Judicial Cooperation Civil Matters" unit at the European Commission's Directorate-General Justice and Home Affairs

*Dr. Aspasia Tsaoussis-Hatzis*
Visiting Professor, Athens Laboratory of Business Administration

# TABLE OF CONTENTS

THE INFLUENCE OF EUROPEAN FAMILY LAW ON THE
FAMILY LAW OF COUNTRIES ACCEDING TO THE EU

UNIFICATION AND HARMONIZATION OF FAMILY LAW
PRINCIPLES: THE UNITED STATES EXPERIENCE

# COMMENCEMENT OF PROCEEDINGS

# EUROPEANISATION OF FAMILY LAW

WALTER PINTENS[*]

## 1. INTRODUCTION

*Ius commune* and Europeanisation have become magic words; they are
on everyone's lips. Comparative law has found a new task, whereby
common modes of thinking are stressed and a common European private
law is promoted.[1] This task will not directly be achieved through
legislation, but, rather, through the didactic elaboration of common
principles. Using the technique employed by the American Restatements
of the law, these principles could serve as the basis for a European
private law.[2]

This idea of a *ius commune* is not new. However, it has little to do with
the *ius commune* based on the *corpus iuris civilis*, which existed in Europe
prior to the advent of state specific legislation[3]; despite the fact that
several legal historians and comparatists have drawn this comparison. The
complexity of today's legal relationships as well as the increase in
technical aspects of the current legal systems preclude a complete
comparison to past centuries. Rather, the current movement is reminiscent
of the ideas of two famous French legal comparatists: *Raymond
Saleilles* (1855-1912) and *Edouard Lambert* (1866-1947). They gave
comparative law a new spark by not limiting its application to mere
national legal questions, but seeking instead to discover a "droit
commun législatif" believing that a "pénétration réciproque de tous les
domaines juridiques nationaux, pour aboutir à une sorte d'unité de

[*] The text is partly based on the following contributions of the author: "Die Europäisierung des Erbrechts", *ZEuP* 2001, 628 ff.; "Die Europäisierung des Familienrechts", in RANIERI (ed.), *Die Europäisierung der Rechtswissenschaft*, Baden-Baden, 2002, 119 ff.; "Grundgedanken und Perspektiven einer Europäisierung des Familien- und Erbrechts", *FamRZ* 2003, 331 ff. The author thanks Koen Vanwinckelen and Justin Aukin for their assistance.
[1] See recently KÖTZ, "Alte und neue Aufgaben der Rechtsvergleichung", *JZ* 2002, 259 ff.
[2] See for instance the activities of the Lando-Commission: LANDO/BEALE, *Principles of European Contract Law*, The Hague/London/Boston, 2000. Hereto ZIMMERMAN, "Principles of European Contract Law Teil I", *ZEuP* 1995, 731 ff. and "Die Principles of European Contract Law. Teile I und II", *ZEuP* 2000, 391 ff.
[3] Regarding the notion of *ius commune*, see HALPÉRIN, "L'approche historique et la problématique du jus commune", *R.I.D.C.* 2000, 717, who rightly states that it rather concerns a jurisprudencial concept to which glossists have contributed, than a homogeneous legal order (in particular p. 727).

doctrine qui domine les législations particulières et dont celles-ci ne doivent sembler que des dérives" was at hand.[4] This movement reached its peak at the 1900 comparative law conference in Paris where the ideas of *Saleilles* and *Lambert* were adopted in a mood of over-optimism and euphoria and where a world law was propagated. This "droit commun universel", however, was limited to "le monde civilisé",[5] which in those days referred exclusively to the european continent.[6]

One hundred years later the ideas of *Saleilles* and *Lambert* are still alive and arouse great interest.[7] Many parallels exist between their ideas and the present-day quest for a *ius commune*. For example, *Saleilles* had in mind, above all, commercial law and its related domains. The present-day quest for a *ius commune* still proceeds from this basis. But important differences remain. The tendency of the 1900 world conference of Paris to focus on the legislative field has not been adopted as a starting point in the current quest for a *ius commune*. Instead, a more spontaneous approximation of law is stressed. In addition, other trends can be discovered in recent years. First, family and succession law, traditionally considered to be marginal areas of comparative law, have come to the fore. The European Union's focus on family and succession law as key areas of a European private international law has brought them into prominence. Today, the Commission deals with substantive family law on the basis of the Laeken Declarations. Second, there is a notion that the *ius commune* will evolve through the use of weak instruments such as restatements and principles leading over several decades to a European civil code, which will one day replace the EURO as the symbol of European integration.[8] Even those who seek to limit a European civil code to the law of obligations and contracts in order to preserve national civil codes, can still envisage the eventual codification of a few common general principles of family and succession law.[9]

Therefore it seems proper (i) to deal with basic questions on the harmonisation of family law, (ii) to analyse the current state of spontaneous

---

[4]   SALEILLES, "Le droit commercial comparé. Contribution à l'étude des méthodes juridiques. A propos d'un livre de M.A. Strafa", *Annales de droit commercial* 1891, 219.

[5]   *Ibid.*, 220-221.

[6]   Lambert even made objections to the common law.

[7]   See JAMIN, "Le vieux rêve de Saleilles et Lambert revisité. A propos du centenaire du congrès international de droit comparé de Paris", *R.I.D.C.* 2000, 733 ff.

[8]   Compare SCHWINTOWSKI, "Auf dem Wege zu einem Europäischen Zivilgesetzbuch", *JZ* 2002, 209-210.

[9]   See recently SCHWINTOWSKI (note 8), *JZ* 2002, 210.

harmonisation and institutional unification of law and (iii) to discuss future possibilities for such harmonisation and unification.[10]

---

[10]    See the voluminous literature on family law: ANTOKOLSKAIA, "Would the harmonisation of family law in Europe enlarge the gap between the law in books and the law in action. A discussion of four historical examples of radical family law reform", *FamPra.ch* 2002, 261 ff.; ANTOKOLSKAIA/DE HONDT/STEENHOFF, *Een zoektocht naar Europees familierecht*, Deventer 1999; BOELE-WOELKI, "De weg naar een Europees familierecht", *Tijdschrift voor familie- en jeugdrecht (FJR)* 1997, 2 ff. and "Comparative research-based drafting of principles of european family law", in FAURE *et al.* (ed.), *Towards a European Ius Commune in Legal Education and Research*, Antwerp/Groningen, 2002, 171 ff.; BRADLEY, *Family Law and Political Culture. Scandinavian Laws in Comparative Perspective*, London 1996 and "Convergence in Family Law: Mirrors, Transplants and Political Economy", *Maastricht Journal of European and Comparative Law (MJ)* 1999, 127 ff.; DE GROOT, "Op weg naar een Europees personen- en familierecht", *Ars Aequi (AA)* 1995, 29 ff. and "Auf dem Wege zu einem europäischen (internationalen) Familienrecht", *ZEuP* 2001, 617 ff.; DE OLIVEIRA, "Een Europees familierecht?", *FJR* 2000, 272 ff.; FALLON, "Droit familial et droit des Communautés européennes", *Revue trimestrielle du droit familial (R.T.D.F.)* 1999, 361 ff.; FURGLER, "L'évolution actuelle et les perspectives d'harmonisation du droit de la famille au sein de l'Europe", *Diritto di Famiglia e della Persone (Dir.Fam)* 1977, 931 ff.; GRANET, "Convergences et divergences des droits européens de la famille", *Droit de la famille (Dr.fam.)* 2000 (Hors-série), 6 ff.; HAMILTON/PERRY (ed.), *Family Law in Europe*, 2nd edition, London 2002; HONDIUS, "Naar een Europees personen- en familierecht", in *Feestbundel De Ruiter*, Zwolle 1995, 173 ff.; JAYME, "Die Entwicklung des europäischen Familienrechts", *FamRZ* 1981, 221 ff.; KUCHINKE, "Über die Notwendigkeit, ein gemeineuropäisches Familien- und Erbrecht zu schaffen", in *Festschrift Söllner*, Munich 2000, 589 ff.; MARTINY, "Europäisches Familienrecht – Utopie oder Notwendigkeit?", *RabelsZ* 1995, 419 ff., "Is Unification of Family Law Feasible or Even Desirable", in HARTKAMP *et al.* (ed.), *Towards a European Civil Code*, 2nd edition, Nijmegen/The Hague 1998, 151 ff., "Die Möglichkeit der Vereinheitlichug des Familienrechts innerhalb der Europäischen Union", in MARTINY/WITZLEB (ed.), *Auf dem Wege zu einem Europäischen Zivilgesetzbuch*, Berlin 1999, 177 ff. and "The Harmonisation of Family Law in the European Community. Pro and Contra", in FAURE *et al.* (this note), p. 190 ff.; MCGLYNN, "A Family Law for the European Union?", in SHAW (ed.), *Social Law and Policy in an Evolving European Union*, Oxford 2000, 223 ff. and "The Europeanisation of family law", *C.F.L.Q.* 2001, 35 ff.; PINTENS, "Rechtsvereinheitlichung und Rechtsangleichung im Familienrecht. Eine Rolle für die Europäische Union?", *ZEuP* 1998, 670 ff., "Over de europeanisatie van het familierecht", *FJR* 1999, 238 ff., "Die Europäisierung des Familienrechts", in RANIERI (ed.), *Die Europäisierung der Rechtswissenschaft*, Baden-Baden 2002, 119 ff. and "Grundgedanken und Perspektiven einer Europäisierung des Familien- und Erbrechts", *FamRZ* 2003, 331 ff.; PINTENS/DU MONGH, "Family and Succession Law in the Euopean Union", in PINTENS (ed.), *Family and Succession Law*, Deventer/Boston 1997; PINTENS/VANWINCKELEN, *Casebook Euopean Family Law*, Leuven 2001, 13 ff.; RIEG, "L'harmonisation européenne du droit de la famille: mythe ou réalité", in *Mélanges von Overbeck*, Fribourg 1990, 473 ff. On succession law: EDENFELD, "Europäische Entwicklungen im Erbrecht", *ZEV* 2001, 457 ff.; LEIPOLD, "Europa und das Erbrecht", in *Festschrift Söllner*, Munich 2000, 647 ff.; PINTENS, "Die Europäisierung des Erbrechts", *ZEuP* 2001, 628 ff.; VERBEKE/LELEU, "Harmonisation of the Law of Succession in Europe", in HARTKAMP *et al.* (ed.), *Towards a European Civil Code*, 2nd edition, Nijmegen/The Hague 1998, 173 ff.

## 2. FAMILY LAW AS OBJECT OF HARMONISATION OF LAW

Traditionally, comparative law, and unification of law in particular, have concentrated on certain areas. These include mainly commercial law and the related domains of civil law, private international law, labour law and intellectual property rights. Family law has rarely been the object of extensive comparative legal studies,[11] and unification has been met with little success in this field. Succession law also has shown a great diversity, which can be expected from a field of law that is rather particularistic and where the mixture of Roman law, customary law, and canon law has led to diverse regulations.[12]

In the last few years, family law (succession law perhaps less so) has become an object of comparative law as well as of harmonisation of law.[13] The principles of equality and non-discrimination adopted by constitutional courts,[14] the Council of Europe and the European Court of Human Rights have played a prominent role. Important sociological changes which have affected marriage and the family, such as the emancipation of women, the equalisation of the rights of illegitimate children and the attention to the child as a legal subject in general,[15] also allow us to recognise common principles, important differences notwithstanding.[16]

---

[11]   See already GANS, *Das Erbrecht in weltgeschichtlicher Entwicklung*, Berlin 1824; UNGER, *Die Ehe in ihrer welthistorischen Entwicklung*, 1850. Hereto ZWEIGERT/KÖTZ, *Einführung in die Rechtsvergleichung*, 3rd edition, Tübingen 1996, 56. BURGE, *Commentaries on Colonial and Foreign Laws, generally and in their conflict with each other, and with the law of England*, 1838, was also significant. It was thought of as a working instrument for the Privy Council in pursuance of foreign law. This book also had great significance for comparative family and succession law, and has been praised by ZWEIGERT/KÖTZ as a basic work of comparative law (p. 55).

[12]   Hereto NEUMAYER, "Einheit in der Vielfalt. Bewegung und Bewahrung im Erbrecht der Nationen", in *Festschrift für Murad Ferid*, Munich 1978, 659 ff. and "Eigenartiges und Altertümliches aus dem vergleichenden Erbrecht", in *Mélanges Piotet*, Bern 1990, 485 ff. For a survey of legislation, see BERGMANN/FERID/HENRICH (ed.), *Internationales Ehe- und Kindschaftsrecht*, Frankfurt (loose-leaf edition); FERID/FIRSCHING/LICHTENBERGER (ed.), *Internationales Erbrecht*, Munich (loose-leaf edition); HAYTON (ed.), *European Succession Laws*, London 1998, PINTENS (ed.), "Family and Succession Law", in BLANPAIN (ed.), *Encyclopaedia of Laws*, Deventer/Boston (loose-leaf edition).

[13]   See the data in note 10.

[14]   Hereto HENRICH, "Familienrechtsreform durch die Verfassungsgerichte", *ZfRV* 1990, 241 ff.; SENAEVE, "Rechterlijke censurering van wetgeving op het vlak van het familierecht op grond van de bescherming van de mensenrechten", in *Opstellen Hoefnagels*, Arnhem 1992, 91 ff.

[15]   See KAUFMANN, *Zukunft der Familie*, Munich 1990; MEULDERS-KLEIN, "La personne, la famille et la loi au sortir du XXe siècle", *J.T.* 1982, 137 ff. and Réflexions sur l'état des personnes, in STORME (ed.), *Personen- en familierecht. Gezin en recht in een postmoderne samenleving*, Ghent 1994, 447 ff.; WORTMANN, "Het familierecht in 2010", *Burgerzaken en recht* 1999, 120 ff.

[16]   MARTINY, in HARTKAMP *et al.* (ed.) (note 11), 162; PINTENS, "Accentverschuivingen in de rechtsvergelijking", in *Liber amicorum Blanpain*, Bruges 1998, 778.

Despite this background, the question often arises whether family law still remains today so culturally specific that an harmonisation would be problematic or even undesired.

Law is clearly a constituent of our culture. So much so that some even assert it must be protected just as we protect our monuments and our landscapes. According to this view, unification and even harmonisation of family law have to be rejected, for they will lead to a loss of an important aspect of one's culture.[17] *Pierre Legrand* even considers the unification of civil law in general as a form of cultural imperialism.[18] But there is a second problem. Currently, comparative law is influenced by postmodernism. Unlike modern comparative law, postmodern comparative law does not emphasise the links between legal systems and institutions, but rather the differences between them.[19] For postmodernists diversity itself becomes a value. By preventing legal institutions from being declared identical all too soon, i.e. without confronting the real differences, this movement definitely has its merits.[20] However, when it exclusively emphasises these differences, it not only endangers comparative law itself, but also denies the fact that law, even though embedded in our culture, is primarily an instrument to regulate human relationships and is not a purpose in itself. In the words of the French lawyer *Demogue*: "Le droit n'est pas fait pour soi-même, mais pour le besoin de l'homme". Cherishing law as a symbol of culture, whatever the circumstances, will inevitably lead to intellectual rigidity and isolate us from the benefits of comparative law and of harmonisation and unification of law.[21]

---

[17]   See CATALA, "La communauté induite aux acquets?", *Les petites affiches* 1992, Nr. 58 (Numéro spécial – 88° Congrès des Notaires de France), 84. Comp. NEUMAYER (note 13), in *Mélanges Piotet*, 485 ff.

[18]   LEGRAND, "Sens et non sens d'un code civil européen", *R.I.D.C.* 1996, 811. See also *Fragments on Law-as-Culture*, Deventer 1999.

[19]   Hereto JAYME, "Osservazioni per una teoria postmoderne della comparazione giuridica", *Riv. dir. civ.* 1997, 813 ff. and "Betrachtungen zu einer postmodernen Theorie der Rechtsvergleichung", Int. Juristenvereinigung Osnabrück, Yearbook 1997-98, 15 ff. See also COLINS, "European Private Law and the Cultural Identity of States", *ERPL* 1995, 353 ff.; ZACCARIA, "I diritto privato europeo nell'epoca del postmoderno", *Riv. dir. civ.* 1997, 367 ff.

[20]   See also the warnings of SCHLESINGER, "The Past and the Future of Comparative Law", *Am. J. Comp. L.* 1995, 447 ff., who rightly states that finding a common core is only possible when the law comparatist is aware of the existing differences between legal systems and does not relativise them too soon.

[21]   PETERS/SCHWENKE, "Comparative law beyond post-modernism", *I.C.L.Q.* 2000, 800, especially, 827 ff.; PINTENS, *Inleiding tot de rechtsvergelijking*, Leuven 1998, 39-40. For a synthesis between Jayme and Legrand, see VAN ERP, *Europees privaatrecht: Postmoderne dilemma's en keuzen. Naar een methode van adequate rechtsvergelijking*, Deventer 1998, 8 ff.

The question thus arises whether the pursuit of harmonisation and unification of law truly threatens our culture. What is there to say against a gradual cultural integration, even in the field of law? Is law still tied to culture to the extent that national protection is required by opposing harmonisation? National family laws have not proven to be resistant to the reception of foreign law. In most European legal systems family law has adopted many reforms of neighbouring countries to the degree that much national individuality and culture has been lost.[22] In the words of *de Oliviera*: "National traditions change themselves from the inside, they do not prevent changes".[23] In 1987, Belgium did not experience a culture shock when it introduced the *mater semper certa est*-principle for establishing the maternity for children born out of wedlock and so replaced the system of acknowledgment. Some countries have proceeded even further and have broken entirely with their tradition. For example, in 1976, Switzerland, at that time a rather conservative country, introduced an affiliation act that can still be considered as one of the most progressive in Europe. Do the Swiss people feel they have lost part of their culture because of this? Why have we lost no part of our cultures by all these reforms? Cultural embeddedment does not mean that we are embedded in a culture to such an extent that we give up our identity when cultural changes occur. If this were so, we would have not only a legal rigidity, but also a cultural rigidity. One has to be able to sometimes go beyond one's culture. The French philosopher *Bernard-Henry Lévy* wrote: "Un démocrate a une culture, une langue, etc. Et fou serait celui qui ferait abandon de cet inestimable bien. Mais être réellement démocrate c'est tenir cette culture, et cette langue, pour des lieux, non de fixation, mais de traversée; c'est renoncer au mythe de la propriété des langues et des cultures pour y accueillir, au contraire, la plus grande quantité possible d'impropriété et de désordre; c'est consentir, en un mot, à un cosmopolitisme raisonné…".[24]

All the reforms have certainly not unified family law in Europe, but they have brought the various legal systems a little closer together and have in particular narrowed the gap between the so-called progressive North and the conservative South. For instance, Italian family law, which was under constant pressure by the Holy See during the *Democrazia Christiana*,

---

[22] In this respect DE GROOT (note 10), *AA* 1995, 31; MARTINY, in MARTINY/WITZLEB (note 10), 179.

[23] DE OLIVEIRA (note 10), 273.

[24] *La pureté dangereuse*, Paris 1994, 256. See also ANTOKOLSKAIA (note 10) 268 ff.; STEENHOFF, Op weg naar een Europees familierecht, in ANTOKOLSKAIA/DE HONDT/STEENHOFF (note 11), 5.

can no longer be considered conservative today. After all, it was the third European legal system after Sweden and Germany to adopt an act on transsexualism.[25] Italy today even has a divorce law in the first place based on the principle of the irretrievable breakdown of marriage, and much lesser on the ground of fault. Italy not only acknowledges the civil effects of a Catholic marriage, but also, if registered in the records of birth, deaths and marriages, those of marriages contracted by Evangelical churches or in accordance with the Adventist, Jewish, Methodist and Waldensist rites.[26] Spain even acknowledges the civil effects of a registered Islamic marriage.[27] After the Revolution of 1975, Portugal has introduced a progressive affiliation law[28] and, since 1998, several Spanish regions have a registered partnership for heterosexuals as well as for homosexuals.

## 3. HARMONISATION OF LAW IN CERTAIN AREAS OF FAMILY LAW

Where do we stand today in the area of harmonisation? This question will be answered by focusing on two fields that are currently a topic of much discussion: the legal matrimonial regime and the registered partnership.

### 3.1. Legal matrimonial regime

European legal matrimonial regimes are divided up into two fundamentally different types.[29] Most systems of the Romanic legal family opt for a limited community system as in the French example,[30] while the German system, followed by Greece, Austria, Switzerland and by some Scandinavian legal systems, are in favour of a system of separation of property combined with a deferred community, a settlement clause or

---

[25]     See PATTI/WILL, *Mutamento di sesso e tutela della persona. Saggi di diritto civile e comparato*, Padua 1986.

[26]     CIAN/TRABUCCHI, *Commentario breve al Codice civile*, 5th edition, Padua 1997, 296 ff.

[27]     See PUIG BRUTAU, *Compendio de Derecho Civil IV*, Barcelona 1990, 21-22.

[28]     See DOS SANTOS, *Direito da Família*, Coimbra 1985, 463 ff.

[29]     Hereto HENRICH, "Zur Zukunft des Güterrechts in Europa", *FamRZ* 2002, 1521; HEN-RICH/SCHWAB (ed.), *Eheliche Gemeinschaft, Partnerschaft und Vermögen im europäischen Vergleich*, Bielefeld 1999.

[30]     This statutory legal regime is also widely spread in Central and Eastern Europe: *e.g.* Czech Republic – § 143 of the Civil Code (hereto HRUŠÁKOVÁ, Czech Republic, in PINTENS (note 12), 161 ff.; Russia – Art. 33-34 of the Family Code (hereto ANTOKOLSKAIA, The 1995 Russian Family Code: A New Approach to the Regulation of Family Relations, *Review of Central and East European Law* 1996, 6648 ff.).

a judicially created settlement claim. In 1998, the Regensburg Colloquium on European matrimonial property law[31] asserted that the differences between both systems will not be easily overcome. Those who support a limited community as a legal regime, emphasise the balance between independence and solidarity as well as the participation by both spouses in the administration of the community, even by the spouse who has no income of its own. In addition, they rightly criticise the complexity of certain deferred community systems. German law[32] provides an extreme example as it admits the complexity of its system by only applying a mathematical settlement of surplus values on divorce, where, upon death, the settlement is replaced with a fixed increase of the inheritance rights of the surviving spouse (§ 1371 BGB). Those who support the deferred community mainly emphasise the great independence that each spouse enjoys during marriage and fear the danger of deadlock when both spouses administer the community, which they consider to be an obstruction of the free market.

However, some of these views are based on misunderstandings and extreme examples. A comparison between France and Germany is perhaps not the most ideal one, for they are both legal systems that take extreme positions. According to the German *Zugewinnausgleich*, the spouse participates not only in the increased value[33] of the other spouse's acquisitions but also of the *Eigengut*, which leads to an extreme solidarity. Swiss law undoubtedly provides a better system. The *Zugewinn* only concerns acquisitions and does not affect the *Eigengut* (Art. 198 ZGB). In this way an equal and justified solidarity is accomplished. The community systems of French and Italian matrimonial property law provide comparable examples. According to French law, all income, including that of the personal property, belongs to the community (Art. 1401 C.c.). In contrast, the Italian *comunione dei beni* offers a more differentiated approach as only the income of community property belongs to the community, while the income of personal property remains separate until the dissolution of the community, at which time it becomes community property provided that it still exists (Art. 177 C.c.it.).[34]

---

[31]  See the book mentioned in note 29.

[32]  See SCHWAB, "Der Zugewinnausgleich in der Krise", in *Festschrift Söllner*, Munich 2000, 1079 ff.

[33]  Except those that are the result of inflation.

[34]  Hereto HENRICH, "Ist eine Neuordnung des Güterrechts angezeigt?", in *Bitburger Gespräche. Jahresbuch 2001*, Munich 2001, 65-66; PATTI, "Eheliche Gemeinschaft, Partnerschaft und Vermögen in Italien", in HENRICH/SCHWAB (note 29), 131 ff.

Matrimonial property law becomes even more complex when English law is taken into account. In principle, English law does not know matrimonial property law. Marriage has no influence on the property of spouses. As a reaction to controversial case law of the House of Lords, which denied a married woman the possibility of acquiring property rights in the family home where she did not invest in the home directly but financed other expenses,[35] the legislature has, since 1970, given the judge the authority to achieve a reallocation of property by issuing property adjustment orders upon divorce.[36] In this way the judge can grant a spouse part of the other spouse's property. The courts are directed to take into account the interests of the children,[37] to achieve a clean break between the parties[38] and to have regard to all circumstances of the case, including the actual and potential income and the financial needs, obligations and responsibilities of each of the parties, as well as the contribution made by them to the welfare of the family.[39] Previous decisions have shown that these rules were interpreted in such a way that the petitioner was secured reasonable requirements. This did not mean that the wealthy spouse had to share his assets equally with the other one, but that the distribution was limited to such a degree as to allow the other spouse to maintain his previous standard of living.[40] In practice, this often amounted to a third of the family assets.[41] The House of Lords overturned this case law in its revolutionary White v. White decision whereby – even if the needs are satisfied – equality is now laid down as a guideline, rather than reasonable requirements.[42] If each spouse contributed equally to the family, then in principle it does not matter which of them earned the money and built up the assets. The Law Lords stated that there should be no bias in favour of the money-earner and against the homemaker and the child-carer. At first the consequences of this decision were not entirely clear, since the House of Lords left a

---

[35]  Petitt v. Petitt [1970] *AC* 777; Gissing v. Gissing [1971] *AC* 886. Hereto LOWE, "The English Approach to the Division of Assets upon Family Breakdown", in HENRICH/SCHWAB (note 29), 48 ff.

[36]  S. 4 Matrimonial Proceedings and Property Act 1970, nowadays replaced by S. 24 Matrimonial Causes Act 1973, modified by Matrimonial and Family Proceedings Act 1984 and by Family Law Act 1996.

[37]  S. 25 (1) Matrimonial Causes Act 1973.

[38]  S. 25a (1) Matrimonial Causes Act 1973.

[39]  S. 25 (2) Matrimonial Causes Act 1973.

[40]  Dart v. Dart [1996] 2 FLR 286.

[41]  See LOWE/DOUGLAS, *Bromley's Family Law*, 9th edition, London 1998, 825-826.

[42]  White v. White [2000] 2 *FLR* 981, especially 989 per Lord Nicholls of Birkenhead, [2000] WLR 1571. Hereto FREEMAN, "Exploring the Boundaries of Family Law in England in 2000", in BAINHAM (ed.), *The International Survey of Family Law 2002*, Bristol 2002, 134 ff.; HODSON, "White: Equality on Divorce?", *Fam Law* 2000, 870 ff.

possibility to depart from equality if there was good reason for doing so. Case law focused on the contribution of the spouses and made adjustments possible so that 60/40 divisions became frequent. But in Lambert v. Lambert the Court of Appeal made it clear that those adjustments are only possible in very exceptional cases.[43] The Court stressed that it is unacceptable to place greater value on the contribution of the breadwinner than that of the homemaker as a justification for dividing the product of the breadwinner's efforts unequally between them. Each contribution should be recognised as no less valuable than the other. Only special contributions can justify an unequal division, but therefore exceptional circumstances are necessary. A good idea, entrepreneurial skill and extensive work are insufficient to establish special contribution. The Court refused to give examples of those exceptional circumstances, but legal writers mention an inheritance or material pre-marriage assets.[44] Everything seems to indicate that marriage, even without matrimonial property law, leads more and more to a kind of deferred community of property.

Some regard matrimonial property law as a technical subject, of which the roots are not too deeply ingrained in the fundamental cultural values of a society, such that unification is possible.[45] However, the divergences as well as the fact that matrimonial property law is interwoven with the law of property interfere with the development of a European legal regime. At most, it will be possible to offer both a regime of community and a regime with a deferred community.[46]

### 3.2. Registered Partnership, Opening of Marriage and Adoption by Same-Sex Partners

Scandinavian regulations on registered partnership have spread all over Europe.[47] A resolution of the European Parliament on equal rights for

---

[43] Lambert v. Lambert [2003] 1 *FLR* 139. Hereto HODSON, GREEN and DE SOUZA, "Lambert – Shutting Pandora's Box", *Fam Law* 2003, 37 ff.

[44] HODSON, GREEN and DE SOUZA (note 43), *Fam Law* 2003, 45.

[45] See already ZAJTAY, *Rechtsvergleichung im ehelichen Güterrecht*, Annales Universitatis Sarviensis 1955, 154 ff.

[46] Compare HENRICH (note 29 and 34), 57 ff.; MARTINY, in HARTKAMP *et al.* (ed.) (note 10), 165.

[47] See the comparative studies of BASEDOW/HOPT/KÖTZ/DOPFFEL (ed.), *Die Rechtstellung gleichgeschlechtlicher Lebensgemeinschaften*, Tübingen 2000; COESTER, "Same-Sex Relationships: A Comparative Assessment of Legal Developments Across Europe", *FamPra.ch* 2002, 748 ff.; JACOB, *Die eingetragene Lebenspartnerschaft im Internationalen Privatrecht*, Cologne 2002, 14 ff.; PINTENS, "Partnerschaft im belgischen und niederländischen Recht", *FamRZ* 1999, 69 ff.; ROY, "Le partenariat civil d'un continent à l'autre", *R.I.D.C.* 2002, 759 ff.; SENAEVE/COENE, *Geregistreerd partnerschap*, Antwerpen 1998; VERSCHRAEGEN, "Gleichgeschlechtliche "Ehen",

homosexuals and lesbians in the European Community of February 8th, 1994 has played an important role.[48] The member states are requested to take action to safeguard an equal treatment of all EC citizens regardless of their sexual orientation, and to eliminate all forms of discrimination based on such orientation. The resolution considers it abusive that some legal systems neither allow homosexual couples to marry nor provide a corresponding legal institution.

But also these new legal institutions, which are less marked by tradition, use different solutions. Belgium,[49] Catalonia, Aragon and Navarra,[50] France[51] and the Netherlands[52] have adopted a statutory regulation for both the heterosexual and homosexual partnership, thus clearly differing from the Scandinavian model that restricts its regulation to the homosexual partnership.[53] Germany has adopted the Scandinavian model,[54] as has a Swiss draft bill.[55] The English Parliament discussed a registered partnership for heterosexuals as well as for homosexuals,[56] but now

---

Vienna 1994 und Nichteheliche Partnerschaft – Eine rechtsvergleichende Einführung", *FamRZ* 2000, 65.

[48]   *OJEC* C 61 (1994), 40. For further resolutions see JAKOB, "Die eingetragene Lebenspartnerschaft im Europarecht", *FamRZ* 2002, 507.

[49]   PINTENS, "Partnerschaft im belgischen en niederländischen Recht", *FamRZ* 2000, 69 ff., especially 71.

[50]   MARTÍN CASALS, "Grundzüge der vermögensrechtlichen Situation von Ehegatten und nichtehelichen Gemeinschaften im spanischen und katalanischem Recht", in HENRICH/ SCHWAB (ed.) (note 29), 293 ff.; SCHLENKER, "Die Stellung gleichgeschlechtlicher Lebensgemeinschaften in Spanien und in spanischen Teilrechtsordnungen", in BASEDOW *et al.* (ed.) (note 45), 145 ff.

[51]   FERRAND, "Das französische Gesetz über den pacte civil de solidarité", *FamRZ* 2000, 517 ff.; LÉCUYER, "Le PACS (Désormais) sous toutes ses cultures", *Dr.Fam.* 2000/1, 4 ff.; RICHARDS, "The Legal Recognition of Same-Sex Couples. The French Perspective", *I.C.L.Q.* 2002, 305 ff.

[52]   BOELE-WOELKI/SCHRAMA, "Die Rechtsstellung von Menschen mit homosexueller Veranlagung im niederländischen Recht", in BASEDOW *et al.* (ed.) (note 45), 51 ff.

[53]   DOPFEL/SCHERPE, "Gleichgeschlechtliche Lebensgemeinschaften im Recht der nordischen Länder", in BASEDOW *et al.* (ed.) (note 45), 7 ff.

[54]   DETHLOFF, "Die Eingetragene Lebenspartnerschaft. Ein neues familienrechtliches Insititut", *NJW* 2001, 2599 ff. and "The Registered Partnership Act of 2001", in BAINHAM (ed.), *The International Survey of Family Law 2002*, Bristol 2002, 171 ff.; KAISER, "Das Lebenspartnerschaftsgesetz", *JZ* 2001, 617 ff.; SCHWAB, "Eingetragene Lebenspartnerschaft. Ein Überblick", *FamRZ* 2001, 385 ff. and *Die eingetragene Lebenspartnerschaft*, Bielefeld 2002.

[55]   Draft bill of November 14th, 2001. Hereto SCHWENZER, "Registrierte Partnerschaft: Der Schweizer Weg", *FamPra.ch* 2002, 223 ff.

[56]   After the House of Lords, in a trail-blazing decision, has given a broad interpretation to the notion "family member" as mentioned in the Rent Act 1977, so that the homosexual partner could continue the tenancy rights of his deceased partner (Fitzpatrick v. Sterling Housing Association Ltd [1999] 3 WLR 1113, [2000] 1 *FLR* 271; hereto FLAUSS-DIEM, "Couples de même sexe et famille. Version anglaise", *Dr.fam.* 2000/12, 8 ff.), the House of Commons
→

government will introduce regulations only for homosexuals. Some legal systems go further by adopting a regulation providing for an asexual partnership between family members, as is the case in Belgium. Here the law allows a partnership *e.g.* between parent and child or between two brothers or sisters, primarily so that the partners can obtain proprietary and tax benefits. However, most legal systems apply impediments to a partnership, which are inspired by those to marriage and rule out to a certain degree the possibility of a partnership between relatives and relatives-in-law.[57]

The consequences of a partnership are regulated very differently. France and Belgium have a partnership with limited consequences. The possibility to unilaterally terminate the partnership renders its modest proprietary statute almost of minor importance. In Denmark, Norway and Sweden, a partnership basically has the same effects as a marriage. Marital property law has general application.[58] Divorce law applies on the dissolution of the partnership.[59] The Netherlands also does not have any proprietary differences between marriage and registered partnership. Thus marital property law is applied to the latter as well. If the partners do not agree on a certain regime, the legal matrimonial regime, *i.e.* a general community of property, will be applied *ipso iure*, thus establishing an extreme solidarity between the partners. A dissolution of the partnership by consent is possible by a joint declaration before the registrar of births, deaths and marriages (Art. 80c, c NBW). However, a unilateral dissolution requires a judicial decision (Art. 80c, d and Art. 80e, 1 NBW). The German *Lebenspartnerschaftsgesetz* also has important proprietary consequences. Marital property law is not applied *ipso iure* as the partners are obliged to make a declaration on their proprietary regime before the establishment of their partnership. The partners can opt for the so-called *Ausgleichsgemeinschaft*, in which the proprietary conditions are comparable with the *Zugewinngemeinschaft*, or for a contractual regime, which must be written down in a notarial deed.[60]

---

discussed a draft on a Relationships (Civil Registration) Bill (Bill 36), which was dropped after some discussion but can be put on the agenda again. Hereto SUMNER, "Will the sky fall in above England? The proposed registered partnership bill", *FJR* 2002, 24 ff. A Civil Partnerships Bill was also pending before the House of Lords, but was withdrawn after the second lecture. The government considers to undertake legislative action.

57  *E.g.* to the 3rd degree in France (art. 515-2 C.c.).
58  DOPFEL/SCHERPE (note 51), 20 ff.
59  DOPFEL/SCHERPE (note 51), 31 ff.
60  Art. 6-7 LPartG. Hereto SCHWAB, *Familienrecht*, 11th edition, Munich 2001, 418-419.

Dissolution is only possible by judicial decision.[61] Also the English proposals strove for a partnership with strong consequences.

Next to the registered partnership, a second tendency becomes obvious, which makes the harmonisation and unification of law more complicated: the opening of marriage. Since April 1st, 2001, the Netherlands is the first European country to have opened marriage up to same-sex partners (Art. 30 NBW) although maintaining the registered partnership.[62] Also in Belgium, Parliament has voted a bill on the opening of marriage to same-sex partners.[63]

Together with the registered partnership and the opening up of marriage, the question of adoption by same-sex partners has arisen. Most legal systems have been averse to such adoptions. This reflects society's hesitancy and the still discussed question of whether such adoptions are consistent with the interests of the children. However, because there are children, whether from former heterosexual relationship of one partner or from artificial insemination, who are being raised in homosexual partnerships, pressure has increased for allowing adoptions by same-sex partners. Ten years after the introduction of a registered partnership, Denmark now allows for adoptions by same-sex partners, but only by a stepparent. A partner in a registered partnership can adopt the child or the adopted child of his partner, unless the adopted child is from a foreign country.[64] The Danish legislator has allowed for such adoptions in order to eliminate disadvantages for these children such as the lack of maintenance or successory claims towards the partner of the parent.[65] The Netherlands is the first country to allow for the adoption of children who do not descend from one partner, although it is limited to domestic children only.[66] A Swedish law of June 2002 is similar to the Dutch law, however, it does allow for the adoption of children from foreign

---

[61] See KAISER, "'Entpartnerung' – Aufhebung der eingetragenen Lebenspartnerschaft gleichgeschlechtlicher Partner", *FamRZ* 2002, 866 ff.
[62] Law of December 21st, 2000, *Staatsblad* January 1st, 2001. See SCHRAMA, "Reforms in Dutch Family Law during the Course of 2001: Increased Pluriformity and Complexity", in BAINHAM (ed.) (note 42), 278 ff.
[63] Law of February 13th, 2003, *Belgisch Staatsblad*, February 28th 2003.
[64] § 4 Law of June 7th, 1989, modified by the Law of June 2nd, 1994. Also NAVARRA: Art. 8 Law of July 3rd, 2000, Bo Navarra July 7th, 2000.
[65] SCHERPE, "Zehn Jahre registrierte Partnerschaft in Dänemark", *DeuFamR* 2000, 34.
[66] Law of December 21st, 2000, *Staatsblad* January 11th, 2001. Hereto ANTOKOLSKAIA, "Recent developments in dutch filiation, adoption and joint custody law", *Familia* 2002, 782 ff.; SCHRAMA (note 62), 289 ff.

countries.[67] By its law of November 8th, 2001 Finland has introduced a registered partnership, but has rejected any possibility for the adoption of children by same-sex partners.[68]

### 3.3. Conclusion

Both examples show similarities and differences. Clearly, neither the establishment of a mainstream nor the creation of a common solution by means of a better law approach have been concluded. European legal matrimonial regimes are divided up into two so fundamentally different systems, that the gap seems unbridgeable. Concerning the registered partnership there is no common core, but a mainstream comes to the fore: most legal systems opt for a strong model with important property consequences so that the gap between marriage and partnership is getting very narrow.

## 4. PERSPECTIVES

### 4.1. The Council of Europe and other International Organizations

To date, the Europeanisation of family law has been a matter of harmonisation. This is due to spontaneous developments whereby case law and legal doctrine have played an important part. Of course, the Council of Europe has met an important goal with its European Convention for the Protection of Human Rights and Fundamental Freedoms and certain other conventions,[69] but other major initiatives should not be expected. Rather than promoting unification of law by international conventions, the Council is seeking to stimulate harmonisation through recommendations of the Consultative Assembly and resolutions of the European Ministers of Justice as well as through scientific meetings.[70] At the international level, two UN treaties are of

---

[67]  Law of June 5th, 2002. See BOGDAN, "Internationale Aspekte der schwedischen Gesetzesnovelle über die Adoption von Kindern durch eingetragene Lebenspartner", *IPRax* 2002, 534-535.

[68]  SAVOLAINEN, "Finnland: Gesetz über die registrierte Partnerschaft", *FamRZ* 2000, 519-520.

[69]  *E.g.* the Luxemburg European Convention on Recognition and Enforcement of Decisions concerning Custody of Children and on Restoration of Custody of Children of May, 20th 1980, ETS No. 105.

[70]  See KILLERBY, "Family Law in Europe. Standards set by the member States of the Council of Europe", in *Liber Amicorum Meulders-Klein*, Brussels 1998, 351 ff.; SCHRAMA, "De Raad van Europa en het familierecht", *FJR* 1998, 54 ff.; VERSCHRAEGEN, "Council of Europe", in PINTENS (ed.) (note 12), 11 ff. Even though the International Commission on Civil Status concluded a number of technical treaties, this organization had practically no success in the field of substantive law. Hereto BISCHOFF, "Harmonisation du droit privé: l'exemple du travail de la Commission Internationale de l'Etat Civil", in *Conflits et harmonisation. Mélanges*

particular importance, the International Treaty on Civil and Political Rights of December 19th, 1966[71] and the Convention of Children's Rights of November 20th, 1989,[72] as well as the Hague Conventions of Private International Law.[73]

More than the Council of Europe, the European Court of Human Rights has served as a catalyst for harmonisation through its decisions and judgments, which have given a rough sketch of European family law.[74] The right to respect for private and family life as laid down in Art. 8 of the ECHR has been of great importance in this regard. The Marckx case[75] has had a controlling influence on the layout of affiliation law, especially regarding the establishment of affiliation *ex parte materna* and the abolition of hereditary discriminations. Several decisions protect the relationship between father and child, even when paternity has not been established. In the Keegan case, the Court ruled that a mother cannot give her child up for adoption without informing the biological father and involving him in the proceedings.[76] In the case of placement of children in foster homes, several decisions have restricted interferences by public authorities and emphasised that any measures implementing a public care decision should always be consistent with the ultimate aim of possibly reuniting the family. Such measures are to be terminated as

---

*von Overbeck*, Fribourg 1990, 117 ff.; MASSIP/HONDIUS/NAST, "International Commission on Civil Status", in PINTENS (ed.) (note 12) 27 ff.; VAN LANGENAEKEN, "Commission Internationale de l'Etat Civil: verwezenlijkingen en perspectieven", in PINTENS (ed.), *Actuele problemen van de burgerlijke stand*, Antwerp/Amsterdam 1979, 56 ff.

[71] 999 U.N.T.S. 171.

[72] U.N.Doc.A/44/49(189).

[73] The Hague Convention on the Civil Aspects of International Child Abduction of October 25th, 1980 above all.

[74] See HOHNERLEIN, "Konturen eines einheitlichen europäischen Familien- und Kindschaftsrechts. Die Rolle der Europäischen Menschenrechtskonvention", *Eur. Legal Forum* 2000, 252 ff.; KUCHINKE (note 10), 592 ff.; SENAEVE, "Van Marckx tot Vermeire. 12 ½ jaar rechtspraak van het Straatsburgse Hof", *FJR* 1991, 195 ff., 224 ff. and 244 ff.; VERSCHRAEGEN, "Council of Europe", in PINTENS (ed.) (note 12), 23 ff.

[75] Series A, No. 31, *FamRZ* 1979, 903, *EuGRZ* 1979, 454, *NJW* 1979, 2449. Hereto JAYME, "Europäische Menschenrechtskonvention und deutsches Nichtehelichenrecht", *NJW* 1979, 2425 ff.; PINTENS, "Menschenrechtskonvention und Privatrecht – Auswirkungen in Belgien", *RabelsZ* 1999, 702 ff.; RIGAUX, "La loi condamnée", *Journal des Tribunaux* 1979, 5113 ff.; STURM, "Das Straßburger Marckx-Urteil zum Recht des nichtehelichen Kindes und seine Folgen", *FamRZ* 1982, 1150 ff.; VOSS, "Belgien: Kindschaft praeter und contra legem", *IPRax* 1986, 120 ff."

[76] ECtHR May 25th, 1994 (Keegan/Ireland), Series A, No. 290. Hereto RUDOLF, "Zur Rechtsstellung des Vaters eines nichtehelichen Kindes nach der EMRK", *EuGRZ* 1995, 110 ff.; O'DONNEL, "The unmarried father and the right to family life: Keegan v. Ireland", *MJ* 1995, 72 ff.

soon as conditions permit.[77] With regard to the hereditary rights of
children born out of wedlock, the Marckx, Inze,[78] Vermeire[79] and
Mazurek[80] cases have eliminated nearly all discrimination.[81]

Despite all these developments, the European Court of Human Rights
will likely have less influence on the approximation of the legal systems
in the future due to the fact that the major discriminations in the fields
of family and, especially, succession law have been eliminated. Thus, it
is debatable whether the Court will maintain its pioneering role. In view
of the increasing number of Member States and their different opinions
regarding human rights, the Court, in general, will probably limit itself
to maintaining minimum standards. Such a decline can already be
noticed in the Mazurek case, in which the Court only examined, in a
proprietary manner, whether Art. 1 of the First Protocol to the ECHR
has been violated, while it rejected an examination on the basis of Art. 8
of the ECHR and the right to respect of family life.[82] This means that
the Court has taken a step back in comparison with its Marckx decision.
Progressive decisions will perhaps become less frequent. A comparison
of the Salgueiro da Silva Mouta case with the Fretté case can illustrate
this. In the case of Salgueiro da Silva Mouta v. Portugal the Court
decided that the refusal to award parental responsibility to a homosexual
man living with another man, on the ground that it is in the child's
interests to grow up in a traditional family environment, is contrary to
the ban on discrimination as laid down in Art. 14 *juncto* Art. 8 of the
ECHR.[83] This ruling provides an expansive interpretation of Art. 14 of
the ECHR and guarantees also protection against discrimination on the
ground of sexual orientation even when Art. 14 only speaks of discrimination on the ground of sex. However, in the recent case of Fretté v. France
the Court has stated that Art. 14 *juncto* Art. 8 of the ECHR is not violated
by the refusal of an adoption on the ground of the adoptant's homosexuality, based on the still differing opinions on adoption by homosexuals
and the fact that the legal systems appear to be in a transitional stage

---

[77] *E.g.* ECtHR March 24th, 1988 (Olsson/Sweden – No. 1), Series A, No. 130, § 81.
[78] ECtHR October 29th, 1987, Series A, No. 126, *ÖJZ* 1988, 177.
[79] EctHR November 29th, 1991, Series A, No. 214-C.
[80] ECtHR February 2nd, 2000, *Dr.fam.* 2000, 20, note DE LAMY, *FamRZ* 2000, note VANWINCKELEN.
The Court has rejected a testing against Art. 8 of the ECHR. See the dissenting opinion of
the judges Loucaide and Tulkens. Hereto GOUTTENOIRE-CORNUT/SUDRÉ, "L'incompatibilité
de la réduction de la vocation successorale de l'enfant adultérin à la Convention EDH," *J.C.P.*
2000 II, No. 10286, 647-648.
[81] Hereto PINTENS (note 10), *FamRZ* 2003, 500.
[82] See note 77. Compare ECtHR October 3rd, 2000 (Camp and Bourimi), No. 28369/95.
[83] ECtHR December 21st, 1999 (Salgueiro da Silva Mouta/Portugal), *IFL* 2000, 33, Rec. 1999-IX,
309.

regarding this matter.[84] Both cases are obviously not entirely comparable. In the Salgueiro da Silva Mouta case there already was an established family life, which must be protected in view of Art. 8 of the ECHR, while in the Fretté case the right to establish a family, in this case by means of adoption, is concerned. This right to establish a family through adoption is not guaranteed by the ECHR. The Court nevertheless emphasises that adoption falls within the application of Art. 8 of the ECHR and that the concept of sexual orientation is covered by Art. 14 of the ECHR. At issue are the competing interests of the adopting parent and the child. The scientific community, particularly experts on childhood, psychiatrists and psychologists, is divided over the possible consequences of a child being adopted by one or more homosexual parents. In addition, there are wide differences in national and international opinion. In the opinion of the Court every Member State is legitimately and reasonably entitled to consider that the right to be able to adopt a child is limited by the interests of the child. This does not mean that the Member States are granted arbitrary discriminatory power, but that they are left a certain margin of appreciation, which is part of every legal system.[85] In the Fretté case, however, one can ask whether this margin is out of proportion, since France has rejected the adoption on the exclusive basis of the applicant's sexual orientation, without weighing the interests of the child against those of the adopting parent. The impression is that the European Court for Human Rights, in cases where there are widely differing opinions in legal systems or in cases regarding controversial matters, no longer pushes the legal frontier forward, but rather tends to take the position of granting Member States a wide margin of appreciation. Provided that most Member States are engaged in a determined attempt to counter all forms of the contested discrimination, the margin of appreciation will be limited or even negated. In those cases the Court's influence will still be important. In the Goodwin case, the Court held that the refusal of the British Government to alter the register of births in case of a post-operative transsexual was a violation of the right to private life (Art. 8). The Court attached less importance than in previous cases[86] to the lack of evidence of a common European approach to the matter, but took into consideration a continuing

---

[84]   ECtHR February 26th, 2002 (Fretté/France), *EHRC* 2002, 259, note JANSSEN/GERARDS, *FamRZ* 2003, 149, *Jurisprudence de Liège, Mons et Bruxelles* 2002, 752, note MARTENS.

[85]   Hereto DELMAS-MARTY/IZORCHE, "Marge nationale d'appréciation et internationalisation du droit", *R.I.D.C.* 2000, 753 ff.

[86]   ECtHR October, 17th, 1986 (Rees/United Kingdom), Series A, No. 106; ECtHR September 27th, 1990 (Cossey/United Kingdom), Series A, No. 184; ECtHR March, 25th, 1992 (B./France), Series A, No. 232-C; ECtHR July, 30th, 1998 (Sheffield and Horsham/United Kingdom), Reports 1998-V, 2011.

international trend in favour not only of increased social acceptance of transsexuals but also of legal recognition of the new sexual identity of post-operative transsexuals. Therefore, the British Government could no longer claim that the matter fell within the margin of appreciation.[87] In the same case, the Court stated that the very essence of the right to marry had been infringed by the refusal of a marriage with a person from the new opposite sex. Even if Art. 12 of the ECHR establishes the right to marry according to the national laws governing the exercise of this right, the reference to the national laws means that the Member States can determine the conditions in which it could be established that gender reassignment had been properly effected. The Member States can also regulate the validity of past marriages and the formalities applicable to future marriages. However, they cannot ban a transsexual from the right to marry under any circumstances.

## 4.2. The European Union

At the European Union level, the European Court of Justice has served as an impetus to harmonisation of law by attributing certain aspects of family law to the freedom of movement.[88] In the Konstantinidis case, the Court ruled that national legislation obliging a Greek national to use, in hisprofession, a written form of his name resulting from its transliteration in the civil registries is incompatible with the right of establishment guaranteed by Art. 52 (now 43) of the EC Treaty if that written form distorts the pronunciation and if such distortion creates a risk of confusion as to the person's identity among his potential clientele.[89] Another example is provided by the Dafeki case where, according to the Court, the freedom of movement for workers requires that the authorities and courts of a Member State must accept certificates concerning personal status issued by the competent authorities of an other Member State unless their accuracy is seriously undermined by concrete evidence

---

[87]   ECtHR July, 7th (Goodwin/United Kingdom), *EHRC* 2002, 708, note JANSSENS/VAN DER VELDE.

[88]   See FALLON (note 10), *R.T.D.F.* 1998, 375 ff.; PINTENS, "Von Konstantinidis bis Grant. Europa und das Familienrecht", *ZEuP* 1998, 843 ff.; ZEYRINGER, "Der Einfluß europäischen Rechts auf das österreichische Personenstandsrecht", *Östa* 1999, 10 ff.

[89]   ECJ March 3rd, 1993 (Konstantinidis/Stadt Altensteig), *CMLR* 1994, 395, note LAWSON, *ECR* 1993, I-1991, *ERPL* 1995, 483, note GAURIER, SCHOCKWEILER, LOISEAU, *Rev.trim.D.H.* 1994, note FLAUSS, *ZEuP* 1995, 89, note PINTENS. See also BASEDOW, "Konstantinidis v. Bangemann – oder die Familie im Europäischen Gemeinschaftsrecht", *ZEuP* 1994, 197 ff.; DE GROOT, "Het Hof van Justitie van de Europese Gemeenschappen waagt zich op het gebied van het namenrecht", *WPNR* 1994, 855 ff.

relating to the individual case in question.[90] In the P. case, the Court criticised the discharge of a transsexual employee, who underwent a gender reassignment, as a contravention to the European Directive No. 76/207 of February 9th, 1976[91] on the equal treatment of men and women with regard to the working conditions. The Court declared itself in favour of an expansive interpretation of this directive, whereby sexual discrimination is not limited to that between men and women but, rather, includes all discrimination on grounds of sex.

These decisions of the Court are very important, as they contribute to the reduction of discrimination and administrative impediments. However, the Court cannot be expected to greatly contribute to a real breakthrough in the field of harmonisation of law. This is exemplified by the Grant case,[92] where the Court decided that a railway company is not obliged to grant the same travel concessions to homosexual partners as to heterosexual partners of its staff members. On the one hand, the Court stated that, given the present state of the law within the EU member states, stable relationships between two persons of the same sex are not regarded as equivalent to marriages or stable relationships outside marriage between two persons of opposite sex. On the other hand, the Court asserted that the principle of equality prohibits discrimination based on the sex of a person but not on a person's sexual orientation. The Court left it to the Council, which, in the light of the Treaty of Amsterdam, is allowed by Art. 13 of the EC Treaty to take appropriate action to eliminate such discrimination. In the case of D. and the Kingdom of Sweden v. Council of the European Union, the Court has for the first time dealt with a registered partnership.[93] The Council rejected an application by an official who lived in a registered partnership with a partner of the same sex, in order to obtain the household allowance provided for in the Staff Regulations of Officials of the European Communities, which is only granted to married officials. The Court stated that statutory arrangements for registered partnership are very diverse and are regarded in the Member States as being distinct from marriage, so that the Community judiciary cannot interpret Staff Regulations in such a way that registered partnerships are treated the

---

[90]   ECJ December 2nd, 1997 (Dafeki/Landesversicherungsanstalt Württemberg), *ECR* 1997, I-6761, *R.C.D.I.P.* 1998, 239, note DROZ.

[91]   ECJ April 4th, 1996 (P./S. and Cornwall County Council), *ECR* 1996, I-2143.

[92]   ECJ December 17th, 1998 (Grant/South-West Trains Ltd.), *ECR* 1998, I-636, *EuZW* 1998, 212, note SZCZEKALLA.

[93]   ECJ May 5th, 2001, *FamRZ* 2001, 1053. Hereto JAKOB (note 48), *FamRZ* 2002, 505 ff. with further references.

same way as marriage. The Court placed its hope on Art. 13 of the EC Treaty and left the initiative to the Community legislator.[94]

Although these decisions do not constitute a breakthrough, they do have practical consequences. The Grant decision created such a stir in Britain that the concerned railway company, in spite of a favourable decision, abolished its discriminatory provisions. The D. decision has also had practical effects. The Commission accepted in the line of the decision that Dutch gay-marriage falls under the concept of marriage as mentioned in the Staff Regulations.[95] This in turn, however, leads to another discrimination. If the national legislature has adopted a far-reaching regulation for the rights of same-sex couples, hereby calling this regulation "marriage", then one enjoys the privileges of the Staff Regulations. If, however, the national legislator designates the same regulation a "registered partnership", then those privileges are not applicable. These decisions and their consequences show that there is a need for developing a family concept on the basis of equality between the sexes.

Basically, the European Union has no competence regarding the unification of family and succession law.[96] The Treaty of Amsterdam has not altered this fact. The Council may take appropriate action to combat discrimination based on sex, racial or ethnic origin, religion or belief, disability, age or sexual orientation, as set out in Art. 13 of the EC Treaty. The approximation of the laws of Member States is only a task for the European Community when it is imperative for the functioning of the common market.[97] The provisions laid down in Art. 94 and 95 EC Treaty[98] on the approximation of laws are thus left outside of consideration since, even using a broad interpretation of the goals of the European Community, there are few rules of family and succession law which directly affect the functioning of the common market, despite the fact

---

[94]　Comp. McGLYNN (note 10), *C.F.L.Q.* 2001, 48.

[95]　Answer Kinnock of October 15th, 2001 in the European Parliament on Question P-2438/01, *OJ* C 93E of April 18th, 2002. See hereto JESSURUN D'OLIVEIRA, "De Europese Commissie erkent het Nederlands huwelijk. Nederlands relatierecht en de Europese Unie", *NJB* 2001, 2035 ff. The administration department of the European Parliament has another opinion. See D'OLIVEIRA, "Het homohuwelijk en de Europese Unie", *NJB* 2002, 973.

[96]　See FALLON (note 10), *R.T.D.F.* 1998, 361 ff.; HAMILTON/PERRY (note 10); McGLYNN (note 10), *C.F.L.Q.* 2001, 36; PINTENS/DU MONGH (note 10), 73; VERBEKE/LELEU (note 10), 181 ff.

[97]　Art. 3 h of the EC Treaty. Hereto OPPERMANN, *Europarecht*, 2nd edition, Munich 1999, 475 with further references.

[98]　Amsterdam version.

that succession law has some economic relevance.[99] The transfer of judicial co-operation in civil matters from the so-called third pillar (co-operation in judicial and legal matters) to the first pillar (community law)[100] does not push the unification of substantive family law much further. Even though Art. 65 of the EC Treaty does not contain a comprehensive enumeration, one could deduce from the measures enumerated in this article as well as from the caption of Title IV EC Treaty that its application is restricted to international family law only.[101] Based on the example of the Council Regulation No. 1347/2000 of May 29th, 2000 on jurisdiction and the recognition and enforcement of judgments in matrimonial matters and in matters of parental responsibility for children of both spouses involved in matrimonial proceedings,[102]

---

[99]   E.g. one could link up with company law and corporate law. Hereto LEIPOLD (note 10), 650; TILLMANN, "Zur Entwicklung eines europäischen Zivilrechts", in *Festschrift Oppenhoff*, Munich 1985, 503.

[100]   Hereto BESSE, "Die justizielle Zusammenarbeit in Zivilsachen nach dem Vertrag von Amsterdam und das EuGVÜ", *ZEuP* 1999, 106 ff.; JAYME/KOHLER, "Europäisches Kollisionsrecht 1997 – Vergemeinschaftung durch "Säulenwechsel"?", *IPRax* 1997, 385 ff.

[101]   Compare BASEDOW, "Das BGB im künftigen europäischen Privatrecht: Der hybride Kodex. Systemsuche zwischen nationaler Kodifikation und Rechtsangleichung", *AcP* 2000, 477.

[102]   *OJ* L 160, June 30th, 2000, 19. This regulation has come into force on March 1st, 2001, thus replacing the so-called Brussels II Convention of May 28th, 1998 on jurisdiction and the recognition and enforcement of judgments in matrimonial matters (*OJ* C 221, June 7th, 1998). Hereto BEAUMONT/MOIR, "Brussels Convention II: A new instrument in family matters for the European Union or the European Community?", *Eur.L.R.* 1995, 268 ff.; BOELE-WOELKI, "Brüssel II: Die Verordnung über die Zuständigkeit und die Anerkennung von Entscheidungen in Ehesachen", *ZfRV* 2001, 121 ff.; DE BOER, "Brussel II: een eerste stap naar een communautair IPR", *FJR* 1999, 244 ff.; EVERALL/NICHOLLS, "Brussels I and II – The Impact on Family Law", *Fam Law* 2002, 674 ff.; GRUBER, "Die "ausländische Rechtshängigkeit" bei Scheidungsverfahren", *FamRZ* 1999, 1563 ff.; HAU, "Internationales Eheverfahrensrecht in der Europäischen Union", *FamRZ* 1999, 484 ff. and "Das System der internationalen Entscheidungszuständigkeit im europäischen Eheverfahrensrecht", *FamRZ* 2000, 1333 ff.; HAUSMANN, "Neues internationales Eheverfahrensrecht in der Europäischen Union", *European Legal Forum* 2000-01, 271 ff.; HELMS, "Die Anerkennung ausländischer Entscheidungen im Europäischen Eheverfahrensrecht", *FamRZ* 2001, 257 ff. and "Internationales Verfahrensrecht für Familiensachen in der Europäischen Union", *FamRZ* 2002, 1593 ff.; JÄNTERÄ-JAREBORG, "Marriage Dissolution in an integrated Europe: The 1998 European Union Convention on Jurisdiction and the Recognition and Enforcement of Judgments in Matrimonial Matters (Brussels II Convention)", in ŠARČEVIĆ/VOLKEN, *Yearbook of Private International Law* 1999, 1 ff.; KOHLER, "Internationales Verfahrensrecht für Ehesachen in der europäischen Union: Die Verordnung "Brüssel II"", *NJW* 2001, 10 ff., "Status als Ware: Bemerkungen zur europäischen Verordnung über das internationale Verfahrensrecht für Ehesachen", in MANSEL (ed.), *Vergemeinschaftung des Europäischen Kollisionsrecht*, Cologne 2001, 41 ff. and "Libre circulation du divorce? Observations sur le règlement communautaire concernant les procédures en matière matrimoniale", in *Estudos Magelhães Collaço*, I, Coimbra 2002, 232 ff.; PIRRUNG, "Unification du droit en matière familiale: la Convention de l'Union européenne sur la reconaissance des divorces et la question de nouveaux travaux
→

one can, pursuant to the Vienna Action Plan and to the Draft Programe of Measures of the Council, expect regulations on the rules of conflict.[103] Regulations on the applicable law in divorce cases, marital property law and succession law are planned.[104] An approximation of law by applying Art. 293 of the EC Treaty on the negotiations between Member States with a view to the equalisation of their nationals also does not provide a solution. Even though the enumeration in this article is not a comprehensive one, Art. 293 of the EC Treaty remains restricted to the equalisation of nationals and also here the rule applies that such treaties should be imperative for the development of the common market.[105] At

---

d'UNIDROIT", *Revue de Droit Uniforme (RDU)* 1998, 629 ff. and "Europäische justizielle Zusammenarbeit in Zivilsachen – insbesondere das neue Scheidungsübereinkommen", *ZEuP* 1999, 834 ff.; PUTZKAJLER, "Das internationale Scheidungs- und Sorgerecht nach Inkrafttreten der Brüssel II-Verordnung", *IPRax* 2001, 81 ff.; SCHACK, "Das neue Internationale Eheverfahrensrecht in Europa", *RabelsZ* 2001, 615 ff.; SPELLENBERG, "Der Anwendungsbereich der EheVGO ("Brüssel II") in Statussachen", in *Festschrift Schumann*, Tübingen 2001, 423 ff., "Anerkennung eherechtlicher Entscheidungen nach der EheGVO", *ZZPInt* 2001, 109 ff. and "Die Zuständigkeit für Eheklagen nach der EheGVO", in *Festschrift Geimer*, Munich 2002, 1257 ff.; STURLÈSE, "Premier commentaire sur un évènement juridique: La signature de la Convention de Bruxelles II ou quand l'Europa se préoccupe des conflits familiaux", *J.C.P.* 1988 I, Nr. 145; VAN DEN EECKHOUT, ""Europees" echtscheiden. Bevoegdheid en erkenningen van beslissingen op basis van de EG-Verordening 1347/2000 van 29 mei 2000", in VAN HOUTTE/PERTEGAS SÉNDER, *Het nieuwe Europese IPR: van verdrag naar verordening*, Antwerpen 2001, 69 ff.; WAGNER, "Die Anerkennung und Vollstreckung von Entscheidungen nach der Brüssel II-Verordnung", *IPRax* 2001, 74 ff.; WATTÉ/BOULARBAH, "Les nouvelles règles de conflits de jurisdictions en matière de désunion des époux", *Journal des Tribunaux* 2001, 369 ff.; WIDMER, "Brüssel II. Die neue EG-Verordnung zum internationalen Eheverfahrensrecht?", *FamPra.ch* 2001, 689 ff. The regulation will be replaced by a broader one (Brussels IIa) that will cover parental authority and visiting rights in all cases. See the proposal by the Commission of May 3, 2002, *OJ* C 203 of August 8, 2002.

[103] Action Plan of the Council and the Commission on how best to implement the provisions of the Treaty of Amsterdam on an area of freedom, security and justice of December 3rd, 1998, *OJ* C 19, January 23rd, 1999 (also published in *IPRax* 1999, 288 ff.); Draft programme of the Council of measures for implementation of the principle of mutual recognition of decisions in civil and commercial matters of January 15th, 2001, *OJ* C 12. Hereto BOELE-WOELKI, "De toekomst van het IPR na het Verdrag van Amsterdam", in *Privaatrecht en Gros. Opstellen aangeboden aan prof. mr. F. Willem Grosheide*, Antwerp/Groningen 2000, 355 ff., especially 368-369; DE BOER (note 102), *FJR* 1999, 244 ff.; HEß, "Die "Europäisierung" des internationalen Privatrechts durch den Amsterdamer Vertrag. Chancen und Gefahren", *NJW* 2000, 23 ff.; JAYME/KOHLER, "Europäisches Kollisionsrecht 1999. Die Abendstunde der Staatsverträge", *IPRax* 1999, 401 ff.; JAYME, "Zum Jahrtausendwechsel. Das Kollisionsrecht zwischen Postmoderne und Futurismus", *IPRax* 2000, 165 ff.; KOHLER, "Interrogations sur les sources du droit international privé européen après le traité d'Amsterdam", *R.C.D.I.P.* 1999, 1 ff. and "Auf dem Weg zu einem europäischen Justizraum für das Familien- und Erbrecht", *FamRZ* 2002, 709 ff.

[104] CLARKSON, "Brussels III – Matrimonial Property European Style", *Fam Law* 2002, 683 ff.

[105] OPPERMANN (note 97), 503.

the very most, Art. 293 of the EC Treaty can serve as a basis for a repeal of rights of retortion.[106]

Art. 18 II of the EC Treaty on the citizenship of the Union is also cited by an author.[107] The Council may adopt provisions to facilitate the exercise of the rights of every citizen of the Union to move and reside freely within the territory of the Member States.[108]Those facilities should protect the freedom of movement, *e.g.* through unification of procedural law.[109] A unification of substantive family and succession law exceeds this goal.

Finally, attention should be drawn to Art. 308 of the EC Treaty by which, if action by the Community should prove to be necessary, in the course of the operation of the common market and neither the objectives of the Community nor the EC Treaty have provided the necessary powers, the Council may, acting unanimously on a proposal from the Commission, and after consulting the European Parliament, take the appropriate measures. *Basedow* has stated that, according to the extent of the necessary harmonisation of the legal systems of the Member States, this article is a legal basis for a European matrimonial regime or a European will.[110] However, Art. 308 of the EC Treaty expressly states that action by the Community should prove necessary to achieve the objectives of the common market. A European matrimonial regime or a European will naturally are desirable and imply a great step in the direction of a Europeanisation of family and succession law, but it is questionable whether they are really necessary for the completion of the common market.

Despite this uncertainty, the European Union has abandoned its previous restraint. With the adoption of the Charter of Fundamental Rights of December 7th, 2000,[111] which is of a mainly programmed aimed

---

[106]   This article expressly mentions "the enjoyment and protection of rights under the same conditions as those accorded by each State to its own nationals" as an exemple.

[107]   Spellenberg, in *Festschrift Schumann* (note 100), 428.

[108]   See also Art. 18 of the EC Treaty. See KLUTH, in CALLIES/RUFFERT, *Kommentar zu EU-Vertrag und EG-Vertrag*, Neuwied 1999, EG-Vertrag Art. 18, Nr. 3.

[109]   KLUTH (note 108), Nr. 15.

[110]   BASEDOW (note 101), *AcP* 2000, 478.

[111]   *OJ* C 364, December 18th, 2000, 1 (also published in *FamRZ* 2001, 78 ff.). Hereto in general DI FABIO, "Eine europäische Charta. Auf dem Weg zur Unionsverfassung", *JZ* 2000, 737 ff.; CARLIER/DE SCHUTTER (ed.), *La Charte des droits fondamentaux de l'Union européenne. Son apport à la protection des droits de l'homme en Europe. Hommage à Silvio Marcus Helmons*, Brussels 2002; SCHRÖDER, "Wirkungen der Grundrechtscharta in der europäischen Rechtsordnung", *JZ* 2002, 849 ff.

nature[112] and reaffirms the rights as they result from the European Convention for the Protection of Human Rights and Fundamental Freedoms and from constitutional traditions, with some enlargement, the Union has acknowledged the importance of the family. Whereas the actions of the Union first of all concerned family policy as a part of social policy, fundamental rights related to family law are now inserted in the Charter, *e.g.* the right to respect for private and family life (Art. 7), the rights of the child (Art. 24) and the rights for the elderly (Art. 25). Artikel 21 prohibits discrimination, expressly including discrimination on the ground of sexual orientation.[113] The citizens of the European Union are no longer being seen as consumers, but as persons with their own rights. This does not imply that the Union now disposes of a legal basis related to family law, but that existing rules can be interpreted in a broader sense.[114]

The presidency conclusions of the Laeken European Council of December 14th-15th, 2001 point out that efforts to resolve the problems arising from differences between legal systems should continue,[115] and the harmonisation of family law is expressly mentioned as an example.[116] Prior to the Laeken European Council, the Ministers of Justice had adopted a report on the need to approximate Member States' legislation in civil matters in which they dealt with family law.[117] In this report, the Council observed that economic considerations, which apply to contract law, cannot be enforced in the same way in other areas of private law such as family and succession law. The Council nevertheless found another legitimate basis for action by anchoring it in the principle of freedom of movement and in the will to establish a real uniform area of freedom, security and justice.[118] The Council does not mention a concrete legal basis. It only points out that, in the event of a necessity

---

[112] But obligatory for the institutions and bodies of the Union and to the member states only when they are implementing Union law (Art. 51).

[113] Hereto SUMNER, "The Charter of Fundamental Rights of the EU and Sexual Orientation", *IFL* 2002, 156, esp. 161-162.

[114] McGLYNN, "Families and the European Union Charter of Fundamental Rights: progressive change or entrenching the status quo?", *E.L.Rev.* 2001, 586; STALFORD, "Concepts of family under EU law – Lessons from the ECHR", *IJLPF* 2002, 411 ff.

[115] Comp. the Tampere European Council of October 15th-16th, 1999, at which already was stressed that "in a genuine European Area of Justice individuals and businesses should not be prevented or discouraged from exercising their rights by the incompatibility or complexity of legal and administrative systems in the Member States" (Nr. 28 of the presidency conclusions).

[116] Nr. 45.

[117] Draft Council Report 13017/01 of October 29th, 2001, adopted at November 16th, 2001.

[118] Nr. 3.

for harmonisation measures, one has to consider the suitability of an institutional framework, especially in regard to Art. 61 ff. of Title IV EC Treaty. The Council clearly has an extension of those articles in mind, but expressly pointed out that the principles of subsidiarity and proportionality as laid down in Art. 5 of the EC Treaty as well as the precise criteria for applying them as laid down in the protocol annexed to the EC Treaty on the application of the principles of subsidiarity and proportionality, should be observed.[119]

It seems that the Council has realised that a unification, which is exclusively restricted to private international law, will not be sufficient to realise its goal of a uniform area of freedom, security and justice. What is more, the Council believes that the development of such an area depends on the extent to which Member States are able to gain confidence in the proper functioning of institutions of other countries, and takes for granted that, in the future, this extent of confidence can be reached by a greater convergence of substantive law.[120] On the basis of a survey of the activities of Community institutions, the Council notes that family law has progressively gained in importance in Community law.[121] The disposing of obstacles to the freedom of movement within the European internal market as well as the warranty of this freedom of movement, which has become more important because of the increasing number of changes of domicile, inevitably lead to interactions between family law and the Community's fields of activity. According to the Council, this development deserves special attention. For that reason it has to be investigated which obstacles resulting from the diversity of legislative provisions of the Member States preclude the principle of freedom of movement.[122] The Council holds the opinion that it is necessary to perform a systematic investigation into which needs exist and that the Commission should draw up a study showing the differences between the legislative provisions of the Member States related to family law that could impair the freedom of movement, and to communicate the findings of this study to the Council on June 30th, 2003 at the latest.[123]

Should this development be welcomed? The fact that the European Union engages into family law, cannot simply be rejected. The probable

---

[119]   Nr. 4.
[120]   Nr. 7.
[121]   Nr. 18.
[122]   Nr. 19.
[123]   Concluding observation f.

unavailability of an ideal rule of competence is the smaller problem, for rules can be made. Instead, one has first to ask whether the European Community is an organisation with the ideal prerequisites and premises to promote harmonisation and unification of family law. Economic views, free movement, realisation of an internal market... they are perhaps not the best starting points. To put it in *Kohler*'s words: "Status als Ware"[124] or family law as product of an economic market.[125] In this case, there is a risk that family law will be downgraded to an auxiliary science of economic law, only serving to realise the economic goals of the Community. Second, the Council makes it a little too easy for itself, as it sees the convergence of substantive law as a possibility to gain confidence in the proper functioning of institutions of the Member States. This requires a lot more. Unification of law, which has been established in back rooms without sufficient participation of the European Parliament and perhaps even of the national parliaments, lacks democratic legitimacy.[126] Unification of law, which has been established without sufficient scientific cooperation, leads to a lowering of quality. A great deal still has to be realised in the judiciary sphere. A real uniform area of law can only function if the education and training of judges reaches a similar level in each Member State. As long as this is not the case, confidence in the proper functioning of the institutions of the Member States is not likely to occur. Thus, there is still a lot of work to be done.

The conclusion can be reached that (i) an institutional unification of substantive family law still has a long journey to go and that this way is currently not advisable, (ii) at first a long phase of spontaneous approximation of laws is necessary and (iii) this harmonisation of family law will be a task for research and education. An intense scientific discussion is necessary.[127] Of course, it goes without saying that the unification of law by international conventions is not entirely out of the question and that quite a lot can be achieved based on the example of the European Convention of May 28th, 1998 on Jurisdiction and the Recognition and Enforcement of Judgments in Matrimonial Matters. Further technical treaties can be concluded based on the example of the International Commission on Civil Status. The case law of the European Court of Human Rights and of the European Court of Justice can still play an important part in eliminating discrimination. However, harmonisation of law will only be successful once there is emphasis on what is common

---

[124] See note 102.
[125] See also MCGLYNN (note 10), 240.
[126] See also KUCHINKE (note 10), 612.
[127] KOHLER (note 103), *FamRZ* 2002, 713.

to the European legal systems and when the differences are placed in perspective rather than denied, thus creating a European consciousness. This can only succeed through education and the evolution of legal doctrine.[128]

Is a spontaneous approximation of law all that is left then? Without a doubt the approximation of law will allow for the rapprochement of legal systems where they are connected with great sociological developments. However, for very technical problems this will not be sufficient. For these matters, only unification by international treaties can in a further stage lead to success. Comparatively speaking, there is as yet little interest. One may presume that this lack of interest is due to ignorance, inadequate information or hesitancy in the face of the technical complexity of family law. Legal doctrine will thus have to stimulate comparative family law, thereby contributing to the Europeanisation and internationalisation of this branch of private law.

## 5.  THE COMMISSION ON EUROPEAN FAMILY LAW

On September 1st, 2001, at an inauguration meeting at the University of Utrecht, six professors[129] established the Commission on European Family Law.[130] Its establishment was based on the idea that family law, with regard to the European citizen's greater mobility, must not fail in a search for a *ius commune* and that the available armamentarium of private international law as well as the legislative and judicial activities of the Council of Europe and of the European Union are not sufficient to reinforce a further harmonisation. The members of the Commission hold the conviction that a certain harmonisation of family law is needed in order to realise a true free movement of persons, and that this harmonisation will reinforce the European identity as well as an efficient uniform area of law. This idea is not entirely new. As early as in the 1920s, the Nordic countries had succeeded in harmonising certain aspects of their family law. During the following years the greater part

---

[128]  PINTENS (note 10), *ZEuP* 1998, 676.
[129]  Prof. KATHARINA BOELE-WOELKI (Utrecht), prof. FRÉDÉRIQUE FERRAND (Lyon), prof. NIGEL LOWE (Cardiff), prof. DIETER MARTINY (Frankfurt an der Oder), prof. WALTER PINTENS (Leuven) and prof. DIETER SCHWAB (Regensburg).
[130]  See the communication note in *ZEuP* 2002, 194. More information on www2.law.uu.nl/priv/cefl. Hereto BOELE-WOELKI, "Divorce in Europe: Unification of Private International Law and Harmonisation of Substantive Law", in *Liber amicorum Joppe*, Deventer 2002, 21 ff. and "Comparative research-based drafting of principles of European family law (note 10)", p. 178 ff.; PINTENS, "Over cultuur, Europa en recht", in *Liber amicorum Herbots*, Antwerpen 2002, 317 ff.

of their family law was unified, sometimes down to the smallest detail, even though Sweden, followed by Finland, have now and then issued more progressive legislation. Today, specific legislation in each Nordic legal system has lead to many differences. But there is still a Nordic model with similar leading ideas and principles in matters as affiliation, parental responsibility, matrimonial property, divorce and cohabitation.[131] This idea is also found in developments in the United States of America, where the fragmentation of family law competence among the different states is considered to be too complex and to be a handicap, which need to be overcome through uniform model laws. Legal doctrine in the United States therefore increasingly advocates a harmonisation of family law by means of federalisation.[132]

Following the example of similar commissions, the Commission on European Family Law consists of two groups: the Organising Committee and the Expert Group. The task of the Organising Committee, consisting of the members at the inauguration meeting, is to set up and co-ordinate the Expert Group, which consists of distinguished experts in the field of family and comparative law from all European Union Member States, Norway and Switzerland, of observers from Central and Eastern Europe and of two independent advisors. The main task for these experts will be to present national reports in preparation for harmonisation projects.

The Organising Committee has long discussed the working method and the fields of family law, which are eligible for harmonisation. For this task, the experiences at the Regensburger Symposia were gratefully used.[133] As a working method, the Commission has opted for the drafting of a set of principles after the example of the Lando-Commission,[134] the UNIDROIT Principles of International Commercial Contracts[135] and the

---

[131] AGELL, "Is there One System of Family Law in the Nordic Countries?", *Eur.J.L.R.* 2001 313. Comp. BRADLEY, *Family Law and Political Culture* (note 10).

[132] See ADLER, "Federalism and Family", *Columbia Journal of Gender and Law* 1999, 197 ff.; LAW, "Families and Federalism", *Washington University Journal of Law and Policy* 2000, 175 ff.; MARTINY, in FAURE *et al.* (note 10), p. 196-197 with further references.

[133] See SCHWAB/HENRICH (ed.), *Entwicklungen des europäischen Kindschaftsrechts*, Bielefeld 1994, 2nd edition, Bielefeld 1996; HENRICH/SCHWAB (ed.), *Der Schutz der Familienwohnung in Europäischen Rechtsordnungen*, Bielefeld 1995; SCHWAB/HENRICH (ed.), *Familiäre Solidarität. Die Begründung und die Grenzen der Unterhaltspflicht im europäischen Vergleich*, Bielefeld 1997; HENRICH/SCHWAB (ed.), *Eheliche Gemeinschaft, Partnerschaft und Vermögen im europäischen Vergleich*, Bielefeld 1999; HENRICH/SCHWAB (ed.), *Familienerbrecht und Testierfreiheit im europäischen Vergleich*, Bielefeld 2001.

[134] See the references in note 2.

[135] BONELL, *An international Restatement of Contract Law. The UNIDROIT Principles of International Commercial Contracts*, New York 1994.

European Group on Tort Law.[136] The Commission has no intention to draft detailed texts of law as the time is not yet ripe. The Commission seeks to apply the method of the American Restaments[137] instead, in order to formulate principles, which form the *ius commune* of the legal systems and could be useful as a source of inspiration to national legislators.[138] This method will not always suffice, as in many fields the differences will be so immense that it becomes impossible to derive common principles from the various national legal systems. In those cases where the solutions provided by each of the national jurisdictions are so different that a common core cannot be found, the Commission will have to propose its own solutions on the basis of a better law approach.[139] Here it has to be examined which interest needs to be protected the most.

The procedure to reach a restatement begins with a questionnaire prepared by the Organising Committee.[140] The experts then answer through national reports. Draft principles are drawn up by one or more members of the Organising Committee, discussed in this Committee and finally presented to the Expert Group.

The choice of a first field of research was not easy. It is often held that harmonisation has the best chance of success in those branches of law which are closely connected to property law, such as marital property law.[141] However, the technical complexity of this field should not be underestimated. In addition, it not only has a close connection to the law of obligations, in which harmonisation becomes apparent, but also to the law of property, which is not always considered to offer great possibilities for harmonisation. The short comparative survey on statutory matrimonial regimes (supra III.2) has shown the difficulty of working out one European statutory matrimonial regime. At most, it will be possible to offer models for different statutory matrimonial regimes, from which the national legislature can choose one.[142] In this regard, several propositions are at hand, each of them being without a doubt very

---

[136]   Hereto SPIER/HAAZEN, "The European Group on Tort Law", *ZEuP* 1999, 469 ff.

[137]   See SCHINDLER, "Die Restatements und ihre Bedeutung für das amerikanische Privatrecht", *ZEuP* 1998, 277 ff.

[138]   See already MARTINY, in HARTKAMP *et al.* (ed.) (note 10), 270.

[139]   In this sense also: ANTOKOLSKAIA (note 10), *FamPra.ch* 2002, 272.

[140]   See the first questionnaire on divorce law: www2.law.uu.nl/priv/cefl/questionnaire.doc. hereto BOELE-WOELKI (note 130), 25-26.

[141]   See already ZAJTAY, *Rechtsvergleichung im ehelichen Güterrecht*, Annalis Universitatis Saraviensis 1955, 154 ff. See also MARTINY, in HARTKAMP *et al.* (ed.) (note 10), 165.

[142]   BOELE-WOELKI (note 130), 23; HENRICH (note 29), 1522.

useful.[143] The Commission has yet another purpose. It searches for a common core and desires to create one set of principles of European family law that are believed to play a key role in the development of national legal systems, but the Commission does not opt for alternative propositions to supplement national family laws.[144] Finally, the Commission has decided to commence activity in the field of divorce law (grounds for divorce and maintenance between former spouses). Parental responsibility has been selected as the second issue. A comparative survey of divorce law does not show evidence of a real approximation of law. However, important tendencies cannot be ignored: the evolution from the principle of culpability to the principle of irretrievable breakdown of the marriage and the limitation of maintenance, be it for a certain time or on a circumstantial basis.[145] As for parental responsibility, the joint custody has found acceptance as a basic model.

The selection of divorce and parental authority fits in well with the activities of the Council and the Commission of the European Union. Following the Brussels Conventions II and IIa, a regulation on the applicable law to divorce cases is to be expected in the near future, thus taking another step in the direction of substantive law.

The establishment of a commission for the harmonisation of family law will seem to be premature for many. Certain scholars will regard its plans as utopian, some will find its propositions too radical, others will find them too modest. However, ideas and points of view quickly develop. What is still a dream today, becomes reality tomorrow. The Lando-Commission has suffered mockery at its beginning, but now, twenty years later, its work is generally praised. The European Commission, for instance, now uses its work as a model.[146] In this way, harmonisation of

---

[143]   See AGELL, "Towards uniforming spouses property rights especially in international marriages", in *Council of Europe, Proceedings of the 3rd European Conference on family law*, Strasbourg 1996, p. 63 ff. and "The division of property upon divorce from a european perspective", in *Liber Amicorum Meulders-Klein*, Brussels 1998, p. 1 ff.; VERBEKE, "Proeve van internationaal huwelijksrecht", in *Van Mourik Bundel*, Deventer 2000, 391 ff.

[144]   Compare the propositions of DE GROOT (note 10), *ZEuP* 2001, 617 ff.

[145]   See AGELL, Grounds and Procedures Reviewed, in WEITZMAN and MACLEAN, *Economic Consequences of Divorce*, Oxford 1992, p. 53 ff.; DUTOIT *et al., Le divorce en droit comparé*, Geneva 2002; MARTINY, in this book 529 ff.; MEULDERS-KLEIN, "La problématique du divorce dans les législations d'Europe occidentale", *R.I.D.C.* 1989, 7 ff.; PINTENS (note 10), *FamRZ* 2003, 336-337.

[146]   See the Communication from the Commission to the Council and the European Parliament on European contract law of July 11th, 2001, COM (2001) 398, *ZEuP* 2001, 963 ff.; also with annexes on internet: http://europa.eu.int/comm/off/green/index_en.htm. See also VON BAR, "Die Mitteilung der Europäischen Kommission zum Europäischen Vertragsrecht", *ZEuP* 2001, 799 ff.

family law is a process that will take several decades. The initiators of the Commission on European Family Law however thought that the time was ripe to take this initiative. Much has spurred them to do this: (i) the great interest in comparative family law, not only in national family law journals, but also in general comparative ones, (ii) the success of the Regensburger Symposia and (iii) the increasing interest of the European Council and the European Commission.

All these developments lead to the conclusion that the creation of a *ius commune* will be more easy and successful in certain branches of law, such as the law of obligations or commercial law, but that the possibility exists in each branch of law, even in the most particularistic ones, such as family and succession law. And thus we find ourselves back at the introduction and with the great French legal comparatist *Edouard Lambert*, who tried to prove that a "droit commun législatif" could play a part in each branch of law. That was precisely the reason, why, in 1903, he had already linked his principal work on the function of comparative law to succession law, stating that "la matière des successions et celle qui, de tout temps, a fourni le milieu de développement la plus favorable au particularisme"[147] and so proving that comparative law can also play a key role in more particularistic areas of the law.

---

[147]   LAMBERT, *La fonction du droit civil comparé*, I, Paris 1903, 2. Hereto JAMIN (note 7), 748 ff.

# PART ONE – ARGUMENTS FOR AND AGAINST UNIFICATION AND HARMONISATION OF FAMILY LAW IN EUROPE

# ARGUMENTS FOR THE UNIFICATION AND HARMONISATION OF FAMILY LAW IN EUROPE

NINA DETHLOFF

## 1. INTRODUCTION

A strange justice that is bounded by a river! Truth on this side of the Pyrenees, error on the other side.[1] Pascal's words show that he probably would not have objected to a uniform family law. Today, however, one is often confronted with the question of why the same law should apply to the legal family ties of both Swedes and Portuguese. The following article will attempt to answer this question.

I will begin my argument by pointing out the difficulties brought about by the current diversity of national family-law regimes in the light of a growing number of cross-border family ties (2.). I will then continue by examining the need for unification arising from the influence of European Community law (3.). Finally, I will seek to demonstrate that a harmonisation of family law is not only necessary but, furthermore, does not lead to a loss of cultural identity (4.).

## 2. CROSS-BORDER FAMILY LIFE

### 2.1. Increase in the number of cross-border family ties

In a Europe that is growing together, family ties increasingly cross one or more national boundaries. The number of binational marriages is growing constantly. Today, more than 15% of those entering into marriage are of different nationalities, often of European states.[2] The same is true for other

---

[1]   Plaisante justice, qu'une rivière borne! Vérité au deça des Pyrénées, erreur au delà. Translation according to: BLAISE PASCAL (1623–1662). *Thoughts. The Harvard Classics.* 1909–14, p. 294; cited at http://www.bartleby.com/48/1/5.html.

[2]   In Germany it is 16.28%, date: 1999, see STATISTISCHES BUNDESAMT (ed.), *Statistisches Jahrbuch 2001*, table 3.26.1, p. 69; in Austria 17.03%, date: 2000, see STATISTIK AUSTRIA (ed.), *Statistisches Jahrbuch Österreichs 2001*, table 2.27, p. 71; in France 13.8%, date: 2000, see BEAUMEL, DOISNEAU, VATAN, "La situation démographique en 2000. Mouvement de la population", table 9, p. 17, in: INSEE (Institut National de la Statistique et des Études Écono- →

relationships, be they same-sex or heterosexual. Children from mixed-national marriages generally possess the citizenship of both parents. Thus, the number of persons with dual or multiple citizenship is growing continually. In addition, the mobility and migration of people is increasing. In the European Union more than 5% of citizens, a figure which amounts to nearly 19 million, do not possess the citizenship of the state in which they live.[3] Of those, almost 6 million are citizens of the Union living in another member state.[4] It is not rare for couples or families – be it jointly or separately – to move their place of residence into a state other than the one in which they formed their relationship or in which their children were born. On average, more than 1.5 million people immigrate into the EU each year (0.5% of the resident population).[5] Add to this the annual migration between EU states, which comes to more than 350,000 a year (0.1% of the resident population);[6] according to surveys[7] and estimates,[8] the real figure is as much as three to five times this number. 54% of immigrants possessed the nationality of a non-EU member state and 18% that of another EU state.[9] The European Union alone has about 25,000

miques) (ed.), *Insee Résultats Société No. 10,* October 2000, http://www.insee.fr/fr/ffc/docs_ffc/iress10.pdf; in Switzerland even 45%, date: 2001, see BUNDESAMT FÜR STATISTIK, http://www.statistik.admin.ch/stat_ch/ber01/du0106.htm. The percentage for divorces is comparable (more than 13%), see STATISTISCHES BUNDESAMT, cited at http://www.verband-binationaler.de, date: 1999.

[3] Eurostat (ed.), *People in Europe,* p. 12, http://europa.eu.int/comm/eurostat/Public/datashop/print-product/EN?catalogue=Eurostat&product=Freeselect1-EN&mode=download.

[4] Eurostat (ed.), *The social situation in the European Union 2001,* p. 30, http://europa.eu.int/comm/eurostat/Public/datashop/print-product/EN?catalogue=Eurostat&product=KE-36-01-702-__-N-EN&mode=download.

[5] THOROGOOD, WINQVIST, Women and men migrating to and from the European Union, in: EUROSTAT (ed.), *Statistics in Focus. Population and social conditions.* 3- 2/2003, p. 1.

[6] See *op. cit.* note 5 on p. 2: Between 1995 and 1998 around 1 in every 1,000 EU citizens changed residence within the EU each year.

[7] According to a survey, 5% of those questioned have taken up residence in another country of the European Union within the last 10 years. See EUROPEAN OPINION RESEARCH GROUP (ed.), *Euro-Barometer Special 54.2, 2001: The social situation in the European Union,* p. 108, http://europa.eu.int/comm/public_opinion/archives/eb/ebs_148_en.pdf. This is equivalent to an annual migration rate of 0.5% of the resident population.

[8] In 1997, about 1 million of the (estimated) 1.4 million legal immigrants are said to have come from a state outside the European Union, see EUROSTAT (ed.), *The social situation in the European Union 2001,* p. 74. This is equivalent to around 0.3% of the resident population.

[9] See THOROGOOD, WINQVIST, "Women and men migrating to and from the European Union", in: EUROSTAT (ed.), *Statistics in Focus. Population and social conditions.* 3- 2/2003, p. 2. The remaining percentage consists of so-called returners, who possess the nationality of the country to which they are migrating.

civil servants, many of whom live in another community state with their partners or families.[10]

As a first step, I would like to address the problems that result from the diversity of national family laws in cross-border family ties (2.2.). Then, I hope to show that these problems cannot be solved through a unification of the international law of civil procedure and rules of conflicts of law alone, but only through a harmonisation of the substantive law (2.3.).

## 2.2. Legal Problems

### 2.2.1. Lack of Legal Certainty and the Costs Associated with the Determination of the Applicable Law

When family ties cross one or more national boundaries – be it because of the citizenship of family members or a change in residence or domicile – it is always necessary to determine which national family law will be applicable. This presents a substantial challenge to lawyers and public notaries who give advice concerning the stipulations of contracts or the likely outcome of legal disputes involving cross-border family situations. The same is true for the courts to which it falls to decide such lawsuits, and for the administrative bodies whose task it is to apply the law. The applicable law in cases in which a foreign element is involved is initially determined by the location where the case is to be decided. The reason for this is that, generally, it is the conflict-of-law rules of the forum that determine which substantive law is to be applied to any specific case.

### A. International Jurisdiction

In cross-border cases the courts or administrative bodies of several states often have international jurisdiction. This is not only the case in the – wide – areas in which international jurisdiction continues to be based on national law, as in disputes concerning parentage, or property-law disputes. Even in those areas where the Brussels Regulation,[11] the Lugano Conven-

---

10  See website of Permanent Representation of the Federal Republic of Germany at the European Union, Bewerben bei EU-Institutionen, http://www.eu-vertretung.de/de/bewerbungen/bewerbung/allgemeines.php.

11  Council Regulation (EC) No 44/2001 of 22 December 2000 on Jurisdiction and the Recognition and Enforcement of Judgments in Civil and Commercial Matters, *OJ* 2001 L 12/1, 16.1.2001.

tion,[12] and in particular the Brussels II Regulation[13] apply, it is often the case that the courts of different states have concurrent international jurisdiction.[14] Thus, for a divorce there is a choice between a large number of alternative fora with equal jurisdiction.[15]

## B. Law of Conflicts

If, in a question of family law, the courts or administrative bodies of several states have international jurisdiction, the applicable law is decided by the conflict-of-law rules of the relevant forum. A lawyer advising in a cross-border case of family law therefore first needs to ascertain the conflict-of-laws rules of all those states that currently – or potentially, in a future legal dispute – have international jurisdiction. In some areas there are Hague Conventions, such as the Hague Convention on Maintenance[16] or the Hague Convention on the Protection of Minors.[17] In some states the relevant conventions have already entered into force, in others they have been ratified, in others signed, and in yet others not even signed.[18] Additionally, there exists a large variety of autonomous laws of conflicts

---

[12] Lugano Convention of 1988 on Jurisdiction and the Enforcement of Judgments in Civil and Commercial Matters.

[13] Council Regulation (EC) No 1347/2000 of 29 May 2000 on Jurisdiction and the Recognition and Enforcement of Judgments in Matrimonial Matters and in Matters of Parental Responsibility for Children of Both Spouses, *OJ* 2000 L 160/19, 30.6.2000.

[14] On concurrent jurisdiction pursuant to Art. 2 and Art. 5 of the Brussels II Regulation, see *e.g.* KROPHOLLER, *Europäisches Zivilprozessrecht*, 7th ed. 2002, introduction to Art. 5, para 2 *et seq.*

[15] For a critical view, see LOWE, "The Growing Influence of the European Union on International Family Law – A View From the Boundary", 56 *Current Legal Problems* 2003 (to be published); for details on the rules of jurisdiction under Art. 2, see BOELE-WOELKI, "Brüssel II: Die Verordnung über die Zuständigkeit und die Anerkennung von Entscheidungen in Ehesachen", *ZfRV* 2001, 121, 123 *et seq.*; SCHACK, "Das neue Internationale Eheverfahrensrecht in Europa", *RabelsZ* 65 (2001) 615, 621-622; KOHLER, "Internationales Verfahrensrecht für Ehesachen in der Europäischen Union: Die Verordnung 'Brüssel II'", *NJW* 2001, 10, 11-12. For a general view of this subject, see *e.g.* SPELLENBERG, "Der Anwendungsbereich der EheGVO („Brüssel II") in Statussachen", in: GOTTWALD, ROTH (eds.), *Festschrift für Ekkehard Schumann zum 70. Geburtstag*, 2001, p. 421; WAGNER, "Die Anerkennung und Vollstreckung von Entscheidungen nach der Brüssel II-Verordnung", *IPRax* 2001, 73.

[16] Convention of 1973 on the Law Applicable to Maintenance Obligations.

[17] Convention of 1961 Concerning the Powers of Authorities and the Law Applicable in Respect of the Protection of Minors.

[18] For the current status of ratification concerning these two conventions, which are already in force in many European states, see the website of the Hague Conference on Private International Law, http://www.hcch.net/e/conventions/index.html. By contrast, the Convention of 1978 on the Law Applicable to Matrimonial Property Regimes is only applicable in the Netherlands, France and Luxembourg.

which decide the applicable law.[19] In some states, like England, Switzerland and the Scandinavian states, or according to some Hague conventions, the determination of the conflict-of-law rules is transplanted into the laws of jurisdiction: if the court or administrative body finds it has international jurisdiction, it applies its own substantive law.[20] Although this removes the need to determine the applicable law (often a lengthy and costly process), in cases of concurrent international jurisdiction the international uniformity of decision-making is disturbed and there arises a substantial danger of forum shopping, which I will address later.[21]

If, however, the applicable law is decided – as it usually is – through the conflict-of-law rules, after having found the relevant source – or sources – of law, one still needs to establish the relevant provision of the conflict-of-law rules. This process, too, can present considerable difficulties. The significant differences in the substantive family laws often cause problems of characterisation, that is, the question under which provision of the conflict-of-law rules a foreign substantive law concept can be subsumed: for example, is the distribution of property after divorce under English law a consequence of the law of divorce or is it a question of the marital law of property or even of maintenance?[22] Which law is to be applied can also depend on whether the law applicable to a preliminary question, such as the validity of a marriage for questions of the legal effects of the marriage or the divorce, is decided independently, that is, decided according to the lex fori, or made dependent on the law applicable to the main question.[23]

---

[19]   For the different principles underlying the establishment of the connecting factors within national conflict-of-law regimes, see *infra* 2.2.2.A.

[20]   See for such a parallelism between international jurisdiction and private international law the Hague Convention of 1961 on the Protection of Minors, the Hague Convention of 1996 on Jurisdiction, Applicable Law, Recognition, Enforcement and Co-operation in Respect of Parental Responsibility and Measures for the Protection of Children (Art. 15) and the Convention of 1965 on Jurisdiction, Applicable Law and Recognition of Decrees Relating to Adoptions (Art. 4). For the authoritativeness of lex fori in foro proprio from a Swiss perspective, *cf.* VISCHER, "Bemerkungen zum Verhältnis von internationaler Zuständigkeit und Kollisionsrecht", in: STOFFEL, VOLKEN (eds.), *Mélanges en l'honneur d'Alfred E. von Overbeck. Conflits et harmonisation*, 1990, p. 349, 367.

[21]   See *infra* 2.2.2.A.

[22]   For the function that such a division of assets has, see LOWE, "The English Approach to the Division of Assets upon Family Breakdown", in: HENRICH, SCHWAB (eds.), *Eheliche Gemeinschaft, Partnerschaft und Vermögen im europäischen Vergleich*, 1999, p. 47, 60; for an interpretation of the term maintenance in Art. 5 (2) of Brussels I Regulation, see ECJ 27. 2. 1997 (van den Boogard/Laumen) *ECR* 1997, I-1147, para 22.

[23]   On the preliminary question in general, see WENGLER, "The Law Applicable to Preliminary (Incidental) Questions", in: DAVID (ed.), *International Encyclopedia of Comparative Law*, vol. III, Chapter 7; SCHURIG, "Die Struktur des kollisionsrechtlichen Vorfragenproblems", in:
→

## C. Determination and Application of Foreign Law

If it has been determined which law of which state or states is to be applied to a case in which a foreign element is involved, in a second step it will be necessary to determine the content of the applicable law. In a number of jurisdictions it falls to the courts to determine the applicable foreign law ex officio.[24] The foreign law in question must be applied in the same way as it is in its home country.[25] Most judges – as in the case of lawyers and public notaries – are not qualified through their training to do so. Lawyers and public notaries run the risk of becoming liable towards their clients as a result of the incorrect application of foreign legislation.[26] In many cases even the texts of the foreign codes of law are likely to be unavailable.[27] In difficult cases, therefore, expert opinions must be obtained.[28] This process is not only time-consuming – a fact which can be especially problematic in family-law cases – but also entails substantial costs for the parties involved.[29] This is the case even if, as in many countries, the determination of foreign law is considered to be a question of fact and

---

MUSIELAK, SCHURIG (eds.), *Festschrift für Gerhard Kegel zum 75. Geburtstag*, 1987, p. 549; specifically on the preliminary question in international family law, see OLLICK, *Das kollisionsrechtliche Vorfragenproblem und die Bedeutung des ordre public unter besonderer Berücksichtigung der deutschen Rechtsprechung zum internationalen Familienrecht*, 1992; FÜLLEMANN-KUHN, *Die Vorfrage im Internationalen Privatrecht*, 1977, p. 36 *et seq.*

[24]  See § 293 ZPO (German Code of Civil Procedure); §§ 3, 4 Austrian Conflict of Laws Act; Art. 14 Italian Conflict of Laws Act. In Switzerland, the duty to make official investigations under Art. 16 Conflict of Laws Act applies only to non-pecuniary claims. From a comparative law perspective SPICKHOFF, "Fremdes Recht vor inländischen Gerichten: Rechts- oder Tatfrage?", *ZZP* 112 (1999) 265, 276 *et seq.*

[25]  Expressly Art. 15 Italian Conflict of Laws Act. From the German point of view, *e.g.* BGH (Bundesgerichtshof) *NJW* 1991, 1419; see also KEGEL, SCHURIG, *Internationales Privatrecht*, 8th ed. 2000, § 15 III, p. 441 *et seq.* From the French point of view, MAYER, HEUZÉ, *Droit international privé*, 7th ed. 2001, no. 191. From the Spanish point of view, SOBRINO, "Der Beweis ausländischen Rechts in der neuen spanischen Zivilprozessordnung vom 7. Januar 2000: Chronik einer Ernüchterung", in: BASEDOW *et al.* (eds.), *Aufbruch nach Europa. 75 Jahre Max-Planck-Institut für Privatrecht*, 2001, p. 685, 694.

[26]  On the liability of lawyers in cases which involve a foreign element, see SCHÜTZE, *Rechtsverfolgung im Ausland*, 3rd ed. 2002, para 22; see also BGH *NJW* 1972, 1044; OLG Hamm *DZWir* 1997, 460, note GRUBER: Anwaltshaftung bei der Anwendung ausländischen Rechts; SIEG, *Internationale Anwaltshaftung*, 1996, p. 118 *et seq.*

[27]  On the problems arising in connection with the application of foreign law, see LANDO, "The eternal crisis", in: BASEDOW (ed.), *Festschrift für Ulrich Drobnig zum 70. Geburtstag*, 1998, p. 361, 362-363.

[28]  For other methods to ascertain the foreign law, see SCHELLACK, *Selbstermittlung oder ausländische Auskunft unter dem europäischen Rechtsauskunftsübereinkommen*, 1997.

[29]  The remuneration of an expert under German law is governed by § 3 para 2, 3 ZSEG (Zeugen- und Sachverständigenentschädigungsgesetz). The cost of an expert opinion may be imposed on the losing party, provided it is covered by § 293 ZPO (German Code of Civil Procedure).

therefore, in principle, is saddled on the parties.[30] The application of foreign law is especially questionable in summary proceedings,[31] which are not uncommon in family-law cases. It is often unclear if and when a court may or ought to abort its efforts to determine the applicable foreign law due to urgency. The fact remains that the determination and application of foreign law in cross-border family-law cases is fraught with substantial uncertainty and entails considerable effort and enormous costs. Decisions are difficult to predict, long-term property dispositions impeded.

### 2.2.2. Loss or Change of Legal Positions

The variety of national family laws in Europe also creates other problems in cross-border family situations. The differences between legal regimes can lead to the loss of legal positions or changes in rights or obligations. There are two reasons for this: first of all, due to differing laws of conflicts and substance, varying results may arise when family-law matters are considered from the point of view of different legal regimes (A). Second, taking up residence in a different state may lead to the applicability of a different law (B).

### A. Lack of Internationally Uniform Decision-Making

In cases that involve a foreign element, family ties must often be judged from the point of view of several legal regimes. Given the substantial differences that exist between the autonomous laws of conflicts and substantive laws, this often leads to divergent results. In the conflict-of-law rules, there still exists a rift between the principle of domicile on the one hand and the principle of citizenship on the other, even though with the

---

[30] Regarding English law, see *e.g.* Lazard Bros & Co v. Midland Bank [1933] *A.C.* 289; Ascherberg, Hopwood & Co v. Casa Musicale Sonzogno [1971] 1 *W.L.R.* 173, 1128 (C.A.); HARTLEY, "Pleading and proof of foreign law. The major European systems compared", 45 *I.C.L.Q.* (1996) 271, 282-283. In France, the duty of establishing the foreign law applicable was originally incumbent on the plaintiff, Cass. civ. 25.5.1948 – (arrêt Lautour), *Revue critique du droit international privé* 38 (1949) 89; Cass. civ. 24.1.1984 – (arrêt Soc. Thinet et Dumez c. Soc. des Etablissements Roque et autres), *Revue critique du droit international privé* 74 (1985) 89. Now such proof has to be supplied by the party that invokes the application of foreign law, Cass. com. 16.11.1993 – (arrêt Soc. Amerford c. Cie Air France et autres), *Revue critique du droit international privé* 83 (1994) 332, note LAGARDE.

[31] See OLG Hamburg *IPRax* 1990, 400; on this subject, MANKOWSKI, KERFACK, "Arrest, einstweilige Verfügung und die Anwendung ausländischen Rechts", *IPRax* 1990, 372, 373-374; see also DETHLOFF, "Ausländisches Wettbewerbsrecht im einstweiligen Rechtsschutz", *RabelsZ* 62 (1998) 286, 290-291; KINDL, "Ausländisches Recht vor deutschen Gerichten", *ZZP* 111 (1998) 177, 184-185; v. WESTPHALEN, "Fallstricke bei Verträgen und Prozessen mit Auslandsberührung", *NJW* 1994, 2113, 2116.

principle of citizenship, the factor of habitual residence is growing in importance.[32] Divergent results also arise if – as in Swiss or English law – the national law is applied on principle if international jurisdiction is found.[33] Here also there is a lack of internationally uniform decision-making.

If one legal regime provides for a legal status unknown to another, or if it makes the creation of a particular legal status dependent on requirements unknown to another, this may lead to the creation of "limping" family-law relationships, that is, legal relationships which exist under one law but are not recognised by another.[34] The result is limping marriages, limping registered partnerships or even limping fatherhoods. Differences in the law of divorce lead to limping divorces. Furthermore a certain status may give rise to quite different legal rights and obligations. For example, under one legal regime, the unmarried parents of a child have joint parental responsibilities by operation of law,[35] under another only the mother has parental responsibilities.[36] Alternatively, there may be a title to the distribution of property after divorce or the separation of a domestic partnership under one law, but not under another.[37]

---

[32] Arguments in favour of a switch to the principle of habitual residence can already be found in NEUHAUS, KROPHOLLER, "Entwurf eines Gesetzes über Internationales Privat- und Verfahrensrecht (IPR-Gesetz)", *RabelsZ* 44 (1980) 326, 335; see also ROHE, "Staatsangehörigkeit oder Lebensmittelpunkt? Anknüpfungsgerechtigkeit im Lichte neuerer Entwicklungen", in: ENGEL, WEBER (eds.), *Festschrift für Dietrich Rothoeft zum 65. Geburtstag*, 1994, p. 1, 28 *et seq.*; JUENGER, The National Law Principle, in: GERKENS *et al.* (eds.), *Mélanges Fritz Sturm*, vol. 2, 1999, p. 1519; HENRICH, "Abschied vom Staatsangehörigkeitsprinzip?", in: HOHLOCH, FRANK, SCHLECHTRIEM (eds.), *Festschrift für Hans Stoll zum 75. Geburtstag*, 2001, p. 437.

[33] A critical appraisal of a parallelism between forum and ius is found in PFEIFFER, *Internationale Zuständigkeit und prozessuale Gerechtigkeit*, 1995, p. 104 *et seq.*

[34] For the term limping relationships, see DORENBERG, *Hinkende Rechtsverhältnisse im internationalen Familienrecht*, 1968, p. 15 *et seq.*

[35] Art. 154 Spanish Civil Code; Art. 373 para 1 Belgian Civil Code; Art. 372 para 2 French Civil Code, provided that parentage was recognized beforehand (Art. 120 Spanish Civil Code; Art. 319 § 1 Belgian Affiliation Act of 1987; Art. 355 *et seq.* French Civil Code). See also Section 4 (1) Children Act 1989, as amended by the Adoption and Children Act 2002.

[36] See § 166 Austrian Civil Code; Art. 298 para 1 Swiss Civil Code. In the absence of declarations of joint parental responsibility, under German law, too, only the mother has parental responsibility, § 1626a para 2 German Civil Code.

[37] For a comparative-law view of the laws governing cohabitation, see Forder, Civil law aspects of emerging forms of registered partnerships, Report on the Fifth European Conference on Family Law, Council of Europe 1999, p. 21-22. See *e.g.* the provisions for the financial consequences of cohabitation in Sweden in the Lag om sambors gemensamma hem (Sambolag=Law governing cohabitation), No. 232 of 1987; and in Norway in the Lov om rett til felles bolig og innbo nå hustandsfelleskap opphører, No. 45 of 1991 (=Law governing the dissolution of a domestic partnership).

To the extent that the validity of such legal positions is the object of court or administrative decisions, limping family-law relationships or contradictory rulings are prevented through the recognition of foreign judgments.[38] So far, this is only ensured in those areas where the Brussels I and II Regulations are applied. The era of limping divorces, at least in those areas where Brussels II applies,[39] is therefore a thing of the past[40] – as are contradictory decisions on parental responsibility for the children of both spouses in cases of divorce.[41] The same has long been true for decisions on maintenance. Limping legal relationships are still created, however, when foreign judgments are not recognised under autonomous national laws[42] or when changes in legal position come about by operation of law.[43] The larger the differences in the conflict-of-law rules and the substantive law, the more often this will be the case. Thus, due to the substantial differences in the law of parentage, limping fatherhoods are often created.[44] It is likely that there are also a number of limping registered partnerships and marriages between same-sex partners.[45] Diverging rulings

---

[38]   In conjunction with Art. 27-30 of the Brussels I Regulation, Art. 11-12 of the Brussels II Regulation which provide that the court second seized shall stay the proceedings.

[39]   Within the EU the Regulation does not apply in Denmark; see Art. 1 para 3 of the Brussels II Regulation.

[40]   Some take a critical view, alleging that this tends to facilitate divorce; see e.g. KOHLER, "Status als Ware: Bemerkungen zur europäischen Verordnung über das internationale Verfahrensrecht für Ehesachen", in: MANSEL (ed.), Vergemeinschaftung des Europäischen Kollisionsrechts. Vorträge aus Anlaß des fünfzigjährigen Bestehens des Instituts für internationales und ausländisches Privatrecht der Universität zu Köln, 2001, p. 47-48; JAYME, "Zum Jahrtausendwechsel: Das Kollisionsrecht zwischen Postmoderne und Futurismus", IPRax 2000, 165, 167-168; SCHACK, "Das neue Internationale Eheverfahrensrecht in Europa", RabelsZ 65 (2001) 613, 616-617.

[41]   See the envisaged widening of the scope of Brussels II by the Proposal for a Council Regulation concerning Jurisdiction and the Recognition and Enforcement of Judgments in Matrimonial Matters and in Matters of Parental Responsibility repealing Regulation (EC) No 1347/2000 and amending Regulation (EC) No 44/2001 in matters relating to maintenance, called Brussels IIa, COM (2002) 222 final/2, whereby issues concerning parental responsibility for all children and also those issues arising in non-matrimonial proceedings will be included.

[42]   Within the scope of the Lugano Convention, judgments are still not recognised if the court of the state of origin has decided a preliminary question, especially one concerning the status of a natural person, in such a way that it conflicts with a rule of the private international law of the state in which recognition is sought, see Art. 27 (4) of the Lugano Convention.

[43]   Especially with respect to the joint parental responsibility of unmarried parents, which exists by operation of law (see supra note 35).

[44]   See for the establishment of parentage from a comparative-law perspective, MEULDERS-KLEIN, "The Status of the Father in European Legislation", 44 American Journal of Comparative Law 1996, 487.

[45]   See for the considerable differences in the conflict-of-law rules and the substantive laws governing registered partnerships DETHLOFF, "Registrierte Partnerschaften in Europa", ZEuP 2003 (to be published). Limping registered partnerships are also created if the dissolution
→

remain frequent in the area of property-law decisions as well; here, too, there are substantial differences in the conflict-of-law rules as well as in substantive law.[46] The enforceability of the rulings in question is then dependent on the place of enforcement, which is largely random.

Limping legal positions can have severe disadvantages for the persons concerned. Many legal regimes tie effects of administrative law to the existence of a certain status. Whether a marriage, registered partnership or a parent-child-relationship exists or not, can be of relevance from the perspective of the law of residence permits, the law of nationality and citizenship, the social law and the tax law.[47] The existence of a legal status can also be a preliminary question for private-law relationships. Where a particular status is not recognised, no rights can be derived from it. The effects of this could potentially continue over several generations as far as nationality, the name, or the law of inheritance are concerned.

### B. Changes in the Applicable Law

Diverging national family law can also bring about a change in rights and obligations in cases where a change of residence to another state leads to the applicability of different laws. The provisions of the conflict-of-law rules are in many areas tied to the actual domicile or habitual residence and are therefore subject to change. If persons – individually, as a couple or as a family – move their domicile or residence to another state, this leads to a change of jurisdiction and so of the applicable law.[48] Legal positions

---

of the partnership is not recognised in another state. Registered partnerships do not fall within the scope of the Brussels II Regulation. Same-sex marriages ought to be included; whether the ECJ will do so, remains to be seen. See for an inclusion de lege ferenda, KOHLER, "Status als Ware: Bemerkungen zur europäischen Verordnung über das internationale Verfahrensrecht für Ehesachen", in: MANSEL (ed.), *Vergemeinschaftung des Europäischen Kollisionsrechts. Vorträge aus Anlaß des fünfzigjährigen Bestehens des Instituts für internationales und ausländisches Privatrecht der Universität zu Köln*, 2001, p. 41, 53.

[46] See AGELL, "The Division of Property upon Divorce from a European Perspective", in: POUSSON-PETIT (ed.), *Liber amicorum Marie-Thérèse Meulders-Klein. Droit comparé des personnes et de la famille*, 1998, p. 1, 7 et seq.; VERBEKE et al., "European Marital Property Law Survey 1988-1994", 3 *European Review of Private Law* 1995, 445.

[47] For the treatment of preliminary questions in public law, see MÜLLER-FREIENFELS, *Sozialversicherungs-, Familien- und Internationalprivatrecht und das Bundesverfassungsgericht*, 1984; SAMTLEBEN, "Zur kollisionsrechtlichen Vorfrage im öffentlichen Recht", *RabelsZ* 52 (1988) 466. For the treatment of preliminary questions in the law regulating the rights and duties of Community civil servants, see KOHLER, "Zum Kollisionsrecht internationaler Organisationen: Familienrechtliche Vorfragen im europäischen Beamtenrecht", *IPRax* 1994, 416; PIRRUNG, "Europabeamtenrecht und Scheidungsfolgen", in: GOTTWALD, JAYME, SCHWAB (eds.), *Festschrift für Dieter Henrich zum 70. Geburtstag*, 2000, p. 461.

[48] Even if nationality is used as a connecting factor, a change in nationality can lead to another law being applicable.

provided for under the law of one state may no longer exist in the new state. This is the case particularly if the law of the new state of residence ties different legal effects to a status. Registered partners, in particular, are in danger of losing their rights through a change of residence.[49] The same is true when a legal regime grants legal protection to factual relationships: for domestic partners who acquire communal property during the time of their cohabitation, as in Hungary[50] or Bosnia-Hercegovina,[51] or in cases where the marital property law is applied to domestic partners – as it is in Croatia to partners who have been living together for three years or more[52] – these effects may cease when the couple takes up residence in another state which does not recognise such automatic legal consequences of living together.

In child law, tying the applicable law to the mutable residence of the child can also have severe consequences: if, for example, unmarried parents have joint parental responsibilities – be it by operation of law as in Spain, Belgium or France,[53] or by declaration as in Germany[54] – the father may, if the residence of the child moves, e.g. to Austria[55] or Switzerland,[56] lose parental responsibility.[57] He may even be unable to regain parental responsibility if the attainment of joint parental responsibility through an administrative or court order requires not only the consideration of the child's welfare but the consent of both parents.[58] The same holds true for registered partners who take up residence in another state after having held joint parental responsibility in the Netherlands.[59] As full parental responsibility of the registered partner is not recognised outside the Netherlands, the partner may lose his or her rights.[60] A change of the child's

---

[49]   See DETHLOFF, "Registrierte Partnerschaften in Europa", *ZEuP* 2003 (to be published).
[50]   § 578/G para 1 Hungarian Civil Code.
[51]   Art. 278 Službeni list Socijalističke republike Bosne i Hercegovine (=Law governing the family) No. 21 of 9.6.1979 as amended on 20.12.1989.
[52]   Art. 262 Narodne novine (=Family Act) No. 162/98, Pos 1993 of 22.12.1998.
[53]   See *supra* note 35.
[54]   § 1626a para 1 no. 1 German Civil Code.
[55]   Sole custody of the mother, § 166 Austrian Civil Code.
[56]   Sole custody of the mother, Art. 298 para 1 Swiss Civil Code.
[57]   Thus in the case of variability of the connecting factor in accordance with Art. 2 of the Hague Convention of 1961 on the Protection of Minors or Art. 21 EGBGB (Introductory Law of the German Civil Code); a different view emerges from Art. 16 para 2, 3 of the Hague Convention of 1996 on the Protection of Children, whereby parental responsibility which exists under the law of the child's habitual residence subsists, regardless of whether it was attributed by operation of law, by agreement or unilateral act.
[58]   § 167 para 1 Austrian Civil Code; Art. 298a Swiss Civil Code.
[59]   Art. 253sa Dutch Civil Code.
[60]   Here, too, the risk of loss only exists in the case of variability of the connecting factor, see supra note 57.

residence may even lead to the loss of legal contact rights which were recognised by the law of the former country of residence.[61] The diverging substantive laws in the area of parental responsibilities for the children of unmarried couples can also lead to problems in instances in which the parents relied on the lack of legal rights and obligations: thus the unmarried mother of a child who moves to France, Belgium or Spain may suddenly find that the father now has joint parental responsibility with her even though she has had no contact with him for a long time.[62]

Moving one's residence can also endanger significant legal positions in the area of property law.[63] Thus in some countries the changes that can be made to a matrimonial property agreement once it has come into effect are limited.[64] Even a couple living in accordance with the legal matrimonial regime of their state of residence cannot be sure of its effects: thus, if a couple moves its place of residence to the United Kingdom, they must face the possibility that in case of divorce a substantially different distribution of marital property will be the consequence than the one envisaged under the original matrimonial property regime.[65]

---

[61] Differences exist within the various legal systems with respect to *e.g.* the question whether and under what circumstances someone other than a parent, such as a grandparent, stepparent or foster parent, has a right of contact with a child, see *e.g.* § 1685 German Civil Code; §§ 44a, 45 Norwegian Children Act (Law No. 7 of 8.4.1981).

[62] See for joint parental responsibility note 35. Since March 2002, French law no longer requires that the parents have cohabitated, Art. 372 para 1 French Civil Code.

[63] This is always the case if the law governing matrimonial property is mutable, as it is *e.g.* in Croatia (Art. 36 II Službeni list SFRJ No. 43/82 of 15.7.1982, adopted in Narodne novine No. 53/91 of 8.10.1991), where in the absence of a joint nationality, the connecting factor is the joint habitual residence. In Switzerland, moving the habitual residence even has a retroactive effect on the matrimonial property regime, Art. 55 Swiss Conflict of Laws Act. Swedish law stipulates that the new residence regulations apply once a person has been domiciled in the country for two years, § 4 para 2 of Act 1990:272 governing certain international questions concerning the matrimonial property regime. In most legal systems, however, the proper law applicable to matrimonial property is immutable in the absence of a choice of law, see *e.g.* Art. 15 EGBGB (Introductory Law of the German Civil Code), § 19 Austrian Conflict of Laws Act.

[64] In the Netherlands, a matrimonial property agreement cannot be amended until one year after the marriage was entered into, Art. 1:118 Dutch Civil Code. Both conclusion and amendment require the approval of a court, which examines whether a reasonable motive has been given, Art. 1:119 Dutch Civil Code.

[65] See Sec. 24 English Matrimonial Causes Act 1973; Sec. 8, 9 Scottish Family Law Act 1976, under which a court may order that the property or the right of use and enjoyment is transferred to the other spouse or to a child. The international jurisdiction of Scottish and English courts follows from the domicile, see Sec. 5 (2) and 7 (2) English Domicile and Matrimonial Proceedings Act 1973. The courts apply the law of the forum.

Finally, substantial differences in the law governing divorce and its legal consequences may cause a relationship, which was established and lived – possibly over a long period of time – in reliance on a particular legal regime, to have entirely different consequences following a change in residence. If, for example, a couple concluded a marriage in a country where divorce can be obtained against the will of the "innocent" party only after three or more years,[66] that party loses the protection it enjoyed when the couple moves to a country where divorce can be obtained against the will of the other party immediately, or after a very brief period of time.[67]

Divergent substantive law also has consequences for the law of maintenance, where the jurisdictional and conflict-of-law rules have already been unified by the Brussels Regulation and Hague Convention on Maintenance, respectively[68]: while a partner may enjoy lifelong financial security at the marital standard of living in the state in which the marriage was concluded, there may be no title to maintenance in the new state of residence,[69] or one which is severely limited in terms of duration, as is the case in Sweden.[70] Conversely, there may result an obligation towards support in the new state of residence where there was none before: for example, in Sweden there exists an obligation to support stepchildren.[71] The Spanish legal regime of Navarra stipulates a right of maintenance at the dissolution of a domestic

---

[66]  In Austria (§ 55 Marriage Act) and Luxembourg (Art. 230 Civil Code) the period is three years. The four-year period stipulated in Art. 114 Swiss Civil Code became the subject of a reform debate only one year after it came into force with effect from 1.1.2000, see FANKHAUSER, "Vom clean break zum fast break? Überlegungen zur geforderten Revision von Art. 114 ZGB", *FamPra.ch* 2002, 471. If none of the spouses was at fault, Greek law, too, requires a period of living apart for four years, Art. 1439 Greek Civil Code.

[67]  Even without separation, a marriage in Sweden can be divorced on unilateral application after a six-month period for reflection, Chapter 5 Sec. 2, 3 Äktenskapsbalken (Marriage Act) 1987:230. The international jurisdiction for divorces in Sweden and the application of Swedish law result from Chapter 2 Sec. 1 and 4 Act 1904:26 governing certain international legal relationships concerning marriage and guardianship.

[68]  The international jurisdiction of the courts of the new country of habitual residence is derived from Art. 5 (2) of the Brussels I Regulation or Art. 5 (2) of the Lugano Convention; the application of the law of the place of residence is derived from Art. 4 of the Hague Convention of 1973 on Maintenance. The harmonisation is, however, disrupted if the law applied to a divorce governs the maintenance obligations, Art. 8 of the Hague Convention of 1973 on Maintenance.

[69]  If no or only limited maintenance is granted in the case of divorce by fault, see *e.g.* §§ 66, 68a Austrian Marriage Act.

[70]  See JÄNTERÄ-JAREBORG, "Swedish report concerning the CEFL questionnaire on grounds for divorce and maintenance between former spouses", http://www2.law.uu.nl/priv/cefl, p. 23, 26.

[71]  Chapter 7 Sec. 5 Föräledrabalken (=Parents Act) 1949:381 of 10.6.1949, incorporated by Act 1978:853.

partnership,[72] as does the law of some Balkan states.[73] And finally, maintenance agreements may be invalid in the new country of residence because they fail the fair and reasonable test.[74]

### 2.2.3. Conclusion

If people, especially when changing their place of residence, lose their status or rights due to diverging family-law regimes in Europe, their habitual confidence in the authority of a certain legal regime could be undermined. In the area of family relationships there is a general interest in the continuity of legal ties. People live their relationships in reliance on the existence of a valid legal relationship, which creates certain rights and obligations.[75] A loss of status or legal position can as seriously harm these rightful expectations as the creation of new obligations.

### *2.3. Solution*

Let us now turn to the question of how the manifold problems of cross-border family ties arising from the divergence of national family laws can be resolved. Does a solution necessitate unification of the substantive law?

As we have seen, the loss of legal positions due to a lack of internationally uniform decision-making can be countered by creating a free movement

---

[72] Art. 5 (4) Ley foral 6/2000 of 3.7.2000 para la igualdad jurídica de parejas estables.

[73] See Art. 3, 226, 221 Narodne novine No. 162/98 Pos 1993 of 22.12.1998 (=Croatian Family Code); Art. 16 para 1, 293 para 1, 287 Serbian Marriage and Family Act of 22.4.1980 as amended on 30.5.1994; Art. 9, 261 para 1, 255 Službeni list SRCG Pos 121, No. 7/89 of 23.3.1989 (=Montenegro Family Code); Art. 14, 246 para 1, 239 Službeni list Socijalističke republike Bosne i Hercegovine (=Bosnian Family Code) No. 21 of 9.6.1979 as amended on 20.12.1989. From a comparative-law perspective, BATTES, "Unterhaltsansprüche aufgrund nichtehelichen Zusammenlebens", in: HOFMANN, MEYER-CORDING, WIEDEMANN (eds.), *Festschrift für Klemens Pleyer zum 65. Geburtstag*, 1986, p. 467.

[74] According to Italian case law, any renunciation of post-divorce maintenance that has been agreed outside the divorce proceedings is invalid, see PATTI, CARLEO, BELLISARIO, "Italian report concerning the CEFL questionnaire on grounds for divorce and maintenance between former spouses", at http://www2.law.uu.nl/priv/cefl, 40. In the Netherlands agreements governing post-divorce maintenance concluded before marriage are invalid, Hoge Raad, 7.3.1980, No. 11538, *NJ* 1980, No. 363; Hoge Raad, 12.1.1996, No. 8682, *NJ* 1996, No. 352. In Switzerland, too, renunciation agreements are subject to control by the court, *cf.* Art. 140 § 1 Swiss Civil Code, where invalidity of the renunciation of maintenance can be derived particularly from Art. 27 Swiss Civil Code, *cf.* HAUSHEER, SPYCHER, KOCHER, Brunner, *Handbuch des Unterhaltsrechts*, 1997, p. 607, para 11.84 *et seq.*; see also SCHWENZER, "Richterliche Kontrolle von Unterhaltsvereinbarungen zwischen Ehegatten", *ZEuP* 1997, 863.

[75] See KROPHOLLER, *Internationales Privatrecht*, 4th ed. 2001, § 21 II 3.

of decisions. So far, the Brussels I and II Regulations have only accomplished this in part, but more regulations could be created under which all family-law decisions, be they status decisions or other court decisions, are generally recognised.[76] If, however, the treatment by the conflict-of-law rules and thus the applicable law continues to vary, such recognition would create a large incentive for forum shopping.[77] Generally – even after unification of the law of jurisdiction – the courts of several states have international jurisdiction. Parties have the ability to choose the forum which applies the substantive law most in their favour. This gives an advantage to the economically stronger party, who is more easily able to afford in-depth legal advice regarding the conflict-of-law rules and the substantive laws of the available fora, as well as the additional costs of a legal dispute in another country. A race to the courthouse could well occur between the parties. This, too, may hamper the equality between the parties, since it is not always possible for both parties to sue[78]: although either party may bring an action in divorce or custody proceedings, in maintenance or distribution of property cases this is only possible if an action for a negative declaration can be brought. The danger of forum shopping is created not only by diverging national conflict-of-law provisions, but also – as mentioned earlier – in cases where the courts of a state, once they have affirmed that they have international jurisdiction, will always apply their own national law. A reduction of concurrent international jurisdictions cannot alleviate this problem without severely limiting access to the courts.

To prevent this situation arising, unification of the family laws of conflicts in Europe would be necessary: so much has been envisaged for the divorce law through the creation of Rome III.[79] Uniform rules on conflict of laws

---

[76]  See Proposal for Brussels IIa (note 41). Also planned are Regulations in the area of matrimonial property, wills and succession, see Action Plan of the Council and the Commission on how best to implement the provisions of the Treaty of Amsterdam on an area of freedom, security and justice – Text adopted by the Justice and Home Affairs Council of 3 December 1998, *OJ* 1999 C 19/1, 10, No. 41 (c).

[77]  See SIEHR, "„Forum shopping" im internationalen Rechtsverkehr", *ZfRV* 25 (1984) 124; SCHACK, *Internationales Zivilverfahrensrecht*, 3rd ed. 2002, para 220 *et seq.*

[78]  For a detailed treatment of this subject, see KROPHOLLER, Das Unbehagen am forum shopping, in: HENRICH, VON HOFFMANN (eds.), *Festschrift für Karl Firsching zum 70. Geburtstag*, 1985, p. 165.

[79]  See Action Plan of the Council and the Commission of 3 December 1998 (note 76). See also the Draft for Rome III by the Deutscher Rat für Internationales Privatrecht, cited by HENRICH, "Wenn Schweizer sich in Deutschland scheiden lassen", in: GEISER *et al.* (eds.), *Privatrecht im Spannungsfeld zwischen gesellschaftlichem Wandel und ethischer Verantwortung. Festschrift für Heinz Hausheer zum 65. Geburtstag*, 2002, p. 235, 241.

constitute the basis for rules of recognition and enforcement.[80] Brussels I was followed by Rome I[81]; the law of marital status and matrimonial property was expressly excluded from Brussels I due to the substantial differences in the conflict-of-law rules and the substantive law.[82] Only unified rules on conflict of laws can ensure internationally uniform decision-making, so that a status existing in one state, whether created by operation of law or based on a court decision, remains in effect in another.

A unification of the conflict-of-law rules would not, however, solve the above-mentioned problems of determining the applicable law. Such unification would make the determination of the relevant source of law less difficult than it is today. However, the problems associated with the variety of substantive laws (how, for example, to characterise legal terms) remain, as does the uncertainty in determining the content of the foreign law and its application along with the effort required to do so. If the current trend towards basing decisions increasingly on the law of habitual residence or domicile continues, it will less often be necessary to determine foreign law; nevertheless the necessity will remain.

Primarily, however, unification of the conflict-of-law rules cannot satisfactorily resolve this latter problem: even if the rules on conflict of laws are unified, a loss of legal positions can arise with a change in residence. Such a loss of legal position will always occur where the connecting factor is not immutable, but where the applicable law is based on the habitual residence in question. An immutable connection is not always possible, however. As far as the existence of a status or a family-law relationship is concerned, any rulings should be guided by the time of inception, so that the status or legal relationship remains in force even with a change in residence. A marriage or registered partnership should remain in effect, no changes should be made to parentage.[83] As far as the legal effects of a status or legal

---

[80]   As also argued by KOHLER, "Status als Ware: Bemerkungen zur europäischen Verordnung über das internationale Verfahrensrecht für Ehesachen", in: MANSEL (ed.), *Vergemeinschaftung des Europäischen Kollisionsrechts, Vorträge aus Anlaß des fünfzigjährigen Bestehens des Instituts für internationales und ausländisches Privatrecht der Universität zu Köln*, 2001, p. 41, 52.

[81]   EC Convention of 1980 on the Law Applicable to Contractual Obligations.

[82]   JENARD, "Report concerning the Convention on Jurisdiction and the Enforcement of Judgments in Civil and Commercial Matters", *OJ* 1979 C 59/1, 10.

[83]   On the matter of parentage, German law in Art. 19 EGBGB (Introductory Law to the German Civil Code) is different; a critical appraisal of the consequences of mutability is found in LOOSCHELDERS, "Alternative und sukzessive Anwendung mehrerer Rechtsordnungen nach dem neuen internationalen Kindschaftsrecht", *IPRax* 1999, 420, 423 *et seq.*; DÖRNER, "Probleme des neuen internationalen Kindschaftsrechts", in: GOTTWALD, JAYME (eds.), *Festschrift für Dieter Henrich zum 70. Geburtstag*, 2000, p. 120, 124 *et seq.*

relationship are concerned, however, integration into the state of residence – through the basing of decisions on the mutable factor of the current habitual residence – must be possible. Existing rights can only partially be upheld by the conflict-of-law rules, such as through a partial immutability or other conservation of vested rights.[84] Only in some areas, such as the matrimonial property regime, can the interest of the parties in integration be accommodated by an increase in choice-of-law opportunities.[85] Besides, even in this case a subsidiary connecting factor is required, a factor that applies in cases where there is no choice of law and which allows the relationship to be adapted to the new legal environment – albeit resulting in a loss of legal effects.

It is worthwhile noting, therefore, that a unification of the conflict-of-law rules – if properly shaped – can prevent a loss of status or of family-law relationship, but not the loss of their effects. This can only be achieved through a harmonisation of the substantive family law. Furthermore, only such a harmonisation can prevent the situation arising in which the person, who claims their rights in court before moving, is better off than the one who does not. The preferential treatment of those who carry their title in their briefcase can lead to an incentive – which is undesirable in terms of reducing the number of disputes – towards asserting one's rights in court early on, before changing residence.[86]

If the differences in family-law regimes only lead to these problems in cross-border family situations, it is worth asking whether it would be possible to limit oneself to the creation of a uniform substantive law for European or

---

[84] On partial mutability in the Hague Convention of 1978 on the Law Applicable to Matrimonial Property Regimes, see AGELL, "The Division of Property upon divorce from a European Perspective", in: POUSSON-PETIT (ed.), *Liber Amicorum Marie-Thérèse Meulders-Klein. Droit comparé des personnes et de la famille*, 1998, p. 1, 16 *et seq.*; see also the important new provision in Art. 16 para 2, 3 of the Hague Convention of 1996 on the Protection of Children, whereby existing parental responsibility subsists after a change of the habitual residence.

[85] See also DE GROOT, "Auf dem Weg zu einem europäischen (internationalen) Familienrecht", *ZEuP (Zeitschrift für Europäisches Privatrecht)* 2001, 617, 623 *et seq.*; in favour of a choice of law in the international regime of matrimonial property for this reason already, BEITZKE, "Zur Reform des Ehegüterrechts im deutschen Internationalprivatrecht", in: LAUTERBACH (ed.), *Vorschläge und Gutachten zur Reform des deutschen internationalen Eherechts*, 1962, p. 89, 90-91.

[86] See JÄNTERÄ-JAREBORG, "Marriage Dissolution in an Integrated Europe: The 1998 European Union Convention on Jurisdiction and the Recognition and Enforcement of Judgments in Matrimonial Matters (Brussels II Convention)", *Yearbook of Private International Law*, 1999, 1, 35.

international cases only.[87] One possibility would be the creation of a uniform European matrimonial property regime accessible only to binational couples or couples who do not possess the citizenship of the state in which they live.[88] To the extent that family-law relationships can be determined through private action, this kind of uniform law for cross-border cases seems feasible. Thus it would be, in my opinion, a commendable effort to harmonise the law in the area of matrimonial property law, where the differences are particularly pronounced, through the creation of a uniform regime. Such a regime should, however, be accessible to everyone – regardless of whether there is a foreign element involved or not. In the extensive area of mandatory law, by contrast, the creation of a uniform law governing exclusively cross-border cases does not represent a solution, as it would be difficult, in many cases, to define the cross-border criterion, especially before the fact. However, differences between the family-law regimes lead to severe problems particularly in this area. To resolve these difficulties it is necessary, if not to unify, then at least to harmonise the substantive law.

## 3. EUROPEANISATION OF THE LAW

Pressure towards a harmonisation of family law is also exerted by the law of the European Community.

### 3.1. Free Movement of People

The EC Treaty guarantees the free movement of people. The freedom of employees protected by Art. 39 ensures the mobility of those who are

---

[87]  For a uniform European private law for cross-border cases in economically oriented areas of law, DROBNIG, "Europäisches Zivilgesetzbuch – Gründe und Grundgedanken", in: MARTINY, WITZLEB (eds.), *Auf dem Wege zu einem Europäischen Zivilgesetzbuch*, 1999, p. 109, 122-123; DROBNIG, "Scope and general rules of a European civil code", 5 *European Review of Private Law* 1997, 489; TILMANN, "Eine Privatrechtskodifikation für die Europäische Gemeinschaft?", in: MÜLLER-GRAFF (ed.), *Gemeinsames Privatrecht in der Europäischen Gemeinschaft*, 2nd ed. 1999, p. 579; BROGGINI, "Was bedeutet heute gemeineuropäisches Vertragsrecht?", *ZfRV* 1997, 221, 229; on the various models for the harmonisation of private law, see also REMIEN, "Denationalisierung des Privatrechts in der Europäischen Union?", *ZfRV* 1995, 116, 121; for an optional European family law DE GROOT, "Auf dem Weg zu einem europäischen (internationalen) Familienrecht", *ZEuP* 2001, 617, 626-627.

[88]  For a property system for international marriages AGELL, "The Division of Property upon divorce from a European Perspective", in: POUSSON-PETIT (ed.), *Liber Amicorum Marie-Thérèse Meulders-Klein. Droit comparé des personnes et de la famille*, 1998, p. 1, 18 *et seq.*; VERBEKE, "Perspectives for an International Marital Contract", 8 *MJ* 2001, 189, 192 *et seq.*; see also BASEDOW, "Das BGB im künftigen europäischen Privatrecht: Der hybride Kodex", *AcP* 200 (2000) 445, 476.

---

working in a dependent position, while the freedom of establishment of Art. 43 ensures the mobility of those who are self-employed.

### 3.1.1. Prohibition of Restrictions

Both freedoms do more than simply prohibit any discrimination based on nationality. The rulings of the European Court of Justice recognise that both freedoms – like the other basic freedoms – establish a general prohibition on the imposition of restraints of any kind.[89] Differences between the legal regimes of the member states, which limit the exercise of the basic freedoms guaranteed by the EC Treaty or make the exercise thereof less attractive, constitute restrictions on the free movement of people, and as such are in need of justification.[90] First and foremost, legal differences must not hinder or prevent a citizen of the Union from leaving their home country in order to exercise an economic activity in another member state and to remain there.[91] While the Court has more closely defined the scope of the product freedoms, especially the freedom of the movement of goods,[92] the freedoms of the movement of people still lack such clarification.[93] One thing alone is clear: not every non-discriminatory

---

[89]  On the free movement of employees ECJ 15.12.1995 (Bosman) *ECR* 1995, I-4921, para 94 *et seq.*; see also ECJ 17.01.2000 (Graf) *ECR* 2000, I-493, para 18; on the freedom of establishment ECJ 31.3.1993 (Kraus) *ECR* 1993, I-1663, para 32 *et seq.*; ECJ 30.11,1995 (Gebhard) *ECR* 1995, I-4165, para 37; for more details on this perspective ROTH, "Die Niederlassungsfreiheit zwischen Beschränkungs- und Diskriminierungsverbot", in: SCHÖN (ed.), *Gedächtnisschrift für Brigitte Knobbe-Keuk*, 1997, p. 729, 731 *et seq.*; EVERLING, "Das Niederlassungsrecht in der EG als Beschränkungsverbot – Tragweite und Grenzen", in: SCHÖN (ed.), *Gedächtnisschrift für Brigitte Knobbe-Keuk*, 1997, p. 607, 608; JARASS, "Elemente einer Dogmatik der Grundfreiheiten II", *EuR* 2000, 705, 708 *et seq.* On the convergence of freedoms BEHRENS, "Die Konvergenz der wirtschaftlichen Freiheiten im europäischen Gemeinschaftsrecht", *EuR* 1992, 145; JARASS, "Elemente einer Dogmatik der Grundfreiheiten", *EuR* 1995, 202.

[90]  ECJ 31.3.1993 (Kraus) *ECR* 1993, I-1663, para 32 *et seq.*; ECJ 30.11.1995 (Gebhard) *ECR* 1995, I-4165, para 37.

[91]  ECJ 15.12.1995 (Bosman) *ECR* 1995, I-4921, para 96.

[92]  See ECJ 24.11.1993 (Keck) *ECR* 1993, I-6131, para 16-17; also subsequently, in particular, ECJ 02.6.1994 (Tankstation 't Heukske and Boermans) *ECR* 1994, I-2199, para 12-13; ECJ 29.6.1995 (Commission/Greece) *ECR* 1995, I-1621; ECJ 13.1.2000 (TK-Heimdienst Sass) *ECR* 2000, I-151, para 25 *et seq.*; a selection of the vast literature on these rulings: ROTH, "Freier Warenverkehr nach 'Keck'", in: HÜBNER, EBKE (eds.), *Festschrift für Bernhard Großfeld*, 1999, p. 929; MADURO, "The Sag of Article 30 EC Treaty: To Be Continued", 5 *MJ* 1998, 298; PICOD, "La nouvelle approche de la Cour de justice en matière d'entraves aux échanges", *RTDE* 1998, 169; WEATHERHILL, "Recent Case Law concerning the free movement of goods: mapping the frontier of market deregulation", 36 *C.M.L.Rev.* 1999, 51; DETHLOFF, *Europäisierung des Wettbewerbsrechts*, 2001, p. 150 *et seq.*

[93]  For a more detailed treatment of the scope of the freedoms DECKERT, SCHROEDER, note ECJ 27.1.2000, C-190/98, *JZ* 2001, 88; NETTESHEIM, "Die europarechtlichen Grundrechte auf wirtschaftliche Mobilität (Art. 48, 52)", *NVwZ* 1996, 342, 343 *et seq.*; RÖTHEL, note ECJ 13.4.2000, C-176/96, *EuZW* 2000, 379, 380.

provision of the receiving state – which makes taking a position and taking up residence in that state less attractive – constitutes a restriction on the free movement of people and as such is in need of justification. As with the other basic freedoms, a distinction must be made between provisions which deny or severely limit access to the market and those provisions whose limiting effects are merely incidental and uncertain.

### 3.1.2. Family-Law Provisions as Restrictions

The question therefore is whether family-law provisions could in any way adversely affect the freedom of movement. Here one must point out that the basic freedoms can impinge on all areas of the national law regimes affecting the exercise of the economic freedoms. Key private-law provisions are not exempted, just as family law is not.[94] The European Court of Justice has already, in the Konstantinidis decision,[95] found that status-law provisions can fall into the ambit of the basic freedoms, in this case, the freedom of establishment. That ruling concerned a, rather rare in family law, indirect discrimination based on citizenship.

Far more often one must ask whether restrictions on the free movement can be a result of the differences in the family-law regimes of member states. Whether, and to what extent, the differences of the laws prevent or hinder the access of employed or self-employed persons to the receiving state, is the decisive factor. In this context it has to be taken into account that the guarantee of free movement in EU law, as expressly stated by the ECR,[96] is to be interpreted in the light of the fundamental right to respect for a person's family life, which is protected by Art. 8 ECHR.[97] If the legal

---

[94] See KOHLER, "L'article 220 du traité CEE et les conflits de juridictions en matière de relations familiales: Premières réflexions", *Riv. dir. int. priv. proc.* 28 (1992) 221, 227 *et seq.*; BASEDOW, "Konstantinidis v. Bangemann – oder die Familie im Europäischen Gemeinschaftsrecht", *ZEuP* 1994, 197, 198-199; DE GROOT, "Auf dem Weg zu einem europäischen (internationalen) Familienrecht", *ZEuP* 2001, 617, 619 *et seq.* SCHACK, "Das neue Internationale Eheverfahrensrecht in Europa", *RabelsZ* 65 (2001) 615, 618, by contrast denies the market relevance of family law as long as the trade in spouses is illegal.

[95] ECJ 30.3.1993 *ECR* 1993, I-1191; *cf.* PINTENS, "Von Konstantinidis bis Grant – Europa und das Familienrecht", *ZEuP* 1998, 843; PINTENS, "Rechtsvereinheitlichung und Rechtsangleichung im Familienrecht. Eine Rolle für die Europäische Union?", *ZEuP* 1998, 670; see also ECJ 2.12.1997 (Dafeki) *ECR* 1997, I-6761.

[96] ECJ 11.7.2002 (Carpenter) *ECR* 2002, I-6279, para 40, note MAGER, *JZ* 2003, 204; ECJ 25.7.2002 (MRAX) *ECR* 2002, I-6591; see TOGGENBURG, "Familienangehörige aus Drittstaaten: Der Schutz des Familienlebens als trompe l'œil-Tor zum Binnenmarkt?", *ELR* 2002, 319.

[97] European Convention of 1950 for the Protection of Human Rights and Fundamental Freedoms.

differences between states lead to a loss of status, this definitely impairs the freedom of movement. Thus the loss of status or of a family relationship for members of non-EU countries could result in their being refused residence in the receiving country. As a result, family life for such a person would be frustrated and the exercise of free movement impeded.[98] Such a loss of status, however – as pointed out earlier – can be avoided through a unification of the international laws of jurisdiction and conflicts. But is it not the case that access to the receiving state may also be hampered if an existing legal relationship has entirely different legal effects in the receiving state than it does in the state of origin? If rights, which existed in the state of origin, are lost in the receiving state or entirely new obligations are created? I have already drawn attention to the fact that serious economic consequences can arise as a result of the loss or creation of support obligations or compensation claims, and to the potentially serious impact on personal relations arising from changes in parental responsibility or contact rights. The decision to settle or to pursue an employment in another member state is influenced by a large number of factors.[99] The authority of a particular legal regime, according to which a family-law relationship with particular effects exists between the parties, is a factor of some importance in this decision. That a transfer fee needs to be paid if a football player transfers to another club – as in the European Court of Justice's Bosman ruling[100] – is likely to restrict his access to the receiving state just as much as does the fact that the same football player following his divorce is required – as would not be the case in his home state – to make a large compensation payment. The effects of the existing, substantial differences in many areas of the substantive family law are in fact certain and direct enough to substantially inhibit the access of both employed and self-employed persons to the market of the receiving state. The greater the differences are, the more likely they are to have a restricting effect. The possibility of a choice of law – which exists in some areas – does not, in my mind, remove such restrictions.[101] After all, even non-

---

[98]   See STALFORD, "The citizenship status of children in the European Union", 8 *The International Journal of Children's Rights* 2000, 101, 105 *et seq.*

[99]   For the socio-economic, public-policy, legal and socio-cultural factors and language barriers influencing mobility, see HANTRAIS, "What is a Family or Family Life in the European Union", in: GUILD (ed.), *The Legal Framework and Social Consequences of Free Movement of Persons in the European Union*, 1999, p. 19, 28-29.

[100]   ECJ 15.12.1995 (Bosman) *ECR* 1995, I-4921.

[101]   Thus especially BASEDOW, "Un droit commun des contrats pour le marché commun", *Revue internationale de droit comparé* 50 (1998) 1, 12-13; LURGER, *Grundfragen der Vereinheitlichung des Vertragsrechts in der Europäischen Union*, 2002, p. 273 *et seq.*; ECJ 24.1.1991 (Alsthom Atlantique) *ECR* 1991, I-107 takes a different view.

mandatory rules of law have mandatory legal effect in a dispute where an autonomous agreement of the parties is absent.

### 3.1.3. Justification Through Public Interest

The restrictions on free movement arising from substantial legal differences are only permissible if they are justified by public interest, are not disproportionate[102] and are furthermore in agreement with the fundamental rights.[103] That they are necessary for the coherence of the system, as has been assumed for provisions in the area of social security law,[104] can hardly be claimed for family law. At best, a few provisions will be suitable, necessary and proportionate in order to fulfil the mandatory requirements in the public interest.

### *3.2. Conclusion*

A harmonisation of the substantive law would enable us to avoid such restrictions on the free movement of people, which are contrary to the EC Treaty. Moreover, such harmonisation would also take into account the general freedom of movement guaranteed by Art. 18 paragraph 1 of the EC Treaty, which applies to all union citizens independent of economic activity.[105] In a Europe of citizens, people are no longer considered primarily as elements of factor mobility within the single market.[106] Thus the relevance of family relationships and of the family-law provisions shaping them is gaining in importance for the realisation of Freedom and Equality in Europe.

---

[102] See *e.g.* ECJ 7.7.1976 (Watson and Belmann) *ECR* 1976, II-1185, para 21-22; ECJ 18.5.1989 (Commission/Germany) *ECR* 1989, 1263, para 20; ECJ 15.12.1995 (Bosman) *ECR* 1995, I-4921, para 104.

[103] As already stated in ECJ 28.10.1975 (Rutili) *ECR* 1975, 1219, para 32; and, more recently, ECJ 11.7.2002 (Carpenter) *ECR* 2002, I-6279, para 40.

[104] See ECJ 28.1.1992 (Bachmann) *ECR* 1992, I-249, para 21 *et seq*; ECJ 28.1.1992 (Commission/Belgium) *ECR* 1992, I-305, para 14 *et seq.*; ECJ 27.6.1996 (Asscher) *ECR* 1996, I-3089, para 56 *et seq.*

[105] See ECJ 17.9.2002 (Baumbast) C-413/99, http://www.curia.eu.int/jurisp/cgi-bin/form.pl?lang=en; on the recent developments in the area of the right to freedom of movement HÜHN, "Freizügigkeit und Unionsbürgerschaft nach Art. 18 EG", *ELR (European Law Reporter)* 2002, 358.

[106] A critical view of the market orientation of European family policies: McGLYNN, "A Family Law for the European Union?", in: SHAW (ed.), *Social Law and Policy in an Evolving European Union*, 2000, p. 223.

## 4. FAMILY LAW AND CULTURAL IDENTITY

Now that we have seen how the growing integration of Europe necessitates a unified law in the area of family law, I would like in conclusion to explore the question of whether family law, which by its nature is rooted in the national legal cultures, prevents such unity. Some have even objected to the unification of those areas of law which are more economically oriented – such as contract law, the general law of obligations or tort law – arguing that private law is far too historically, politically and, most importantly of all, culturally anchored in the societies of the different states.[107] A unified private law would therefore, so runs the argument, result in a loss of cultural integrity. Does this also – or perhaps even particularly – apply to family law?

It is true that law has always a cultural context. Neither the economically oriented private law nor family law can be viewed as independent of culturally shaped values or ideals. It embodies certain concepts, for example, of just distribution, the role of the state in the enforcement of law, or the balance between freedom and commitment.[108] This cultural anchor, however, poses no obstacle to the harmonisation of family law.[109] In the area of family law, in particular, there are religious, historical and cultural roots common to Europe. From a historical perspective, parts of family law, at least, especially the law of marriage, have tended to be uniform throughout Europe.[110] In this area more than in others it would be possible to talk about a ius commune based on canon law.[111] It was only after the secularisation of family law that the law became fragmented and displayed an increasing variety in national laws.

---

[107]   LEGRAND, "The impossibility of Legal Transplants", 4 *MJ* 1997, 111, 116 *et seq.*; LEGRAND, "Against a European Civil Code", 60 *Modern Law Review* 1997, 44; COLLINS, "European Private Law and the Cultural Identity of States", 3 *European Review of Private Law* 1995, 353, 363.

[108]   See LURGER, *Grundfragen der Vereinheitlichung des Vertragsrechts in der Europäischen Union*, 2002, p. 34.

[109]   PINTENS, "Grundgedanken und Perspektiven einer Europäisierung des Familien- und Erbrechts – Teil 1", *FamRZ* 2003, 329, 351-352; a different opinion is expressed in GAUDEMET-TALLON, "Droit privé et droit communautaire", *Revue du marché commun et de l'Union européenne* 2000, 228, 240.

[110]   COING, *Europäisches Privatrecht*, vol. 1, 1985, p. 224; MÜLLER-FREIENFELS, *Ehe und Recht*, 1962, p. 13; ANTOKOLSKAIA, "Would the Harmonisation of Family Law in Europe Enlarge the Gap between the Law in the Books and the Law in Action?", *FamPra.ch* 2002, 261, 278.

[111]   See ANTOKOLSKAIA, "The "better law" Approach and the Harmonisation of Family Law", in this book, p. 159 *et seq.*; a general appraisal of the notion of a European ius commune COING, *Europäisches Privatrecht*, vol. 1, 1985, p. 7 *et seq.*; ZIMMERMANN, "Das römisch-kanonische ius commune als Grundlage europäischer Rechtseinheit", *JZ* 1992, 8; VAN CAENEGEM, *An historical introduction to private law*, 1992, p. 45 *et seq.*

That the process of secularisation shows many similarities, is of far greater importance than these common historical and religious roots. The trend is going in the same direction, though at different speeds.[112] This development is marked most of all by an increasing liberalisation of divorce, equal rights for women and men, less discrimination against children born out of wedlock and their parents, and the growing importance of the child's welfare and the recognition of the rights of children.[113] On the rise is joint custody for children after divorce,[114] and there is a growing tendency to give legal relevance to factual relationships – between partners as well as between parents and children.[115] Thus, family law in Europe today is based on a number of common basic principles. Overall one can therefore find – in spite of substantial differences in certain aspects – a convergence of family-law regimes which is an expression of concurring basic values. These basic values have found their legal expression predominantly in the European Convention on Human Rights, which in the past decades has had a sustained influence on the development of national family-law regimes.[116] They also find expression today in the Charter of Fundamental

---

[112] ANTOKOLSKAIA, "The Process of Modernisation of Family Law in Eastern and Western Europe: Difference in Timing, Resemblance in Substance", 4.2 *EJCL* 2000, 2, http://ejcl.org/ejcl/42/art42-1.html; AGELL, "Legal Policy, Technique and Research in Family Law – Some Comparative Aspects", 8 *BYU Journal of Public Law* 1993, 145; BRADLEY, "Convergence in Family Law: Mirrors, Transplants and Political Economy", 6 *MJ* 1999, 127, 130 *et seq.*

[113] See *inter alia* JAYME, "Die Entwicklung des europäischen Familienrechts", *FamRZ* 1981, 221, 223 *et seq.*; WILLEKENS, "Long Term Developments in Family Law in Western Europe: an Explanation", in: EEKELAAR, NHLAPO (eds.), *The Changing Family. International Perspectives on the Family and Family Law*, 1998, p. 47; MÜLLER-FREIENFELS, "The Unification of Family Law", in: MÜLLER-FREIENFELS, *Familienrecht im In- und Ausland*, vol. 1, 1978, p. 79, 107 *et seq.*; BOELE-WOELKI, "The Road towards a European Family Law", 1.1 *EJCL* 1997, 8 *et seq.*, http://ejcl.org/ejcl/11/art11-1.html; see also PINTENS, "Die Europäisierung des Erbrechts", *ZEuP* 2001, 628, 635 *et seq.*

[114] HENRICH, "Entwicklungslinien des deutschen Kindschaftsrechts im europäischen Kontext", in: SCHWAB, HENRICH (eds.), *Entwicklungen des europäischen Kindschaftsrechts*, 1996, p. 187, 194-195.

[115] For an intensive treatment of this subject SCHWENZER, *Vom Status zur Realbeziehung*, 1987, p. 171, 253 *et seq.*; for the Scandinavian countries AGELL, "Is there one system of Family Law in the Nordic Countries?", 3 *European Journal of Law Reform* 2001, 313, 315 *et seq.*

[116] On the importance of the ECHR in family law KILLERBY, "Family Law in Europe", in: POUSSON-PETIT (ed.), *Liber Amicorum Marie-Thérèse Klein. Droit comparé des personnes et de la famille*, 1998, p. 351, 355 *et seq.*; HOHNERLEIN, "Konturen eines einheitlichen europäischen Familien- und Kindschaftsrechts. Die Rolle der Europäischen Menschenrechtskonvention", *Eur. Legal Forum* 2000, 252; Kuchinke, "Über die Notwendigkeit, ein gemeineuropäisches Familien- und Erbrecht zu schaffen", in: KÖBLER, HEINZE (eds.), *Europas universale rechtsordnungspolitische Aufgabe im Recht des dritten Jahrtausends. Festschrift für Alfred Söllner zum 70. Geburtstag*, 2000, p. 589, 592 *et seq.*; on the effect of the ECHR on German law ELLGER, "Europäische Menschenrechtskonvention und deutsches Privatrecht", *RabelsZ* 63 (1999) 625; KOPPER-REIFENBERG, *Kindschaftsrechtsreform und Schutz des Familienlebens nach Art. 8 EMRK*, 2001.

Rights.[117] There is therefore a foundation of a common legal culture in Europe, which allows us to speak of a European cultural identity in this respect.[118] This common European legal and cultural foundation exists despite the general rift between Common Law and Civil Law, especially as this rift does not seem to be as wide in family law as it is in other areas of private law.[119]

Moreover, in most European states the significance, for family law, of – sometimes-differing – political values and morals is on the decline. Family law is no longer, as was much more the case in the past, shaped predominantly by certain basic convictions: most European countries increasingly take social realities into consideration.[120] Family law is now primarily concerned with solving comparable social problems – increasingly, though still far from sufficiently – on the basis of interdisciplinary studies.[121] But even if the social reality in Europe is not nearly as homogenous as it was in the Nordic countries when their family law was coordinated,[122] at least the underlying conditions in the European industrial states are comparable. Thus not only are the economic and social circumstances increasingly similar, the demographic trends of decreasing birth rates and increasing life expectancy are also converging. In spite of certain regional variations and time differentials, the forms of family life across Europe are changing substantially: the number of marriages is in decline; the number of factual

---

[117]    Charter of Fundamental Rights of the European Union, *OJ* 2000 C 364/1, 18.12.2000, http://www.europarl.eu.int/charter/pdf/text_de.pdf. See inter alia LENAERTS, DE SMITJER, "A "Bill of Rights" for the European Union", 38 *C.M.L.Rev.* 2001, 273, 289; McGLYNN, "Families and the European Union Charter of Fundamental Rights: progressive change or entrenching the status quo?", 26 *E.L.Rev.* 2001, 582; GIJZEN, "The Charter: A Milestone for Social Protection in Europe?", 8 *MJ* 2001, 33.

[118]    See for an emerging European identity as one of multiple identities LAYTON-HENRY, "Insiders And Outsiders in the European Union: The Search for a European Identity and Citizenship", in: GUILD (ed.), *The Legal Framework and Social Consequences of Free Movement Persons in the European Union*, 1999, p. 49.

[119]    On the differences between common law and civil law in family law AGELL, "Legal Policy, Technique and Research in Family Law – Some Comparative Aspects", 8 *BYU Journal of Public Law* 1993, 145, 146 *et seq.*; on the problems of harmonising law of common-law and civil-law systems in general ZIMMERMANN, "Das römisch-kanonische ius commune als Grundlage europäischer Rechtseinheit", *JZ* 1992, 8, 13 *et seq.*; ZIMMERMANN, "Heard melodies are sweet, but those unheard are sweeter...", *AcP* 193 (1993) 121, 123 *et seq.*

[120]    See MARTINY, "Europäisches Familienrecht – Utopie oder Notwendigkeit"?, *RabelsZ* (1995) 419, 439; on private law in general LURGER, *Grundfragen der Vereinheitlichung des Vertragsrechts in der Europäischen Union*, 2002, p. 213.

[121]    As already stated in MÜLLER-FREIENFELS, "The Unification of Family Law" in: MÜLLER-FREIENFELS (ed.), *Familienrecht im In- und Ausland*, vol. 1, 1978, p. 79, 101 *et seq.*

[122]    See AGELL, "Is There One System of Family Law in the Nordic Countries?", 3 *European Journal of Law Reform* 2001, 313.

---

partnerships and extramarital births is rising. Divorce rates are increasing, as are the consequent numbers of single parent and reconstituted families. Furthermore, families are increasingly reduced from three to two generations.[123]

I would like to point out two further important trends for the shaping of family law; both are in evidence in all European states, but differ to a large degree in terms of their extent. First, gainful employment amongst women has increased not only in general,[124] but in particular among women with children.[125] There are, however, considerable differences in this area, which are, of course, significant for the law of maintenance and marital property. On the one hand, in countries like Denmark or Greece childcare has virtually no influence on the level of employment among women.[126] On the other hand, in countries like Germany or the Netherlands only slightly more than 60% of the women who care for children are gainfully employed, whereas 80% of those who do not care for children are gainfully employed.[127] In these countries the employment situation of a woman caring for a child is substantially affected: in the Netherlands almost 80% of women who care for children and are in gainful employment work part-time; in Germany the corresponding figure is just above 50%.[128]

Secondly, a functional shift has occurred across Europe from the family to societal institutions. Of course here, too, the degree to which social security benefits or childcare facilities have replaced or complemented familial obligations differs enormously.[129] One of the causes of this is diverging family policies in different countries, which of course are in turn

---

[123] For more details on these developments in general HANTRAIS, LETABLIER, *Families and Family Policies in Europe*, 1996, p. 15 *et seq.*

[124] The employment rate of women increased by about 5% between 1990 and 2000, see EUROSTAT (ed.), *The social situation in the European Union 2002*, p. 25.

[125] The number of double-income households with children increased substantially in all member states between 1992 and 2000; they now account for 60% of all gainfully employed households with children, *cf.* FRANCO, WINQVIST, "Women and men reconciling work and family life", in: Eurostat (ed.), *Statistics in focus No. 3-9/2002. Population and social conditions*, p. 2.

[126] EUROPEAN COMMISSION, EUROSTAT (ed.), *The life of women and men in Europe – A statistical portrait. Data from the years 1980-2000*, p. 59, table 67, employment of women aged between 20-49 years who had children in their care or no children in their care, date: 1998.

[127] *Op. cit.* (note 126).

[128] *Op. cit.* (note 126) p. 64, table 74, Employment of women aged between 20-49 years in part-time and full-time employment, date: 1998.

[129] See for the recent trends in state support for families in Europe GAUTHIER, *The State and the Family. A Comparative Analysis of Family Policies in Industrialized Countries*, 1996, p. 163 *et seq.* (cash benefits), 172 *et seq.* (maternity und parental leave benefits), 180 *et seq.* (child-care facilities).

caused by differences in the political, social and cultural traditions and in economic circumstances.[130] When taking a long-term view, however, it is likely that a convergence in this area will come about – taking also into account the influence of the family policy of the European Union, whose aim it is to improve the compatibility of family and gainful employment.[131] Until this has been achieved, any harmonisation would have to take into account these differences by making any provisions suitably flexible.

I mentioned earlier that family law today is predominantly shaped by the given social reality, which is in many ways similar throughout Europe. This excludes, of course, a few areas that are of particular sensitivity from a political or religious point of view. Questions such as the legal recognition of same-sex partnerships or the attitude towards modern medical reproduction techniques are influenced predominantly by moral and ethical convictions, which differ substantially from country to country. Even in these sensitive areas certain common trends can be observed, as is illustrated by the widespread creation of new legal institutions of registered partnership. The variety of national provisions in these ideological battlefields is exceptionally large.[132] The result is an increase in cross-border relationships through the creation of "registration havens" or "fertility tourism". In these cases, in particular, – as I have already indicated – the large diversity of provisions severely impedes mobility.[133] Harmonisation in such areas would thus be especially difficult to achieve, the gain of – at least – partial harmonisation correspondingly great.

Generally, however, family law is concerned with finding solutions to the many questions of couple- and parent-child-relationships, which adequately reflect real life. Here, in particular, comparative legal studies, which are a prerequisite of any harmonisation, are of inestimable value.[134] It is

---

[130]  For a discussion using Sweden as an example WILLEKENS, "Long Term Developments in Family Law in Western Europe: an Explanation", in: EEKELAAR, NHLAPO (eds.), *The Changing Family*, 1998, p. 47, 68-69.

[131]  HANTRAIS, LETABLIER, *Families and Family Policies in Europe*, 1996, p. 116 *et seq.*

[132]  See BASEDOW, HOPT, KÖTZ, DOPFFEL (eds.), *Die Rechtsstellung der gleichgeschlechtlichen Lebensgemeinschaften*, 2000; COESTER, "Same-Sex Relationships: A Comparative Assessment of Legal Developments Across Europe", *FamPra.ch* 2002, 747, 751 *et seq.*; DETHLOFF, "Registrierte Partnerschaften in Europa", *ZEuP* 2003 (to be published); PINTENS, "Grundgedanken und Perspektiven einer Europäisierung des Familien- und Erbrechts – Teil 1", *FamRZ* 2003, 329, 335-336.

[133]  See *supra* 2.2. For the Community Law aspects of modern medical reproduction techniques FLAUSS-DIEM, "Insémination post mortem, droit anglais et droit communautaire", in: POUSSON-PETIT (ed.), *Liber Amicorum Marie-Thérèse Meulders-Klein. Droit comparé des personnes et de la famille*, 1998, p. 217, 223.

[134]  KÖTZ, "Alte und neue Aufgaben der Rechtsvergleichung", *JZ* 2002, 257, 259 *et seq.*

important to realise that harmonising family law in Europe does not entail the tearing of foreign systems from a cultural context that is very different and subsequently transplanting them.[135] The aim is, rather, to start from common fundamental values and to discover, through a process of cross-fertilisation, the most appropriate solutions.

## 5.  CONCLUSION

Summing up, it can be said that a harmonisation of family law in Europe – whether on the level of the European Union or the Council of Europe[136] – would represent a great gain: in cross-border relationships the enormous difficulties and costs involved in the application of law would cease. People could rely on the continuity of their family relationships when changing their residence. Free movement in Europe would no longer be hampered through the substantial differences in the substantive law. To achieve this, full unification of the law is not necessary, but harmonisation of family law is. An important contribution to this process can and must be made by academia. Academia alone can lay the foundations to ensure that one day a European Civil Code might encompass family law. European families need a harmonised European family law.

---

[135]  On the application of mirror- and transplant-theories in family law BRADLEY, "Convergence in Family Law: Mirrors, Transplants and Political Economy", 6 *MJ* 1999, 127.
[136]  In detail see PINTENS, "Europeanisation of Family Law", in this book, p. 3 *et seq.*

# A FAMILY LAW FOR EUROPE? SOVEREIGNTY, POLITICAL ECONOMY AND LEGITIMATION

DAVID BRADLEY

## 1. INTRODUCTION

The Commission on European Family Law is an academic initiative. Its declared objective is to launch a pioneering theoretical and practical exercise in relation to harmonisation of family law in Europe.[1] In fact, in the Commission itself, this spirit of analysis and investigation slips into an assumption that harmonisation can be achieved. It has been stated that the Commission will identify the "common core" of legal policy and there are indications that it will also propose models of "better" family law.[2] And the working method of the Commission is to isolate specific issues: it has selected divorce and maintenance between former spouses as the initial project, and sought information on law and reform proposals from European jurisdictions through an extensive questionnaire.[3]

Almost 25 years before the Commission was established, Kahn-Freund gave an uncompromising assessment of prospects for this type of venture in a colloquium examining "New Perspectives for a Common Law of Europe."[4] He judged the attempt to construct a European family law a "hopeless quest" and implied that difficulties would remain.[5] His overall conclusion was that projects of this type appeared to involve the work "more of a Sisyphus than a Hercules."[6]

Kahn-Freund not only regarded construction of a pan-European family code a practical impossibility, but also opposed development of common

---

[1] Commission on European Family Law <http://www2.law.uu.nl/priv/cefl/index1.asp>.
[2] BOELE-WOELKI, "Comparative Research Based Drafting of Principles of European Family Law", in M. FAURE *et al.* (eds.), *Towards a European Ius Commune in Legal Education and Research* (Antwerp: Intersentia, 2002) 171, 180.
[3] *Ibid.* 182.
[4] KAHN-FREUND, "Common Law and Civil Law – Imaginary and Real Obstacles to Assimilation", in M. CAPPELLETTI (ed.), *New Perspectives for a Common Law of Europe* (Leyden: Sijthoff, 1978) 138.
[5] *Ibid.* 141.
[6] *Ibid.* 142.

principles of private law which were not required for functioning of an economic community. He placed family law in this category. In general, his view was that harmonisation was unnecessary for the political, economic and cultural future of Europe.[7]

This was not a parochial position. Kahn-Freund argued that the strength of Europe lay in the diversity of nation states and that this should continue to be recognised in distinct legal traditions.[8] Resolution of problems caused by divergence in family laws should, he suggested, be achieved through private international law.[9] Moreover, he considered that the United States, Canada and the United Kingdom, demonstrated that a successful economic or political community, or close federation, did not require harmonisation of either family law, or general legal systems.[10]

The environment in which the Commission on European Family Law is working has changed significantly since this negative assessment. "Top down" pressure at the European level is clearly discernible. The European Parliament has re-iterated its support for a code of private law.[11] There is growing concern within the Council over differences in national family laws undermining free movement.[12] The Council has referred to establishment of an area "of freedom, security and justice."[13] It is also significant that a programme to identify "best practice" in European welfare policy is underway.[14] Welfare models, like family law, are commonly viewed as closely associated with national identity.

This momentum to link family law with broader objectives[15] has been accompanied by direct intervention from European institutions on key aspects of legal policy. In Goodwin v UK,[16] the European Court of Human Rights recast the foundations of the institution of marriage. The Brussels II initiative in private international law includes divorce proceedings and

---

[7]   *Ibid.* 139-142.
[8]   *Ibid.* 168.
[9]   *Ibid.* 141.
[10]  *Ibid.* 141-2.
[11]  EC OJ 1989 C158, 400; OJ 1994 C205, 518.
[12]  Draft Council Report 13017/01 of 29.10.2001 adopted on 16.11.2001.
[13]  *Ibid.*
[14]  TELÒ, "Governance and Government in the European Union," in M.J. RODRIGUES (ed.), *The New Knowledge Economy in Europe* (UK, Cheltenham: Edward Elgar, 2002) 242 *et seq.*
[15]  See McGLYNN, "A Family Law for the European Union", in J. SHAW (ed.), *Social Law and Policy* (Oxford: Hart, 2000) 223; McGLYNN, "The Europeanisation of family law" (2001) 13 *CFLQ* 35.
[16]  [2002] 2 FLR 518 (ECHR).

---

was implemented by EC regulation.[17] And although Article 13 EC has no direct application to the legal status of same-sex relationships, it at least raises an inference that this status should be improved. In fact, this argument has been advanced in some jurisdictions.[18] More broadly, the Charter of Fundamental Rights of the European Union has the potential to make a wide-ranging impact on legal policy applied to domestic relationships.[19]

Accompanying what appears to be the somewhat inexorable "Europeanisation" of family law, is the perception, in some quarters, that "bottom up" convergence of legal policy is occurring. For example, Pintens and Vanwinckelen, strong advocates of harmonisation, emphasise common tendencies in European family laws, arising spontaneously between jurisdictions themselves, albeit with limitations attributable to different legal traditions.[20]

This paper responds to the call from the Commission on European Family Law to examine the project which it has initiated. In doing so, the paper introduces a perspective which is not particularly well developed in writing on harmonisation. It is important to move beyond abstract analysis and generalised accounts of family laws, not least in relation to assumptions about convergence. The paper therefore includes three case studies to support its principal arguments. The general aim is to counter the view that convergence and barriers to harmonisation can be considered primarily, if not exclusively, from a legal standpoint. It is imperative in this particular field of law to adopt a broader approach. The studies in this paper are detailed and are intended to provide a chronology of family law: to look back to the immediate past; to examine contemporary developments; and to anticipate future legal policy. The purpose is to emphasise an issue of paramount importance in the debate on harmonisation, i.e. the continued influence of political and institutional factors on the evolution and structure of laws regulating domestic relationships.

---

[17]    McELEAVY, "The Brussels II Regulation: How the European Community has moved into family law" (2002) *51 ICLQ* 883.

[18]    SCAPPUCCI, "Italy Walking a Tightrope Between Stockholm and the Vatican", in R. WINTEMUTE and M. ANDENÆS (eds.), *Legal Recognition of Same-Sex Relationships* (Oxford: Hart, 2001) 519, 525.

[19]    For a sceptical view, see McGLYNN, "Families and the European Union Charter of Fundamental Rights" (2001) 26 *E.L.Rev.* 582.

[20]    W. PINTENS and K. VANWINCKELEN, *Casebook: European Family Law* (Leuven: Leuven UP, 2001) 13 *et seq.*

David Bradley

It is not an objective here to argue the merits of a European family law, nor is the intention to consider what new competence is required to establish this.[21] The paper focuses on three issues. First, why was harmonisation judged so impossible by Kahn-Freund, and what barriers remain today, so far as European jurisdictions themselves are concerned? In general, what is at stake for nation states in the Commission's project? The argument in this paper is that family law is a component of political economy – the concept is outlined below.[22] A case study will demonstrate that this was readily apparent when Kahn-Freund made his forthright assessment a quarter of a century ago.

The second issue examined in the paper is the degree of convergence of family laws and whether earlier obstacles to a uniform law are receding. In the recent past, family law was considered unsuitable for inclusion in a European Civil Code.[23] However, if convergence is in fact occurring, harmonisation is not more problematic than other areas of legal policy – if anything it is somewhat easier.

This paper argues that the convergence thesis is an over-simplification. To support this, it includes a study of contemporary legal policy in the Nordic countries. Nordic co-operation has been judged remarkably successful by some commentators.[24] Developments in the Nordic region may, perhaps, be considered a prototype for a European family law,[25] not least as the Helsinki Agreement of 1962 provided for the greatest possible uniformity in private law.[26] This paper will indicate that there is, in fact, significant divergence in Nordic family law systems and that, to date at least, Nordic co-operation does not provide a model for broader harmonisation.

The third issue examined here is the problem of legitimation, used in this context to mean the justification advanced for putting forward particular laws.[27] On what basis can the Commission on European Family Law support

---

[21] See LOOKOFSKY, "The Harmonization of Private and Commercial Law" 39 *Sc.St.L.* 111, 114-116.
[22] Pp. 69-71.
[23] HONDIUS, "Towards a European Civil Code" in A.S. HARTKAMP *et al.* (eds.), *Towards a European Civil Code* (Dordrecht, Nijhoff, 1994. 1st edn.) 1, 4.
[24] See p. 81 below.
[25] K. ZWEIGERT and H. KÖTZ, *An Introduction to Comparative Law* (Oxford: Clarendon Press, 1998) 284.
[26] Art. 4, Treaty of Co-operation between Denmark, Finland, Iceland, Norway and Sweden; BERNITZ, "Nordic Legislative Cooperation in the New Europe" 39 *Sc.St.L.* 29, 33.
[27] For a broader approach, see SCHMID, "Legitimacy Conditions for a European Civil Code" (2001) 8 *MJ* 277.

68

Intersentia

its recommendations? This question will remain regardless of the status of the body proposing harmonisation; whether its proposals are intended to be a code or non-binding, general principles; and whether or not it relies on opinions from respondents in particular jurisdictions.

Convergence in legal policy is not only considered, in some quarters, as holding out prospects of success for the Commission, but is also seen as solving problems of legitimation by providing models of "better" law. The position in this paper is that the concepts of a "common core" of legal policy and "better" family law have little, if any, validity. A further case study will demonstrate this in relation to the changing agenda of family law.

In conclusion, the paper notes the absence of precedents for the attempt to introduce a family law for Europe and considers the significance of the initiative from the Commission on European Family Law.

## 2. 'DEEPLY EMBEDDED" FAMILY LAW

### 2.1. Political Economy and Sovereignty

The problems involved in harmonising legal policy applied to domestic relationships are commonly seen as more acute, than in other fields. Family law appears to lack even initial criteria for unification, comparable to commercial practice or efficiency for contract law. And whereas proposals to develop a European system of securities regulation[28] require reconciliation of particular types of financial market, family law is commonly presented as reflecting deeply embedded differences between states themselves.[29]

While this does appear to be a widespread perception, there is a lack of clarity as to what ties a family law so closely to the jurisdiction in which it operates.[30] For example, Antokolskaia has referred to adherence to

---

[28]  See A. LAMFALUSSY, *Final Report of the Committee of Wise Men in the Regulation of European Securities Markets* (Brussels, 15.2.2001) http://europe.eu.int/comm/internal_market/en/finance/general/lamfallusyen.pdf.

[29]  PINTENS and VANWINCKELEN, *op. cit.*, n 20, 15.

[30]  The view of the Council of the European Union is that family laws are "very heavily influenced by... culture and traditions," *op. cit.* n 12. Müller-Freienfels identifies moral, religious, social, political, psychological, historical and social factors: see MÜLLER-FREIENFELS, "The Unification of Family Law" (1968) 16 *Am. J. Comparative Law* 175. However, Grossen has dismissed tradition and religion as factors impeding comparative analysis and reform of family laws: see GROSSEN, "The Contribution of Comparative (or Foreign Law) Studies to Family Law Reform", in G. HAND and C.J. MCBRIDE (eds.), *Droit Sans Frontières* (Birming-

---

tradition and ideology as part of the "cherished cultural heritage" of individual jurisdictions, and has rejected these factors as barriers to a European family law.[31] So far as these particular factors are concerned, her judgement appears correct. Traditional influences on legal policy cannot be immutable. A salient illustration is the development towards full marital capacity for same-sex partnerships, which has been achieved in the Netherlands,[32] proposed in Belgium,[33] and also advocated by a prominent politician in Spain.[34] Neither, of course, will cultural attitudes necessarily endure. Referenda on abortion and divorce in the Republic of Ireland provide evidence of this.[35] There are also examples from Eastern Europe of the displacement of ideological influences on legal policy. Thus, religious marriage is now recognised in the Czech Republic and Lithuania.[36] In addition, former, socialist aversion to treating family law as a branch of civil law[37] is no longer a feature of the new Lithuanian Civil Code.[38]

Tradition, ideology and culture do not, by themselves, present insurmountable obstacles to development of a European law. However, advocates of harmonisation, who focus on the roots of legal policy in a particular jurisdiction, and on family law as a manifestation of heritage, adopt too limited a view. The emphasis in this type of approach is misplaced. It ignores, or at least underplays, the active, contemporary and continuing function of family law as a component of political economy.

Laws regulating domestic relationships are capable of serving a wide range of objectives. At their narrowest, developments in family law support the status of interest groups involved in implementation of legal policy –

---

ham: Holdsworth Club, 1991) 95, 97. And PINTENS and VANWINCKELEN suggest resistance to harmonisation indicates attachment to "cultural baggage", *op. cit.*, n 20 14,15.

[31] ANTOKOLSKAIA, "A European Civil Code and the New Dilemmas for the Harmonisation of Family Law" (forthcoming 2003) *European Review of Private Law.*

[32] See pp. 91-2 below.

[33] DE SCHUTTER and WEYEMBERGH, "'Statutory Cohabitation' Under Belgian Law: A Step Towards Same-sex Marriage?", in WINTEMUTE and ANDENÆS, *op. cit.*, n 18, 465, 473.

[34] See p. 95 below.

[35] English "Ireland 1982-94" in T.W. MOODY and F.X. MARTIN (eds.), *The Course of Irish History* (Dublin: Mercier Press, 2001) 306, 316-7; KEOGH, "Ireland at the Turn of the Century: 1994-2001", *ibid.* 321, 336.

[36] HRUŠÁKOVÁ, "Czech Republic", in W. PINTENS (ed.), *International Encyclopaedia of Family and Succession Law* Vol 1 (The Hague, Kluwer) 76-8; Article 3.24 Civil Code of Lithuania, adopted in 2000.

[37] ANTOKOLSKAIA, "The 1995 Russian Family Code", (1996) 22 *Review of Central and East European Law* 635, 637-9.

[38] Book 3, Civil Code of Lithuania.

extensive powers vested in the English judiciary illustrate this. At its broadest, a family law can maintain national or regional identity. An example is the commitment to Swedish laws in Finland, when it was an autonomous Grand Duchy of Russia, and Finland's association with the Scandinavian countries after independence.[39]

Central to the function of family law as an aspect of political economy is its role in attempting to establish norms, influence opinion and reinforce a particular system of social organisation. The principles of social order implicit in a national family law will tend to define morality in terms of individual responsibility and a traditional concept of the family or, alternatively, will emphasise collectivism and egalitarianism. Legal policy will reflect the degree of commitment to religious values on the part of the state and, in addition, the extent to which the state is prepared to intervene in family autonomy. At issue will be the approach to gender equality and commitment to pluralism, not least in relation to ethnic groups and sexual orientation. Family law will also complement taxation, social and labour market policies. Consequently, it will have implications for income and class equality.

Inevitably, family law reform will be keenly contested by political interests, which will be constrained by, as well as attempting to dictate, public opinion. Social structure will also have an impact on values and mores and will influence legal policy in a particular jurisdiction. Montesquieu's references to climatic conditions have limited appeal today,[40] but factors as basic as geography and a country's geo-political position will also play a part, at some level, in determining a system of family law.

The essential point is that family law is an indispensable medium to promote political objectives. This is a constant, although there will inevitably be shifts in ideology, cultural attitudes and the balance of political power. At issue, therefore, in the construction of a family law for Europe is abandonment of an aspect of national sovereignty, less apparent perhaps than a state's social welfare model or fiscal policy, but no less important.

---

[39]   BRADLEY, "The Antecedents of Finnish Family Law", (1998) 19 *Jo of Legal History* 94, 98.
[40]   A.M. COHLER *et al.* (eds.), *The Spirit of the Laws* (Cambridge: CUP. 1989) 233-4.

David Bradley

## 2.2. Politics and Family Law Reform in a Period of Transition: Case Study

Kahn-Freund gave his pessimistic verdict on harmonisation in the late 1970's, at a time of wide-ranging transformation of family law in Europe. Post-war expansion of welfare states and their clientele had produced:

> "a transition from a perception of events mainly in terms of religion or morality... from charitable feeling to social consciousness. The state [had] become the abstract, universal and anonymous caretaker of all members of society."[41]

Pressure for family law reform intensified in the post-war period and complemented this general change in mentality. At issue was displacement of the established order, expressed in laws applied to domestic relationships and, in particular, the religious component of legal policy. There was ample scope for new laws to further political objectives within individual jurisdictions. And within Europe itself, there was the potential, in this period of transition, for family law reform to indicate differences between nation states. In the event, this potential was fully realised.

Reforms in Sweden provide a reference point for developments elsewhere. Directives approved by the Social Democrat Government in 1969, decreed the comprehensive secularisation of family law.[42] The same year, illegitimate children acquired full inheritance rights. Pioneering legislation was enacted to extend marital capacity to transsexuals in 1972. And the following year a Committee of the Swedish Parliament endorsed the proposition – remarkable for its time – that "from society's point of view, cohabitation between two persons of the same sex is a perfectly acceptable form of family life."[43]

A radical revision of marriage and divorce law was introduced in 1973. An indication of the general tenor of the reform is the fact that marriage between half brothers and sisters was permitted in certain cases.[44] (By some accounts, Swedish reformers had entered the "zone of horror."[45]) The new

---

[41] DE SWAAN, "Welfare State", in J. KRIEGER (ed.), *The Oxford Companion to the Politics of the World* (Oxford. OUP, 2001), 903. 907.
[42] *Abstract of Protocol on Justice Department Matters* (1969) (English translation), and see below pp. 81-2.
[43] YTTERBERG, "From Society's Point of View, Cohabitation Between Two Persons of the Same Sex is a Perfectly Acceptable Form of Family Life", in WINTEMUTE and ANDENÆS, *op. cit.*, n18, 427, 428.
[44] Chapter 2, S3, Marriage Code of 1987.
[45] M.A. GLENDON, *The Transformation of Family Law* (Chicago: Chicago UP, 1989) 57.

72

Intersentia

divorce law specified no grounds or waiting periods for spouses who agreed on divorce and had no children under 16. In other cases, six months consideration was required, but even this was waived where there had been two years separation. Nor was there any check on reconciliation or necessity to resolve disputes relating to support, property or children, before divorce was obtained.[46]

Enactment of the most liberal abortion law in Western Europe followed in 1974.[47] And in 1978, financial support obligations on divorce were reduced to a minimum to complement expansion of the public sector and an active labour market policy for women.[48] All these developments in Swedish family law embodied the "socialist offensive" of the early 1970's.[49]

There were, however, limits to the reforms. Swedish Social Democrats had learned never to move too far in advance of public opinion.[50] Thus, a proposal to limit recognition to civil marriage was not implemented.[51] And despite the declaration of support for same-sex relationships, a bill to equalise the homosexual and heterosexual ages of consent failed in 1971. Contrary to the situation in the Netherlands, referred to below, its sponsor was informed that it would be political suicide to present this proposal.[52]

In the Netherlands, prophetically in view of the recognition of same-sex marriage some thirty years later, parity in the age of consent for homosexuals and heterosexuals was enacted in advance of Sweden and many other European jurisdictions. This step was taken in 1971.[53] However, although non-confessional parties had strengthened their position in the Dutch legislature, developments in this period reflected a different ethic to that underpinning Swedish reforms.

---

[46]    Chapter 5, SS1, 2, 4 Marriage Code of 1987.
[47]    LINDHALL, "Sweden", in B. ROLSTON and A. EGGERT (eds.), *Abortion in the New Europe* (Westport: Greenwood Press, 1994) 237, 239.
[48]    D. BRADLEY, *Family Law and Political Culture* (London: Sweet and Maxwell, 1996) 81-2.
[49]    PONTUSSON, "Sweden: After the Golden Age", in P. ANDERSON and P. CAMILLER (eds.), *Mapping the West European Left* (London: Verso, 1994) 23, 27.
[50]    H. MILNER, *Sweden: Social Democracy in Practice* (London. OUP, 1989) 63.
[51]    GLENDON, *op. cit.*, n 45, 75.
[52]    RYDSTRÖM, "Between Men and Animals: Homosexuality, Bestiality, and Criminal Law in Sweden 1864-1978", in *Kriminaliteten er ikke hva den var - Avviket i historisk lys.* (Rapport fra NSfKs 42. forskerseminar, Bergen, Norge 2000).
[53]    MOERINGS, "The Netherlands", in D.J. WEST and R. GREEN (eds.), *Socio-Legal Control of Homosexuality* (New York: Plenum Press, 1997) 299, 302.

There was no comparable, far-reaching secularisation of legal policy or social engineering in the Netherlands. Divorce was liberalised, but retained traditional features, which were also apparent in laws regulating marital capacity.[54] Provisions governing financial support on divorce did not indicate a commitment to eroding traditional family roles, to the same extent as in Sweden.[55] Nor did developments in related areas signal a shift to transforming women's role in the public sphere. Thus, abortion on request became a reality but it was impossible to liberalise abortion legislation at this stage.[56]

Tolerant attitudes to homosexuality have been attributed to a "politics of accommodation" in the Netherlands.[57] Reform of the homosexual age of consent was the product of, or at least facilitated by, increasingly liberal public opinion.[58] One view of Dutch political culture in the early 1970's was that:

> "[f]inally the dikes burst, and a society which had distinguished itself by constant reflection upon the restrictive traditional teachings of orthodox theology became a very permissive society indeed within a few years." [59]

Revision of the Civil Code in France was the subject of deep-rooted controversy in this period. Conservative politicians viewed reform relating to illegitimate children in 1972 as "a revolution in the civil law,"[60] and as drastically undermining the legitimate family, notwithstanding the fact that the child of an adulterous relationship still had inferior succession rights.[61] Divorce reform raised the prospect of pitting conservative, Catholic interests against Republicanism – the "two Frances" as Rheinstein put it.[62] Carbonnier, who formulated the divorce law enacted in 1975, foresaw

---

[54]   The law referred to irretrievable breakdown, not divorce as an entitlement, and included a modest fault component: DE RUITER, "The Reform of Family Law in the Netherlands", in A.G. CHLOROS (ed.), *The Reform of Family Law in Europe* (Deventer: Kluwer, 1978) 19, 36-7. For capacity, see Arts. 31-42 Civil Code which, inter alia, retained a different marriage age for men and women and also some prohibited degrees of affinity.

[55]   DE RUITER *ibid.* 38-9.

[56]   KETTING, "Netherlands", in ROLSTON and EGGERT, *op. cit.*, n 47, 173, 175.

[57]   SCHUYF AND KROUWEL, "The Dutch Lesbian and Gay Movement", in B.D. ADAM et al (eds.), *The Global Emergence of Gay and Lesbian Politics* (Philadelphia: Temple UP, 1999) 158.

[58]   KOOY, "The Netherlands", in R. CHESTER (ed.), *Divorce in Europe* (Leiden: Martinus Nijhoff, 1977) 97, 101.

[59]   *Ibid.* 102.

[60]   MARTIN and THÉRY, "The PACS and Marriage and Cohabitation in France" (2001) 15 *IJLPF* 135, 144.

[61]   M.A. GLENDON, *State, Law and Family* (Amsterdam: North Holland, 1977) 90; FOYER, "The Reform of Family Law in France", in CHLOROS, *op. cit.*, n 54, 75, 101.

[62]   GLENDON, *op. cit.*, n 45, 160.

this.[63] The result was an elaborate compromise, combining a liberal divorce regime, albeit with reconciliation requirements for those in agreement, alongside fault grounds and lengthy separation periods, for those who were not.[64]

A modernising, centre-right administration was initially responsible for abortion reform in France but, not surprisingly, this proved controversial in a society in which the birth rate had been a constant preoccupation.[65] The new law was liberal, although less so than Swedish legislation, in failing to establish unambiguously abortion as a right.[66] A traditional approach to the status of women and the more conservative of the "two Frances," referred to above, also influenced marriage law.[67] Nor was there any development on Dutch lines to equalise the homosexual and heterosexual ages of consent. A provision from the Vichy era, which discriminated against same-sex relationships, remained in force.[68]

In the Federal Republic of Germany, an illegitimacy reform, enacted after prompting from the Constitutional Court, gave an indication of subsequent developments. In contrast to the political climate in Sweden, it was impossible, or considered undesirable, to allow full equality in relation to inheritance. However, the form of discrimination differed from French law.[69] Pressure for divorce reform intensified with the formation in 1969 of a Social Democrat-led coalition. The Chancellor struck a more guarded note than the Swedish Government by emphasising the importance of settling "ideological differences" over divorce and protecting dependents.[70]

The Government produced proposals for divorce reform in 1970, but ideological differences did surface. There was persistent controversy in the legislature.[71] Conciliation was necessary to reconcile the Bundestag and

---

[63]  GLENDON, *op. cit.*, n 61, 204.
[64]  FOYER, *op. cit.*, n 61, 106,7.
[65]  MOSSUZ-LAVAU, "Abortion Policy in France under Governments of the Right and Left" (1973-84) 86, in J. LOVENDUSKI (ed.), *The New Politics of Abortion* (London, Sage. 1986) 86, 88,9; DOWD, "Envisioning Work and the Family" (1989) 26 *Harvard Journal of Legislation* 312, 330. For a contemporary indication, see *Le Figaro* 15.10.2001 "Les Françaises championes d'Europe de la fécondité."
[66]  LATHAM, "Reform and Revolution", in E. LEE (ed.), *Abortion Law and Politics Today* London: Macmillan Press, 1998, 130, 131.
[67]  GLENDON, *op. cit.*, n 61, 30.
[68]  F. LEROY-FORGEOT, *Histoire juridique de l'homosexualité en Europe* (Paris: Presses Universitaires de France, 1997) 108 n 1.
[69]  BOHNDORF, "The New Illegitimacy Reform in Germany" (1970) 19 *ICLQ* 299, 306-7.
[70]  Policy statement of 28/10/69: *Keesing's Contemporary Archives* 1969-70, 23702.
[71]  GLENDON, *op. cit.*, n 61, 218.

more conservative Bundesrat.[72] A late electoral gain for the Christian Democrats further affected the structure of the legislation.[73] Conservative interests also secured a symbolic, although incongruous declaration that "marriage is for life," as the opening provision of the law.[74] Nor did controversy end when the reform was finally enacted in 1976. The detail of a hardship defence had been closely scrutinised: a subsequent challenge to the Constitutional Court resulted in removal of a time bar on its operation.[75] There was no pressure as in France for reconciliation procedures on divorce, but a requirement to resolve ancillary issues, in specified circumstances, was introduced.[76] In this respect, and in relation to divorce grounds, the result was an altogether more conservative reform than in Sweden.

Prospects for a comprehensive revision of German marriage law were unfulfilled.[77] In contrast to the position in Sweden, reform was incremental.[78] A suggestion from a member of the Committee, charged with producing proposals, is that a programme which touched on the issue of civil marriage still remained sensitive a century after the Kulturkampf.[79] The law enacted in 1976 did, however, eliminate traces of formal inequality between husband and wife, which remained in the Civil Code, and was also intended to limit support obligations.[80] One view is that this latter issue was more contentious than divorce itself.[81] In the event, the emphasis on self-sufficiency and independence for women was much less pronounced than in the Swedish reform.[82] The issue that, above all, polarised political opinion, was abortion. Constitutional challenges from Christian Democrats and state governments to the rights-based law enacted in 1974, which had been supported by the Social Democrats, were successful. The Federal Constitutional Court annulled the measure, inter alia, on the grounds that experience under fascism necessitated affirmation of human life.[83]

---

[72] D. DUMUSC, *Le divorce par consentement mutuel dans les législations européennes* (Genève: Librarie Droz, 1980) 158.

[73] GLENDON, *op. cit.*, n 45, 178.

[74] RHEINSTEIN and GLENDON, "West German Marriage and Family Law Reform" (1978) 45 *University of Chicago LR* 519, 520, 521.

[75] GLENDON, *op. cit.*, n 45, 180.

[76] RHEINSTEIN and GLENDON *op. cit.* n 74, 551.

[77] MÜLLER-FREIENFELS, "The Marriage Law Reform of 1976 in the Federal Republic of Germany" (1979) 28 *ICLQ* 184, 184-5.

[78] See n 217 below.

[79] Letter on file from Professor Müller-Freienfels to the author.

[80] See former A1356; GLENDON, *op. cit.*, n 45, 219.

[81] GLENDON, *ibid.*, 178.

[82] *Ibid.*, 219-221.

[83] KOMMERS, "Abortion and Constitution" (1977), *Am. J. Comp. Law* 255, 272.

In contrast to this politically charged process in the Federal Republic of Germany, reforms in England were de-politicised. Laws relating to abortion, homosexuality and divorce were all Private Member's measures – too sensitive for the Labour Government of the day to sponsor directly.[84] The status of illegitimate children was also improved, but in contrast to the contemporaneous Swedish law, full inheritance rights were withheld.[85] And unlike the position in the Netherlands, the age of consent for homosexuals remained significantly higher than for heterosexuals.[86]

Whereas reform in the Federal Republic of Germany produced a no-fault divorce regime, English law combined modified matrimonial offences, lengthy separation periods and a restricted hardship defence – there was no constitution to override Parliament on this latter issue.[87] English polity and its system of family law was founded on institutions – the Monarchy, Parliament, Established Church, represented by its bishops in the House of Lords, and the common law.[88] And abortion legislation, unlike reforms in Sweden, France and the Federal Republic of Germany, was also noticeably ambiguous. It was too problematic to clarify this in a society in which inequality and differences in social class were institutionalised. One judgement was of a "typically British pragmatic compromise."[89]

The Government did take the initiative in securing abandonment of a proposal in Parliament for community property.[90] And the Law Commission subsequently rejected the German *Zugewinngemeinschaft* in favour of wide discretionary powers for the courts on divorce.[91] Nor was there any reference, at this time, to independence after divorce in the legislation governing financial support. The judiciary, rather than Parliament, developed policy. This followed earlier precedents and was a further element in lowering the profile of politically controversial issues and limiting social change.[92]

---

[84]   B.H. LEE, *Divorce Law Reform in England* (London: Peter Owen, 1974) 89; LATHAM, *op. cit.*, n 66,136; J. WEEKS, *Sex, Politics and Society* (London: Longman,1981) 267.

[85]   S14 Family Law Reform Act 1969.

[86]   I.e. 21 as against 16.

[87]   S.M. CRETNEY and J. MASSON, *Principles of Family Law* (London: Sweet and Maxwell. 2002) 275-297.

[88]   J. HABGOOD, *Church and Nation in a Secular Age* (London: Darton, 1983) 40-1.

[89]   LYON and BENNETT, "Abortion – Whose Decision" (1979) 9 *Family Law* 35, 49.

[90]   KIRALFY, "The English Law", in A. KIRALFY (ed.) *Matrimonial Property* (Leiden: Sijthoff, 1972) 180, 181-2.

[91]   Law Commission *Family Law: First Report on Family Property* (London: HMSO, 1973) 18-9.

[92]   J. EEKELAAR and M. MACLEAN, *Maintenance after Divorce* (Oxford: Clarendon Press, 1986) 8-18.

Differences between England and the Republic of Ireland were also plainly visible. Provisions relating to family law in De Valera's Catholic Constitution of 1937 – most prominently the ban on divorce – had served to emphasise independence.[93] And a further constitutional amendment would be introduced in 1983 to "copperfasten" restrictions on abortion.[94]

The delayed modernisation of Italian family law after fascism, and difficulties over divorce reform in post-Franco Spain, underscored the political significance of legal policy at this time. Family law reform in Italy in the 1970's offered ample opportunity for political capital to be won and lost. The gap between fascist norms, still expressed in the Civil Code, and the actual situation of families, not least those denied divorce, appeared to be growing.[95] Divorce reform enabled members of the small Radical Party to present themselves as champions of civil rights – "they made the most of it."[96] (The campaign included a hunger strike outside Parliament by the Radical's First Secretary.[97]) Christian Democrats opposed divorce and cast themselves as champions of the family and society.[98] However, divorce was introduced and the Christian Democrats' attempt to annul the reform by a referendum has been judged one of their most important post-war defeats.[99]

The divorce referendum demonstrated the importance of accommodating women's interests. The Christian Democrat and Communist Parties united to support a reform which repealed anachronisms in marriage law.[100] Illegitimate children also acquired enhanced rights. Public opinion required that they should not suffer unduly for their parents' misdemeanours,[101] but the 1948 Constitution, a compromise between Communists and Christian Democrats,[102] struck a cautious balance in protecting the "legitimate" family. This was carried forward to the new law.[103]

---

[93] LYNCH, "The Irish Free State and the Republic of Ireland 1921-66", in MOODY AND MARTIN, *op. cit.*, n 35, 272, 277.
[94] O'BRIEN, "Abortion Law in the Republic of Ireland", in E. LEE (ed.), *Abortion Law and Politics Today* (London: Macmillan Press, 1998) 110, 111.
[95] L. CALDWELL, *Italian Family Matters* (London: Macmillan, 1991) 78.
[96] M. CLARK, *Modern Italy* (London: Longman, 1984) 381.
[97] *Ibid.*
[98] CALDWELL, *op. cit.*, n 95, 82.
[99] D. SASSOON, *Contemporary Italy* (London: Longman, 1986) 107.
[100] *Ibid.* 108, 9.
[101] LIBRANDO, "The Reform of Family Law in Italy," in CHLOROS, *op. cit.*, n 54, 151, 164.
[102] SASSOON, *op. cit.*, n 99, 201,4.
[103] LIBRANDO, *op. cit.*, n101, 165.

The final political contest over family law reform in this period involved abortion. A Christian Democrat proposal in 1976, which continued to define abortion as a crime, was supported by neo-fascists but alienated Communists. An election became inevitable.[104] The abortion law, which followed, enabled the Christian Democrats, once more, to claim a role as defenders of the family and the Communists stepped back from demanding abortion on request.[105]

The advent of democracy in Spain necessitated repeal of fascist laws. However, those drafting the democratic Constitution were alive to possible political controversy and adopted a cautious position on issues such as divorce.[106] A new law was enacted in 1981: public opinion was no barrier to this.[107] However, the governing coalition fell apart a year later. "The issue which, above all others, sealed its fate was divorce."[108]

Family law reform in Europe in this period of transition was central to political programmes and ambitions and dictated by the strength of political parties. The precise form of legislation was contested by competing political interests. Moreover, in particular instances, national constitutions determined both the direction and detail of reforms.

Abortion law falls outside orthodox, narrow, academic classifications of family law and does not form part of initiatives for harmonisation – the Commission on European Family Law must be grateful for that. However, even the brief account above demonstrates the interdependence of legal policy and how closely, in political terms, abortion was associated with other issues.

The function of family law as a component of political economy is unmistakable in this period – as are differences between jurisdictions and the role of legal policy as an indicator of national sovereignty. Kahn-Freund's view of the futility of harmonisation appears fully justified at the time it was made. What then has changed?

---

[104]   P. GINSBORG, *A History of Contemporary Italy* (London: Penguin, 1990) 373.
[105]   *Ibid.* 394; CALDWELL, *op. cit.*, n 95, 109.
[106]   DE USSEL, "Family Ideology and Political Transition in Spain" (1991) 5 *IJLF* 277, 292.
[107]   *Ibid.* 278.
[108]   J. HOOPER, *The New Spaniards* (London: Penguin, 1987) 183.

## 3. FAMILY LAW AND SOCIAL CHANGE

### 3.1. Convergence?

Even in the 1970's, a body of academic opinion asserted or implied that family laws were converging.[109] And at first sight, this does appear to be confirmed by subsequent developments. For example, in 1978, Glendon identified the trend to limit restrictions on marital capacity,[110] and Pintens and Vanwinckelen note that the Federal Republic of Germany and Italy have followed Sweden in recognising transsexual marriage.[111]

In 1985, David and Brierly concluded that "even in family law... there has been, in a very concrete way, a true concordance of legislative developments and not merely a generally similar tendency," and gave developments in matrimonial property law as an illustration.[112] The same year, Scottish law was reformed: it has been suggested that this took "a major step towards a system of deferred community property."[113] And in England, the government has now raised the question whether legislation should include a reference to equal division of assets on divorce.[114]

Kahn Freund himself noted in 1974 "intensive" and "rapid" assimilation of ideas and institutions in family law, and referred to the "remarkable" acceptance of divorce for breakdown.[115] However, he also questioned whether this would ever be accepted in Dublin.[116] In the event, the Irish Constitution has been amended and, moreover, the Family Law (Divorce) Act 1996 is a no-fault law.[117] In the late 1980's, Glendon appeared to despair of finding common ground between Irish and other European family laws, not least because of the constitutional position, noted above.[118] However,

---

[109]   See, eg, CHLOROS, "Preface" to Chloros, *op. cit.*, n 54, vii.
[110]   GLENDON, *op. cit.*, n 61, 25.
[111]   PINTENS and VANWINCKELEN, *op. cit.*, n 20, 14.
[112]   R.DAVID and J.C. BRIERLY, *Major Legal Systems in the World Today* (London: Stevens, 1985) 7.
[113]   CLIVE, "The financial consequences of divorce: reform from the Scottish perspective", in M.D.A. FREEMAN (ed.), *State, Law and the Family* (London: Tavistock, 1984) 196, 204.
[114]   Home Office, *Supporting Families* (London: HMSO, 1998) 38.
[115]   KAHN-FREUND, "On Uses and Misues of Comparative Law" (1974) 37 *Modern Law Review* 1, 14.
[116]   *Ibid.* 15.
[117]   WARD, "Republic of Ireland", in C. HAMILTON and A. PERRY (eds.), *Family Law in Europe* (London: Butterworths, 2002) 359, 376.
[118]   GLENDON, "Irish Family Law in Comparative Perspective" (1987) 9 *Dublin University Law Journal* 1; see p. 78 above.

a judicial decision subsequently recognised abortion rights in specified circumstances, and this has been confirmed by referendum.[119]

Finally, with regard to extra-marital relationships, one view in 1980 was that "illegitimacy is on the way out."[120] As evidence of this, full succession rights have been established under German and English law[121] and the discriminatory provision in French law, referred to above, which restricted the claims of children born in adulterous relationships, has recently been abolished.[122] The widespread introduction of registered partnership laws indicates legitimation of informal cohabitation. And if regions of Spain are able to legislate for same-sex relationships, it may perhaps be inferred that an end to the great disputes and divisions in family law is in sight.[123]

This view of convergence is misconceived. The "three great trends" in family laws "towards liberty, equality and secularity"[124] are clearly visible, but they are no more than general trends. The demand for rights – to marry, divorce, in relation to equality in marriage and for extra-marital and same-sex relationships – strikes directly at traditional legal policy. All jurisdictions have had to respond to this. However, the nature of that response and structure of reforms has varied significantly.

The study below tests convergence in the Nordic countries. The view of Pintens and Vanwinckelen is that:

> "[t]oday, the greater part of [Nordic family law] is unified, sometimes down to the smallest detail, even though Sweden, followed by Finland, have now and then issued more progressive legislation."[125]

If there are in fact significant differences in Nordic family laws, notwithstanding close ties in the region, this must substantially undermine assessments of broader convergence elsewhere in Europe, and may not augur well for the Commission on European Family Law.

---

119   O'BRIEN, *op. cit.*, n 94, 113.
120   CLIVE, "Marriage an Unnecessary Legal Concept?" in J. EEKELAAR and S. KATZ (eds.), *Marriage and Cohabitation in Contemporary Societies* (Toronto: Butterworths, 1980) 71.
121   FRANK, "Germany: Parentage Law Reformed", in A. BAINHAM (ed.), *The International Survey of Family Law 1997* (The Hague: Kluwer, 1999) 167, 169; S18 Family Law Reform Act 1987 (England).
122   Law 2001-1135 of 3 December 2001.
123   See PINTENS and VANWINCKELEN, *op. cit.*, n 20, 16.
124   CLIVE, *op. cit.*, n 120, 73.
125   PINTENS and VANWINCKELEN, *op. cit.*, n 20, 14.

## 3.2. Divergence in Nordic Family Laws: Case Study

There has been a tendency to overstate the impact of Nordic[126] co-operation in the field of family law. For example, the matrimonial property reforms of the early 20th Century are commonly seen as a principal achievement of the first phase of co-operation. There were, however, differences in the retrospective application of the new laws which were important in practice.[127] And a limited revision of illegitimacy law in Sweden, at this time, supports the view that it was, in some respects, conservative in comparison with the rest of Scandinavia.[128]

So far as contemporary legal policy is concerned, all the Nordic countries have now enacted marriage and divorce reforms, but the latest round of co-operation has been judged a failure. One view from the head of the Norwegian Marriage Committee is that:

> "one cannot characterise the Nordic law co-operation as particularly successful... It seems the ambition to achieve uniformity in legislation has not been sufficiently strong, while at the same time the political undertones have become more marked where marital law is concerned. This has frustrated efforts to arrive at uniform rules."[129]

And if further evidence of divergence is needed, it can be found in the fact that in 1998, Nordic Ministers of Justice instigated a new investigation of prospects for harmonisation of family law.[130] Moreover, the co-ordinator of this investigation has suggested that its success will depend exclusively on political considerations.[131]

The reference above to "political undertones" can be taken to apply to the Directives for reform, endorsed by Sweden's Social Democrat Government in 1969, referred to above.[132] These stipulated that family legislation would be used to achieve a society where "equality between men and women is a reality" and, in addition, required legitimation of unmarried cohabita-

---

[126] The term "Nordic" is used here to include Sweden, Denmark, Norway and Finland, whereas "Scandinavia" in this text excludes Finland.

[127] NISKANEN, "Marriage and Gendered Property Rights in Early Twentieth-Century Rural Sweden", in K. MELBY et al (eds.), *The Nordic Model of Marriage and the Welfare State* (Copenhagen: Nordic Council of Ministers, 2000) 69, 70,1.

[128] VERNEY, "The Foundations of Modern Sweden" (1970) 20 *Political Studies* 42, 59.

[129] LØDRUP, "Norway" (1988-9) 27 *J. Fam. L.* 253, 254.

[130] I am grateful to Professor Anders Agell for information.

[131] AGELL, "Is There One System of Family Law in the Nordic Countries?" (2001) 3 *European Journal of Law Reform* 313, 329.

[132] P. 72.

tion.[133] Travaux préparatoires for divorce reform also stated that the law could not, and should not, influence attitudes to marriage.[134]

Sweden cast itself as a pioneer and broke with Nordic co-operation.[135] The result was the radical reforms of the 1970's, outlined above.[136] They have been followed subsequently by the Cohabitees (Joint) Homes Act of 1987, which also applies to same-sex relationships, and by registered partnership legislation, amended in 2002, to open up adoption to same-sex couples.[137] This latest measure permits adoption of children from overseas.

These reforms demonstrate the dominance of the Social Democratic Party and its "rational," secular enterprise. Religious values, expressed in family law, have been abandoned. In their place, social order is to depend on collectivism. Past mistakes – on sterilisation, for example – are scrutinised by government-appointed commissions and society moves on.[138]

All this requires social engineering. It has been suggested that a faith in the state, inherited from the period of benign absolutism, is a pervasive feature of Scandinavian political culture.[139] This appears particularly marked in Sweden: the new law on same-sex adoption is a salient indicator. The report of the government commission, which preceded the measure, found that, of those who expressed a firm view, a majority was opposed to adoption of children from overseas.[140] Those countries, which sent children to Sweden, were also polled and it was concluded that they were unlikely to accept same-sex couples.[141] Nothing daunted, the Swedish legislature sanctioned overseas adoption.[142]

There has been no corresponding development in other Nordic countries. Political and institutional influences on legal policy are clearly apparent in the two areas which the Commission on European Family Law is currently considering, i.e. divorce and post-divorce maintenance.

---

[133]   Abstract of Protocol on Justice Department Matters (1969).
[134]   Entry into and Dissolution of Marriage (SOU 1972:41) (English Summary).
[135]   AGELL, *op. cit.*, n 131, 315; Bernitz, *op. cit.*, n 26, 40.
[136]   Pp. 72-73.
[137]   SALDEEN, "Sweden", in HAMILTON and PERRY, *op. cit.*, n 117, 619, 656-8.
[138]   *Steriliseringfrågen I Sverige 1935-1975: Ekonomisk ersättning* (SOU 1999:2); *Steriliseringfrågen I Sverige 1935-1975: Historisk belysning Kartläggning Intervjuer* (SOU 2000:20).
[139]   P. BALDWIN, *The Politics of Social Solidarity* (1990) 71, n 51.
[140]   *Children in Homosexual Families* (English Summary) (SOU 2001:10) 17.
[141]   *Ibid.* 18-19.
[142]   I. FROMAN, *Two parents of the same sex* (Stockholm: Swedish Institute, 2003).

The Swedish divorce reform of 1973 and maintenance law of 1978 have not been adopted in Norway. The Norwegian Marriage Committee considered and rejected the Swedish divorce model.[143] Under the Marriage Law of 1991, divorce after legal separation is the principal procedure. There is an unqualified right to a separation and to divorce one year thereafter. A narrowly defined fault ground has also been retained. An additional requirement, which originated in the Norwegian legislature, is that spouses who have children under 16 participate in mediation before judicial separation or divorce.[144] In the Nordic context, this is a conservative divorce regime. On post-divorce support, Norwegian law stipulates, as a general rule, that marriage should not have consequences after it has broken down. However, the law also refers to an order where ability to ensure adequate support has been reduced by child-care or household tasks, subject to a three year limit in ordinary cases.[145]

Progressive elements, including the Liberal Party in the early 20th Century, and Labour subsequently, have had a significant impact on family law reform, but the Norwegian Labour Party has not enjoyed the dominant position of its Swedish counterpart.[146] Moreover, the strength of a traditional counter-culture in Norway is apparent in the standing of the Christian People's Party.[147] The result is a more conservative slant, than in Sweden, on sensitive issues of legal policy.

For example, in addition to the provision for spousal support, noted above, a traditional perspective on the role of women is apparent in marital property and abortion laws.[148] On one view, there has been a relatively slow "modernisation" of motherhood in Norway.[149] The development of rights for unmarried heterosexual cohabitation has also proved more problematic than in Sweden: this is apparent in the development and structure of the Joint Households Law.[150] In addition, the present government, which includes the Christian People's Party, has defended an administrative

---

[143] LØDRUP, "Norway: The New Marriage Act" (1992-3) 31 *J.Fam.L.* 411.
[144] S26 Marriage Act, which states that the aim is mediation.
[145] SS 79,81 Marriage Act.
[146] BRADLEY, *op. cit.*, n 48, 178-82.
[147] *Ibid.* 186.
[148] S31 Marriage Act; BRADLEY, *op. cit.*, n 48, 199-200; and see AGELL, "Family Forms and Legal Policies" 38, *Sc.St.L.*198, 201 for judicial decisions on marital property.
[149] A. LEIRA, *Welfare States and Working Women* (Oslo: NUP, 1992) 57.
[150] BRADLEY, *op. cit.*, n 48, 213-7.

practice which restricts adoption by a partner in a same-sex relationship.[151] All this is at odds with developments in Swedish family law.

Denmark's divorce reform in 1989 also bears few of the hallmarks of Swedish radicalism in the early 1970's. Judicial separation can be obtained unilaterally and followed by divorce after six months, where spouses agree, or after one year where they do not. Matrimonial offences are limited, but still provide an alternative route to divorce.[152] And Danish maintenance law places less emphasis on restricting support than Swedish legal policy. The formal position is that, in the absence of very special circumstances, maintenance can be ordered for a limited period, which is not normally to exceed 10 years.[153] Nor has Denmark followed the Swedish line and regulated informal heterosexual cohabitation.[154]

The influence of the Danish Social Democratic and Radical Liberal Parties is apparent in a range of progressive reforms.[155] However, a tradition in which society is identified with the state has been less in evidence, and social democracy has been weaker than in Sweden. Nor have developments in Danish family law been conditioned by social engineering to the same extent. Thus, contemporary abortion law is more restrictive, and measures such as banning physical punishment of children have been introduced somewhat more reluctantly, than in Sweden.[156] This less directive approach is also apparent in other spheres, for example the approach to gender equality.[157] (Alcohol policy is a further indicator.[158]) Regulation in Denmark, it has been suggested, has a "pragmatic" character.[159]

---

[151] The Adoption and Registered Partnership Acts were amended in 2001 to allow a same-sex partner to adopt the other's child. Although no age limit was specified, adoption authorities introduced a requirement, when granting approval in this situation, that the child should be 12 years old. I am grateful to Professor Tone Sverdrup for information.

[152] NIELSEN, "Denmark," in HAMILTON and PERRY, op. cit., n 117, 63, 78.

[153] Ibid. 80.

[154] Ibid. 90.

[155] Abortion law was reformed in 1937 and 1973 in advance of Sweden. More recently, Denmark has pioneered registered partnerships and step-parent adoption in same-sex relationships.

[156] BRADLEY, op. cit., n 38, 143; NIELSEN and FROST, "Children and the Convention: The Danish Debate", in M. FREEMAN (ed.), Children's Rights a Comparative Perspective (Brookfield Vt: Dartmouth, 1996) 65, 77.

[157] BRADLEY, op. cit., n 48, 147-8.

[158] KNUDSEN and ROTHSTEIN, "State Building in Scandinavia" (1994) 26 Comparative Politics 203, 216-7.

[159] KNUDSEN, "State Building in Scandinavia", in T. KNUDSEN (ed.), Welfare Administration in Denmark (Institute of Political Science: University of Copenhagen, 1991) 9, 95.

The argument that political economy and institutions determine the structure of legislation and response to social change is reinforced by a comparison of Finnish and Swedish family law. Divergence in these two jurisdictions assumes an added significance, given their common legal heritage and strong association.[160] Nor are there merely random differences – there is a consistent pattern.

The Swedish General Code of 1734 remained in force when Finland was part of the Russian Empire. However, on a range of issues, including guardianship of unmarried women, revision of marriage law and the right for a married woman to control her earnings, family law was modernised more slowly than in Sweden.[161] And an illegitimacy reform, introduced in Finland after independence, has been judged a more limited measure than other Nordic laws.[162] This is unremarkable, given the fact that White Finland had been victorious in the Civil War.

The Finnish Marriage Act of 1929 closely followed Sweden's Marriage Code of 1920, but policy on marriage age, prohibited degrees of relationship and divorce was conditioned by the values of a predominantly agrarian society.[163] And in the 1930's, there were moves to impose criminal penalties on those living in extra-marital relationships.[164] Sterilisation laws were introduced in both countries. However, "reform eugenics" and a commitment to "scientific" progress inspired Swedish measures, whereas in Finland this element was absent.[165] There was also a slower and more limited reform of abortion law in the post-war period.[166]

This conservatism is apparent in contemporary legal policy. A report from Finland's Family Law Reform Committee in 1972 proposed far-reaching revision of divorce law.[167] But there was limited enthusiasm to implement this recommendation in a society in which social democracy was weaker

---

[160]   See, eg, AARNIO, "Introduction" to J. PÖYHÖNEN (ed.), *An Introduction to Finnish Law* (Helsinki, Finnish Lawyer's Publishing Company, 1993) 3, 5; MODEEN, "La Droit Finlande Scandinave" (1993) 45 *Revue Internationale de Droit Comparé* 783, 794.

[161]   BRADLEY, *op. cit.*, n 39.

[162]   THERBORN, "The Politics of Childhood", in G. CASTLES (ed.), *Families of Nations* (Aldershot: Dartmouth, 1993) 241, 259.

[163]   BRADLEY, *op. cit.*, n 39, 102-5; HEISKAMO, "Women's Voices and the Marriage Act", in K. MELBY *et al.* (eds.), *Ægteskab i Norden fra Saxo til i dag* (Nordisk Ministerråd: København. 1999) 211, 220-2.

[164]   BRADLEY, *op. cit.*, n 39, 105-6.

[165]   *Ibid.* 108-9.

[166]   BRADLEY, "Equality and Patriarchy: Family Law and State Feminism in Finland" (1998) 26 *International Journal of the Sociology of Law* 197, 203-4.

[167]   BRADLEY, "Politics, Culture and Family Law in Finland" (1998) 12 *IJLPF* 288, 295.

than in Sweden, and in which the Centre (formerly Agrarian) Party had been a pivotal force. Finland experienced a cultural revolution of sorts at this time, but urbanisation – "the great migration" from the countryside – was a recent phenomenon.[168]

Marriage and divorce laws were eventually revised in 1987, but Savolainen has distanced the new laws from Swedish reforms:

> "The [Finnish] Government Bill did not attempt to follow any particular coherent philosophy or ideology. Instead most proposals were based upon purely pragmatic considerations."[169]

Aspects of the Marriage Act of 1987 were controversial, but the overall structure of the legislation is a manifestation of "consensus politics," in Finland in the 1980's.[170] Consequently, the drive to secularise marriage law has been less marked than in Sweden. Finnish divorce law is also marginally more restrictive.[171] And on support, the Marriage Act states, that "when a spouse is deemed to be in need of maintenance, the court may order the other spouse to make payments which are considered reasonable with a view to his or her ability and other circumstances" with or without a time limit.[172] This is of academic importance, given the labour market activity of women in Finland, but the point is that there has been no integrated strategy, as in Sweden, to use legal policy to promote equality. Thus, Finnish law also stipulates that spouses are entitled to decide whether to engage in gainful activity outside the home.[173] Related provisions in Swedish law were judged undesirable and have been repealed.[174]

The fact that abortion law in Finland is, for the most part, an indicator rather than a rights-based model is consistent with this general approach.[175] And, as in the other Nordic countries, family law complements areas of social policy. Thus, a home care allowance has been introduced in Finland,

---

[168] ALESTALO, "Sociological Perspectives on the Post-War Development of Finnish Society", in V. STOLTE-HEISIKANEN (ed.), *Sociology in the Context of Social Change* (University of Tampere: Dept. of Sociology, 1989) 19, 27-9. BRADLEY, *op. cit.*, n 167, 293.

[169] SAVOLAINEN, "Finland: The New Marriage Act Enters Into Force" (1988-9) 11 *Journal of Family Law* 127.

[170] BRADLEY, *op. cit.*, n 167, 297.

[171] *Ibid.* 302-3.

[172] S48 Marriage Act.

[173] S2 Marriage Act.

[174] AGELL, "Can and Should Family Law Influence Behaviour?", in J. EEKELAAR and T. NHLAPO (eds.), *The Changing Family* (Oxford: Hart, 1998) 132.

[175] BRADLEY, *op. cit.*, n 166, 208.

whereas this type of measure has been resisted by Social Democrats in Sweden on the grounds that it reinforces inequality.[176]

Nor is there legislation regulating heterosexual cohabitation in Finland.[177] Decriminalisation of homosexuality has also been slower than in Sweden.[178] The Finnish registered partnership law, enacted in 2001, differs significantly from Swedish legislation.[179] First, it denies registered partners the automatic right to adopt a common name. Second, there is no provision for a ceremony on registration. Travaux préparatoires confirm that the aim was to distance partnership status from marriage, and the restriction relating to names is clearly intended to have the same effect. The third, much more prominent distinction is the absence of any provision for same-sex adoption. These limitations were important: they were necessary to ensure consensus in the government coalition,[180] and may also have served to ensure enactment of the partnership law, which was a close run thing.[181]

From one perspective, divergence in family law in Finland and Sweden reflects a fundamental difference in political economy. In Sweden, secular policies on divorce, homosexuality, abortion and in relation to the role of women, complement establishment of an "advanced," social democratic welfare model.[182] Equality has been an "almost tedious theme"[183] in social democratic propaganda, but one (possibly dated) view is of the welfare state as a device to allow Swedish elites to maintain their position and subdue demands for genuine equality.[184]

Finland attained the status of an "advanced" welfare state in the 1980's, but development was slower and welfare provision has been less extensive than in Sweden.[185] There are, however, also assessments that Finland is one of

---

[176]  BRADLEY, *op. cit.*, n 48, 86; Bradley, *op. cit.*, n 166, 206.
[177]  LUOMARANTA, "Finland" in Hamilton and Perry, *op. cit.*, n 117, 232, 244.
[178]  BRADLEY, "Comparative Family Law and the Political Process" (1999) 26 *Journal of Law and Society* 175, 186-8.
[179]  SAVOLAINEN, "The Finnish and the Swedish Partnership Acts – Similarities and Divergencies" in BOELE-WOELKI and FUCHS (eds.), *The Legal Recognition of Same-Sex Couples in Europe*, (EFL series No. 1, Intersentia-Antwerp), 2003, 24.
[180]  I am grateful to Markku Helin for information.
[181]  Voting was 99 to 84, 1 abstention, 15 absent: See SAVOLAINEN, *op. cit.*, n 179.
[182]  BRADLEY, "Family Laws and Welfare States", in MELBY, *op. cit.*, n 127, 37.
[183]  DAHL, "Those Equal Folk", in S.R. GRAUBARD (ed.), *Nordem: The Passion for Equality* (Oslo: NUP. 1986) 97, 101.
[184]  F. PARKIN, *Class, Inequality and Political Power* (London: MacGibbon and Kee, 1971).
[185]  ALESTALO AND UUSITALO, in P. FLORA (ed.), *Growth to Limits* (Berlin: de Gruyter, 1986) 203, 265.

the most egalitarian societies in the industrialised world.[186] There has been less inclination than in Sweden to engage in social engineering in areas such as family law reform, and perhaps less need to do so.

Although, in comparative terms, liberal laws have been introduced in the Nordic countries, there is limited convergence.[187] Variations in legal policy are not isolated occurrences, but are apparent throughout each Nordic system of family law and are attributable to differences in political economy. The inference that there is similar divergence in other European family laws is confirmed below.

## 4. PROBLEMS OF LEGITIMATION

### 4.1. Family Law Reform, Modernity and 'Better" Law

The convergence thesis has been interpreted as providing a basis for legitimating selection of particular models for a European family code, where there is no "common core" of legal policy or consensus on human rights.[188] As family laws are evolving in the same direction, the argument runs, "better" law represents modernity, to which all jurisdictions will eventually move.[189] Swedish law would appear to be the paradigm.[190]

This approach implies that, in each jurisdiction, legal policy can be located on a continuum, which extends from laws embodying remnants of canon law and religious principles at one extreme, to the model for a new ius commune, based on secular rationalism and Enlightenment values at the other. From this standpoint, all that appears to be in issue in dictating the pace of reform is a contest between "conservative" and "progressive" interests over law as an aspect of cultural heritage.[191] Thus, Antokolskaia has argued that:

> "differences that colour the map of the current European family laws are directly linked to the difference in the timing of this modernisation of family law... [T]he infamous diversity of family laws within Europe is mainly a difference in the level of modernity of the family laws in various countries in Europe." [192]

---

[186]  *The European* 8 May 1997, 5.
[187]  AGELL, *op. cit.*, n 131, 328-9.
[188]  On the latter issue, see ANTOKOLSKAIA, *op. cit.*, n 31.
[189]  *Ibid.*
[190]  *Ibid.* "Principles [could be elaborated] upon the highest standard of modernity achieved in present-day European family law."
[191]  *Ibid.*
[192]  *Ibid.*

In fact, there is no simple trajectory to modernity and "better" law which resolves problems of legitimation. Nor, on many issues, is there any easily identifiable, or uncontroversial, "common core" of legal policy. And far more is at stake in the development of family laws than attachment to, or rejection, of cultural heritage.

It seems important to distinguish between formation of legal policy by the Commission on European Family Law on the basis of objective criteria and policy formation in accordance with the subjective and intuitive judgments of its members. As the case study below indicates, objective standards to legitimate recommendations from the Commission are lacking.

## 4.2. From a Moral to an Economic Agenda in Family Law: Case Study

The boundaries of family law shift in response to social and demographic change. Inevitably, some issues cease to be significant in political terms – formal equality between husband and wife in marriage is an obvious example – but new controversies emerge. As in the 1970's, and with contemporary legal policy in the Nordic countries, family law in the rest of Europe remains a powerful medium to further a range of political objectives.

In proposing laws for inclusion in a European Code, the Commission on European Family Law must take decisions that impinge on labour market and fiscal policies and social security provision. In addition, the Commission must select between competing political and institutional traditions and principles of social organisation expressed in legal policy.

This is apparent even in areas where consensus might appear assured. For example, it is now axiomatic that all children should have the same rights, regardless of their parents' marital status. However, Sweden and other Nordic countries operate a mandatory paternity procedure, which applies whenever a child is born to an unmarried woman. In England, this has been considered and rejected.[193] English policy involves direct pressure to establish paternity only where a woman is in receipt of state benefits.[194] This reflects a weaker orientation to the state than in the Nordic countries, and also a less egalitarian approach and greater concern with public expenditure.

---

[193] THE LAW COMMISSION *Family Law: Illegitimacy* (London: HMSO, 1982) 146,7.
[194] SS 6, 46 Child Support Act 1991, as amended by S3 Child Support, Pensions and Social Security Act 2000.

90

German law used to have something similar to Nordic procedures in its provisions for official guardianship, but these were repealed after re-unification.[195] However, it remains the case that both Nordic and German laws sanction compulsory tests in paternity disputes, whereas this is exceptional among European jurisdictions.[196] Proposing a model for paternity law therefore involves endorsing a strong state ethic or, alternatively, a commitment to individual liberty.

The problem of legitimation is clearly acute in issues such as the rights of same-sex partners. Development of legal policy here involves a political contest as to whether sexual activity in general, and homosexuality in particular, constitutes a danger to society. The prize is destruction or retention of a religious concept of marriage. Establishing a quasi-marital or marital status for same-sex relationships represents a seminal change. It carries in its wake legitimation of heterosexual cohabitation. This in turn undermines restrictions on marriage and divorce. All this involves the de-institutionalisation of traditional family law.

Many of the features of family law reform in the 1970's have re-emerged in the introduction of registered partnership laws and same-sex marriage in the Netherlands. In some jurisdictions, national constitutions have had a decisive impact on legal policy. In others, partnership legislation has reflected differences in political processes, public opinion and the strength of political interests.

Divergence in the Nordic countries in relation to registered partnerships and heterosexual cohabitation has been noted above. In the Netherlands, the establishment of same-sex marriage has accompanied legalisation of prostitution[197] and liberal legislation on euthanasia. None of this, it has been argued, would have been possible without displacement of the Christian Democrats in 1994 and formation of a left-liberal, "purple coalition."[198] This latter administration initially rejected same-sex marriage, but its re-constitution after the 1998 elections depended on an explicit

---

[195]  FRANK, *op. cit.*, n 121, 168.
[196]  FRANK, "Compulsory Physical Examination for Establishing Paternity" (1996) 10 *IJLPF* 205.
[197]  See GOULD, "The Criminalisation of Buying Sex: The Politics of Prostitution in Sweden" (2001) *Jnl. Soc. Pol.* 437 for the markedly different approach in Sweden. This demonstrates the link between family law and other aspects of political economy and also differences between these two jurisdictions.
[198]  R.B. ANDEWEG and G.A. IRWIN, *Governance and Politics in the Netherlands* (Basingstoke: Palgrave, 2002) 112.

agreement to open up marriage.[199] The approach in the Dutch legislature to a spectrum of issues in the same-sex marriage and adoption proposals graphically demonstrates divisions between political parties and their concern with the precise form of the legislation.[200] Comparatively liberal public opinion assisted advocates of same-sex marriage, as was the case with decriminalisation of homosexuality in 1971.[201] Once again, however, social engineering has not been apparent to the same extent as in Sweden. Thus, Dutch law does not permit adoption from overseas.[202]

Prior to the drive for same-sex marriage in the Netherlands, political differences had already surfaced in proposals for registered partnership legislation for heterosexual and same-sex relationships. The Christian Democrat-led administration, in office before 1994, supported a model that differentiated the partnership institution from marriage.[203] The new government took a different approach and in 1997 the Ministry of Justice described marriage and partnership as "equivalent... [t]he consequences are virtually identical."[204] In fact, the State Secretary emphasised that registered partnerships "under the law, are given a separate and equal place to that of marriage."[205]

In France, political interests divided over the PACS, which was introduced in 1999.[206] In the vote in the National Assembly, there was a split almost exactly on party lines.[207] However, those on the left were initially wary of public opinion. And when, after some prevarication, the content of the proposal was settled, the Minister of Justice, in direct contrast to her counterpart in the Netherlands, was keen to distance the PACS from

---

[199] FORDER, "The Netherlands", in A. BAINHAM (ed.), *The International Survey of Family Law 1997* (The Hague: Kluwer, 2000) 239, 248.

[200] For analysis of the positions adopted by D66, the Green-Left Party, CDA, PvdA, VVD and strict and stricter Protestant factions in the First and Second Chambers, see FORDER, "The Netherlands", in A. BAINHAM (ed.), *The International Survey of Family Law 2001* (The Hague: Kluwer, 2001) 301-320; SCHRAMA, "The Netherlands", in A. BAINHAM (ed.), *The International Survey of Family Law 2002* (The Hague: Kluwer 2002) 277-302.

[201] VAN DEN AKKER, "Primary Relations in Western Society", in P. ESTER *et al.* (eds.), *The Individualising Society* (Tilburg: Tilburg UP, 1993) 97, 114.

[202] REINHARTZ, "The Netherlands", in HAMILTON and PERRY, *op. cit.*, n 116, 436, 462.

[203] FORDER, "The Netherlands", unpublished paper to 5th European Conference on Family Law, The Hague 1999.

[204] Ministry of Justice, *Registered Partnership* (The Hague, 1997) 3.

[205] *Press Release* 22.5.1997.

[206] BRADLEY, "Regulation of Unmarried Cohabitation in West-European Jurisdictions" (2001) 15 *IJLPF* 22, 35.

[207] *Ibid.*, 44 n42.

marriage. Marriage is fundamentally different, she argued.[208] In fact, the structure of the French and Dutch models does differ in major respects.[209] The PACS developed once again as a challenge between the "Two Frances."[210] One further institutional consideration, peculiar to France, which influenced the measure, was the commitment to an inclusive concept of citizenship.[211] Prior to the PACS, it had been a priority to deny a specific, homosexual group identity.[212] The legislation endorsed this approach by including a range of relationships.

In contrast, a major concern in drafting a partnership law in the Federal Republic of Germany was to exclude heterosexual cohabitation, in order to comply with the requirement in the Basic Law to protect marriage.[213] A further factor, which determined the content of the legislation, was that conservative interests in the Bundesrat blocked provisions within their competence.[214] There was also limited enthusiasm, within the Federal Government itself, to acknowledge links with children.[215] Moreover, the law as originally drafted, clearly established that a same-sex partnership would be inferior to marriage.[216] The legislation differs significantly from

---

[208]   STEINER, "The spirit of the new French registered partnership law" (2000) 12 Child and Family Law Quarterly 1, 4.

[209]   BRADLEY, op. cit., n 206, 28-37. This divergence is consistent with other aspects of marriage law, e.g. age and prohibited degrees of relationship: compare REINHARTZ in HAMILTON and PERRY, op. cit., n 117, 443 and CHAUVEAU ibid. 256. In addition, gender re-assignment and transsexual marriage were recognised in the Netherlands in 1984: in France this has been much more problematic: see ICCS, Transsexualism in Europe (Strasbourg: Council of Europe, 2000) 14-5.

[210]   MARTIN and THÉRY, op. cit., n 60, 154; see p. 74 above.

[211]   VELU, "Faut-il 'pactiser' avec l'universalisme?" (1999) 7 Modern and Contemporary Politics 429.

[212]   FILLIEULE and DUYENDAK, "Gay and lesbian activism in France: Between integration and community- oriented movements", in B.D. ADAM et al. (eds.), The Global Emergence of Gay and Lesbian Politics (Philadelphia: Temple University Press, 1999) 185, 204.

[213]   THORN, "The German Law on Same-Sex Partnerships", in BOELE-WOELKI and FUCHS (eds.), The Legal Recognition of Same-Sex Couples in Europe, (EFL series No. 1, Intersentia-Antwerp), 2003, 84.
         And see ibid. for the subsequent, liberal judgement of the Federal Constitutional Court.

[214]   Ibid.

[215]   Federal Ministry of Justice "Legislation on Same Sex Partnerships" para. 1.2 <http://www.bmj.bund.de>

[216]   This is apparent in the term "life partnership," the absence of an obligation relating to conjugal life, the fact that the Zugewinngemeinschaft does not apply automatically, more limited maintenance obligations and pension-sharing rights than in marriage and, in particular, the fact that a registered partnership does not preclude marriage: see THORN, op. cit., n 213; DETHLOFF, "The Registered Partnership Act of 2001", in A. BAINHAM (ed.), The International Survey of Family Law 2002 (The Hague: Kluwer 2002) 171-180.

Dutch and Swedish partnership law.[217] All this confirms suggestions that the measure was of limited importance for the Social Democrats – not seen as a vote winner – but necessary to honour an agreement with the Greens, their coalition partners who, in any event had originally advocated same-sex marriage.[218]

English law now provides for same-sex adoption[219] but, as yet, there is no partnership legislation, nor has there been comprehensive revision of the status of heterosexual cohabitation. Although this may appear incongruous, it is consistent with earlier traditions of de-politicisation and the generally cautious approach of governments of either party to marriage law reform.[220] The adoption measure originated as a Private Member's proposal and did not form part of the Government's adoption bill. Nor was the Government keen to take over partnership bills introduced by Private Members.[221] It has, however, now stated that it will go ahead, but the responsible Minister has referred to "complex considerations."[222] The legislation may therefore differ from Dutch and Swedish law. It is also a moot point whether heterosexual relationships will be included. This has proved politically sensitive in the past.[223] And Labour itself has stated that:

> "marriage is still the surest foundation for raising children and remains the choice of the majority of people in Britain. We want to strengthen the institution of marriage…"[224]

In Ireland, the constitutional framework for enhanced rights for same-sex partners has been judged "unpromising."[225] The absence of initiatives in this area is consistent with the refusal to allow transsexual marriage.[226] In

---

[217] The process of reform on other aspects of marriage law is consistent with this approach: compare, for example, the comprehensive reform of Swedish marriage law in 1972 and 1973 described at pp. 72-73 above, with the establishment in Germany of transsexual marriage in 1980, following a decision of the Federal Constitutional Court, and the much later abolition of prohibited degrees of affinity in 1997.

[218] THORN, *op. cit.*, n 213.

[219] SS 49, 144(4) Adoption and Children Act 2002.

[220] The most prominent manifestation is the approach to transsexualism: see generally, BRADLEY, "Comparative Law, Family Law and Common Law" (2003) 3 *Oxford Journal of Legal Studies* 127, 131-2.

[221] *Ibid.*

[222] Minister for Social Exclusion, 6 December 2002 <http://www.labour.org.uk/gaypartnerships/>.

[223] BRADLEY, *op. cit.*, n 206, 40.

[224] HOME OFFICE, *op. cit.*, n 114, 5.

[225] FLYNN, "From Individual Protection to Recognition of Relationships?", in WINTEMUTE and ANDENÆS, *op. cit.*, n 18, 590, 591.

[226] Re Foy, Attorney General and Foy (Judgement of McKechnie J 9.7.2002).

Italy, recognition of a right to marry for transsexuals in 1982, followed a decision of the Constitutional Court and the ferment in family law reform in the 1970's described above.[227] Establishment of rights for same-sex relationships appears to be of an entirely different order. This has been supported predominantly by deputies on the left and has been "on and off the Italian political agenda."[228] Anti-discrimination legislation has come to the fore and provoked fierce debate and strong opposition from Christian Democrats.[229]

In regions of Spain such as Catalonia, introduction of the Law on Stable Unions which applies to same-sex and heterosexual relationships, has served distinctive political objectives in enhancing regional autonomy. The legislation complements other aspects of Catalonian particularism, including enactment of a Family Code.[230] The structure of the Law on Stable Unions is equally distinctive in that it excludes social security and other rights, which are within the remit of central government. The law was clearly drafted with care in other respects. Thus, same-sex couples are denied the right to adopt, which is available to heterosexual partnerships as well as married couples, while same-sex partners have acquired inheritance rights, which are denied to their heterosexual counterparts.[231] Public opinion has not proved a barrier to these measures, any more than it impeded divorce reform 20 years ago.[232]

At the national level in Spain, the contest between opposing political interests over partnership legislation has involved the same objectives as in other jurisdictions; i.e. to enhance or limit comparisons with marriage in the proposals which have been put forward.[233] The programme from the Secretary General of the Socialist Party to open up marriage to same-sex couples, if it wins the next election, is linked to abortion reform and a law on euthanasia.[234] Family law will therefore be at the centre of political debate.

---

[227] Pp. 78-79.
[228] SCAPPUCCI, *op. cit.*, n 18, 518, 526.
[229] *Ibid.* 528.
[230] MARTÍN-CASALS, "Same-Sex Partnerships in the Legislation of Spanish Autonomous Communities" in BOELE-WOELKI and FUCHS (eds.), *The Legal Recognition of Same-Sex Couples in Europe,* (EFL series No. 1, Intersentia-Antwerp), 2003, 54.
[231] I. SALAS, "The Law on Stable Unions", in WINTEMUTE and ANDENÆS, *op. cit.*, n 18, 505.
[232] P. 79 above. S.P. MANGEN, *Spanish Society After Franco* (Basingstoke, Palgrave, 2001) 129 *et seq.*
[233] BRADLEY, *op. cit.*, n 204, 26.
[234] MARTÍN-CASALS, *op. cit.*, n 230.

There is no "common core" in European registered partnership legislation. Rather, there are complex laws which cover different relationships and rights, and which are finely tuned to political interests and public opinion in the jurisdictions in which they operate. In recommending "better" law, the Commission on European Family Law will have to determine whether it will equate the partnership model closely with marriage, and further the process of de-institutionalisation, referred to above. The alternative is to stigmatise homosexuality to a greater or lesser extent. It is difficult to see a basis on which this decision will be taken, other than personal opinion within the Commission.

Same-sex marriage appears the most contentious issue which confronts the Commission, but it cannot be assumed that even its initial project is unproblematic, merely because major divorce reforms in Europe were enacted over two decades ago.[235] For example, as noted above, Swedish law imposes minimal controls on divorce where there are children.[236] Official reports advise that: "staying together just for the sake of the children is rarely a good idea."[237] Conservative interests in other jurisdictions are perhaps unlikely to endorse this sanguine approach. This is not to make a judgement on whether divorce does or does not affect children, but simply to note that Swedish policy is consistent with social democratic ideology, and may not be considered "better" law elsewhere.[238]

In any event, divorce law does not simply involve spouses or their children. From a political and institutional standpoint, the question is whether legislation should attempt to reinforce an image of divorce as prejudicial to society. It was this issue which was negotiated in the detail of the French reform of 1975, which occupied political parties in Germany in their protracted dispute over the structure of the 1976 law, and which subsequently split the Spanish government.[239] It remains a live issue today. Thus, the English Law Commission has rejected Swedish law as this "represents the abdication of the State from any responsibility for determining whether a divorce should be granted."[240] And in France, a recent proposal for divorce reform has proved controversial. Conservatives in the Senate have

---

[235] See above pp. 72-80.
[236] Pp. 72-73.
[237] SOCIALSTYRELSEN, *Getting Divorced* (Stockholm: NBHW, c2000.) 1.
[238] See D. POPENOE, *Disturbing the Nest* (New York; De Gruyter, 1988) 335.
[239] See pp. 74-79.
[240] LAW COMMISSION, *Facing the Future* (London: HMSO, 1988) 32.

opposed a proposal from the National Assembly to limit reliance on fault.[241] Moreover, the present right wing administration – not surprisingly – appears to favour modest reform.[242] Nor are fault grounds necessarily retrogressive: the inclusion of violent conduct as a ground for divorce in Norwegian law emphasises the seriousness of domestic violence.[243]

The Commission must sift through the complex variations in European divorce laws, which encompass different matrimonial offences and defences, separation and waiting periods of varying lengths, and distinct requirements relating to mediation and resolution of ancillary issues. There is no obvious "common core" on these issues. In proposing a model for harmonisation, the Commission on European Family Law has to take a political decision, with no apparent basis for its legitimation.

It also appears problematic to isolate particular areas of legal policy as the Commission seeks to do. Conservative interests may, for example, oppose a liberal measure on divorce as the precursor to other "progressive" laws. The degree to which elements of a family law system were interdependent in the 1970's, has been noted above.[244] There is no reason why there should not be similar linkage today.

If Swedish law is to be the model for the Commission, how many jurisdictions outside the Nordic region will adopt its policy on marital capacity, which not only permits marriage between half-brothers and sisters, in certain circumstances, but also, for the present at least, allows marriage between adoptive parents and children?[245] Even on the most basic question, such as formalities for marriage, there is no obvious "better" law. The Commission faces a formidable task here. It cannot be argued that a system which recognises only civil marriage is technically superior. A majority of West-European countries recognise civil and religious marriage.[246] Does this constitute the "common core?" If so, the Commission must recommend that the Federal Republic of Germany and France allow religious marriage and reverse policies adopted in the Kulturkampf and Revolution. The alternative is for the Commission to recommend that religious marriage should not be recognised. This may be accepted in Sweden, if only

[241] FERRAND, "Grounds for divorce and maintenance between former spouses" <http://www2.law.uu.nl/priv/cefl/Reports/pdf/France02.pdf.>
[242] Le Monde 18. 12. 2002 "La notion de divorce pour faute ne sera pas modifiée."
[243] S23 Marriage Act.
[244] Pp. 72-79 above.
[245] SALDEEN, op. cit., n 137, 624.
[246] See HAMILTON and PERRY, op. cit., n 117 passim.

to establish same-sex marriage. However, it is likely to be problematic not just in England where there has been continued deference to the Church on the issue of formalities for marriage,[247] or in Italy where religious marriage was established in the 1929 Concordat,[248] but also in other Nordic countries where the position of State Churches is recognised in national constitutions.[249]

Since the Reformation, policy on issues such as divorce and, more recently, the status of extra-marital and same-sex relationships has provided a sensitive indicator of political developments in European jurisdictions. This epoch may be drawing to a close as secularisation of society and demographic change undermine the "moral" agenda in family law. However, this area of legal policy will continue to provide a site to advance political interests and objectives.

Economic issues will become more prominent in the future. The extent to which society, or individuals and families, should provide child support, or meet the cost of dependency in informal cohabitation, will remain controversial, as will property and housing entitlements on divorce. Pension division is likely to become increasingly important. Child custody and contact laws, and compulsion to mediate rather than litigate in family disputes, will also remain sensitive issues, not least for women who head lone-parent families. Variations in family law will not be eliminated, so long as there are independent nation states, with different welfare models and taxation policy.

At present, jurisdictions such as England and the Federal Republic of Germany have not followed Sweden in restricting financial support on divorce to reinforce the labour market participation of women.[250] English law was reformed in 1984, but the legislature did not provide a clear principle on this issue.[251] This is not simply a product of the common law tradition. Social engineering in English family law has been at a premium. In general, there has been a reactive response to social change, in contrast

---

[247]   BRADLEY, *op. cit.*, n 220.

[248]   T.G. WATKIN, *The Italian Legal Tradition* (Aldershot UK: Ashgate, 1977) 170.

[249]   Article 62, Constitution of the Republic of Iceland; S4 Danish Constitution; Art 2 Norwegian Constitution.

[250]   Gender equality has been considered a pre-requisite to prosperity in Sweden: SOMMESTAD, *Gender Equality – a Key to our Economic Prosperity?* (Stockholm: Swedish Institute, 2001) 432.

[251]   S25 (2)a Matrimonial Causes Act 1973, as amended.

to the proactive approach in Sweden.[252] In the Federal Republic of Germany, a reform in 1986 did limit support rights, but here also there were differences with Swedish policy. Thus, an objective was to protect maintenance debtors from the inability of former spouses to find employment.[253] This reform also re-introduced fault, which has no place in Swedish law.[254] It is difficult to see how it is possible for the Commission on European Family Law to legitimate, or even propose, a recommendation for harmonisation, given the different contexts in which laws in this area operate.

There are also significant variations in legal policy relating to marital property and employment pensions. In fact, the close assimilation of property regimes, described by David and Brierly, is limited. Sweden retains a near universal property regime, but this was rejected in the Federal Republic of Germany in favour of an acquests system.[255] Moreover, there is a wide divergence between German and English legal policy. In England, the government has yet to legislate for equal division of assets on divorce, although the judiciary has been moving hesitantly towards this.[256] The fact that it is has proved extraordinarily difficult to acknowledge equality as a basic value in English family law is itself an indicator of political culture and traditions. In the Federal Republic of Germany "equal entitlement... in all marital property forms part of the constitutionally protected essence of marriage."[257] When (or if) legislation is enacted in England, it is likely to involve a much weaker commitment to equality. And it is almost certain to differ from Swedish law, both in the scope of judicial discretion to depart from equality, and in the provision for housing women and children after

---

[252] GIBSON, "Changing Family Patters in England and Wales over the Last Fifty Years", in J. EEKELAAR and S. KATZ (eds.), *Cross Currents* (Oxford: Clarendon Press, 2000) 32-55; Bradley, *op. cit.*, n 182, 37, 54-66.

[253] FRANK, "Germany" (1987-8) *Journal of Family Law* 101, 103-4.

[254] GLENDON, *op. cit.*, n 45, 222.

[255] See DAVID and BRIERLY, *op. cit.*, n 112, above, who refer incorrectly to the Swedish matrimonial property regime of participation in acquests.

[256] White v White [2000] 2 FLR 981 (HL); Cowan v Cowan [2001] 2 FLR 192 (CA); Lambert v Lambert [2003] 1 FLR 139 (CA).

[257] VOEGELI and WILLENBACHER, "Property Division and Pension Splitting in the FRG", in L.J. WEITZMAN and M. MACLEAN (eds.), *Economic Consequences of Divorce* (Oxford: Clarendon Press, 1992) 163, 166. There is also much less emphasis on transfer of housing after divorce in German law: see T. HONORÉ, *The Quest for Security* (Stevens: London, 1982) 67; P. GOTTWALD, D. SCHWAB and E. BÜTTNER, *Family and Succession Law in Germany* (The Hague: Kluwer, 2001) 64.5.

divorce.[258] This area of family law complements welfare provision. An "advanced" welfare state on Nordic lines has not been established in England; welfare policy here has been vulnerable to neo-liberal pressure in the recent past.[259]

With regard to employment pensions, in Sweden as a general rule, these are excluded from property division as non-transferable assets. This approach is also compatible with gender policy.[260] In contrast, a pension-splitting regime was introduced in the Federal Republic of Germany in 1976. This is consistent with the principle of subsidiarity in the "state corporatist" welfare model.[261] And the scheme is intricate – "the law covers probably the most complicated matters ever legally regulated."[262] In England, however, the courts have recently acquired wide discretionary powers to re-allocate pensions.[263] There is no "common core" here. What is a "better" pension splitting law – the Swedish, German or English model? Can the Commission legitimate proposals relating to division of pensions and other aspects of marital property which impact on social security and welfare provision, and consequently taxation?

### 4.3. The Fallacy of the 'Common Core" and 'Better" Family Law

The three studies in this paper demonstrate that family law is integral to the political economy of nation states. The fallacy in presenting concepts of a "common core" and "better" law as the basis for legitimating components of a European code lies in failing to consider the political and institutional dimension of legal policy, or in downgrading this dimension to a relatively unimportant aspect of heritage. This is a law-dominated perspective, which also accounts for over-simplified assessments of

---

[258] See Chapter 11 S8 and Chapter 2 S1 Marriage Code. And for the mechanistic guidelines available to Swedish courts, see AGELL, "The Division of Property Upon Divorce From a European Perspective", in J. POUSSIN-PETIT (ed.), *Liber Amicorum Marie Thérèse Meulders-Klein* (Bruxelles: Bruylant, 1988) 1, 10.

[259] CLARKE AND LANGAN, "Restructuring Welfare: The British Regime in the 1980's", in A. COCHRANE and J. CLARKE (eds.), *Comparing Welfare States* (London : Sage Publications, 1993) 49, 69 *et seq.* Compare Ministry of Industry, Employment and Communications (Sweden) *Towards Full Employment* (Stockholm, 2001) p. 3: "It is thanks to welfare and equality that this country is prospering."

[260] Chap 10 S3 Marriage Code. The position is different for private pensions and savings schemes: see now SALDEEN, "Sweden", in BAINHAM (ed.), *The International Survey of Family Law 1995* (The Hague: Kluwer, 1997) 477, 488. I am grateful to Margareta Brattström for information.

[261] ALBER, "Germany" in FLORA, *op. cit.*, n 185, 1, 4.

[262] VOEGELI and WILLENBACHER, *op. cit.*, n 257, 176.

[263] CRETNEY and MASSON, *op. cit.*, n 87, 412-5.

convergence and the view that harmonisation is simply a technical exercise to solve problems of private international law.

Family law cannot, in any real sense, be viewed as private law, involving merely the rights of parties to domestic relationships *inter se*.[264] It would be an unusual, if not unique, politician who did not have views on issues such as marriage, divorce, extra-marital relationships and homosexuality, the welfare of children and whether the family or the state should support dependants. And it is a fair assumption that policy on these issues will continue to differ between jurisdictions.

Legal policy applied to domestic relationships offers ample scope for the acquisition of power and profit; for establishment of ideologies which satisfy personal prejudice and psychological needs; and for the presentation of particular definitions of reality. Friedman touches on this in his general depiction of law as:

> "an organised system of social control... a mirror held up against life. It is order: it is justice; it is also fear, insecurity, emptiness; it is whatever results from the scheming, plotting, and striving of people and groups with and against each other."[265]

In fact, this appears a precise description of the nature and functions of family law. Kahn-Freund advised that:

> "those interested in the harmonisation of law in Europe should give serious consideration to the need for studying each rule and each institution not as a piece of legal history or dogmatic reasoning or organisational technique, but as the outcome of the social and political history and the social and political environment in which they grew and exist."[266]

This advice remains as valid today, as when it was offered 25 years ago, subject to one clarification. Family laws do not simply operate in a particular social or political context, but form part of an integrated political design.

---

[264] See MEULDERS-KLEIN, "Quelle unité pour le droit de la famille en Europe? (2000) 438 *Revue du marché Commun et de L'Union Européene* 328.

[265] M.A. FRIEDMAN, *A History of American Law* (New York: Simon & Schuster, 1973) 595.

[266] KAHN-FREUND, *op. cit.*, n 4, 168.

David Bradley

## 5. CONCLUSION

It is important to appreciate both the novelty and significance of the task on which the Commission on European Family Law is engaged.

It may be reassuring for advocates of harmonisation to look back to canon law and the ius commune – "the first unification of European law," as it has been described.[267] However, the ambit of canon law was restricted; its main focus was on marriage and Christian doctrine relating to sexual activity.[268] And even within areas of direct concern to the mediaeval Church, there was a diversity of approach. This was the case, for example, in resistance to the canon law doctrine of free consent to marry. The exigencies of family life in the mediaeval period must have necessitated parental control over marriage in many cases. The result was a proliferation of devices to maintain family authority.[269]

In the 20th Century, the strongest potential for harmonisation was perhaps within the Eastern bloc after World War II, rather than in the Nordic countries. However, communist ideology did not result in uniform family laws. For those countries within the Soviet sphere of influence, differences remained on issues such as age for marriage, divorce and marital property.[270] Far less did fascism produce convergence. Franco annulled the divorce law introduced in Spain under the Second Republic, whereas in Germany, divorce grounds were extended in the interests of National Socialism.[271] Nor do post-communist family laws reflect a uniform approach. The introduction of religious marriage in the Czech Republic and Lithuania has been referred to above. This step was not taken in the Russian Family Code of 1995.[272] There are, in addition, differences in relation to divorce: in contrast to Russian law, the Lithuanian Civil Code has re-introduced fault grounds.[273]

With regard to the significance of the project undertaken by the Commission on European Family Law, harmonisation will not simply have

---

[267] R.C. VAN CAENEGEM, *European Law in the Past and Future* (Cambridge, CUP, 2002)
[268] M. SHEEHAN, *Marriage, Family and Law in Medieval Europe* (Buffalo, Toronto UP, 1996) 246.
[269] KORPIOLA, "Controlling Their Children's Choice", in K. MELBY *et al.* (eds.), *Ægteskab i Norden fra Saxo til i dag* (Copenhagen: Nordic Council of Ministers, 1999) 71.
[270] PAP, "Socialist Law", in CHLOROS, *op. cit.*, n 54, 227.
[271] R. PHILLIPS, *Putting Asunder* (Cambridge: CUP, 1988) 541, 547-50.
[272] ANTOKOLSKAIA, "The 1995 Russian Family Code" (1996) 22 *Review of Central and East European Law* 635, 643.
[273] Article 3.26 Civil Code of Lithuania. This may pose additional problems for the Commission on European Family Law.

102

Intersentia

implications for private international law. If the Commission proposes a status for unmarried heterosexual cohabitation and same-sex partnerships, which is taken up, this will extend the application of existing decisions of the European Court of Justice relating to free movement, and increase pressure for a more liberal approach from the Court itself.[274] Enhanced rights for same-sex relationships would also complement Article 13 EC. In addition, a family law code could confirm commitment to liberal values in the European Union and add substance to the Charter of Fundamental Rights.[275]

Behind all this is a broader objective. As family law is a central component of political economy in European nation states, harmonisation will mark a significant step towards an ever closer political union. To date, top down Europeanisation of legal policy has involved a cautious accommodation of sovereignty. The judgement in Goodwin v UK[276] was based on the broad consensus reached in European jurisdictions on gender re-assignment, and followed a series of decisions which allowed the United Kingdom a margin of appreciation on this issue.[277] The programme to resolve problems of private international law through initiatives such as Brussels II is proceeding by stages. The official commentary on the (non-binding) Charter of Fundamental Rights pointedly leaves open the question whether Article 9 could lead to same-sex marriage.[278] Moreover, arguments that Article 13 EU sets a standard for family law must acknowledge that, even apart from the limited scope of this provision, its application is hedged in with restrictions.[279]

These and similar concessions to sovereignty in the future will be unnecessary if a uniform law is established. Behind the rhetoric of "better" law and an "area of freedom, security and justice," harmonisation of family law is a political exercise and should be recognised as such. This paper has not argued in principle against a European law – perhaps this should be emphasised. All it has sought to indicate is that accounts of convergence are exaggerated; that objective criteria for legitimating components

---

[274] McGLYNN, "The Europeanisation of family law" (2001) 13 *CFLQ* 35, 47.
[275] See *ibid.* 48 for the contrary view that a European code may have a conservative orientation and perpetuate exclusion and inequality in domestic relationships.
[276] [2002] 2 FLR 518 (ECHR)
[277] Rees v UK [1987] 2 FLR 111; Cossey v UK [1991] 2 FLR 492; Sheffield and Horsham v UK [1998] 2 FLR 928.
[278] Explanations relating to the Charter of Fundamental Rights of the European Union: http://ue.eu.int/df/docs/en/EN_2001_1023.pdf
[279] SUMNER, "Going Dutch: A Comparative Analysis and Assessment of the Gradual Recognition of Homosexuality with respect to the Netherlands and England" (2002) 9 *MJ* 29, 49-50.

of a common code are not available; and that what is at issue in the construction of a family law of Europe is the negation of a vital aspect of the nation state.

# TOWARDS A EUROPEAN CIVIL CODE ON FAMILY LAW? ENDS AND MEANS

MARIE-THÉRÈSE MEULDERS-KLEIN

## 1. INTRODUCTION

Drawing on the title of Hartkamp's book: "Towards a European Civil Code" (1998),[1] and in an attempt to gauge to what extent such a move might be justified, this report takes a serious look at the hypothesis of the unification of the family law of European countries by means of a common Civil Code or otherwise. However, I immediately wish to point out that I am by no means "opposed" to the idea of seeking ways to achieve as far as possible a "harmonization" of family laws in Europe. It all depends on the aims pursued and the means used to attain them. Hence my first remark will deal with the ambiguity of the title of the programme read as a whole: "Harmonization AND Unification of Family Law in Europe".

I propose therefore to spell out my thinking as follows. After an initial exploratory overview of the project and its potential ends, and after underlining the specificity of family law in relation to other branches of private law, I intend in a second part to offer an analysis of the technical feasibility of its implementation in European law. And, finally, in a third part, I will deal with its political desirability and its potential repercussions.

## 2. DEFINING THE ENDS

### 2.1. A matter of terminology

First of all, what are we actually talking about? I ask the question because simultaneous use is made of terms such as *harmonization, unification, codification* and, finally, a "European Civil Code" leading to a *Ius commune*. The fact is, though, that these different terms do not cover the same realities.

---

[1]     A. HARTKAMP *et al.* (eds.), *Towards a European Civil Code,* 2nd revised and expanded edition, Kluwer Law International 1998.

*Harmonization* implies a concern to reconcile the preoccupations and the interests of the various systems so as to avoid conflicts and clashes. This is the gentle approach involving neither coercion nor constraint, but rather goodwill and dialogue with due respect for all concerned and their specific positions, without any attempt to impose a uniform solution on all of them. Harmonization is not uniformization.

*Unification*, on the contrary, means the voluntary or imposed uniformization of different systems and thus postulates greater sacrifices, *a fortiori* if they result from measures of constraint. Moreover, Community language does not generally use this term but rather that of "*approximation*".

As to *codification*, this is a legal technique consisting either of the formal compilation of pre-existing texts such as the Justinian codes or the old Scandinavian codes, which is of no direct relevance to our present purpose; or of the drawing up of a structured and coherent code resulting from entirely new legislative work designed technically and symbolically to unify the law of a Nation State in a legal monument identical for all and binding by definition.[2] This is clearly the most radical means.

As for the return of a long tradition of *Ius commune* in Europe, here again, words are misleading. The "*Ius Commune*" of the Mediaeval Universities was not positive law but rather a search for universal principles of justice, existing side by side with a host of local laws. Ingeniously built on the fiction of the flexible "Immemorial Custom of England" and the reasoning of the judges construing case by case rules in accordance with the needs which were felt, the English Common Law system was designed to underpin royal power throughout the kingdom only, and it is still totally allergic to codification notwithstanding the missions entrusted to the Law Commission by the Law Commission Act (1965).[3] And finally on the Continent, the great modern codifications, such as the French Civil Code of 1804 and, a century later, the German Bürgerliches Gesetzbuch (1900), were designed first and foremost to unify their Nation States: two giants, but as different from one another as a chateau on the Loire and a Gothic cathedral,

---

[2]     G. CORNU, *Vocabulaire juridique* Capitant, Presses Universitaires de France, Paris, 2002, V° Code. See also G. CORNU, "Un Code civil n'est pas un instrument communautaire", Dalloz, 2002, n°4, Chronique, p. 351-352.

[3]     See for instance after the Law Commission Act H.R. HAHLO, "Here Lies the Common Law: Rest in Peace", *Mod. Law Review*, Vol. 30, 1967, pp.241-262; H.R. HAHLO, "Codifying the Common Law: Protracted Gestation", *MLR*, Vol.38, 1975, pp. 23-30; S.M. CRETNEY, "The Codification of Family Law", *MLR*, Vol. 44, 1981, pp. 1-20, apologizing for the delay. Today there is still no codification.

albeit both members of the Roman-Germanic family, because each of them so much mirrors the genius which is peculiar to its people.

Thus far, it is not quite correct to assert that Civil Law and Common Law countries have ever had a common legal tradition in the sense of similar rules on the basis of Roman Law, especially in the field of contract.[4] Nor is it realistic to believe that political debates surrounding family issues have now died down, since the silence of public opinion may just as well mean either resignation to or fear of political uncorrectness.[5]

## 2.2. The matter of aims

The second question is what might be the aims of and the reasons for drawing up a European civil code or whatever kind of unification extending even into the sanctuary of substantive family law?

One can think of many such motives:
- First of all, utilitarian and practical reasons that are understandable in economic terms such as contracts, liability, securities, or in procedural terms, but also bound up with the mobility of people within the European space, the increased number of binational or multinational families, and that of family conflicts as a result of the greater fragility of couples. The objective would then be to simplify their legal problems and their lives, as well as those of lawyers, by unifying substantive and procedural rules, whatever the content of the rules.
- It may also be a matter of political reasons on the part of European leaders wishing to strengthen their authority in the Member States of the European Union under the cover of the "new space of freedom, security and justice" and of the will to give the new citizens of the Union a feeling of identity and citizenship which they are far from possessing so far and that has no concrete content as yet.[6] It was also Napoleon's

---

[4]   Cf. R. ZIMMERMANN, "Roman Law and European Legal Unity", in HARTKAMP, *op.cit.*, pp. 21-39.
[5]   S. D. MARTINY, "Is Unification of Family Law Feasible or even Desirable?" in HARTKAMP, *op. cit.*, pp. 151-1 especially pp. 164-165.
[6]   See the Draft Council Report 13017/01 of 29.10.2001 adopted on 16.11.2001 on the necessity to approximate Member States' legislations in Civil matters, including Family Law, Marriage and the Law of Succession, according to which "*the enshrinement of the principle of free movement of persons and the desire to create a genuine area of freedom, security and justice could provide an alternative justification for the introduction of measures in these areas*".-On this deliberate invasion of Community Law into the field of Family Law see H. GAUDEMET-TALLON, "Droit privé et droit communautaire: Quelques réflexions", *Revue du Marché Commun*, 2000, p. 228. See also P. MCELEAVY "The Communautarisation of Family Law: A Case of too much Haste, too little Reflexion?", in this book, pp. 504-521.

political ambition to cement the unity of France with the Civil Code of the French and that of Bismarck in order to achieve a similar aim with the German Civil Code.

- And, finally, philosophical, ideological or moral reasons may be involved as well, in order to promote or impose, directly or indirectly via a common system of law, the ideal model of what the "modern" family should be in such civilized nations as ours, as we shall see further. Or rather a combination of these three kinds of ends.[7]

### 2.3. Specificity of Family Law

However, it is in this context that I wish to emphasize that family law is unlike any other branch of the law.

Contrary to an often held view, family law is not merely "private" law concerning only individuals and their private interests, for it lies also at the interface between the social and private spheres, and no society – any more than individuals themselves – would have been able to survive or to continue to do so without rules capable of introducing order within human relationships by creating bonds of parentage and affinity as sources of identity and solidarity, but also of prohibitions and limits. This is why family law is not a neutral branch of the law left entirely at the disposal of the parties. In most countries it is indeed looked upon as belonging at least in part to the area of "public order".

Furthermore, the family is not a mere collection of individuals, each equipped with his or her own rights. It is rather a nucleus of privileged relationships between beings who are very close to one another, which lends the family a dimension other than that of "Privacy" in the American meaning of the term.[8] But it is at the same time the place of loves and

---

[7] On these trends see especially K. BOELE-WOELKI, "The road towards a European Family Law", Electronic Journal of Comparative Law, 1997; K. BOELE-WOELKI, "Comparative Research–based Drafting of Principles of European Family Law"; D. MARTINY, "The Harmonization of Family Law in the European Community: Pro and contra" in M. FAURE, I. SMITS & H. SCHNEIDER, *Towards a European Ius Commune in Legal Education and Research*, Intersentia, 2002, at pp. 170-185 and pp. 191-201; M. ANTOKOLSKAIA *et al.*, *Een zoektocht naar Europees Familierecht*, Nederlandse Vereniging voor Rechtsvergelijking, n° 59, Kluwer, 1999; W. PINTENS, "Europeanisation of Family Law", in this book at p. 3; and generally speaking the work of the *Commission on European Family Law* (an unfortunately misleading name which might lead to confusion with the European Commission of the European Union itself).

[8] On this topic see especially M.A. GLENDON, *Rights Talk: The Impoverishment of Political Discourse*, New York Press, 1991. See also on the opposition between Human Rights as the fundamental entitlements of the lone individual, and the family as a group and the core of social relationships, A.J. ARNAUD, "Philosophie des droits de l'homme et droit de la famille", in

hatreds, and of the most violent tensions between the freedoms and the rights of its members. "Private life" within the meaning of individual freedom and "family life" within the meaning of a close community may thus clash at the cost of the deepest distresses and the greatest injustices. Such is the paradox and dilemma of Article 8 of the European Convention on Human Rights which protects both of these two concepts at the same time.[9] For family law is not a *Lex mercatoria*. It is a body of law made up of flesh and blood. In so far as the family is the nucleus of any society, family law is the hard core of any legal culture.

Finally, as has already been said, family law is – even still today – characterized by its diversity, deeply rooted in peoples' history, culture, mentalities and values. A long experience in analyzing, teaching and writing about every aspect of the evolution of European legislations in family matters from a comparative point of view from the 1960s up to the present enables me to bear witness to the fact that, despite converging trends towards more equality and more freedom, national differences create clear dividing lines, not only between Common Law and Civil Law countries, Northern and Latin countries, but also between countries so close to one another as France, Germany and the Netherlands[10] and even between Nordic countries.[11] Here lies also the avowed reason why, despite more or less converging sociological patterns, it is so difficult to extract from them a "common core" that might serve as a basis for unification.[12]

Philosophies and religions may account for this to some extent. This holds true for English liberalism and utilitarianism, Scandinavian realism, French idealism, and also strong reactions against Puritanism in countries where

---

F. DEKEUWER-DEFOSSEZ (ed.), *Internationalisation des droits de l'homme et évolution du droit de la famille*, Librairie Générale de Droit et Jurisprudence (L.G.D.J.), Paris, 1996, pp. 1-25.

[9]    See especially M.T. MEULDERS-KLEIN, "Vie privée, vie familiale et droits de l'homme" and "Internationalisation des droits de l'homme et évolution du droit de la famille: Un voyage sans destination." in M.T. MEULDERS-KLEIN, *La Personne, la Famille et le Droit - 1968-1998: Trois décennies de mutations en Occident*, Bruylant, Brussels, 1999, at pp. 467-493 and 495-525.

[10]    See M.T. MEULDERS-KLEIN, *La Personne, la Famille et le Droit... op.cit.*, at note 9.

[11]    See A. AGELL, "Is there One System of Family Law in the Nordic Countries?" *European Journal of Law Reform*, Vol. 3, n° 3, 2001, pp. 313-330; D. BRADLEY, *Family Law and Political Culture. Scandinavian Laws in Comparative Perspectives*, Sweet & Maxwell, London, 1996; D. BRADLEY, "Convergence in Family Law: Mirrors, Transplants and Political Economy", 6 *MJ* 2 (1999), pp. 127-150; D. BRADLEY, "A Family Law for Europe? Sovereignty, Legitimation and Political Economy", in this book at p. 65.

[12]    Cf. M. ANTOKOLSKAIA, "Human Rights as a Basis for the Harmonisation of Family Law?" in *Human Rights and Family Life*, Proceedings of the 11th World Conference of the International Society of Family Law, 2-7 August 2002, Copenhagen/Oslo, for publication, and M. ANTOLOLSKAIA, "The "Better Law" Approach and the Harmonisation of Family Law", this book at p. 159.

it has prevailed. However, other deep-seated differences, such as the attachment to biological truth in Germany and the Nordic countries, as opposed to will and affective bonds in France as the basis for the establishment of parentage, find their roots solely in the history of peoples and their unconsciousness.[13] The German Federal Constitutional Court was thus prompted in 1988[14] to enshrine as guaranteed by the Constitution the right for each individual to know his or her biological origins by all available means, including compulsory biological checks,[15] and to secure accordingly the legal establishment of paternity, even against a pre-established legitimate affiliation actually experienced by the individual concerned.[16] For its part France admits the mother's right to conceal her name in the birth certificate, mendacious recognitions and false "possession of status", and rejects any idea of compulsion in the matter of biological evidence of paternity.[17] Similarly, when it comes to divorce, given a subtle balance between grounds, procedures and legal effects, no two European countries have the same laws.[18] The rules governing the family name, matrimonial property, inheritance, and, last but not least, "registered partnership", bear witness to the same cultural diversity.

There is a need to be aware of this before imposing on peoples the uniformization of their laws in such a sensitive area.

## 3.  MEANS: THE LEGAL FEASIBILITY OF UNIFICATION

Notwithstanding what has just been said, I shall now look at the legal means that might be used to achieve the harmonization and most of all the

---

[13]   See for a comparative approach M.T. MEULDERS-KLEIN, "Fondements nouveaux du concept de filiation" and "La place du père dans les législations européennes" in La Personne, la Famille et le Droit, *op. cit.* at note 9, pp. 153-184 and pp. 231-284, especially pp. 251-265; R. FRANK, "Die unterschiedliche Bedeutung der Blutverwandschaft im deutschen und französischen Familienrecht", *FamRZ* 1992, pp. 1365-1372; A. ERIKSON & A. SALDEEN, "Parenthood and Science. Establishing and contesting Parentage" in J. EEKELAAR & P. ŠARČEVIĆ (eds.), *Parenthood in Modern Society*, Martinus Nijhoff, 1993, pp. 75-92.

[14]   BVerfG 18 January 1988, *NJW* 1988, p. 3010. See also on the mother's obligation to reveal the natural father's name to her illegitimate child, BVerfG. 6 May 1997, *FamRZ* 1997, 869; R. FRANK & T. HELMS, "Der Anspruch des nichtehelichen Kindes gegen seiner Mutter auf Nennung des leiblichen Vaters", *FamRZ* 1997, pp. 1258-1263.

[15]   See R. FRANK, "Compulsory Physical Examination for Establishing Parentage", *Int. Journal of Law, Policy and the Family* 10 (1996) pp. 205-218.

[16]   BVerfG. 31 January 1989, *NJW* 1989, p. 891.

[17]   See M.T. MEULDERS-KLEIN, "Réflexions sur les destinées de la possession d'état" pp. 185-208, "Les empreintes génétiques et la filiation" pp. 209-229 and "La place du père dans les législations européennes", pp. 231-265 in *La Personne, la Famille et le Droit*, *op.cit.* at note 9.

[18]   See M.T. MEULDERS-KLEIN, "La problématique du divorce dans les législations d'Europe occidentale" in *La Personne, la Famille et le Droit*, *op.cit.* note 9, pp. 53-119.

"unification" of domestic family laws in Europe. Two paths are indeed available that could lead to that end: a "high road" and a "low road", or a gentle way and a hard way, gradually taking us from *Soft Law* to *Hard Law*.

### 3.1. From Soft Law ...

The soft way is the path of interstate dialogue on the basis of comparative studies and restatements.

To begin with, there are of course spontaneous convergences bound up with the sociological development of ideas and behaviours and the progressive adjustment of state legislations as determined by their own peculiarities. However, to become effective, a deliberate harmonization of legislations necessarily requires a resort to conventions. These may cover rules for conflicts of law in Private International Law or substantive law and legal cooperation, by means of bilateral or multilateral treaties. At the overall European level, the chief architect of this method is undeniably the *Council of Europe* which, already for some considerable time, has been attempting to find such means of approximation and standards so that they might serve as model reforms for national legislations and encourage them to cooperate, without compelling member States to adopt uniform laws that might give rise to internal political and social resistance. To this end the Council has commissioned comparative studies, set up standing committees of experts, convened international conferences on family law, drawn up recommendations and draft conventions opened for the signature of member States, currently 44 in number.[19] To these instruments should of course imperatively be added the achievements of the *Hague Conference on Private International Law* and of the *International Commission on Civil Status*. This work is still in progress. However, there is a need here to recognize the immense difficulty of giving concrete form to reforms of substantive family law in so many different laws on a subject by subject basis, given the internal logic binding the latter so closely together, be it a matter of marriage, divorce, affiliation, name, parental authority, marriage, matrimonial property or inheritance, substantive law and procedural law, as well as constitutional law, social and economic policy, taxation and labour law and so on, and this notwithstanding the shared general principles that may be put forward.

---

[19]    See on these numerous activities the comprehensive Document of the COUNCIL OF EUROPE: *Pour construire ensemble l'Europe du Droit*, Directorate General of Legal Affairs, January 2002. See also M. KILLERBY, "Family Law in Europe: Standards set by the Member States of the Council of Europe" in *Liber Amicorum M.T. Meulders-Klein –Droit comparé des Personnes et de la Famille*, Bruylant, Brussels, 1998, pp. 351-378.

## 3.2. to Hard Law

At the same time, however, as we know, it was through the case-law of the European Court of Human Rights (ECHR) that a form of constraint was laid down for the first time in the field of family law by the landmark judgment in the case of Marckx v. Belgium (1979) and the discovery of a *positive obligation* on States to amend their civil law so as to bring their law into line with the requirements of Articles 8 and 14 of the Convention in order – and rightly so – to enable the child born out of wedlock to enjoy from birth a *"normal family life"*, that is, to have affiliation established first with its mother (Marckx v. Belgium, 1979) then with its father ( Johnston v. Ireland, 1986) and with the same effects (Mazurek v. France, 2000). But it is the child which makes the family, and not the couple. Since then, the Court has delivered many decisions concerning the "right to respect of family life", including "the right to marry and found a family" (Article 12). Here we enter the field of the case-law through the judicial review of the conventionality of domestic laws and even of national Constitutions,[20] albeit with *relative res judicata authority* only, at least in principle. But even if authors admit the indirect existence of a general obligation of the States to abide by the Strasbourg Court's judgments in the name of *res interpretata*,[21] it obviously does not entail an obligation to unify the laws of member States, each of which remains free to determine how it contemplates applying the principle that has been construed (art. 53 ECDH). In any event, what is involved is a case-by-case pattern of development and an unpredictable piecemeal approach depending on unforeseeable majorities of judges.

More unexpectedly, however, European Community law has also penetrated the field of national family law, firstly through the case-law of the Court of Justice of the European Communities concerning the "free movement of goods, persons, services and capital" which is necessary for the "good functioning of the internal market" in keeping with its own internal logic, but also by way of reference to Human Rights that the Court interprets freely as "general principles" since the Community itself has never ratified as such the European Convention on Human Rights for various legal, practical and political reasons.[22] So far the Luxembourg Court has observed

---

[20]  On this very thorny question See J. ROBERT, "Constitutional and International Protection of Human Rights: Competing or Complementary Systems?", General Report to the IXth Conference of European Constitutional Courts, *Human Rights Law Journal* Vol. 15, N° 1-2, 1994, pp. 1-23.

[21]  See F. SUDRE, *Droit international et européen des droits de l'homme,* 5th ed. Presses Universitaires de France (PUF), Paris, 2001, pp. 450-470, n° 263-275.

[22]  See F. SUDRE, *op.cit.* at note 20, pp. 103-107, n° 72 and pp. 140-141, n° 94.

great prudence in this matter. However, when the Charter of Fundamental Rights of the European Union proclaimed at the Nice Summit in December 2000 in a different, more vague and broader wording than that of the European Convention on Human Rights itself, becomes binding – and even failing this – the Court's power of coercion will undoubtedly extend further into family matters thus entailing additional risks of divergent interpretations between the two European Courts, so much the more so as article 52.3 of the Charter allows the Court of Justice to provide more extensive protection than the ECHR.[23] And this will not result in a coherent unification of European family law. Far from it, for the superimposition of three different national and supranational normative orders and three sorts of judicial scrutiny of the constitutionality and conventionality of domestic laws will serve only to emphasize and add further complexity to the process of law-making, interpretation and application of the law in the member States.[24]

What then is needed to bring about a European unification of domestic substantive family law? Clearly, it will mean turning towards Statute law. However, despite increased urging by the European Parliament, Commission and Council to embark on this course, the European Union is presently not empowered to legislate by regulation or directive in this field, since – apart from that vested in judicial cooperation in civil and international private law matters on the basis of Articles 65 and 67 of the EC Treaty – the family branch of civil law does not fall under the exclusive or even the peripheral jurisdiction of the Community institutions in accordance with Articles 3 and 5 of the EC Treaty. On the contrary, under Article 94 of the EC Treaty, the extension of this jurisdiction to include the approximation of national legislations dealing with family issues would require a *unanimous* decision of the Council on the basis of a proposal by the Commission and after consultation with the European Parliament and the Economic and Social Committee, and this only insofar as the matter involves legislative, regulatory or administrative provisions of member States "directly affecting the establishment and operation of the common

---

[23] See Judge M. WATHELET, "Le point de vue d'un juge à la Cour de Justice des Communautés européennes" in J.Y. CARLIER & O. DE SCHUTTER, *La Charte des droits fondamentaux de l'Union européen – son apport à la protection des droits de l'homme en Europe*, Bruylant, Brussels, 2002, pp. 241-250.

[24] On this superimposition, see M.T. MEULDERS-KLEIN, "Family Law, Human Rights and Judicial Review in Europe: Heterogeneity and Complexity", Keynote paper delivered at the XIth World Conference of the International Society of Family Law on Family Life and Human Rights, Copenhagen/Oslo, 2-7th August 2002. See also J.Y. CARLIER & O. DE SCHUTTER (eds.), *La Charte des droits fondamentaux de l'Union européenne, op.cit.* at note 23.

market".[25] Furthermore, Article 67 point 5 EC Treaty, as added by the Treaty of Nizza (2000) explicitly excludes "family law issues" from the application of article 251 EC Treaty (codecision procedure). All this is all the more subject to the principles of *subsidiarity* and *proportionality* (Article 5.2 of the EC Treaty and Protocol n° 7 annexed to the Amsterdam Treaty). Given the diversity of the member States and the imminent enlargement of the European Union to 25 countries, it is unlikely that such unanimity could be found to waive the power of their parliaments to legislate in such a sensitive area.

However, even supposing that such unanimity could be reached among the Community institutions and that experts responsible for drawing up the draft were able to find a "common core" and to agree on the wording of an overall or partial European codification of family law, to what extent would such an enterprise be politically and socially advisable?

## 4. POLITICAL DESIRABILITY OF A UNIFIED EUROPEAN FAMILY LAW

Politically speaking, one cannot be but surprised at the route travelled from the purely economic and social objectives of the earlier European treaties to the gradual infiltration of domestic substantive family law.[26] Questions have also been asked more recently as to the motives underlying the appearance of a "European Charter of Fundamental Rights" as a competitor of the European Convention on Human Rights at the Nice Summit of 2000.[27] The explanation no doubt lies in the fact that in the meantime Community policies have evolved and changed in nature, from a vast single market to a centralized political and civil community. However, whereas there is no doubting economic and political advantages accruing from accession to the Union for the candidate States, if the interest of European citizens is to be aroused for that new "space of freedom, security and justice" they are offered, the need was no doubt felt to hold out to them a promise of additional rights by means of an expanded catalogue of fundamental rights simultaneously and symbolically announced as a kind of *Bill of Rights* making up the Preamble of a future European Constitution in a more or less federating structure. However, there is nothing to show that these citizens, any more than the States, are seeking a Family Civil

---

[25]   …unless a far-reaching political interpretation of these words, or of the promise of "a new space of freedom, security and justice" would be used as a tool to expand the discretionary jurisdiction of the Union to regulate any potential matter, as we have seen before…

[26]   See M. FALLON, "Droit familial et droit des Communautés européennes", *Revue trimestrielle de droit familial* (Belg.) 1998, pp. 400; H. GAUDEMET-TALLON, *op.cit.* at note 6.

[27]   See J.Y. CARLIER & O. DE SCHUTTER, *op.cit.* at note 23.

Code that would be identical from London to Ankara. One might rather fear that they might suddenly discover in such a Code the unwanted aggressive hand of a centralizing authoritarianism which at the end of the day would leave national Parliaments with less freedom to legislate than that enjoyed by the States of the United States of America, which in any case have an entirely different history. We are confronted here with a danger of totalitarian thinking that has nothing to do with respect for legal pluralism, national cultures and self-determination as it is so often asserted. Still, in terms of political desirability, one may well wonder about the future of the democratic process of law-making – even setting aside the specific case of the Common Law countries – if the drawing up and the adoption of a European Civil Code – or regulation – were to become the *prerogative* of the European Institutions over the heads of national Parliaments. Indeed, even though the European Parliament is supposed to represent the peoples of the member States, how could 750 MEPs validly represent more than 450 million citizens? Further, if I am well informed, the linkage between the European Parliament, currently endowed with increasing powers, and national parliaments in the legislative process of the Union is at present unclear and poor.[28]

The question is all the more interesting as, once it has been adopted, the future "European Family Code" will not remain engraved in stone. Family law is indeed very much akin to a patient who cannot keep still while undergoing treatment. The instrument will therefore need periodic revision in accordance with the same procedures, not to mention the remedies that people still unhappy about the protection of their rights and liberties will not fail to invoke before one or other of the two European Courts, thus furthering its evolution towards even more freedoms and rights.[29] I therefore very much fear that the venture will turn out to be tantamount to building a cathedral on quicksand.

Finally, in order to avoid this sort of endless headlong pursuit regardless of whether it is with or without codification, we might ask ourselves from the outset which "Better Law" or "Best Model" might serve as a basis for

---

[28] Protocol n° 13 on the Role of National Parliaments in the Union annexed to the Treaty of Amsterdam.

[29] See especially C. MCGLYNN, "A Family Law for the European Union?" in J. SHAW (ed.), *Social Law and Policy in an European Union*, Hart, Oxford, 2000, pp. 223-241; C. MCGLYNN, "Families and the European Union Charter of Fundamental Rights: Progressive change or entrenching Status quo?" (2001) 26 *E.L.Rev.Dec*, Sweet & Maxwell and Contributors, pp. 582-598; C. MCGLYNN, "Human Rights and Family Law", in this book p. 217; I. SUMNER, "The Charter of Fundamental Rights of the European Union and Sexual Orientation", *International Family Law*, Nov. 2002, pp. 156-165.

this European legislative purpose if no "common core" is to be found.[30] The reply that I discovered in the report presented this summer in Oslo by Masha Antokolskaia at the XIth World Congress of the International Society of Family Law would be the "most permissive law" because even the case-law of the Strasbourg Court and that of Luxembourg in the field of Human Rights are fettered by the "margin of appreciation" enjoyed by the States and by the divergence of opinions of judges still insufficiently "modern" in their outlook.[31] However, even if this "ideal model", whose author insists should not be mandatory, were to be adopted, it is by no means certain that it would make civil law and the lives of citizens, lawyers and judges any easier, because the greater the freedom of choice of individual lifestyles, the more the laws are fragmented, at least if – with all due respect – we consider the fantastic complexity of the new Dutch family law in matters of marriage, cohabitation, registered partnership, step-families, the family name, adoption, affiliation, parental authority, etc. and the array of scenarios for which it provides.[32] Moreover, it has already been proven that the greatest individual autonomy is not the best guarantee of equality and happiness for all, in whatever field it might be, but especially in family matters, and first of all for children who are the first victims of this general disarray. The economic, social and psychological costs might be too high. Accordingly, one can hardly help thinking at the end of this review that this combination between political goals and ideological bias casts some doubts on the validity of the enterprise as a sound policy.

## 5. CONCLUSION

I will therefore conclude by saying that there is an urgent need to clarify the debate and to raise it to the level of an authentic political reflection. Such a hotchpotch of objectives and so many things left unsaid in economic, political and ideological terms mean that we can hardly expect to be confronted with a transparent democratic scheme. Whatever his or her nationality, no European citizen would be able to find a way out of such a maze of rival political institutions, standard-setting sources and national and international jurisdictions and to gain a clear view of what it is really all about. Finally, being overkeen to regulate everything on so confused a basis carries the risk of undermining the democratic process of law-

---

[30]  See M. ANTOKOLSKAIA, "The "Better Law" Approach and Harmonisation of Family Law", in this book, p. 157.

[31]  See M. ANTOKOLSKAIA, op.cit. at note 12.

[32]  See W. SCHRAMA, "Reforms in Dutch Family Law During the Course of 2001: Increased Pluriformity and Complexity", *International Survey of Family Law 2002*, Family Law, pp. 277-303.

making, Community law, Human rights and Family law at the same time. I believe therefore that the best democratic path towards an approximation of domestic legislations dealing with family relationships, is not that of the unrealistic scheme to establish a uniform civil code, nor that of constraining Community regulations and directives, but rather the reasonable, pluralistic and flexible path of open democratic dialogue and the voluntary acceptance of satisfactory solutions, possibly on the basis of restatements, respectful of the values and cultures of all European citizens.

# TOWARDS A EUROPEAN *IUS COMMUNE*: THE CURRENT SITUATION IN OTHER FIELDS OF PRIVATE LAW

EWOUD HONDIUS[*]

## 1. INTRODUCTION

This volume deals with the feasibility of the harmonisation of family law in Europe. Exceptionally, this particular article will not deal with family law. Rather, upon the request of the organisers, it will focus on efforts to harmonise other areas of private law. In an earlier publication I briefly analysed the need for the harmonisation of family law in Europe.[2] With regard to contract law and other private law (No. 2), there are already a number of directives, regulations (No. 2.1) and communications (No. 2.2) and there is a growing body of case law (No. 2.3). There are also a number of private efforts (No. 3); the projects of Lando (No. 3.1), Gandolfi (No. 3.2), Trento (No. 3.3), Spier and others (No. 3.4) Van Gerven (No. 3.5), Schulze (No. 3.6) and Grundmann (No. 3.7) are some of the best known among such projects.

There are also some notable non-achievements (No. 4). First of all, somewhat surprisingly, there is no consensus as to a firm basis for the codification of private law in the European Treaty (No. 4.1). Even those who think that there is such a basis, hesitate in forcing such a Code down the throats of non-consenting partners (No. 4.2). Most surprising is the unfriendly attitude of trade and industry to European harmonisation (No. 4.3). Even within the academic community, there is some outright hostility (No. 4.4). Will this opposition be overcome (No. 5)? There are a number of concerns. First, although there is a growing body of Community case law on questions of private law, it is still very limited when compared to domestic case law (No. 5.1). It is of major importance that the present ongoing harmonisation projects take into account the forthcoming arrival

---

[*] This paper represents "work in progress". Part of it was published earlier in: MICHAEL FAURE, JAN SMITS, HILDEGARD SCHNEIDER (eds.), *Towards a European ius commune in Legal Education and Research*, Antwerp: Intersentia, 2002, p. 39-55.

[2] EWOUD HONDIUS, "Naar een Europees personen- en familierecht", in: *Drie treden/Opstellen aangeboden aan Job de Ruiter*, Zwolle: Tjeenk Willink, 1995, p. 173-181.

of a number of new member states in the European Union (No. 5.2). Which areas of private law should be covered in a harmonisation project (No. 5.3)? Finally, a number of technical questions will be dealt with (No. 5.4).

In my conclusions, I shall return come back to the important role of academics in the discussion on harmonisation (No. 6).

## 2. ACHIEVEMENTS ON AN OFFICIAL LEVEL

Having set the tone for this paper, I now turn to its first aspect, devoted to the development of a European private law in areas other than family law. The past decade has witnessed a spectacular growth of interest in developing a European private law. This has occurred first of all on an official level: directives and regulations (No. 2.1), communications (No. 2.2) and case law (No. 2.3).

### 2.1. From directive to regulation

The European Union has four instruments available for harmonisation: treaties, regulations, directives and recommendations. Until recently, directives were the main vehicle for the harmonisation of private law. The many directives on consumer protection are a good example. Their main advantage was, and remains, that they enable member states to integrate a directive's substance in the form of national legislation. The drawbacks are twofold: first, – an often time-consuming – transposition is needed to implement these instruments, and second, the adaptation to domestic law may lead to – sometimes major – divergences. It is therefore of some importance that as of late the regulation seems to score better in Brussels. Where directives are concerned, the European Court is now stricter in surveying their correct transposition.

### 2.2. The Communication on Contract Law

On 11 July 2001, the European Commission published its "Communication of the Commission to the Council and the European Parliament on Contract Law".[3] With this Communication, the Commission sought a discussion on the desirability, the feasibility and the necessity of a European Law of Obligations, not only between academics but also in business circles. To this effect, the Commission first sketched the then current state of affairs. So far, the discussion has been very academic, between partisans

---

[3]     COM(2001) 398 definitive, <http://europa.eu.int/comm/off/green/index_nl.htm>.

and antagonists, between those who advocate codification and those who seek a Restatement, technicians and advocates of a legal cultural identity.

Four options have been offered to us by the Commission. In the first place, we can simply do nothing and leave the conclusion of contracts to the market forces, which may arrive at industry-wide model contracts for cross-border transactions. A second solution is to promote the development of Principles, such as the Lando Commission's Principles of European Contract Law. In this respect, the Commission sees a role for itself (p. 17). In this respect one may also think of Euro-wide general conditions. A third option is to improve the quality of existing European regulation. In this respect, the Commission mentions two examples: the SLIM project – which stands for "Simpler Legislation for the Internal Market" – and the possibility of extending the scope of application of a number of consumer protection directives to non-consumer transactions. A fourth and final option exists in promoting a text with "provisions on general questions of obligations" (p. 19). Here, the Commission is thinking of a directive, regulation or recommendation, which may run from fully optional to wholly mandatory. The last-mentioned solution would replace domestic law, while an option regulation would come next. The Commission does not exclude the existence of even more options.

Those who have read the Communication without any pre-existing ideas, will have been disappointed. Is this all there is to say? The Communication contains 64 pages, but 43 thereof are Enclosures. In the remaining 21 pages, the Commission does mention four interesting options, but nowhere does it pronounce an opinion itself. Could the Commission not have provided some guidance to the discussion? And yet, to end with this impression would not be entirely correct. The major importance of the Communication is that it has put the subject of a European Civil Code on the political agenda, something which, to date, has only been touched upon by academics, and which may now turn into a political issue on which trade and industry and other pressure groups will take a stance. To some extent, this has indeed been the case, witness the many reactions to be found on the Commission's website.

Which of the four options will be preferred by which groups, seems self-evident. The Lando Commission[4] has always, like its sister working group that drafted the UNIDROIT Principles for International Commercial Contracts, been in favour of a Restatement. The Study group for a

---

[4]    No. 3.1 below.

European Civil Code directed by Christian von Bar may have opted for a Code (the fourth option), but the fact that this group is actually the heir to the Lando Commission with the presence in its midst of a fair number of Restatement proponents, make a compromise between the two strands plausible.[5] Gandolfi's Academy,[6] finally, which like the Lando Commission is quoted in the Communication, clearly sees its draft as a draft codification and not as a Restatement. Gandolfi, however, is not very clear as to the entry into force of his Code: "le groupe de travail ne s'est pas expressément posé le problème de la voie par le truchement de laquelle l'avant-projet pourra devenir un code en vigueur pour les citoyens de l'Union européenne" (p. LVII). In short, the choice between a Code and a Restatement is where the discussion between academics, a solitary legrandist notwithstanding, will lie. My own preference lies with a Restatement (the second option): it would be at variance with all forms of respect (*comity*) to force a code upon the English and the Irish.[7]

The non-thinking part of trade and industry will most probably prefer the option of not doing anything (option 1); the thinking part will look ahead and will choose between a Code and a Restatement. It finally appears useful not to opt for only one solution, but rather to extend the scope of application of a number of directives and to simplify the chosen terminology.

The Communication did achieve what it purported to do: it led to a highly interesting discussion. A major event was the conference organised by SECOLA (Society for European Contract Law) in Leuven in November 2001, just two weeks before the Laeken Summit. The volume containing conference papers[8] contains reactions to the Communication from Andreas Schwartze, who advocates empirical research, Hugh Beale who points to the cultural differences between trade and industry in England and France: "the Germans are likely to see the contract as a way of building trust whereas in England, contract and trust are seen as being mutually exclusive and reference to the contract is likely to destroy the commercial relationship" (p. 71), Geraint Howells, who pleads for a general revision of consumer contract law, Bernard Tilleman and Bart Du Laing, who also

---

[5]   CHRISTIAN VON BAR, OLE LANDO, "Communication on European Contract Law: Joint Response of the Commission on European Contract Law and the Study Group on a European Civil Code", *European Review of Private Law* 2002, p. 183-248.

[6]   No. 3.2 below.

[7]   See No. 4.2 below.

[8]   STEFAN GRUNDMANN, JULES STUYCK (eds.), *An Academic Green Paper on European Contract Law*, The Hague: Kluwer Law International, 2002, 432 p.

advocate an evaluation of the present European rules, and Josef Drexl, who favours total harmonisation.

Massimo Bianca (who is in charge of sales in the Gandolfi group) sees a role for the Gandolfi project in a future Code. Christian von Bar ("Even law professors must learn to play in teams"), Jürgen Basedow, Mauro Bussani, Martijn Hesselink, Giuseppe Gandolfi, Ole Lando, Ugo Mattei ("The new European Code should be hard, minimal, not limited to contracts, and process oriented") and Hans-Peter Schwintowski ("Das *Europäische Zivilgesetzbuch* könnte ein zweiter Baustein – after the euro, EH – auf dem Wege zur Verinnerlichung der Idee *Europa* in den Herzen der europäischen Bürger sein"), Roger Van den Bergh ("Forced Harmonisation of Contract Law in Europe: Not to be continued"), Hugh Collins and Norbert Reich wrote the papers in the Third Chapter of the SECOLA volume.

The fourth chapter contains the papers by Stefan Grundmann and Wolfgang Kerber, U. Drobnig, Gerrit de Geest, Christian Kirchner, Jan Smits, Walter van Gerven and Thomas Wilhelmsson.

### 2.3. Case-law of the European Court of Justice

The recent case law of the European Court of Justice shows the increasing importance of private law. Two examples are Heininger and TUI. In Heininger, a couple had taken out credit to the tune of DM 150,000 (approx. euro 75,000) in 1990 in order to purchase an apartment. Eight years later, the Heiningers cancelled the credit agreement, alleging that they had been led into the agreement by an intermediary who had visited them on his own initiative. This meant – according to the Heiningers – that the German Door-to-Door Sales Act applied, and since the bank had not observed its duty to inform the credit taker of his cooling-off period, that period still ran. The German courts totally disagreed with the Heiningers' contention, but they at least allowed them to ask the opinion of the European Court, which in its wisdom finally allowed the Heininger claim.[9]

TUI is perhaps even more interesting.[10] An Austrian family had booked a holiday in Turkey, where their ten-year old daughter Simone fell ill from salmonella poisoning. Simone was confined to bed for the remaining part of the holiday and her parents claimed compensation. Compensation was

---

[9]  Case C-481/99, Heininger/Bayerische Hypo- und Vereinsbank.
[10]  Case C-168/00, Leitner/TUI.

duly awarded, but the amount did not include anything for the missed holiday ("entgangene Urlaubsfreude"). The appellate court, the *Landesgericht* Linz, thereupon wanted to know from the European Court whether this interpretation of the package travel directive was correct – which according to the Court was not the case. The notion of "immaterial damage" should be interpreted in a uniform way, preferably in a broad sense, so as to allow compensation for "entgangene Urlaubsfreude".

The development of a European jurisdiction reminds one of the growth of American law. In the 1980s, Cappelletti directed a European University Institute-based research project into the question of what Europeans could learn from American federalism. In a recent English language publication, Van Erp has again taken up this question.[11] On the basis of the case law of the American *Supreme Court*, Van Erp analyses to what extent the European Court contributes to the development of European Private Law. In both instances, the author discerns a two-tiered approach: "Only after examination of its own authority under the EC Treaty can the Court decide if it will create a substantive rule of private law itself or leave the matter to the courts of the member states, be it within certain limits. As such, this approach is not different from the common analysis of the US federal common law cases, where also a two-pronged test is used" (p. 57).

## 3. ACHIEVEMENTS BY PRIVATE GROUPS

It is not only on an official level that harmonisation of private law has been attempted. Well-known are the efforts of private groups such as those of Lando (No. 3.1), Gandolfi (No. 3.2), Trento (No. 3.3), Spier and others (No. 3.4) and Van Gerven (No. 3.5), Schultze (No. 3.6) and Grundmann (No. 3.7).

### 3.1. The Lando Commission; its Unidroit counterpart and the Von Bar succession

Of the various private efforts at the harmonisation of private law in Europe, Ole Lando's Commission on European Contract Law is no doubt one of the best known. The Commission started its well-documented work in the 1980s. It resulted in the publication of the first part of its Principles of European Contract Law, consisting of General Provisions, Terms and

---

[11]   J.H.M. VAN ERP, *European Union Case Law as a Source of European Private Law/A Comparison with American Federal Common Law, preadvies Nederlandse Vereniging voor Rechtsvergelijking,* Deventer: Kluwer, 2001, p. 1-58.

Performance of the Contract, Non-Performance and Remedies in General, and Particular Remedies for non-Performance.[12] In 2000, Part II followed (integrated with Part I).[13] Meanwhile, in 2001 a third part was completed. It consists of chapters on assignment, assumption of debt, compound interest, conditional obligations, illegality, joint liability, prescription and set off. This Part, which will once again be integrated with Parts I and II, is expected to be published in 2003.

By a strange coincidence, the Commission on European Contract Law was not the only group to embark upon a harmonisation project. In Rome, the Institute for the Unification of Law (UNIDROIT) started a very similar project, which in 1994 resulted in the publication of Principles for International Commercial Contracts.[14] There has always been some competition between the two projects, probably for the better. But the most striking conclusion from a comparison between the two is their obvious similarity. Not only are the adopted solutions often the same or similar, but the very choice of the subjects dealt with, the style of drafting and the order of the chapters are all very much alike. This in itself is not so strange, if only because of the personal connections – at least five members served on both Commissions. Two formal points on which the two sets of Principles differ relate to their scope of application. The UNIDROIT Principles only deal with commercial contracts, whereas the PECL are applicable to all con-tracts, including consumer transactions and private contracts. An obvious difference is that the Lando Principles only cover (Western) Europe, while UNIDROIT has a global scope of application. This geographical feature does perhaps explain why the PECL's highly acclaimed system of national Notes could not work in the case of UNIDROIT.

On one point, the UNIDROIT Principles have met with more success than PECL: UNIDROIT and the President of its Working Group, Michael Joachim Bonell, have always succeeded in having the better publicity. This, and the fact that in the end the UNIDROIT Principles were published first, may explain the apparent edge that they still have with regard to their practical application. Indeed, there is an increasing number of arbitral

---

[12] OLE LANDO, HUGH BEALE (eds.), *Principles of European Contract Law/Part I*, Dordrecht: Nijhoff, 1995.

[13] OLE LANDO, HUGH BEALE (eds.), *Principles of European Contract Law/Parts I and II*, The Hague: Kluwer, 2000.

[14] Principles of International Commercial Contracts, Rome: UNIDROIT, 1994, also available in many other languages, including Arabic, Dutch, French, German, Italian and Spanish. See M.J. BONELL, *A New Approach to International Commercial Contracts/The UNIDROIT Principles of International Commercial Contracts*, The Hague: Kluwer, 1999.

awards which are based on the Principles for International Commercial Contracts, and they have also influenced new legislation in Central and Eastern Europe.[15]

One of the weaknesses of the Lando project is that it is very much a one-man effort. At one time it was hoped that Hugh Beale would prove to be the successor once Ole Lando – born in 1922 – would step down, but his appointment as a Law Commissioner prevented him from taking over. With the Commission on European Contract Law having held its final meeting in Copenhagen in February 2001, the question was raised as to how to deal with practical issues such as copyright. For this purpose, a four-member commission has been appointed, consisting of Eric Clive (Scotland), Ole Lando (Denmark), André Prüm (Luxembourg) and Clause Witz (France).[16] More importantly, another group has presented itself – and been accepted – as the spiritual heir to the Lando Commission.

In 1997, under the then Dutch presidency of the European Union, a conference on a European Civil Code was held in Scheveningen, the seaside resort of The Hague. Although the conference was not in favour of drafting a European Code that would be binding upon all Member States, it was precisely that which Christian von Bar agreed to look into. The Study Group that Von Bar has set up includes several members of the former Lando Commission. Von Bar succeeded in securing sufficient funds to set up a number of teams of young researchers in Germany and the Netherlands.[17]

### 3.2. Gandolfi

So much publicity has been given to the *Principles of European Contract Law*, that one nearly forgets that there are other projects as well. Perhaps the second best known project is the one initiated by the Italian Romanist Giuseppe Gandolfi. Around 1990, Gandolfi started with his major work, a Code of Contract Law, based on the Italian *Codice civile*.[18] Until recently, the project was chiefly known for the fact that one of its members had acknowledged that he had belonged to a mixed committee of the English

---

[15] See for Lithuania: VALENTINAS MIKELENAS, "Unification and Harmonisation of Law at the Turn of the Millennium: the Lithuanian Experience", *Revue de droit uniforme* 2000, p. 243-260.
[16] The group also serves as the Editing Group.
[17] See CHRISTIAN VON BAR, "Die Study Group on a European Civil Code", in: *Festschrift Dieter Henrich*, Gieseking, 2000, p. 1-12.
[18] Why the Italian Code (1942), and not the more modern Dutch Civil Code (1992)? Gandolfi's answer: because the Dutch Code has not yet generated case law and a code without case law is like potatoes without gravy.

and Scottish *Law Commissions* and to have elaborated a draft Contract Code. Gandolfi immediately saw to it that this "MacGregor Code" was published and so it was spared the fate of oblivion.[19] Another consequence was that next to the *Codice civile* the MacGregor Code would serve as the guideline for the work of the Gandolfi Academy. In 2002, the Academy published its Draft Code ("avant-projet").[20] The subject matter is close to what the Lando Principles deal with. On three points, the Gandolfi Draft Code is different, however. First, whereas the Lando Principles are a team effort, the Gandolfi Code has been drafted by one man, Giuseppe Gandolfi, albeit guided by his *Académie des privatistes européens*. Then, an attractive feature, the text enters into a discussion on the two sets of Principles and on the ideas of Gandolfi's colleagues: "Les contributions des Académiciens". Finally, the project has been drafted in French.

### 3.3. Trento

Another private project is the Trento Common Core of European Private Law, directed by Mauro Bussani and Ugo Mattei. The project is based on the ideas of the two Rudi's: Rodolfo Saco and the late Rudi Schlesinger. Every July, a large band of young (at heart) lawyers gather in the beautiful North Italian town of Trento. Each meeting begins with a plenary session,[21] but then it is back to the core issue: the development of a common core of private law. Two volumes have so far been published. The first volume to be published as a fruit of the project, is the one on Good Faith edited by Zimmermann and Whittaker.[22] The volume comprises thirty cases, which are all dealt with from the point of view of sixteen jurisdictions – the fifteen EU jurisdictions, including Norway and Scotland, but excluding Luxembourg. This analysis is preceded by a general introduction by the two Editors, historical surveys by Schermaier on Roman law and Gordley on *ius commune*, and a comparative paper on the American reception of *good faith* by Summers. The book ends with concluding remarks by Zimmermann and Whittaker. What kind of cases does the book deal with? An

---

[19]   H. MCGREGOR, *Contract code drawn up on behalf of the English Law Commission*, Milan/London, 1993.

[20]   GIUSEPPE GANDOLFI (ed.), *Code européen des contrats/Avant-projet, Livre premier*, Milan: Giuffrè, 2001, 576 p.; see: HANS JÜRGEN SONNENBERGER, "Der Entwurf eines Europäischen Vertragsgesetzbuchs der Akademie Europäischer Privatrechtswissenschaftler – ein Meilenstein", *Recht der Internationalen Wirtschaft* 2001, p. 409-416.

[21]   See the collection of papers read at plenary sessions in MAURO BUSSANI, UGO MATTEI (eds.), *Making European Law/Essays on the "Common Core" project*, Università degli Studie di Trento, 2000.

[22]   REINHARD ZIMMERMANN, SIMON WHITTAKER, *Good Faith in European Contract Law*, Cambridge: Cambridge University Press, 2000, 720 p.

example is the following: "case 1, courgettes perishing": "Barchester Chemicals Ltd. is a producer of agricultural and domestic fertilisers. Cecil is a market gardener and buys directly from Barchester's a quantity of one of their products, "Growright 100", for use on his courgettes. Owing to the high content of salt in this product, the plants' vegetation perishes: it is clear that this would not have happened if Cecil had been advised to give the plants large quantities of water at the time of administering the product. What claims does Cecil have against Barchester?" (p. 171). This has nothing to do with good faith, a Dutch reader may object, and indeed that is what the Dutch reporter Van Erp observes (p. 192). All the same, he concludes that Barchester was bound to inform Cecil, as is the case under Belgian, French and German law, but then on the basis of good faith. The common law reaches the same result by the technique of "implied terms". This is in line with the general conclusion that, of the thirty cases, eleven are solved in exactly the same way in all jurisdictions; nine are solved in exactly the same way in most of the jurisdictions and only in ten cases are there clear differences. Surprisingly, to the Editors, it is not the common law that is the odd man out. "Instead, we often find a smaller legal jurisdiction out on a limb, this being particularly noticeable as regards the Nordic legal systems and Irish law. One possible reason for this may be that where a legal system by its size tends to engender less litigation there are fewer occasions on which courts are presented with facts suitable to test or to clarify the application of exiting legal rules" (p. 655).

A disadvantage of teamwork such as that in the Trento project is that it may take a long time to finish. This is apparent from the fact that the national reports in the Zimmermann/Whittaker volume have been concluded in 1997. Fortunately, the general report does reflect later developments. The disadvantage is also discernible in the second volume, which was published on *Enforceability of Promises*.[23] The Editor of this volume is the American comparatist and legal historian James Gordley. The volume looks into the question of to what extent promises are binding. In modern continental law, this question is usually answered in the affirmative, as opposed to Roman law and the *common law* with its *consideration* requirement. The book comprises fifteen cases, which are dealt with from the point of view of twelve European jurisdictions (Denmark, Finland, Luxembourg and Sweden are missing, but Scotland once again receives special attention). Contrary to the Editor's expectation, the differences are greater than he had anticipated. An example is the gift. In most European jurisdictions

---

[23]   J. GORDLEY (ed.), *The Enforceability of Promises in European Contract Law*, Cambridge: Cambridge University Press, 2001, 478 p.

its validity is still dependent upon the fulfilment of a form requirement. Usually, the form required is a notarial deed, but in Portugal, Scotland and Spain an ordinary deed is sufficient. In England and Wales, the promisor should make a "deed under seal" – it is sufficient (but not in Ireland) that he declares the deed to have the object of being such a deed, or he must establish a trust. Gordley did find *something* in common: "We did find that, generally, these results reflect similar underlying concerns" (p. 371).

### 3.4. Spier and Koziol and others

One of the more active private groups that are engaged in the development of "Principles" of European Private Law is the Spier/Koziol group. Before publishing a set of Principles, the group sets out to discover any common ground between the various jurisdictions. The questionnaire method used is very much akin to that of the Trento Common Core project, to be discussed in No. 8 below. It is highly commendable that the group does not keep the results of the questionnaire approach to itself, but is willing to share the finds with others through publication. In an *ERPL* Survey, I already mentioned three of the group's publications. By 2002, another four had been published. No. 4 deals with causation.[24] It contains ten national reports and a comparative analysis. The national reports deal with the same 24 cases each. The ten jurisdictions covered are Austria (Koziol), Belgium (Cousy, Vanderspikken), England and Wales (Rogers), France (Galand-Carval), Germany (Magnus), Greece (Kerameus), Italy (Busnelli, Coman-dei), South Africa (Neethling), Switzerland (Widmer) and the United States (Schwartz). The comparative analysis demonstrates how much the jurisdictions have in common, but also how much they differ on other points.

I have given this overview by way of example. Outside the realm of Contract Law, various other private projects may be mentioned. In the area of Tort, there is a group that includes Helmut Koziol (Vienna) and Jaap Spier (Tilburg/Maastricht), which strives for harmonisation.[25] Principles have also been developed for the Law of Trusts by the Kortmann group.[26] A set

---

[24]  J. SPIER (ed.), *Unification of Tort Law: Causation*, European Centre of Tort and Insurance Law, The Hague: Kluwer, 2000, 161 p.

[25]  See JAAP SPIER and OLAV A. HAAZEN, "The European Group on Tort Law ("Tilburg Group") and the European Principles of Tort Law", *Zeitschrift für Europäisches Privatrecht* 1999, p. 469-493. Meanwhile, the centre of the group has gravitated to Vienna (Helmut Koziol).

[26]  D.J. HAYTON, S.C.J.J. KORTMANN, H.L.E. VERHAGEN (eds.), *Principles of European Trust Law*, The Hague: Kluwer Law International – W.E.J. Tjeenk Willink, 1999.

of draft directives on Procedural Law has been drafted by a group chaired by Marcel Storme.[27]

## 3.5. Casebooks

"I had a dream". The Leuven – and formerly: Maastricht – based Walter Van Gerven would probably add: "that once there shall be a time when lawyers all over Europe share a common thesuarus of case law". An era when Donoghue v Stevenson, Hühnerpest en Jeand'heur are not just known locally in England, Germany and France, but in all European countries. Van Gerven's dream has resulted in two casebooks. The first to appear was "Tort Law".[28] Here four jurisdictions are compared on the basis of annotated cases. These jurisdictions are England and Wales, France, Germany and Europe. Other European jurisdictions are mentioned only occasionally. Earlier, one single Chapter from this book had already been published separately – "Scope of Protection" (1998). When that Part was published, the question could be raised how many thousands of pages the final volume would contain. The Editors have been able to limit the size to a little under 1,000 pages, first by limiting the number of decisions from jurisdictions other than the four major ones, and second, by referring to Maastricht University's website[29] for further information and for the text in the original language. The Chapters added as compared with the earlier book include General Topics, Liability for One's Own Conduct, Causation, Liability for the Conduct of Others, Liability not Based on Conduct, Defences, Remedies, and the Impact of Supranational and International Law.

This is a highly readable book. Tort law really comes to life through cases. A disadvantage, as with the teamwork involved in the Trento series, is that the outcome is very much dependent upon the punctuality of all co-operators. This is evident in the second volume that appeared in the series, the one on Contract Law, edited by Hugh Beale.[30] The book deals with the notion of Contract, the relation with Tort and Restitution, pre-contractual liability, the binding force of contracts, offer and acceptance, validity, *vices de consentement*, unfair contract terms, interpretation, *imprévision*, remedies,

---

[27]   M.L. STORME (ed.), *Approximation of Judiciary Law in the European Union*, Dordrecht: Kluwer, 1994.

[28]   WALTER VAN GERVEN, JEREMY LEVER, PIERRE LAROUCHE (eds.), *Tort Law*, Common Law of Europe Casebooks, Oxford: Hart, 2000, 969 p.

[29]   <http://www.rechten.unimaas.nl/casebook>.

[30]   HUGH BEALE and others (eds.), *Contract Law*, Oxford: Hart, Casebooks on the Common Law of Europe, 2002, 993 p.

third parties and assignment. As in the Tort volume, these subjects are illustrated by cases taken mainly from English, French and German law. Other cases have been taken from Australia, Belgium, Italy (6), the Netherlands (4), and Switzerland, but Austria, Greece, the Nordic countries, Portugal, Scotland and Spain remain unrepresented. Unlike the Tort volume, the one on Contract Law does not have a companion website with the original text. This is a handicap for those readers who prefer a text in the original language.

A third casebook yet to appear is a volume on "Judicial Review of Administrative Action".

Van Gerven is not the only Editor of casebooks. The "Casebook Europäisches Privatrecht" comprises 19 cases from the European Court of Justice in the area of private law.[31] Cases reported are for instance Francovich, Cassis de Dijon and Bosman. The interest of the casebook lies in the fact that these cases are annotated from a European, English, German, French and Italian perspective. Earlier, the same publishers published a "Casebook Europäisches Verbraucherrecht".[32] These are only some recent examples[33] of casebooks that will most certainly contribute to a growing common thesaurus of European cases.

### 3.6. The acquis communautaire group

An active centre for the promotion of an exchange of ideas is based in Münster. The *acquis communautaire* group has indeed been able, under the spirited leadership of Reiner Schulze and Hans Schulte-Nölke, to begin a number of highly interesting projects.

### 3.7. SECOLA

Another German who has been active over the past years is Stefan Grundmann, presently of Erlangen. His SECOLA association has held a number of lively conferences in Rome, Leuven and London. The Leuven meeting has already been mentioned above.

---

[31] REINER SCHULZE, ARNO ENGEL, JACKIE JONES (eds.), *Casebook Europäisches Privatrecht*, Baden-Baden: Nomos, 2000, 425 p.
[32] HANS SCHULTE-NÖLKE, REINER SCHULZE, JACKIE JONES (eds.), *A Casebook on European Consumer Law*, Oxford: Hart, 2000, 320 p.
[33] An earlier example is INGEBORG SCHWENZER, MARKUS MÜLLER-CHEN, *Rechtsvergleichung/Fälle und Materialien*, Tübingen: Mohr, 1996, 352 p.

## 4.  NON-ACHIEVEMENTS

The achievements then, at first sight, seem overwhelming. A decade of efforts, especially at NGO level, has resulted in a common core of academic writing on most parts of private law in Europe. Still, much remains to be done. In this part, I will indicate some non-achievements during the past decade.

### 4.1. *Constitutional competence*

First of all, surprisingly, there is no consensus as to a firm basis for the codification of private law in the European Treaty. The 1997 Scheveningen Conference, the results of which were published in the *European Review of Private Law*, clearly indicate the diversity of scholarly opinion on this point, with a slight majority being of the opinion that the Treaty offers no such competence.

### 4.2. *Comity*

The minority, which is of the contrary opinion, would nonetheless not wish to force a European Civil Code upon down the British and the Irish. The principle of comity argues against this. An alternative to the Code movement of Von Bar and others would perhaps be a Restatement. The Code v Restatement discussion is an ongoing debate, even within groups such as the Von Bar Commission.

### 4.3. *The business community*

When in 1980 the Vienna Sales Convention (CISG) was adopted, the academic community welcomed this major achievement towards world trade. But world trade itself could not have been less interested. After the entry into force of the CISG, most major businesses would opt out of the Convention. Only those businesses that were unaware of the Convention would be bound by it. This lack of interest in the CISG has never failed to amaze academics. Why not be glad with a neutral set of rules when one party is based in China and the other in Germany?

A similar unpleasant surprise – from an academic point of view – is the lack of interest on the part of European trade and industry in the private efforts at harmonisation presented above. So rare is the interest of the business community, that whenever there is an arbitral award in which the Unidroit Principles are referred to, this is overall reported as another example of the importance of these Principles.

## 4.4. The academic community

Above I have suggested that the academic community is enthusiastic about the harmonisation movement. I should now perhaps add that, first, not all scholars feel comfortable with the movement towards European harmonisation and, second, that there is some outright hostility. First, perhaps the majority of University lecturers up until the present time prefer to stick to domestic law, often because of unfamiliarity with European law. I suggest that these lecturers will soon be forced by directives and case law to readjust their classes or else they will outplace themselves. The second group is more interesting. It consists of those who are familiar with the movement but rather – or in their views: because of that – are very much against the present methods of harmonisation. Such opponents include a number of English authors – Hugh Collins,[34] Tony Weir[35] –, transatlantic-born jurists – the Canadian Legrand[36] –, and even some Dutch authors, such as Jan Smits[37] from Maastricht University. I would suggest that it is the essence of academia that there be debate, so the opponents actually do contribute to harmonisation by making the partisans aware of their faulty reasoning.

## 5. WE SHALL OVERCOME? SOME CONCERNS

What should one do with regard to the non-achievements just summed up? The constitutional impediment only looks like a minor one: if a qualified majority so wishes, the Giscard d'Estaing Commission on a European Constitution may elaborate an amendment to the European Treaty. The comity principle can be taken care of by offering member states a Restatement – or a Model Code – instead of forcing them to swallow a code.

How can we to make business aware of the advantages – and disadvantages – of harmonisation? Seminars and the like seem to be the proper answer. Easily readable commentaries may equally serve to raise the business interest. The academic community will finally be forced by market forces to provide the legal education and to carry out the legal research that live up to today's requirements.

---

[34] H. COLLINS, "European Private Law and the Cultural Identity of States", *ERPL* 1995, p. 353-365.
[35] T. WEIR, "Die Sprachen des europäischen Rechts: Eine skeptische Betrachtung", *ZEuP* 1995, p. 368.
[36] PIERRE LEGRAND, "Against a European Civil Code", 60 *Modern Law Review* 44-63 (1997).
[37] JAN SMITS, *The Making of European Private Law*, Antwerp: Intersentia, 2002.

Although there are ways to overcome the present non-achievements, there is reason for some concern.

### 5.1. Case-law

First, although there is a growing body of Community case law on questions of private law, it is still very limited as compared with domestic case law. What is now important is that *domestic* case law on questions of European private law be reported in other jurisdictions and other languages. Only in this way may lawyers of other nationalities learn of such cases.

### 5.2. Geographical

There are a number of ongoing research projects on private law in Europe, mentioned elsewhere in this paper. It is of major importance that these projects already take into account the forthcoming arrival of a number of new member states.

### 5.3. Subject-matter

There is now little doubt that Contract Law is a major target for harmonisation. Contract Law is close to two other areas: Securities and Tort Law. Once one harmonises Contract Law, Securities are bound to follow. This then raises the difficult question of whether or not the remainder of Property Law (including the transfer of real property) should follow suit. Only in the case of *Intellectual* Property is harmonisation self-evident. With the decreasing importance of the demarcation between Contract Law and Tort Law, it seems inevitable, as the Lando and Unidroit working groups found, that some Tort Law will also have to be harmonised. The problem here is the entwinement with Social Security, which so far remains very different in European jurisdictions.

When we talk about Contract Law nowadays, this includes Commercial Contract Law. As the Italians have long realised, the distinction between a separate Civil Law and Commercial Law is no longer desirable.

Two growth areas of harmonisation, after the Tampere summit, are Civil Procedure and Private International Law. On the other hand, the recent formation of a Study Group on European Family Law will still have great barriers to overcome. Inheritance Law will likewise resist Europeanisation for some time.

Finally, we should always be aware of the growing co-operation of Private Law and Anti-trust Law, which is already harmonised, and Administrative Law, which is not.

### 5.4. Technical

In the preceding text I have already mentioned a number of technical problems which will keep us occupied over the present decade, such as the form of harmonisation: Regulation v. Directive, Code v. Restatement. There are other technical problems, such as the question of a single fabric – should we accept the increasing dichotomy between domestic law and European law within one legal system.

## 6. CONCLUSION: THE ROLE OF ACADEMICS

Private law is rapidly becoming European in outline. This lays a heavy burden upon the shoulders of academics. First, and most important, is the training of future generations of students. The European Union's successful Erasmus programme has paved the way. The Bologna Declaration aims to do the same.[38] Academic staff should also themselves engage in exchange. It is important to engage in an exchange of intellectual ideas in Europe. To this end, we should learn to express ourselves in other European languages.

In our teaching, we should promote the common stock of legal thinking: Savigny, Maitland and Pothier. We should also promote the development of a common stock of landmark cases and in the drafting of common projects. More in general, common research projects such as that of the Commission on European Family Law may be the cornerstone for increased harmonisation.

### BIBLIOGRAPHY 2000-2002

GUIDO ALPA, EMILIO NICOLA BUCCICO (eds.), *La riforma del codici in Europa e il progetto di codice civile europeo*/Materiali dei seminari 2001, Milan: Giuffrè, 2002, 247 p.

M.V. ANTOKOLSKAIA, W.A. DE HONDT, G.J.W. STEENHOFF, *Een zoektocht naar Europees familierecht*, Report Nederlandse Vereniging voor Rechtsvergelijking, Deventer: Kluwer, 1999.

---

[38] Although the Dutch experience shows that the development of bachelor and master programmes may actually endanger some of the exchange programmes set up in the last century.

HEINZ-DIETER ASSMANN, GERT BRÜGGEMEIER, ROLF SETHE (eds.), *Unterschiedliche Rechtskulturen – Konvergenz des Rechtsdenkens/Different Legal Cultures – Convergence of Legal Reasoning*, Baden-Baden: Nomos, 2001, 126 p.

CHRISTIAN VON BAR, "Die Study Group on a European Civil Code", in: *Festschrift Dieter Henrich*, Bielefeld: Gieseking, 2000, p. 1-12.

JÜRGEN BASEDOW (ed.), *Europäische Vertragsrechtsvereinheitlichung und deutsches Recht*, Tübingen: Mohr, 2002, 281 p.

JÜRGEN BASEDOW, "Codification of Private Law in the European Union: the making of a Hybrid", *ERPL* 2000, p. 35-49.

HUGH BEALE and others (eds.), *Contract Law*, Oxford: Hart, Casebooks on the Common Law of Europe, 2002, 993 p.

GIANNANTONIO BENACCHIO, VIVIANA SIMONI (eds.), *Repertorio di diritto comunitario civile e commerciale (legislazione – dottrina – giurisprudenza)*, Padova: Cedam, 2001, 741 p.

GIANNANTONIO BENACCHIO, *Diritto privato della Communità Europea/Fonti, modelli, regole*, second ed., Padova: Cedam, 2001, 542 p.

KLAUS PETER BERGER, "Europäisches Gemeinrecht der Methode", *Zeitschrift für Europäisches Privatrecht* 2001, p. 4-29,

KLAUS PETER BERGER, *Transnational Commercial Law in the Age of Globalization*, Rome, 2001, 29 p.

ULF BERNITZ, Mot en europeisk civillag?, *Europarättslig Tidsskrift* 2001, p. 469-474.

GERRIT BETLEM, EDWARD H.P. BRANS, "The Future Role of Civil Liability for Environmental Damage in the EU", 2 *Yearbook of European Environmental Law* 183-221 (2002).

P. BIAVATI, "Diritto comunitario e diritto processuale civile italiano fra attrazione, autonomia e resistenze", *Il Diritto dell'Unione Europea* 2001, p. 717-748.

D. BUSCH, *De middellijke vertegenwoordiging in Europa*, Ph.D. Thesis Utrecht, Deventer: Kluwer, 2002, 471 p.

MAURO BUSSANI, UGO MATTEI (eds.), *Making European Law/Essays on the "Common Core" project*, Università degli Studie di Trento, 2000.

R.C. VAN CAENEGEM, *European Law in the Past and the Future/Unity and Diversity over Two Millennia*, Cambridge: Cambridge University Press, 2002, 175 p.

CLAUS-WILHELM CANARIS, ALESSIO ZACCARIA (eds.), *Die Umsetzung von Zivilrechtlichen Richtlinien der Europäischen Gemeinschaft in Italien und Deutschland*, Berlin: Duncker & Humblot, 2002, 253 p.

CAROLINE CAUFFMANN, "De Principles of European Contract Law", *Tijdschrift voor Privaatrecht* 2001, p. 1231-1309.

ANTHONY CHAMBOREDON, CHRISTOPH SCHMID, "Pour la création d'un "Institut européen du droit"/Entre une unification législative ou non législative, l'emergence d'une science juridique transnationale en Europe", *Revue internationale de droit comparé* 2001, p. 685-708.

GÉRARD CORNU, "Un code civil n'est pas un instrument communautaire", *Dalloz* 2002, Chronique p. 351-352.

IWAN DAVIES, "Retention of Title Clauses and Non-Possessory Security Interests: A Secured Credit Regime within the European Union?", in: Iwan Davies (ed.), *Security Interests in Mobile Equipment*, Dartmouth: Ashgate, 2002, p. 335-373.

J.H.M. VAN ERP, *European Union Case Law as a Source of European Private Law/A Comparison with American Federal Common Law*, preadvies Nederlandse Vereniging voor Rechtsvergelijking, Deventer: Kluwer, 2001, p. 1-58.

J.H.M. VAN ERP, J.M. SMITS (eds.), *Bronnen Europees privaatrecht*, The Hague: Boom, 2001, 431 p.

JOACHIM G. FRICK, "Die UNIDROIT-Prinzipien für internationale Handelsverträge", *Recht der internationalen Wirtschaft* 2001, p. 416-422.

GIUSEPPE GANDOLFI (ed.), *Code européen des contrats/Avant-projet, Livre premier*, Milan: Giuffrè, 2001, 576 p.

KERSTIN GEIST, *Die Rechtslage bei Zusendung unbestellter Waren nach Umsetzung der Fernabsatzrichtlinie/Eine rechtsvergleichende Untersuchung unter Berücksichtigung des deutschen, schweizerischen, österreichischen und englischen Rechts*, PhD thesis Konstanz 2002, Konstanz: Hartung-Gorre, 2002, 270 p.

J. GORDLEY, *ed.*, *The Enforceability of Promises in European Contract Law*, Cambridge: Cambridge University Press, 2001, 478 p.

INGO GROSSKINSKY, *Außervertragliche Produkt- und Umwelthaftpflicht – Paralellität oder Autonomie?*, Frankfurt 2002, 251 p.

STEFAN GRUNDMANN, JULES STUYCK (eds.), *An Academic Green Paper on European Contract Law*, The Hague: Kluwer Law International, 2002, 432 p.

ANDRÉ HERWIG, *Der Gestaltungsspielraum des nationalen Gesetzgebers bei der Umsetzung von europäischen Richtlinien zum Verbrauchervertragsrecht*, Frankfurt 2002, 266 p.

MARTIJN W. HESSELINK, *The New European Legal Culture*, Deventer: Kluwer, 2001, 103 p.

M.W. HESSELINK, G.J.P. DE VRIES, *Principles of European Contract Law*, Deventer: Kluwer, 2001, 189 p.

MARTIJN HESSELINK and others, *European Review of Private Law* 2002/1, p. 1-151.

MARTIJN W. HESSELINK, *The New European Private Law/Essays on the Future of Private Law in Europe*, The Hague: Kluwer Law International, 2002, 283 p.

BURKHARD HEß, "Aktuelle Perspektiven der europäischen Prozessrechtsang-leichung", *Juristen-Zeitung* 2001, p. 573-583.

E.H. HONDIUS, A.W. JONGBLOED, R.CH. VERSCHUUR (eds.), *Van Nederlands naar Europees procesrecht?!/Liber amicorum Paul Meijknecht,* Deventer: Kluwer, 2000, 363 p.

EWOUD HONDIUS, ANETA WIEWIÓROWSKA-DOMAGALSKA, "Europejski kodeks cywilny (Analiza prac Grupy Stuyjnej)", *Panstwo i Prawo* 2002, p. 27-36.

CHRISTOPHE JAMIN, DENIS MAZEAUD (eds.), *L'harmonisation du droit des contrats en Europe,* Paris: Economica, 2001, 178 p.

NILS JANSEN, "Auf dem Weg zu einem europäischen Haftungsrecht", *Zeitschrift für Europäisches Privatrecht* 2001, p. 30-65.

KONSTANTINOS D. KERAMEUS, "Angleichung des Zivilprozeßrechts in Europa/Einige grundlegende Aspekte", *RabelsZ* 2002, p. 1-17.

B.A. KOCH, H. KOZIOL (eds.), *Unification of Tort Law: Strict Liability,* The Hague: Kluwer, 2002, 444 p.

HUGO J. VAN KOOTEN, *Restitutierechtelijke gevolgen van ongeoorloofde overeenkom-sten/Een rechtsvergelijkende studie naar Nederlands, Duits en Engels recht,* Ph.D. thesis Utrecht, Deventer: Kluwer, 2002, 368 p.

JACQUES LAFFINEUR, "L'évolution du droit communautaire relatif aux contrats de consommation", *Revue européenne de droit de la consommation* 2001/3, p. 19-42.

OLE LANDO, "My life as a lawyer", *Zeitschrift für Europäisches Privatrecht* 2002, p. 508-522.

FRIEDERIKE LEHMANN, *Die Rezeption des europäischen Verbraucherschutzes im österreichischen Recht,* Frankfurt 2002, 301 p.

YVES LEQUETTE, "Quelques remarques à propos du projet de code civil européen de M. von Bar", *Dalloz* 2002, p. 2202-2214.

MARCO B.M. LOOS, "Towards a European Law of Servcie Contracts", *ERPL* 2001, p. 565-574.

BRIGITTA LURGER, *Grundfragen der Vereinheitlichung des Vertragsrechts in der Europäischen Union,* Vienna: Springer, 2002, 599 p.

ULRICH MAGNUS (ed.), *Europäisches Schuldrecht Verordnungen und Richtlinien – European Law of Obligations Regulations and Directives – Droit Européen des Obligations Règlements et Directives,* Berlin: Sellier, 2002, 850 p.

ULRICH MAGNUS, JAAP SPIER (eds.), *European Tort Law/Liber amicorum for Helmut Koziol,* Frankfurt am Main: Lang, 2000, 350 p.

ALAIN MARCIANO, JEAN-MICHEL JOSSELIN, *The Economics of Harmonizing European Law,* Cheltenham: Edward Elgar, 2002.

BASIL S. MARKESINIS, *The Coming Together of the Common Law and the Civil Law/The Clifford Chance Millennium Lectures,* Oxford: Hart, 2000, 255 p.

BASIL S. MARKESINIS, HANNES UNBERATH, *The German Law of Torts,* fourth ed., Oxford: Hart, 2002, 1050 p.

DIETER MARTINY, "The Harmonization of Family Law in the European Community. Pro and Contra", in: Michael Faure, Jan Smits, Hildegard Schneider (eds.), *Towards a European ius commune in Legal Education and Research*, Antwerpen: Intersentia, 2002, p. 191-201.

J.M. MILO and others, "Special Series on Trust", *European Review of Private Law* 2000/3, p. 421-544.

P. NÈVE, *Eigendomsvoorbehoud*, Preadvies Nederlandse Vereniging voor Rechtsvergelijking, Deventer: Kluwer, 2000.

HERMAN NYS, *Patiënt in Europa*, inaugural address Maastricht, 2000, 28 p.

GEORGE PANAGOPOULOS, *Restitution in Private International Law*, Oxford: Hart, 2000, 274 p.

PASCAL PICHONNAZ, *La compensation*, Fribourg: Éditions universitaires, 2001, 726 p.

ANDREA PINNA, "Drafting a civil code for Europe – aims and methods", *Tilburg Foreign Law Review* 2002/4, p. 337-357.

J. MICHAEL RAINER (ed.), *Europäisches Privatrecht/Die Rechtsvergleichung*, Frankfurt: Lang, 2002, 485 p.

INGO SAENGER, REINER SCHULZE (eds.), *Der Ausgleichsanspruch des Handelsvertreters/Beispiel für die Fortentwicklung angeglichenen europäischen Rechts*, Baden-Baden: Nomos, 2000, 197 p.

SIXTO A. SÁNCHEZ LORENZO, *Derecho privado europeo*, Granada: Comares, 2002, 362 p.

HARRIËT N. SCHELHAAS (general editor) *et al.* (eds.), *The Principles of European Contract Law and Dutch Law/A Commentary*, Nijmegen: Ars Aequi/The Hague: Kluwer, 2002, 471 p.

JOCHEN NIKOLAUS SCHLOTTER, *Erbrechtliche Probleme in der Société Privée Européenne*, Ph.D. thesis Heidelberg 2001, Frankfurt: Lang, 2002, 340 p.

CHRISTOPH SCHMID, Legitimitätsbedingungen eines Europäischen Zivilgesetzbuchs, *Juristen-Zeitung* 2001, p. 674-683.

E.J.H. SCHRAGE (ed.), *Unjust Enrichment and the Law of Contract*, The Hague: Kluwer, 2001, 492 p.

HANS SCHULTE-NÖLKE, REINER SCHULZE, JACKIE JONES (eds.), *A Casebook on European Consumer Law*, Oxford: Hart, 2000, 320 p.

REINER SCHULZE, ARNO ENGEL, JACKIE JONES (eds.), *Casebook Europäisches Privatrecht*, Baden-Baden: Nomos, 2000, 425 p.

KATHARINA SIEGEL, *Produkthaftung im polnischen, tschechischen und slowenischen Recht*, Frankfurt 2002, 166 p.

LIONEL D. SMITH (ed.), *Restitution*, Dartmouth: Ashgate, 2001, 565 p.

JAN M. SMITS, *The Good Samaritan in European Private Law/On the Perils of Principles without a Programme and a Programme for the Future*, inaugural address Maastricht, Deventer: Kluwer, 2000, 50 p.

J.M. SMITS, "How to predict the differences in uniformity between different areas of a future European private law? An evolutionary approach", in: Alain Marciano, Jean-Michel Josselin (eds.), *The Economics of Harmonizing European Law*, Cheltenham: Elgar, 2002, p. 50-70, <http://www-edocs.u-nimaas.nl/abs/pr02001.htm>.

Jan SMITS, *The Making of European Private Law/Toward a Ius Commune Europaeum as a Mixed Legal System*, Antwerpen: Intersentia, 2002, 306 p.

J.M. SMITS, R.R.R. Hardy, "De toekomst van het Europees contractenrecht", *WPNR* 6513 (2002).

J. SPIER (ed.), *Principles of European Tort Law: Causation*, The Hague: Kluwer, 2000.

J. SPIER (ed.), *Unification of Tort Law: Causation*, European Centre of Tort and Insurance Law, The Hague: Kluwer, 2000, 161 p.

VERICA TRSTENJAK, "Evropski Civilni Zakonik – Moznost, nujnost ali utopija?", *Pravnik, Ljubljana*, let. 56 (2001), 11-12, p. 675-700.

MARK VAN HOEKE EN FRANCOIS OST (eds.), *The Harmonisation of European Private Law*, Oxford: Hart, 2000, 255 p.

STEFAN VOGENAUER, *Die Auslegung von Gesetzen in England und auf dem Kontinent*, 2 vols., Tübingen: Mohr Siebeck, 2001, 1481 p.

STEPHEN WEATHERILL, "The European Commission's Green Paper on European Contract Law: Context, Content and Constitutionality", *Journal of Consumer Policy* 2001, p. 339-399.

JOHANNES CHRISTIAN WICHARD, "Europäisches Markenrecht zwischen Territorialität und Binnenmarkt", *Zeitschrift für Europäisches Privatrecht* 2002, p. 23-57.

WILLEM J.H. WIGGERS, *International Commercial Law/Source Materials*, The Hague: Kluwer/Allen & Overy Legal Practice, 2001, 881 p.

REINHARD ZIMMERMANN, *Roman Law, Contemporary Law, European Law/The Civilian Tradition Today*, Clarendon Law Lectures, Oxford: Oxford University Press, 2001, 197 p.

REINHARD ZIMMERMANN, SIMON WHITTAKER, *Good Faith in European Contract Law*, Cambridge: Cambridge University Press, 2000, 720 p.

REINHARD ZIMMERMANN, *Comparative Foundations of a European Law of Set-Off and Prescription*, Cambridge: University Press, 2002, 182 p.

# PART TWO –
# METHODOLOGICAL ASPECTS

# METHODOLOGICAL ASPECTS OF HARMONISATION OF FAMILY LAW

INGEBORG SCHWENZER[*]

## 1. INTRODUCTION

Let me start by assuming that we all have reached the same answer to the open question of whether it is desirable to harmonise or even unify family law. That we all agree that the answer is yes. And that we further agree that this ambitious endeavour is feasible.[1] But even if we do come this far, our problems are not over. Indeed, it is here that I want to begin today: What methodological problems will we face as we start harmonising (or even unifying) family law?

"Methodos", the Greek notion, means "the way to something", the systematic procedure to reach a certain goal. Thus, my analysis will be extremely practical. So let me take you on an adventurous journey of unifying family law, and let us see what pitfalls await us along the path.

---

[*] The author is grateful to Professor Dr. h.c. Carol Bruch (University of California, Davis, US) for a critical reading of the manuscript as well as to lic. iur. Michelle Cottier MA (Basel) for her valuable research assistance.

[1] The more recent literature is predominantly optimistic: ANTOKOLSKAIA, MARIA V., "Would the Harmonisation of Family Law Enlarge the Gap between the Law in the Books and the Law in Action?", *Die Praxis des Familienrechts (FamPra.ch)* 2002, 261-292; BOELE-WOELKI, KATHARINA, "The Road Towards a European Family Law", *Electronic Journal of Comparative Law*, Vol. 1.1 November 1997; MARTINY, DIETER, "Is Unification of Family Law Feasible or Even Desirable?", in: HARTKAMP, ARTHUR *et al.* (eds.), *Towards a European Civil Code*, 2nd ed., The Hague etc. 1998, 151-171; PINTENS, WALTER/VANWINCKELEN, KOEN, *Casebook European Family Law*, Leuven 2001, 15; PINTENS, WALTER, "Rechtsvereinheitlichung und Rechtsangleichung im Familienrecht. Eine Rolle für die Europäische Union?", *Zeitschrift für Europäisches Privatrecht* 1998, 670-676; RIEG, ALFRED, "L'harmonisation européenne du droit de la famille: mythe ou réalité?", in: STOFFEL, WALTER A./VOLKEN, PAUL (eds.), *Conflits et harmonisation, Liber amicorum Alfred E. von Overbeck*, Fribourg/CH 1990, 473-499.

## 2. STARTING POINT: THE COMPARATIVE METHOD

I am convinced that comparative law must be our starting point.[2] But the comparative method has come under attack in recent years. Postmodernists blame comparative law for being trapped in cultural frameworks,[3] for being extremely conservative[4] and for not adequately considering the non-legal framework within which society functions.[5] Although there is quite a bit of truth in this critique, abandoning comparative law altogether would mean throwing the baby out with the bathwater. Instead, especially in family law, we can benefit from these insights by always keeping value questions in mind and by enriching the comparative method with an interdisciplinary approach. I will come back to this suggestion later.

## 3. LAW IN BOOKS – LAW IN ACTION

It goes without saying that the comparative method cannot confine itself to the law as it is found in books but must also reveal the law as it appears in action.[6] Indeed, in this respect, family law is similar to the law of obligations, the century-old domain of comparative law.[7]

Still, let me give some examples drawn from family law to demonstrate the practical importance of this principle.

---

[2] See also BOELE-WOELKI, KATHARINA, "The Road Towards a European Family Law", *Electronic Journal of Comparative Law*, Vol. 1.1 November 1997, 7.

[3] See PETERS, ANNE/SCHWENKE HEINER, "Comparative Law Beyond Post-Modernism", *International and Comparative Law Quarterly* 49 (2000), 800, 802. For an example of the opening of comparative law to the "global perspective" see EDGE, IAN (ed.), *Comparative Law in Global Perspective*, Ardsley NY 2000.

[4] *E.g.* MICHAELS, RALF, "Im Westen nichts Neues?, 100 Jahre Pariser Kongress für Rechtsvergleichung – Gedanken anlässlich einer Jubiläumskonferenz in New Orleans", *Rabels Zeitschrift für ausländisches und internationales Privatrecht* 66 (2002), 97, 109.

[5] *E.g.* LEGRAND, PIERRE, "European Legal Systems are not Converging", *International and Comparative Law Quarterly* 45 (1996), 60 ff.

[6] BOELE-WOELKI, KATHARINA, "The Road Towards a European Family Law", *Electronic Journal of Comparative Law*, Vol. 1.1 November 1997.

[7] First studies in comparative family law have been published from the 1960s on, see MÜLLER-FREIENFELS, WOLFRAM, *Ehe und Recht*, Tübingen 1962; NEUHAUS, PAUL HEINRICH, "Europäisches Familienrecht?: Gedanken zur Rechtsvergleichung und Rechtsvereinheitlichung", in: VON CAEMMERER, ERNST *et al.* (eds.), *Vom deutschen zum europäischen Recht: Festschrift für Hans Dölle*, Tübingen 1963, Vol. 2, 419-435; RHEINSTEIN, MAX, *Marriage stability, divorce, and the law*, Chicago 1972. The International Society of Family Law has been founded as late as in 1973. Concerning the history of comparative law see ZWEIGERT, KONRAD/KÖTZ, HEIN, *Einführung in die Rechtsvergleichung*, 3rd ed., Tübingen 1996, 1 ff.

As we all know, in most national statutes the notion of fault has lost its importance as a ground for divorce.[8] In some countries, however, it still plays a role when it comes to the consequences of divorce, especially regarding post-divorce spousal support.[9] Let us take, for example, Germany on the one hand and England on the other. According to § 1579 No. 6 of the German BGB, post-divorce spousal support can be reduced or even denied if there has been *manifestly gross, one-sided misconduct* on the part of the spouse seeking support. In England, pursuant to Sec 25 (2) (g) of the MCA,[10] the conduct of the parties, that is fault, is one of several factors that the court must take into account when deciding upon the financial consequences of divorce. Taken these provisions at face value, one would suppose, that the German courts would consider fault much less frequently than the English courts. But as early as in 1973 the English Court of Appeal[11] decided that a reduction or even denial of a financial provision should only be thought of in case of obvious and gross misconduct – that is, if granting financial relief would be "repugnant to anyone's sense of justice". This formula sounds pretty similar to the wording of the German statute. Can one then suppose that an identical case will be decided alike in the two countries? Not at all. Apparently judges in Germany and England differ considerably in what they consider to be obvious and gross misconduct. Thus there are many German court decisions discussing whether adultery amounts to such misconduct,[12] whereas in England, as in many other Anglo-American legal systems, it almost seems that nothing short of an attempted murder of the obligor spouse will suffice.[13]

One further difference is to be noted: In Germany "obvious and gross misconduct" may only be invoked against the requesting spouse, i.e. in almost all cases the wife,[14] whereas in England and other Anglo-American legal systems it works both ways. It is possible to increase an award if the obligor's behaviour amounted to obvious and gross misconduct, especially

---

[8]   See DUTOIT, BERNARD *et al.*, *Le divorce en droit comparé. Vol. 1: Europe*, Geneva 2000.

[9]   See HINDERLING, REGULA, *Verschulden und nachehelicher Ehegattenunterhalt: eine rechtsvergleichende Untersuchung zum schweizerischen, US-amerikanischen und deutschen Recht*, Basel 2001.

[10]  Matrimonial Causes Act 1973.

[11]  See *Wachtel v. Wachtel* [1973] Fam. 72 = [1973] 2 W.L.R. 366.

[12]  See MAURER, HANS ULRICH, commentary on § 1579 No. 48, in: *Münchener Kommentar zum Bürgerlichen Gesetzbuch*, 4th ed., Munich 2000 ff.

[13]  England: see LOWE, NIGEL/DOUGLAS, GILLIAN, *Bromley's Family Law*, 9th ed., London/Edinburgh/Dublin 1998, 840f.; United States: see AMERICAN LAW INSTITUTE, *Principles of the Law of Family Dissolution: Analysis and Recommendations*, Newark/San Francisco 2002, 84 f.

[14]  This amounts to an indirect or factual discrimination of women, see DETHLOFF, NINA, "Reform of German Family Law – a Battle against Discrimination", *European Journal of Law Reform* 3 (2001), 221-241.

---

in cases of domestic violence by the husband against the wife[15] – cases that in general do not entail any additional financial consequences under German law.

Only if one is aware of such discrepancies in interpretation can one usefully discuss the relevance of fault in post-divorce spousal support.

Let me draw your attention to another feature of family law that illustrates the differences between the law in books and the law in action: Court decisions reflect but a very small percentage of family law resolutions. Thus probably in most countries 90 per cent of all divorce proceedings or even more end with a separation or divorce agreement that resolves the financial issues.[16] It is these agreements and not court decisions that determine the life of most divorcees, although of course they are bargained for in the shadow of the law.[17] If one wants to get a clear picture of the consequences of divorce in a given country, then, one has to examine the reality of such agreements and – going even a bit further – the role of the professions involved in negotiating them.[18]

## 4. THE FUNCTIONAL APPROACH

In family law as in the classical fields of comparative law, or even more so, the starting point has to be the functional approach.[19] There is little sense in comparing institutions, but it is absolutely necessary to ask what the underlying problem is that a certain legal provision is aimed to redress.

---

[15] England: *Jones v Jones* (1976) Fam 8 = (1975) 2 W.L.R. 606; Australia: see *e.g.* BAILEY-HARRIS, REBECCA, "The Role of Maintenance and Property Orders in Redressing Inequality: Re-Opening the Debate", *Australian Journal of Family Law* 12 (1998), 3, 15 ff.

[16] In Norway, Denmark and Iceland, the spouses can choose in the case of an agreement the procedure of administrative divorce, see DANIELSEN, SVEND, "The Scandinavian Approach: Administrative and Judicial Resolutions of Family Conflicts", in: MEULDERS-KLEIN, MARIE-THÉRÈSE (ed.), *Familles & Justice*, Bruxelles 1997, 139, 151 ff.; SCHWENZER, INGEBORG, "Registerscheidung?", in: GOTTWALD, PETER/JAYME, ERIK/SCHWAB, DIETER (eds.), *Festschrift für Dieter Henrich*, Bielefeld 2000, 533, 534.

[17] MNOOKIN, ROBERT H./KORNHAUSER, LEWIS, "Bargaining in the Shadow of the Law: The Case of Divorce", *Yale Law Journal* 88 (1979), 950 – 997.

[18] See *e.g.* BASTARD, BENOIT/CARDIA-VONÈCHE, LAURA, "Inter-professional tensions in the divorce process in France", *International Journal of Law and the Family* 9 (1995), 275-285; EEKELAAR, JOHN/MACLEAN, MAVIS/BEINART, SARAH, *Family Lawyers. The Divorce Work of Solicitors*, Oxford 2000.

[19] See ZWEIGERT, KONRAD/KÖTZ, HEIN, *Einführung in die Rechtsvergleichung*, 3rd ed., Tübingen 1996, 33.

Let me give you one example, the question of pension splitting for husband and wife at divorce, that is the equalisation of pension rights accrued during marriage. Germany pioneered in these fields, expressly providing for pension splitting as early as 1976.[20] It was not until recently that other countries followed suit, for example, the Netherlands in 1995,[21] and England[22] and Switzerland[23] in 2000. Still, even today, there are many legal systems that do not split pensions at divorce, although they all face the same factual problem: the wife who took care of the family and was not employed outside the home (at least not full-time) and therefore accumulated lesser pension rights than her husband, who worked full-time at higher pay. But focussing only on explicit pension splitting rules would lead to a totally wrong impression. In many legal systems the difference in spouses' pension rights is taken care of by property distribution upon divorce. Pension rights accumulated during the ongoing marriage are regarded as marital property and may thus be divided upon divorce, be it equally or according to the discretion of the court.[24] In still other legal systems differences in accumulated pension rights have to be taken into account in setting post-divorce spousal support awards.[25] This leads us to the conclusion that an overall understanding of how countries deal with the inequality of spouses' work-related retirement accumulations can be achieved only by considering all the economic consequences at divorce: explicit rules on pension splitting, matrimonial property law in general, and spousal support, at least.

Yet another family law example may be mentioned here. The possibility of premarital contracts to regulate the economic consequences of divorce is currently a hotly debated topic.[26] A country's treatment of the issue can be fully understood only against the background of its matrimonial property and spousal support regimes. Even if one finds that spouses are free to agree upon a regime of separate property, it is possible that a country's courts may provide relief outside family law that circumvents the agreement, yet avoids any overt control of its contents. Well known is, for

---

[20]   § 1587-1587p BGB.
[21]   Art. 94 para. 4, 155 BW.
[22]   Welfare Reform and Pensions Act 1999.
[23]   Art. 122-124 CC.
[24]   *E.g.* in Sweden: Chapter 10, § 3 para. 3 Marriage Act. United States: AMERICAN LAW INSTITUTE, *Principles of the Law of Family Dissolution: Analysis and Recommendations*, Newark/San Francisco 2002, § 4.08 sec. 1 (a).
[25]   *E.g.* in France: Art. 272 CC.
[26]   See COURVOISIER, MAURICE, *Voreheliche und eheliche Scheidungsfolgenvereinbarungen – Zulässigkeit und Gültigkeitsvoraussetzungen*, Basel 2002; SCHWENZER, INGEBORG, "Richterliche Kontrolle von Unterhaltsvereinbarungen zwischen Ehegatten", *Zeitschrift für Europäisches Privatrecht* 1997, 863-873.

example, the longstanding tradition of Anglo-American courts, which make use of trust doctrines when family law does not provide suitable remedy.[27] In other countries fictitious employment contracts or partnerships are popular tools to compensate wives who helped build up their partners' businesses and find themselves without any legal title to the proceeds when it comes to divorce.[28]

These examples may suffice to illustrate the functional comparative method and how it applies in the field of family law.

## 5. CONVERGING TENDENCIES

Once we have come this far and are able to analyse the underlying problematic fact patterns and identify their solutions, however disguised they may be, we will find quite a number of converging tendencies in European family law.[29] As early as the 1970s a German author labelled this trend "Uniform Law Through Evolution".[30] Because these legal changes only reflect socio-demographic developments in familial behaviour, let me recall the major changes that have taken place in Western industrialised states during recent decades.

The most salient feature is the rise in the divorce rate. Since the 1970s, it has more than doubled nearly everywhere.[31] In many countries, the probability of divorce has now reached 40 to 50 per cent. In Scandinavia, however, a certain stagnation at this high level has been observed since the 1980s, indicating that the saturation point might now have been reached. The high number of divorces brings about manifold further developments. These are, on one hand, the rapid increase of children living in stepfamilies and, on the other, the growing number of single-parent families. This is closely linked to the phenomenon described as the feminisation of

---

[27]  See *e.g.* CRETNEY, STEPHEN M., "Family Law", 4th ed., London 2000, 144 ff.

[28]  See SCHWENZER, INGEBORG, "Restitution of Benefits in Family Relationships", *International Encyclopedia of Comparative Law*, Vol. X: Restitution – Unjust Enrichment and Negotiorum Gestio, Chapter 12, Tübingen/Dordrecht/Boston/Lancaster 1997, 27 ff.

[29]  The most prominent voice dismissing the convergence thesis is LEGRAND, PIERRE, "European Systems are not Converging", *International and Comparative Law Quarterly* 45 (1996), 52-81.

[30]  LUTHER, GERHARD, "Einheitsrecht durch Evolution im Eherecht und im Recht der eheähnlichen Gemeinschaft", *Rabels Zeitschrift für ausländisches und internationales Privatrecht* 45 (1981), 253-267.

[31]  See COUNCIL OF EUROPE, *Recent demographic developments in Europe*, Strasbourg 1998, T2.5; KAMERMAN, SHEILA B./KAHN, ALFRED J., *Family Change and Family Policies in Great Britain, Canada, New Zealand, and the United States*, Oxford (UK) 1997.

poverty.[32] Indeed, studies of poverty have shown that in many countries divorce constitutes a much higher risk factor for women than for men[33] and that women living alone with children are especially touched by poverty.[34]

Other features are the increase in age at first marriage and the general decrease in marriages. Taking the example of France, this means that today only approximately 56 per cent of all women below the age of 50 have ever married, compared to approximately 92 per cent of all women of this age group who had married at least once in 1970.[35]

Simultaneously, cohabitation has increased in all countries, in some places dramatically indeed. In the Scandinavian countries, cohabitation can be considered an actual alternative to marriage, whereas in many other countries non-marital unions are of shorter duration and frequently are formalised when children are born.[36]

A general decline in fertility rates can also be observed. Since about 1965, the reproduction rate of the population has fallen to a below-replacement level in all developed countries.[37] On the other hand, the number of out-of-wedlock births has increased dramatically in recent decades. In some countries, namely in Scandinavia, it has reached a level between 50 and 65 per cent.[38]

These demographic developments have nevertheless not occurred to the same extent or at the same pace in all European countries.[39] Large

---

[32] In the great majority of the states of the European Union, women are more at risk of poverty than men, see EUROSTAT, *The life of women and men in Europe*, 2002 edition, 99.
[33] See for Switzerland: LEU, ROBERT E./BURRI, STEFAN/PRIESTER, TOM, *Lebensqualität und Armut in der Schweiz*, Berne 1997.
[34] In most countries of the European Union, over 40% of all women living alone with a child had an income below 60 % of the median in 1997, see EUROSTAT, *The life of women and men in Europe*, 2002 edition, 100.
[35] See COUNCIL OF EUROPE, *Recent demographic developments in Europe*, Strasbourg 1998, T2.2.
[36] "Kindorientierte Eheschliessung", see NAVE-HERZ, ROSMARIE, "Familiale Veränderungen seit 1950", *Zeitschrift für Sozialisationsforschung und Erziehungswissenschaft* 4 (1984), 45-63.
[37] See ROTHENBACHER, FRANZ, "Social Change in Europe and its Impact on Family Structures", in: EEKELAAR, JOHN/NHLAPO, THANDABANTU (eds.), *The Changing Family*, Oxford (UK) 1998, 3, 5.
[38] Norway 48,6 per cent in 1997, Denmark 46,3 per cent in 1996, Iceland 65,2 per cent in 1997: COUNCIL OF EUROPE, *Recent demographic developments in Europe*, Strasbourg 1998, T 3.2.
[39] ROTHENBACHER uses the term "the contemporaneity of the non-contemporaneous" to describe this phenomenon: ROTHENBACHER, FRANZ, "Social Change in Europe and its Impact on Family Structures", in: EEKELAAR, JOHN/NHLAPO, THANDABANTU (eds.), *The Changing Family*, Oxford (UK) 1998, 3, 21.

differences remain, with Scandinavian countries at one extreme and the Latin countries and Ireland at the other.[40]

Family law could not and has not stayed unresponsive to these profound socio-demographic changes. As MARTINY once wrote: "The basic issues [have been] resolved".[41] International Conventions, such as the European Convention on Human Rights[42] and the UN Convention on the Rights of the Child, have contributed a lot in settling central questions.[43]

Converging tendencies can be found in the substantive law of divorce. In almost all countries marital breakdown is if not the only, at least the central ground for divorce, and notions of fault have been largely banned.[44] Even the consequences of divorce in most parts of Europe no longer depend upon fault.[45] Discrimination against illegitimate children has been abolished in most countries.[46] Formal equality between the spouses has also been implemented.[47] There is widespread consensus that the person who renders the homemaker's services and therefore refrains from gainful employment has a right to participate in the wealth accumulated during

---

[40]  See HÖPFLINGER, FRANÇOIS, "Haushalts- und Familienstrukturen im intereuropäischen Vergleich", in: HRADIL STEFAN/IMMERFALL STEFAN (eds.), *Die westeuropäischen Gesellschaften im Vergleich*, Opladen 1997, 97-138.

[41]  MARTINY, DIETER, "Is Unification of Family Law Feasible or Even Desirable?", in: HARTKAMP, ARTHUR *et al.* (eds.), *Towards a European Civil Code*, 2nd ed., The Hague etc. 1998, 151, 164.

[42]  The latest example for the impact of the ECHR are the judgements of the European Court of Human Rights in the cases Goodwin v. UK and I. v. UK (11 July 2002) introducing the right of transsexuals to marry. The judgement of Marckx v. Belgium (13 June 1979) had a comparable impact concerning the equality of children born out of wedlock with children born to married parents, see PINTENS, WALTER/VANWINCKELEN, KOEN, *Casebook European Family Law*, Leuven 2001, 16 ff.

[43]  See VLAARDINGERBROEK, PAUL, "Trends in the Development of Family Law in Europe – Comparative Perspectives", in: KAUFMANN, FRANZ-XAVER *et al.* (eds.), *Family Life and Family Policies in Europe*, Vol. 2, Oxford 2002, 120 ff.; MCGLYNN, CLARE, "The Europeanisation of family law", *Child and Family Law Quarterly* 13 (2001), 35-49; KILLERBY, MARGARET, "The Council of Europe's Contribution to Family Law (Past, Present and Future)", in: LOWE, NIGEL/DOUGLAS, GILLIAN (eds.), *Families Across Frontiers*, The Hague/Boston/London 1996, 13-25.

[44]  In some countries fault remains a ground for divorce among others, most importantly France (Art. 242 CC, Art. 243 CC), Belgium (Art. 229 CC, Art. 231 CC), Austria (§ 49 Ehegesetz), England (Sec. 1 (2) (a)-(c) MCA 1973).

[45]  An exception is Belgium, where fault excludes the right to maintenance after divorce (Art. 301 § 1 CC).

[46]  In the Netherlands and Belgium, the *Marckx*-case (ECHR 13 June 1979, Series A, No. 31) has given an important impulse for the reform in favour of illegitimate children; see PINTENS, WALTER/VANWINCKELEN, KOEN, *Casebook European Family Law*, Leuven 2001, 18 f.

[47]  See HENRICH, DIETER/SCHWAB, DIETER (eds.), *Eheliche Gemeinschaft, Partnerschaft und Vermögen im europäischen Vergleich*, Bielefeld 1999.

---

150

marriage, including pensions.[48] The last few years even show a converging tendency to provide a legal institution for same-sex partners.[49]

But all these are mere tendencies, and it would be premature to think that one can build uniform rules on these tendencies.

## 6. DIFFERENT CODIFICATION TECHNIQUES

The differences between the legal systems are already present when it comes to codification techniques. Due to historical developments, we find significant differences between the common law and the continental legal systems.

In the common law tradition, there are fewer rules for relationships in intact family. Instead the law focuses on conflict situations.[50] In contrast, the continental systems tend to set up abstract rights and duties for intact family,[51] although it is perfectly clear for continental lawyers, too, that they come into play only when the personal relationship is no longer functioning. The differences in practice are, accordingly, not as big as they may initially seem.

Another salient characteristic of common law statutes is their use of legal definitions,[52] something unknown to continental statutes. When developing uniform rules that are to be applied by persons from different legal backgrounds who may associate different meanings to a term, such legal definitions might prove extremely helpful.

Let me call your attention to a third point on which national family law statutes differ considerably. It is the amount of discretion given to the courts. Take the financial consequences of divorce, for example, one of

---

[48]  See HENRICH, DIETER, "Vermögensregelung bei Trennung und Scheidung im europäischen Vergleich", *Zeitschrift für das gesamte Familienrecht* 2000, 6 f.

[49]  See COESTER, MICHAEL, "Same-Sex Relationships: A Comparative Assessment of Legal Developments Across Europe", *Die Praxis des Familienrechts (FamPra.ch)* 2002, 748-764; JAKOB, DOMINIQUE, "Die eingetragene Lebenspartnerschaft im Europarecht", *Zeitschrift für das gesamte Familienrecht* 2002, 501-508; see also the contributions in *European Journal of Law Reform* 3 (2001), Nr. 3, Special Issue on Family Law.

[50]  SCHEIWE, KIRSTEN, *Kinderkosten und Sorgearbeit im Recht*, Frankfurt/M 1999, 330.

[51]  Examples are norms concerning the duties of the spouses: Netherlands: Art. 81 and 83 para. 1 BW; France: Art. 212 and Art. 215 para. 1 CC; Sweden: Chapter 1, § 2 Marriage Act; Belgium: Art. 213 CC.

[52]  See *e.g.* England: sec. 3 (meaning of "parental responsibility"), sec. 8 (definition of residence, contact and other orders with respect for children) Children Act 1989.

the central concerns of contemporary divorce law. As I already mentioned, according to English law the court may make financial orders, having regard to a number of factors, which permits case-by-case analysis. The leading cases of *White v. White*,[53] *Cowan v. Cowan*[54] and *Lambert v. Lambert*[55] have produced some long awaited guidelines[56] but a great deal of discretion is still left to the courts.[57] A rather similar situation can be found in the Scandinavian countries.[58] Once again, however, the continental legal systems show a different picture. As far as matrimonial property regimes are concerned, they all employ hard and fast rules,[59] defining exactly what goods have to be taken into account, at what time the respective properties have to be evaluated, and what the share of each spouse will be. As to spousal support, although many continental legislators also defer to the discretion of the court,[60] there are other approaches as well. Take, for example, German law. In the German Civil Code seven provisions regulate in detail when support is to be ordered by the court.[61] In practice so-called maintenance guidelines[62] are issued by the appellate courts that specify the amount of support due in a given case down to Euro and Cent.

Which of the two paths should a uniform or harmonised law follow when it comes to the financial consequences of divorce? Blanket clauses that give much leeway to judges might receive wide approval. But that is at the same time their biggest shortcoming. As blanket clauses permit broad differences in interpretation, nothing would have to change, and every national court

---

[53]    [2001] 1 All ER 1, [2000] 2 FLR 981.

[54]    [2001] EWCA Civ 679, [2001] 2 FLR 192.

[55]    [2002] EWCA Civ 1685, [2003] 1 FLR 139.

[56]    See EEKELAAR, JOHN, "The Politics of Pragmatism: Family Law Reform in England and Wales", *European Journal of Law Reform* 3 (2001), 297, 304; HODSON, DAVID/GREEN, MIRANDA/DE SOUZA, NADINE, "Lambert – Shutting Pandora's Box", [2003] *Fam Law*, 37-45.

[57]    See also DEWAR, JOHN, "Reducing Discretion in Family Law", in: EEKELAAR, JOHN/NHLAPO, THANDABANTU (eds.), *The Changing Family. Family Forms & Family Law*, Oxford 1998, 231-250.

[58]    The Scandinavian laws contain rules to avoid "unreasonable results" in the application of the principle of equal division of property, see AGELL, ANDERS, "Is there One System of Family Law in the Nordic Countries?", *European Journal of Law Reform* 3 (2001), 313, 327.

[59]    See HENRICH, DIETER, "Vermögensregelung bei Trennung und Scheidung im europäischen Vergleich", *Zeitschrift für das gesamte Familienrecht* 2000, 6-12; AGELL, ANDERS, The Division of Property Upon Divorce From a European Perspective, in: POUSSON-PETIT, JACQUELINE (ed.), *Droit comparé des personnes et de la famille*, "Liber amicorum Marie-Thérèse Meulders-Klein", Bruxelles 1998, 1-20; see also the contributions in: HENRICH, DIETER/SCHWAB, DIETER (eds.), *Eheliche Gemeinschaft, Partnerschaft und Vermögen im europäischen Vergleich*, Bielefeld 1999.

[60]    See France: Art. 272 CC; Switzerland: Art. 125 CC.

[61]    § 1570-1576 BGB.

[62]    Most influential are the Düsseldorf guidelines (*Düsseldorfer Tabelle*), the version of 1 January 2002 is published in *Zeitschrift für das gesamte Familienrecht* 2001, 810 ff. or on www.famrz.de.

could go on adjudicating much as under its prior national rule.[63] There is yet another strong argument against blanket clauses for financial matters: In the bargaining context they work against the economically weaker party, who settles for less than under hard and fast rules.[64] This is why the Principles of the Law of Family Dissolution[65] worked out by the American Law Institute and published recently now expressly define what marital property is,[66] what share each spouse will get[67] and how post-divorce spousal support is to be calculated.[68] The Principles even recommend the employment of mathematical formula for some of these purposes.[69]

## 7. DIVERGENCES DUE TO DIFFERENT STRUCTURES OF ADMINISTRATION OF JUSTICE AND THE LAW OF PROCEDURE

Major differences between legal systems exist regarding the structures of administration of justice.[70] This may have a strong effect on substantive law. Thus, for example, the level of protection afforded to the weaker party by a requirement that a marriage contract be notarised depends upon the relevant law for notaries. Are notaries members of the legal profession or not; are they obliged to counsel the parties or do they simply authenticate the signatures on a written agreement? The effectiveness of the law of child protection also differs according to whether youth authorities are filled by professionals or laypersons.[71] Likewise it is highly important whether a country provides for family courts[72] and a specialised bar[73] or whether

---

[63]   See concerning contract law KÖTZ, HEIN, "Alte und neue Aufgaben der Rechtsvergleichung", *Juristen Zeitung* 57 (2002), 257, 259.

[64]   SCHEIWE, KIRSTEN, *Kinderkosten und Sorgearbeit im Recht*, Frankfurt/M 1999, 365; MNOOKIN, ROBERT H./KORNHAUSER, LEWIS, "Bargaining in the Shadow of the Law: The Case of Divorce", *Yale Law Journal* 88 (1979), 950, 977 ff.

[65]   AMERICAN LAW INSTITUTE, *Principles of the Law of Family Dissolution: Analysis and Recommendations*, Newark/San Francisco 2002 (in the following: ALI Principles).

[66]   § 4.03-4.08 ALI Principles.

[67]   § 4.09-4.12 ALI Principles.

[68]   Chapter 5 ALI Principles.

[69]   *E.g.* § 5.04 ALI Principles recommends to establish a rule that applies "a specified percentage to the difference between the incomes the spouses are expected to have after dissolution". This percentage is called the durational factor because it increases with the marriage's duration, see ALI Principles, 816 f.

[70]   See the contributions in: MEULDERS-KLEIN, MARIE-THÉRÈSE (ed.), *Familles & Justice*, Bruxelles 1997.

[71]   Switzerland for example knows a system of local child protection authorities with high lay participation, whereas France has a system of professional "juge des mineurs".

[72]   Examples are the specialised family courts in Germany, Portugal or Spain, see *e.g.* SCHWAB, DIETER, "Le droit de la famille et la justice en Allemagne", in: MEULDERS-KLEIN, MARIE-THÉRÈSE (ed.), *Familles & Justice*, Bruxelles 1997, 105, 108; DE SOUSA, MACHADO ALEXANDRE,

judges may even be laypersons[74] and whether legal counsel is provided and required in family law matters.[75] Finally the level and the frequency of mediation, as well as the professions of persons who practise it,[76] influence family law in action.

## 8. DIVERGENCES DUE TO DIFFERENT FAMILY POLICIES AND FAMILY REALITIES

Having reached this stage of analysis, we can tackle the substantially differing solutions among several national legal systems. How do we react, for example, once we discover that in one country parents owe support to their adult children who are still students, but in another country support obligations are due only for minor children? The explanation for this limitation can possibly be found in publicly funded scholarships that young adults can benefit from. Yet another example: If a legal system does not at all provide pension sharing at divorce, this need not mean, that women are left without means for their old age. It may instead be that women in that country do not need pension splitting or other financial provisions because they have very high employment rates accompanied by public care for children and/or state guaranteed income.[77] Or it is even conceivable that kinship relations and family networks still function so well that women are not left in poverty.[78]

This leads us to differences in family realities. When it comes to joint custody for children after divorce established as a rule, it makes a big difference whether fathers take a truly active role in children and family

---

[73] Portugal, in: HAMILTON, CAROLYN/PERRY, ALISON (eds.), *Family Law in Europe*, 2nd ed., London 2002, 521, 523; ROCA, ENCARNA, Spain, in: HAMILTON, CAROLYN/PERRY, ALISON (eds.), *Family Law in Europe*, 2nd ed., London 2002, 587, 590.

[73] See EEKELAAR, JOHN/MACLEAN, MAVIS/BEINART, SARAH, *Family Lawyers. The Divorce Work of Solicitors*, Oxford 2000.

[74] An example is the family proceedings court in England and Wales, see HAMILTON, CAROLYN, "England & Wales", in: HAMILTON, CAROLYN/PERRY, ALISON (eds.), *Family Law in Europe*, 2nd ed., London 2002, 97.

[75] *E.g.* § 78 of the German Law on civil procedure (Zivilprozessordnung) states a requirement to be represented by a lawyer in divorce and related matters before the family courts.

[76] See CONSEIL DE L'EUROPE, *La médiation familiale en Europe: actes, 4e Conférence européenne sur le droit de la famille, 1er-2 octobre 1998*, Strasbourg 2000.

[77] This is the case in Scandinavia, see LEIRA, ARNLAUG, "The modernisation of motherhood", in: DREW, EILEEN/EMEREK, RUTH/MAHON, EVELYN (eds.), *Women, Work and the Family in Europe*, London/New York 1998, 159, 168.

[78] This is the case in Southern Europe, see FLAQUER, LLUÍS, "Is there a Southern European model of family policy?" in: PFENNING, ASTRID/BAHLE, THOMAS (eds.), *Families and Family Policies in Europe*, Frankfurt/M 2000, 15-33.

work during the ongoing family[79] – as it seems to be more and more the case in Scandinavia[80] – or not, as in Southern Europe, where patriarchal patterns still dominate.[81]

As these examples demonstrate, to get an overall picture of working family law is possible only if we include research on other areas of law that are elements of national family policies such as social law, labour law and tax law. European countries encompass a wide variety of family policies, ranging from Sweden that supports families with the declared aim of reaching gender equality, to Switzerland that defines family as a private matter without need of public support.[82] Having this in mind, it is more or less a question of technicalities how to reconcile the different areas of law concerned. Likewise, before we start harmonising or even unifying family law, we need insights from sociology of law, family sociology and psychology.[83] Indeed, this interdisciplinary exchange is indispensable.

---

[79]  As to the beneficial effects of fathers' participation in family work see *e.g.* HERLTH, ALOIS, "The New Fathers: What Does it Mean for Children, Marriage and for Family Policy?", in: KAUFMANN, FRANZ-XAVER *et al.* (eds.), *Family Life and Family Policies in Europe*, Vol. 2, Oxford 2002, 299-320.

[80]  See BJÖRNBERG, ULLA, "Family orientation among men", in: DREW, EILEEN/EMEREK, RUTH/MAHON, EVELYN (eds.), *Women, Work and the Family in Europe*, London/New York 1998, 200-207.

[81]  See GIOVANNINI, DINO, "Are fathers changing?", in: DREW, EILEEN/EMEREK, RUTH/MAHON, EVELYN (eds.), *Women, Work and the Family in Europe*, London/New York 1998, 191-199.

[82]  See *e.g.* KAUFMANN, FRANZ-XAVER, "Politics and Policies towards the Family in Europe: A Framework and an Inquiry into their Differences and Convergences", in: KAUFMANN, FRANZ-XAVER *et al.* (eds.), *Family Life and Family Policies in Europe*, Vol. 2, Oxford 2002, 419-490; PFENNING, ASTRID/BAHLE, THOMAS (eds.), *Families and Family Policies in Europe*, Frankfurt/M 2000; COMMAILLE, JACQUES/DE SINGLY, FRANÇOIS (eds.), *The European Family*, Dordrecht/Boston/London 1997; FUX distinguishes the following family policy regimes: The etatistic family policy aims at supporting gender equality and providing benefits for a variety of living arrangements (*e.g.* Sweden). The familialistic family policy aims at balancing the income situation between parents and stimulating reproductive behaviour (*e.g.* France). The individualistic family policy defines family as a private matter (*e.g.* Switzerland); see FUX, BEAT, "Which Models of the Family are Encouraged or Discouraged by Different Family Policies?" in: KAUFMANN, FRANZ-XAVER *et al.* (eds.), *Family Life and Family Policies in Europe*, Vol. 2, Oxford 2002, 363, 385 ff.

[83]  See already KAHN-FREUND, OTTO, "On uses and misuses of comparative law", *Modern Law Review* 37 (1974), 1, 27, quoted in BRADLEY, DAVID, "Convergence in Family Law: Mirrors, Transplants and Political Economy", *Maastricht Journal of European and Comparative Law* 6 (1999), 127, 129.

## 9. DIVERGENCES DUE TO DIFFERENT VALUE SYSTEMS

Finally, most of the divergences in national family laws and family policy can only be attributed to different value systems.[84] Why does one country rely upon post-divorce and kinship support duties, for example, while another provides public support?[85] Why are there still so many countries that do not provide adequate rules for the breakdown of non-marital unions?[86] Why are there still differences in parentage law for children born within and outside of wedlock?[87] Why are premarital agreements scrutinised by courts in one country, but not in others?[88] I could go on putting such questions endlessly.

Certainly all depends on the relevant value system. But what are the crucial issues that determine so many outcomes in family law as well as in the surrounding areas linked to family policy?

In my opinion three basic points determine the orientation of all national family laws: The importance of marriage as a basis of family law, gender issues, and the conceptual dualism of private and public spheres.

The first central question is whether and if so to what extent family law is still firmly based on marriage. Many rules can only be explained as attempts to protect the institution of marriage despite the contrary needs of parties who are involved.[89] In this context, form is often more important than substance. Surely, there has been a constant process of deinstitutionalisation of family relationships in all countries during recent decades,[90] fuelled in part by the ever-growing importance of human rights. But major differences between countries still exist.

---

[84] See ANTOKOLSKAIA, MASHA, "Family Values and Harmonisation of Family Law", in: MACLEAN, MAVIS (ed.), *Family Law and Family Values*, Oxford (forthcoming).

[85] The latter is especially the case in Scandinavia, see BRADLEY, DAVID, *Family Law and Political Culture*, London 1996, 259.

[86] See RUBELLIN-DEVICHI, JACQUELINE, *Des concubinages dans le monde*, Paris 1990.

[87] Differences especially concern the establishment and contestation of paternity, see SCHWENZER, INGEBORG, Empfiehlt es sich, das Kindschaftsrecht neu zu regeln?, Gutachten A für den 59. Deutschen Juristentag – Hannover 1992, Munich 1992, 21 ff.

[88] See SCHWENZER, INGEBORG, Richterliche Kontrolle von Unterhaltsvereinbarungen zwischen Ehegatten, *Zeitschrift für Europäisches Privatrecht* 1997, 863-873.

[89] Examples are the still existing differences in parentage law between children born within and outside of wedlock or the spouses' obligation to choose a common family name.

[90] See WILLEKENS, HARRY, "Long-term Developments in Family Law in Western Europe: an Explanation", in: EEKELAAR, JOHN/NHLAPO, THANDABANTU (eds.), *The Changing Family*, Oxford (UK) 1998, 47, 55 ff.

The second crucial issue is the gender aspect of family law. It is true that all norms directly discriminating against women have been banned from family law statutes.[91] Thus formal equal rights have been widely achieved. The remaining task is to track down subtle cases of indirect discrimination and achieve substantially equal opportunities, taking into account existing social inequalities.[92] Sensitivity to this goal still differs greatly among countries.[93]

The third key question is closely linked to the first and the second: it centres on the conceptual dualism of private and public spheres. Are the tasks of bringing up children and caring for those who are not able to earn their own living by gainful employment private in nature? Or are enabling and motivating women to re-enter the workforce (by providing day care and the like) or encouraging men to engage in childrearing by granting generous father's leave public tasks?[94] Is the exclusion of all financial adjustments upon divorce in a premarital contract or a separation agreement a private affair?[95] How about domestic violence in the ongoing relationship?

All these examples demonstrate that deinstitutionalisation of family relationships and growing awareness of gender issues in family law go hand in hand with the family moving more and more to the public sphere. The aim of family law, in my opinion, is on the one hand not to hinder people in their quest for individually satisfying family structures and, on the other hand, to protect the interests of the vulnerable when individuals fail in that quest.

---

[91]  For the history of gender inequality in family law see *e.g.* DÖLEMEYER, BARBARA, "Frau und Familie im Privatrecht des 19. Jahrhunderts", in: GERHARD, UTE (ed.), *Frauen in der Geschichte des Rechts*, Munich 1997, 633 ff.

[92]  See DETHLOFF, NINA, "Reform of German Family Law – a Battle against Discrimination", *European Journal of Law Reform* 3 (2001), 221-241; SCHEIWE, KIRSTEN, *Kinderkosten und Sorgearbeit im Recht*, Frankfurt/M 1999, especially 327 ff.

[93]  See KÜNZLER, JAN, "Paths Towards a Modernization of Gender Relations, Policies and Family Building", in: KAUFMANN, FRANZ-XAVER *et al.* (eds.), *Family Life and Family Policies in Europe*, Vol. 2, Oxford 2002, 252-298.

[94]  BASEDOW underlines the link between the equality of women and men in the workplace according to European Community law and equality in family law, see BASEDOW, JÜRGEN, "Konstantinidis v. Bangemann oder die Familie im Europäischen Gemeinschaftsrecht", *Zeitschrift für Europäisches Privatrecht* 1994, 197-199.

[95]  See the important decision of the German *Bundesverfassungsgericht*, BVerfG, 1 BvR 12/92 of 6.2.2001, 31 (see www.bundesverfassungsgericht.de).

## 10. CONCLUSION

Let me come to a close. I have taken you on the mental journey that I believe must undergrid the unifying process in family law. I have had to omit very important questions, such as, what kind of instrument are we aiming at – a convention, a directive, a model law, principles or guidelines? But I did so deliberately. Because I think the utmost importance has to be given to the process of unification itself. First, we must employ the well-known comparative law approach; next, we need to undertake an interdisciplinary discussion; and, finally, we have to sit together and resolve important values issues. Only then can we start drafting. The challenges entail quite a few methodological problems – but I am convinced that we can shoulder them.

# THE 'BETTER LAW" APPROACH AND THE HARMONISATION OF FAMILY LAW

MASHA ANTOKOLSKAIA[*]

## INTRODUCTION

Until recently the main dilemmas concerning the harmonisation of family law were connected to the principal question whether or not such a harmonisation is feasible and desirable.[1] It would be premature to say that a broad consensus already exists in Europe concerning the necessity for family law harmonisation. While the popularity of the idea of such harmonisation has been notably increasing throughout the last decade, the resistance to it has also grown. The establishment of the *Commission on European Family Law (CEFL)*[2] has somewhat shifted the emphasis of the attention from this purely academic debate to more functional issues. Consequently, new, more practical questions have been added to the old ones. One of these questions constitutes the central subject of this paper: the problems surrounding the employment of the so-called "better law" method while drafting harmonised family law.

In order to delineate these problems I will first reiterate the two main methods of drafting harmonised law: the "common core" and the "better law" method, and I will point to the general difficulties related to their application. Then I will provide an overview of the use of these methods by the groups and commissions that already have a great deal of experience in the field of private law harmonisation in Europe. I will try to show what lessons could be drawn from this experience. After that I will explain why

---

[*]   This article expresses the personal opinion of the author and not that of the Commission on European Family Law. This research has been made possible by a fellowship from the Royal Netherlands Academy of Arts and Sciences.

[1]   See for instance: D. MARTINY, "Is Unification of Family Law Feasible or Even Desirable?" In: *Towards a European Civil Code*, A. Hartkamp *et al.* (eds.), Ars Aequi Libri, Nijmegen, 1998, p. 159. D. MARTINY, "Die Möglichkeit der Vereinheitlichung des Familienrechts innerhalb des Europäischen Union", in: D. MARTINY, N. WITZLEB (eds.), *Auf dem Wege zu einem Europäischen Zivilgesetzbuch*, Berlin, 1999, p. 177-189; M. ANTOKOLSKAIA, I. DE HONDT, G. STEENHOFF, *Een zoektocht naar Europees familierecht*, Preadvies voor de Nederlandse Vereniging voor rechtsvergelijking, Kluwer, Deventer, 1999.

[2]   Established on 1 September 2002. For more information see the website of the *CEFL*: http://www2.law.uu.nl/priv/cefl.

I expect that the main problem in the application of the "better law" method: justifying the choice for the "better rule", will manifest itself more strongly with the harmonisation of family law. I will also consider the possibility to use the shared European notion of family rights in order to facilitate such a justification. Finally, two different strategies for the drafting of *Principles of European Family Law* will be discussed. The first is to draft *common core based Principles* with a low level of modernity and innovation, using the "common core" method only. The second is to draft non-binding *Principles* based upon the highest standard of modernity achieved in present-day European family law, using the "better law" method. I will argue in favour of this latter option.

To illustrate my argumentation I will consistently use divorce law as an example, as the grounds for divorce are one of the two subjects chosen by the *CEFL* for the first round of its activities.

## 1. 'COMMON CORE" AND 'BETTER LAW" METHODS: WHAT IS THE PROBLEM?

### 1.1. Two methods

The term "harmonisation" seems to suggest that the harmonised rules will be derived from existing laws rather than invented by the drafters. This, however, can only be true to a limited extent. While elaborating the rules of harmonised law the drafters basically have three choices. They can make use of a rule that is common for all or most of the relevant jurisdictions; they can select a rule that represents a minority or even only one jurisdiction; or they can formulate a new rule themselves. The use of a common rule denotes the so-called "common core" method.[3] The choice for a minority rule or the elaboration of a new rule is distinctive of the "better law" method.

### 1.2. The 'common core" method and its limits

The "common core" method seems easiest to use, because it makes justifying the choice of a particular rule very simple: the rule has been chosen merely because it represents a majority of the jurisdictions. That is why all drafters always try to "restate", as far as possible, the already existing common core of the legal solutions to a particular problem. The

---

[3]    The term "common core" method is used in this article without referring to the specific methodology as developed within the Trento project on the Common core of European Private law.

common rule extracted in this way is then used for elaborating the harmonised law. For example, one can extract the rule that nowadays no European country has fault as the only possible ground for divorce. However, almost no harmonisation activity could be solely based on the "common core" method. The very need for harmonisation already indicates that not all the rules in the field in question are common; otherwise the whole harmonisation exercise would be superfluous. Sometimes the application of the "common core" method requires one further step. The rules represented in different national laws could be formulated in a technically different way, although pursuing the same functional result. In this case the application of the "common core" method needs to be combined with the method of functional equivalence. The drafters have to extract the functionally equivalent common rules from the shell of technically different national terms.

However, a common denominator on the level of functional equivalence is also not always found. Sometimes even the opposite is true: functionally different legal phenomena hide behind similar legal concepts. For instance, the divorce laws of both Ireland and Sweden are based upon the concept of non-fault divorce. The use of the same conceptual language suggests similarity between those laws. In reality, however, the Swedish divorce "on demand" in some instances without a waiting period and without having to disclose the reasons for the divorce, and the Irish divorce, requiring four years of separation and having to convince the court that the marriage has irretrievably broken down, are the opposite extremes on the scale of varieties within European divorce law. Thus, in such cases one could better speak of a functional "disequivalence" instead of a functional equivalence.

The experience of drafting harmonised private law for Europe has shown that the "common core" method, extensively used in the elaboration of the American Restatements,[4] can much less be relied upon for drafting the European *Principles*. While the drafters of the American Restatements could in principle restate the common core of the existing case law, the main difference is that the drafters of the Principles "could not do so because

---

[4]    Although the drafters of the Restatements could also not simply limit themselves to restating the common core. On the use of the "better law" approach in drafting the American Restatements see: W. GRAY, A. ARBOR, " Pluribus Unim: A Bicentennial Report of Unification of Law in the United States", 50 *RabelsZ* 1986, p. 119; A. ROSETT, "Unification, Harmonisation, Restatement, Codification and Reform in International Commercial Law", 40 *Am. J. Comp. L.* 1992, p. 689 and 693; R. HYLAND, "The American Restatements and the Uniform Commercial Code", in: *Towards a European Civil Code*, 1998, p. 63 and 65.

of divergences in the laws of the nations even within the European Union itself".[5] It should be added that even if a common core can be found, it does not necessarily represent a satisfactory solution.

Both the aforementioned situations demonstrate the limits of the "common core" method. In the first case no common core can be extracted at all, because too much diversity exists not only at the level of the technical solutions, but also at the level of functional equivalents. In the second case a common core does exist, but this common denominator lies below the drafters' requirement as to the quality and the modernity of the law they wish to make. The solution in both cases is to move towards the "better law" method and either to select the "better" rule among the diverging rules existing in the national jurisdictions, or to engineer a better rule if no existing solution seems satisfactory.

## 1.3. The 'better law" method and the problem of justifying the choices made

The application of the "better law" method is much more complicated than that of the "common core". Although the former leaves more room for creative drafting, it invokes the troublesome problem of justifying the choices made. This problem concerns, of course, not only the drafters of harmonised law, but is equally relevant for the drafting of domestic law. The obvious difference is that the drafting of domestic laws always involves the national legislature, which has the political authorisation to act in behalf of the population of its country. The drafters in the commissions and groups which are active in the field of the harmonisation of European private law on the contrary, are self-appointed, and neither represent their governments, nor have they been appointed by any supranational organisation. So they cannot rely on any political authorisation, and the only source of authority that they can invoke is their academic reputation. That, on the one hand, gives them the freedom to make their choices on the basis of purely academic considerations. On the other hand, this lack of authorisa tion makes the drafters very susceptible as soon as they dare to choose for a particular rule which is not common to the majority of the European countries. How can they justify their choice if they, for example, choose for divorce, based solely on the irretrievable breakdown of marriage? On what grounds should one accept their judgment that this rule is better than, for instance, a mixed system of fault and non-fault grounds for divorce?

---

[5]   A. HARTKAMP, "Principles of Contract Law" in: *Towards a European Civil Code*, 1998, p. 108.

## 2. PRACTICAL EXPERIENCE WITH THE USE OF THE 'COMMON CORE" AND 'BETTER LAW" METHODS

In order to foresee what kinds of complications could arise from the application of the "better law" method while drafting harmonised family law, it is helpful to look at the experience already built up by the groups and commissions who have already been engaged in the harmonisation of private law in Europe for quite some time.

### 2.1. The Commission for the UNIDROIT Principles for International Commercial Contracts

The UNIDROIT *Principles for International Commercial Contracts*[6] were, in the words of Bonell, the Chairman of the Commission: "not intended to unify existing national laws, but rather to enunciate common principles and rules to the existing legal systems and to select the solutions that are best adopted to the special requirements of international commercial contracts".[7] However, in spite of this commitment to keep as close as possible to the "common core" method, some "clearly innovative solutions"[8] appeared to be unavoidable. Bonell summarises this balance between the "common core" and "better law" methods by using the terms "tradition" and "innovation".[9] He underlines that the UNIDROIT *principles* represent a mixture of both and that only when there are "irreconcilable differences between the various domestic laws"[10] does the "common core" method fail to be successful, and that the "best solutions" are to be chosen "even if those solutions still represent a minority view".[11] As criteria for the selection of these "best solutions" the "special needs of international trade"[12] are bound to be involved.[13] What those "special needs" precisely imply is not clarified, but, on the basis of the terminology that Bonell uses, a plausible

---

[6]  The UNIDROIT Commission on the *Principles for International Commercial Contracts* started its work in 1980. The UNIDROIT *Principles* are designated as non-binding Principles, intended to provide general rules for commercial contracts with an international dimension. The scope of the Commission's harmonisation activities is worldwide.

[7]  M. BONELL, "Unification of Law by Non-Legislative Means: The UNIDROIT Draft Principles for International Commercial Contracts", 40 *Am. J. Comp. L.* 1992, p. 622.

[8]  *Ibid.*, p. 123.

[9]  M. BONELL, *An International Restatement of Contract Law. The UNIDROIT Principles of International Commercial Contracts*, Transnational Publications, New York, 1997, p. 16.

[10]  M. BONELL, *An International Restatement of Contract Law*, 1997, p. 16.

[11]  *Ibid.*

[12]  *Ibid.*

[13]  See also: *Principles for International Commercial Contracts*, UNIDROIT, Rome, 1994, p. viii.

interpretation could be that the drafters were more concerned with the economic efficiency of the rules than with their ideological connotations.

## 2.2. The Lando Commission on European Contract Law

The members of the probably best-known group, the Lando Commission on European Contract Law,[14] made use of the "common core" and "better law" methods in a rather similar way. Here too, there was tension between the inclination to remain as close as possible to the common core and the desire for improvement. Lando and Beale confirmed the intention of the drafters to restate the common core of European contract law, but at the same time they stated that "the Principles are also intended to be progressive".[15] Therefore they recommended moving over to a "better law" method not only in the case of "irreconcilable differences between the various domestic laws",[16] as the drafters of the UNIDROIT Principles declared to have done, but also when this would provide a "more satisfactory answer than that which is reached by traditional legal thinking",[17] as represented in the national laws. Which criteria they used for measuring this "progressiveness" was not specified.

## 2.3. The European Group on Tort Law

The particular nature of the method used by the European Group on Tort Law[18] is that, compared to the above-mentioned Commissions, it relies less on the "common core" method and seems to be more ready to find a remedy in the use of "the better law" method. The initiator of the project, Spier, and another member, Haazen, stated this quite explicitly in their article published in 1999: "An approach that relies *solely* upon 'the common core' is bound to be unsuccessful. First of all, it is precisely because of the divergence in the European law of torts that there is little European tort law capable of being 'restated' as the existing common core."[19] They

---

[14] *The Lando Commission* was set up in 1982. The purpose of the Commission is the development of general provisions intended to be equally applicable to both commercial and non-commercial contracts and to cover international as well as domestic cases. The territorial scope of these Principles is limited to the European Union.

[15] O. LANDO, H. BEALE, *Principles of European Contract Law*, 2000, p. xxii.

[16] M. BONELL, An *International Restatement of Contract Law*, 1997, p. 17.

[17] O. LANDO, H. BEALE, *Principles of European Contract Law*, 2000, p. xxii.

[18] The European Group on Tort Law, aimed at the harmonisation of the law of torts started its activity in 1992. The Principles of Tort Law are not intended to be a binding instrument. The scope is limited to a number of European jurisdictions.

[19] J. SPIER, "The European Group on Tort Law", *A Civil Code for Europe*, Coimbra editora, Coimbra, 2002, p. 62. *ZEuP* 1999, p. 480.

further remark that: "A *common core* of tort law, or of any other part of law, is, however, not necessarily more *modern*."[20] Spier and Haazen describe the Principles on European Tort Law in a similar fashion as Bonell has done with respect to the UNIDROIT Principles,[21] as a mixture of rules selected "for reasons of their being *common* to all or most jurisdictions, and those that were picked as "best" (whereby it seems reasonable to equate "modern" with "best")."[22] Using "modernity" as a criterion for selecting the best rule, they refrain, however, from any further elaboration of this matter and only acknowledge the complexity of the problem.[23] Economic efficiency is mentioned by Spier and Haazen as an expected result of harmonisation itself,[24] but they are silent as to its suitability as a criterion for the selection of better rules.

## 2.4. The Commission on European Family Law

The newly established Commission on European Family Law has already devoted some attention to the problem of combining the "common core" and "better law" methods. The Organising Committee of the *CEFL* has decided that: "the main goal should be to distil common rules. However, there will be cases where the *CEFL* will have to propose alternative solutions and will decide to elaborate innovative "better law"."[25]

## 2.5. Hiding behind 'technical choices"

The preceding sketch shows that all the commissions and groups which are engaged in drafting *Principles* of European private law, without exception employ the "common core" method as well as the "better law" one. Yet, most of them do not elaborate on the problem of justification and present their choices as being merely technical[26] and not as ideology-laden ones. However, the vision of the economically related areas of private

---

20    J. SPIER, O. HAAZEN, "The European Group on Tort Law ("Tilburg Group") and the European Principles of Tort Law", *ZEuP* 1999, p. 480.
21    M. BONELL, *An International Restatement of Contract Law*, 1994, p. 14.
22    J. SPIER, O. HAAZEN, "The European Group on Tort Law", *ZEuP* 1999, p. 480.
23    J. SPIER, O. HAAZEN, "The European Group on Tort Law", *ZEuP* 1999, p. 481.
24    J. SPIER, O. HAAZEN, "The European Group on Tort Law", *ZEuP* 1999, p. 486.
25    K. BOELE-WOELKI, "Comparative Research Based – Drafting of Principles of European Family Law", in: M. FAURE *et al.* (eds.), *Towards a European Ius Commune in Legal Education and Research*, (Ius Commune Europaeum), 40, Intersentia, Antwerpen 2002, p. 180.
26    ZWEIGERT and KÖTZ present private law, with the exception of such value-laden areas as family and succession law, as "relatively unpolitical". K. ZWEIGERT, H. KÖTZ, *An Introduction to Comparative Law,* 3rd ed., Clarendon Press, Oxford, 1998, p. 40.

law as "technical" was recently persuasively contested.[27] It was also observed that "those projects end up by advocating seemingly neutral ideas which have so far confined them within the narrow limits of areas of law in which no open value choices are, or seem to be, made (mainly contract law)".[28] In practice all the groups and commissions have implicitly made the ideological choices inherent in the "better law" method, but their participants have been understandably reticent in openly acknowledging this fact.

## 3. FAMILY LAW: THE SAME PROBLEMS BUT TO A GREATER EXTENT

The major difficulty inherent in the drafting of *Principles* for family law seems to be caused not by the different nature of the problem of justification but by the much greater extent thereof.

### 3.1. The scarcity of a common core

First, it is widely acknowledged that, in spite of far-reaching convergence, the differences between the various European countries with respect to family law are still very significant and therefore the common core is less obvious than in the economically related area of private law. The law on divorce is quite a good example in this respect. If we define "common core" very rigidly, it will mean that a common core can only be established to the extent that a certain rule exists in all the European countries. In this case the search for a common core for the law on the dissolution of marriage will not be successful, since a right to obtain a full divorce is not common for all the European counties: this right does not exist in Malta. If we define "common core" more loosely, we will find countries with divorce based solely on the irretrievable breakdown of marriage (like the Netherlands, Russia, Sweden; England and Wales, Ireland etc) and countries with mixed grounds for divorce (like Belgium, France, Austria, Poland etc).

A further analysis of the first group shows that it is also far from homogenous. This group includes countries where the breakdown of the marriage, in some instances, no longer needs to be proved: if the spouses state that their marriage has broken down, the competent state officials have to take this for granted. Those countries (like, for instance, Russia, Sweden, the

---

[27] D. KENNEDY argues that all relevant choices, even in the "technical" fields like contract law, are always ideology-laden. *A Critique of Adjudication (fin de siècle)*, Harvard University Press, Cambridge Massachusetts, 1997.

[28] M. BUSSANI, ""Integrative" Comparative Law Enterprises and the Inner Stratification of Legal Systems", 1 *ERPL* 2000, p. 91.

Netherlands) have in fact left the concept of the irretrievable breakdown of marriage largely behind. Divorce on the ground of the irretrievable breakdown of the marriage has de facto basically become divorce "on demand". In other countries (for instance, Italy, Ireland, Spain, England and Wales) proving the irretrievable breakdown is still of vital importance, as otherwise the court is empowered to dismiss a divorce application.[29] In several of these countries the irretrievable breakdown can only be proven with the existence of certain formal conditions defined by law (for example: separation of a certain duration,[30] a conviction for certain crimes, non-consummation etc). In other countries the judge is free in his or her estimation of all the presented evidence. Some other countries, like for instance, England and Wales, although they call their divorce ground "irretrievable breakdown of marriage", in fact have a mixed system, as the conditions necessary for establishing the irretrievable breakdown include such fault grounds as adultery or unreasonable behaviour.

Even this superficial overview can illustrate that it is hard to find much true common core even among those countries that formally base their divorce law on the irretrievable breakdown of marriage. This scarcity of a common core will force the drafters of harmonised law much more often to leave aside the "common core" method and to employ the "better law" one.

### 3.2. More ideology-laden choices

Secondly, the ideological dimension of family law is far more explicit than in the "technical" areas of private law, and therefore it is out of the question to maintain that the drafters in choosing their "better law" are merely involved in technicalities and not in the making of ideology-laden choices. This makes the need to explicitly justify policy decisions much more prominent. As almost every choice in family law is connected to the adherence to some ideological commitments, the drafters inevitably will have to take sides in a highly politicised discourse.

On this point I will, for the time being, leave aside the "better law method", and make some suppositions concerning the roots of the strong ideological dimension of family law.

---

[29]   For instance, Irish law explicitly states that: "The court must be satisfied that there is no reasonable prospect of a reconciliation between the spouses" Section 5 (1) (b) of the Family (Divorce) Act of 1996.

[30]   In some countries this has to be of considerable length, for instance in Ireland – four years, in Italy – three years.

## 4. THE IDEOLOGICAL DIMENSION OF FAMILY LAW

The variety of rules in the so-called technical areas of private law can sometimes be explained by the fact that in different countries diverging technical solutions were made in order to solve the same problems and to achieve the same goals. In so far as the goals are the same, it is possible to use the quasi-neutral criterion of efficiency for selecting the best solution to achieve them.[31] However, even in the economically related areas of private law the same goals not always are pursued. It is widely acknowledged that many differences between the various solutions, for example with respect to consumer protection, are more than mere technical differences.

In family law not only the positive law, but also the very goals to be achieved, are frequently different and sometimes even opposite to each other. A good example thereof is provided by David Bradley, who has compared the objectives of the divorce reform in Sweden in 1973 and those of the failed attempt to dispense with the covered fault grounds in the divorce law of England and Wales.[32] The purpose of the Swedish reform was to make divorce as easy as possible. It was clearly stated that "legislation should not under any circumstances force a person to continue to live under a marriage from which he wishes to free himself".[33] In contrast, the objectives of the English Family Reform Act of 1996 were "supporting the institution of marriage, saving marriages and saving cost."[34] Obviously, if the goal is to make divorce more easily available, the measures that are the most efficient for attaining this objective will be quite different from those that are necessary for "saving marriages". Therefore in family law, before one can investigate the most efficient way to attain a certain goal, one will have to make a choice between the controversial goals, represented in various national jurisdictions.

---

[31] For a critical analysis thereof see: U. MATTEI, *Comparative Law and Economics,* The University of Michigan Press, 1996, p. 101-121. Mattei's conclusion that 'law is not the product of the will of a lawmaker [...but...] the outcome of a competitive process between legal formants' (*ibid.,* p. 120) seems not to apply to family law. This is because the development of legal rules in family law is hardly influenced by factors such as competition and the need to strive towards efficiency, but is rather strongly influenced by the political and ideological preferences of the legislators, judges and other lawmakers and adjudicators of the law.
[32] D. BRADLEY, "Convergence in Family Law: Mirrors, Transplants and Political Economy", 6 *MJ* 1999, p. 135-136.
[33] Ministry of Justice of Sweden, Abstract of Protocol on Justice Department Matter, 1969, p. 7.
[34] D. BRADLEY, "Convergence in Family Law: Mirrors, Transplants and Political Economy ", 6 *MJ* 1999, p. 136.

## 4.1. The ideological connotation of the 'cultural constrains" argument

Why is the situation in family law not like that in the economically related areas of private law? The differences between the various systems of family law and the underlying family ideology are often presented as reflecting the different national cultures. Because the "family law concepts are especially open to influence by moral, religious, political and psychological factors; family law tends to become introverted because historical, racial, social and religious considerations differ according to country and produce different family law systems".[35] This perception of the differences between the family laws as part of the unique and cherished national cultural heritage has formed the essence of a cultural constraints argument, widely employed against the harmonisation of family law.[36] The cultural constraints argument gives rise to at least three questions: what are the origins of the diversity of family law in Europe?; are the divergent family laws and the underlying ideologies really the unique products of the development of the particular national cultures?; and does the whole population of each European country share one and the same family culture?

## 4.2. The origins of diversity. The ius commune of family law

If one looks at the current multicolour pallet of family laws in Europe, one could hardly imagine that this diversity did not always exist. However, around a millennium ago the whole of the Occident had one and the same law on marriage and divorce and some related issues. The *ius commune* of family law, in contrast to other fields of private law, was not Roman law as rediscovered in the Middle Ages and developed in the European universities since the 12th century,[37] but the uniform medieval canon family law. Again unlike the economically-related areas of private law, this *ius-commune* was equally shared until the Reformation by the Western European civil and common law countries as well as by the Scandinavian region and the Eastern European countries with a Catholic tradition. The Orthodox Eastern European countries were, strictly speaking, never part of this *ius commune*.

---

[35]   W. MÜLLER-FREIENFELS, "The Unification of Family Law", 16 *Am. J. Comp. L.* 1968-69, p. 175.
[36]   On this argument see for instance: G. DE OLIVEIRA "A European Family Law? Play it again, and again … Europe!", *A Civil Code for Europe*, Coimbra editora, Coimbra, 2002, p. 127; M. HOHNERLEIN, "Konturen eines einheitlichen europäischen Familien- und Kindschaftsrecht – die Rolle der Europäischen Menschenrechtskonvention", 4 *European Legal Forum* 2000-01, p. 252.
[37]   See: R. ZIMMERMANN, "Roman Law and European Legal Unity", *Towards a European Civil Code*, 1998, p. 21-32.

This *ius commune* took shape within the framework of the first attempt to unify family law that occurred in Europe.[38] This unification represented the final point in the gradual replacement of the wide spectrum of pre-Christian marriage and divorce law, characterised by its informal rules as to the formation of marriage, easy divorce, tolerance towards concubinage and the acceptance of illegitimate children, by an entirely new set of uniform canon law rules. Many legal concepts (marriage as a sacrament, the indissolubility of marriage, strict monogamy and the exclusion of illegitimate children from the family) which were influential in some parts of Europe until deep into the 20th century, were vested or developed during that time.

The uniformity of canon marriage and divorce law only lasted until the Reformation. The roots of the current diversity therefore lie in the regulations of the different Protestant Churches and the secular laws of the advancing national states. But the end for uniformity did not mean the end of the dominance of the ecclesiastical concepts of the Middle Ages. Although the Protestant countries rejected the sacral character of marriage and the principle of its indissolubility, most of the canon heritage survived. As Glendon puts it: "secular government simply took over much of the ready-made set of the canon law".[39] With the differentiation within the Church and the Enlightenment, ideological pluralism increased, and it became increasingly difficult for the state to justify the canon law concepts, which it had inherited. Nonetheless, they were upheld for a considerable period of time, much longer than other medieval political and religious dogmas. Subject to serious discussion for the first time during the Enlightenment and the French Revolution, they again ruled almost uncontested for a long time thereafter. They remained an inseparable part of the status quo. They only came under serious fire towards the end of the 19th century. The 20th century witnessed a wave of revolutionary changes in the field of family law. In the Scandinavian countries and the Soviet Union family law was rapidly and radically reformed during the first decades thereof. During the first two decades of the 20th century the progress of the so-called Nordic co-operation[40] resulted in the co-ordinated drafting and

---

[38] The unification process evolved slowly through the centuries, before accelerating at the time of the reforms of Pope Gregory VII and it was almost complete by the end of the 12th century. However, the final point was only reached in the 16th century at the Council of Trent.

[39] M. A. GLENDON, *The Transformation of Family Law,* The University of Chicago Press, Chicago and London, 1989, p. 31.

[40] Nordic cooperation exemplifies the most successful attempt at the harmonisation of family law in Europe. On the course of this cooperation, see: R. DAVID, "The International Unification of Private Law", in: *International Encyclopaedia of Comparative Law,* vol. 2, 65, chapter 5, Mohr, Tübingen, 1971, p. 181-185.

enactment of legislation allowing divorce on the ground of the irretrievable breakdown of marriage.[41] In Russia non-fault divorce - the easiest in Europe at that time - was introduced immediately after the Bolshevik Revolution of 1917.[42] The Southern European countries needed almost the entire century in order to achieve the same level of modernity: divorce in Italy was only introduced in 1970, in Ireland in 1996 and Malta remains the last European country not to allow a full divorce. The remainder of Europe fell somewhere in between.[43]

The essence of this reformation of family law was to leave behind the surviving concepts introduced into family law at the time of the medieval canon unification. This reformation was generally promoted by the liberal-progressive wing and opposed by the conservatives. Thus in the 19th and 20th centuries family law issues frequently appeared in the middle of progressive-conservative debate.[44] Liberation from the medieval heritage occurred in all European countries without exception and in some countries it is not entirely complete even today. As I pointed out elsewhere,[45] the driving forces and the direction were the same everywhere, but the process was far from synchronised in the different countries. From the beginning of the 20th century onwards, a rather clear distinction can be made between countries in the vanguard and those in the rearguard. These differences could be linked with the dissimilar balance of power between the progressive and conservative political forces in European countries, different religious backgrounds and other factors.[46]These differences that colour the map of the current European family laws are

---

[41]    T. SCHMIDT, The Scandinavian Law of procedure in Matrimonial Causes, in: J. EEKELAAR, N. KATZ (eds.), *The Resolution of Family Conflicts*, Butterwoths, Harvard, 1984, p. 80.

[42]    See: M. ANTOKOLSKAIA, "De ontwikkeling van het Russische familierecht vanaf de Bolsjewistische revolutie: een poging tot verklaring", 70 *Tijdschrift voor Rechtsgeschiedenis* 2002, p. 137-151.

[43]    This of course is a rather simplistic sketch of a more complicated situation. Eastern European law was not modern in all respects. Portugal was the first country where radical reform, albeit not long-lasting, had taken place. In some other countries the modernity of family law differed significantly from one particular institution to the other.

[44]    For instance, equality of women, civil marriage and liberal divorce had been perceived as matters of the highest political priority since the second half of the 19th century and the first decade of the 20th century.

[45]    M. ANTOKOLSKAIA, "Development of Family Law in Western and Eastern Europe: Common Origins, Common Driving Forces, Common Tendencies", 1 *Journal of Family History*, vol. 28, p. 52-69.

[46]    For the attempts at explanation see: H. WILLEKENS, Explaining Two Hundred Years of Family Law in Western Europe, in: H. WILLEKENS (ed.), *Het gezinsrecht in de sociale wetenschappen*, Vuga Uitgeverij B.V, 's-Gravenhage, 1997, p. 59-95.

---

directly linked to the difference in the timing of this modernisation of family law.

The point I am trying to make is that the infamous diversity of family laws within Europe is mainly the result of the difference in the level of modernity of the family laws in various countries in Europe. The family law situation in each country is, on the one hand, not unique because almost every country is passing the same stages in its development on the way towards modernising family law. On the other hand, this situation is unique in the sense that it is coloured by the particularities of this development (speed; intensity) specifying only this particular country. Using this analysis one might dare to predict that the countries with less modern family law will reach the current level of the vanguard countries in due time.

However, this prediction hardly calls for the harmonisation of family law. First, by the time the rearguard will have reached the current level of the vanguard, the vanguard countries will probably already be far above this level, and then the diversity will persist. Zeno could ask whether or not Achilles could overtake a tortoise, but he would probably agree that a tortoise could hardly ever overtake Achilles. Secondly, no one can say to, for instance, Ireland: "sooner or later you will have the same divorce law as Sweden now does, so why lose time, why not introduce a modern harmonised family law right away?" It is quite obvious that "moral and political reforms must be initiated from within each culture"[47] and cannot be forced from outside.

### 4.3. The conservative –progressive divide in Europe

The conservative-progressive discourse colours not only the differences in the modernity of family law in various European countries, but also the distinctions in the appreciation of family law situations within each particular country. In family law cultural differences do not only lie along state borders but are present in every particular European country. I am not even referring to the growing multiculturalism resulting from immigration from non-European countries. What I mean is that even the innate population in each particular European country is split into various different "cultures", reflected in corresponding ideologies. The "culture" of an urban family of highly educated young professionals differs significantly from the "culture" of a rural family of middle-aged traditional

---

[47]    W. HOLLEMAN, The Human Rights Movement. Western Values and Theological Perspectives, Praeger, New York, 1987, p. 211.

farmers in any European country, be it Ireland, Sweden, Malta or the Netherlands. The modernity of family patterns and family culture differs greatly from one social environment to another. Rothenbacher concisely labelled this phenomenon "the contemporaneity of the noncontemporaneous".[48] Each country has of course a predominant culture, which is generally the culture of the majority of the population or the *élites dirigeante*.[49] This predominant culture is usually reflected in the pertinent family laws. Following this reasoning one can suggest the existence of a progressive-conservative divide in Europe, based on the presence of a conservative and a progressive pan-European ideology of family morals. Each of those ideologies has its own rank and file in each European country. Sometimes this is a majority, sometimes a tiny stratum. The countries with modern family laws also have a population group with a conservative family "culture" and the countries with conservative family laws always have population groups that represent the most modern views on family life. The members of the affiliated cultural groups understand each other across the borders, often looking abroad to support their ideas, and they repeatedly call on the European courts to adjudicate their confrontations with their compatriot opponents. This allows the suggestion that the ideas of Pierre Legrand, one of the best known adepts of law as an emanation of culture, who perceives the "cultureness" of law only from a national perspective,[50] or from the perspective of the common law/civil law dichotomy,[51] are not entirely valid for family law.

## 5. SHARED NOTION OF FAMILY RIGHTS AND JUSTIFYING THE 'BETTER LAW"

### 5.1. Additional need for political legitimation

The suggested link between the level of modernity of family law and the appreciation thereof with the conservative–progressive divide means that many decisions concerning the "better" family law rule for harmonised family law will involve an ideology-laden choice. In making this choice the

---

[48]   F. ROTHENBACHER, "Social Change in Europe and its Impact on Family Structures", in: J. EEKELAAR, N. THANDABUTU, *The Changing Family. International Perspectives on the Family and Family Law*, Hart Publishing, Oxford, 1998, p. 21.

[49]   I am indebted to E. ÖRÜCÜ for this term. See her *Critical Comparative Law: Considering Paradoxes for Legal Systems in Transition*. Preadvies voor de Nederlandse Vereniging voor Rechtsvergelijking, Kluwer, Deventer, 1999, p. 86.

[50]   He speaks in this sense of the "Frenchness" of French law. P. LEGRAND, *Fragments on Law-as-Culture*, W.E.J. Tjeenk Willink, Deventer, 1999, p. 5.

[51]   P. LEGRAND, *Fragments on Law-as-Culture*, 1999, p. 64.

drafters of the harmonised law will necessarily have to take sides in the progressive-conservative discourse and make value judgments in respect of the choices made by the national legislators. Under these circumstances the self-appointed drafters will be likely to search for all support that they can discern in the practices of the recognized European institutions. The most obvious option for the justification of "better rules" for harmonised family law is to use the shared European notion of human rights relating to the family. This is a relatively safe road to follow, because this shared notion as vested in the European Convention on Human Rights and developed in the related case law of the European Court of Human Rights, the European Court of Justice and in the recent European Charter of Fundamental Rights of the European Union, could provide certain and acknowledged reference points to justify the policy-laden choices of the drafters of harmonised family law.

### 5.2. The European courts are also searching for justification

But the drafters might be rather disappointed when following this road. The case law of the ECHR and the ECJ shows that both courts often also seek legitimation for their value judgements in the common core: the European "consensus" or the "common European standard". The literal texts of all three articles of the European Convention on Human Rights relating to family rights: 8 (protection of family life), 12 (right to marry and to found a family) and 14 (prohibition of discrimination) do not always provide relief. Thus the ECHR, in deciding cases, has to go beyond the literal text and to interpret it "in the light of present-day conditions."[52] The same applies to the practices of the ECJ. The long road towards the recognition of EU capacity in respect of human rights[53] and especially those relating to family law, and the subjection of the protection of the family to the economic goals of the Union, casts its shadow on the development of EU policy regarding family rights.[54] The ECJ is also restrained by the subsidiarity principle and often seeks additional authorisation in the consensus argument.[55] Since the political mandates

---

[52]  *Marckx v. Belgium.* Judgement of 13 June 1979, Series A, no. 31, para. 41.

[53]  See for instance: P. ALSTON (ed.), *The EU and Human Rights,* Oxford University Press, Oxford, 1999, p. 9-11; A. VON BOGDANDY, "The European Union as a Human Rights Organisation? Human Rights and the Core of the European Union", *37 Common Market Law Reviews* 2000, p. 1317.

[54]  N. NEUWAHL, A. ROSAS, *The European Union and Human Rights,* Nijhoff, The Hague, 1995, p. 221-230; C. MCGLYNN, "A Family Law for the European Union", in: J. SHAW (ed.), *Social Law and Policy in an Evolving European union,* Oxford Hart, 2000, p. 229-232.

[55]  On the use of this argument see, for example: C. MCGLYNN, "A Family Law for the European Union", in: *Social Law and Policy in an Evolving European Union,* p. 226.

of the ECHR and the ECJ are indubitable only within the margins of the European Convention, and the EU legislation respectively, they need additional sources of authorisation every time they employ an extensive or even contra legal interpretation. Seeking such authorisation both courts generally refer to the consensus or the "common European standard" among the Contracting States.[56] However, an overall consensus or common core almost never exists, otherwise the very case would never appear before the court. The Courts have to decide cases in a Europe divided into conservative-progressive family ideologies,[57] and the composition of the judges, representing the Contracting States, also reflects this divide. One thing and another oblige the Courts to be cautious in using their power.

### 5.3. Johnston v. Ireland: no right to divorce

Searching for political legitimation sometimes results in a rather low level of protection. My choice for the consistent use of divorce law as an illustration throughout this article leads us to a rather discouraging example. In divorce law the level of the shared notion of protection of family rights seems to be as low as the lowest common denominator. A good illustration of the scale of the political tension under which the European courts have to pursue their goals is provided by one of the classic family law ECHR cases: *Johnston and others v. Ireland*.[58] As is well known, in the *Johnston* case an Irishman, who many years previously had obtained a judicial separation from his first wife, and his second partner challenged the Irish law that did not permit full divorce and remarriage.[59] Some four days before the final deliberation in the Johnston case, the overwhelming majority of the Irish population rejected divorce in a referendum. Therefore the absence of divorce had just acquired the highest political legitimation.[60] There was also almost no possibility that the Irish government would acquiesce in any intervention of the ECHR. The court faced a difficult political dilemma. It finally refused to provide a dynamic

---

[56] G. CAROZZA, "Propter Honoris Respectum: Uses and Misuses of Comparative Law in International Human Rights: Some Reflections of the Jurisprudence of the European Court of Human Rights", 73 *Notre Dame L. Rev. 1217*, 1998, p. 1231-1232.

[57] In the *Handyside* case the ECHR has acknowledged that "it is not possible to find in the domestic laws of the various Contracting States a uniform European conception of morals". *Handyside v. the United Kingdom* Judgement of 7 December 1976, Series A no 24, para. 48.

[58] *Johnston and others v. Ireland*. Decision of 18 December 1986, Series A, no. 112,

[59] *Johnston and others v. Ireland*. Decision of 18 December 1986, Series A, no. 112.

[60] P. MAHONEY has stressed that "the Court (and the Commission) should be careful not to allow that machinery to be used so as to enable disappointed opponents of some policy to obtain a victory in Strasbourg that they have been unable to obtain in the elective and democratic forum in their own country. "Marvellous Richness of Diversity or Invidious Cultural Relativism?", 19 *Human Rights Law Journal 1,* 1998, p. 3.

interpretation of art. 12. Instead, the Court referred to the *travaux préparatoires* of the Convention, in order to argue that the omission of the right to dissolve a marriage was deliberate.[61] The Court stated, without any reference to the relevant laws of the Member States, that "having regard to the diversity of the practices followed and the situations obtaining in the Contracting States, the notion's requirements will vary considerably from case to case". Remarkable indeed, considering that at that moment only two member States – the defendant Ireland and Malta – had not introduced full divorce, thus the "great majority" of the states did share a consensus upon this matter. Accordingly, the ECHR proclaimed divorce law to be "the area in which the Contracting Parties enjoy a wide margin of appreciation in determining the steps to be taken to ensure compliance with the Convention".[62] As a result, the Court refused to recognise the right to dissolve a marriage as a right protected under the ECHR. Ireland finally introduced divorce in 1996, but the *Johnston* case has never been overruled, as this issue was never brought before a European court again. Malta still has no full divorce.

The right to divorce is, of course, quite an extreme example. Because family rights are developed by the ECHR on an unsystematic case-to-case basis, the level of protection that is actually attained in various fields of family law is also quite uneven. It varies from the lowest common denominator in respect of divorce (it is quite plausible that *Johnston* would now be decided differently, however) to one of a high degree, as in the most recent cases with respect to the rights of post-operative transsexuals.[63] However, the average of a "narrow and traditional" concept of the family as developed in ECHR case law was rightly summarised by McGlynn.[64]

### 5.4. European Charter: still no right to divorce

The Charter of Fundamental Rights of the European Union[65] is important for our enquiry because it is alleged to represent "a fully up-to-date *Ius*

---

[61]  *Johnston and others v. Ireland.* Decision of 18 December 1986, Series A, no. 112, paras. 52–53.

[62]  *Johnston and others v. Ireland.* Decision of 18 December 1986, Series A, no. 112, para. 55.

[63]  See for example the recent cases *Goodwin v. the United Kingdom* and *I. v. the United Kingdom*, where the ECHR finally acknowledged that the refusal to provide legal recognition to the new gender identity of post-operative transsexuals violates both art. 8 and art.12 of the Convention. See respectively: *Goodwin v. the United Kingdom*, Decision of 11 July 2002, and *I. v. the United Kingdom*, Decision of 11 July 2002, http://hudoc.echr.coe.int/hudoc.

[64]  C. McGlynn, "Families and the European Union Charter of Fundamental Rights: progressive change or entrenching the status quo?", 26 *European Law Review* 2001, p. 587-593.

[65]  [2000] *OJ* C364/1.

*Commune Europaeum* of human rights protection in Europe".[66] The purpose of the Charter is "to strengthen the protection of fundamental rights in the light of the changes in society, social progress and scientific and technological developments by making those rights more visible in the Charter". Therefore, in contrast to the more than 52-year old Convention upon which it is built, the Charter could reasonably be expected to reflect the current level of the existing shared notion of family rights. At least with respect to family rights however, almost all of these expectations have remained unjustified.

Article 7 of the Charter has the same meaning and scope as the corresponding article 8 of the ECHR.[67] According to article 53 of the Charter, if the articles of the Charter coincide with those of the ECHR, they should be given the same interpretation. That means that they should also be interpreted in the light of the case law of the ECHR.[68] However, if Community law provides more extensive protection, the Charter should be interpreted in the light of this law.[69] That means that the level of protection may not drop below the level of protection guaranteed by the ECHR and the relevant case law, but it may be higher. Surprisingly enough, article 9, the counterpart of article 12 of the ECHR, also contains no right to dissolve a marriage. We do not know whether this was a deliberate omission or simply an oversight. Anyhow, the introduction of this right would not have been superfluous, because Malta is waiting on the candidates' list.

The aforementioned example shows that the Charter, at least in relation to family rights, is largely based on the same "common ground" as the case law of both courts.[70] The European institutions have hardly gone any further than the vague text of the Convention, and have not even sufficiently reflected the achievements of the case law of the European courts. That might have happened not because of unwillingness.[71] A more plausible reason could be the same conservative-progressive divide that has

---

66    "The EU Charter of the Fundamental Rights – Some Reflections on its External Dimension", Editorial, 1 *MJ* 2001, p. 3.
67    M. GIJZEN., "The Charter: A Milestone for Social Protection in Europe?", 1 *MJ* 2001, p. 57.
68    F. LENAERTS, E. DE SMIJTER, "A "Bill of Rights" for the European Union, 38 *Common Market Law Reviews* 2001, p. 296.
69    For more on this issue see: M. GIJZEN, "The Charter: A Milestone for Social Protection in Europe?", 1 *MJ* 2001, p. 54.
70    C. MCGLYNN, "Families and the European Union Charter of Fundamental Rights: progressive change or entrenching the status quo?", 26 *European Law Review* 2001, p. 598.
71    The unsuitability of the minimalist approach to the development of EU human rights protection law is clearly shown by N. NEUWAHL, A. ROSAS, *The European Union and Human Rights,* Nijhoff, The Hague, 1995, p. 58-63.

so often precluded both European courts from going beyond the common ground. Because of this divide a higher level may simply have not been politically feasible. It is probably still to some extent true that "the Community, when attempting to draw a list of human rights, would necessarily take a minimalist approach and be able to agree only on the lowest common denominator of such rights."[72]

### 5.5. The shared notion of family rights provides no relief

It is quite clear that, in spite of all the advantages of invoking the shared notion of family rights for the justification of "better law" choices, there remains a serious obstacle along this road. The problem is that certain rights cannot acquire the status of human rights that are recognised throughout the Union, precisely because of the differing ideas thereon within Europe. Both the ECHR and the ECJ repeatedly refer to the "common ground" when acknowledging the existence of a certain right. The European Charter has not changed this picture to any great extent. Therefore the drafters of harmonised law, when trying to evoke the shared vision of human rights in order to justify their choices, will very soon find themselves moving in a kind of vicious circle. They have to select or create "better rules", because there is too little common core to build upon. In order to justify the "better rule" they invoke the shared notion of human rights, but the judicial institutions responsible for delineating such a notion often go no further than the common core. In this way they return to where they have started.

Apart from the downplaying influence of the consensus argument, the conventional level of the protection of family rights is almost never the highest among the Contracting States, because the Convention only guarantees the minimum level of protection and creates a kind of "floor", below which Contracting States cannot drop. Meanwhile, "the differences above this "floor" may still exist without injuring anyone's human rights."[73] The same is true for Community law.[74]

My conclusion is that the level of modernity of human rights-based *Principles* would be unsatisfactorily low. The drafters of the *Principles* should

---

[72] N. NEUWAHL, A. ROSAS, *The European Union and Human Rights*, Nijhoff, The Hague, 1995, p. 16.

[73] N. JOHNSON, "Recent Developments: the Breadth of Family Law Review Under the European Convention on Human Rights", 36 *Harv. Int'l L.J.* 513, 1995, lexis.

[74] N. NEUWAHL, A. ROSAS, *The European Union and Human Rights*, Nijhoff, The Hague, 1995, p. 247.

of course invoke the shared notion of human rights in every case when Community law or the case law of the ECHR reaches a sufficient level, but this might not often be the case.

## 6.  HARMONISATION AS A MOVEMENT TOWARDS MORE MODERN FAMILY LAW?

Does the impossibility of finding any solid external source for justifying the choice of "better" rules for harmonised family law make the harmonisation of family law impossible? I do not think so. First, it remains possible to try to avoid the problems connected with the use of the "better law" method and to attempt to build the *Principles* on the common core only. Second, there is the more ambitious but promising alternative to face the challenges of the "better law" method and to employ it while elaborating the *Principles*. This would be a very complicated enterprise, vitally dependent upon whether or not it will be feasible to make credible value judgments in respect of various family law rules and concepts, and to convincingly justify the selection of the "better" ones.

### 6.1. *Common core-based Principles*

The first option is to try to escape the whole problem of justifying "better law" and to build the *Principles* upon the thin layer of a common core already existing between various European jurisdictions plus the achievements of the case law of both European Courts. If we interpret the "common core" not too strictly, then in respect of divorce we could disregard Malta and even *Johnston*, and acknowledge that there is a common ground to include the right of divorce in such *Principles*. Further, there is a sufficient *common core* for certain minimum requirements, for instance that fault should not be the exclusive ground for divorce; that a "guilty" spouse should not be precluded from applying for divorce; that matrimonial fault should not automatically lead to the loss of custody of minor children; and so on. Such *Principles* could even serve as a model for binding EU law, because they would hardly introduce anything new. At the same time, in anticipation of the accedence of new members, they would certainly not be useless. For Malta for instance, such binding law would mean that it would have to introduce divorce in order to comply with the EU law. Such *common core-based Principles* would in fact only do what the European Charter failed to accomplish in respect of family law. They would define the lowest level of protection, below which the EU members would not be allowed to go, while they would remain completely free to ensure a higher level of protection in their domestic laws. Later on, both the

European Courts might carefully try to raise the standard of minimum protection little by little.

In spite of all the advantages of common core-based harmonisation, the problem described above remains: certain rights cannot acquire the status of human rights that are recognised throughout the Union because of the differing ideas thereon within Europe. The consequences seem to be that the level of modernity of *common core-based Principles* would be quite low. The fact that there was not enough consensus even to make the European Charter a binding instrument clearly shows that the promotion of *common core-based Principles* would still be an extremely difficult task.

### 6.2. 'Better law" Principles

The second, more demanding, option is to elaborate the *Principles* using the "better law" method. This implies that the drafters are prepared to take sides and to express value judgements. They have to dare to pronounce openly why they, for instance, prefer the Swedish permissive divorce law above the restrictive Irish one or *vice versa*. As the situation in family law in Europe is typified by the progressive-conservative discord, there could be as many visions of what is the "better" family law, as there are nuances within the spectrum of this discourse. In theory, a truly conservative drafting group may also wish to design and promote *Principles* built upon the most conservative solutions represented in the European jurisdictions. However, *Principles* that would try to turn back the hand of time would probably have very little chance to be taken seriously.

My personal preference would be to draft non-binding *Principles* based upon the highest standard of modernity achieved in present-day European family law. Such *Principles* would clearly go beyond the level of the shared European notion of human rights. Although a certain amount of subjectivity would be inevitable in the drafting, some methods could diminish the risk of estimations based purely on the personal preferences of the drafters. Putting the various existing family law solutions into a historical perspective would provide the necessary guidance for assessing the level of modernity of different solutions and to identify the most modern ones.

An objective argument in favour of high-standard *Principles* seems to be the fact that modern would-be *Principles* are generally more permissive and would therefore leave the more conservative groups within the population with the freedom to follow their own pattern of behaviour.[75] For instance, if one finds divorce unacceptable due to one's religious convictions, a law permitting divorce does not force anyone to dissolve a marriage. Even if one is divorced by one's spouse, one could abstain from remarrying out of respect for the indissolubility of marriage. *Principles* built upon a conservative "culture" would, on the contrary, necessarily be rather restrictive. Conservative family law always tends to subject the population groups representing the minority "cultures" to the restrictions of that law, although they do not share its underlying convictions.[76] Therefore these minorities often have the feeling that their minority rights are being infringed in an undemocratic manner. That is the main objective advantage of permissive law over restrictive law in the context of ideological controversy. This is the most important reason why the *Principles* of European family law should be progressive and possibly absorb the most modern solutions achieved in various European countries. Therefore I feel a great deal of sympathy to McGlynn's assumption that harmonised family law has to be *"utopian"* and *"libertarian"*.[77]

## CONCLUDING REMARKS

My conclusions are that the use of the "better law" method is just about inevitable in elaborating harmonised family law. At the same time, almost no objective criteria can be found in order to justify the choice as to why the drafters consider the rule that they have selected to be the "better" one. As the diversity of family laws in Europe is politically and ideologically coloured, any possible justification would be subjective, depending on the convictions of the drafters. The conservative-progressive discord among the European countries, but also within every particular country, means

---

[75] Conservative-minded persons could of course have ideological difficulties in accepting a progressive law, even if it does not touch them directly. For instance, one well-known Dutch family law professor was so discontent with the prospect of same-sex couples being able to enter into a marriage, that he declared his intention to dissolve his own happy marriage in the Netherlands in order to recelebrate it immediately in another country that does not have the possibility for homosexual couples to marry.

[76] A good example is the first Irish divorce referendum of 1986, when 63.5% of the voters voted against the introduction of divorce and 36.5% voted in favour. (C. JAMES, "Ireland Welcomes Divorce: The 1995 Irish Divorce Referendum and The Family (Divorce) Act of 1996", 8 *Duke Journal of Comparative & International Law* 1997, lexis). As divorce is not compulsory, the result of the referendum meant that the majority of the Irish population denied the minority the right to dissolve their marriage, and imposed its view even upon the non-Catholic part of the population (about 8%), which did not share the Catholic notion of the indissolubility of marriage.

[77] C. MCGLYNN, "A Family Law for the European Union?", in: *Social Policy in the Evolving European Union*, p. 241.

that whatever *Principles* would be drafted, they would never answer the expectation of every country within Europe and every section of the population within each country. But neither do domestic family laws.

Under these circumstances I would be inclined to accept the challenges of the "better law" method and to draft non-binding *Principles* upon the highest standard of modernity. Obviously, in this approach the non-binding nature of the *Principles* would be crucial. Any attempt to "emancipate" citizens against their will would be paternalistic, disrespectful and doomed to failure in any democratic society. I am in no way advocating a kind of crusade aiming to enforce libertarian *Principles* of family law upon the European population. The task of the *Principles* should merely be to highlight and to make more transparent the achievements in the legal solutions for family law problems, which have already been attained in different parts of Europe or have been elaborated by the drafters. At most they would give the promoters of the modernisation of domestic family laws some additional moral support. Modern *Principles*, and the extensive comparative research on which they would be based, could save the national governments, the courts and the European institutions a great deal of time and money. Because such *Principles* would not be intended to be binding, and would be deemed to serve only as models, they would be no more of a threat to the national cultures and national sovereignty than a good comparative law survey.

# PART THREE –UNIFICATION OF PRIVATE INTERNATIONAL LAW IN FAMILY MATTERS

# UNIFICATION OF PRIVATE INTERNATIONAL LAW IN FAMILY LAW MATTERS WITHIN THE EUROPEAN UNION

Mário Tenreiro* and Monika Ekström*

## 1. LEGAL BASIS FOR JUDICIAL CO-OPERATION IN FAMILY LAW MATTERS

This article will provide a brief overview of the judicial co-operation within the European Union in the field of family law. It will first deal with the question of the legal basis for such co-operation and, in particular, whether judicial co-operation in the field of family law is necessary for the proper functioning of the internal market in the sense of Article 65 of the Treaty. It will also describe the most recent developments in the ongoing negotiations on the draft Regulation that is sometimes referred to as the "Brussels II bis Regulation".

The entry into force of the Amsterdam Treaty vested the Community with competence in matters of judicial co-operation in order to progressively establish an area of freedom, security and justice. Article 61(c) stipulates that the Council shall adopt measures in the field of judicial co-operation in civil matters as provided for in Article 65. Article 65 specifies that the civil measures in question shall have cross-border implications and be necessary for the proper functioning of the internal market. The measures shall include, inter alia, improving and simplifying the recognition and enforcement of decisions in civil and commercial cases and promoting the compatibility of the rules applicable in the Member States concerning conflict of laws and jurisdiction. Article 67 lays down the applicable procedure for decision-making.

The Community action in the area of judicial co-operation in family law has given rise to certain criticism. In particular, some commentators have

---

* This article is based on the speech delivered by Monika Ekström who replaced Mário Tenreiro at the conference held in Utrecht on 11-14 December 2002 on the theme "Perspectives for the unification and harmonisation of family law in Europe" organised by the Commission on European Family Law. This article does not express the official position of the European Commission, but the personal opinion of the authors.

argued that (a) family law, as such, falls outside the scope of Articles 61 and 65, and (b) to the extent that family law falls within the scope of Article 65, such measures are, in any event, not necessary for the proper functioning of the internal market.

The European Court of Justice has consistently held that the legal basis for a certain measure must be based on objective factors, which are liable to judicial review. Those factors include, in particular, the aim and content of the measure.[2] Each measure must be analysed to verify whether these criteria have been met. The argument that family law would not, as such, fall under Articles 61 and 65 would seem to be difficult to sustain with the entry into force of the Nice Treaty. This Treaty amends Article 67 in order to provide for a co-decision procedure for measures provided in Article 65 *with the exception of aspects relating to family law* (emphasis added). The amendment implies that the rule of unanimity will continue to apply in family law matters.

The question whether family law measures in the field of judicial co-operation are necessary for the proper functioning of the internal market raises several issues. It could first be noted that Article 65 does not refer to the functioning of the internal market, but rather to the "proper" functioning of the internal market. This would seem to suggest that the measure does not have to be indispensable for the functioning of the internal market as such, but only for its "proper" functioning. There is, as yet, no case law from the European Court of Justice, which would clarify how the criterion of necessity is to be interpreted and applied in the context of Article 65. Some guidance may, however, be found in the case law of the Court of Justice on Treaty provisions, which contain similar expressions. In this respect we can refer to Article 93 of the EC Treaty, which stipulates that the Council shall adopt provisions for the harmonisation of indirect taxes to the extent that such harmonisation is "necessary to ensure the establishment and the functioning of the internal market...". Advocate General Mischo stated that the Council has the power of appreciation as regards the necessity of the measures to be taken under this Article.[3] Although the cited Opinion cannot be directly transposed to the application of Article 65, it does suggest that a necessity criterion relating to the functioning of the internal market is in general not an absolute concept; it rather gives the Council a certain level of discretion.

---

[2]   Case C-271/94, Parliament v. Council, ECR [1996] I-1689, paragraph 14.
[3]   Opinion of 25.02.1999 in Case 166/98, Socridis v. Receveur principal des douanes, paragraphs 53-54.

The concept of the "internal market" is not limited to the free movement of goods, but comprises the four freedoms, i.e. the free movement of goods, persons, services and capital. The free movement of persons has resulted in the increasing mobility of citizens to move between the Member States, which in turn has resulted in an increasing number of couples of different nationalities as well as couples residing in a Member State other than that of their nationality. Against this background, the adoption of Regulation (EC) No. 1347/2000 ("the Brussels II Regulation")[4] was considered a necessary measure in the sense of Article 65, since differences in the national rules on jurisdiction and enforcement hampered the free movement of persons and the sound operation of the internal market.[5] A person could, for instance, be reluctant to accept a job offer and move to another Member State if that Member State would not recognise a prior judgment issued by a court in another Member State on family law matters, such as divorce or parental responsibility.

The arguments submitted above do not of course mean that the Community has unlimited powers to legislate in the area of judicial co-operation in family law under Article 65. Substantive family law measures in principle fall outside the scope of this Article. Neither does it imply that all measures in the field of judicial co-operation in family law matters having cross-border implications could be considered necessary for the proper functioning of the internal market. An assessment of the necessity thereof must be made in each specific case. It is ultimately the choice of the Council to assess to what extent they consider a certain measure to be necessary for the proper functioning of the internal market in the light of its aims and content.

## 2. THE PROGRESSIVE CREATION OF A COMMON JUDICIAL AREA IN THE FIELD OF FAMILY LAW

### 2.1. The Programme of mutual recognition

In 1999 the European Council in Tampere endorsed the principle of mutual recognition of judgments as a cornerstone for the creation of a common judicial area. The Council invited the Commission to work towards the progressive abolition of the concept of exequatur. As a first

---

[4]    Council Regulation (EC) No. 1347/2000 of 29 May 2000 on jurisdiction and the recognition and enforcement of judgments in matrimonial matters and in matters of parental responsibility for children of both spouses, *OJ* L 160, 30.06.2000, p. 19.

[5]    Recital 4 of Regulation (EC) No. 1347/2000.

step, the Council mentioned as areas of priority, uncontested claims and, in the field of family law, maintenance claims and visitation rights.[6]

In accordance with the mandate of the Tampere Council, the Commission and the Council prepared a joint Programme on mutual recognition of judgments,[7] which was adopted on 30 November 2000 by the Justice and Home Affairs Council. The Programme foresees the implementation of the principle of mutual recognition through the progressive abolition of the exequatur for all decisions in civil and commercial matters. Its ultimate goal, to be achieved in three stages, is the abolition of all intermediate measures for the recognition of judicial decisions between the Member States. As a result, judicial decisions will no longer be treated differently or be subject to additional procedures because they are issued in another Member State. The Programme identifies five areas in which progress should be made. Three of these areas concern family law: decisions on matrimonial matters and on parental responsibility (Area II), decisions on property rights arising out of separation between married and unmarried couples (Area III) and decisions on wills and succession (Area IV).

The Programme constitutes the European Commission's main working programme in the field of judicial co-operation in civil matters and to a large extent determines its agenda. Although the Council has set out very far-reaching ambitions in the Programme, progress has so far been relatively slow, due to various factors.

## 2.2. Existing EC legislation –the Brussels II Regulation

The co-operation between Member States in the field of private international law in family law matters is currently regulated by Council Regulation No. 1347/2000,[8] commonly referred to as the "Brussels II Regulation". This Regulation, which was adopted on 29 May 2000 and which entered into force on 1 March 2001, contains rules on jurisdiction, recognition and enforcement of decisions on divorce, legal separation and marriage annulment. It also applies to decisions on parental responsibility to the extent that they are issued in the context of a matrimonial proceeding and

---

[6]   Points 33 and 34 of the Tampere conclusions.

[7]   Programme of mutual measures for the implementation of the principle of mutual recognition of decisions in civil and commercial cases, *OJ* No. C 12 of 15.01.2001, p.1. The title of the programme as published incorrectly refers to a "draft programme", although the programme has indeed been adopted.

[8]   Council Regulation (EC) No. 1347/2000 of 29 May 2002 on jurisdiction and the recognition and enforcement of judgments in matrimonial matters and in matters of parental responsibility for children of both spouses, *OJ* No. L 160 of 30.06.2000, p. 19.

concern children that are common to both spouses. This article will not further deal with this Regulation.

### 2.3. Proposed EC legislation –the Commission proposal of 3 May 2002

### 2.3.1. Background

Very shortly after the adoption of the Brussels II Regulation, the French Presidency submitted an initiative aimed at facilitating the exercise of cross-border access rights through the abolition of the exequatur for decisions concerning access rights to children below the age of sixteen. To counter-balance the direct enforceability of decisions on access rights, the French initiative provided certain guarantees that the child would automatically return at the end of a visiting period in another Member State. The scope of the initiative was linked to the Brussels II Regulation. The discussions showed that it was difficult to make progress on the French initiative as long as the scope of the Brussels II Regulation remained limited as regards decisions on parental responsibility. It was considered unsatisfactory that a large part of the decisions on parental responsibility was not covered by the Regulation, either because the decisions concerned children of unmarried couples or because they were not issued in the context of divorce proceedings.

Against this background, the Justice and Home Affairs Council concluded in November 2000 that a further examination of the French initiative should be pursued in parallel with the extension of the scope of application of the Brussels II Regulation, so as to ensure the equal treatment of all children. The Commission undertook to present a proposal to this effect and presented a working document in March 2001,[9] which formed the basis of a public hearing in June 2001. The public hearing, which was widely attended, showed the need for action, in particular to ensure the child's right to maintain contact when the parents live in different Member States. It also showed the need for action to secure the return of the child not only in cases of access rights, but also in all cases of child abduction. On the basis of the comments and submissions, in September 2001 the Commission submitted a draft Regulation on parental responsibility extending the scope of application to all decisions on parental responsibility.[10] It also

---

[9]    Mutual recognition of decisions on parental responsibility, 27.03.2001, *COM* (2001) 166 final.
[10]   Proposal for a Council Regulation on jurisdiction and the recognition and enforcement of judgments in matters of parental responsibility, *OJ* No. C 332 of 27.11.2001, p. 269.

dealt with the question of child abduction through provisions on jurisdiction and the return of the child. In this regard the proposal was based on the notion underlying the French initiative, but went a step further by extending the rules on the return of the child to all cases where the child had been unlawfully removed from one Member State to another. The reason for including child abduction in the proposal was that it did not seem logical to apply stricter rules for the return of the child when the child does not return at the end of a visiting period than when a child does not return due to abduction. The aim was to develop Community rules, tailored to a common judicial area and based on the principle of mutual recognition, that would effectively deter child abduction.

The discussions showed the need to review the question of parental responsibility in its entirety. Rather than presenting a modified proposal, the Commission took the rather unusual initiative of withdrawing its previous proposal from September 2001 and presenting a new one. The new proposal, which was presented on 3 May 2002, brings into one text the Brussels II Regulation, the French initiative on access rights and the Commission proposal of September 2001.[11] It extends the principle of mutual recognition and enforcement in Brussels II to all decisions on parental responsibility. It also elaborates a solution for the return of abducted children and abolishes the exequatur procedure for access rights as well as for the return of abducted children. As regards matrimonial matters, the proposal does not introduce any changes, but adopts the provisions from the Brussels II Regulation on this subject. The latter Regulation will be repealed with the adoption of the new proposal, which adopts the provisions of the Regulation.

### 2.3.2. The question of child abduction

When the proposal was first presented, Member States were divided regarding the necessity and desirability of introducing separate rules on the question of child abduction. Certain Member States claimed that there was no need for Community action in this field, since the existing 1980 Hague Convention on child abduction[12] is in force in all the Member States and functions well. Other Member States shared the view of the European Commission that it was possible and indeed desirable to create even more ambitious rules on child abduction within the European Community. The negotiations finally ended in a deadlock situation and a compromise

---

[11]    This Commission proposal was officially withdrawn on 6 June 2002, *COM* (2002) 297 final.
[12]    Convention of 25 October 1980 on the Civil Aspects of International Child Abduction.

proved to be necessary in order to advance the discussions. During the second half of 2002, the Danish Presidency, in close co-operation with the Council, therefore devoted its efforts to elaborating a compromise on the question of child abduction. The successful work of the Danish Presidency enabled the Justice and Home Affairs Council to reach an agreement on 29 November 2002 on two different, but interrelated, questions. First, an agreement was reached on the rules on child abduction to include a future Regulation. Second, an agreement was reached on the decision to authorise the Member States to sign the 1996 Hague Convention on child protection[13] in the interest of the Community.[14]

In short, the agreement ensures that the 1980 Hague Convention on child abduction will continue to apply within the European Community. However, the future Regulation will add a number of rules intended to complement and reinforce the application of the Convention within the Community. The rules relate to jurisdiction, the procedure for the return of the child and the enforcement of a subsequent decision on custody issued in the country of origin.

The rule on jurisdiction seeks to ensure that there is no artificial transfer of jurisdiction to the courts of the Member State to which the child has been abducted, for the benefit of the abductor. Thus, the courts in the Member State where the child was habitually resident immediately before the abduction retain jurisdiction also after the abduction. Jurisdiction may shift to the courts of the Member State to which the child has been abducted only under very strict conditions to ensure that the non-abducting parent always retains the possibility to seize the court in the Member State where the child was habitually resident before the abduction in order to ensure that this court has the last word in deciding on the case. Thus, jurisdiction may only shift if all possessors of parental responsibility have acquiesced in the abduction or the child has resided in the other Member State for at least one year and the non-abducting parent has not lodged a request for return under the 1980 Hague Convention within that period of time or the court of origin has issued a decision confirming that the child shall not return. Jurisdiction may also shift if, following a decision

---

[13]  Convention of 19 October 1996 on Jurisdiction, Applicable Law, Recognition, Enforcement and Co-operation in Respect of Parental Responsibility and Measures for the Protection of Children.

[14]  A Commission proposal to this effect had been submitted on 20 November 2001, *COM* (2001) 680 final.

on non-return, the case has been transferred to the competent court of origin, but the parties do not wish to commence proceedings.

As stated above, the 1980 Hague Convention will continue to apply within the Community in cases of child abduction. However, the agreement provides that the Community judges shall apply certain principles relating to the procedure when they deal with requests for the return of a child pursuant to Article 12 of the 1980 Hague Convention. In those cases, the judges shall use the most expeditious procedures available under national law and shall decide whether or not the child shall return within a period of six weeks from the date on which the court was seized, unless this proves to be impossible. In addition, the person having applied for the return of the child shall have the opportunity to be heard during the procedure. The child shall also be given the opportunity to be heard during the proceedings unless this is inappropriate having regard to his or her age and maturity. Moreover, a court cannot refuse to return a child on the basis of Article 13(b) of the 1980 Hague Convention if it is established that adequate arrangements are provided to secure the protection of the child after its return. When a court has delivered a decision on non-return pursuant to Article 13 of the 1980 Hague Convention, it shall inform the competent court of origin of its decision within one month. The court of origin or the central authority must then give the parties the opportunity to make submissions within three months.

Finally, the agreement foresees that a subsequent decision delivered by the courts of origin and which entails the return of the child will be directly enforceable in the Member State to which the child has been abducted. The exequatur procedure is thus abolished in these cases provided that the decision is accompanied by a certificate issued by the court of origin. This document shall certify that the parties and the child have been given an opportunity to be heard and that the court of origin has taken account of the reasons for and evidence underlying the decision on non-return delivered by the court in the Member State to which the child has been abducted.

The agreement on child abduction provided a welcome impetus to the discussions on the future Regulation. Although a number of issues remain to be discussed, it is foreseeable that the new Regulation could be adopted during 2003.

Progress was also made with regard to the 1996 Hague Convention on child protection, where a decision was taken to authorise the Member States to sign the Convention in the interest of the Community. As a second step, the European Commission will submit a proposal for a decision authorising the Member States to ratify the said Convention within six months after the adoption of the decision on signature, *i.e.* at the latest in June 2003.

### 2.4. Envisaged EC legislation

As stated above, the Programme on mutual recognition foresees further action in the area of judicial co-operation in the field of family law. Thus, it is foreseen that future legal instruments will be drawn up on jurisdiction, recognition and enforcement of judgments relating to property rights arising out separations between married and unmarried couples (Area III) and to wills and successions (Area IV). The European Commission has instigated studies in these two areas, which are of great interest to the everyday lives of citizens. The studies will be followed by a thorough consultation procedure to allow all interested parties to submit comments.

The European Commission has also instigated a study on the practical problems resulting from the non-harmonisation of conflict of law rules on divorce. This study will also be followed by public consultation to ascertain whether there is a need for Community action to harmonise the conflict of law rules of the Member States in this respect. A White Paper on this subject is likely to be published during 2003.

# UNIFICATION OF INTERNATIONAL FAMILY LAW IN EUROPE –A CRITICAL PERSPECTIVE

MAARIT JÄNTERÄ-JAREBORG

## 1. INTRODUCTION

### 1.1. The topic

Special European family law for cross-border situations is today, rather unexpectedly, a reality. In the political rhetoric of the European Union, unified rules on various international family law matters are claimed to be essential for integration in Europe. They respond to the European citizen's justified expectations on what the Union should do for him or her. The citizen shall be able to count upon that judgments rendered in one Member State will be recognised in the other Member States. In addition, the citizen shall have access to justice within the whole Union. From the citizen's point of view it shall, further, not matter in which Member State proceedings are initiated. Whereas the first two objectives are directly related to the "free circulation of judgments" and jurisdiction within the EU, the last one seems to require that the same law be applied within the whole Union. More generally, the vision is establishing a "genuine judicial area in the EU where freedom, security and justice prevail".

The legal basis for this development is found in the EC Treaty, as revised by the Amsterdam Treaty, Articles 61c, 65 and 67. The Action Plans of the EU for the implementation of the Amsterdam Treaty include several family law projects, but limited to cross-border situations.[1] The prevailing opinion is correspondingly that the EU lacks competence in respect of substantive family law. Hence, it is at present not possible for the EU to start unifying

---

[1]     See: "Action Plan of the Council and Commission on how to best implement the provisions of the Treaty of Amsterdam on an area of freedom, security and justice", *Official Journal* No. C 19 of 23 January 1999, p. 1. See also: "Programme of measures for implementation of the principle of mutual recognition of decisions in civil and commercial matters", *Official Journal* No. C 12 of 15 January 2001, p. 1. The programme includes actions in the following four areas of family law: (1) Brussels I Regulation (= maintenance), (2) Brussels II Regulation (= marriage dissolution and parental responsibility) and family situations arising through relationships other than marriage, (3) rights of property arising out of a marital relationship and the property consequences of the separation of an unmarried couple, (4) wills and succession.

or harmonising substantive family law. On the other hand, the door is not closed for such measures in the future. – Should we as family law scholars (as well as citizens of Europe) rejoice at the EU's attempts to pay special attention to the citizen's (presumed) needs? Or is there reason for us to light lamps of warning, urging the institutions of the EU to initiate and support new measures only after thorough analysis of the real needs? Personally, I can envisage many advantages with a European cooperation in family law. However, the manner in which this cooperation is at present carried out within the EU is alarming.

Evaluating the ongoing development in the EU requires an overview of what has been achieved so far, as well as scrutiny of what is planned for the near future. In this contribution I will, in respects of the achievements, focus on the so-called *Brussels II Regulation*, i.e., Council Regulation (EC) No 1347/2000 on jurisdiction and the recognition and enforcement of judgments in matrimonial matters and in matters of parental responsibility for children of both spouses. I will also touch upon the work in progress since July 2000 to extend the scope of the Brussels II Regulation to cover all situations of parental responsibility. This project is commonly called *Brussels IIa* or *Brussels II bis*. In addition, I will comment upon the plans to enact unified choice of law rules for divorce, sometimes called the *Rome III* project. In that connection, also harmonisation of substantive divorce law in the EU will be touched upon, although at present this is not within the legislative competence of the EU.

### 1.2. Remarks on the used terminology

This contribution is about "international family law" in the EU, by which I mean "the private international law of the family". I use this concept in a broad sense, covering the issues of *(a)* jurisdiction, *(b)* choice of the applicable law, *(c)* recognition and enforcement of foreign judgments on family law, and *(d)* international judicial assistance in the field of family law, *e.g.*, returning of unlawfully abducted children to their home State. It is also possible to label this area of law as "the private law for cross-border situations within the family".

When discussing the EU's present or planned activities in international family law, I systematically talk about *unified rules of private international law*, irrespective of which of the above-mentioned issues is at stake. In private international law *unification* – where appropriate – is the only worthwhile approach. An advantage of unified rules is that the States concerned are only expected to grant judicial assistance, or recognise or enforce foreign judgments, on the same conditions. Further, a foreign State's jurisdiction is easier to accept where the same jurisdictional rules apply in the other concerned States. Uniformity of result (= uniform decisions) can be achieved where the States concerned apply identical choice of law rules, leading in each State to the application of the same law. In the field of substantive family law, where I believe it would be an advantage if the EU in the future were given a certain legislative competence, I refer to *harmonisation of substantive (domestic) family law*. In this field unification, resulting in identical rules in the Member States, is hardly feasible or even desirable. Considering that the societies are becoming more and more similar, economically and socially, and that family law has to respond to the same needs all over Europe, harmonisation, on the other hand, could in certain areas be a plausible alternative. There is today growing support for harmonisation of substantive family law within the EU.

### 1.3. Evaluating the importance of the various issues

In my opinion, the various issues of international family law cannot be placed on an equal footing with each other. A readiness to *recognise and enforce foreign judgments* forms traditionally the cornerstone of cross-border cooperation; the needs in family law are the same in this respect. However, the most successful international instruments, when evaluated on the basis of the number of ratifications, deal with *international judicial assistance*. An excellent example in this respect is the 1980 Hague Convention on the civil aspects of international child abduction, to which 72 States had acceded by the end of December 2002. The content of the rules on *jurisdiction* is closely connected with States' readiness to recognise and enforce foreign judgments. Granting jurisdiction only in situations with a close connection to the State where proceedings are initiated increases the prospects of the judgment's recognition and enforcement abroad. In comparison, the content of the rules on *choice of law* (conflict of laws) is in my opinion of a much more limited importance. I will try to illustrate this point when commenting upon the planned *Rome III Regulation* on unified choice of law rules on divorce.

## 2. BEFORE BRUSSELS II –A RETROSPECT

The relevance given to cross-border family law issues since the Amsterdam Treaty entered into force on 1 May 1999 has come as a total surprise to many, including both specialists in Community law and in family law. Considering the central part played by the free movement of workers in the European integration, it has, however, never been possible to fully separate Community law from family law.[2]

When negotiations were initiated in the late 1950s between the then six Member States, the aim being to draft a Convention ensuring reciprocal recognition and enforcement of judgments, family law was not excluded. When the Convention was finally adopted in 1968 – Convention on jurisdiction and the enforcement of judgments in civil and commercial matters, *Brussels I Convention* – family law proceedings had been dropped out, with the exception of those relating to *maintenance*.[3] This delimitation was found necessary due to the divergences among the legal systems of the Member States in both substantive family law and family conflict of laws. Including family law proceedings would have jeopardised the Convention's aim of (semi) automatic recognition, as explained in the Jenard Report.[4] This outcome seems to have been generally accepted also by the States later joining the Community, the notion being that the Community is primarily engaged in the economic sphere.

In 1990, the Member States took further actions of their own in the field of maintenance by adopting the Convention on the simplification of procedures for the recovery of maintenance payments. This Convention is essentially very similar to the United Nations' Convention on the Recovery Abroad of Maintenance, adopted in New York in 1956. It has been criticised for being totally unnecessary[5] and has not entered into force. Some years later, much more ambitious steps were taken. The Maastricht Treaty serving as the legal basis, time was now considered ripe to extend the scope of the Brussels I Convention to other family law proceedings. This extension resulted in the adoption of an independent

---

[2]  Family issues come into play in policies such as providing social protection and raising the standard of living and quality of life, as well as in relation to fundamental rights. The link between the freedom of movement and aspects of family law has been acknowledged by the EC Court in several of its rulings. See W. PINTENS & K. VANWINCKELEN, *Casebook European Family Law*, 2001.

[3]  According to Article 1.2, the Convention shall not apply to (1) the status or legal capacity of natural persons, rights of property arising out of a matrimonial relationship, wills and succession. – When the Brussels I Convention was adopted, there were still countries in Europe, *e.g.*, the founding Member State Italy, where the law did not permit divorce.

[4]  Report on the Convention on jurisdiction and the enforcement of judgments in civil and commercial matters (signed at Brussels on 27 September 1968), by P. JENARD. Published in: *Official Journal* No C 59 of 5 March 1979, p. 10. The legal basis of the Convention was Article 220 (now 293) of the EC Treaty.

[5]  See: M. SUMAMPOUW, "The EC Convention on the Recovery of Maintenance: Necessity or Excess?", in: *Law and Reality. Essays on National and International Procedural Law in Honour of Cornelis Carel Albert Voskuil*, 1990, pp. 315-336.

Convention in 1998, namely the Convention on jurisdiction and the recognition and enforcement of judgments in matrimonial matters, *i.e.*, the so-called *Brussels II Convention*.[6] After the Amsterdam Treaty had entered into force, this Convention was in all relevant respects converted into a Council Regulation, *i.e.*, the above-mentioned Brussels II Regulation. This Regulation entered into force on 1 March 2001 in the then Member States of the EU, with the exception of Denmark.[7]

## 3. THE BRUSSELS II REGULATION

### 3.1. Special community rules or global rules?

When drafting rules of its own in the field of private international law the EU inevitably treads on the toes of other actors in this field. There is less room both for national (= autonomous) rules and for rules originating from international cooperation in other fora. Most affected is undoubtedly the Hague Conference on private international law, which since 1893 has been working on the harmonisation (unification) of rules of private international law.[8] The results of this work are demonstrated in form of numerous Hague Conventions, adopted in the course of the years. As long as the activities of the EC/EU were directly linked with the internal market there were natural reasons for preferring special rules for the Member States to autonomous rules or, *e.g.*, rules adopted in Hague Conventions.[9] With respect to cross-border transactions, both the Brussels I Convention

---

[6]   See: A. BORRÁS, "Explanatory Report on the Convention, drawn up on the basis of Article K.3 of the Treaty of the European Union, on Jurisdiction and the Recognition and Enforcement of Judgments in Matrimonial Matters", *Official Journal* No. C 221 of 16 July 1998, p. 27.

[7]   In accordance with Articles 1 and 2 of the Protocol on the position of Denmark, annexed to the Treaty of Amsterdam, Denmark does not participate in cooperation included within Title IV of the new EC Treaty, including judicial cooperation in civil matters. Denmark's special position is connected with its opposition to "communitarisation" of the concerned areas. Also the United Kingdom and Ireland enjoy a special position in this respect, but may "opt into" the various legislative initiatives. So far, both States have fully participated in the new civil law cooperation.

[8]   See: C.C.A. VOSKUIL, "Preface", in: *The Influence of the Hague Conference on Private International Law. Selected Essays to Celebrate the 100ᵗʰ Anniversary of the Hague Conference on Private International Law*, 1993. – According to Article 1 of The Statute of the Hague Conference, in force since 15 July 1955, unification is the objective: "La Conférence de La Haye a pour but de travailler à l'unification progressive des règles de droit international privé."

[9]   All the Member States of the EU have, *e.g.*, ratified the Brussels I Convention and the Rome I Convention. The Member States have, on the other hand, refrained from ratifying potentially competing Hague Conventions, such as the 1986 Convention on the law applicable to contracts for the international sale of goods.

and the Rome Convention on the law applicable to contractual obligations (*Rome I*, 1980) have been important.

In respect of international family law the situation is more complicated. Firstly, the link with the internal market is clearly weaker, and the criteria put forth in Articles 61.c and 65 of the EC Treaty are also strongly in favour of restraint. Measures in the field of judicial cooperation in civil matters are to be taken only where they are *necessary for the proper functioning of the internal market*.[10] This, surely, can only exceptionally be the case in family law? The ongoing legislative activities within the EU suggest, on the contrary, a flexible interpretation, which would seem to make it possible to take measures in respect of practically all cross-border family law matters.

Secondly, families with links to the territory of the EU are split all over the world, making family conflicts global in character. Many Member States have a large foreign population originating from a third State, *i.e.*, a non-member State, where they may still be citizens. Many citizens of the Member States are also living on a more or less permanent basis in third States, *e.g.*, in North America, Asia or Australia. This being the case, global cooperation addressing the resulting legal problems should be given high priority.[11] Again, the ongoing activities in the EU suggest that the institutions of the EU, and also several Member States, attach high value to special community rules also in this area.

### 3.2. A clash with existing Hague Conventions

All the Member States of the EU are members to the Hague Conference on private international law. In particular when seen as a group, the EU Member States have had an enormous influence in the drafting of the Hague Conventions. Some of these Conventions have also turned highly successful and received a huge number of accessions from all parts of the world.[12] Some others, on the contrary, have not even received the mini-

---

[10]   In addition, Article 65 requires that there must be cross-border implications.

[11]   Only where such cooperation cannot succeed because of fundamental differences in moral values or because the States" legal traditions are inconsistent with each other, there is reason to prefer a legal cooperation with geographically much more limited effects. The so-called "cultural constraints" argument is much more vitally present in global cooperation than in regional cooperation between basically very similar States.

[12]   The Convention on the conflicts of laws relating to the form of testamentary dispositions (1961), the Convention abolishing the requirement of legalisation for foreign public documents (1961) and the Convention on the service abroad of judicial and extrajudicial documents in civil and commercial matters (1965) can be given as examples. Examples of later, highly successful Hague Conventions are the Convention on the civil aspects of

mum amount of accessions to enter into force. Generally speaking, the Member States of the EU have during the last decades been very selective in choosing which Conventions to ratify. Further, they have made their decisions individually. As a result, there is at present only one Hague Convention that has been ratified by *all* the Member States of the EU, namely the Convention on the civil aspects of international child abduction. Several other Hague Conventions have, however, been ratified by a great majority of them. – The drafting of the Brussels II Convention and its sequel in form of the Brussels II Regulation and later proposals, demonstrates how differently the Member States value the work of the Hague Conference.

As its title indicates, the Brussels II Regulation is limited to proceedings relating to the dissolution or weakening of the marital bond and proceedings on parental responsibility, arising on the occasion of matrimonial proceedings between the child's parents. Included are rules on jurisdiction and on the recognition and enforcement of (other) Member States' judgments. This choice of issues meant the EU starting to legislate in areas where there already existed a multitude of Conventions, adopted mainly at the Hague Conference and ratified by many of the Member States. In particular the following Conventions should be mentioned: the 1970 Convention on the recognition of divorces and legal separations (*Hague Divorce Convention*),[13] the 1961 Convention on jurisdiction and applicable law in respect of protection of minors (*1961 Hague Child Protection Convention*),[14] the 1980 Convention on the civil aspects of international child abduction (*1980 Hague Child Abduction Convention*) and the Convention on jurisdiction, applicable law, recognition, enforcement and cooperation in respect of parental responsibility and measures for the protection of children (*1996 Hague Child Protection Convention*). Also the European Convention on recognition and enforcement of decisions relating to custody of children and restoration of care of children, adopted at the Council of Europe in 1980, should be mentioned.[15]

---

international child abduction (1980) and the Convention on protection of children and cooperation in respect of intercountry adoption (1993).

[13] Of the Member States of the EU Denmark, Finland, Italy, Luxembourg, Netherlands, Portugal, Sweden and the United Kingdom have ratified this Convention.

[14] Of the Member States of the EU Austria, France, Germany, Italy, Luxembourg, Netherlands, Portugal and Spain have ratified this Convention.

[15] All the Member States of the EU have ratified this Convention. In principle, this Convention provides a more comprehensive tool for recognition and enforcement of judgments on parental responsibility than the Brussels II Regulation. In the relations between the Member States, this Convention, as well as the majority of the other above mentioned instruments, is superseded by the Brussels II.

Considering this abundance of existing instruments, the new European civil law cooperation made possible by the Amsterdam Treaty got a very bad start. The need for it and its legitimacy have been questioned from the very beginning, many doubting that the Brussels II Regulation, has anything to add of value.

### 3.3. Being short-sighted has a price

Several of the Member States which are parties to the Hague Divorce Convention were of the opinion that that Convention already provided a sufficient tool for the recognition of foreign divorces.[16] Problems caused by "limping divorces" within the Union could easily be solved if all the Member States were to ratify that Convention. Such problems were manifest not least in French-German relations, due to the lack of mutual recognition of divorce decrees.[17] The French-Spanish initiative to include parental responsibility, i.e. questions of custody and access rights,[18] was opposed on the ground that the Hague Conference had already adopted several instruments in this area.[19] It turned out, however, that the Member States outside the Hague Divorce Convention were not willing to ratify it, and that also in respect of parental responsibility the majority of the Member States were in favour of drafting special community rules.

A comprehensive political compromise, reached in December 1997, resulted in the inclusion of both proceedings. The Member States objecting to merging these issues were compensated by various concessions relating to the content of the adopted rules. Additional rules on jurisdiction in matrimonial proceedings were adopted, and in other respects the new community rules were largely modelled on the Hague Divorce Convention and the 1996 Hague Child Protection Convention.[20] The

---

[16]   In particular the Nordic Member States of the EU and the UK took this line of reasoning.

[17]   See: P. MCELEAVY, "The Brussels II Regulation: How the European Community has Moved into Family Law", *International and Comparative Law Quarterly* 2002, pp. 889-890.

[18]   The French-Spanish initiative was based on adjusting the new instrument to these States' national systems on divorce proceedings. Another aim was to add the "value" of the new instrument by extending its scope further than that of, *e.g.*, the 1970 Hague Divorce Convention.

[19]   In this respect, the Nordic Member States and the UK had support among several other Member States.

[20]   This development is described more in detail by M. JÄNTERÄ-JAREBORG in "Marriage dissolution in an integrated Europe: The 1998 European Union Convention on jurisdiction and the recognition and enforcement of judgments in matrimonial matters (Brussels II Convention)", *Yearbook of Private International Law*, Volume I 1999, pp. 6-27.

Hague Child Abduction Convention was left intact, and Belgium, the only Member State outside the Convention, was put under pressure to ratify it.[21]

What is then the value added by the Brussels II Regulation? Personally, I would claim that it is very limited and that the disadvantages outweigh the advantages. The Regulation has brought about some improvements on a general EU-level in respect of matrimonial proceedings. It has set aside exorbitant national rules on jurisdiction and, where correctly applied, prevents concurrent divorce proceedings from taking place in different Member States. Exclusive jurisdiction to dissolve the matrimonial bond belongs to the competent court first seized. This can save the spouses costs, caused by competing divorce proceedings. Also the temptation of initiating proceedings in more than one State is reduced.[22] Judgments dissolving a marriage and originating from a Member State are now valid within the whole Union. In particular from point of view of those Member States where foreign divorces were not initially recognised this is a clear improvement. It could, however, also have been achieved by enacting more flexible autonomous rules on recognition in those States or through their ratification of the Hague Divorce Convention.

On the other hand, including parental responsibility was a mistake. Linking parental responsibility (solely) to matrimonial proceedings consolidates obsolete notions, by making the legal position of the child dependent of its parents and treating children born in a marriage differently from other children. In modern child law, on the contrary, the child is treated as a separate holder of rights, independent of its parents, its birth in or out of wedlock being irrelevant. Once the Regulation was adopted it was immediately evident that it was out of date and in need of improvement. Ever since, enormous efforts have been made to "improve" the adopted rules on parental responsibility.

### 3.4. Exequatur precedes enforcement –a shortcoming or a necessity?

Among the judgments covered by the Brussels II Regulation, only judgments on the exercise of parental responsibility can require enforce-

---

[21] Belgium ratified the Convention in 1999.

[22] This is true in respect of proceedings aiming at the dissolution or the weakening of the marital bond. Considering that related issues, which normally are settled in connection with divorce proceedings, are outside the scope of the Regulation, it may still be in a spouse's interest to initiate proceedings relating to such ancillary matters in another Member State than the State of divorce. In such case, the spouses will still be forced to engage in proceedings related to the marriage dissolution in more than one Member State. See below, under section 5.2.

ment.[23] In this respect, one could well have expected tailor-made rules, based not only on the often-repeated notion of "mutual trust among the Member States" but also, in particular, on the best interests of the child. A judgment on custody or access rights can never be "final", excluding a review due to changed circumstances. Instead, the rules on enforcement were directly modelled on those of the Brussels I Convention,[24] dealing with completely different types of judgments, normally in commercial matters, and limited to an "in-between" procedure known as the *exequatur.* Before a judgment can be enforced in another Member State it must – on the application of any interested party – be declared enforceable there. This requirement of *exequatur* causes, naturally, both delay and inconvenience to concerned parties. Further problems are caused by the fact that there are no rules on how the enforcement is to take place, once the judgment has been declared enforceable in the requested Member State. In my opinion, this deficiency is more serious than the complications caused by *exequatur.*

### 3.5. How should enforcement take place?

As mentioned above, the Regulation says nothing on how the enforcement is to take place once the judgment has been declared enforceable in the requested Member State. Two alternative approaches would seem to be possible in this respect. One is to regard the outcome of *exequatur* as binding, meaning that once the exequatur is granted in the requested Member State, then that State has an obligation also to enforce the judgment in question. The scope of that State's autonomous law on enforcement is then limited to "technicalities" and the manner of enforcement, *e.g.*, the penalties available in case of non-compliance.

Another alternative is to surrender enforcement fully to the law of the Member State of enforcement, including their prevailing substantial conditions for enforcement. These conditions may pay regard to factors

---

[23]  The other judgments included concern divorce, legal separation or marriage annulment, i.e., the marital (civil) status of the spouses. Such judgments are not enforceable.

[24]  This outcome is essentially explained by the fact that the rules on enforcement were not part of the political compromise reached among the Member States in December 1997. After the compromise, the Member States were generally unwilling to enter into any discussions on additional questions, such as the content of the rules on enforcement. Adopting the rules of the Brussels I Convention on enforcement was facilitated also by the fact that also the 1996 Hague Child Protection Convention requires enforcement to be preceded by *exequatur.* See: M. JÄNTERÄ-JAREBORG, "A European Family Law for Cross-Border Situations – Some Reflections Concerning the Brussels II Regulation and its Planned Amendments", in *Yearbook of Private International Law*, Volume IV, 2002, pp. 67-82.

such as the judgment's compatibility with the child's best interests in changed circumstances or the child's objection to the enforcement, and are likely to differ among the Member States of the EU. In Sweden, the court examining an application for enforcement may refuse enforcement, if it is of the opinion that the circumstances have manifestly changed, the child's best interests requiring a review of the judgment.[25] Hence, a judgment may well be enforceable in its State or origin and even be declared enforceable in another Member State, *e.g.*, Sweden, in accordance with the Brussels II Regulation (the Regulation's conditions of recognition being fulfilled), but will, still, not be enforced there.[26]

## 4. THE FRENCH PROPOSAL TO FACILITATE THE EXERCISE OF RIGHTS OF ACCESS

In July 2000, only one month after the adoption of the Brussels II Regulation, France presented a detailed proposal aimed at facilitating the exercise of rights of access.[27] This proposal consisted, essentially, of two parts. The first was to abolish *exequatur* in respect of judgments relating to access rights. The second aimed at securing the prompt and unconditional return of a child who is retained in another Member State following the exercise of access rights. Originally, the proposal covered only judgments within the scope of the Brussels II Regulation, *i.e.*, judgments given on the occasion of matrimonial proceedings between the child's parents. Later on, when the proposal was substituted by more comprehensive proposals by the Commission, all judgments on access rights were included.

In the following, my intention is not to go into any details of the French proposal but only to comment upon it on a level of principles. I do not distinguish between the French proposal and the subsequent proposals by the Commission,[28] replacing and extending the former. In respect of

---

[25]   Code on Parents and Children (*Föräldrabalken*), Chapter 21 Section 6.
[26]   In the Swedish discussion, it has not been considered plausible to treat foreign judgments on parental responsibility more binding than corresponding Swedish judgments, when examining an application on enforcement: "Foreign judgments cannot be allowed to take a VIP lane at the expense of the interest and welfare of the child." See: M. JÄNTERÄ-JAREBORG, *supra* note 24.
[27]   See: Initiative of the French Republic with a view to adopting a Council Regulation on the mutual enforcement of judgments on the rights of access to children, in: *Official Journal* C 234 of 15 August 2000, p. 7.
[28]   In September 2001, the Commission put forth a proposal on parental responsibility, covering all children and without link to matrimonial proceedings. See: Proposal for a Council Regulation on jurisdiction and the recognition and enforcement of judgments in matters of parental responsibility, in: *Official Journal* No. C 332 of 27 November 2001, p. 269. A later proposal by the Commission of 3 May 2002 replaces this proposal. See: Proposal for a

the issues discussed here, these proposals are essentially the same. They are commonly called "Brussels IIa" or Brussels II bis".

## 4.1. The effect of abolishing exequatur

Abolishing *exequatur* means canalising all control of the enforceability of another Member State's judgment on the court or other authority in charge of the enforcement itself. This can save both time and money. It can also spare the parties from the confusion caused by different conclusions if *exequatur* is first granted in the requested Member State but, afterwards, *enforcement* is refused there (see above 3.5). Abolishing *exequatur* is also in line with the frequent references to "mutual trust" as the basis for the new civil law cooperation. Where mutual trust prevails there should be no need of an additional procedure checking the conditions for recognition and enforceability.

However, by focusing on *exequatur*, a more important aspect has been lost, namely the enforcement itself. In my opinion, this is an illustrative example of the EU's lack of ability (or will) to identify the real key issues.[29] Abolishing the exequatur doesn't prevent situations from arising where enforcement is refused in the requested State due to there prevailing (national) rules on enforcement, although the judgment is enforceable in its State of origin. In such a case, it is misleading to refer to a free movement of judgments. Real progress can be made only when the EU is prepared to enter into discussions in sensitive areas where Member States' outlook may differ from each other. If the Member States are not willing to accept that the final outcome – enforcement or not – may depend on the domestic law on enforcement of the requested Member State (= substantial conditions in that law), then efforts must be made to harmonise these rules, at

---

Council Regulation concerning jurisdiction and the recognition and enforcement of judgments in matrimonial matters and matters of parental responsibility repealing Regulation (EC) No 1347/2000 and amending Regulation (EC) No 44/2001 in matters relating to maintenance, published in: *Official Journal* No. C 203 of 27 August 2002. The aim is a single instrument covering marriage dissolution and parental responsibility.

[29]  The Commission's proposal from May 2002 contains a meaningless provision on this issue: "The enforcement procedure is governed by the law of Member State of enforcement", Article 50. It remains unclear whether the scope of this provision is limited to purely procedural issues (= manner of enforcement) or even covers such discretion as the court of enforcement in the requested Member State may enjoy, under there prevailing law on enforcement. The second alternative would seem to require more detailed drafting. Compare this drafting with Article 28 of the 1996 Hague Child Protection Convention: "Enforcement takes place in accordance with the law of the requested State to the extent provided by such law, taking into consideration the best interests of the child." This provision would seem to give room for substantial considerations.

least with respect to cross-border situations.[30] Surprisingly, the EU has so far only been prepared to discuss abolishing *exequatur* in respect of judgments on access rights, but not custody rights.[31]

### 4.2. The return of unlawfully retained children

The second part of the proposal gave rise to a tough battle, dividing the Member States into those arguing in favour of the continued application of the Hague Child Abduction Convention, and those in favour of special community rules also in this respect.[32] No convincing reasons were ever given in support of such rules, apart from general claims of inefficiency of the Hague Child Abduction Convention and abuse of its grounds for refusal to return the child to its State of habitual residence. It was also alleged to be common practice for a court in the State of refuge, after refusal to return the child, to readily assume jurisdiction in respect of parental responsibility. Rumours, on the other hand, alleged that the origin of the proposal was to be found in the dissatisfaction felt by France on how Germany was applying the Hague Convention in relation to France. Generally, the Convention was operating very well, also within the EU.[33]

The resulting deadlock was finally solved through a political compromise reached on 28 November 2002. The Hague Child Abduction Convention will continue to be applicable. It was also agreed that in case of wrongful removal or retention of a child, the Courts of the Member State of the habitual residence of the child keep their jurisdiction until the child has acquired habitual residence in another State.

---

[30] In that case Member States such as Sweden would have to accept that different notions may apply in cross-frontier cases compared with domestic situations, see above note 26. – In the discussion relating to the scope of Article 65 of the EC Treaty, it has not been excluded that it could provide a legal basis for *limited harmonisation* of both substantive civil law and the law of civil procedure. See: M. HELLNER, "The Limits to Judicial Cooperation in Civil Matters: Taking Legality Seriously", in: *Wege zum Europäischen Recht*, 2002, pp. 17-18.

[31] The final aim is, however, to abolish *exequatur* for all decisions. See: "Programme of measures for implementation of the principle of mutual recognition of decisions in civil and commercial matters", *Official Journal* No. C 12 of 15 January 2001, p. 1.

[32] A short description of the two subsequent proposals by the Commission, in respect of child abduction, is given by P. WINKLER VON MOHRENFELS, "Von der Konfrontation zur Kooperation. Das europäische Kindesentführungsrecht auf neuem Wege", *Praxis des Internationalen Privat- und Verfahrensrechts* 2002, pp. 374-375. Winkler von Mohrenfels regards, in fact, the Commission's latter proposal as superior to the present rules. He is not concerned about the disadvantages of applying one set of rules to child abduction among the EU Member States and another (= the Hague Child Abduction Convention) to (other) Convention States.

[33] See: P. MCELEAVY, *supra* note 17, pp. 903-904.

Assessing the value of this part of the French proposal and in the subsequent proposals by the Commission, one should not forget that also the 1996 Hague Child Protection Convention contains special rules on jurisdiction for such situations. None of the Member States of the EU has been able to ratify that Convention, since external competence in this area belongs partly to the EU as a result of the Brussels II Regulation.[34] The conclusion is that enormous efforts needed to be made to achieve something that, essentially, already was there.

## 5. UNIFIED CHOICE OF LAW RULES ON MARRIAGE DISSOLUTION –THE ROME III

### 5.1. Fear for forum shopping and forum racing

The action plans of the EU include the adoption of uniform choice of law rules to marriage dissolution. The planned Regulation, known as the *Rome III*, is aimed at supplementing the Brussels II Regulation. The alternative grounds on jurisdiction in matrimonial proceedings, contained in the Brussels II, are feared to encourage the spouses to both *forum shopping* and *forum racing*. This means choosing forum on the basis of what best suits the plaintiff's interests, in which respect the law applied to divorce in the alternative States of forum may be of great importance. Under the Brussels II the competent court first seized will have exclusive competence. As a result, both spouses may find it necessary to "race to court" in order to be the first one to initiate proceedings.

An illustrative example could be dissolution of a marriage between spouses who are Swedish citizens but habitually resident in Ireland. If the wife wants to divorce without delay but the husband opposes this, it is surely in the wife's interest to initiate divorce proceedings in a Swedish court. Article 2 of the Brussels II grants Swedish courts jurisdiction (on the basis of the spouses' joint citizenship). According to the autonomous Swedish choice of law rules on divorce, forum law is applicable. In Swedish law, marriage is regarded as a voluntary union that any spouse may at any time freely

---

[34] The political compromise of November 2002 covers authorisation of the Member States of the EU to sign and, later on, to ratify the 1996 Hague Child Protection Convention. Such proposals have been repeatedly on the table, but they have not been adopted due to other controversies, in particular relating to the 1980 Hague Child Abduction Convention and plans to replace it by special community rules. This example illustrates how different questions are linked to each other to put pressure on Member States to achieve a certain outcome. When also the 1996 Hague Convention is in force in the Member States, community rules shall in the EU Member States' mutual relations take precedence before the 1996 Hague Convention.

terminate by divorce.[35] The question of guilt is totally irrelevant, and proof on an irretrievable breakdown is not required. Where one of the spouses objects to divorce, the divorce shall be granted on a renewed application after a period of reconsideration of six months. The legal consequences of divorce do not need to be assessed in connection with divorce proceedings, but can be postponed till after the divorce decree.

If divorce proceedings were first initiated in Ireland – Article 2 grants also Irish courts jurisdiction on the basis of the spouses' habitual residence – it would take the wife much longer to receive the desired divorce against her husband's will.[36] Under the circumstances it might in fact be in the husband's interests to be the first one to initiate divorce proceedings – but in Ireland – to prevent the wife from having access to a quick divorce. Although he cannot prevent the divorce from gradually being granted, he can delay it by "racing" to an Irish court.

Calculations of this kind would be useless if the courts of all the Member States were to apply the same law to the marriage dissolution. At present, it is not a question of unifying the domestic laws of divorce within the EU, but achieving a uniform result through unified choice of law rules. Irrespective of in which Member State the proceedings are initiated, the same choice of law rules would apply leading to the application of the same State's substantive divorce law. Hence, it is claimed that the Brussels II must be supplemented by a Rome III Regulation.

### 5.2. Procedural provisions relating to divorce and its legal consequences must be taken into account

Although this argument in favour of unified choice of law rules at first may seem convincing it becomes problematic when the law on divorce is scrutinised closer. Everywhere in Europe, save Malta, the law permits divorce but on very different conditions. Not only the grounds for divorce are different but also other conditions for divorce, such as that the spouses must have reached an agreement on the legal consequences of the divorce.[37] Further, in each State, the law contains procedural provisions on divorce proceedings, adjusted to the law on divorce prevailing in that

---

[35] See: "Report of Sweden" by M. JÄNTERÄ-JAREBORG in: *European Family Law in Action*, Volume I: Grounds for Divorce, Commission on European Family Law, 2003.

[36] It is assumed that an Irish court having jurisdiction in divorce proceedings applies Irish law to the divorce application.

[37] In some Member States of the EU, there are also special preconditions for divorce relating, *e.g.*, to the duration of the marriage, unknown in the other States.

State, but difficult or even impossible to apply where another State's law is applicable.

Suppose that a Rome III Regulation did exist, and that according to it Irish law, as the law of the State of habitual residence of the spouses, is applicable to the divorce. According to Irish law, the spouses must have lived apart from one another for at least four years.[38] The court must also be satisfied that there is no reasonable prospect of reconciliation between the spouses. In addition the court must be satisfied that such provision, as the court considers proper, exists or will be made for the spouses and any dependent members of the family. For a Swedish court to be able to apply Irish law, the procedural provisions in Swedish law relating to divorce would require thorough changes. Such changes would also be necessary in Irish law, for an Irish court to be able to apply Swedish law to divorce.[39] Unless a new *European notion* on public policy (*ordre public*) is introduced, application of foreign law is likely to get blocked also on grounds of national public policy all over Europe. To give an example, foreign rules giving effect to a spouse's fault to marriage dissolution are contrary to Swedish public policy and cannot be applied in Sweden.

In many Member States, a divorce can be granted only on condition that the spouses have reached an agreement on all (or certain of) the legal consequences of divorce. In some other Member States, no such conditions exist. The domestic law on the legal consequences of divorce differs greatly among the Member States, not least in respect of post divorce maintenance and division of the spouses' assets. The rules on jurisdiction, recognition and enforcement in the Brussels II Regulation do not extend to these ancillary issues, with the result that in these respects concurrent jurisdiction and conflicting judgments are not avoided. Forum shopping is not as simple or objectionable as is often claimed. In the Swedish-Irish case mentioned above, the wife wanting a divorce may also be eager to receive generous financial provision on divorce. If the divorce proceedings take place in Sweden, Swedish courts will have jurisdiction.[40] Her prospects of receiving maintenance after divorce are likely to be much more limited

---

[38] See: "Report of Republic of Ireland" by G. SHANNON, in: *European Family Law in Action*, Volume I: Grounds on Divorce, Commission on European Family Law, 2003.

[39] Were the plans for a Rome III Regulation to proceed, there may well be support for the application of the law of the spouses' joint citizenship to divorce.

[40] In respect of maintenance, this follows of the Article 5.2 in the *Brussels I Regulation* (Council Regulation No 44/2001 on jurisdiction and the recognition and enforcement of judgments in civil and commercial matters). In respect of matrimonial property, the autonomous Swedish rules grant jurisdiction, i.a., in connection with matrimonial proceedings taking place in Sweden.

than if an Irish court decided on the matter. Also from her point of view, it may in the end turn out best to initiate divorce proceedings in Ireland.[41]

All this calls for reflection. It is generally believed that the main dispute between the spouses is not the divorce itself, but the legal consequences of a divorce. Little would be gained by merely unifying the rules of choice of law to divorce application. Instead, the whole "package" consisting of marriage dissolution and the legal consequences of divorce would need to be addressed.[42] It seems that the proposers of a Rome III Regulation have not paid proper attention to all its consequences and links with other issues.[43] European integration and European citizens would, probably, benefit more of a harmonisation of European divorce law, including the law on the legal consequences of divorce.[44]

## 6. WHAT LESSONS CAN BE LEARNED?

I want to emphasise that I do not categorically or out of principle reject all unification of international family law in the Member States of the EU. I admit that the EU is in such a position and now also equipped with such

---

[41] Problematic is not least Article 8 in the 1973 Hague Convention on the law applicable to maintenance obligations. According to this provision, the law applied to divorce shall in a Contracting State in which the divorce is granted or recognised, govern the maintenance obligations between the divorced spouses and the revision of decisions relating to these obligations. Of the Member States of the EU France, Germany, Italy, Luxembourg, Netherlands, Portugal and Spain have ratified this Convention. Considering that in Sweden maintenance to a spouse after divorce is exceptional and, if granted, aimed only for a transitional period following the divorce, it may often be in the wife's interest not to have the divorce proceedings take place in Sweden. See: "Report of Sweden" by M. JÄNTERÄ-JAREBORG, in: *European Family Law in Action*, Volume II: Maintenance, Commission on European Family Law, 2003. – This example shows that it is misleading to concentrate only on the grounds for divorce. Instead, a divorce must be seen as a package consisting of the dissolution of the marital bond and the legal consequences of the divorce.

[42] The various aspects of divorce were, however, addressed in the "Questionnaire on the law applicable to divorce (Rome III)", sent to the Member States.

[43] Worthwhile to remember in this connection is also the history behind the adoption of Article 18 in the Brussels II Regulation. This Article confirms the formal equality of the laws on marriage dissolution in the EU. Its inclusion, as a result of the political compromise reached in December 1997, was of utmost importance for in particular Sweden and Finland because of their liberal laws on marriage dissolution, both in domestic and cross-border situations. Forcing uniform choice of law rules on the Member States would, thus, conflict with an essential condition for the adoption of the Brussels II Regulation.

[44] As Boele-Woelki reminds us, "conflict of law rules generally ensure no more than that a legal situation is always subject to a national law and that even unified private international law cannot overcome the diversities of substantial national law". See: K. BOELE-WOELKI, "Comparative Research-Based Drafting of Principles of European Family Law", in: *Towards a European Ius Commune in Legal Education and Research*, 2002, p. 174.

powers, that it has good prospects of achieving results in areas where no other organisation can succeed. Where Community enactments turn out to be necessary, Regulations are a superior instrument of reaching the objectives rapidly and in a uniform manner. My criticism is based on the *choice of areas of international family law* where special Community rules have been adopted (*Brussels II*) or where legislative activities are under preparation (*Brussels IIa*). In addition, I find *serious faults in how the new civil law cooperation is organised and carried out* in the EU.

### 6.1. Article 65 requires restraint

According to Articles 61.c and 65 of the EC Treaty, measures may be taken in situations with cross-border implications, but only where they are necessary for the proper functioning of the internal market. In addition, it follows of the EC Treaty that the principles of subsidiarity and proportionality always must be respected. Measures can never be justified without a thorough investigation of the real problems, their nature and origin and the resulting disturbances on, precisely, "the proper functioning of the internal market". In family law, the free movement of persons must be affected.[45] Where the problems can be solved more appropriately through other methods, the EC Treaty does not provide a legal basis for new legislation.

### 6.2. Identifying the problems and available methods

In estimating the need of special community rules for cross-border family law matters, special attention should be given to factors such as the following.

(1) Are the alleged problems common to the Member States in general or manifest only in the relations among some of them? What is the origin of these problems?

(2) What are the shortcomings of the existing national (autonomous) rules or international treaties in force in the Member States?

(3) What international instruments exist (or are planned) in the concerned areas to which the Member States of the EU could accede? Do the purposes behind these instruments correspond with the needs of cross-border cooperation in the EU?

---

[45]     *De lege ferenda*, this link to the proper functioning of the internal market, through the free movement of persons (workers), is hardly sufficient. There must be scope for other reasons to unify or harmonise family law. As Pintens points out, family law should not be degraded into an auxiliary science of economic law, only serving the economic goals of the Community. See W. PINTENS's contribution, "Europeanisation of Family Law" in this book, p. 3.

Having in mind the Brussels II Regulation and the ongoing work to supplement it (or replace it) by a new instrument covering parental responsibility in all situations, one must conclude that so far measures have been taken in areas where special community rules were in no way urgent or necessary. Nor were the alleged problems common to all the Member States, but rather only to some of them. Although certain Member States seem to have decided against rules adopted at the Hague Conference on private international law, other Member States have been strongly in favour of them. As a result, the new community rules differ only in some respects from the Hague rules. Much effort and strain has, simply, led to very little results of added value. It is surprising and unfortunate that the new cooperation was initiated in precisely those areas of international family law where the Hague Conference, in the opinion of many Member States, has been able to adopt well-balanced and progressive instruments. It had been better to start with globally difficult issues but with a strong link to the European integration, such as cohabitation without marriage, matrimonial property rights and inheritance.[46]

### 6.3. Working methods

In my opinion, special community rules should be an *ultima ratio*, to be used only where other methods are not available or have failed. At present, on the contrary, the impression is that such rules are by some Member States regarded as a *sola ratio*, or *prima ratio*. This position seems to be shared by the Commission.

It is evident that in the future projects must be chosen with greater care and respect to the strict conditions for judicial cooperation in this area. Problematic issues should be jointly identified in an unbiased dialogue among the Member States and the institutions of the EU. If, *e.g.*, a large number of the Member States prefer Hague rules, then this is an argument speaking strongly against special community rules. To abstain may in fact be better than to adopt rules, differing in some respects from those in other international instruments. Although special community rules may in

---

[46] These areas are all included in the action plans for the civil law cooperation, *supra* note 1. In these areas, the prospects of a global organisation succeeding in the unification of rules of private international law are limited. Unmarried cohabitation is on the agenda of the Hague Conference of private international law, but without priority. The Convention concerning the international administration of estates of deceased persons (Hague 1973), the Convention on the law applicable to matrimonial property regimes (Hague 1978) and the Convention on the law applicable to succession to the estates of deceased persons (Hague 1989) have been ratified only by a few States.

substance be "better" than other rules, the price is an increasing confusion in the legal practice each time a new set of rules in adopted.[47]

The legislative cooperation should be organised in another form than (at present) frequent one-day meetings in the concerned working parties. Very little can be achieved during one day, and no time is available for any real dialogue. Still, it has so far taken years to adopt any instrument.[48] Using the national languages puts the delegates in the hands of interpreters, preventing general, direct communication. It is also evident that the quality of the preparatory work needs to be improved, requiring a staff of genuine experts in the Commission.[49] The insufficient preparatory work, and also the lack of a dialogue, has made so-called political compromises necessary for achieving any results. No Member State is in the end really satisfied, but many Member States are relieved after having avoided an outcome that in their eyes would have been a "pure disaster".[50] Referring to the "political will" of the Member States as the "engine" for the EU's new activities in international family law gives the impression of a dynamic process with clear goals. In essence, however, this political will is limited to giving preference to alleged common goals, each consenting Member State expecting to be compensated in return.

---

[47] The national courts and legal practitioners are already facing difficulties in identifying the right "source of law", which may be community rules, convention-based rules or national (autonomous) rules. Differences in substance between these rules cause irritation and may make it more difficult to foresee the outcome.

[48] Opinions differ on when the work started with what later on became the Brussels II Regulation. In any case, it took more than four years to draft the Brussels II Convention and, formally, two more years before it could be transformed into a Regulation. The French proposal, later on replaced by the Commission's proposals on Brussels IIa, was initiated in early July 2000. It is estimated to take at least till the end of 2003, probably longer, before the new Regulation can be adopted.

[49] At present, the preparations are essentially based on comparative studies, *e.g.*, by a group of academics, whose tender was chosen by the Commission. In comparison, the working methods of the Hague Conference on private international law are clearly superior. Although national experts are consulted and play a central role also at the Hague Conference at all stages of the work, the Permanent Bureau's contribution is essential.

[50] As an example can be mentioned the political compromise of 28 November 2002 not to replace the 1980 Hague Child Abduction Convention by special community rules in the Member States mutual relations. Another example is the inclusion in the Brussels II Regulation of a provision (Article 18) not allowing a Member State to refuse recognition of a judgment on marriage dissolution on the basis that that judgment would not have been possible in the requested State. Without this provision, modelled on Article 6.2 of the 1970 Hague Divorce Convention, the new instrument would have been impossible from, *e.g.*, the Swedish and Finnish points of view.

## 6.4. The content of mutual trust

The EU and its Member States must venture to identify the real key issues of relevance for their cooperation. My impression is that at present much remains on the level of political rhetoric, without being reflected in the adopted rules. Instead, the adopted rules remain traditional in approach.

One example is the frequent reference to mutual trust among the Member States as the basis for the new measures. Still, *exequatur* is required and its abolishment is at present proposed only in respect of judgments on access rights![51] In inter-Scandinavian relations, a judgment rendered in one Scandinavian State is directly enforceable in the other Scandinavian States as if it were a domestic judgment. In comparison, the requirement of *exequatur* among the Member States of the EU seems to reflect a profound mistrust. Nor have the Member States ventured a discussion on the content of the free circulation of judgments within the EU. Does it at the stage of enforcement mean equalising the judgment and a corresponding domestic judgment, or does it require giving the judgment the same effects as in its State of origin all over the EU? Since positions are believed to differ, it is considered better to leave the matter open, permitting each Member State to choose its own interpretation until the EC Court comes with a preliminary ruling on the issue.

My other example relates to the content of the community rules. So far they have been modelled on other already existing international instruments, but with some novelties of their own. Does this mean that the EU can succeed only as a "copycat", without venturing more radical approaches? Also this state of affairs is in my opinion largely explained by serious shortcomings in how projects are initiated and prepared in the EU. Where from the beginning several Member States are opposed to the adoption of new rules – or a detailed proposal put forth without these States having been consulted – these States are not likely to agree to any other rules than those modelled on already existing ones.

## 6.5. A comparison with Scandinavian cooperation

A close legislative cooperation within substantive (domestic) family law was initiated among the Scandinavian States already in the 1910s, resulting in closely harmonised legislation in particular in marriage law.[52] In respect

---

[51] The final aim is, however, to abolish *exequatur* for judgments.
[52] The term "Scandinavian States" is here used for Denmark, Finland, Iceland, Norway and Sweden. These States are also commonly called "Nordic States" and their mutual cooperation for "Nordic cooperation".

of the law on inheritance[53] the attempts to harmonise failed, still contributing to mutual understanding of the reasons behind divergent national
approaches. This, is turn, facilitated the subsequent cooperation in the
field of international family law.

In the early 1930s, three Conventions were adopted introducing unified
rules of international family law for inter-Scandinavian relations. Of these
Conventions, two are still in force, namely the 1931 Convention on
marriage, adoption and guardianship, and the 1934 Convention on
inheritance, wills and administration of the estates of deceased persons.
The third Convention, also from 1931, on the recovery of maintenance,
was in 1962 replaced by a new inter-Scandinavian Convention in the field.
Considering the present legislative activities within the EU, the Scandinavian experiences should be of interest.

In Scandinavia, the basis for unified rules of international family law was
the harmonisation of substantive family law or – in certain areas – an insight into why such harmonisation could not be achieved. The States were
able to agree on such rules of private international law for their mutual
relations that still today seem superior to other rules.
(1)   The grounds of jurisdiction are limited, and are often based on a
      fixed hierarchy.[54] The main ground of jurisdiction is the habitual
      residence (of the spouses', of the deceased, etc.).
(2)   The competent authority applies, as a rule, the law of the State of
      habitual residence (of the main person/persons), which normally is
      also the law of the forum. Where the habitual residence changes from
      one Scandinavian State to another, also the applicable law changes.
      In respect of inheritance, a concerned party may request application
      of the law of nationality of the deceased, if the habitual residence in
      the new State has not lasted for at least five years.
(3)   Judgments rendered in one Scandinavian State are recognised
      automatically in the other Scandinavian States, without any examina-
      tion of the ground of jurisdiction or the substance of the judgment.
      In many cases, there are no grounds at all permitting refusal of
      recognition.

---

[53]   In Scandinavia, the law of inheritance is normally qualified as a part of family law.
[54]   In this respect, the rules on jurisdiction in matrimonial proceedings, contained in the 1931
       Convention, were changed as a result of the adoption of the Brussels II Regulation, and its
       Article 36.2. In essence, the 1931 Convention is in this respect a duplication of the
       jurisdictional grounds contained in the Brussels II. On the other hand, the Convention's
       rules on recognition are left intact. See: M. JÄNTERÄ-JAREBORG, *supra* note 24.

(4)  A judgment rendered in one Scandinavian State and enforceable in its State of origin is directly enforceable in the other Scandinavian States, as if it were a domestic judgment of that State. The applicant may directly turn to the authority in charge of enforcement in the State where he or she wants the judgment to be enforced. No *exequatur* exists and no certificates on the judgment are required.

The ongoing legislative activities in family law within the EU have given the Scandinavian States reason to recognise the value of their own achievements within both substantive and international family law. Note that the Scandinavian States could already 70-80 years ago agree on such solutions that still today are considered progressive and included in the agenda of the EU! This insight has renewed the Scandinavian States' interest on mutual cooperation in family law.[55]

---

[55]  In 2000 and 2001, Conventions on the revision of the 1931 Convention and the 1962 Convention (on recovery of maintenance) were adopted. These Conventions, reflecting developments within the EU and EES, in form of the adoption of the Brussels II Regulation and the Brussels I and Lugano Conventions (maintenance), have also entered into force. At present, a revision on the rules relating to spouses' matrimonial property relations is under preparation. – In the field of substantive family law, under the auspices of the Ministers of Justice of the Scandinavian States, an academic group, consisting of leading Scandinavian professors in family law, has recently (2002) put forth two comprehensive preparatory studies on the possibilities of harmonising the rules on marriage, divorce and inheritance. A third study is expected in 2003, dealing with prospects for harmonisation in child law.

# PART FOUR –UNIFICATION AND HARMONISATION OF FAMILY LAW: DIFFERENT PERSPECTIVES

# CHALLENGING THE EUROPEAN HARMONISATION OF FAMILY LAW: PERSPECTIVES ON 'THE FAMILY"

CLARE MCGLYNN

## 1. INTRODUCTION

The central argument of this chapter is that the harmonisation of family law within the European Union must be resisted for so long as the concept of "family" which underpins EU law remains a traditional one which is exclusionary and discriminatory in its effects. This limited concept of "family" has been reproduced and legitimated by the European Court of Justice through its jurisprudence, primarily in the fields of free movement of persons and sex equality law. In addition, recent legislative initiatives in the areas of free movement, asylum and immigration appear to reinforce the approach of the Court. Furthermore, it does not appear that the Charter of Fundamental Rights is likely to bring about any radical changes in this field, especially while it remains of persuasive force only.

## 2. THE COURT OF JUSTICE AND 'THE FAMILY"

The concept of "family" which has been developed by the Court of Justice in its jurisprudence in the fields of free movement of persons and sex equality law is one which is based on the traditional "nuclear" family: that of a married heterosexual union, in which the husband is head of the family and principal breadwinner and the wife is primary carer. It is also a conceptualization of family which reinforces the notion of children as dependents and appendages to the "family". Thus, the jurisprudence of the Court not only privileges specific family forms, principally heterosexual marriage, but also legitimates a particular sexual division of labour and responsibility within families.

The concept of family was first addressed in the Court's jurisprudence on the free movement of workers when the Court was asked to interpret the rights of workers to bring their "family" with them as they move states to take-up work. Regulation 1612/68 entitles a worker to be accompanied by members of their "family", including their "spouse". In *Netherlands v Reed*, the Court was asked whether the term "spouse" included a heterosexual cohabitee.[1] The Court held that for the purpose of the grant of free movement "family rights", the term "spouse" is limited to married persons and does not therefore include cohabitees. A European "family", therefore, entails heterosexual partnerships which are accorded the status of "family" only via marriage.

Equally, whereas marriage bequeaths the status of "family", divorce appears to take it away. In *Diatta v Land Berlin* the Court implied that on divorce, a spouse's right of residence could be revoked.[2] The Court appears to be privileging a traditional form of "family", that of marriage, and any rights granted to the spouse are only valid so long as the couple remain married. In this way, the rights of the spouse are "parasitic"; that is, the spouse has no rights of their own, but derives rights from their husband or wife. It has been argued, therefore, that the apparent aim of EU law is to privilege, and encourage the movement of, those families which provide the "infrastructure for men's mobility",[3] that is, the availability of a (preferably full-time) wife. Furthermore, the Court's limited interpretation of the concept of "worker", on which many free movement rights are based, effectively excludes all informal/unpaid care work. This significantly limits the rights of many women to exercise free movement and where they do so, will render them dependent on a male "worker". This pattern of the Court's jurisprudence has led Isabella Moebius and Erika Szyszczak to argue that the free movement provisions are based on a "male breadwinner family model" which "reproduces and reinforces traditional patterns of gender relations and dependency within the family".[4]

This articulation of the concept of "family" in the area of free movement of persons has been entrenched in recent judgments relating to the rights of gays and lesbians under the Community's sex equality laws. *Grant v South West Trains* involved a claim of sexual orientation discrimination against a company which granted benefits to an employee's husband/wife or "opposite sex" cohabitee.[5] Lisa Grant argued that this constituted discrimination against her as she lived with a woman cohabitee and was not

---

[1] Case 59/85 *Netherlands v Reed* [1986] ECR 1283.

[2] Case 267/83 *Diatta v Land Berlin* [1985] ECR 567.

[3] Kirsten Scheiwe, "EC Law's Unequal Treatment of the Family: the case law of the European Court of Justice on rules Prohibiting Discrimination on the Grounds of Sex and Nationality" (1994) 3 *Social and Legal Studies* 243 at 251.

[4] Isabella Moebius and Erika Szyszczak, "Of Raising Pigs and Children", (1998) 18 *Yearbook of European Law* 125 at 144, 148.

[5] Case C-249/96 *Grant v South West Trains* [1998] IRLR 165.

therefore entitled to the extra benefits. The particular issue was whether the principle of equal pay for women and men could be extended to cover discrimination on the grounds of sexual orientation. The Court refused to extend the reach of the equal pay principle, stating that there was a lack of consensus among member states about whether "stable relationships between persons of the same sex may be regarded as equivalent to stable relationships between persons of the opposite sex".[6] It continued that member states held this position "for the purpose of protecting the family".[7] Apparently, same sex partnerships do not constitute a "family", nor are they deemed worthy of the protection of Community law.

The Court of First Instance relied on this expression of the limits of Community law when faced with the argument that same sex partners, registered as a partnership under national laws granting similar rights to those of married partners, should be treated as "spouses".[8] It held that "Community notions of marriage and partnership exclusively address a relationship founded on civil marriage in the traditional sense of the term".[9] This approach was upheld on appeal to the Court of Justice which declared that gay and lesbian relationships, even ones registered under national law, remain legally distinct from "marriage" and therefore cannot be treated in the same way as marriage.[10] Thus, individuals and partnerships that do not conform to this normative family model, even those whose relationship may closely approximate the "male breadwinner" model of "coupledom",[11] such as in *Netherlands v Reed* and *Grant*, fall outside the remit of Community law.

In addition to the privileging of particular family forms, the Court of Justice has also engaged in a construction of the appropriate roles of women and men within families. This ideology of familial roles is, I have suggested elsewhere, based on a dominant ideology of motherhood which constructs a normative model of women and motherhood, the foundation of which is the perceived natural, universal and unchanging nature of women's role within families and particularly their primary role in care work.[12] The

---

6    *Grant*, para 35.
7    *Grant*, para 33.
8    Case T-264/97, *D and Sweden v Council* [1999] ECR II-1, para 26.
9    *Ibid.*
10   C-122, 125/99, *D and Sweden v Council* [2001] ECR I-4319, para 37.
11   CARL STYCHIN, "Consumption, Capitalism and the Citizen: Sexuality and Equality Rights Discourse in the European Union", in JO SHAW (ed.), *Social Law and Policy in an Evolving European Union*, (Oxford: Hart, 2000).
12   See CLARE MCGLYNN, "Ideologies of Motherhood in European Community Sex Equality Law" (2000) 6 *European Law Journal* 29.

mother-child relationship is privileged, it being considered to be sacrosanct and pivotal to the emotional and physical well-being of the child, based on the now discredited theories of mother-infant bonding.[13] Accordingly, childcare is seen to be the primary responsibility of women, and if paid employment is taken-up, it should take second place to the woman's responsibilities within the home. This ideology was developed by the Court in the mid-1980s[14] and has been strengthened in recent years.[15] In essence, the Court has upheld different treatment on account of motherhood (and not biological differences regarding the capacity to give birth), arguing that the privileging of motherhood over fatherhood does not constitute unlawful sex discrimination. In doing so, the Court reinforces sexual divisions of labour in which childcare is always the responsibility of mothers, ignoring any conception that the father may also have a legitimate need and/or desire for a period of leave. Fatherhood is thereby limited, by implication, to a breadwinning role, with the assumption that a man's primary commitment and identification should be with paid work, rather than care work.

Finally, the concept of "family" developed and reproduced by the Court is also one which has tended to reinforce the notion of children as dependants.[16] The original omission of children from the EEC is historically understandable in view of its original economic orientation. However, the validity of this justification has progressively weakened as more and more measures have been adopted which affect children and as the movement for children's rights has become ever more powerful and international. However, despite this omission from the Treaty, by the late 1960s, in the field of free movement of persons, the Community first adopted measures which concerned children.[17] Children were recognised as "obstacles" to free movement and so were accorded rights in order to

---

[13] For a detailed discussion of these theories and their impact on Community law and the dominant ideology of motherhood, see *ibid.*

[14] Case 163/82 *Commission v Italian Republic* [1983] ECR 3273; case 184/83 *Hofmann v Barmer Ersatzkasse* [1984] ECR 3047.

[15] Case C-243/95 *Hill and Stapleton v The Revenue Commissioners and the Department of Finance* [1998] 3 CMLR 81; case C-218/98 *Abdoulaye v Renault*, [1999] IRLR 811 (see further Clare McGlynn, "Pregnancy, Parenthood and the Court of Justice in *Abdoulaye*", 25 (2000) *European Law Review* 654) and case C-476/99 *Lommers v Minister van Landbouw, Natuurbeheer en Visserij*, judgment of 19 March 2002.

[16] LOUISE ACKERS and HELEN STALFORD: "Children, Migration and Citizenship in the European Union: Intra-Community Mobility and the Status of Children in EC Law" (1999) 21 *Children and Youth Services Review* 987 and *A Community for Children? Children, Citizenship and Migration in the European Union* (Ashgate), forthcoming 2003.

[17] For a full discussion, see HELEN STALFORD, "The Citizenship Status of Children in the European Union" (2000) 8 *International Journal of Children's Rights* 101-131.

facilitate the movement of their parents. Thus, rights to education, and to other social and tax advantages, were extended to the children of persons exercising their Community law free movement rights.[18] Importantly, however, these rights and entitlements were not given to children qua children, but were designed to facilitate the economic ambitions of the free movement of persons provisions.

Despite such inauspicious beginnings, the Court of Justice has taken steps in recent years to extend the scope of children's Community law entitlements. In doing so, the Court has reduced, to a limited extent, the requirement for "dependency" and has potentially created space for future rulings which grant entitlements to those who are not economically active, including children.[19] Nonetheless, such jurisprudential feats do not remove the fact that the child's rights remain parasitic: children are only extended rights so long as the parent is or was exercising Community law rights. As Helen Stalford makes clear, these rights are "not accorded to migrant children as independent citizens, but rather, are contingent upon their familial, dependent link with an adult who qualifies under the free movement provisions".[20] Furthermore, Stalford argues that the parasitic nature of these rights also "enhances the vulnerability of children" whose "destiny and access to rights is entirely contingent on their parents".[21]

I am arguing, therefore, that the Court has constructed a concept of "family" which forms the normative basis for its jurisprudence when faced with questions demanding a definition and interpretation of the concept of "family". The Court has reproduced, and thereby legitimated, a concept of family which is exclusionary and reactionary and one which limits the opportunities of women, men and children. Not only does this concept of family limit the potential of the Community's free movement and sex

---

[18] Articles 12 and 7(2) of Regulation 1612/68.

[19] In case C-7/94 *Lubor Gaal* [1996] ECR I-1031 the Court extended educational benefits to a child who did not comply with the age limits or dependency requirements of the relevant provisions. Instead, the mere fact of the child's status as the biological child of an EU migrant worker was deemed sufficient to entitle him to educational benefits. In addition, in case C-85/98 *Sala* [1998] ECR I-2691 the Court also appeared to extend the potential scope of Community law entitlements to those who are not economically active, a ruling which might potentially be used to advance children's claims. See further, Stalford *supra* note 17 at 114-116.

[20] STALFORD, *supra* note 17 at 110.

[21] STALFORD, *supra* note 17 at 110. This picture is supported by empirical research demonstrating the partial and parasitic nature of children's entitlements under the free movement provisions and the consequent vulnerability of the children of migrants, discussed in Helen Stalford, "The developing European agenda on children"s rights" (2000) 22 *Journal of Social Welfare and Family Law* 229-236, at 234-235.

equality laws, but, in the context of this chapter, the argument is that as jurisdiction in the family law field develops, it is of great concern that this "family" model may form the basis for an emerging EU family law.

## 3. THE COURT OF JUSTICE: A CHANGE IN DIRECTION?

The concept of "family" discussed above is not only normatively undesirable, but is also out of step with the empirical realities of family life across the European Union. Are there indications, therefore, that the approach of the Court is changing, for the better?

In the recent case of *Eyüp*, the Court held that a (heterosexual) cohabitee could be deemed to be a "member of the family" for the purposes of calculating a qualifying period for residence rights.[22] Although the Court did not go so far as to say that a cohabitee is a "spouse", a step towards that position was taken. However, although *Eyüp* represents some forward movement, particular attention must be paid to the peculiar facts of the case. The couple in question were married, divorced but continued to live together, and then remarried. Thus, the period of unmarried cohabitation was sandwiched between periods of marriage. In addition, the Court appeared to place significance on the nature of the relationship which subsisted during the period of unmarried cohabitation, namely that Mrs Eyüp "devoted herself essentially to household tasks"[23] and only "occasionally" took "short-term jobs".[24] Moreover, at all times, Mr Eyüp "maintained his family".[25]

There appears, therefore, to be a number of central features upon which the Court based its ruling: the cohabitation closely resembled marriage; children were born during the period of cohabitation; Mr Eyüp maintained his family; and Mrs Eyüp was primarily engaged in caring for the children. It is not clear what weight was placed on each of these factors, but it seems likely that they will be important factors to be considered in subsequent cases. Following from this examination of the facts, the Court simply stated that the period of cohabitation "cannot be regarded as an interruption of their joint family life" and that accordingly Mrs Eyüp could be deemed to be a "member of the family".[26] Thus, at best, the judgment implies that a cohabitee may come within the concept of "member of the family". But

---

[22] Case C-65/98 *Eyüp*, judgment of 22 June 2000, para 36.
[23] *Eyüp*, para 12.
[24] *Eyüp*, para 32.
[25] *Eyüp*, para 32.
[26] *Eyüp*, para 36.

it appears likely that initially only some cohabitees may benefit from such a ruling, most likely heterosexual cohabitees who can demonstrate significant levels of commitment via children, marriage and dependency.

Nonetheless, there may be another important factor at work in this case. Advocate General La Pergola examined, in considerable detail, the jurisprudence of the European Court of Human Rights on the article 8 right to respect for private and family life and its implications in this case. He opined that as a "general principle" including the cohabitee of a worker within the concept of "member of the family", "contradicts neither the spirit nor the purpose" of the relevant provision.[27] Noting that the European Court of Human Rights had held there to be family life deserving of respect in circumstances displaying a lesser degree of stability than the facts in question,[28] the Advocate General opined that not to hold Mrs Eyüp to be a "member of the family" would constitute a breach of her fundamental rights, as detailed in article 8 of the European Convention of Human Rights (ECHR). Although the Court of Justice did not explicitly take up the Advocate General's reasoning in this case, it was perhaps influential. Indeed, in the subsequent case of *Carpenter*, the Court itself engaged in a detailed analysis of article 8 of the ECHR, this time ruling that step-children fell within the scope of the concept of "family" for the purpose of free movement rights.[29] By the time of the *Carpenter* judgment, the EU had adopted the Charter of Fundamental Rights which includes the right to respect for family life, reproduced from the ECHR, though the Court of Justice conspicuously failed to refer to it.

Post-*Eyüp* and *Carpenter*, we can see that the Court of Justice is more willing to engage with the jurisprudence of the European Court of Human Rights on the article 8 right to family life and is employing it in a positive fashion to extend the rights of individuals. Nonetheless, in *Eyüp* both the Court and the Advocate General stressed the particular nature of the facts, discussed above. There is a clear presumption of heterosexuality in this case, with the implication that a gay or lesbian couple would not find it as easy to bring themselves within the relevant definition. Partly, this would be due to the continuing reluctance of the European Court of Human Rights to hold that gay and lesbian couples can constitute family life for the purposes of article 8. It is also not possible to be entirely confident of the approach of the Court of Justice to cohabiting couples who have never married each

---

[27]   *Eyüp*, Opinion of Advocate General La Pergola, of 18 November 1999.
[28]   *Eyüp*, Opinion of Advocate General La Pergola, para 23.
[29]   Case C-60/00 *Carpenter v Secretary of State for the Home Department*, judgment of 11 July 2002, paras 38-44.

other, whose length of cohabitation is comparatively short, who do not have any children or who both work and are therefore financially independent. Accordingly, although *Eyüp* represents a success of sorts, in that it is a step on from *Netherlands v Reed*, the "family" which has been recognised is one which although does not demonstrate the formal bond of marriage, does exhibit the features of a traditional marriage, most particularly a sexual division of labour and the inherent economic dependence of the woman partner.

Nonetheless, in terms of extending the concept of "member of the family" to include heterosexual cohabitees, the future has to be positive. For the Court of Justice to ignore both the changing realities of family life *and* the jurisprudence of the European Court of Human Rights would be breathtaking indeed. The European Court of Human Rights has made it clear that heterosexual unmarried relationships do enjoy the protection afforded by the right to respect for family life, as clearly recognised by the Advocates General in *Carpenter*, *Baumbast* and *Eyüp*.[30] The Union not only refers to the European Convention for its human rights inspiration, but it has also specifically incorporated such rights into the Union Charter. At the very minimum, therefore, so that the Union is compliant with the human rights norms of the Court of Human Rights, it must grant similar protection to heterosexual cohabiting relationships.

The Court of Justice will have the opportunity to move things forward in the forthcoming *Pathminidevi* case.[31] This case concerns the interpretation of the Community regulation ensuring social security protection for migrants and their families. The Court is being asked whether a partner who cohabits with an employed partner in a relationship "similar to marriage and who looks after and raises the couple's child" can be regarded as a "member of the family". It would seem incredible if the Court would not acknowledge that such a person is a "member of the family" and indeed would be out of line with the jurisprudence of the European Court of Human Rights if it did not. This is not a judgment about the concept of "spouse" which would remain, but about the concept of "family" and thus makes it easier for the Court of Justice to respond positively in this case.

---

[30] This much is noted, without a fanfare, by Advocate General Geelhoed in *Baumbast* where he notes that under article 8 ECHR "relationships of sufficient permanence stand on the same footing" as marriage. Case C-413/99 *Baumbast and R v Secretary of State for the Home Department*, Opinion of 5 July 2001, para 59.

[31] Case C-407/99 *Pathminidevi v Landeskreditbank*.

There is also change on the horizon in relation to the rights of children within the EU. The Charter of Fundamental Rights has considerably enhanced the role and status of children and is discussed further below. But recent judgments of the Court of Justice have also begun to recognise the rights of children. In *Baumbast* the Court granted a right of residence to a former spouse, with whom the children of the former marriage lived, on the basis of the Community educational rights of the children.[32] This meant that the children were entitled to continue exercising the educational rights derived from the rights of their father as a Community migrant. Although the logic of the judgment remains within a free movement and economic paradigm, it does nonetheless extend further rights to children, almost independent of their parents.

The approach of the Court in *Baumbast* is matched in *Humer* and *Carpenter*. In *Humer* the Court allowed a child to claim maintenance from her father, even though she had never migrated and this right was denied to her under Austrian law.[33] This case is important as the Court recognised the child's individual right to claim maintenance. Moreover, the relevant Regulation[34] did not specifically provide for circumstances post-divorce, but the Court held that this was not a sufficient basis for refusing to interpret the regulation in a favourable way towards the child. Finally, in *Carpenter* the Court recognised that a step-child was a member of the "family" for the purposes of Community law. Together, these judgments represent a shift in emphasis, away from the "parasitic" nature of children's rights, towards an approach which recognises children as individuals and "rights-bearers", albeit that the progress is slow.

Overall, there are indications that the Court is moving towards a more egalitarian concept of family, one which is more in tune with the approach of the European Court of Human Rights and which recognises the realities of family life within the EU today. Whether the Charter of Fundamental Rights will fasten the pace of change is considered below.

---

[32]  *Baumbast* supra note 30.
[33]  Case C-255/99 *Anna Humer*, judgment 5 February 2002.
[34]  Regulation 1408/71 entitles the migrant worker to apply for family benefits.

## 4. THE CHARTER OF FUNDAMENTAL RIGHTS AND 'THE FAMILY"

### 4.1. General provisions on 'the family"

The general approach of the EU to families and family life is now laid down in the Charter of Fundamental Rights which establishes the principles on which the Union is founded. There are two general provisions in the Charter which relate to families.[35] The first of these two provisions is to be found in article 7 which provides that: "Everyone has the right to respect for his or her private and family life, home and communications." This article is a close repetition of article 8 of the ECHR. Although the Court of Justice has referred to article 8 of the ECHR in its jurisprudence,[36] arguably with little effect until very recently, this is the first time that this provision has been made so explicitly a part of the EU's rights regime. The other central provision is to be found in article 33(1) which states that: "The family shall enjoy legal, economic and social protection." This article is the first direct reference to the EU's role regarding families, or rather "the family". In particular, the focus is on "the family" as a unit to be protected in its own right, rather than exploited in the pursuit of other goals. Article 33(1), therefore, represents recognition of the fact that EU law does impact on families and expresses an aim to seek to "protect" them.

These provisions raise the question as to what will constitute a "family" for the purposes of EU law and the Charter? The first step towards answering this question is by analysing the existing ECHR jurisprudence on the "right to private and family life", now included in article 7 of the Charter.[37] The ECHR jurisprudence on this right is extensive, but tends to show that the "respect" extended to family life varies according to a hierarchy of relationships. Heterosexual marriage is at the top of the hierarchy, being a protected state and one within which there is always "family life". In second place are cohabiting heterosexual relationships. Thus, the European Court of Human Rights has stated that: "the notion of "the family" ... is not confined solely to marriage-based relationships and may encompass other de facto "families" where the parties are living together

---

[35]   See further CLARE MCGLYNN, "Families and the European Charter of Fundamental Rights: progressive change or entrenching the status quo?" 26 (2001) *European Law Review* 582.

[36]   For example, case 249/86, *Commission v Federal Republic of Germany* [1989] ECR 1263; case 12/86, *Demirel* [1987] ECR 3719.

[37]   Article 52(3) of the Charter states that where a Charter provision corresponds to that from the ECHR, the jurisprudence of the ECHR is to be followed, while allowing the Union to provide "more extensive protection".

outside of marriage".[38] Therefore, where a child is born outside of marriage, there may still be a "family unit".[39] In order to make a determination of whether a particular situation constitutes "family life", the European Court of Human Rights has ruled that a number of factors may be relevant, including: "whether the couple live together, the length of their relationship and whether they have demonstrated their commitment to each other by having children together or by any other means".[40] Therefore, so long as the cohabiting relationship is closely assimilated to marriage, it may gain some "respect" and protection.

It used to be clear that at the bottom of the hierarchy were gay, lesbian and transgender relationships. However, as a result of the judgment of the European Court of Human Rights in *I v UK* and *Goodwin v UK*,[41] it is arguable that the relationships of transgender persons have been elevated, in the hierarchy, above gay and lesbian partnerships. The Court in *Goodwin* held that the right to privacy and the right to marry had been breached by the UK government because of its refusal to allow a change in the birth certificate of a post-operative transgendered individual and therefore refused the right to marry in the chosen gender. This groundbreaking judgment introduces for the first time a definition of marriage which is not based on biological sex. The impact of this judgment is yet to be felt, but it seems clear that the grant of the right to marry to transgender partnerships does mark such relationships out from gay and lesbian partnerships and may pave the way for greater familial rights in due course.[42]

At the bottom of the hierarchy remain gay and lesbian partnerships for which there appears to be little respect extended and even less protection.[43] Homosexual unions do not currently fall within the scope of the right to respect for family life,[44] although there is some evidence that this position may be changing.[45]

---

[38]   *Keegan v Ireland*, (1994) 18 EHRR 343, para. 43.
[39]   *Ibid.*
[40]   *X, Y and Z v UK*, (1997) 24 EHRR 143, para 36.
[41]   Application no 28957/95, judgment of 11 July 2002.
[42]   At present, article 8 of the ECHR does not require a state to recognise in law the parental role of a transgender father, thereby rejecting the notion that a transgender parent can enjoy "family life": *X, Y and Z v UK*, (1997) 24 EHRR 143. It may be that this restrictive approach to the family relationships of transgender individuals changes.
[43]   Albeit that there has been important successes in rendering unlawful the most egregious examples of discrimination against homosexuals, *e.g. Dudgeon v UK*, 4 EHRR 149.
[44]   *Kerkhoven v Netherlands*, application no 15666/89 (19 May 1992).
[45]   *Salgueiro da Silva Mouta*, application no 33290/96 (1 December 1998).

It is clear, therefore, that the concept of "the family" in the ECHR jurisprudence is relatively narrow and traditional, albeit with some recognition of relationships outside of marriage, particularly where they are closely assimilated to marriage. As article 7 of the Charter "corresponds" to article 8 in the ECHR, article 52(3) applies which requires that the "same" interpretation must be given to the Charter provision. On this reading, article 7 of the Charter is to be read in a similarly restrictive and traditional manner. However, the Charter further states that the jurisprudence of the Convention need not be followed where EU law offers "more extensive" protection.[46] In addition, the preamble to the Charter states that it aims to "strengthen the protection of fundamental rights" in the light of "changes in society" and "social progress".[47] Would broadening the scope of "the family", to include cohabiting relationships, both same sex and heterosexual, not constitute more "extensive protection"? It is certainly arguable that such an interpretation does afford more "extensive" protection, bringing hitherto excluded relationships within the protective frame of the Charter. This is even more so in view of the changing demographic situation of the EU in which relationships outside of marriage are increasingly common.

However, the likely expansion of the scope of article 7 to include relationships outside of marriage looks unlikely. The Court of Justice, as discussed above, has itself privileged heterosexual marriage in its jurisprudence and has refused to extend the protective shield of Community law to other forms of family life.[48] Thus, as well as article 7 regarding the "respect for family life" bearing a limited interpretation, it seems that the approach to article 33(1), that is which families will enjoy "protection", will be very similar.[49]

---

[46]    [2000] OJ C364/1 of 18.12.2000, article 52(3).

[47]    *Ibid*, preamble.

[48]    McGLYNN, *supra* n 35.

[49]    Article 33(2) of the Charter states that to reconcile professional and family life, individuals must have access to paid maternity leave, to parental leave and must not be dismissed for a maternity related reason. Although an earlier version of the Charter included a "right to reconciliation", which could have been used to broaden the scope of the provision and perhaps initiate a change in the traditional parental roles of women and men, the final version of the Charter replicates existing Community law and provides little opportunity for development. Article 33(2) is not likely, therefore, to effect any change in the interpretation of article 33(1). On article 33(2) of the Charter, see CLARE McGLYNN, "Reclaiming a Feminist Vision: the reconciliation of paid work and family life in European Union law and policy" (2001) 7 *Columbia Journal of European Law* 241.

## 4.2. The right to marry

As well as the general provisions of the Charter discussed above, there are more specific family rights detailed in the Charter, including in article 9 the "right to marry" which provides that: "The right to marry and the right to found a family shall be guaranteed in accordance with the national laws governing the exercise of these rights." This provision echoes article 12 of the ECHR, but it differs in significant ways. Most importantly, article 12 of the ECHR states that it is "men and women" that have the right to marry. Arguably, the removal of the qualifier "men and women" from the Charter article may have a significant impact on the interpretation of this provision.

Until the judgment of the Court of Human Rights in *Goodwin* in 2002, it seemed that this article, and its restrictive interpretation by the ECHR demonstrated, yet again, the privileged status of heterosexual marriage.[50] However, the *Goodwin* judgment has changed perceptions and provides possibilities for radical change. In *Goodwin*, the European Court of Human Rights held that the right to marry must be extended to post-operative transgender individuals. In other words, marriage was no longer confined to biological sex. From the perspective of the EU, a particularly interesting aspect of the European Court of Human Right's judgment was its reference to article 9 of the Charter. The European Court of Human Rights was surveying the changing nature and ideas of marriage throughout Europe and cited article 9 of the Charter as being an example of a move away from a biological determination of marriage, because of its removal of the qualifier "men and women" from its text. Thus, article 9 of the Charter was used by the European Court of Human Rights to signal change and to justify its progressive interpretation of article 12 ECHR and the right to marry.

Therefore, the Charter has had the indirect effect of facilitating change in the jurisprudence of the ECHR. As the Charter is to be interpreted in accordance with the jurisprudence of the ECHR, in time, the impact of the *Goodwin* judgment in EU law should be felt. The irony here is that the Advocate General in *D v Council* rejected arguments that the Charter could be used to broaden the concept of "spouse", relying on the jurisprudence of the European Court of Human Rights reiterating the biological imperative of marriage. While the judgment in *Goodwin* would not necessarily mean that the term spouse requires re-interpretation to cover same-sex couples, it seems more than likely that it will have to be re-

---

[50]     *I v UK* (Application no 25680/94); *Goodwin v UK* (Application no: 28957/95).

interpreted to cover transgender partnerships. The biological and heterosexual foundations of marriage are crumbling.[51]

### 4.3. The rights of the child

In the traditional family, children played a subservient role to a (male) head of the family. This relationship of dependency has been seen as an essential and necessary one, with power over the child's life resting almost exclusively with parents. Children, in this conceptualization, had no rights, role or entitlements beyond those of the family, which inhere in the parents. Until the adoption of the Charter, EU law largely replicated this approach to children and their rights, as discussed above.[52]

Accordingly, the inclusion of an article detailing the rights of the child in the Charter marks a step away from a traditional conceptualisation of family, towards an understanding of children as rights-bearers and equal citizens.[53] Thus, the article on the rights of the child is highly symbolic in representing a positive step forward for the Union and its approach to families and family life. Indeed, this is also an area in which there has been a considerable advantage in drafting the Union's own Charter, rather than simply adopting the ECHR, with its singular lack of reference to the rights of the child.

Article 24 of the Charter, setting out the rights of the child, largely reproduces central elements of the United Nations Convention on the Rights of the Child, in particular the principle of the "best interests of the child". In addition, there is a careful balancing between rights of autonomy and self-determination and paternalistic rights of protection. Thus, protection *and* empowerment are found in article 24. The inclusion of the "best interests" principle in the Charter means that for the first time the child's interests are to be considered in all areas of policy which "relate" to children.[54]

---

[51] Note, however, the judgment of the European Court of Human Rights in *Frette* in which it refused a claim by a gay man that the French government's refusal to allow him to adopt a child breached his right to respect for family life: application no. 36515/97, judgment of 26 February 2002.

[52] HELEN STALFORD, "The citizenship status of children in the EU", 8 (2000) *International Journal of Children's Rights* 101.

[53] See further CLARE MCGLYNN, "Rights for Children: the potential impact of the European Union Charter of Fundamental Rights" 8 (2002) *European Public Law* 387.

[54] It is arguable that the "primacy" to be given to the best interests of the child may not be a sufficient safeguard, in view of the Union's track record in giving precedence to economic and market rights, over civil and political rights. See further MCGLYNN *ibid.*

In sum, therefore, the inclusion of provisions on the rights of children is a substantive step forward in ensuring that children are no longer invisible in the Union. Children's interests are to be taken into consideration in all policies relating to them, their voices are to be heard in actions concerning them and they are to be extended protection where necessary. These provisions will certainly provide support for those demanding a more integrated and thoughtful approach to children in the Union. In addition, with the Union developing its competence in the family law field, these provisions ensure a necessary focus on children's rights within families.

Accordingly, the adoption of the Charter offers mixed blessings in respect of the concept of "family" and development of family rights. The Charter employs a concept of "family" which privileges marriage, with only a few exceptions. This replicates the status quo under the ECHR and existing Community law jurisprudence, with the Charter offering little possibility for future development. Similarly, in at least one case so far, *D v Council*, the Charter has been used to entrench the status quo. Thus, although the Charter claims to be founded on the "universal values" of "human dignity, freedom, equality",[55] it remains the case that this is only dignity, freedom and equality for some, not all. Thus, the Charter has only succeeded in bringing the EU closer to some of its citizens. Some children may benefit, but those living outside the traditional nuclear family remain marginalised and largely excluded from many of the entitlements and "benefits" of EU membership.

## 5. LEGISLATIVE INITIATIVES AND DEFINITIONS OF 'FAMILY"

An analysis of the concept of "family" in EU law requires not just an examination of the jurisprudence of the Court of Justice and the impact of the Charter of Fundamental Rights, but also recent legislative initiatives. These recent initiatives provide a useful indication of the approach of the Union institutions and member states to the concept of family.

### 5.1. Free movement of persons

In the area of free movement of persons, the Commission has proposed the adoption of a new regulation which would replace Regulation 1612/68 and therefore provide a new definition of "family".[56] However, the

---

[55]    [2000] *O.J.* C364/1 of 18.12.2000, preamble.
[56]    Commission, "Proposal for a European Parliament and Council Directive on the rights of citizens of the Union and their family members to move and reside freely within the territory of the Member States", *COM* (2001) 257.

opportunity of modernising and liberalising the definition of family in relation to the free movement of persons has not been taken up. The proposal does little more than simply establish in legislative form the principles set out by the Court of Justice in *Netherlands v Reed*. In other words, the limited concept of spouse remains, subject only to a principle of non-discrimination where existing national rules grant rights to non-married partners.

There is some movement in relation to the adverse impact of divorce on the rights of a spouse, especially one who is a third country national. Following *Diatta*, it has been assumed that a divorced spouse would loose all rights which they had as a spouse of a Community national.[57] The proposed new regulation would grant an extension to the existing residence rights of a divorced third country national, subject to a number of qualifying conditions, including being in employment and having sufficient financial resources. While this represents some movement, it is hardly groundbreaking. The requirement of sufficient financial resources is particularly open to criticism, especially in view of the financial strains that divorce places on most families.

Accordingly, the measures proposed by the Commission fail to address the criticisms of the existing limited concept of family employed in the field of free movement of persons. Heterosexual marriage is again given primacy, with few concessions to cohabiting couples or those who divorce. It is clearly arguable that a strict interpretation of these provisions would clash with the jurisprudence of the ECHR which recognises de facto relationships and which limits deportations in some circumstances.[58] Moreover, what the Commission fails to recognise, in drafting this proposal, is that it is the existing limited definition of family which constitutes a restriction on the free movement of persons. Perhaps energies would be better spent seeking to remove such limitations before seeking to extend the family laws of the EU on the basis that this is necessary to facilitate free movement.

### 5.2. Family law

The only measure of EU family law thus far adopted, Regulation 1347/2000, only covers the breakdown of marriages and the consequences

---

[57]  Case 267/83 *Diatta v Land Berlin* [1985] ECR 567.
[58]  See further HELEN STALFORD, "Concepts of Family under EU Law: lessons from the ECHR", (2002) 16 *International Journal of Law, Policy and the Family* 410.

for joint children.[59] Stepchildren and children of unmarried couples are excluded from this legislative regime. Although this position will be somewhat ameliorated when the proposed replacement Regulation is adopted,[60] it nonetheless exemplifies a worrying trend. The lowest common denominator forms the basis for measures – agreement on provisions relating to marriage and to joint children. Only thereafter is action taken in relation to others. But what happens when further agreement is not reached? Then, we are left with a situation in which the rights and entitlements of children vary depending on the marital status of their parents. This is a deplorable situation and one which violates the principles of non-discrimination and the declarations of the ECHR that children should not be adversely treated for being born out of wedlock. Even where further measures are proposed, as now, a hierarchy has still been established and which is causing and will continue to cause undue hardship in many cases.

## 5.3. Asylum and immigration

The Union's competence in the field of asylum and immigration law has been increasing in recent years, particularly since the development of a legislative programme to support the creation of an area of freedom, justice and security, an aim established by the Treaty of Amsterdam. Existing Community legislation in this area maintains the axis between marriage and family, with the 1990 Dublin Convention referring to "family member" as spouse and minor children.[61] This privileging of marriage has been largely reproduced in four recent measures, one of which, the Temporary Protection Directive has already been adopted.[62] However, whereas these measures do continue to privilege marriage, it is with some significant exceptions.[63]

---

[59]  See further HELEN STALFORD, "Regulating Family Life in Post-Amsterdam Europe", (2003) 28 *European Law Review* 39.
[60]  Proposal for a Council Regulation concerning jurisdiction and the recognition and enforcement of judgments in matrimonial matters and in matters of parental responsibility repealing Regulation (EC) No 1347/2000 and amending Regulation (EC) No 44/2001 in matters relating to maintenance, *COM* (2002) 222 final/2, 2002/0110 (CNS).
[61]  The Convention came into force in 1997: *OJ* C 254/1.
[62]  Council Directive 2001/55/EC of 20 July 2001 on minimum standards for giving temporary protection in the event of a mass influx of displaced persons and on measures promoting a balance of efforts between member states in receiving such persons and bearing the consequences thereof, [2001] *OJ* L 212/12. This measure does not apply to Ireland or Denmark.
[63]  See further, MARK BELL, "We are family? Same-sex partners and EU migration law", 9 (2002) *Maastricht Journal of European and Comparative Law* 335.

The Temporary Protection Directive defines family members as: "the spouse of the sponsor or his/her unmarried partner in a stable relationship, where the legislation or practice of the Member State concerned treats unmarried couples in a way comparable to married couples under its law relating to aliens; the minor unmarried children of the sponsor or of his/her spouse, without distinction as to whether they were born in or out of wedlock or adopted".[64] Although there is considerable ambiguity in this definition, for example what constitutes a "stable relationship", it nonetheless represents a symbolic recognition that unmarried partners constitute families. The definition of family in the Temporary Protection Directive is reproduced in the final draft of the Reception Conditions Directive.[65]

In "Dublin II", unmarried couples are only included if "the legislation of the Member State responsible treats unmarried couples in the same way as married couples, provided the couple was formed in the country of origin".[66] This definition is considerably more restrictive than that in the Temporary Protection Directive. Finally, the Qualification for Refugee Status proposal defines family members as "the spouse of the applicant or his/her unmarried partner in a stable relationship, where the legislation or practice of the Member State concerned treats unmarried couples in a way comparable to married couples".[67] Such a provision is closer to the text of the Temporary Protection Directive, although it still varies in requiring a comparison between the treatment of married and unmarried couples is not simply in the law relating to aliens, but national law or practice in general.

The problem with these definitions is twofold. First, they maintain a privileging of marriage, in that marital relationships always constitute families. Secondly, the rights of unmarried partners will vary considerably

---

[64] Paragraph 1(a).
[65] Commission, "Proposal for a Council Directive laying down minimum standards on the reception of applicants for asylum in Member States", COM (2001) 181; Council, "Council Directive laying down minimum standards for the reception of asylum seekers in Member States", Ref 9098/02, Brussels, 17 June 2002. Ireland and Denmark are not participating in this proposal.
[66] Commission, "Proposal for a Council Regulation establishing the criteria and mechanisms for determining the Member State responsible for examining an asylum application lodged in one of the Member States by a third country national", COM (2001) 447. Denmark is not participating in this proposal, article 2(i).
[67] Commission, "Proposal for a Council Directive laying down minimum standards for the qualification and status of third country nationals and stateless persons as refugees, in accordance with the 1951 Convention relating to the status of refugees and the 1967 Protocol, or as persons who otherwise need international protection", COM (2001) 510. Denmark is not participating in this proposal.

between the member states depending on that state's recognition of such partners. Nor is it clear why such different definitions are included in the different proposals.

In relation to immigration and third country nationals, the main measure is the Family Reunification Directive.[68] This measure provides rights of family reunification to spouses and minor children.[69] The right to reunification for unmarried partners, or partners in a registered relationship, is, however, permissive. Member states "may" authorise the entry of such persons but are not obliged to do so.[70] This marks a clear differentiation from the rights of married or unmarried partners, leaving the discretion to member states to admit unmarried partners. Although there is clearly some recognition of unmarried partners, it remains as a second-class status. Furthermore, the rights of unmarried partners in this instance is considerably less than those afforded in the context of asylum measures.

Accordingly, the reforms in the field of immigration and asylum, although recognising in part the diversity of family forms, still privileges heterosexual marriage, effectively marginalizing those who fall outside this norm.

## 6. CONCLUSIONS

The EU is embracing a new agenda in the field of family law. Already one regulation has been adopted, with many more on the horizon. This is a new field of endeavour for the EU and one which will herald considerable controversy. The debate regarding the advantages or disadvantages of EU action in this field is underway. This essay focuses on one aspect of this debate, namely the concept of family which presently underpins EU law. The argument is that this concept of family is exclusive and discriminatory and marginalises those who do not conform to the "ideal family" of EU law. Moreover, it is a concept of family which is out of touch with the changing nature of families within the EU. Finally, in many respects, the approach of the Court of Justice is out of step with that of the European Court of Human Rights. A family law for the European Union, grafted onto this basis, does not bode well for the future of those families outside the norm. A family law of the European Union should embrace and respect diversity.

---

[68]   Council Directive on the Right to Family Reunification, final text agreed on 27 February 2003. The Long-Term Residents Directive defines family by reference to the Family Reunification Directive, Commission, Proposal for a Council Directive concerning the status of third country nationals who are long-term residents', *COM* (2001) 127.

[69]   Article 4(1) and (2).

[70]   Article 4(3).

This is the reality of the EU's protection of "the family" and family life and this is the limited impact of the Charter. My final question is: do we really want to develop a family law for the European Union on this foundation?

# THE INFLUENCE OF EUROPEAN FAMILY LAW ON THE FAMILY LAW OF COUNTRIES ACCEDING TO THE EU

## The example of Poland

Andrzej Mączyński

An evaluation of the Polish family law currently in force [*lex lata*] requires a brief presentation of its evolution. Up to the end of 1946 on a considerable part of Polish territory, in the field of family law the laws of those countries which these lands formed part before Poland regained its independence in 1918 were still in force. In the southern territories it was Austrian law, in the west and north – German law, and in the east– Russian law (from before the Bolshevik Revolution). There was a special situation in the central part of Poland (the so-called Kingdom of Poland), where the basic source of civil law was the Napoleonic Code, with its First Book and Title 5 of the Third Book having been replaced by the civil code of the Kingdom of Poland (1825), which in itself was based on the Napoleonic Code, while the field of matrimonial law had been replaced with the provisions imposed in 1836 by the tsarist authorities, similar to those which were in force in Russia. Temporarily in the far south Hungarian law had been in force, which was soon replaced by the law, which was binding in the remainder of the area – namely Austrian law.

The effort to replace all the above-mentioned provisions with a uniform system of Polish regulations had had limited success up until the outbreak of the Second World War. In the field of family law – apart from the abolition of some evidently archaic regulations – only some very interesting drafts may be mentioned: a draft matrimonial personal law, a draft matrimonial property law, a draft for relationships between parents and children and a draft register of civil status law. They were all elaborated by the Codification Commission, which had been established in 1919. On the basis of these drafts some statutory decrees were issued in 1945 and 1946, thanks to which new uniform regulations concerning family law in its entirety came into force in the state as a whole, as well as regulations for a register of civil status. Their content corresponded to the principles

established in the liberal-democratic countries of Europe. Within the domain of matrimonial law the following principles were introduced:
- the exclusively civil format for contracting a marriage (although emphasising that the rule did not exclude the observance of a religious ceremony before or after the civil form);
- a reduction in the number of factors excluding a marriage (matrimonial impediments) – thus as a consequence a reduction in the number of grounds for the nullification of marriage;
- equality of spouses as regards their personal and property rights as well as their relationships with children;
- finally, the possibility to dissolve a marriage by a decree of divorce delivered by a state court (even one which had been contracted when the former provisions were in force).

Temporarily – for a period of three years – the possibility to dissolve a marriage on the unanimous request of childless spouses was introduced. In the field of matrimonial property law a system for dividing the acquired property of spouses was introduced, which had been modelled on the legislation of the Scandinavian countries, especially the Swedish Act of 6th November 1920. It was considered to comprehensively guarantee the equality of spouses' rights. However, extensive possibilities for an alternative regulation by way of a marriage settlement were permissible, and this was done by means of a valid contract concluded before or after contracting a marriage.

In the field of parental law, there were separate regulations depending on whether a child had been born in or out of wedlock. As regards a child's parentage, both voluntary recognition and the judicial establishment of paternity were provided.

The above-mentioned regulations were soon found to be not sufficiently *progressive* by the then authorities and they were thus replaced with the Family Code of 1950. The Code was the result of Polish-Czechoslovak cooperation, aimed at the unification of the family laws of both neighbouring states. Too hasty drafting resulted in many essential issues being left unregulated, and numerous lacunae had to be filled by the judicature. Thus, the intended uniformisation was not achieved in practice. The Family Code was based on the principles, which soon after its promulgation were given voice in the provisions of the 1952 Constitution of The People's Republic of Poland. These principles were, for example:

- equal rights for men and women in all domains of life, the provision which expressed this principle being the general principle of equal rights of all citizens;
- no detriment to a child's rights because it was born out of wedlock;
- the state cares for and protects marriage and the family, with emphasis being placed on caring for families with many children as well as on the mother and the child;
- separation of church and state;
- separation of school and church.

These principles mirrored the ones adopted in the constitutions of other states with a "people's democracy". It is to be emphasized, however, that in Poland some extreme solutions from earlier and contemporary Soviet law were not adopted. The influence of the official ideology was definitely more apparent in other code regulations, such as the ones regarding compulsory education, than in the Family Code itself.

Regulations adopted in the Code shaped some institutions of family law somewhat differently from previously binding regulations. Thus, as the statutory system of matrimonial property rights, the system of joint property was adopted, although with possibilities for its exclusion, limitation or extension. In the field of parental law separate provisions regarding children born out of wedlock disappeared. The presumption of the mother's husband's paternity was retained, as well as two other ways of establishing paternity, namely voluntary recognition and the judicial establishment of paternity. The system for contracting adoption was replaced by a judicial system. Only a minor could be adopted and it was emphasized that the adoption had to serve the child's interests.

The institutions of family law which were shaped as mentioned above were laid down in the 1964 Family and Guardianship Code, which came into force on 1st January 1965. The Code established the basic source of Polish family law. Irrespective of the intentions of its drafters, the Code is currently assumed not to amount to a separate codification from the simultaneously adopted Civil Code and should be considered as only a formally distinct book of the Civil Code of 1964.

Before 1989, some provisions of the Family and Guardianship Code were twice amended, in 1975 and 1986. The most essential changes concerned the regulation of the effects of divorce (as far as the matrimonial home was concerned), and adoption (a third type of adoption was added to the two already existing forms, which were described as "complete" and "incomplete"). This third type, called "total", was characterized by the impossibility of dissolution as well as by the concealment of the child's real origin). Some changes were made in the field of spouses' names, the limitation of paternal authority and spouses' liability for obligations.

The amendment of the Constitution adopted in 1976 did not change the basic principles of family law, although some changes were made in the provisions. For example, the provision banning discrimination against children born out of wedlock was formulated in the form of the a guarantee of equal rights regardless of marital origin. Some provisions were added obliging parents to raise their children in such a way so that they become honest and conscious citizens of the People's Republic of Poland, while at the same time the principle of the state's obligation to care for the upbringing of the younger generation was preserved.

When characterizing the above-mentioned period of Polish family law development we must point to the total lack of influence exerted by regulations adopted at that time in Western Europe. Regulations adopted in Polish law differed to a greater or lesser extent from solutions that were predominant in Western countries. However, as changes were introduced in those systems, the differences grew narrower. We should also remember another characteristic feature of the legal systems of countries with so-called *real socialism*, namely the essential divergence between what was written and what took place in practice, a considerable gap between *law in books* and *law in action*. Nonetheless, it has to be stressed that as far as Polish family law was concerned – both in the field of theory and in practice – communist ideology never in fact excessively permeated it. The traditionally strong influences of the Catholic Church on Polish society were of significantly more importance.

The influence of legal regulations adopted by the Council of Europe became possible after the political breakthrough of 1989, in particular after Poland was admitted to the Council. A few years earlier Poland had acceded to the Hague Conference of Private International Law, and was then admitted to the International Commission on Civil Status (ICCS). The first sign of interest in regulations adopted in European law was the publication of the Polish translation of the full text of conventions and recommendations of the Council of Europe together with explanations and commentaries on the relationship between them and the Polish provisions, which were prepared by a Polish specialist. The collection was issued in 1994 and was followed by analogous collections of legal acts issued by the Council of Europe as well as the European Communities concerning various branches of the law. The problem of European standards has become the subject of doctrinal studies and has also been taken into consideration in university handbooks and in practical commentaries. It is generally assumed that Polish family law in its present form in principle fulfils European standards.

Poland acceded to all the family law conventions prepared within the framework of the Council of Europe, namely:
– The European Convention on Placement of Children;
– The European Convention on the Legal Status of Children Born out of Wedlock;
– The European Convention on Recognition and Enforcement of Decisions Concerning Custody of Children and Restoration of Custody of Children.

By means of this accession Poland took advantage of the possibility to notify objections where the Polish family law currently *in force* differs from the content of the conventions. Poland is also a party to the UN Convention on the Rights of the Child, having contributed a great deal to its elaboration.

The essential aspect of that period was the resolution and entry into force of the new Constitution in 1997. It is based on principles that are entirely different from those which were previously binding. In Chapter One, including fundamental principles, there is Article 18, in which institutions that are protected by the state are enumerated. They are: marriage, which is defined as a relationship between a man and a woman, the family, maternity and parenthood. The adoption of the Constitution provision which ensures protection only for the marital relations between a man and a woman, took place during the final stages of the legislative process and it was evidently intended to exclude the possibility of legalising homosexual partnerships. The same underlying notion provided the basis for excluding a provision guaranteeing common equality (article 32) as regards sexual orientation. Numerous provisions included in Chapter Two of the Constitution ("Rights and freedoms of man and citizen") are of significance for family law. Article 47 guarantees the right to protection of family life. Article 71 lays down the obligation to respect the interests of the family, ensuring special assistance from the public authorities in cases of family problems and assistance for mothers before and after the birth of a child. Some provisions (articles 48 item 1, 53 item 3, 70 item 3) concern the parents' right to raise a child according to their own convictions, with due respect, however, for the child's freedom of conscience and for its own convictions. The notion of state care, which is laid down in the provisions, can be considered as a leftover from former communist times. According to article 48 item 2 the limitation and deprivation of parental rights is only admissible in those situations provided in the statute. Article 72 concerns the legal position of a child. In item 1 a child is guaranteed the protection of its rights. Item 2 bestows a right to protection and assistance on the part of the public authorities to a child deprived of parental care. The terminology used in the Constitution is also very characteristic – the traditional term "parental authority" (as is used in the Family and Guardianship Code) has been replaced by the term "parental care". Finally, item 3 imposes on public authority agencies, as well as on persons responsible for a child, the obligation to hear and respect a child's opinion when establishing its rights. In comparison with the previous Constitution there is no provision guaranteeing equality of rights for children born in and out of wedlock, since it was not found to be necessary to provide that which is obvious when faced with the principle of equality, which is firmly established in social awareness. The same is true as regards the state's guarantees for the performance of maintenance rights and obligations.

Despite the above-mentioned differences, the entry into force of the new Constitution did not give rise to any contradictions between constitutional norms and the hitherto prevailing family law.

Amendments adopted in the Family and Guardianship Code after the political breakthrough of 1989 were the result of various factors. The changes concern the individual institutions of family law, such as contracting a marriage, separation and adoption. None of them has been the result of the necessity to remove any essential contradictions between Polish family law provisions and European law.

The first chronological amendment was the change in the provisions concerning adoption, adopted in 1995. Its inspiration was the entry into force of the UN Convention on the Rights of the Child. It was pointed out that its article 21 considers an adoption resulting in the transfer of a child abroad to be a measure, which should only be applied if there is no possibility to provide childcare in the state of origin. By adopting an extremely rigorous interpretation of that provision, which ignores even the main principle of the interests of the child, provisions were included in the Code, which effectively excluded the possibility for a child domiciled in Poland to be adopted abroad. This new Polish regulation is to be applied if either the adopter or the adoptee is a Polish citizen. It must also be remembered that Poland is a party to the Hague Convention of 29th May 1993 on Protection of Children and Co-operation in Respect of Intercountry Adoption. At the same time numerous changes were made in the provisions regulating adoptions, among other things widening the possibility of establishing total adoption.

Another amendment to the Family and Guardianship Code (1998) is first of all connected with the entry into force of the Concordat between the Holy Apostolic See and Poland. The former Concordat of 1925, which was broken by the Polish authorities after the Second World War, made no mention of family law. In the Concordat concluded in 1993, ratified in 1998, there is a provision that is aimed at providing a dispensation to persons intending to contract a marriage under both canon and state laws from the necessity of having to undergo two marriage ceremonies. All the provisions under Polish law concerning impediments to marriage as well as the registration of marriage have however been retained. Statutory regulation, however, is still a requirement for other religious forms of marriage whose legal status is regulated in a separate statute. Thus, not every marriage contracted in the religious form in Poland is effective with reference to the state. The admittance of this new form for contracting a marriage corresponds with new provisions in Poland's neighbouring states, such as Lithuania and the Czech Republic. The original feature of the Polish regulation is the requirement to make a separate declaration including the spouses' intention that the marriage which they conclude in a religious form should also have effect under civil law. The ratification of the Concordat did not result in a necessity to amend any other regulation concerning matrimonial law. In particular a marriage contracted in a religious form may be dissolved by a state court. A divorce awarded by a state court has no effect within ecclesiastical (canon) law.

The same amendment adopted some other changes in matrimonial law that are aimed at aligning Polish law with some international treaties. The point was to achieve complete equality between spouses concerning their surnames. The most important change consists of the adoption of the rule according to which if there is no spousal declaration concerning the surname, each of them preserves his and her previous surname, while under the former regulation the wife adopted the name of her husband. The statutory marriageable age was also changed. By restoring the regulation that was in force until 1965, the marriageable age was made equal at 18 years for men as well as for women, although the court can permit a 16-year old woman to marry (a different proposition, modelled on the German regulation, according to which a man of 16 can also obtain such permission was rejected). To fulfil Poland's international obligations, the Family and Guardianship Code was amended by including a regulation concerning the influence of a defective declaration on the validity of a marriage. The lack of such a provision had been criticised for quite some time. Doctrine had pointed to incompatibility with the UN Convention on Consent to Marriage, Minimum Age for Marriage and Registration of Marriages of 1962, which equated the contracting of a marriage with expressing a complete and free wish to do so.

Another change also concerns matrimonial law. It is not connected with the fulfilment of Poland's international obligations, and its adoption gave rise to many disputes. It concerns the adoption of judicial separation (1999). The separation is decided by the court in the case of "the complete disintegration of matrimonial life". Thus the ground for separation is more lenient than the ground for divorce, the latter including – in addition to complete disintegration – permanent disintegration. Separation has in principle the same effects as divorce. The most important difference lies in the impossibility of contracting a new marriage by a separated spouse. A decision on separation does not exclude the dissolution of marriage through a divorce. When introducing the institution of separation into the Family and Guardianship Code no changes were made to the provisions regulating divorce.

Some already drafted or proposed amendments in Polish family law are also worth mentioning. In 1994 draft changes to the divorce regulation were lodged by a group of Members of Parliament. They provided that when the spouses have no children, the sole prerequisite for divorce should be the request of one of the spouses to dissolve the marriage. According to the draft, in such cases the court would not be obliged to establish whether matrimonial life has actually disintegrated or which of the spouses – if any – is responsible for this disintegration. The opinion of the other spouse was to be – according to the draft – of no relevance. Those proposing the draft justified the postulated changes with the need to protect each spouse's right to privacy. However, the draft was generally considered to deprive the non-culpable spouse of protection, not to take into account the social significance of marriage and even to be immoral and was eventually – in the course of legislative proceedings – rejected by Parliament during the following year. Since then the idea of liberalizing the provisions regulating the grounds for divorce has never resurfaced.

To date, no other important and carefully prepared draft concerning a radical change in matrimonial property law has been considered. Since economic relations have changed and the standards of living have become based on personal economic activity rather than hired labour, the system of joint property attained by the spouses is no longer apt, which tends to recommend change. The system of joint property attained by the spouses, which has been in force up until now, as well as the rules of property management, are no longer suitable. Changes to parental law have also been planned, although which direction this should take has not yet been determined. It is also proposed to regulate issues concerning non-marital relationships.

While comparing Polish law with European standards it is worth mentioning the specific regulation concerning the spouses' rights to an apartment, which is the subject of Recommendation R (81)15 of the Council of Europe. Polish law already contains some legal relationship rights to use an apartment. Such rights usually concern renting, ownership and some specific rights connected with membership of a housing co-operative society. The regulations regarding the equal rights of both spouses to an apartment in which they reside were adopted in 1974 initially concerning rented apartments. In 1982 a similar, but more detailed, regulation was adopted in the Law on Co-operative Societies. The essence of the regulation consists of creating a joint property of a special kind, which encompasses an apartment and exists irrespective of the system of matrimonial property, thus also in the case of a system of separate estates within matrimony. Such a regulation is currently to be found among the provisions on the renting of apartments in the Civil Code (2001) as well as in the Act on Housing Co-operative Law (2000). In Polish law there are also provisions regulating apartment issues between ex-spouses as well as ones that aim to protect the widow or widower who does not "possess" a right to the apartment in which he or she resides.

For the sake of completeness some remarks concerning private international law are also required. Poland is a country with a long tradition of statutory regulation of private international law. The Polish statute of 1926 was a highly regarded achievement on the part of Polish legal thought. It had a strong influence on both statutes adopted by other countries and bilateral conventions concluded between countries of Central and Eastern Europe after the Second World War. Its provisions concerning matrimonial law remained despite the influence of the Hague Conventions of 1902 and 1905 although Poland itself was not a party to either of them. The basic connecting factor within the scope of matrimonial law was citizenship. The ability to contract a marriage was to be considered according to the national law of each of the spouses, while personal and property relations between the spouses, as well as divorce and judicial separation were to be determined according to the common national law of both spouses, and if there was no such law then according to the last common national law. For the statutory matrimonial property system, however, husband's *lex patriae tempore celebrationis matrimonii* was to be applied. In norms concerning the competence of parental law there were separate regulations depending on whether a child had been born in or out of wedlock.

Because some of these regulations had become archaic, a new statute was adopted in 1965. The new statute, which remains in force today, attaches essential importance to national law (*lex patriae*). In matrimonial law it consistently applies the law that has the closest connection with both spouses. It principally concerns both the personal and property effects of the marriage. Within this scope the common national law of both spouses is applicable if the spouses are not nationals of the country in which they both have their place of residence (not necessarily a common one). Finally, when spouses with no common citizenship do not live in the same country, Polish law is applicable. Such a "cascade of laws" is also relevant as regards divorce.

The main rule of parental law is the application of the national law of the child. The judicial establishment of paternity is subject to the national law of the child from the time of its birth, while fathering a child is subject to the child's *legi patriae* at the time of fathering. The regulation of the applicable law is the same whether or not the child is born in or out of wedlock.

However, in adoption law there is another rule in force: namely, the application of the national law of the adopter, not the adoptee. Such a regulation is justified by the interest of the adoptee – it is aimed at increasing the chances that the adoption judgement will be recognized abroad.

To sum up: it can be stated that despite the isolation of the Polish family law system during most of its post-War progress from what was occurring during that time in The West, as a final result its content does not differ from the standards established by the Council of Europe. Thus Poland's accession to the Council of Europe did not result in the necessity to reject the family law that was previously in force.

# UNIFICATION AND HARMONIZATION OF FAMILY LAW PRINCIPLES: THE UNITED STATES EXPERIENCE

NANCY G. MAXWELL

## 1. OVERVIEW OF THE STATE/FEDERAL RELATIONSHIP IN THE CONTEXT OF FAMILY LAW

Family law issues in the United States, particularly the issues currently under study by the Commission on European Family Law – grounds for divorce and spousal support – are matters generally reserved to the individual states.[1] This situation has resulted in numerous conflicts among the states, particularly within the last 100 years, as the U.S. population became increasingly mobile. A good example of the complexities of the U.S. situation is the current inconsistency among the states concerning the legal status of same-sex couples, a topic that has received a great deal of discussion in the papers presented at this conference. On one extreme is the state of Vermont, where the 2000 state legislature created civil unions, a legal equivalent to heterosexual marriages.[2] On the other extreme are the states that continue to criminalize same-sex sexual activity as sodomy.[3] Therefore, if a same-sex couple living in Kansas were to travel to Vermont and enter into a civil union, when the couple returns to Kansas and engages in certain types of sexual activity, the couple would be committing criminal acts. To complicate this situation, the U.S. Congress has passed legislation, known as the Defense of Marriage Act,[4] which refuses federal recognition to same-sex marriages, should any state authorize these marriages.[5]

---

[1]  "We disclaim altogether any jurisdiction in the [federal] courts of the United States upon the subject of divorce, or the allowance of alimony . . . ." Barber v. Barber 62 U.S. (21 How.) 582, 584 (1859).

[2]  VT. STAT. ANN. tit. 15, §§ 1201-1207 (2000).

[3]  See the sodomy/sexual misconduct statutes from the following jurisdictions: Kansas, Kan. Stat. Ann. § 21-3505 (2001), Missouri, Mo. Ann. Stat. § 566.090 (West 2002), Oklahoma, Okla. Stat. Ann. tit. 21, § 886 (West 2002), Rhode Island, R.I. Gen. Laws § 11-10-1 (2002), Texas, Tex. Penal Code Ann. § § 21.01(1), 21.06 (Vernon 2001).

[4]  Defense of Marriage Act, 28 U.S.C. § 1738C (2001).

[5]  No state in the United States has opened marriage to same-sex couples. Vermont has created a parallel institution to marriage through its civil union legislation. Thirty-six states have passed legislation limiting marriage to one man and one woman. NATIONAL GAY AND LESBIAN TASK FORCE, "Specific Anti-Same-Sex Marriage Laws in the U.S.", at http://www.ngltf.org/downloads/marriagemap0601.pdf.

As one can see, this situation can result in serious conflicts that could have devastating consequences on individuals' personal lives and intimate relationships.

In examining efforts to unify and harmonize the grounds for divorce and spousal support, a historical overview of the situation in the United States over the last 100 years provides an important context to understanding the current status of these legal issues in the U.S. states.

## 1.1. State statutes and case law control within the jurisdiction of each state

Initially, it is important to understand that when a party, who is seeking a divorce or an order of spousal maintenance, meets the jurisdictional requirements of the state where the action is filed, then that state court applies its own substantive law, even though the other party to the marriage may be a resident of another state. This fact has resulted in forum shopping and a long history of migratory divorce in the United States. Therefore an important issue in the history of divorce in the United States has been determining whether a state, which has granted a divorce, had the proper jurisdiction to do so. It is only those divorce decrees, issued by a state court with proper jurisdiction, that will be granted recognition and enforcement in the sister states, according to the full faith and credit clause of the United States Constitution.[6] Consequently there has been a great deal of litigation over the issue of whether a sister state must recognize and enforce another state's divorce decree, particularly if there is great disparity between the two states' substantive law.

## 1.2. Divorce jurisdiction

### 1.2.1. Full faith and credit and migratory divorce

The United States Supreme Court became involved in establishing the jurisdictional basis for divorce through the interpretation of the "full faith and credit" clause of the United States Constitution. This clause states "Full Faith and Credit shall be given in each State to the public Acts, Records, and judicial Proceedings of every other State."[7] The Court interpreted this clause as it applies to divorce jurisdiction in the 1906 case of Haddock v. Haddock.[8] In that case a couple was married in New York, but shortly

---

[6]    U.S. Const. art. IV, § 1.
[7]    *Id.*
[8]    201 U.S. 562 (1906).

thereafter the husband moved to Connecticut, where he obtained a divorce. According to the Supreme Court decision, the Connecticut divorce decree was not deserving of full faith and credit because New York was the marital domicile state and the wife remained a New York resident. As a result, the state of New York did not have to recognize or enforce the Connecticut divorce decree. This rule was highly criticized, particularly as the U.S. population became more mobile and the phenomenon of migratory divorces became more prevalent.

Migratory divorce was the result of great discrepancies between the states concerning the grounds for divorce and inconsistencies in the length of time one must be domiciled within a state before filing for a divorce. Citizens who resided in states that had very strict grounds for divorce, and who had adequate financial resources to do so, would travel to states where the grounds for divorce were lenient and the time periods were short. These individuals would live within the second state long enough to meet the minimum time necessary to establish domicile. Then they would file for and obtain a divorce,[9] only to return to their home states as a divorced person. This was what occurred in the well-known Williams line of cases in which the state of North Carolina prosecuted a man and a woman for bigamous cohabitation. The couple, who were married to other individuals and resided in North Carolina, traveled to Nevada, where they obtained divorces and then married one another, returning to live together in North Carolina. The state prosecutor's argument in the criminal trial for bigamous cohabitation was that the couple's divorces in Nevada were not worthy of recognition in North Carolina under the Supreme Court's interpretation of the full faith and credit clause in the Haddock case, because North Carolina was the marital domicile and the defendants' spouses remained in North Carolina.

In the first case of Williams I,[10] however, the U.S. Supreme Court reversed the Haddock case, holding that if a party was actually domiciled in the state that granted the divorce, then the divorce decree was worthy of full faith and credit. Because the state of North Carolina had failed to provide evidence on the issue of whether the parties were, in fact, domiciled in the

---

[9]    Generally, in this scenario the party filing for divorce would give notice to his or her spouse of the divorce action by publishing a written notice in a local newspaper, which had the practical effect of no actual notice at all because the other spouse remained in the marital domicile state. If, however, the couple agreed to the divorce, then the filing spouse would file a document signed by the other spouse submitting to the jurisdiction of the divorce court.

[10]   Williams v. North Carolina, 317 U.S. 287 (1942).

state of Nevada at the time of the divorce, the Nevada divorce decree carried the presumption that it was a valid decree deserving full faith and credit. After a retrial, the case was again appealed to the Supreme Court and, in the Williams II decision,[11] the Court modified its earlier holding. In Williams II the Court held that a court in a second state could decide for itself whether the party obtaining a divorce decree was, in fact, domiciled in the first state. However, if the first state had made a determination in the divorce decree that the party was domiciled there, that determination was entitled to "respect and more" in the second state. Thus the party attacking the decree in a second state carried the burden of proving the absence of domicile. The proof of domicile is based on two factors: one's physical presence within a state, coupled with that person's intent to remain within the state. The practical impact of Williams II was that the person attacking the court's finding of domicile had the difficult burden of disproving another person's state of mind. This decision resulted in two states having valid jurisdiction to issue divorces – the state in which the plaintiff spouse had established a new domicile, as well as the marital domicile state, assuming the other party to the marriage remained domiciled there.[12]

### 1.2.2. Due process challenges and migratory divorces

In 1975 a woman seeking a divorce in Iowa challenged the constitutionality of an Iowa statute that required a person to be domiciled within the state for one year prior to filing for a divorce.[13] The litigant alleged that this waiting period denied her due process of the laws under the U.S. Constitution. The Supreme Court disagreed, finding that Iowa had a legitimate interest in making certain its decrees were not subject to attack under the full faith and credit clause under the Williams cases. The court cited the Williams case, stating that "until such a time as Iowa is convinced that appellant intends to remain in the State, it lacks the 'nexus between person and place of such permanence as to control the creation of legal relations and responsibilities of the utmost importance.'"[14] Therefore each state was allowed to determine how long a person must remain within the state in order to establish domicile before filing for a divorce.

---

[11] Williams v. North Carolina, 325 U.S. 226 (1945).

[12] For a detailed discussion of migratory divorce, see HOMER CLARK, *The Law of Domestic Relations in the United States*, § 12.2 (2d ed. 1988).

[13] Sosna v. Iowa, 419 U.S. 393 (1975).

[14] *Id.* at 407, citing Williams v. North Carolina, 325 U.S. 226, 229 (1945).

## 1.2.3. Personal jurisdiction and orders of spousal support

The cases discussed up to this point involved *ex parte* divorces – in other words, the other spouse was domiciled in another state and was not present before the divorce court. The issue in these cases was limited to whether a state court had proper jurisdiction to alter the party's status from a married person to a divorced person. The U.S. Supreme Court determined that these cases involved limited *in rem* jurisdiction, the *res* being the status of the party. In order for a divorce court to require a party to pay spousal maintenance, however, the court must have personal jurisdiction over the party. General rules of civil procedure require a person to have some "nexus" or connection to a state before that state's courts can assert personal jurisdiction over the person. One exception to this rule is when the defendant, who is not a resident of the state in which the law suit is brought, submits to that state's jurisdiction over him or her.

This was the situation in a 1948 United States Supreme Court case involving the issue of the recognition and enforcement of a divorce decree where the non-domiciled spouse actually participated in a divorce action in a state other than the marital domicile. In Sherrer v. Sherrer[15] the wife left the marital domicile state of Massachusetts and moved to Florida. After living in Florida for the requisite period of time to establish domicile under the Florida divorce statutes, the wife filed for divorce. The husband entered his appearance in the Florida divorce action, opposing the divorce and claiming the wife was not a bona fide domiciliary of Florida. At the time of trial, however, the husband did not present evidence concerning the issue of whether his wife was domiciled in Florida. Ultimately the Florida court granted the wife a divorce. The husband then brought a suit in Massachusetts attacking the validity of the Florida divorce. On appeal, the United States Supreme Court held that the husband was prevented by the principle of res judicata[16] from attacking the Florida divorce action. By submitting to the jurisdiction of the Florida court, the Florida divorce court had obtained personal jurisdiction over the husband. The United State Supreme Court held that a divorce decree was a valid decree when 1) the defendant had participated in the divorce proceedings, 2) he had been

---

[15]    334 U.S. 343 (1948).

[16]    A result similar to the application of the principle of res judicata occurs under the doctrine of estoppel. Under this equitable doctrine, a person who has participated in obtaining a judgment is estopped from attacking that judgment in a later proceeding. The policy behind res judicata is that there must be finality in litigation once a party has had the opportunity to present his or her case. The policy behind estoppel, however, is one of a personal disability, preventing someone from challenging the validity of a judgment that he or she actively procured. See CLARK, *supra* note 12, at § 12.3.

accorded full opportunity to contest the jurisdictional issues and 3) the decree was not susceptible to collateral attack in the courts of the state that rendered the decree.

Another general rule of civil procedure for obtaining personal jurisdiction over a defendant is through personal service of process. This occurs when a plaintiff, who is domiciled in another state, is able to serve the defendant with a lawsuit when the defendant happens to be physically present within the borders of plaintiff's domicile state. There had been some debate over the issue of whether personal service would be sufficient, under the due process clause, to establish personal jurisdiction over a defendant in a divorce action if the defendant had no connection with the state. According to this debate, it was questioned whether a state could impose its substantive laws concerning spousal maintenance, child support and property division on a defendant who had no "nexus" with the plaintiff's domicile state other than coincidently being within that state's borders. That issue was resolved in 1990 in the case of Burnham v. Superior Court of California[17] in which the U.S. Supreme Court applied the general rule, finding that personal service was sufficient to establish personal jurisdiction. Consequently, if the plaintiff is able to lure the defendant within the borders of his or her new state of domicile and personally serve the defendant, then the defendant will be bound by the substantive law of that state, including the laws concerning the award of spousal maintenance.

To summarize, a state court's divorce decree must be given full faith and credit in all other states if the divorce is issued by the marital domicile court, assuming at least one party to the marriage remains within the state. In addition, a decree that merely alters the status of the parties, i.e. a simple decree of divorce, also is entitled to full faith and credit if it is issued in a state in which the plaintiff is a bona fide domiciliary. Finally, a court has jurisdiction to grant spousal maintenance when that court has personal jurisdiction over the debtor. Personal jurisdiction can be established if the debtor is personally served within the borders of state where the action for support is filed, or if the debtor has submitted to the jurisdiction of the court. Given this situation, it is conceivable that there may be concurrent jurisdiction in two different states to grant the divorce if the parties to the marriage have different domicile states. In addition, it is possible that a state granting the divorce may not have jurisdiction to issue an order for spousal support if the debtor is not subject to personal jurisdiction within that state. For example, if a couple's marital domicile is the state of Kansas

---

[17]    495 U.S. 604 (1990).

and the wife leaves Kansas and becomes a domiciliary of Texas, both Texas and Kansas would have jurisdiction to grant her a divorce, but Texas would not have jurisdiction to order the husband to pay her spousal support if the husband does not come within the borders of Texas and he refuses to submit voluntarily to the jurisdiction of the Texas divorce court. In order to get an order of spousal support, the wife would be required to bring the support action in the courts of Kansas, where she could obtain personal service over her husband. In that situation, the Texas court would apply Texas divorce law[18] in granting the divorce, but the Kansas court would apply Kansas law in determining spousal support. Both decrees, under the full faith and credit clause, must be recognized and enforced in all the states.

## 1.2.4. Failure to enforce orders of spousal support

Although a court may have jurisdiction to issue a spousal support order, historically this did not necessarily result in a sister state enforcing the order against a debtor resident. Only those decrees that are "final orders" are covered under the full faith and credit clause of the U.S. Constitution. Many spousal support orders are subject to modification, based on changed circumstances of the parties. Therefore, it was not uncommon for a state to refuse to enforce a sister state's original support order because the order was not "final" or a state allowed the debtor to seek a modification of the first state's original order. This resulted in decrees being issued in different states with different amounts being ordered, leaving courts in a quandary as to which order should be recognized and enforced. For example, assume that the couple was divorced in the marital state of New York and the New York court ordered the man to pay $500 a month in spousal support. The man then moves to Kansas and stops making the spousal support payments. The woman brings the New York order to a Kansas court, seeking enforcement of the New York order. The Kansas court may determine that the New York judgment is not a final judgment in the state of New York, because the New York court has the power to modify the decree upon a showing of a material change in circumstances, and the Kansas court refuses to enforce the order. Or another possibility is that the Kansas court may allow the man to file a motion to modify the New York order, reducing the amount to $300 a month, based on a material change in circumstances. Even if the man pays the $300 a month in Kansas, he remains in arrears in New York for the additional $200 each month, in continuous violation

---

[18] Texas divorce procedure is highly unusual because it provides for a jury trial. Tex. Fam. Code Ann. § 6.703 (Vernon 1998).

of the New York order. The woman could then seek enforcement of the New York arrearage in Kansas, putting the Kansas court in a position of having to choose between the contradictory orders.

### 1.3. Federal limitations on state power –access to divorce courts and sexual equality issues

As shown in the prior discussion, the U.S. Supreme Court's rulings on the full faith and credit clause have had little effect on harmonizing the grounds for divorce or the law of spousal support. Neither have the rulings resulted in uniformity in the recognition or enforcement of sister state decrees. There are two decisions, however, that have had a national impact on state laws.[19] The first case, Boddie v. Connecticut[20] involved a constitutional challenge against a Connecticut statute that required a mandatory payment of filing fees before one could file an action for divorce. A group of indigent women sued the state, alleging that the requirement of the filing fee prevented them from obtaining a divorce. The petitioners alleged that they were being denied due process of the law because the filing file requirement prevented them from having access to the only remedy available to them to end their marriages, divorce. The Supreme Court agreed, striking down the statute as a violation of the due process clause; "a State may not, consistent with the obligations imposed on it by the Due Process Clause of the Fourteenth Amendment, pre-empt the right to dissolve this legal relationship without affording all citizens access to the means it has prescribed for doing so."[21] Therefore, state statutes cannot prevent access to the divorce court by requiring a filing fee, if a person is unable to pay the fee.[22]

The second case, Orr v. Orr,[23] involved a constitutional challenge of Alabama's spousal maintenance statute, which authorized the court to award support to a wife but was silent about an award to a husband. The

---

[19] There have been a number of U.S. Supreme Court cases that have impacted substantive family law principles. See generally VICTORIA MIKESELL MATHER, "Commentary: Evolution and Revolution in Family Law", 25 *St. Mary's L. J.* 405, 417-27 (1993). However, because the initial investigation of the CEFL concerns the grounds for divorce and spousal support, these other cases are not discussed here because they are outside the scope of this article.

[20] 401 U.S. 371 (1971).

[21] *Id.* at 383.

[22] To comply with this constitutional mandate a state statute may provide that an affidavit of poverty may be filed with the divorce action, showing an inability to pay the fee. See Kan. Stat. Ann. § 60-2001 (Supp. 2002). However, some courts assess the filing fee at the end of the proceedings, after granting the divorce, thereby creating a debt to the court. See Davis v. Davis, 623 P.2d 1369 (Kan. App. 1981).

[23] 440 U.S. 268 (1979).

Alabama Supreme Court interpreted the statute as authorizing support only in favor of the wife. The U.S. Supreme Court struck down the statute because it violated the equal protection clause of the U.S. Constitution,[24] based on impermissible sex discrimination. As a result, all state statutes and courts must use sex neutral considerations in awarding spousal support.

## 2. ATTEMPTS TO UNIFY AND HARMONIZE SUBSTANTIVE FAMILY LAW

### 2.1. Early attempts – The Uniform Marriage and Divorce Act

An obvious way to deal with problems of forum shopping is for the states to have similar substantive laws. The National Conference of Commissioners on Uniform State Laws (NCCUSL) was formed for this purpose, to draft uniform or model acts, which would be presented to the individual state legislatures for consideration and, hopefully, enacted without amendments. In the 1960s, NCCUSL began work on the Uniform Marriage and Divorce Act (UMDA). Perhaps the best description of the 1970 Uniform Act, when it was presented to the American Bar Association, was that its provisions were a hybrid between the "common core" and the "better law" approach.[25] The most significant evidence of the better law approach was the proposal to eliminate fault as a factor in granting the divorce as well as in awarding spousal maintenance, child support and dividing the couple's property. The Commissioners were influenced by the no-fault movement in Europe and in California[26] and the movement's rationale that divorce should not place blame, but rather focus on effective ways to resolve the issues that result from the breakdown of a marriage.

Unfortunately, the 1970 version of the UMDA met with strong opposition in the House of Delegates of the American Bar Association (ABA) and actually resulted in the ABA proposing another uniform act in opposition to the NCCUSL's proposal. The NCCUSL amended the UMDA in 1971 and again in 1973, during which time there were acrimonious debates until, finally, in early 1974, the American Bar Association approved the 1973 version of the UMDA.[27] The main focus of the disagreement was that

---

[24]  U.S. Const. amend. XIV, § 1.
[25]  See MASHA ANTOKOLSKAIA, "The "better" law approach and the harmonisation of family law", in this book, p. 157.
[26]  HERMA HILL KAY, "Equality and Difference: A Perspective on No-Fault Divorce and its Aftermath", 56 *U. Cin. L. Rev.* 1, 45 (1987).
[27]  See generally, HARVEY L. ZUCKMAN, "Commentary: The ABA Family Law Section v. The NCCUSL: Alienation, Separation and Forced Reconciliation Over the Uniform Marriage and Divorce Act", 24 *Cath. U. L. Rev.* 61 (1974).

the 1970's version of the Act did not define a specific ground for divorce; rather the Act used a series of procedural steps that the court applied in determining whether the marriage had broken down. This issue was resolved in the 1973 version in which a compromise provision required a finding that the marriage was irretrievably broken, either through evidence that "(i) the parties have lived separate and apart for a period of more than 180 days next preceding the commencement of the proceeding, or (ii) there is serious marital discord adversely affecting the attitude of one or both parties toward the marriage."[28] Another provision of the Act stated that a finding of irretrievable breakdown "is a determination that there is no reasonable prospect of reconciliation."[29] According to the Commissioners' Comment the "legal assignment of blame is here replaced by a search for the reality of the marital situation: whether the marriage has ended in fact."[30] In addition, if the parties established that the marriage was irretrievably broken, "the court is not authorized to make a contrary finding because of the impact of the dissolution of the marriage on the minor children."[31]

There were two other significant changes in the UMDA, one involving property division and the other dealing with spousal support. The 1970 version of the Act proposed a modified community property concept, a concept that existed in a minority of states, generally those states located in the southwestern part of the country, as well as Louisiana, states that were influenced by the civil law of Spain or France. The 1973 version, however, adopted the "equitable division" concept, which was followed in the majority of the states. This concept gives a great deal of discretion to the court in determining the division of the property.

In the area of spousal support, which the drafters referred to as "maintenance," the new provisions narrowly limited the award only to those situations in which the court found that the spouse receiving maintenance lacked sufficient property to provide for his or her needs and was unable to support himself or herself through appropriate employment or was the custodian of a child whose condition or circumstances made it appropriate that the custodian not be required to seek employment outside the home.[32] In determining maintenance, the UMDA set out six factors the court

---

[28]    Unif. Marriage & Divorce Act § 302 (amended 1973) 9A *U.L.A.* 200 (1998).
[29]    Unif. Marriage & Divorce Act § 305(c), 9A *U.L.A.* 242 (1998).
[30]    *Id.* § 305(c), cmt.
[31]    *Id.*
[32]    Unif. Marriage & Divorce Act § 308(a), (amended 1971, 1973) 9A *U.L.A.* 446 (1998).

should consider in making the award. Specifically, the section stated the following:

> "The maintenance order shall be in amounts and for periods of time the court deems just, without regard to marital misconduct, and after considering all relevant factors including: (1) the financial resources of the party seeking maintenance, including marital property apportioned to him, his ability to meet his needs independently, and the extent to which a provision for support of a child living with the party includes a sum for that party as custodian; (2) the time necessary to acquire sufficient education or training to enable the party seeking maintenance to find appropriate employment; (3) the standard of living established during the marriage; (4) the duration of the marriage; (5) the age and the physical and emotional condition of the spouse seeking maintenance; and (6) the ability of the spouse from whom maintenance is sought to meet his needs while meeting those of the spouse seeking maintenance."[33]

The Commissioners' Comment stated that it was their intention to encourage the court to provide for the financial needs of the spouses through the division of the property rather than by an award of spousal support,[34] a clear departure from the current status of the law. Although the number of cases in which spousal support is awarded has remained at approximately 15%, the introduction of no-fault divorce resulted in spousal payments having shorter time limits, as opposed to the previous open-ended awards that generally continued until death of either party or remarriage of the spouse receiving support.[35] The impact of this change has had significant negative consequences on the economic status of former wives and children in their custody and has been referred to as the "feminization of poverty."[36]

At the same time the ABA was balking at adopting the UMDA, many state legislatures began to embrace the idea of no-fault divorce. Some states adopted portions of the 1970, 1971 and 1973 versions of the Act or adopted provisions of the California Family Law Act, which influenced the drafters of the UMDA.[37] Some states adopted major portions of the various acts, while others merely added a no-fault ground to the statutory list of grounds for divorce. Only 8 states ultimately adopted either the 1970, 1971 or 1973

---

[33] *Id.* § 308(b).
[34] *Id.* § 308, cmt.
[35] MARSHA GARRISON, "The Economic Consequences of Divorce: Would the Adoption of the ALI Principles Improve Current Outcomes?", 8 *Duke J. Gender L. & Pol'y* 119 (2001).
[36] *See generally,* LENORE WEITZMAN, *The Divorce Revolution,* 337-43 (New York, Free Press; London, Collier Macmillan 1985).
[37] KAY, *supra* note 26, at 50-56.

versions of the UMDA,[38] but the no-fault divorce revolution had impacted every state in the Union. By 1985, all state legislatures had enacted some form of a no-fault ground for divorce, most having done so before the end of the 1970s. Eliminating fault as a factor in spousal support was not as successful; currently 29 states permit the court to consider some form of marital fault in determining spousal support, with 7 of these states allowing a total ban on support if a potential recipient committed adultery.[39]

## 2.2. Recent developments

### 2.2.1. Unifying the Uniform Acts –The Joint Editorial Board for the Family Law Acts

The UMDA has not been met with broad acceptance among the states, although many of the concepts contained in the Act can be found in numerous state statutes or judicial decisions. Other NCCUSL uniform acts dealing with family law, however, have been widely adopted in the states.[40] Even with these acts, however, the state legislatures have amended key provisions, resulting in reduced uniformity than had been anticipated. Recently NCCUSL established a Joint Editorial Board for the Family Law Acts (JEB), with the purpose of reviewing the effectiveness of current acts and to recommend amendments that would remove the lack of uniformity among the states. The JEB also is charged with determining and recommending the areas of family law in which new uniform acts may be drafted in the future.

### 2.2.2. Transforming spousal support to compensatory payments – The American Law Institute's Principles of the Law of Family Dissolution

The American Law Institute (ALI) is well-known for its work on the Restatements of the Law, which synthesize legal principles into the majority and minority positions among the states. The ALI also has been involved in drafting model acts, as well, presenting the model act as the "better law" in a particular subject area.[41] It is this second function that prompted the

---

[38]   Unif. Marriage & Divorce Act (amended 1971, 1973), 9A *U.L.A.* 169 (1998).

[39]   For current charts on the factors for awarding spousal support in the U.S., see Chart 1 at http://www.abanet.org/family/familylaw/tables.html.

[40]   For example, see the Unif. Child Custody Jurisdiction Enforcement Act, 9 *U.L.A.* 649 (1998); Unif. Interstate Family Support Act, 9 *U.L.A.* 235 (1998); Unif. Premarital Agreement Act, 9 *U.L.A.* 35 (2001).

[41]   J. Thomas Oldham, "The American Law Institute's Principles of the Law of Family Dissolution: Its Impact on Family Law", 7 *Tex. J. Women & L.* 161 (1998).

ALI Project on Family Dissolution to study and ultimately propose the Principles of the Law of Family Dissolution. As is noted in the Forward of the 1997 draft, the "current disarray in family law" prompted the Institute to draft principles that would "give greater weight to emerging legal concepts" than a Restatement.[42] In the Principles, the drafters do not address the growing debate about the efficacy of no-fault divorce,[43] but rather focus on such areas as property division, spousal support, child support and child custody, within the context of both marital and non-martial relationships. Recognizing that the majority of family dissolutions reach the courts with a negotiated settlement, the goal of the drafters was to create presumptions and formulas that would make the negotiation process, as well as a decision by a court, predictable, consistent and reliable.[44] After approximately 10 years of study, the ALI adopted the final draft of the Principles in May of 2000, which were officially published in 2002.

Chapter 5 deals with spousal payments; the innovative nature of the Chapter is immediately identifiable by its title, "Compensatory Spousal Payments." The goal of the drafters was to shift the focus of spousal payments from a needs-based analysis to one of compensatory entitlements. According to § 5.03, compensatory awards should equitably allocate the financial losses that one or both of the spouses may suffer when, at dissolution, the family is divided into separate economic units. This section sets out the circumstances in which there should be a compensatory payment.

(2)   The following compensable losses are recognized in Topic 2 of this Chapter:

    (a)   In a marriage of significant duration, the loss in standard of living experienced at dissolution by the spouse who has less wealth or earning capacity (§ 5.04).

    (b)   An earning capacity loss incurred during marriage but continuing after dissolution and arising from one spouse's disproportionate share, during marriage, of the care of the marital children or of the children of either spouse (§ 5.05).

---

[42]   GEOFFREY C. HAZARD, *ALI Principles of the Law of Family Dissolution: Analysis and Recommendations*, Forward (Proposed Final Draft Part I, 1997).

[43]   OLDHAM, *supra* note 41, at 162.

[44]   "A core recommendation of Chapter 5 [Compensatory Spousal Payments], however, is the establishment of presumptions and guidelines to provide predictability and consistency . . . ." IRA MARK ELLMAN, "Chief Reporter's Forward to Principles of the Law of Family Dissolution: Analysis and Recommendations", xix (*Am. Law Inst.* 2000). See also, GARRISON, *supra* note 35, at 123.

  (c) An earning capacity loss incurred during marriage but conti-
    nuing after dissolution, and arising from the care provided by
    one spouse to a sick, elderly, or disabled third party, in ful-
    fillment of a moral obligation of the other spouse or of both
    spouses jointly (§ 5.12).
(3) The following compensable losses are recognized in Topic 3 of this
  Chapter:
  (a) The loss either spouse incurs when the marriage is dissolved
    before that spouse realizes a fair return from his or her invest-
    ment in the other spouse's earning capacity (§ 5.15).
  (b) An unfairly disproportionate disparity between the spouses in
    their respective abilities to recover their pre-marital living
    standard after the dissolution of a short marriage (§ 5.13).[45]

Although these factors for triggering a payment may be found in either
current statutory law or in judicial decisions, the Principles require a state
to create a percentage-based presumption, both as to the duration of the
payment and the value of the payment. A major criticism of the Principles,
however, is that they merely provide a formula without offering any
appropriate percentages. For example, under § 5.04, a compensable loss
occurs when a person, married to someone with significantly greater wealth
or earning capacity, suffers a loss in the standard of living that person
would otherwise experience, and the marriage is of sufficient duration that
equity requires that some portion of the loss be treated as the spouses' joint
responsibility. The provision continues by stating that there should be a
statewide rule "under which a presumption of entitlement arises in
marriages of specified duration and spousal income disparity."[46]

The weakness of the Principles, however, is their failure to provide
specificity. Instead § 5.04 states that the value of the award "should be
determined by a rule of statewide application that sets a presumptive award
of periodic payments calculated by applying a specific percentage to the
difference between the incomes the spouses are expected to have after
dissolution."[47]This percentage is called the durational factor, which "should
increase with the duration of the marriage until it reaches a maximum
value set by the rule."[48] Under § 5.06 an award under this previous section
can be for a specific time or can be indefinite, but a presumption arises that
the term should be indefinite "when the age of the obligee, and the length

---

[45] A.L.I., *Principles of the Law of Family Dissolution* §§ 5.03(2), (3) (2002).
[46] *Id.* § 5.04.
[47] *Id.*
[48] *Id.*

of the marriage, are both greater than a minimum value specified in the rule.'[49] If this presumption does not apply, however, then "the term is fixed at a duration equal . . . to the length of the marriage multiplied by a factor specified in the rule . . .'[50] It becomes readily apparent that the amounts of the awards from state to state will vary greatly, depending on the numerical value of the factors and the percentages each state adopts.

The practical results of the Principles are difficult to determine because of this lack of specificity. In general, though, one might be able to predict that in long term marriages, in which there is significant income disparity, a presumption of indefinite payments is more likely. In marriages that involve minor children, the formula also suggests that payments will be ordered, even in marriages of short duration. Both of these results would change the current trend in spousal support payments in the United States.[51]

### 2.2.2. A minor retreat from no-fault divorce –Covenant marriages

Three states, Louisiana, Arizona and Arkansas, have retreated from no-fault divorce by adopting legislation referred to as "covenant marriages."[52] Under these statutes, if the couple signs a covenant marriage agreement when they marry, they voluntarily restrict the grounds for divorce to fault-based grounds, or, in the alternative, they agree to live separate and apart for a specified period of time before being able to file for a divorce. The rationale behind covenant marriages is that no-fault divorce has made divorce too easy, resulting in a myriad of societal problems, which are blamed on easy divorce. According to this rationale, if couples agree when they marry that they will only divorce if fault grounds exist or they have been separated for the required period of time, then there will be more commitment to the marriage, fewer divorces, thereby lessen these societal ills. Although covenant marriages have been recently enacted, the initial statistics show that few couples opt for the covenant marriage alternative. Most covenant marriages have been the result of couples who are already

---

[49]   *Id.* § 5.06
[50]   *Id.*
[51]   GARRISON, *supra* note 35, at 130-31. Professor Harry D. Krause notes that the ALI Principles "would on the one hand, impose greatly increased financial responsibility on divorce (thus strengthening marriage) when, on the other hand, the same ALI recommendations would allow most marital responsibilities to be negated by voluntary marital contract [under Chapter 6, Domestic Partners and Chapter 7, Agreements], thus weakening marriage." HARRY D. KRAUSE, "Marriage for the New Millennium":, 34 *Fam. L. Q.* 271, 293 (2000).
[52]   La. Rev. Stat. Ann. § 9:307 (1991), Ariz. Rev. Stat. § 25-903 (1999), Ark. Code Ann. § 9-11-808 (2001).

married converting their prior marriages to covenant marriages. One possible negative result of covenant marriages may be the recurrence of migratory divorces, should a person in a covenant marriage wish to terminate the marriage but he or she does not care to wait the required time period for living separate and apart and neither party has committed a fault ground for divorce. This individual can easily travel to another state, establish domicile and then obtain a divorce under that second state's no-fault grounds.

## 3. THE UNIFICATION AND HARMONIZATION OF LAWS RECOGNIZING AND ENFORCING SISTER STATE DECREES

Unlike the history of the UMDA, several uniform acts have been widely adopted, with little amendment or variation among the states. These uniform acts deal with establishing jurisdiction for support[53] and child custody cases,[54] and for the interstate enforcement of any order issued in compliance with the uniform acts. The U.S. Congress is primarily responsible for the successful enactment of these uniform acts, because Congress has required a state to adopt the acts in order to receive certain federal funds. For example, every state has adopted the Uniform Interstate Family Support Act (UIFSA), because only those states that have adopted this Act will receive federal funds to assist the state agencies in collecting child support. Although the main focus of UIFSA is the enforcement of child support orders, spousal support orders also are covered under the Act. The Act prevents numerous states from issuing inconsistent orders of spousal support, which was discussed previously in section 1.2.4. According to § 211 of UIFSA, once a court, which has appropriate personal jurisdiction, grants a spousal support award, that court continues to retain jurisdiction to modify the support order, to the exclusion of all other courts in the United States. This statute prevents courts in other states from modifying the original support order; instead the other courts are required to enforce the original order.[55] Consequently, where the uniform acts have failed in unifying and harmonizing substantive family law principles, Congress, with its control over the disbursement of federal funds to the states, has been

---

[53]  Unif. Interstate Family Support Act, 9 *U.L.A.* 235 (1998).
[54]  Unif. Child Custody Jurisdiction Enforcement Act, 9 *U.L.A.* 649 (1998).
[55]  Another uniform act that has been widely accepted deals with enforcement of other states' decrees, the Uniform Enforcement of Foreign Judgments Act, 13 *U.L.A.* 160 (2002), which has been enacted in 48 states. On the other hand, the Uniform Divorce Recognition Act, 9 *U.L.A.* 23 (1999) promulgated in 1947 to deal with migratory divorce, was adopted in only one state; the NCCUSL withdrew this second Act in 1978 as obsolete.

highly successful in persuading the state legislatures to adopt uniform acts setting out jurisdictional and enforcement provisions for spousal support orders.

## 4. CURRENT STATUS OF U.S. LAW CONCERNING THE GROUNDS FOR DIVORCE AND THE LAW OF SPOUSAL SUPPORT

In order to track family law within the different states, the American Bar Association's family law journal, the Family Law Quarterly, publishes an annual survey, Family Law in the Fifty States, which updates the current status of the law. One of the features of the survey is a series of charts that set out the general legal principles of each state in key areas. Among these charts is a chart covering the grounds for divorce and residency (domicile) requirements (Chart 4) and a chart on spousal support factors (Chart 1). These charts also are easily accessible on-line on the ABA website.[56] According to the chart on ground for divorce, 16 states have no-fault as the sole ground for divorce, 31 states have added a no-fault ground to the traditional fault grounds for divorce, 10 states have incompatibility as a ground for divorce, 25 states have as a ground for divorce living separate and apart for a specified period of time and 38 states also provide for a judicial decree of separation. The longest requirement for domicile before a court has jurisdiction to grant a divorce is one year, but several states have no specific time requirement; these states merely require a party to show he or she is a bona fide domiciliary.

The spousal support chart sets out that 39 states have a statutory list of factors the court considers in awarding support, 24 states do not consider marital fault as a factor as opposed to 29 states in which marital fault is a factor.[57] In addition, 41 states consider the standard of living of the couple in making an award and in 27 states the status of a spouse as a custodial parent is a relevant factor in making a spousal support order.

Although the Family Law Quarterly simplifies the difficult task of determining the laws in the various states, the lack of unification and harmonization of family law principles in the United States makes the work of a family law attorney a very localized and specialized practice.

---

[56] See http://www.abanet.org/family/familylaw/tables.html.
[57] Some states have statutes that state marital fault is not a factor in awarding spousal maintenance, although the court may consider dissipation of marital assets as a factor in awarding spousal support. These states are included in the number of states that use traditional fault factors, i.e. adultery, in determining support awards.

## 5.  WHAT CAN BE LEARNED FROM THE UNITED STATES EXPERIENCE?

There are several observations that can be made about the experience of the United States in attempting to unify and harmonize family law principles. First of all, formal attempts to unify substantive family law principles have been, for the most part, unsuccessful, as can be seen from the ABA hostility toward the proposed Uniform Marriage and Divorce Act. This hostility existed in spite of the fact that every state had representation on the NCCUSL, the drafters of the UMDA. One might come to the conclusion that if the U.S., with a national identity for its citizens, is incapable of producing a uniform act that is acceptable to all of the states, it is far less likely that the European Union, with its great diversity of cultures and populations among its member countries, will be successful in unifying and harmonizing family law principles. Part of this observation is true. Studies have shown that even if a legislative body enacts changes in family law principles, if the law does not reflect the public values and familial expectations, true change will not occur.[58] On the other hand, while the ABA and NCCUSL were embroiled in acrimonious debates over the elimination of marital fault in the UMDA, state legislatures began to enact statutes that adopted no-fault divorce grounds, with the majority of the states doing so in less than a 10 year period. Although the state statutes were not uniform in language, they were uniform in adopting a clear departure from former legal principles about family dissolution. A similar convergence of legal principles in Europe is highly likely, because of the emergence of a more clearly recognizable European identity and citizenry, coupled with the rapid cross-pollenization that is occurring through electronic research and communication.

In addition, adoption of uniform acts that recognize and enforce sister state decrees of divorce and spousal support have been highly successful in the U.S., in part because states want to be assured that their decrees will be given full faith and credit, and in part because of the control the U.S. Congress has over federal funds paid to the states. Finally, the Supreme Court has become more actively involved in protecting due process and equal protection rights of U.S. citizens, thereby establishing a minimum standard of protecting and recognizing individual rights in the family law arena. Therefore, some advances toward harmonization of family law principles in the U.S. have occurred through the use of all three models being debated at this conference – on the level of substantive legal changes,

---

[58]   GARRISON, *supra* note 35, at 123.

in the area of procedural recognition and the enforcement of foreign decrees and, finally, through the use of individual (human) rights.

That is not to say that there are not major differences among the states in family law principles. There is existing in the United States, at the same time, movements toward harmonization and unification, as well as distinct movements that create irreconcilable conflicts among the states and their citizens. Take, for example, the situation posed at the beginning of this article of the same-sex couple who go to Vermont and form a civil union, which is a parallel legal institution to marriage. In one such case in the U.S. the couple later sought a dissolution of the civil union in the state of Connecticut. The appellate court refused to recognize the civil union and denied any relief to the parties.[59] Without this recognition, the only way the couple can legally dissolve the relationship is for one of them to return to Vermont, establish domicile for at least 6 months, and then petition the Vermont court for a dissolution of the civil union. The irony of the Connecticut court decision is that it makes civil unions much more enduring and difficult to exit than heterosexual marriage. By applying the logic behind covenant marriages – i.e. if the institution is difficult to exit, then it should create more commitment by the couple to make the relationship work – one could argue that the Connecticut court is in fact strengthening Vermont civil unions by refusing to dissolve them! This result might be humorous, but for the fact that these are real people's lives – and the irreconcilable legal conflicts of persons who are treated as though they have a parallel institution to marriage in one state and are deemed criminal sodomites in another state, have real emotional, psychological, and financial consequences for these parties and any children they may be raising together. It is because of these very real consequences that the work of the Commission on European Family Law is important and commendable – for it is the real lives of real people that matter.

---

[59]    Rosengarten v. Downes, 802 A. 2d 170 (Conn. App. 2002).

**PART FIVE –SPECIFIC ISSUES**

**1. NEW PROBLEMS OF COHABITATION**

# STRENGTHENING THE TIES THAT BIND: PROPOSALS FOR A CHILD-CENTERED EUROPEAN DIVORCE LAW

ASPASIA TSAOUSSIS-HATZIS[*]

## 1. INTRODUCTION

At the end of the 1960s, divorce reformers in Europe and the United States initiated sweeping changes in divorce law, introducing no-fault grounds for the dissolution of marriage. The new statutes either permitted divorce on the basis of a long period of separation or on grounds of the irretrievable breakdown of the marital relationship. Over thirty years have passed since this strong no-fault wave swept across both sides of the Atlantic – and over these years it has become obvious, through an overwhelming body of empirical evidence, that this so-called "silent revolution"[1] had perhaps the largest number of silent victims than any other revolution in the 20th century. In the United States alone, no-fault divorce led to the impoverishment of millions of women and children.

What is interesting is that the academics, legal practitioners and judges who initiated the reforms had modest goals: they believed that the removal of fault grounds would simply modernize the process of divorce, reducing the adversarial character of divorce proceedings and protecting their integrity, which was threatened by the collusion of couples, a necessary evil under fault regimes. Despite the good intentions of the reformers, the net effect of no-fault legislation was that it lifted most (if not all) barriers to exit from marriage. On the level of symbolic legal expression, no-fault divorce provided a signal to prospective spouses that marriage was not a lifelong commitment after all. As a result, spousal commitment norms were weakened,[2] bringing about a gradual erosion of parental commitment

---

[*] I am indebted to Anders Agell, Ismini Androulidakis-Dimitriadis, Masha Antokolskaia, Brian Bix, Katharina Boele-Woelki, Olga Dyuzheva, Aristides Hatzis, Nancy Maxwell, and Ian Sumner for their helpful comments. Address all correspondence to: atsaoussi@abanet.org.
[1] The term was coined by HERBERT JACOB (1988).
[2] An example of a spousal commitment norm is the standard of sexual fidelity in marriage. The sanctions against the violation of this norm have varied in different social periods and time settings, but the content of the norm has remained relatively unchanged over time.

Intersentia

271

norms.[3] The no-fault divorce reform dismantled what was an internally coherent system under traditional marriage: a closely interwoven bundle of intrafamilial commitment norms.[4]

Because marriage and family life fall within the domain of intimate relationships, the behaviour of parents and children is governed by informal social norms. Thus, the legal regulation of parental responsibilities creates problems of enforcement. Family law prescribes parental duties and intervenes when parents deviate from accepted norms.[5] Some social norms of parental obligations are more easily implemented, because there is greater consensus regarding their social desirability. For example, legislation applying more stringent standards for the enforcement of child support obligations has met with minimal resistance or controversy. By contrast, other norms cannot be successfully enforced, because they are not well defined. Commitment norms in the broader sense (encompassing both spousal commitment and parent-to-child commitment) present an illustrative example.[6]

These hazy norms are the object of this paper. An overview of the relevant social science literature, which will be presented here, suggests that no-fault divorce has erased the lines that had in the past made these norms recognizable and comprehensible to married men and women. The resulting confusion over which norms to follow in marriage has led to increased family disruption, with all its manifested harmful effects on children. I propose that one way to make commitment norms more concrete and thus legally enforceable, is the introduction of covenant marriage statutes in the context of a unified European marriage law. In parallel, in order to take full account of alternative forms of family life, I would recommend that an analogous dual regime be instituted for registered partnerships.[7] By enhancing the contractual freedom of spouses

---

[3]     According to SCOTT (2000: 1908), commitment norms deter selfish behaviour and encourage the alignment of individual interest with that of the spouse or child.

[4]     SCOTT (2000) posits that family law and marital norms formed an internally coherent system for enforcing parental and spousal obligations; this system "has been dismantled through reforms that can fairly be described as *deregulation* of marital commitment norms" (*id.* at 1905).

[5]     For example, when parents deviate from minimum standards of care, when they violate compulsory school attendance laws, etc. the state intervenes under child abuse laws.

[6]     SCOTT (2000: 1910) explains that commitment norms express as general standards of behaviour what each spouse can expect of the other; because the marital obligation is broader in scope and intimacy than the business partnership or friendship, commitment norms are often particularized in concrete behavioural rules.

[7]     As observed by BUCKLEY and RIBSTEIN (2000: 30), marriage substitutes can facilitate the recognition of same-sex relationships by private parties without extending the full panoply of government subsidies. They further argue that allowing the states to offer a variety of

and partners in regulating the consequences of the formation and dissolution of their union, family law would serve an important pedagogic function: it would direct them towards assuming increased responsibility in their intimate relationships and maintaining a higher standard of care for any children born from their union, be it marriage or any other form of partnership (or domestic relationship).[8]

## 2. CHILDREN AT RISK: SOME ALARMING EVIDENCE

The well-known political theorist William Galston observes "for economic, emotional and developmental reasons, marriage is the most promising institution yet devised for raising children and forming caring, competent, responsible adults" (Galston 1996: 323). Taken from the standpoint of the economic well-being of children, overwhelming empirical evidence indicates that the intact two-parent family is generally preferable to all available alternatives (McLanahan and Garfinkel 1989). First and foremost, the presence of two parents reinforces the function of social control performed by the family. Two parents provide more supervision and support to the children than one parent ever can, but also better and more effective supervision, as each parent serves as a check on the other's tendency to be too permissive or too authoritarian.

For legal sociologists, a second major reason why marriage continues to be the only family arrangement which guarantees "top quality" child-rearing is the presence of the father. Margaret Brinig (2000) explains that in marriage, men are better able to monitor their children's behaviour and to interact with them on a regular basis. This allows fathers to act as role models and to develop more solid emotional bonds with their children. Married men also provide the income that furnishes their children with a sense of economic security.

A series of empirical studies show a steady connection between the absence of fathers and poverty, juvenile delinquency, teenage promiscuity and child

---

marriage rules can lead to "an evolution toward consensus" which will accommodate both sides of the marriage debate: both covenant marriage and same-sex unions (*id.* at 33-36).

[8]    Heterosexual cohabitation and same-sex partnerships (registered or informal) are the two most prevalent "alternative" family forms in the European Union. BRADLEY (2001: 42) argues that in many West-European jurisdictions, the "introduction of a legal status for heterosexual cohabitation has operated to facilitate recognition of same-sex partnerships". See also COX (2000).

abuse (Margolin and Craft 1989; Blankenhorn 1995; Popenoe 1996).[9] A recent policy study from the U.K. found that the children of single and cohabiting parents are more likely to suffer physical abuse than the children of married couples (Kirby 2002). Children of fatherless families are twice as likely to have behavioural problems, perform less well in school, become sexually active at a younger age, suffer depression and turn to drugs, smoking and heavy drinking.[10]

Divorce itself is a traumatic event for children, causing stress that is harmful to their emotional well-being (McLanahan and Sandefur 1994).[11] A recent overview of empirical studies (Fagan and Rector 2000) suggests that children whose parents have divorced exhibit more health, behavioural, and emotional problems, are involved more frequently in crime and drug abuse, and have higher rates of suicide.[12] These harmful effects have their impact on children even after they have become members of a reconstituted household formed after the remarriage of one divorced parent. Children living in stepfamilies are three times more likely to run away from home than children living with both their natural parents; children in single-parent families are twice as likely to do so (Rees and Rutherford 2001). Finally, researchers at the Institute for Research on Poverty found that a disruption in family structure is associated with more attendance problems during high school and with school continuation decisions after high school (Bethke and Sandefur 1998: 3).

The overall result of these studies seems to be that children from divorced families are on "average" somewhat worse off than children who have lived in intact families. However, Amato (1994) reminds us that these average differences do not mean that *all* children in divorced families are worse off than all children in intact families. Hetherington (1993) finds important variations relating to these average differences: on a measure of behavioural problems, she reports that 90 percent of adolescent boys and girls

---

[9]   However, child abuse is correlated with many other factors, like income and educational levels. The presence of a father *per se* cannot guarantee that the child will not be abused. In fact, there is empirical evidence to suggest that in the United States, child abuse is more frequent in husband-dominated households (BARTLETT and HARRIS 1998: 575).

[10]   It is characteristic that sociologists reviewing the literature identify as the single most important factor in the many social problems presently confronting our societies "the failure of fathers, the fact that men have abandoned their role in the family" (VITZ 2000).

[11]   AMATO and BOOTH (1991) conclude that individuals experiencing "low-stress" parental divorces did not differ appreciably from those who grew up in happily intact homes.

[12]   The correlation between divorce and suicide has long been recognized in the United States and more recently in several European countries. For a series of comparative and cross-national studies, see esp. STACK (1997) and (1998).

in intact families were within the normal range on problems and 10 percent had serious problems that would generally require some type of help; in divorced families, 74 percent of the boys and 66 percent of the girls were in the normal range and 26 percent of the boys and 34 percent of the girls were in the problematic range. In short, although most children in divorced families do not need help, more children in this group than in intact families are likely to need help.

Perhaps more alarming than these behavioural problems are the effects of divorce on children's economic well-being, which have been amply documented over the last few decades.[13] Children of single-parent families, especially those headed by women, are at a disproportionately higher risk of poverty than children of intact families.[14] A recent comprehensive review of over 200 British and American longitudinal studies (Rodgers and Pryor 1998) confirmed that children of separated families tend to grow up in households with lower incomes, poorer housing and greater financial hardship than intact families. They also tend to achieve less in socio-economic terms as adults than children from intact families.

There is also a growing body of evidence on the long-term effects of parental divorce on adult children, as social scientists have increasingly turned their attention to the continuing effects of a parental divorce on individuals over their adult life course.[15] For example, Wallerstein *et al.* (2000) who followed children of divorce in the United States over a period of twenty-five years, found that experiencing divorce has lasting effects in adulthood, affecting personality, the ability to trust, and the ability to cope with change. Other empirical studies associate parental divorce with several other problems in young adults, such as low educational attainment and early childbearing (McLanahan and Sandefur 1994), more premarital

---

[13]  See *e.g.* WALLERSTEIN and KELLY (1980), FURSTENBERG *et al.* (1983), FURSTENBERG (1990) (for a discussion on the changes in the kinship system of children in stepfamilies), FURSTENBERG and CHERLIN (1991), SELTZER (1991, 1994) and more recently THOMPSON and AMATO (1999).

[14]  In the United States, children living with single mothers are five times as likely to be poor as those in two-parent families.

[15]  See especially CHERLIN *et al.* (1998: 247). See also AMATO and KEITH (1991a; 1991b), AMATO *et al.* (1995), AQUILINO (1994), and CHASE-LANSDALE *et al.* (1995) (finding that experiencing a parental divorce before the age of 16 was associated with poorer mental health, but concluding that 89 percent of children of divorce did not suffer clinically significant psychological problems as young adults). For a similar meta-analysis of divorce-related research in West Germany, see in particular RIEHL-EMDE (1992). Longitudinal studies have revealed that young women from divorced families face several psychological difficulties in late adolescence and young adulthood. See KALTER *et al.* (1985); KALTER (1987).

---

cohabitation (Cherlin et al. 1995; Thornton 1991), early marriage and divorce,[16] even a shorter life span.[17]

In its latest report, UNICEF's International Child Development Centre (in cooperation with the Centre for Europe's Children) announced that child poverty rates have increased one-and-a-half times more than the overall poverty rate in the 18 European countries covered by the Report. In all these countries, there are about 150,000 more children affected annually by divorce than there were at the end of the 1980s, bringing the total to more than one million children each year. In the former Communist countries, child poverty has been increasingly associated with a rise in the number and share of single-parent households.[18] This is why in a recent report on child poverty, the European Children's Trust recommended that rather than direct aid, the West should help the expansion of services preventing family breakdown.[19]

The Human Development Sector Unit of the World Bank reports that the dramatic increase in the numbers of children at risk in Central Europe is attributable to dysfunctional family relations and parental inability to provide for children.[20] As a result, the percentage of children aged three years and under who are placed in infant homes has risen over the last few years. Another indicator of greater family vulnerability is the increase in the number of street children.

---

[16] National statistics show that divorce runs 60 percent higher for white women (and 35 percent higher for white men) who are from divorced families than for those from intact families. See especially GLENN and KRAMER (1987); McLANAHAN and BUMPASS (1988); WALLERSTEIN and BLAKESLEE (1989); McLANAHAN and SANDEFUR (1994).

[17] One recent public health report showed a shorter life span among adults whose parents divorced when they were children (SCHWARTZ 1995).

[18] Centre for Europe's Children, "Children at Risk in Central and Eastern Europe: Perils and Promises", Economies in Transition Study, Regional Monitoring Report No. 4, International Child Development Centre UNICEF, Florence, Italy.

[19] According to a report by the European Children's Trust, fifty million children are living in poverty in Eastern Europe and the former Soviet Union. The economic meltdown in 1998 brought about a collapse of any safety nets provided by the old regime. [FIONA WERGE, "Child Poverty Soars in Eastern Europe", BBC News, October 11, 2000].

[20] Statement by ANNETTE DIXON, Director of the Human Development Sector Unit (Europe and Central Asia Region) of the World Bank Group, delivered at the Conference on Children Deprived of Parental Care: Rights and Realities, Budapest, Hungary, October 22-24, 2000.

## 3. THE CONFLICTING INTERESTS OF PARENTS AND CHILDREN UPON DIVORCE

International family law recognizes children's autonomy and their status as independent legal actors. Children have distinct civil, political, economic and social rights under international conventions like the *United Nations Convention on the Rights of the Child*. This becomes particularly important when the interests of parents and children conflict, which is typically the case when parents decide to divorce or when adults lack the ability to be good parents. At the same time, family law acknowledges that children require special legal protection, so that their basic interests and primary needs are fully met. The widely recognized principle of the "best interests of the child" is safeguarded in international conventions (like the Hague Convention of 1996)[21] and in European conventions, as well as in European Community legal instruments and case law.[22]

Since World War II, children's rights in Europe have considerably expanded. The European Community has no doubt played a crucial role in this direction, drafting legal instruments that safeguard children's rights, directing member states to sign and ratify international conventions and taking all appropriate measures for children's empowerment to exercise their lawful rights. One such measure is the appointment of a special Ombudsman for children, who informs them of their rights, counsels them, and may even take legal action on their behalf.

In recent years, children have been granted procedural rights in family proceedings. The object of the European Convention on the Exercise of Children's Rights (signed in Strasbourg on Jan. 25, 1996) was to facilitate the exercise of these procedural rights by ensuring that children are, themselves or through other persons or bodies, informed and allowed to participate in such proceedings, in particular those involving the exercise of parental responsibilities such as residence and access to children.

---

[21]  On 20/11/2001, the Commission of the European Communities presented a proposal for a council decision authorizing the Member States to sign in the interest of the European Community the Convention on Jurisdiction, Applicable Law, Recognition, Enforcement and Cooperation in respect of Parental Responsibility and Measures for the Protection of Children (the Hague Convention, which was concluded on October 19, 1996).

[22]  For example, the Parliamentary Assembly's Recommendation No. 1121 (1990) on the Rights of Children stipulates that children, as human beings who have not attained their majority, "are in need of special assistance, care and protection".

Council Regulation (EC) No. 1347/2000 of May 29, 2000 (better known as *"the Brussels II Convention"*)[23] lays down rules on the jurisdiction, automatic recognition and simplified enforcement of judgments in matrimonial matters and matters of parental responsibility for the children of both spouses. On May 3, 2002, the Commission adopted a Proposal for a Council Regulation concerning jurisdiction and the recognition and enforcement of judgments in matrimonial matters and in matters of parental responsibility, repealing Regulation (EC) No. 1347/2000 and amending Regulation (EC) No. 44/2001 in matters relating to maintenance [COM (2002) 222].[24] The Commission proposes to extend the principle of mutual recognition to all decisions on parental responsibility, abolishing *exequatur* for rights of access, and devising a solution for the return of the child in cases of abduction.

Children rely on adults, most commonly their parents, to make important decisions influencing their lives: their living arrangements, their place of residence, their education, to name but a few. It has been suggested that in this sense, parents act as fiduciaries or trustees of their offspring (Scott and Scott 1995).[25] An expansive interpretation of the term "parental responsibility" as this is used in the legal instruments of the European Union, is fully congruous with this view. Recommendation 1121 (1990) of the Parliamentary Assembly on the Rights of Children recognizes that parental powers on children are derived from "a duty for their protection". Furthermore, in its Preamble, the European Convention on the Exercise of Children's Rights (signed in Strasbourg on Jan. 25, 1996) recognizes the importance of the parental role in protecting and promoting the rights and best interests of children.

---

[23]   *Official Journal* L 160 of 30/06/2000.

[24]   This Proposal integrates the provisions on parental responsibility of Council Regulation (EC) No. 1347/2000, the Commission proposal on parental responsibility presented in September 2001 (*OJ* C 332 of 27.11.2001) and the French initiative on rights of access presented in July 2000 (*OJ* C 234 of 15.8.2000).

[25]   In a similar vein, children are viewed as stakeholders in their parents' marriage. "If children are treated as the key stakeholders in their parents' marriage and as those most at risk in the dissolution of the marriage, then parents, clergy, therapists, judges, and policymakers will be more likely to attend to the claims and interests of children" (WHITEHEAD 1997: 190). Parents arguably have the moral expectation that if they invest in their children, the children will return the favour by providing support and protection in the parents' old age. Such an implicit contract between parent and child was described by WILLIAM BLACKSTONE in the late 18th century. This contract prescribed the parents' duty to provide support, protection, education, discipline and religious instruction in return for the child's duty to provide wages during minority and support and protection in the parents' old age, honour and reverence, subjection, and obedience (BRINIG 1994: 299-300).

The parents' decision to divorce represents a classic case of conflicting interests between adults and children. Under the perspective of children's autonomy, there is a conflict of interests in the strict sense, manifested as a clash of individual rights: the parents' right to divorce, and the child's right to live in an intact home. Under the "parental responsibility" perspective, parents violate their implicit fiduciary agreement to act jointly as care-providers for the child and to provide an environment of emotional stability and economic security.[26]

If we adopt a children's rights perspective, it is obvious that the adults' rights to divorce supersede the children's rights to an intact home in every legal system in the world. The emerging priority of individualism and personal autonomy in both family law and family life since the 1970s has "left the matter of creating and terminating marriages largely to individual choice". (Hafen 1998: 103). Furthermore, after divorce, children cannot enforce contracts regarding child support, visitation or child custody. Since children cannot act as autonomous agents in divorce proceedings, the principle of autonomy is of limited use in this analysis.

A better basis for explaining children's status in divorce is by reference to children's interests. In beginning to formulate an interest-based approach, we turn our attention to another perspective, which views the marriage contract under the prism of economic analysis and children as third parties. As third parties, they do not have a say over how the contract is realized, or over how and when it will end, but have a definite "vested" moral and material interest in the preservation of the marriage. Divorce creates negative externalities (unfavourable third-party consequences) to any children born to the marriage.

Parents and children may have divergent interests, but they also have important shared interests in the continuation of the family and in enjoying the benefits deriving from membership in the family unit. This large area of shared interests may be best understood when thinking of the family in contract terms. The special relationship binding parent and child is a mix of love, altruism, and reciprocity that rests on an implicit covenant

---

[26] Parents also violate their duties as care-providers when they abuse their children, either verbally or physically. In such cases, divorce undoubtedly serves the children's best interests, in a very real sense salvaging children from a highly dysfunctional home environment. In the United States, domestic violence is an aggravated social problem. Recently, a group of studies in Colorado found that nearly one-quarter of welfare applicants reported current domestic abuse; three quarters of them reported that the abuser was the father of their children (GRALL 2000).

between them. Marriage is then predicated on a bilateral exchange of promises to perform.[27] When they become parents, the marital partners are bound by an implied commitment to support their minor children.

Gary Becker, recipient of the 1992 Nobel Prize in Economics for his pioneering work on the family, had in the early 1980s emphasized the benefits of gender-specific specialization within the family unit.[28] He stressed that it is in the joint interest of marital partners to specialize in the joint family production process in such a way as to maximize the output of family "goods", such as children, prestige and esteem, health, education, safety and altruism (Becker 1991). Therefore, children are family-specific and family-produced goods;[29] at the same time, they are connected to other such family-produced goods in an inextricable fashion.

When divorce disrupts family life, children are cut off from these goods and are deprived of any benefits attached to them. They can no longer lay claim to the family's name, prestige or social standing.[30] What is worse, the parents' joint production of social and human capital ceases upon divorce (Teachman et al. 1997). The parents' joint investment in the children's human capital is interrupted, and as a result, children of divorce receive investments unilaterally, from the custodial parent, who has already suffered precipitous losses in his or her economic and social status. Child support payments, even when they are collected regularly, cannot compensate the children for this loss in the flow of social capital.

## 4. STRENGTHENING MARRIAGE FOR THE SAKE OF CHILDREN

Over the last two decades, the negative repercussions of no-fault divorce on women and children in the United States have manifested themselves

---

[27] A basic corollary of contractual freedom is the principle of liability (*pacta sunt servanda*).

[28] But see OKIN (1989) for an approach to the traditional family based on justice rather than on efficiency. See also CARBONE (2000: 227-241) for an interesting analysis of different philosophical approaches to the two-parent family.

[29] Children are the most significant measurable example of *a public good within marriage* (WEISS and WILLIS 1985: 268), or what BECKER calls a "family" commodity (BECKER 1974: 320). If husband A and wife B have two children, the number of children enjoyed by A is the same as the number of children enjoyed by B – two. Within marriage, A cannot choose to have fewer children so that B can have more.

[30] One of the greatest social theorists of the 20th century, JAMES COLEMAN, had called attention to this aspect of the two-parent family. COLEMAN (1990: 595-597) had argued that the presence of both parents in the household is the leading indicator of social capital in the home and that the absence of a parent dramatically deprives the child of many of the benefits associated with the social networks of the absent parent.

with great intensity, alarming social scientists and legal theorists. The ongoing scholarly debate, which is informed by empirical findings and in turn informs marriage and divorce reform policy, has increasingly been launched from the front of a "children-first approach". In the past ten years, many no-fault critics began to advocate restrictions on adult freedom to divorce to protect children from palpable psychological and economic harms (Younger 1981: 88-90; Scott 1990: 29-37; Wardle 1991: 101-102, 113-115). In response, several state legislatures examined the possibility of imposing a modest limitation on the ability of a couple to terminate their marriage if children were involved.

In an effort to reduce high divorce rates, a number of states enacted covenant marriage legislation. The mixed legal system of Louisiana was the first to enact a "Covenant Marriage Act" on July 15, 1997.[31] Arizona was next, with the *Arizona Covenant Marriage Law of 1998*, followed by Arkansas in 2001 (*Covenant Marriage Act of 2001*). Twenty more states are currently in the process of considering the passage of covenant marriage laws, having already introduced relevant bills.[32]

Covenant marriage may generally be described as a voluntary contract between a man and a woman whereby they agree to "opt-out" of the system of no-fault divorce.[33] Covenant marriage legislation allows couples to choose between "regular" or fortified marriage contracts. Covenant marriage laws essentially introduce a dual marriage, dual-divorce system (LaBauve 1997: 424-425). Under one system, the married couple is allowed to obtain a no-fault divorce in six months. Those who choose the more durable form of marriage (the so-called "convenant marriage") could dissolve their union only upon proof that the other spouse has committed adultery, or been imprisoned for a felony, or abandoned the home for a year and refuses to return, or committed sexual or physical abuse on a spouse or a child of one of the spouses. In addition to these four fault grounds, the Covenant Marriage Act includes a no-fault ground by which

---

[31]    On July 15, 1997, the Governor of Louisiana MIKE FOSTER signed House Bill 756 thereby creating Act 1380 (or the "Covenant Marriage Act") establishing "covenant marriages" in Louisiana. It was passed by the state legislature on June 23, 1997, was signed into law on July 15, 1997 and took effect on August 15, 1997.

[32]    Legislation is (or has been) actively proposed in Alabama, California, Georgia, Indiana, Iowa, Kansas, Maryland, Minnesota, Mississippi, Missouri, Ohio, Oklahoma, Oregon, Nebraska, South Carolina, South Dakota, Tennessee, Texas, Virginia, West Virginia and Washington state. In fact, legislation has passed one house, but not both, in Oregon, Georgia, Texas and Oklahoma.

[33]    Already-married couples may designate their marriage to be a covenant marriage.

either spouse in a covenant marriage may obtain a divorce by living "separate and apart" and without reconciliation for a period of two years.[34]

Covenant marriage acts require the couple to recite a declaration in which, among other things, they state that "marriage is a covenant between a man and a woman who agree to live together as husband and wife for so long as they both may live". The prospective spouses further declare that "they have received premarital counselling on the nature, purposes, and responsibilities of marriage" and that if they experience marital difficulties, they will commit themselves to take all reasonable efforts to preserve their marriage.

The covenant marriage acts have met with strong criticism. Some opponents (*e.g.* Kramer 1997) point out that the return to a fault-based option for marriage is out of touch with the nation's traditional values (self-expression, self-fulfilment, self-reliance) and thus invites couples to latch themselves on to a morality that the broader culture does not support. Others, like Krause (2000: 292), characterize the advocates of covenant marriage as "defenders of the past trying to resurrect a concept of marriage that has not been practiced for a generation" and point out that the new laws still provide couples with plenty of opportunity for divorce. Finally, the actual number of couples who have opted for a covenant marriage is currently lower than expected.[35]

Although it is too soon to determine whether these covenant marriage laws will achieve their expected goals,[36] it is certain that providing an option

---

[34]   This particular provision has been criticized as allowing the easy dissolution of a covenant marriage. LABAUVE (1997: 440) writes: "With the availability of living separate and apart for two years as a ground for divorce, the dissolution of a covenant marriage merely requires a greater degree of patience. Further, counseling is an obstacle to obtaining a divorce, but one that can be overcome".

[35]   One year after the introduction of the covenant marriage act (in 1998), a total of 39,544 marriages occurred in Louisiana; of those marriages, only 609 were covenant marriages [*Source*: Louisiana State Center for Health Statistics, National Center for Health Statistics]. In Arizona, in the first 25 months after the enactment of covenant marriage, less than 1 percent of marriages had been covenant marriages. Statewide, 755 marriages were conducted each week. Of these, only two are covenant marriages. Thirteen out of 15 Arizona counties recorded almost no covenant marriage activity in the past 25 months [*Source*: *Arizona Citizen*, March 2001, p. 2].

[36]   Local community premarital counselling programmes have yielded promising results, reportedly reducing divorce rates as much as five to six times faster than the declining divorce rates at the national level (FAGAN 1999: 23). Because local churches have undertaken much of this type of counselling, the continuing debate tends to run along the dividing lines of secularity and non-secularity. For example, covenant marriage critics question the name of the union at issue ("covenant marriage"), which harbours deep religious overtones.

for a stricter form of marriage performs an important educative function, since it directs spouses towards premarital counselling, as well as a signalling function, alerting couples to the possibility of a different kind of marriage premised on commitment. Both of these functions can play a key role in promoting marital stability and ensuring a more harmonious home environment for the rearing of children. Moreover, covenant marriage is an institution that lies within the area of shared interests between adults and children in marriage and divorce. On the one hand, it expands the available options that adult men and women can choose from to regulate their marital relationship and thus it is fully compatible with their individual rights and freedoms, more particularly with the right to personal autonomy. On the other hand, it provides a safety net to children, by minimizing the risk of family disruption.

To be more specific, I identify four major reasons why the option for a covenant marriage should be given serious consideration in any future effort to reconstruct European family law in ways that better serve the interests of children:

(1) According to Buckley and Ribstein (2001), the most significant function of a covenant marriage is to protect spouses and particularly children from the opportunistic spouse who seeks an easy marital dissolution under current no-fault divorce law.[37] It protects against the risk of unilateral opportunism first of all by making divorce available only with the consent of both spouses or upon proof of fault. Katherine Spaht, one of the drafters of Louisiana's covenant marriage law, explains that "[T]he covenant marriage legislation seeks to restore some bargaining power, or leverage, to 'innocent' spouses who have kept their promises and desire to preserve the marriage". (Spaht 2002: 107-108).

A covenant marriage statute has the effect of a "property" rule[38] that forces the wage earner who seeks divorce to buy his way out of the marriage and allows the other spouse to name her price (to evaluate what she stands to lose by divorce). By contrast, under no-fault divorce regimes, the financially weaker spouse is protected by the provisions

---

[37] The spouse who invests more heavily in children usually foregoes valuable opportunities to develop skills that could be sold in employment markets. The spouse who is freed from childcare responsibilities can work outside the home and contribute financially to the marriage. These asymmetric investments, which are reinforced by gender roles, create high risks of opportunism: The "working" spouse (typically the male breadwinner) can withdraw from the marriage after reaping much of the advantage of specific investment in the children, but *before* making his financial contribution. See mainly BECKER *et al.* (1977), COHEN (1987) and SCOTT (1990).

[38] For this distinction, see the classic work by CALABRESI and MALAMED (1972).

on maintenance and child support, that represent a kind of "liability rule". In this case, the spouse depends on legal rules and on their judicial interpretation for an evaluation of her contribution within the marriage. There is strong evidence to suggest that married women, especially homemakers, are not adequately compensated for these investments (Holden and Smock 1991).

(2) A second important function of a covenant marriage is that it encourages the spouses' investment in marriage and in raising children: under a no-fault regime, the spouses tend to under-invest in what economists call "marriage-specific capital". This under-investment might take the form of a weaker emotional commitment to each other and to their children, or it might translate into the partners offering each other little material support or making fewer or no joint material investments, such as buying a house.

(3) A third advantage of a covenant marriage is its "signalling" function for prospective spouses.[39] Agreeing to the possibility of covenant marriage sends out useful information to a prospective spouse. More particularly, it sends a strong signal of commitment and thus facilitates matches between mates who are compatible. Men and women who believe that an important characteristic of a future spouse is his or her commitment to the marriage can locate such a spouse in less time and at lower cost (financial or emotional) under a covenant marriage regime. In economic terms, we would say that prospective spouses under covenant marriage regimes can save on transaction costs in their search for partners in the marriage market.[40] The result is that more efficient matches will occur, making for higher quality marriages. The benefits for any children born to these marriages are clear.

(4) Finally, a covenant marriage statute may act as a deterrent for a divorce surplus, by effectively preventing a significant number of failed marriages. If covenant marriage can reduce divorce rates, then

---

[39] For an early application of the signalling theory to marriage, see BISHOP (1984). More recently, see TREBILCOCK (1999) and the important work of ERIC POSNER on social norms (POSNER 2000), but especially POSNER (1999: 260-262), observing that a menu of marriage options may give rise to signalling problems with third parties: for example, how can the public know whether a particular marriage is a "high-commitment marriage" or in fact one where the parties have contracted to accept "free love" – and hence, how are members of the community to know when to sanction certain behaviours? ROWTHORN (2002: 143-144) concedes that the introduction of a covenant marriage gives rise to interesting signalling issues. For example, how will the existence of a covenant marriage affect the signalling function of ordinary marriage? The answer to this and other questions depends "on the future popularity of covenant marriage".

[40] They "filter out" bad prospective spouses, on the basis of the criterion of willingness to make a commitment.

from a children's interests perspective, this is a socially desirable goal, since a greater number of children are effectively maintained within intact families.

For all these reasons, I propose that covenant marriage should be introduced as an optional marital regime in a future "harmonized" or unified European Family Law. National legislatures should examine the possibility of enacting choice-of-law rules that give the parties the power to specify which marriage regime applies. The requirement that couples receive marriage counselling both prior to marriage and prior to divorce should also be given due emphasis. The Louisiana House of Representatives considered counselling to be the most important weapon for divorce prevention (Carriere 1998: 1703). The purpose of counselling is to help men and women develop realistic expectations for healthy relationships, to understand the meaning of commitment, and to learn some interpersonal skills that can make marriage succeed.

The more general idea of importing more elements of contract law into marriage law[41] would no doubt promote cooperation within marriage by reinforcing informal social norms of reciprocity and discouraging opportunistic behaviour.[42] "Contracts are not as unstable as marriage, in part because the parties understand that the commitment will be legally enforced" (Scott 2000: 1903). Thus, marriage contracts could in the long run reduce the number of divorces, as spouses would be encouraged to invest in the welfare of their families.[43] Furthermore, the increasing contractualization of marriage could have important spill-over effects into other forms of family life, like *de facto* families resulting from cohabiting partnerships, either heterosexual or same-sex. Unmarried partners who exhibit a stronger sense of overall commitment to the partnership would be far better protected under a regime that allows a greater degree of contractual freedom for intimate relationships.

---

[41] "The movement of the progressive societies has hitherto been a movement from Status to Contract". See MAINE 1970 [1861]: 170.

[42] Discussing premarital contracts, WAX (1998: 629) points out that even if a couple did not start out from positions of equal outside options and equal extramarital welfare, "the ability to negotiate a binding antenuptial agreement would still have salutary effects, because it would arrest the bargaining squeeze and eliminate the potential for opportunism that it presents".

[43] As noted by BECKER and NASHAT BECKER (1997: 105), "contracts that increase the security of wives could even reduce the number of divorces by encouraging women who are not interested in pursuing a career to have children earlier and withdraw from the labor force longer while caring for young children".

Aspasia Tsaoussis-Hatzis

Finally, it should be noted that there is a clearly discernible trend toward the privatisation of divorce law across Europe. The recent reform of Swiss divorce law constitutes a characteristic example: under the Federal Act of 1998 reforming the requirements for contracting a marriage and the statutes on divorce, privatisation is a central point. The Swiss judge will normally no longer inquire into the private life of spouses before granting them a divorce; the mutual agreement of the spouses has become the fundamental ground for divorce (Guillod 2000: 359-360).

## 5. PROBLEMS OF ENFORCEMENT OF PRIVATE MARITAL AGREEMENTS

The enactment of an option for covenant marriage is likely to encourage the private ordering of the consequences of marriage and divorce. An increasing number of couples will draft private agreements attaching monetary penalties to divorce, or regulating child custody in case of divorce.

As with all other contractual obligations, problems may arise concerning the enforcement of these agreements.[44] On one level, the existence of a statutory option for covenant marriage will not be a sufficient guarantee that promises made under the effect of this statute will not be breached. On another level, courts might be hesitant to enforce covenant marriages both because of the judicial burden to supervise performance, or because of paternalism concerns about holding the parties to onerous obligations (Buckley and Ribstein 2000: 28).

Courts are generally hard-pressed to enforce any agreement that can be seen as threatening the mandatory and absolute nature of the right to divorce.[45] A way to sidestep this problem is to enact statutes that permit divorce but provide for liquidated damages in some circumstances.[46] A "statutory standard form contract" is more efficient: since its terms are

---

[44] SCOTT (2000: 1917) makes a useful distinction: "The parties understand that marital norms will be enforced on four levels: through individual precommitment to abide by the obligations, through both spousal and community sanctions, and ultimately (if informal mechanisms fail) through legal enforcement".

[45] However, according to BUCKLEY and RIBSTEIN (2000: 28), the expansion of free contracting rights suggests that the courts might overcome their reluctance over time. See also HAAS (1988).

[46] "Even if courts hesitate fully to enforce durable marriages, legislatures might fill the gap by promulgating statutory standard form contracts that spouses could enter into when they marry requiring the party seeking a divorce to pay damages in some circumstances". (BUCKLEY and RIBSTEIN, id.).

mandatory, it provides a greater degree of certainty to the parties with regard to its enforcement. It also reduces the likelihood of potential re-negotiation and thus contributes directly to the increased stability of the relationship.

The contractual approach has already been made available for cohabiting couples in several European jurisdictions. To begin with, the Pacte Civil de Solidarité (PACS), introduced in France in 1999, permits both heterosexual and same-sex partners to regulate by, private contract, their reciprocal obligations of support and assistance, both personal and financial.[47] Furthermore, the Danish registered partnership authorizes a standard form for same-sex couples that provides for such aspects as property in marriage, inheritance, support and maintenance – but not rules relating to children such as custody rights or adoption.[48] It seems clear that the registered partnership laws of the Scandinavian countries aim to regulate the same kinds of legal problems, which arise after the dissolution of heterosexual marital unions.[49]

European family policy needs to look for the common ground between traditional marriage and registered partnership: a shared value that figures prominently on the agenda of both sides of the "marriage debate" is the concern for the fate of children. A characteristic example of a jurisdiction that has successfully constructed family policy on this solid common ground is Norway: cohabiting Norwegian couples who have children together or have lived together for at least two years have many of the same rights and obligations to social security, pensions and taxation as their marital counterparts (Noack 2001).[50] Thus, it would be a serious mistake

---

[47]  The PACS is registered before the *tribunal d'instance*. Its termination similarly takes place either by mutual agreement communicated to this tribunal or unilaterally (a PACS automatically terminates if one party marries). Any household items acquired after the conclusion of the PACS are presumed to be owned in equal shares – as are other items of property. However, these are the default provisions: the law on the PACS leaves room for private agreements in the area of property relations. On termination, there is no default provision for financial assistance or compensation, similar to that available upon divorce. See generally STEINER (2000).

[48]  For a discussion of the domestic partnership laws in Denmark, Sweden and the Netherlands, see GRAHAM-SIEGENTHALER (1998). See also PEDERSEN (1991-92), for an analysis of the rules regulating the separation of same-sex couples in Denmark.

[49]  Of course, as noted by BRADLEY, political culture is a key determinant of legal policy on cohabitation; for example, institutionalized tolerance in the Netherlands "appears to have produced a pragmatism which permeates family law and is wholly consistent with the introduction of registered partnerships" (*id.* at 32).

[50]  NOACK (2001: 115) explains that a main reason why recent amendments have incited little controversy, making the process of converting cohabitation from deviant to normal behavior in Norway a smooth and pragmatic adaptation to the changing nuptiality patterns, is that

for European policymakers to become consumed in "marriage wars", missing out on the opportunity to construct a marriage law predicated on a unifying normative model: that of the responsible adult partner and parent.

The trend for the contractualization of European marriage law should be encouraged, as it currently seems to be the one that is best suited to encompass and lend legal validation to the full spectrum of familial arrangements. Freedom of contract as applied to interpersonal relationships is congruous with the recent conceptualizations of "family" as a series of everyday practices, what Weeks et al. (2001: 199) call "practices of freedom".[51] Sociologists studying the family have repeatedly called attention to the fluidity of family structures and intimate relationships. As families are going through a period of transition from one set of norms to another, "families of blood" will increasingly be replaced by "families of choice" (*id.* at 11).

European marriage law should be restructured along two major axes:
(a) the expanded freedom of the partners to enter into voluntary agreements regarding the consequences of marriage and divorce,[52] and
(b) if divorce occurs and children are involved, the introduction of statutes orienting the courts to enforce those aspects of the marital contract that are in the child's best interests. Thus, parents will be prevented from using contract as a mechanism for eschewing family-based financial obligations. This new normative model of increased responsibility will hopefully lead to greater stability of both marital and non-marital relationships.

---

the target of the reforms has been only the most marriage-like cohabitations. "To equalize cohabiting couples with common children and cohabiting couples whose relationship has lasted for some time has probably been an important contribution to restoring a fair distribution of rights and obligations in the society". (*Id.*) Of course, Norway has one of the highest cohabitation rates in Europe: the proportion of cohabiting Norwegian women aged twenty to thirty-nine is more than twice the percentage in Great Britain.

[51] As explained by WEEKS *et al.* (2001: 38), "We live family rather than dwell within it. [...] Family is what we do".

[52] This includes the freedom to renegotiate when changed circumstances make particular aspects of the original agreement onerous for one party. Discussing recent trends of cohabitation in Germany, OSTNER (2001: 92) notes that "[T]he shift towards *Lebensformen* stresses options and choices and hence the possibility continuously to revise past decisions".

## 6. CONCLUSION

Maclean and Eekelaar (1997) argue that parenthood, rather than marriage, is emerging as the central mechanism through which moral principles are converted into legal and social obligations. "Whatever the changes in lifestyles, the real purpose of giving special legal status to marriage and family remains what it has always been: The provision of our first-choice setting for the protection and raising of children" (Krause 2000: 299).

Covenant marriage statutes offer an option for reinforcing parenthood, because they can "bundle together" spousal commitment and parental commitment norms. Such statutes may act as an effective deterrent for divorce, may effectively protect children, and may have multiple incentive effects on other marriages.[53] Furthermore, if covenant marriage statutes are designed with a strong emphasis on contractual freedom, they will pave the way for a growing legal recognition of the rights and obligations governing "alternatives to marriage".[54]

Regardless of the existing marital regime, there will always be a number of marriages that will be entered into hastily – marriages that exemplify the well-known expression "marry in haste, repent at leisure". But a greater number of married couples will be *educated* into marriage, and a greater number of spouses will be protected from opportunistic partners seeking a low-cost exit to family responsibilities. A general culture that has gone from divorce destigmatization to divorce acceptance needs more precise legal definitions of what marriage is and what it entails. More importantly, family law should strengthen norms of parental obligation, encouraging parents to identify their own interest with that of their children.

Family policy within a unified Europe should adopt and promote any and all measures designed to reinforce parents' active and continued involve-

---

[53] Incentive effects are discussed by BRINIG and BUCKLEY (1998a), who point out that the courts have apparently failed to see that their dissolution decisions have important incentive effects on other marriages.

[54] It seems that a necessary stage of this course towards full recognition is the situation whereby "free unions" achieve legal status by imitating the legal effects of marriage. The paradox is the trade-off that appears to exist between legal recognition and social recognition. A greater degree of legal recognition is actually a pyrrhic victory, since it has served to fortify the traditional matrimonial model. Describing the process by which the "*union libre*" in France became a non-deviant alternative to formal marriage, GLENDON (1977: 91) writes of traditional marriage: "No longer bothering to look down on its adversaries, it has transformed them in its own image". This danger can be minimized by a legislative expansion of the contractual freedom of all marriage-like relationships (including traditional marriage).

ment in their children's upbringing. If such measures strengthen the two-parent family, this should not be viewed by the legislator as a goal that is incompatible or even disparaging to alternative forms of family life. The question should not be how to substitute marriage, but how to promote emotional maturity and economic sufficiency in any family arrangement that includes children.[55]

Schneider (1992) has posited that in family law, the state does not intervene directly, but rather creates or (more often) supports social institutions which are thought to serve desirable ends. He describes this as the "channelling function" of family law. Building on this idea, Carbone (1997) has argued that the challenge for public policy is the rebuilding of a family-friendly infrastructure that forges the link between state policy and a moral code that takes children's interests into account.

The introduction of covenant marriage in European family policy will arguably prove more effective compared to the United States, because the European Union can boast of a strong infrastructure of family support.[56] European countries have generally provided the proper incentives for the maintenance of the intact family. A prime example is the fact that most European economies have fiscal policies of support for marriage, through joint taxation. Furthermore, two of the most significant social problems associated with marital stability, namely domestic violence and poverty, have mobilized the concern of official European Union organs and many other organizations that have taken measures towards their alleviation.[57]

---

[55] This is the idea that KRAUSE expresses so appropriately in the epilogue to his article (KRAUSE 2000: 298): "Come to Think of It, Marriage Isn't Really the Important Issue –Children Are". OSTNER (2001: 92) observes that in Germany, the notion of plurality of living forms and options has entered the political arena, having shaped the meaning of parenthood and the family: "A family is where children are".

[56] In the spring of 1998, CERIDWEN ROBERTS, Director of the Family Policy Studies Centre, had remarked: "The USA offers no model of family well-being for us to follow. Family breakdown indicators of divorce, extra marital births, child poverty, mental illness, school underachievement, crime and disorder and welfare dependency are distressingly high. And the US infrastructure of family support is low. There is no equivalent of child benefit, few people have access to significant paid maternity leave, the quality of formal child care is largely unregulated and millions of children have no access to free quality health care;", "A budget for all families?", Editorial in *Family Policy*, Bulletin of the Family Policy Studies Centre, Spring 1998.

[57] Discussing the American government's use of welfare reform legislation to carve out a stronger role in promoting marriage, KOPPELMAN (2002: 13) writes that preventing domestic violence "is a key reason that many liberals oppose a welfare policy that rewards those who marry or punishes those who do not". Women's advocacy groups also oppose such efforts. LAURIE RUBINER, of the National Partnership for Women and Families, comments: "The mission of welfare reform should be to reduce poverty and help people achieve economic

For both cultural and political reasons, the European safety net has been extended to include actions towards the resolution of these problems in a manner that has proven more successful than similar efforts undertaken in the United States.

More importantly, comparative family law has facilitated the borrowing and exchange of "workable" and effective legal institutions between European countries. A primary example is the joint custody regime of Sweden,[58] introduced by Bill 1997/1998, which entered into force on October 1, 1998. The Bill places greater emphasis on the principle of the best interests of the child and aims to assist parents in reaching agreements concerning custody and access to children (Saldeen 2000: 352). This regime can function as a model for other EU memberstates, as it has been shown to lead to increased involvement in children by both parents after family break-up (Bernhardt 1996). Germany also introduced joint custody as the default regime in 1997.[59]

Therefore, the establishment of joint custody as the preferred regime is another pro-family measure that a unified European Family Law should consider adopting in order to ensure continued cooperation between the former spouses in making important decisions about their children.[60] As

---

independence, not to engage in social engineering or discrimination against families that do not meet a particular ideal about family composition…" (id.).

[58] In Sweden, after divorce or separation, parents retain joint custody of their children according to a law introduced in 1983, unless one of them files for the annulment of joint custody. Since October 1998, the court can decide about continued joint custody according to the child's best interest even if one of the parents objects. The court also has the power to decide on the child's place of residence (including joint physical custody) against the will of one of the parents. However, an unintended negative consequence of this regime appears to be the rise in the divorce rate: a recent study found a significant (30%) increase in the risk of family disruption since the introduction of joint custody for children (OLÁH 2001). OLÁH explains this increase as follows: "Perhaps as the new rule gave parents a better chance to remain an active parent even if the children did not live with them permanently after the family breakup, parents felt less obligated to stay in a union which they found unsatisfactory". (id. at 124).

[59] In September of 1997, because of rising concern over bitter and often public custody disputes, the German Parliament passed a new "Childhood Rights Bill", with a majority that crossed all party boundaries. Under the Bill, in cases of separation, the custody of the children should not be assigned to one of the parents, but rather to both of them – regardless of whether they are married or not. MATUSSEK (1997: 84) writes that "the goal of the new Bill, to share parenting and custody between both parents, presupposes a wealth of goodwill – and that is often precluded in the fight over the child".

[60] Important issues that parents have to agree upon include the children's residence, education, extracurricular activities, etc. See SELTZER (1991) for an overview of custody arrangements with respect to their influence on children's well-being. Finally, see MACCOBY and MNOOKIN (1992), whose study suggests that once divorce proceedings are over, both

noted by Schiratzki (1999: 27), the presumption of joint custody in all cases except in cases of abuse or real animosity discourages litigation; instead, it encourages parents to seek cooperation talks and to work out custodial arrangements that serve the child's best interests. Joint custody laws have been correlated with lower divorce rates (as predicted by bonding theories), as well as with higher child-support ratios (as predicted by monitoring theories).[61]

The Nordic countries have offered viable models of reconciling workplace and domestic responsibilities, and lessons can be learned from France and Austria in terms of improved child support policies. Despite existing problems, the welfare umbrella in the European Union has been more inclusive of those segments of the population that are in greater need of social protection. This will no doubt facilitate EU countries in reaching consensus about adequate family policy for a unified Europe. More importantly, a comprehensive welfare system geared to the resolution of other social problems closely connected to the quality of family life, will guarantee a more effective implementation of family policy.

Policymakers across Europe would readily agree that the nurture of children should be a primary objective of every civilized society.[62] But it might prove more difficult to reach agreement on the values, which our civilized European societies should embrace and promote.[63] Encouraging institutions that allow adults to be better care-providers for their children requires a clear shift in our prioritisation of values: it requires that we recognize the limits of individual autonomy for the sake of those who

---

mothers and fathers drifted toward more traditional residential arrangements, in which mothers had primary child-care responsibility.

[61] See BRINIG and BUCKLEY (1998b). For an earlier feminist defence of joint custody, see BARTLETT and STACK (1986), arguing that the affirmative assumption that both parents will take important roles in the care of their children is essential to any realistic reshaping of gender roles within parenthood.

[62] The Parliamentary Assembly of the European Union characteristically notes that a society's vitality depends on the opportunities it offers its younger generation for growth and development in safety, self-realization, solidarity and peace [Recommendation No. 1121 (1990)].

[63] American social scientists and commentators agree that American society places individual autonomy high in the ranking of social values. THEODORA OOMS (2002) observes: "Most people regard decisions to marry, divorce, and bear children as intensely private. Any policy proposals that hint at coercing people to marry, reinforcing Victorian conceptions of gender roles, or limiting the right to end bad marriages are viewed as counter to American values of individual autonomy and privacy".

depend on us for care and protection.[64] The question then is, "can we be civilized enough to put our children first?"

## BIBLIOGRAPHY

AMATO, PAUL R. 1994. "Life-span Adjustment of Children to their Parents' Divorce." *The Future of Children* 4: 143-164.

AMATO, PAUL R. and ALAN BOOTH. 1991. "Consequences of Parental Divorce and Marital Unhappiness for Adult Well-Being." *Social Forces* 69: 895-914.

AMATO, PAUL R. and BRUCE KEITH. 1991a. "Parental Divorce and Adult Well-Being: A Meta-Analysis" *Journal of Marriage and the Family* 53: 43-58.

AMATO, PAUL R. and BRUCE KEITH. 1991b. "Parental Divorce and the Well-Being of Children: A Meta-Analysis." *Psychological Bulletin* 110: 26-46.

AMATO, PAUL R., S.L. LOOMIS and ALAN BOOTH. 1995. "Parental Divorce, Marital Conflict, and Offspring Well-being During Early Adulthood." *Social Forces* 73: 895-915.

BARTLETT, KATHARINE T. and CAROL B. STACK. 1986. "Joint Custody, Feminism, and the Dependency Dilemma." *Berkeley Women's Law Journal* 2: 9-41.

BARTLETT, KATHARINE T. and ANGELA P. HARRIS. 1998. *Gender and Law: Theory, Doctrine, Commentary.* 2d ed. New York: Aspen Law and Business.

BECKER, GARY S. 1974. "A Theory of Social Interactions." Journal of Political Economy 82: 1063-1093.

BECKER, GARY S. 1991. *A Treatise on the Family.* 2d ed. Cambridge, MA: Harvard University Press.

BECKER, GARY S., ELISABETH M. LANDES and ROBERT T. MICHAEL. 1977. "An Economic Analysis of Marital Instability." *Journal of Political Economy* 85: 1141-1187.

BECKER, GARY S. and GUITY NASHAT BECKER. 1997. *The Economics of Life: From Baseball to Affirmative Action to Immigration, How Real-World Issues Affect Our Everyday Life.* New York: McGraw-Hill.

BERNHARDT, E.M. 1996. "Non-Standard Parenting Among Swedish Men." In: U. BJÖRNBERG and A.-K. KOLLIND (eds.), *Men's Family Relations,* pp. 91-102. Stockholm: Almquist & Wicksell International.

---

[64] BUCKLEY and RIBSTEIN (2001: 574) point to the symbolic value of a covenant marriage, as "states endorse the primacy of commitment and responsibility over individual freedom and love". Although this is a nascent attempt to reverse the tide of no-fault divorce in America, it is a good beginning. As ROWTHORN (1999: 688) observes: "Britain and other European countries could follow this example, rather than wait until things get as bad as they are in America".

BETHKE, LYNNE and GARY SANDEFUR. 1998. "Disruptive Events During the High School Years and Educational Attainment." Discussion Paper no. 1168-98, August 1998. Institute for Research on Poverty.

BISHOP, WILLIAM. 1984. "'Is He Married?' Marriage as Information." *University of Toronto Law Journal* 34: 245-263.

BLANKENHORN, DAVID. 1995. *Fatherless America: Confronting Our Most Urgent Social Problem.* New York: Basic Books.

BRADLEY, DAVID. 2001. "Regulation of Unmarried Cohabitation in West-European Jurisdictions –Determinants of Legal Policy." *International Journal of Law, Policy and the Family* 15: 22-50.

BRINIG, MARGARET F. 1994. "Finite Horizons: The American Family." *International Journal of Children's Rights* 2: 293-315.

BRINIG, MARGARET F. 2000. *From Contract to Covenant: Beyond the Law and Economics of the Family.* Cambridge, MA: Harvard University Press.

BRINIG, MARGARET F. and F.H. BUCKLEY. 1998a. "No-Fault Laws and At-Fault People." *International Review of Law and Economics* 18: 325-340.

BRINIG, MARGARET F., and F.H. BUCKLEY. 1998b. "Joint Custody: Bonding and Monitoring Theories." *Indiana Law Journal* 73: 393-427.

BUCKLEY, FRANK H. and LARRY E. RIBSTEIN. 2000. "A Choice-of-Law Solution to the Marriage Debates." Working Papers in Law and Economics: Working Paper No. 00-11 (Jan. 2000). George Mason University School of Law.

BUCKLEY, FRANK H. and LARRY E. RIBSTEIN. 2001. "Calling a Truce in the Marriage Wars." *University of Illinois Law Review* 2: 561-610.

CALABRESI, GUIDO and DOUGLAS MELAMED. 1972. "Property Rules, Liability Rules, and Inalienability: One View of the Cathedral." *Harvard Law Review* 85: 1089-1128.

CARBONE, JUNE. 1997. "Choosing Between Children's Rights and Triage: Children, the Changing Family and the State". A paper presented at the 9th International Conference on Socio-Economics, Montreal, Canada, July 5, 1997.

CARBONE, JUNE. 2000. *From Partners to Parents: The Second Revolution in Family Law.* New York: Columbia University Press.

CARRIERE, JEANNE LOUISE. 1998. "'It's Déjà Vu All Over Again': The Covenant Marriage Act in Popular Cultural Perception and Legal Reality." *Tulane Law Review* 72: 1701-1748.

CHASE-LANSDALE, P. LINDSAY, ANDREW J. CHERLIN, and KATHLEEN E. KIERNAN. 1995. "The Long-Term Effects of Parental Divorce on the Mental Health of Young Adults: A Developmental Perspective" *Child Development* 66: 1614-1634.

CHERLIN, ANDREW J., KATHLEEN E. KIERNAN and P. LINDSAY CHASE-LANSDALE. 1995. "Parental Divorce in Childhood and Demographic Outcomes in Young Adulthood." *Demography* 32: 299-318.

CHERLIN, ANDREW J., P. LINDSAY CHASE-LANSDALE, and CHRISTINE MCRAE. 1998. "Effects of Parental Divorce on Mental Health throughout the Life Course." *American Sociological Review* 63: 239-249.

COHEN, LLOYD. 1987. "Marriage, Divorce, and Quasi Rents; or, 'I Gave Him the Best Years of My Life'." *Journal of Legal Studies* 16: 267-303.

COLEMAN, JAMES S. 1990. *Foundations of Social Theory.* Cambridge, MA: Cambridge University Press.

COX, BARBARA J. 2000. "The Little Project: From Alternative Families To Domestic Partnerships To Same-Sex Marriage." 15 *Wisconsin Women's Law Journal* 77-92.

FAGAN, PATRICK F. 1999. "How Broken Families Rob Children of Their Chances for Future Prosperity." Washington, DC: Heritage Foundation, Backgrounder No. 1283, June 11, 1999.

Fagan, Patrick F. and ROBERT RECTOR. 2000. "The Effects of Divorce on America." Washington, DC: Heritage Foundation, Backgrounder No. 1373.

FURSTENBERG, JR., FRANK F. 1990. "Divorce and the American Family." *Annual Review of Sociology* 16: 379-403.

FURSTENBERG, JR., FRANK F. and ANDREW J. CHERLIN. 1991. *Divided Families: What Happens to Children When Parents Part.* Cambridge, MA: Harvard University Press.

FURSTENBERG, JR., FRANK F., JAMES L. PETERSON and CHRISTINE NORD. 1983. "The Life Course of Children of Divorce: Marital Disruption and Parental Contact." *American Sociological Review* 48: 656-668.

GALSTON, WILLIAM A. 1996. "Public Morality and Public Policy: The Case of Children and Family Policy." *Santa Clara Law Review* 36: 313-323.

GLENDON, MARY ANN. 1977. *State, Law and Family: Family Law in Transition in the United States and Western Europe.* Amsterdam and New York: North-Holland Pub. Co.

GLENN, NORVAL D. and KATHRYN KRAMER. 1987. "The Marriages and Divorces of the Children of Divorce." *Journal of Marriage and the Family* 49: 811-825.

GRALL, TIMOTHY. 2000. "Child Support for Custodial Mothers and Fathers, 1997." *Current Population Reports*, October 2000, pp. 60-212. Washniton, D.C.: U.S. Census Bureau.

GRAHAM-SIEGENTHALER, BARBARA E. 1998. "Principles of Marriage Recognition Applied to Same-Sex Marriage Recognition in Switzerland and Europe." *Creighton Law Review* 32: 121-146.

GUILLOD, OLIVIER. 2000. "Switzerland: A New Divorce Law for the New Millennium." Andrew Bainham ed., *The International Survey of Family Law 2000*, pp. 357-368. Bristol, UK: Jordan Publishing.

HAAS, THEODORE F. 1988. "The Rationality and Enforceability of Contractual Restrictions on Divorce." *North Carolina Law Review* 66: 879-930.

HAFEN, BRUCE C. 1998. "The Legal Definition and Status of Marriage." In CHRISTOPHER WOLFE ed., *The Family, Civil Society and the State*, pp. 99-117. Lanham, MD: Rowman & Littlefield.

HETHERINGTON, E. MAVIS. 1993. "An Overview of the Virginia Longitudinal Study of Divorce and Remarriage With a Focus on the Early Adolescent." *Journal of Family Psychology* 7: 39-56.

HOLDEN, KAREN C. and PAMELA J. SMOCK. 1991. "The Economic Costs of Marital Dissolution: Why Do Women Bear A Disproportionate Cost?" *Annual Review of Sociology* 17: 51-78.

JACOB, HERBERT. 1988. *Silent Revolution: The Transformation of Divorce Law in the United States.* Chicago: University of Chicago Press.

KALTER, NEIL. 1987. "Long-Term Effects of Divorce on Children." *American Journal of Orthopsychiatry* 57: 587-600.

KALTER, NEIL, BARBARA RIEMER, ARTHUR BRICKMAN, and Jade W. Chen. 1985. "Implications of Divorce for Female Development." *Journal of the American Academy of Child Psychiatry* 24: 538-544.

KIRBY, JILL. 2002. *Broken Hearts: Family Decline and the Consequences for Society.* London: Centre for Policy Studies.

KOPPELMAN, JANE. 2002. "Promoting Marriage as Welfare Policy: Looking at a Public Role in Private Lives." National Health Policy Forum Issue Brief No. 770/February 15, 2002. Washington, D.C.: The George Washington University.

KRAMER, PETER D. 1997. "Divorce and Our National Values." (Editorial) *New York Times*, Aug. 29, 1997, at A23.

KRAUSE, HARRY D. 2000. "Marriage for the New Millennium: Heterosexual, Same Sex – Or Not at All?" *Family Law Quarterly* 34: 271-300.

LABAUVE, MELISSA S. 1997. "Covenant Marriages: A Guise for Lasting Commitment?" *Loyola Law Review* 43: 421-442.

MACCOBY, ELEANOR E. and ROBERT H. MNOOKIN. 1992. *Dividing the Child: Social and Legal Dilemmas of Custody.* Cambridge, MA: Harvard University Press.

MACLEAN, MAVIS and JOHN EEKELAAR. 1997. *Parental Obligation: A Study of Parenthood Across Households.* Oxford: Hart Publishing.

MAINE, HENRY SUMNER. 1970 [1861]. *Ancient Law (Its Connection with the Early History of Society and Its Relation to Modern Ideas).* 10th ed. Frederick Pollock ed. Gloucester, MA: Peter Smith.

MARGOLIN, LESLIE and JOHN L. CRAFT. 1989. "Child Sexual Abuse by Caretakers." *Family Relations* 38: 450-455.

MATUSSEK, MATTHIAS. 1997. "Verlierer sind die Manner." [Men Are the Losers]. *Der Spiegel*, Nov. 17, 1997, at 84-89.

MCLANAHAN, SARA and LARRY BUMPASS. 1988. "Intergenerational Consequences of Family Disruption." *American Journal of Sociology* 94: 130-152.

MCLANAHAN, SARA S. and IRWIN GARFINKEL. 1989. "Single Mothers, the Underclass, and Social Policy." *Annals of the American Academy of Political & Social Sciences* 501: 92-104.

MCLANAHAN, SARA and GARY SANDEFUR. 1994. *Growing Up With a Single Parent: What Helps, What Hurts?* Cambridge, MA: Harvard University Press.

NOACK, TURID. 2001. "Cohabitation in Norway: An Accepted and Gradually More Regulated Way of Living." *International Journal of Law, Policy and the Family* 15: 102-117.

OKIN, SUSAN MOLLER. 1989. *Justice, Gender, and the Family.* New York: Basic Books.

OLÁH, LIVIA Sz. 2001. "Policy Changes and Family Stability: The Swedish Case." *International Journal of Law, Policy and the Family* 15: 118-134.

OOMS, THEODORA. 2002. "Marriage Plus." *The American Prospect*, Vol. 13, no. 7, April 8, 2002.

OSTNER, ILONA. 2001. "Cohabitation in Germany – Rules, Reality and Public Discourses." *International Journal of Law, Policy and the Family* 15: 88-101.

PEDERSEN, MARIANNE H. 1991-92. "Denmark: Homosexual Marriages and New Rules Regarding Separation and Divorce." *Journal of Family Law* 30: 289-293.

POPENOE, DAVID. 1996. *Life Without Father: Compelling New Evidence that Fatherhood and Marriage Are Indispensable for the Good of Children and Society.* New York: Martin Kessler Books.

POSNER, ERIC A. 1999. "Family Law and Social Norms." In Frank H. Buckley ed., *The Fall and Rise of Freedom of Contract.* 256-274. Durham, NC: Duke University Press.

POSNER, ERIC A. 2000. *Law and Social Norms.* Cambridge, MA: Harvard University Press.

REES, GWYTHER and CELIA RUTHERFORD. 2001. "Home Run: Families and Young Runaways". The Children's Society.

RIEHL-EMDE, ASTRID. 1992. "Ehescheidung und ihre Folgen: Bericht óber Forschungsliteratur." *Familiendynamik* 1992 (4): 415-434.

RODGERS, BRYAN and JAN PRYOR. 1998. *Divorce and Separation: The Outcomes for Children.* York, England: The Joseph Rowntree Foundation.

ROWTHORN, ROBERT. 1999. "Marriage and Trust: Some Lessons from Economics." *Cambridge Journal of Economics* 23: 661-691.

ROWTHORN, ROBERT. 2002. "Marriage as a Signal." In Antony W. Dnes and Robert Rowthorn eds., *The Law and Economics of Marriage and Divorce,* pp. 132-156. Cambridge, UK: Cambridge University Press.

SALDEEN, ÅKE. 2000. "Paternity and Custody: Sweden", In Andrew Bainham ed., *The International Survey of Family Law 2000,* pp. 351-356. Bristol, UK: Jordan Publishing.

SCHIRATZKI, JOHANNA. 1999. "Custody of Children in Sweden: Recent Developments.", In Peter Wahlgren ed., *Legal Issues of the Late 1990s [Scandinavian Studies in Law, volume 38],* pp. 255-262. Stockholm: The Stockholm University Law Faculty.

SCHNEIDER, CARL E. 1992. "The Channeling Function in Family Law." *Hofstra Law Review* 20: 495-532.

SCHWARTZ, JOSEPH. 1995. "Sociodemographic and Psychosocial Factors in Childhood as Predictors of Adult Mortality." *American Journal of Public Health* 85: 1237-1245.

SCOTT, ELIZABETH S. 1990. "Rational Decisionmaking about Marriage and Divorce." *Virginia Law Review* 76: 9-94.

SCOTT, ELIZABETH S. 2000. "Social Norms and the Legal Regulation of Marriage." *Virginia Law Review* 86: 1901-1970.

Scott, Elizabeth S. and ROBERT E. SCOTT. 1995. "Parents as Fiduciaries." Virginia Law Review 81: 2401-2476.

SELTZER, JUDITH A. 1991. "Legal Custody Arrangements and Children's Economic Welfare." *American Journal of Sociology* 94: 895-929.

SELTZER, JUDITH A. 1994. "Consequences of Marriage Dissolution for Children." *Annual Review of Sociology* 20: 235-266.

SPAHT, KATHERINE SHAW. 2002. "Louisiana's Covenant Marriage Law: Recapturing the Meaning of Marriage for the Sake of the Children." In Antony W. Dnes and Robert Rowthorn eds., *The Law and Economics of Marriage and Divorce,* pp. 92-117. Cambridge, UK: Cambridge University Press.

STACK, STEVEN. 1997. "A Comparative Analysis of the Effect of Domestic Institutions on Suicide Ideology." *Journal of Comparative Family Studies* 28(3): 304-319.

STACK, STEVEN. 1998. "Marriage, Family, and Loneliness: A Cross-National Study." *Sociological Perspectives* 41(2): 415-432.

STEINER, EVA. 2000. "The Spirit of the New French Registered Partnership Law: Promoting Autonomy and Pluralism or Weakening Marriage?" *Child and Family Law Quarterly* 12: 1-14.

TEACHMAN, JAY D., KATHLEEN PAASCH and KAREN CARVER. 1997. "Social Capital and the Generation of Human Capital." *Social Forces* 75:1343-1360.

THOMPSON, ROSS A. and PAUL R. AMATO. 1999. The Postdivorce Family: Children, Parenting and Society. Beverly Hills, CA: Sage.

THORNTON, ARLAND. 1991. "Influence of the Marital History of Parents on the Marital and Cohabitational Experiences of the Children." *American Journal of Sociology* 96: 868-894.

TREBILCOCK, MICHAEL J. 1999. "Marriage as a Signal." In Frank H. Buckley ed., *The Fall and Rise of Freedom of Contract*. 245-255. Durham, NC: Duke University Press.

VITZ, PAUL C. 2000. *Faith of the Fatherless: The Psychology of Atheism*. Dallas, TX: Spence Publishing Company.

WALLERSTEIN, JUDITH S. and JOAN B. KELLY. 1980. *Surviving the Breakup: How Children and Parents Cope with Divorce*. New York: Basic Books.

WALLERSTEIN, JUDITH S. and SANDRA BLAKESLEE. 1989. *Second Chances: Men, Women, and Children a Decade After Divorce*. New York: Ticknor & Fields.

WALLERSTEIN, JUDITH S., SANDRA BLAKESLEE and JULIA M. LEWIS (2000). *The Unexpected Legacy of Divorce: A Twenty-Five Year Landmark Study*. New York: Hyperion.

WARDLE, LYNN D. 1991. "No-Fault Divorce and the Divorce Conundrum." *Brigham Young University Law Review* 1991: 79-142.

WAX, AMY L. 1998. "Bargaining in the Shadow of the Market: Is There A Future for Egalitarian Marriage?" *Virginia Law Review* 84: 509-672.

WEEKS, JEFFREY, BRIAN HEAPHY and CATHERINE DONOVAN. 2001. *Same Sex Intimacies: Families of Choice and Other Life Experiments*. New York: Routledge.

WEISS, YORAM and ROBERT J. WILLIS. 1985. "Children as Collective Goods and Divorce Settlements." Journal of Labor Economics 3: 268-292.

WHITEHEAD, BARBARA DAFOE. 1997. *The Divorce Culture*. New York: Alfred A. Knopf.

YOUNGER, JUDITH T. 1981. "Marital Regimes: A Story of Compromise and Demoralization, Together with Criticism and Suggestions for Reform." *Cornell Law Review* 67: 45-102.

# VARIATIONS ON THE THEME OF STATUS, CONTRACT AND SEXUALITY: AN ITALIAN PERSPECTIVE ON THE CIRCULATION OF MODELS

MATTEO BONINI-BARALDI[*]

## 1. INTRODUCTION

In January 2002 the Law Commission of Canada made public its report entitled "*Beyond Conjugality*":[1] its aim is best summarized as follows:

> "instead of simply arguing that some relationships that are currently excluded (such as non-conjugal relationships) should be included, we are of the view that it is time to fundamentally rethink the way in which governments have relied on relational status in allocating rights and responsibilities".[2]

What does it mean to "fundamentally rethink" the relevance of personal relationships in the juridical experience? Which values – if any – should substitute the existing ones, and through what means? What are the effects and the risks of different approaches? As is known, there are mainly two legal categories – summarised by the keywords of status and contract – that provide a theoretical framework for this debate. In this paper I intend to present some variations on these well-studied concepts.

Several areas of family law show their influence. The current trend towards deregulation, for example, is founded upon more private autonomy: less reciprocal duties between spouses, recognition and enforcement of prenuptial agreements, incentives to mediate. Also, systems that allow divorce by consent tend to emphasise the contractual nature of marriage and the consequent freedom of the parties to terminate it by mutual agreement.

---

[*]   I am grateful to Larry Cata Backer at Pennsylvania State University, Dickinson School of Law, Bruce MacDougall at the University of British Columbia and Kees Waaldijk at the University of Leiden for their precious comments on earlier drafts of this paper.
[1]   LAW COMMISSION OF CANADA, *Beyond Conjugality* (Ottawa, 2001), available on-line at www.lcc.gc.ca.
[2]   LAW COMMISSION OF CANADA, *supra*, 29.

What we call "recognition" of family models occurs through the use of these legal categories – almost inevitable and certainly culturally prescribed – that in the abstract carry values which are either market – oriented (isolation and conflict) or gendered and hierarchical (dominance and supremacy) and are traditionally linked to opposite ethics, of which the family and the market would be an expression: cooperation v. competition, altruism v. individualism. However, it has been pointed out that family and market (or status and contract) cannot be viewed in the light of an exclusionary logic, because the interconnection between each other has influenced their redefinition and reciprocal construction.[3]

Whichever the choice for regulating family relationships (a few of which are discussed in this paper), fundamental rights recognised as general principles of the EU (recently codified in the Charter of fundamental rights) remind us of the importance of acknowledging the dynamics that drive the censorship of gay and lesbian families; those values make it crucial to avoid reiterating the imposition of silence. In this paper I will first sketch a theoretical background by analyzing a few aspects of contract and status arguments as related to family law; second, I will trace a rough categorization of legislation existing in European countries, and features of the Italian regulation of marriage as well as cohabitation; third, I will analyze the use that European legislation makes of those concepts.

I will conclude that as legislative examples from many countries multiply, the blending that is the result of expanding the reach of the law presents both opportunities and pitfalls for gays and lesbians. In the midst of that whirling construction of systems of law (and, indeed, of normative ethics), where status and contract have both been bolstered, some have attempted to reiterate the view that new regulation (fortunately, they say) lacks the capacity to attract same-sex couples within the "family".[4] In some instances, the injection of more pluralism in the field of the family has truly shaken academics and political actors (France) or still prevents any law reform (Italy), because of the traditional rigidity of the categories (such as status, legitimacy, etc.) on which the system is founded. Community measures that touch upon the family are in turn influenced by developments occurring at the national level.

---

3   MARELLA, M.R., "Il diritto di famiglia fra status e contratto: il caso delle convivenze non fondate sul matrimonio", in *I contratti di convivenza*, ed. by ZOPPINI, A. and MOSCATI, E., (Turin: Giappichelli, 2002) 71, at 104.

4   See *infra*, section 3.

## 2. RELEVANT THEORETICAL CONCEPTS: STATUS AND CONTRACT

Traditional views hold that common law systems place more emphasis on private autonomy, while continental civil law systems accentuate the relevance of public interest. Legally, perhaps, the distinction may be summarized by two keywords: contract and status. The concept of status is deemed to be politically linked to republicanism or communitarianism; it provides fixed and exclusive social and legal boundaries.[5] Legally, it is the sum of rights and responsibilities of the individual that depends on his or her position in the family and in society.[6] It may be seen as a tool to distribute legal capacity, an attribute of "persons" only, on the basis of characteristics defined by the being, rather than the having as in ancient times. Contract, in turn, is defined as democratic and is based on an abstract identity such as the liberal and autonomous self. It allows intentional arrangements of the marketplace and inventiveness of social choice.[7] Rights and responsibilities find their source, on the one hand, in the will of the law, on the other in the will of the parties.

In the context of legal recognition of same-sex families contract, the symbol of freedom and autonomy, might become in certain instances an instrument for redressing subordination caused by values of gender supremacy and heterosexism embedded in the traditional family; in this respect, it could be said that status has played an important role as an instrument for curtailing individual rights. However, the argument has been made that the former is too weak a device for altering power relations existing in society, especially those between men and women; the use of status techniques, therefore, would appear as a minimum safeguard for the weaker partner and as a legitimization of state benefits. It is also possible to imagine that civil status is not limited to the married/unmarried dichotomy, but is able to embrace more options (in Canada: the common law partner; in Europe: the registered partner and others).

The attitude of the political and legal system towards new family models and relationships between adults is magmatic, while the emphasis on (heterosexual) spousal status is reaffirmed by conservative arguments as

---

[5] GOLDBERG-HILLER, J., "'Making a Mockery of Marriage'. Domestic Partnerships and Equal Rights in Hawai'i", in *Sexuality in the Legal Arena*, ed. by Stychin, C., and Herman, D. (London: The Athlone Press, 2000) 113.

[6] ALPA, G., *Status e capacità: la costruzione giuridica delle differenze individuali* (Rome-Bari: Laterza, 1993), at 44.

[7] GOLDBERG-HILLER, J., *supra*, at 116.

a paradigm of excellence, in the light of which same-sex couples are incapable of nothing more than a simulacrum of marriage.[8] New legislative schemes tend to generate conflicting messages.

What conclusion should one draw when a reinterpretation of discrimination (even where progressive laws have been enacted) is made possible by the use of the concept of "contract" that, on the contrary, in our culture carries expectations of more possibilities once foreclosed by the rigidities of status? And what notions of freedom does the use of contract (or its interpretations) in family law entail?

Cohabitation has traditionally been the domain of "contract", freedom, and personal autonomy. However, a distinguished Italian scholar remarked in an article written as early as 1980 that the "legitimate" and the "natural" family were the object of two opposite trends that were both contributing to bringing them closer: deregulation *vis-à-vis* the former, and juridification *vis-à-vis* the latter.[9] In other words, there seems to be both a well-established trend toward deregulation within marriage (considered today as a "privatized" institution as far as the nature of the act is concerned: a contract based on free consent, which embraces respect for the rights of the individual as a person, and rejects the unity of the family as a paramount public good) and a "need for status" with regard to unmarried (opposite-sex or same-sex, more accentuated in the latter) cohabitation.

In Canada, for example, the need to protect the weaker partner who made contributions to a de facto relationship was met in the 1970s on the ground of public policy (through doctrines of constructive trust or unconscionability), somewhat restraining the autonomy of unmarried partners to consider themselves wholly outside the law (family law). In the 1980s and 1990s the legislatures adopted the more far-reaching choice of ascribing spousal status to unmarried opposite-sex partners who cohabited in a marriage-like relationship for a definite amount of time. This choice contributes to the blurring of boundaries between *de jure* and *de facto* relationships, because a factual situation such as living together in a marriage-like relationship becomes the source of a status, which entitles subjective positions *vis-à-vis* third parties (and possibly among partners, too, *e.g.* as far as support obligations are concerned). This evolution from normative to functional definitions of the family is shared by some European countries where

---

8    CALHOUN, C., "Making Up Emotional People. The Case of Romantic Love", in *The Passions of Law*, ed. by Bandes, S. (New York, London: New York University Press, 1999), 217, at 218.

9    ROPPO, E., "La famiglia senza matrimonio. Diritto e non-diritto nella fenomenologia delle libere unioni", (1980) I, *Rivista trimestrale di diritto e procedura civile* 697.

concerns for public policy have been met with the use of legislative models based on (or creating) status (Scandinavian laws). What was the domain of freedom has been subject to regulation applying automatically in order to protect public interests, such as the prevention of exploiting the weaker party; values of responsibility and reciprocal solidarity dominate over individual freedom.

In these reforms it is possible to read a consolidation of spousal status (individual choices with regard to family arrangements are recognized *and* become automatically regulated). In this sense, juridification is understood as an empowering tool, which is able to bring about more equity and social justice.[10] In US common law, however, the courts have had fewer problems in achieving equitable results by enforcing private agreements between unmarried partners that, in Italian case law, were first considered to be against good morals and subsequently have been overwhelmed by the doctrine of *obbligazioni naturali*.[11]

Some would argue that marriage is not private because it is still the only available means for acquiring many public benefits. It is true that marriage is at the core of what we define as spousal status, which provides obligations that find their source in the law itself (*ipso jure*), not in terms freely chosen by the parties. The point of contact, here, is that in both cases what the law seems to value most is, other than the presence of formality, the constant reiteration of the *relationship* that lies at the heart of both marriage and cohabitation: *e.g.* the treatment of children (once called "legitimate" and "natural") is nowadays much the same, both relationships can be dissolved and, in many instances, both are an entitlement to public benefits.

Some have proposed that this relationship could be protected through the application of contractual norms of which critical legal scholars have demonstrated the constant tension between individual interests and the protection of expectations and trust generated in the other party. The proposal is therefore founded upon the idea that contract law is not completely individualistic; on the contrary, it acknowledges several

---

[10]   Nevertheless, there have certainly been many forms of criticism aimed at what ought to be considered marriage-like, and some authors have pointed out the lack of certainty that has resulted from the recognition of cohabitation: DOUGLAS, G., "Cohabitation and Parenthood – From Contract to Status?", in *Cross Currents: Family Law and Policy in the US and England*, ed. by S. KATZ, J. EEKELAAR and M. MACLEAN (Oxford:Oxford University Press, 2000), 231; RYDER, B. & COSSMAN, B., "What is Marriage-Like Like? The Irrelevance of Conjugality" (2001) 18 *Can. J. Fam. L.* 269 ff.

[11]   MARELLA, M.R., *supra*, at 123.

situations that could be used to regulate an ongoing relationship (*e.g.* excessive benefit or unfair advantage as stated in art. 4:109 of the European principles of contract law). As far as intra-family torts are concerned, the argument has been made that the termination of cohabitation by one partner could not only amount to a tortious act (loss of stability), but could also give rise to "an independent claim for breach of contract damages".[12] The matter seems to be relevant as far as the movement of persons across borders is concerned. Depending on the qualification of the relationship in the contract/status continuum, rules of private international law could lead to the application of different substantive laws (*e.g.* the law of contract in lieu of the law of marriage).

## 3. THE USE OF STATUS AND CONTRACT IN EUROPEAN COUNTRIES' PARTNERSHIP LEGISLATION

As far as same-sex couples are concerned, in continental Europe national legislatures have acted in a variety of ways (while some have not acted at all) but all within a rather shared framework. It is well known that in Northern European countries equality for same-sex partners has been identified by means of access to an institution which, although referred to differently from marriage and separate from it, is based on the choice to publicly celebrate and register a private commitment (or contract). I call this model an *institutional recognition* similar to marriage, as opposed to the *interpretive* recognition that has been preferred in Canada[13] (and other common law jurisdictions in Australia) where a *de facto* situation produces automatic legal consequences in its external relations – *i.e.* public benefits – or upon ending the relationship. Registered partnership schemes have been framed as close as possible to marriage, mirroring, for example, the same impediments. To elaborate on the civil status issue, it has been

---

[12]   PATTI, S., "Intra-Family Torts", in *International Encyclopedia of Comparative Law*, vol. IV, *Persons & Family* (Dordrecht, Boston, Lancaster: J.C.B. Mohr (Paul Siebeck), Tubingen and Martinus Nijhoff Publishers, 1998), 3 at 25.

[13]   The avenue chosen has been that of expanding the definition of "spouse". By the mid and late 1990s, when same-sex couples first succeeded in their challenges to this definition, considerable parts of family law and of the welfare system included unmarried opposite-sex cohabitants. The most common strategy to date has been to remain within this system of recognition, based on ascription of spousal status to unmarried partners. Nevertheless, the federal legislature has introduced a new status, that of common-law partner, and is considering more changes as a result of recent rulings in marriage cases in Ontario and Quebec: *Halpern* v. *Canada (Attorney General)*, 12 July 2002, www.sgmlaw.com/userfiles/filesevent/file_1413620_halpern.pdf; *Hendricks* v. *Québec (Procureur Général)*, 6 September 2002, www.jugements.qc.ca/cs/200209fr.html. Quebec has also enacted a civil union law that affords same-sex couples many of the rights and responsibilities emanating from marriage.

forbidden for registered partners to marry a different person without filing a prior application for the dissolution of their union. The provision might be explained by emphasizing that the system resembles a celebration and entails the recognition of status, incompatible with the married status precisely because it is so *similar* to it. These schemes are almost exclusively available to same-sex couples (except in the Netherlands). This again emphasizes their nature as substitutes for marriage in cases where the partners are not allowed to marry; of course, they have been criticized precisely because they have been an instrument for avoiding the opening up of marriage to same-sex couples. The Dutch law of marriage, which allows same-sex couples to celebrate a valid civil marriage, today symbolizes at best the institutional model.[14]

Unlike Canada, in many European countries there has never been such a tight link between same-sex couples and unmarried opposite-sex couples (different is the situation in the Netherlands and other Scandinavian countries). In fact, while approaches to the latter phenomenon vary considerably among countries, newer schemes used for tackling the former (*e.g.* registered partnership) show greater similarities.[15]

Even within a relatively homogeneous legal scenario, European countries today present a variety of statutes concerning partnership recognition that, in turn, reflect different attitudes regarding *de facto* relationships and homosexuality. In general, I would argue that what has been called the "need for status" of relationships outside the reach of the law clashes in certain instances with the inherent heterosexual values upon which the family order was built. Contract, on the other hand, could be too weak a challenge to those values, because it leaves existing dynamics of power untouched. Mixed solutions have also appeared.

In Italy, despite the recent appointment of two Arcigay-Arcilesbica militants as MPs in the 2001 national parliamentary elections, gay and lesbian advocates face difficulties in dealing with mainstream political discourses. Stychin has distilled these discourses with clarity with regard to the French situation. In his view, which *mutatis mutandis* can be extended to Italy as well (and possibly to other continental countries), in France the political discourses employed by the rhetoric of Republicanism are less centred on identities and communities.[16] The idea of the generality and universality

---

[14] Act of 21 December 2000, *Staatsblad* 2001, n. 9 and 10, in force since 1 April 2001.

[15] FORDER, C., "European Models of Domestic Partnership Laws: The Field of Choice" (2000) *Can. J. Fam. L.* 371, at 391.

[16] STYCHIN, C., "Civil Solidarity or Fragmented Identities? The Politics of Sexuality and Citizenship in France" (2001) 10:3 *Soc. & Leg. Studies* 352.

of the law theoretically requires that no particular group enjoys legislation specifically designed for it, neither for conferring privileges nor for imposing burdens or disadvantages. The central concept, Republicanism, entails several assumptions, such as the prohibition of the "politicization of identities", the "central role of the state", an "assimilationist model of citizenship" and the need for individuals to transcend their particular affiliation, a "clear differentiation between public and private spheres" and the privatization of cultural difference, as well as a universalist, neutral, liberal vision of the Republic. Equality is expressed through the language of universality, which resists any claims to difference. The new form of contract (PACS) passed for regulating certain aspects of the "*vie commune*" has finally been adopted in the name of "social utility" rather than individual rights. The work of some European scholars in the field of the family is nowadays focused on showing that human rights (such as equality, or respect for private life) are paramount in a pluralistic context, and should assist the legislature in enacting appropriate legal reforms.[17]

However, as remarked by Borrillo, the French legislators have forcefully emphasized the (moral) differences between heterosexuality and homosexuality, which have underpinned the need to "dematrimonialize" the new PACS as far as possible, allowing the observer to conclude that a certain kind of universality might conceal a hierarchy.[18] Again, the view of many is that any lesser status than the married one does not satisfy substantive equality.

My understanding is that the PACS was meant to be "quasi-matrimonial", but due to violent parliamentary opposition it has been downgraded to a form that refuses rational encapsulation. It is now a hybrid scheme that does not satisfy either advocates or opponents. First, if it was meant to be recognition of same-sex *families*, this element has been wiped out by allowing non-conjugal couples to stipulate the agreement (later corrected by the interpretation of the Conseil Constitutionnel, but still present in the Belgian law on *cohabitation légale*). In fact, as both Stychin and Borrillo report, some components of the Senate committee had forcefully advised that the PACS had to be open to same-sex couples only, so that the concept of the (real, heterosexual) family and that of other kinds of partnerships would not become confused. If equality was the purpose, it is clear that the

---

17    For example LOCHAK, D., "Egalités et differences. Reflexions sur l'universalité de la regle de droit", in *Homosexualités et Droit*, ed by BORRILLO, D. (Paris : Presses Univeritaires de France, 1998) 42.

18    BORRILLO, D., "Pluralisme Conjugal ou Hiérarchie des sexualités? La Reconnaissance Juridique des Couples Homosexuels dans l'Union Européenne" (2001) *McGill L. J.* 875 ff.

PACS fell short of any recognition of equal rights. Second, if it was not meant to acknowledge the status of gays and lesbians within the family and the community, it is unclear (as indeed conservatives maintained) why it contains certain provisions so similar to the impediments to marriage.

If, on the one hand, solutions based on contract are to be given greater weight, because they are in accordance with the general trend toward de-institutionalization and because they avoid trapping same-sex couples in outdated and heterosexist values, on the other hand restrictive interpretations cast a shadow on its usefulness. It may be recalled that Belgian rules on *cohabitation légale* have been inserted in the third book of the civil code, concerning the acquisition of ownership. An Italian author has disassembled the structure of the French *pacte* in order to demonstrate that same-sex couples may not be considered families from the legal perspective adopted in the French law.[19] In fact, he recalled that the *pacte* does not modify the civil status of either party, it does not carry any consequences for children and there is no obligation to "moral" assistance. Although there is an obligation to provide "material" assistance, the content of this obligation may be determined by the parties themselves. As far as termination is concerned, unilateral dissolution is allowed, without notice, even by the subsequent marriage of one party with another person. The opinion of the *Conseil Constitutionnel* delivered in the aftermath of the new law clarifies that the *pacte* is only a "contrat nouveau…étranger au mariage".[20] The conclusion of some has been that contract law is applicable, not family law. The interpretation of doctrinal categories in such a way can only descend from a clear antipathy toward same-sex couples and takes the flexibility of contract law down the road of further exclusion.

## 4. HUMAN RIGHTS AND SEXUALITY IN ITALY

Although feminist thought has deep roots in recent social, political, and academic history, in Italy there has certainly been less exposure to the vast amount of feminist and homosexual studies that have problematized concepts of sexual identity, heterosexuality and the family. Nevertheless, marriage today has a very different meaning than decades ago, when the unity of the family dominated individual rights. When dealing with family issues, legal scholars must take into account a peculiar constitutional provision, section 29 of the 1948 Constitution which states that: "The

---

[19]   VITUCCI, P., "'Dal dì che nozze…' Contratto e diritto di famiglia nel pacte civil de solidarité" (2001) *Familia* 713 ff.

[20]   Decision of 9 November 1999, n. 99-419 DC, in Journal Officiel of 16 November.

Republic recognizes the rights of the family as a natural society based upon marriage". The reach of the law in this realm has always been considered with suspicion, as many distinguished scholars recalled when a far-reaching reform of Italian family law was enacted in 1975.[21]

The constitutional rule assisted many Catholic views that favoured a precise link between an ideologically – driven idea of "nature" and a gendered and heterosexual model of family relationships.[22] Today, several scholars acknowledge this interpretation of section 29 as being particularly outdated.[23] Many are more inclined to interpret it as a recognition of family models that exist within the realm of social behaviour (as opposed to state laws), and to embrace concepts of the family which are less centred around the presence of the formal act of marriage; rather, the family is seen as being based on the "private" element of affection and consent and as a "formazione sociale" that deserves protection according to section 2 of the Constitution.[24] However, some politicians and legal scholars fiercely use section 29 as a bar to any possible recognition of family units that are different from marriage, in some instances even if they are heterosexual. Interestingly, section 29 does not expressly dictate who is able to marry -and could ironically be interpreted so that, should gays and lesbians be allowed

---

[21]    CIAN, G., Introduzione al *Commentario alla riforma del diritto di famiglia*, ed. by CARRARO, L., OPPO, G., TRABUCCHI, A. (Padova: CEDAM, 1977) I, 1, at 23; SANDULLI, A.M., Rapporti etico-sociali, art. 29, in *Commentario al diritto italiano della famiglia*, ed. by CIAN, G., TRABUCCHI, A., OPPO, G. (Padova: CEDAM, 1992), I, at 3.

[22]    A famous article by JEMOLO, A.C., "La famiglia e il diritto", in *Pagine sparse di diritto e storiografia* (Milan: Giuffré, 1957), at 222 ff. was aimed at demonstrating that the "family" is a pre-juridical experience, "an island that the sea of the law may touch, but only slightly touch" because it is rooted in affection, instincts, morals, and religion, not law.

[23]    The debate is well exemplified in the works of BESSONE, M., *Rapporti etico-sociali, Commentario della Costituzione*, directed by Branca (Bologna-Rome: Zanichelli-Società Editrice del Foro Italiano, 1976) sub arts 29-31; RESCIGNO, P., *Persona e Comunità*, II, (Padova: CEDAM), 1988; ALAGNA, P., *Famiglia e rapporti tra coniugi nel nuovo diritto*, 2nd ed., (Milan: Giuffré, 1983); GRASSETTI, C., "I principi costituzionali relativi al diritto familiare", in *Commentario sistematico alla Costituzione italiana*, I, (Firenze: Barbera 1950), at 290 ff.; GRASSETTI, C., "Famiglia (diritto privato)", in *Novissimo Digesto Italiano*, VII, (Turin: UTET, 1965).

[24]    "The Republic recognizes and guarantees the inviolable rights of man, both as an individual and as a member of the social groups in which one's personality finds expression, and it requires the performance of imperative political, economic, and social duties". See SESTA, M., "Privato e pubblico nei progetti di legge in materia familiare", in *Studi in onore di P. Rescigno*, II, *Diritto Privato*, 1, *Persone, famiglia, successioni e proprietà* (Milan: Giuffré, 1998), p. 811 ff.; FERRANDO, G., "La famiglia senza matrimonio", in *Famiglia e servizi*, ed. by DELLA CASA, F., DOGLIOTTI, M., FERRANDO, G., FIGONE, A., MAZZA-GALANTI, F., SPALLAROSSA, M.R. (Milan: Giuffré, 2001), at 105 ff.; BESSONE, M., ALPA, G., D'ANGELO, A., FERRANDO, G., SPALLAROSSA, M.R., *La famiglia nel nuovo diritto*, 5th ed., (Bologna: Zanichelli, 2000) at 69 ff.; SCALISI, V., "La 'famiglia' e le 'famiglie'", in *La riforma del diritto di famiglia dieci anni dopo* (Padova: CEDAM, 1986), at 270 ff.

to marry, their partnership would be (morally and) legally more justifiable than heterosexual unmarried cohabitation (if what matters is marriage).

When I say, as many Italian scholars do, that marriage is a "privatized" institution I look at the meaning that the "person" has acquired within the democratic Constitution. Marriage and the family may no longer be understood as vehicles for (at least overtly) injecting into people's lives state-approved values and moral teachings, as the fascist dictatorship (and indeed many other fairly liberal legal systems) had attempted to do. The new democratic values reflect a particular concept of the "person" and its legal ramifications. It is commonly pointed out that the "person" should be considered at the core of the system of fundamental rights as a value in itself (*principio personalistico*).[25] In accordance with the Catholic and leftist traditions that had a significant influence on Italian constitutional legislation and legal scholarship after 1948, this bundle of ethical and social values (the "person") is not seen by section 2 as embodying abstract values of isolation. It is, on the contrary, envisaged as the centre of a multitude of social relations. In this view, the Constitution attempted to promote the guarantee of human rights, including those to personal and sexual identity,[26] as concerning the person "both as an individual and as a member of the social groups" where he or she develops his or her own personality.

A discussion on status and contract in the brief terms allowed by this paper may have more sense, if it means anything at all, when it assumes at its core the needs of this "social person". As I have argued elsewhere,[27] this objective may justify the connection between freedom to marry and *droits de la personne*; this leads to viewing gay and lesbian families as authentic manifestations of one's own personality. What this means is that the state should be responsible not only for guaranteeing a negative freedom (from) but also for recognizing freely chosen relationships (the freedom of). Of course, as it often happens, laying down this principle is the beginning, and not the end, of an intricate discussion. Just recently some scholars have begun to acknowledge in their work that the difference in sex is an underlying theme of marriage, and that this requirement might be at odds

---

[25] BARBERA, A., Principi fondamentali, art. 1-12, in *Commentario della Costituzione*, a cura di Branca, *sub* art. 2, (Bologna-Rome: Zanichelli-Società editirice del Foro Italiano, 1975); BALDASSARRE, A., Diritti inviolabili, *Enciclopedia giuridica*, (Rome: Treccani, 1989), vol. XI.

[26] The Courts have been quite active in this field: see *Corte Costituzionale*, 3 February 1994, n.13 (1994) II *Consiglio di Stato* 137; *Corte di Cassazione* 22 June 1985, n. 3769 (1985) *Foro italiano* 2211; see also *Corte di Cassazione* 9 June 1998, n. 5658 (1998) *Corriere giuridico* 1168.

[27] BONINI-BARALDI, M., "Società pluraliste e modelli familiari: il matrimonio fra persone dello stesso sesso in Olanda" (2001) *Familia* 419.

with the constitutional value of equality.[28] Recent bills on "unione domestica registrata" and "patto civile di solidarità" adopt approaches which are similar to those outlined above and it could be predicted that an eventual parliamentary debate will be fairly sanguine on these points.

The position of cohabitation outside marriage has been vigorously debated, starting from a conference held in Pontremoli in 1975, and today more open and accepting attitudes are largely shared. First of all, the civil code, revised in 1975 as far as family relationships are concerned, does not distinguish between the treatment of children depending on the married status of their parents. Natural parents, if they live together, may jointly exercise parental rights (section 317*bis* It. civil code). In one instance when two unmarried partners ended their relationship, the court granted joint custody to both parents.[29] However, equal rights have been denied in many instances. Two arguments support this conclusion. First, the *Corte di Cassazione* has held that a constitutional claim based on section 3 (principle of equality) was ill founded because de facto relationships are not similar to the legitimate family (because of a lack of stability and commitment).[30] The original petition sought to apply to an unmarried partner of a business owner section 230*bis* of the civil code, a groundbreaking rule introduced in 1975 in order to provide maintenance rights and decision-making rights to the married spouse and other relatives that work in the family or in the family business of an entrepreneur (and the Italian economy is largely based on small-scale family businesses).

Second, as many authors have held, it is necessary to respect the autonomy of unmarried partners who have freely chosen to remain outside the legal realm.[31] This constitutes a major difference with the approach of other European countries. The legislature has been reluctant to impose or ascribe the legal regulation of marriage to *de facto* cohabitants, albeit through judicial intervention piecemeal recognition has been given, for example, in cases of damages for wrongful death.[32] However, only a generic legal relevance has been created (through the extension of general areas of law, such as liability rules, social security rules, etc.), with the exclusion of a

---

[28]  FERRANDO, G., "Il matrimonio", in *Trattato di diritto civile e commerciale*, diretto da Cicu, A., and Messineo, F., (Milan: Giuffré, 2002), V, at 276 ff.

[29]  *Tribunale minorenni Perugia*, 16 January 1998 (1998) 4 *Famiglia e diritto* 376.

[30]  *Corte di Cassazione*, 2 May 1994, n. 4204 (1995) I, 1 *Giurisprudenza italiana* 845.

[31]  GAZZONI, F., *Dal concubinato alla famiglia di fatto* (Milan: Giuffré, 1983); FERRANDO, G., "La famiglia senza matrimonio", in *Famiglia e servizi, supra*, at 113, holds that the problem of the legal scholar and of the courts in the field of cohabitation is that of reconciling *freedom* and *responsibility*.

[32]  *Corte di Cassazione*, 10 March 1994, n. 2322 (1995) I, 1 *Giurisprudenza italiana* 1370.

specific legal relevance in the realm of family relations. When the right to housing was concerned (a right which is considered to be fundamental in the Italian tradition), the right of the unmarried partner to be substituted as a tenant in the rental contract after the death of the original tenant has been justified by the Constitutional Court because of the amplitude of such a right.[33] Housing should be granted to the heirs or relatives who used to live with the deceased tenant and to the unmarried partner, too, the Court stated. However, it also held that it is the situation descending from sharing a residence that deserves protection: the unmarried partner was included because of this reason, not because the partner was considered to be part of the "family". The protection of *de facto* families has been, in this instance, incidental and indirect, and some scholars have praised this approach as a paradigm that entitles individuals to rights or benefits regardless of their spousal status.[34]

In recent legislation, unmarried (opposite-sex) partners have gained the right to obtain parental leave from work[35] and restraining orders in case of domestic violence.[36] No regulation exists as far as maintenance duties or property division upon the ending of a relationship are concerned. In this field Italian case law has abandoned the former qualification of contributions from one partner to the other or to the couple as gifts during the relationship (evidence of which was often problematic) and is nowadays consistent in applying the doctrine of *obbligazioni naturali*.

What is the significance of this doctrine and what developments could be expected as far as the legal recognition of same-sex couples is concerned? As it has been pointed out, both contract and status have been -in certain areas- the legal basis for achieving similar results: *e.g.* in common law jurisdictions agreements between partners have been taken more seriously and the courts have attached rights and obligations to them which are just as significant as those afforded by legislation, i.e. in Sweden, (such as contractual damages, contractual licence, proprietary estoppel, etc.).[37] What I consider important is to highlight that (especially) underlying judicial decisions are policy considerations that reflect (or contribute to produce, some would say) existing values with respect to, for example, the economic assessment of family labour. With respect to this delicate issue

---

[33]    *Corte Costituzionale*, 7 April 1988, n. 404, (1988) I, 1 *Giurisprudenza italiana* 1627.
[34]    FERRANDO, G., "Convivenze e modelli di disciplina", in *Matrimonio, Matrimonii*, ed. by D'ANGELO, A. and BRONETTA-D'USSEAUX, F. (Milan: Giuffré, 2000), at 307.
[35]    Act n. 53/2000, *Gazzetta ufficiale* 13/3/2000 n. 60.
[36]    Act n. 154/2001, *Gazzetta ufficiale* 28/4/2001 n. 98.
[37]    MARELLA, M. R., *supra*, at 105.

in Italy, for example, judges have always upheld the concept of gratuity for any work done in the (legitimate) family, because market paradigms could not be applied to a community based on moral and ethical values that promoted altruism and solidarity. Consistently, they treated the work of the unmarried cohabitant as being equally non-economically valuable. The shift occurred in 1975 when the family law reform reversed this presumption by stating very clearly that the spouse (and other family members) who works in the business of the other spouse (or, as the courts have clarified over the years, works in the house but performs tasks that might be functional to the running of the company) is entitled to patrimonial and other rights.

As mentioned, the courts have repeatedly denied that the same rule (art. 230 bis Italian civil code) applies to relations between unmarried partners, governed by the scheme of *obbligazioni naturali*. If, prior to the law reform, both kinds of family were treated similarly, subsequently the parallelism came to an end, with no reasonable justification (other than the plain meaning of words used in art.230 bis). The consequence is that contributions to the family when marriage is present are legal duties (art. 143 It. civ. code) and work carried out for the business of the (legal) spouse must thereby be compensated (art. 230 bis). On the other hand, the unmarried partner has no right to economic contributions or to compensation for the work done in the family or family business. Whatever was given by one partner to the other is considered as a contribution to the performance of duties which are binding on a moral or social level; therefore, it is not required by law (but, when done, it is not subject to restitutory remedies). At least when no specific (written) contract can be demonstrated, arguments based on freedom and "contract" in Italian case law provide only very minimal protection, in contrast to the more significant solutions arrived at by the common law courts.

## 5. EUROPEAN CITIZENSHIP: SOME IMPLICATIONS FOR FAMILY LAW

I am under the impression that the "need for status" claimed by supporters of same-sex marriage has fuelled – especially in the United States – a resurgence of the rhetoric on spousal status that appeared to be dormant or bypassed by a trend toward convergence of married and de facto families. It therefore becomes crucial to reassess the extent to which spousal status is assumed as the paradigm for conferring rights descending from European citizenship. While a thorough analysis is beyond the scope of this article,[38] at least three examples come to mind: the case of D v. *Council*, the proposed directive on the right of citizens of the Union and their family members to move and reside freely within the territory of the Member States(complemented by the parallel with growing initiatives regarding immigration law), and the General framework directive against discrimination in employment and occupation (2000/78/EC).

First, in D v. *Council* the Court of first instance ruled that the term "spouse" in Council staff regulations could not be interpreted as encompassing (Swedish) registered partners.[39] The Court of Justice upheld the decision[40] and, as it has been remarked, carved out a European definition of what constitutes "spouse" (and of marriage) which is distinct from that of any particular state,[41] whereas civil status only depends on national law. Contrary to the hopes of those who would view the development of partnership legislation in many European countries as an incentive towards a more inclusive definition of spouse,[42] art. 13 of the EC Treaty, forbidding discrimination on the ground of sexual orientation, did not assist the Court in reversing the judgement. As it has been highlighted, the most problematic area is that of the movement of registered couples from Member States that allow a quasi-matrimonial status to Member States that do not.[43] This becomes even more problematic when the alternative status is less than quasi-matrimonial.

For the purposes of free movement of individuals within the Union several developments are underway.[44] The latest proposal for a directive on free movement of European citizens contains a definition of "family member"

---

[38] An inventory of EC regulations and directives referring to "marriage" or "spouse" has been made by the Dutch Government's "Commission on the opening up of civil marriage to persons of the same sex" and it found more than forty such pieces of legislation. See WAALDIJK, K., "Towards the Recognition of Same-Sex Partners in European Union Law: Expectations Based on Trends in National Law", in *Legal Recognition of Same-Sex Partnerships. A Study of National, European and International Law*, ed. by WINTEMUTE, R., and ANDENAES, M., Oxford-Portland Oregon, 2001, 637 at 644.

[39] Case T-264/97 *D.v. Council* [1999] *Reports of European Community Staff Cases* (ECR-SC) II-1.

[40] Cases C-122/99P and C-125/99P [2001] ECR I-4319.

[41] BELL, M., *Anti-Discrimination Law and the European Union* (Oxford: Oxford University Press, 2002), at 103.

[42] WAALDIJK, K., "Towards Equality in the Freedom of Movement of Persons", in *After Amsterdam: Sexual Orientation and the European Union* (Brussels: ILGA-Europe, 1999), at 43.

[43] BELL, M. *supra*, at 100.

[44] See BELL, M., "We are Family? Same-Sex Partners and EU Migration Law" (2002) 9 *MJ* 4, 335.

(art. 2 (2)),[45] as referring to: "(a) the spouse, (b) the unmarried partner, if the legislation of the host Member State treats unmarried couples as equivalent to married couples and in accordance with the conditions laid down in any such legislation". This proposal incorporates changes that occurred at the national level as far as partnership legislation is concerned. The explanatory memorandum makes the argument that (married) spouses and unmarried partners should be treated equally with respect to the right of residence when legislation of the host Member states treats unmarried couples as equivalent to married couples.

Similar developments were an ingredient of the previous proposal to amend art. 10 of Regulation (EEC) 1612/68 (now merged in the mentioned proposal on the right of Union citizens to move and reside freely) which would have afforded the worker (who is a national of another Member State) the right to install in a Member state: (a) "his spouse or any person corresponding to a spouse under the legislation of the host Member State (...)"; and (c) "any other member of the family of the worker (...) who is dependent on the worker or is living under his roof in the Member State whence he comes".[46] As it has been argued, the definition proposed in 1998 could have been inadequate in redressing issues of discrimination between registered partners and married spouses (the right to install was limited to a small number of Member States), as well as between married spouses and unmarried cohabitants (the word "family" being subject to narrow interpretations).[47] These aspects have been partially tackled by the 2001 proposal, which seeks to equate married and unmarried partners, although it remains a problem of understanding an undefined "equivalent treatment" in the legislation of the host Member State.

According to the provisional report of the Committee on Citizens' Freedoms and Rights, Justice and Home Affairs (rapporteur Santini) of 25 September 2002, the European Parliament would favour a more restrictive definition of family member. "Spouse" should be defined as "heterosexual"; and "de facto and de jure couples" (registered partners, partners registered under less thorough schemes and unregistered de facto cohabitants, I would say) should also be encompassed by the definition of "family member" if the host Member State "recognizes" such couples. While the attempt to include unmarried partners (both registered and un-

---

[45]  *COM* (2001) 257 – 2001/111 (COD), *OJ* [2001] C 270/150, Proposal for a European Parliament and Council Directive on the right of citizens of the Union and their family members to move and reside freely within the territory of the Member States.

[46]  *COM* (1998) 294 final – 98/229 (COD), *OJ* [1998] C 344/9.

[47]  WAALDIJK, K., *supra*, at 45.

registered) as family members should be praised, both the text proposed by the Commission and the proposed parliamentary amendment seem to reiterate the view that the term "spouse" may only refer to legally married partners, with the exclusion of, *in primis*, registered partners. As is made clear by the accompanying text of the proposed amendment, this stems from the decision of the Court of Justice in *D* v. *Council*. However, it could be argued that art. 2(2) of the proposal could adopt, for the purposes of the directive, a definition of "family member" and of "spouse" that is capable of taking into account the legal choices made in several Member States. This would be consistent with the *ratio* of several registered partnership laws, as indicated in previous sections of this paper, whereas as far as less comprehensive or regional partnership schemes are concerned the situation remains doubtful.

Significantly, the final Santini report of 23 January 2003 – approved by Parliament on the 11th of February – revolutionized the previous definition. Three categories would now qualify as "family members": "a) the spouse, irrespective of sex, according to the relevant national legislation"; "aa) the registered partner, irrespective of sex, according to the relevant national legislation"; "b) the unmarried partner, irrespective of sex, with whom the applicant has a durable relationship, if the legislation or practice of the host and/or home Member State treats unmarried couples in a corresponding manner to married couples and in accordance with the conditions laid down in any such legislation". The proposed amendments give rise to a number of issues. Firstly, this definition of "spouse" would embrace same-sex legally married spouses, according to the marriage laws of The Netherlands and Belgium. However, it is unclear whether the reference to "relevant national legislation" is made to the law of the home Member State (which would allow Dutch and Belgian couples to move and reside freely in any Member State), of the host Member State (which would only allow Dutch spouses to move to Belgium and vice versa), or to the law of both (as under letter b). Secondly, the status of "registered partner" is overtly recognised in the same manner as it is under domestic law, that is as an entity "separate but equal" to marriage; in fact, "spouse" continues to be only the person legally married, although registered partners acquire an autonomous consideration on an equal footing. The same set of considerations seen above with respect to the applicable law can be extended to registered partnership. Thirdly, unmarried partners would be granted freedom of movement, irrespective of sex, when the legislation or practice of the *host* or the *home* Member State treats them correspondingly with married couples. This amendment is of crucial importance because it permits to carry the status of "unmarried partner", acquired and recognized in the home Member State, to any other Member State, even where it has little legal content (although limited to aspects concerning immigration). In general, if the reference to the "relevant national legislation" can optimistically be taken to recall the legislation of the home Member State, the parallel could be made with a sort of "full faith and credit" clause, and with aspects of recognition of divorces in the past (which was, nevertheless, a voluntary choice): the host State would not (and could not) be forced by Community measures to provide a status for its own citizens that it is (as yet) unwilling to provide, but it would be required to recognize that status when it has been acquired elsewhere in the Union. This approach appears to be most in accordance with the spirit of the law relating to the free movement of persons.

Although not technically a component of the European citizenship chapter, it is worth mentioning a number of proposals developed as part of the large chapter regarding immigration of third-country nationals. An earlier version of a proposal for a Directive on family reunion rights defined "family member" as "the applicant's spouse, or an unmarried partner living in a durable relationship with the applicant, if the legislation of the Member State concerned treats the situation of unmarried couples as corresponding to that of married couples".[48] As already remarked, the reference to the equivalent treatment of married and unmarried couples in the legislation of the host Member State is highly ambiguous because it is not always clear when equivalent treatment occurs, especially in the case of unregistered cohabitants. A third proposal readdressed the definition in completely different terms: a family member would only be the (legally married) spouse or the minor children (art. 4(1)).[49] Unmarried partners could be admitted, at the discretion of the Member State, when the relationship could be shown to be long-term (art.4(3)). The discretionary possibility of authorizing entry and residence also characterizes the position of registered partners, for which the requirement of showing a long-term relationship does not apply. The latter proposal is significantly more restrictive: the explanatory memorandum justified this choice on the ground of the "diversity in national legislation concerning those enjoying the right to family reunification". It appears, therefore, that a "minimum common denominator" approach has been adopted, possibly

---

[48]  Commission, Proposal for a Council Directive on the right to family reunification, *COM* (1999) 638, art. 5(1)(a). See BELL, M., *supra*, at 99. Amended by *COM*(2000) 624 final – 1999(258) (CNS), *OJ* [2001] C 62/99.

[49]  Amended proposal for a Council Directive on the right to family reunification *COM*(2002) 225 final – 1999/258 (CNS), *OJ* [2002] C 203/136.

an expression of the Council's unwillingness to embrace any broader definition for the purposes of immigration.

Other proposals in the field of asylum and refugees adopt a definition of "family member" that embraces both the legally married spouse and the unmarried partner in a stable relationship. Some variations in language occur: the recognition of the latter would occur "if the legislation of the Member State where the application has been lodged or is being examined treats unmarried couples in the same way as married couples"[50] or "in a way comparable to married couples".[51] The former proposal was adopted by the Council on 27 January 2003, and it contains the same definition of "family member", although it refers to the legislation of the Member State "concerned".[52] With regard to the latter proposal, the European Parliament's final Report of 8 October 2002 has proposed adding to the definition of family member the principle of gender neutrality, making it explicit that a "spouse" or an "unmarried partner" should be determined "irrespective of gender". Furthermore, a proposal on the status of long-term residents who are third-country nationals refers back to the family reunification proposal (for determining the "family member" of third country nationals) or to the free movement of persons proposal (for Union citizens).[53]

Finally, The General framework directive against discrimination at the workplace (2000/78/EC) contains a non-binding statement related to marital status. In fact, Recital 22 holds that anti-discriminatory provisions of the directive should not go as far as encompassing benefits granted on the basis of marital status ("the Directive is without prejudice to national laws on marital status and the benefits dependent thereon"). This Recital could be read as a limitation on the efficacy of equality legislation, which

---

[50] Proposal for a Council Directive laying down minimum standards on the reception of applicants for asylum in Member States COM(2001) 181 final – 2001/91 (CNS), OJ [2001] C 213/286, art. 2(d); Proposal for a Council Regulation establishing the criteria and mechanisms for determining the Member State responsible for examining an asylum application lodged in one of the Member States by a third-country national COM(2001) 447 final – 2001/182 (CNS), OJ [2001] C 304/ 192, art. (2) (with reference to the "State responsible"). The latter was adopted by the Council on 18 February 2003, but the final text could be examined at the time of writing.

[51] Proposal for a Council Directive on minimum standards for the qualification and status of third country national and stateless persons as refugees or as persons who otherwise need international protection COM(2001) 510 final – 2001/207 (CNS), OJ [2002] C 51/325, art. 2.

[52] Council Directive 2003/9/EC of 27 January 2003 laying down minimum standards for the reception of asylum seekers, OJ [2003] L 31/18.

[53] Proposal for a Council Directive concerning the status of third country nationals who are long-term residents COM(2001) 127 final – 2001/74 (CNS), OJ [2001] C 240/79, art. 2.

should stop at the doorstep of the family, as if the two were incompatible. This underlying assumption has been well documented by the work of Canadian scholars on so called human rights codes, which presented similar (binding) exceptions. It goes without saying that many cases of discrimination at the workplace towards gay and lesbian persons are based on the non-recognition of their families. The directive apparently does little to tackle this issue, although it is predictable that its ban will apply to a situation in which benefits are provided by the employer to unmarried different-sex partners, but not to same-sex partners, a case of sexual orientation discrimination following the decision of the Court of Justice in *Grant*.[54]

## 6. CONCLUSION

In conclusion it may be observed that a binary logic founded on exclusionary concepts of status and contract has proved to be inadequate, whereas more nuanced analyses capture reality more accurately. Today, the prevalent normative paradigm allows for more private autonomy and solutions based on contract law (less reciprocal duties, prenuptial agreements, incentives to mediate, living wills, damages for termination, gross disparity, etc.) but also allows for strong legal rules as far as child custody and protection are concerned. There is, thus, some room for a variety of approaches, while the process of law reform seems to depend on extralegal factors such as predominant categories in the given national culture. The political latitude for embracing changing needs will also influence the balance between status and contract.

In some instances, however, the interconnection between these two key concepts might be suspect if it is based on the procrastination of moral judgements on homosexuality. Perhaps both are necessary and useful in today's discourses on partnership recognition, or perhaps neither of them. In addition, the diachronic dimensions should be kept in mind: legal systems have often begun with explorations in some direction, and have subsequently added or substituted additional measures. Interesting solutions could be those that allow the creation of several statuses, so that the diversity existing in society could be adequately reflected (including non-conjugal arrangements).

EC employment and anti-discrimination law (as well as law in other areas, as seen) might have far-reaching implications for family law, but it falls

---

[54] Case C-249/96, *Grant* v. *South West Trains Ltd.*, [1998] ECR I-621.

short of thorough significant recognition of same-sex couples. As it has been highlighted, most forms of differential treatment occur both between legally married spouses and registered partners (a form of direct discrimination on the basis of sexual orientation or civil status), and between legally married and unmarried (different or same-sex) partners (a form of indirect discrimination on the ground of sexual orientation in the latter case).[55] Building on art. 13 of the Treaty establishing the European Communities and on the provisions of the General framework directive against discrimination in employment and occupation, it has been possible to predict that if the interpretation of the directive embraces these two forms of discrimination (in the field of employment), other EC legislation will be interpreted or amended in the same direction, because it would not be logical for the EU to maintain discriminatory legislation once the same practices have been forbidden for employers.[56]

While national legislatures or courts have deregulated the institution of marriage (especially as far as the capacity to marry and the ongoing relationship are concerned), they have attached more consequences to unmarried cohabitation (especially when children are present), and have recognized the need for the status of same-sex couples through diverse registered partnership schemes; EC legislation, in turn, remains bound to a very traditional and heterosexual definition of the "spouse". The incorporation of new partnership laws in the Member States seems to follow a slow process and appears to be minimal, especially in the light of the above mentioned proposals: registered partners would still be considered as unmarried partners and their legal recognition would be subject to the existence of "equivalent treatment" between married and unmarried partners in the host Member State (for the purposes of free movement).

The expansion of the model based on status (*e.g.* through the ascription of spousal status to unmarried opposite- and same-sex couples) or the creation of new statuses (*e.g.* registered partners) could appear as a culture-

---

[55] WAALDIJK, K., "Towards the Recognition of Same-Sex Partners in European Union Law: Expectations Based on Trends in National Law", *supra*, at 645.

[56] *Ibid.*, at 647. This conclusion emphasizes the legal policy of both the national and the European legislatures. In fact, an area of particular concern is the nature of rights recognized by the legal system. Scholars have become more concerned with the nature and the type of recognition, analyzing the distinction between individual and public rights, which reflected the extent of the recognition afforded to gays and lesbians in different spheres of life. To elaborate, other scholars criticize anti-discrimination legislation -such as the paradigm offered by the General framework directive- when it only applies to employers, leaving unaffected the legal invisibility of same-sex couples *vis-à-vis* public benefits (*e.g.* social security, health, immigration, etc.).

specific option of legal policy, whose transplantation could give rise to some criticism,[57] therefore less subject to circulation. The same could be said for the choice of allowing (legal spouses and) cohabitants to exercise more "contractual" options and for applying contractual remedies to situations generated in such cohabitations.

However, today it is widely acknowledged that the recognition of same-sex couples, unlike other matters in family law, is a human rights or fundamental rights issue that calls into action the constitutional values of equality and freedom (to marry),[58] as well as legal personhood and capacity. The promotion of these values cannot be seen as an academic exercise, but rather as a legal duty arising out of national constitutions, the Charter of fundamental rights of the EU and, with some disparity, the ECHR (recently the cases of *Christine Goodwin*[59] and *Salgueiro*[60]).

---

[57] BRADLEY, D., "Convergence in Family Law: Mirrors, Transplants and Political Economy" (2001) Oxford U Comparative L Forum 2, originally published in (1999) 6 *Maastricht Journal of European and Comparative Law* 127.

[58] WINTEMUTE, R., *Sexual Orientation and Human Rights: The United States Constitution, the European Convention, and the Canadian Charter*, Oxford, 1997.

[59] *Christine Goodwin* v. *UK*, 11/07/2002, appl. n. 28957/95, concerned the right of a post-operative transsexual to marry a person of a gender which is different to that which has been acquired.

[60] *Salgueiro da Silva Mouta* v. *Portugal*, 21/12/1999, appl. n. 33290/96, concerned the right of a father not to be denied custody of his child solely because of his homosexuality.

# DOMESTIC AND CONFLICT DIFFICULTIES INHERENT IN REGULATING THE NEW ORDER

JANEEN M. CARRUTHERS[*]

## INTRODUCTION

Those who study demographic trends have recently indicated that the proportion of the adult population in Great Britain who are in a cohabiting relationship has risen from 9.6% in 1990 to 17.3% in 2000.[1] This increase seems to mirror trends throughout Europe, and it is evident that the lawmakers in each jurisdiction are taking note of changing social attitudes. It is not the task or objective of this author to attempt to explain these trends, less so to describe the demographic projections; rather the objective of this paper is to assess the impact (actual and potential) of these social changes upon the development and operation of rules concerning the conflict of laws.

The paper, which is written from the perspective of Scots law, and through the eyes of a Scots lawyer – though, inevitably now, against the backdrop of E.U. harmonisation – will seek to address some of the conflict of laws issues which are likely to flow from the emergence, and growing (internal law) regulation, of new models of domestic relationship.

## 1. IS OUR 'DOMESTIC" HOUSE IN ORDER? INTERNAL RULES OF SCOTTISH PRIVATE LAW

Before examining the conflict of laws aspects, it may be useful to provide a résumé of the internal rules of Scottish private law concerning the constitution and consequences of domestic relationships.

---

[*] The author wishes to record her thanks to Dr Elizabeth B. Crawford, University of Glasgow, for comments on an earlier draft of this paper. Many of the remarks made, and views expressed, in this paper derive from the National Report for Scotland concerning "The Property of Married and Cohabiting Parties", submitted in May 2002 to the T.M.C. Asser Institute, The Hague, by Dr Crawford and the current author.

[1] The Times, 10 November 2002. Correspondingly, it seems that the marriage rate is declining – in 2001 there were 29,621 marriages in Scotland, compared with over 41,000 in 1951. The decline in the number of marriages, however, appears to be levelling out at around 30,000 per annum. (Scotland's Population 2001 – The Registrar General's Annual Review of Demographic Trends) (October 2002).

## 1.1. Marriage

Marriage,[2] in the eyes of Scots law, is a voluntary union, potentially of lifelong duration, between one man and one woman, to the exclusion of all other parties.[3] There is provision for two types of marriage: *regular*, constituted, according to statute, by religious or civil ceremony,[4] and *irregular*, constituted, according to the Scots common law, by cohabitation with habit and repute.[5]

As to the proprietary and financial consequences of marriage, as a general rule, marriage has no effect on the property rights of spouses:[6] the regime in Scotland is one of separation of property.[7] Marriage does, however, create an obligation of aliment or maintenance between spouses.[8] When

---

[2] See generally CLIVE, E M, *The Law of Husband and Wife in Scotland* 4th ed., (1997). Also THOMSON, J M, *Family Law in Scotland* 4th ed., (2002), Chapters 1 – 5.

[3] *Hyde v. Hyde & Woodmansee* [1866] L.R. 1 P&D 130.

[4] Marriage (Scotland) Acts 1977 and 2002. See CLIVE, *op. cit.*, Chapter 4.

[5] See CLIVE, *op. cit.*, Chapter 5. "If a man and woman who are free to marry each other cohabit as husband and wife in Scotland for a considerable time and are generally regarded as being husband and wife they are presumed to have consented to be married, even if only tacitly, and, if the presumption is not rebutted, will be held to be married by cohabitation with habit and repute." (Scottish Law Commission Discussion Paper, No. 85, *Family Law: Pre-Consolidation Reforms* (1990) [hereinafter "SLC No. 85"], paragraph 2.2) This type of marriage is generally used as a means by which to confer rights of succession, or entitlement to financial provision, on one party to the relationship. Cases still arise regularly for decision: *Campbell v. Campbell* (1866) 4 M. 867; *Wallace v. Fife Coal Co.* 1909 S.C. 682; *Nicol v. Bell* 1954 S.L.T. 314; *Low v. Gorman* 1970 S.L.T. 356; *Shaw v. Henderson* 1982 S.L.T. 211; *Donnelly v. Donnelly* 1992 S.L.T. 13; *Kamperman v. McIver* 1994 S.L.T. 763; *Dewar v. Dewar* 1995 S.L.T. 467; and *Walker v. Roberts* 1998 S.L.T. 1133. The Scottish Law Commission (hereinafter "SLC") has emphasised that this form of marriage " ... is not available to couples who have lived together without ever pretending to be married or acquiring the reputation of being married. " (SLC, No. 85, paragraph 2.5.) Although the SLC recommended, in 1992, that marriage by cohabitation with habit and repute should be abolished as from the date of implementing legislation (Scottish Law Commission No. 135 (1992), *"Report on Family Law"* [hereinafter "1992 Report"], Recommendation 42), the Scottish Executive has indicated that it does *not* intend to implement the SLC recommendation. Accordingly, this type of marriage shall "... be retained for the foreseeable future." (Scottish Executive White Paper, *Parents and Children* (2001), paragraph 10.4/5) Irregular marriages by declaration *de praesenti*, or by promise *subsequente copula*, are no longer available (Marriage (Scotland) Act 1939).

[6] Family Law (Scotland) Act 1985 (hereinafter "1985 Act"), section 24(1).

[7] See CLIVE, *op. cit.*, Chapter 14, and THOMSON, *op. cit.*, Chapters 4 and 5.

[8] 1985 Act, section 1(1): Obligation of aliment.
(1) From the commencement of this Act, an obligation of aliment shall be owed by, and only by–
(a) a husband to his wife;
(b) a wife to her husband;
(c) a father or mother to his or her child;
(d) a person to a child (other than a child who has been boarded out with him by a local or other public authority or a voluntary organisation) who has been accepted by him as a child of his family.

a marriage ends in divorce, Scots lawyers turn to a sophisticated statutory system of financial provision.[9] The philosophy essentially is clean break, the basic principle being fair division of the net value of matrimonial property.[10] Where a marriage ends by death rather than by divorce, at least one third (and up to one half) of the deceased's net moveable estate is ring-fenced for the surviving spouse.[11] In cases of intestacy, the surviving spouse is entitled to "prior rights" out of the deceased's estate. Subject to certain monetary limits, the survivor may claim an interest in a qualifying dwelling house, and to furniture and plenishings, and in addition he/she has a cash entitlement.[12] Satisfaction of prior rights of succession will, in many instances, exhaust the deceased's estate.

---

(2) For the purposes of this Act, an obligation of aliment is an obligation to provide such support as is reasonable in the circumstances, having regard to the matters to which a court is required or entitled to have regard under section 4 of this Act in determining the amount of aliment to award in an action for aliment.

[9] 1985 Act, sections 8 – 22. See CLIVE, *op. cit.*, Chapter 24, and THOMSON, *op. cit.*, Chapter 7.

[10] 1985 Act, section 9(1)(a). The basic order is for payment of a capital sum, but in certain circumstances, orders may be made for the transfer of property from either party to the marriage to the other party, or for the making of a periodical allowance, or for an incidental order. The principles which the court shall apply in deciding what order for financial provision, if any, to make are narrated in section 9, *viz.*:
(1) The principles which the court shall apply in deciding what order for financial provision, if any, to make are that–
(a) the net value of the matrimonial property should be shared fairly between the parties to the marriage;
(b) fair account should be taken of any economic advantage derived by either party from contributions by the other, and of any economic disadvantage suffered by either party in the interests of the other party or of the family;
(c) any economic burden of caring, after divorce, for a child of the marriage under the age of 16 years should be shared fairly between the parties;
(d) a party who has been dependent to a substantial degree on the financial support of the other party should be awarded such financial provision as is reasonable to enable him to adjust, over a period of not more than three years from the date of the decree of divorce, to the loss of that support on divorce;
(e) a party who at the time of the divorce seems likely to suffer serious financial hardship as a result of the divorce should be awarded such financial provision as is reasonable to relieve him of hardship over a reasonable period.
In terms of section 8(2)(b), the order must, in addition, be reasonable having regard to the parties' resources.

[11] Legal rights of *ius relictae/relicti* cannot be defeated by testamentary disposition. The entitlement is to one-half of the deceased's net moveable estate if the deceased leaves a spouse only, and to one-third in the event of his/her being survived by children. Legal rights are an *alternative* to any testamentary bequest, and may *not* be taken in addition thereto. Legal rights are exigible both in cases of testacy and intestacy. See generally MESTON, M C, *The Succession (Scotland) Act 1964*, 4th ed. (1993).

[12] Succession (Scotland) Act 1964, sections 8 and 9.

## 1.2. Cohabitation

The position under internal Scots law regarding the constitution and proprietary and financial consequences of cohabitation stands in contrast to that concerning marriage. There is no distinct, or developed, body of internal Scots law that regulates the rights and obligations of unmarried, cohabiting couples. Various statutes refer *incidentally* to cohabitation, and to the rights of cohabitants, but such provision as exists has been introduced entirely on a token or piecemeal basis.[13] Although there is no distinct body of law which regulates the rights and obligations of unmarried, cohabiting couples, nevertheless, Scots law *recognises the existence* of cohabiting couples, for various purposes including social security, tenants' rights, taxation, occupancy rights, delictual damages, criminal defences, and mental health.[14]

Accordingly, at present, the legal consequences of cohabitation, *per se*, are very limited, and few rights and obligations attach to cohabitants by virtue of cohabitation. Cohabitation has no effect on the property of cohabitants. There is no maintenance obligation between cohabitants. There is no procedure by which to terminate a cohabiting relationship, and upon cessation of cohabitation, a cohabitant has no statutory entitlement to seek financial provision, or to redistribution or equalisation of property; general principles of property law apply. At very best, though seldom successful, a cohabitant may seek a compensating payment, via principles of unjustified enrichment.[15] The law on unjustified enrichment, however, is not easy to determine, or to apply, and the result of such a claim will usually be

---

13   *E.g.* Damages (Scotland) Act 1976, sections 1 and 10(2), as amended by the Administration of Justice Act 1982, section 14(4); Matrimonial Homes (Family Protection) (Scotland) Act 1981, section 18; Mental Health (Scotland) Act 1984, section 53(5); Social Security Act 1986, section 20(11); Housing (Scotland) Act 1988, section 31(4); Finance (No 2) Act 1988, section 42; Adults with Incapacity (Scotland) Act 2000, section 87(1); and Mortgage Rights (Scotland) Act 2001.

14   Scottish Law Commission Discussion Paper No. 86, (1990) *The Effects of Cohabitation in Private Law* [hereinafter "SLC No. 86"], paragraph 1.9. *E.g.* Social Security Act 1986, section 20(11); Housing (Scotland) Act 1988, section 31(4); Finance (No 2) Act 1988, section 42; Matrimonial Homes (Family Protection (Scotland) Act 1981, section 18; Damages (Scotland) Act 1976, sections 1 and 10(2) – amended by the Administration of Justice Act 1982, section 14(4); *McDermott v. H M Advocate* 1973 J.C. 8; *McKay v. H M Adv* 1991 S.C.C.R. 364; Mental Health (Scotland) Act 1984, section 53(5); and Adults with Incapacity (Scotland) Act 2000, section 87(1).

15   See generally CARRUTHERS, J M, "Unjustified Enrichment and the Family: Re-visiting the Remedies" 2000 *S.L.P.Q.* 5(1) 58. *E.g. Newton v. Newton* 1925 S.C. 715; and *Shilliday v. Smith* 1998 S.C. 725.

unpredictable.[16] In the event of death, a surviving cohabitant has no rights of intestate succession in the estate of the deceased, and no claim for legal rights.

In internal Scots law, therefore, the status of cohabitant, if status it be, attracts few legal incidents/property consequences. Nonetheless, there is no bar to private contractual or testamentary arrangement.[17]

### 1.3. Proposals for Reform

In a recent poll, 66% of a representative sample of U.K. adults thought that couples who live together for two or more years should enjoy the same rights as a married couple. 74% favoured the option of registered partnerships for heterosexual couples, whilst 61% thought that such an option should be extended to same-sex couples.[18]

In the 2001/02 session of the Westminster Parliament, two (English) Bills were put (separately, and respectively) before the House of Commons, and the House of Lords: first, the Relationships (Civil Registration) Bill 2001,[19] and secondly, the Civil Partnerships Bill 2002.[20] Both Bills seek to reform the law of England and Wales relating to cohabitants, by providing a system of registered partnerships applicable to heterosexual and same-sex cohabitants alike, and conferring upon registered partners significant rights and obligations concerning (among other things) property, financial provision, and succession.[21] Parliamentary progress is proving to be very slow: the Relationships (Civil Registration) Bill "ran out of time" in the 2001/02 session of Parliament, and Lord Lester intimated that he would

---

[16]     In 1990, the SLC concluded that, "It seems clear that to leave the law as it is would be to leave most cohabitants without effective claims for financial provision or redistribution of property on termination of their relationship." (SLC No. 86, paragraph 5.6).

[17]     There is no statutory regulation of cohabitation contracts *per se*, and such contracts would be subject to general principles of contract law. In 1990, the SLC expressed the hope that the courts would not now regard such contracts as contrary to public policy: "Given that cohabitation is already recognised for various legal purposes ... such a view would be highly questionable." (SLC No. 86, paragraph 9.1) See also WALKER, D M, *The Law of Contracts and Related Obligations in Scotland*, 3rd ed., (1995), paragraph 11.42.

[18]     NOP World Poll conducted for *Panorama*.
        See http://news.bbc.co.uk/1/hi/programmes/panorama/2506369.stm

[19]     Introduced to the House of Commons by JANE GRIFFITHS, MP (Reading, East). A copy of the Bill is available at www.publications.parliament.uk/pa/cm200102/cmbills/036/2002036.pdf.

[20]     Introduced to the House of Lords by Lord Lester of Herne Hill. A copy of the Bill is available at www.publications.parliament.uk/pa/ld200102/ldbills/041/2002041.pdf.

[21]     Full commentaries are available in respect of both Bills at House of Commons Research Paper 02/17 (19 March 2002): http://www.parliament.uk/commons/lib/research/rp2002/rp02-017.pdf.

not be proceeding with the Civil Partnerships Bill pending publication of the results of a cross-departmental Government review of the likely impact of the proposed reforms. The impact study is being conducted by the Cabinet Office.[22] On 6 December 2002, Social Exclusion Minister Barbara Roche advised that the Government's preparatory study was not yet complete, and that the final consultation document is not likely to be produced until summer 2003. Nevertheless, the Minister has voiced her general support for a partnership registration scheme, available to heterosexual and same-sex couples.[23]

Since 1999, responsibility for Family Law in Scotland has vested in the devolved Scottish, rather than the central Westminster, Parliament.[24] The Scottish Executive has consulted widely on matters of Family Law.[25] For the time being, Scots law is taking a guarded approach to new models of domestic relationships.[26] In 1999, the Scottish Executive indicated that it does not seek to equate the legal effects of cohabitation and marriage: "The Executive does not plan to set up a regime of property sharing on separation or on succession which is equivalent to that applying to married couples. Couples who cohabit are making an active choice not to marry, or are not free to marry. That difference must be acknowledged and respected by appropriate differences in the legal consequences of cohabitation."[27]

The latest Scottish proposals recommend only minimal change.[28] At the time of writing, draft legislation is still awaited; the Executive is proceeding cautiously.

---

[22]   Lord Lester has stated that, when the Government review is complete, he will request that a Select Committee of the House of Lords examine the issue of reform. (Press Release, 14 February 2002: www.stonewall.org)

[23]   http://www.ukonline.gov.uk/NewsRoom/NRArticle/0,1169,203387~801b22~fs~en,00.html.

[24]   The Scottish Executive assumed administrative and policy responsibility for these matters (Scottish Office Home Department consultation paper, *Improving Scottish Family Law* (1999) [hereinafter "*ISFL*"]. These proposals are based largely on the recommendations in the 1992 Report.) (*ISFL*, paragraph 4.3)

[25]   *E.g. Parents and Children, op. cit.*

[26]   "[Legal intervention] ... should neither undermine marriage, nor undermine the freedom of those who have deliberately opted out of marriage." (1992 Report, paragraph 16.1).

[27]   *Parents and Children*, paragraph 7.1.

[28]   *Parents and Children*: The presumption of equal shares in household goods, and in money and property derived from housekeeping or similar allowance, should apply, with modifications, to cohabitants (Proposals 12 and 13); measures offering protection from violence should be extended to vulnerable cohabitants (Proposal 16); where the relationship ends by separation, a cohabitant should be able to apply for financial provision from an ex-partner where there has been economic disadvantage (Proposal 14); and where the relationship ends by death, a surviving cohabitant should be able to apply to a court for a discretionary provision from the deceased's estate (Proposal 15).

Janeen M. Carruthers

## 1.4. Same-Sex Relationships

Consistently throughout the 1990s, Scots law reform agencies avoided tackling directly the issue of same-sex marriage and cohabitation.[29]

As has been mentioned already, parties to a valid marriage celebrated in Scotland must be of opposite sexes.[30] This is a mandatory provision, which cannot be overridden by a countervailing rule of the parties' personal law(s). But it may be subject, possibly, to ECHR-inspired amendment to take account of transsexuals.

It has been plainly stated that it is *not* the Executive's policy to introduce same-sex marriage into Scotland,[31] and the Executive's definition of cohabitation *excludes* same-sex relationships.[32] Whilst one or two domestic statutes do confer limited rights on same-sex as well as on heterosexual couples,[33] as far as the wider programme of reform of Family Law is

---

[29] SLC No. 85, paragraph 3.5; 1992 Report, Recommendation 45.
[30] Marriage (Scotland) Act 1977, section 5(4)(e). We await the impact of the ECHR decision in *Goodwin v. United Kingdom* [2002] 2 F.L.R. 487. The applicant in this case had undergone gender re-assignment surgery and lived in society as a female, although remained for legal purposes male. The applicant claimed that refusal to give legal recognition to her gender re-assignment was a violation of her right to respect for her private life, and a violation of her right to marry. The European Court of Human Rights held that there had been violations of Articles 8 and 12 of the ECHR. In particular, the Court held that it was artificial to assert that post-operative transsexuals had not been deprived of the right to marry because they were able to marry a person of their former opposite sex – the applicant lived as a woman and would only wish to marry a man, but had no way of doing so. The Court held that the applicant was entitled to claim that the very essence of her right to marry had been infringed.
[31] *Parents and Children*, paragraph 6.4.2: "While we fully recognise that a same-sex partnership may have similar characteristics to a partnership between opposite sex cohabitants, it is not the Executive's policy to introduce same-sex marriage into Scotland."
[32] SLC No. 86, paragraph 1.2; 1992 Report, p115, note 2. The SLC has articulated the view that heterosexual cohabitation "... is statistically more important and in relation to which there is currently the greater demand for reform." (1992 Report, paragraph 16.3).
[33] See NORRIE, K McK, "Sexual Orientation and Family Law" in SCOULAR, J (ed.), *Family Dynamics: Contemporary Issues in Family Law* (2001), p. 151: "There are other statutes, such as ... the Rent (Scotland) Act 1984 and the Children (Scotland) Act 1995 ... ... in which concepts such as "family" and "household" are wide enough to allow the courts, if they are so minded, to include within their terms same-sex relationships." *E.g.* Adults with Incapacity (Scotland) Act 2000, section 87(1); and Mortgage Rights (Scotland) Act 2001, whereby entitlement to apply to a court for suspension of enforcement by a creditor of his security rights over domestic properties extends to "a person living with the debtor or the proprietor as husband or wife or in a relationship which has the characteristics of the relationship between husband and wife except that the persons are of the same sex ..." (Section 1(2)(c)) See also in English law, in relation to succession to a tenancy, *Fitzpatrick v. Sterling Housing Association Limited* [1999] 3 W.L.R. 1113; the point is now met statutorily in Scotland in the Housing (Scotland) Act 2001.

concerned, the prospective legislative focus in Scotland is firmly, and exclusively, on heterosexual cohabitation.[34]

## 2. AWAITING FOREIGN VISITORS: RULES OF SCOTTISH INTERNATIONAL PRIVATE LAW

For those who cherish the traditional model of marriage, the Scottish house is in good order. For proponents of alternative models of domestic relationship, the house, it seems, is rather small, and to more liberal foreign eyes, the house may appear somewhat bare in terms of relevant domestic and conflict provision.

It is against this background that Scottish courts, like their European equivalents, must prepare to adjudicate upon disputes which raise, in a conflict of laws setting, questions concerning the rights and obligations of cohabitants. Regardless of the approach of internal Scots law to the fact of cohabitation, it is inevitable that conflict of laws issues will soon present themselves in a Scottish forum, requiring the Scottish lawmakers to articulate (and first to formulate!) rules to deal with a new legal order evolving abroad. It is only a matter of time until courts across Europe, and beyond, will be called upon to untangle the personal and proprietary cross-border consequences of domestic relationships which lack an immediate, or even an analogous, counterpart in the internal *lex fori*. Novel questions will inevitably ensue. In the remainder of this paper, it is proposed to address three such questions; one of jurisdiction, one of choice of law, and one of recognition.

### 2.1. A Question of Jurisdiction

There are no special rules of jurisdiction in Scots law which pertain to disputes between unmarried couples concerning either personal or property issues. At present, it is the approach of Scots law to treat an unmarried couple as strangers in law. The Scottish rules of jurisdiction[35] would permit the Scottish court *qua situs* of moveable property to assert, declare, or determine proprietary or possessory rights therein, and jurisdiction would likewise be exercised *qua situs* of immoveable property. Rules have recently been put in place, in terms of Brussels II,[36] for the

---

[34]   1992 Report, paragraph 16.3.
[35]   Civil Jurisdiction and Judgments Acts 1982 and 1991, section 20 and Schedule 8.
[36]   Council Regulation (EC) No 1347/2000 on Jurisdiction and the Recognition and Enforcement of Judgments in Matrimonial Matters and in Matters of Parental Responsibility for Children of Both Spouses. See also Proposal (adopted by the European Commission on 17 May 2002) concerning Jurisdiction and the Recognition and Enforcement of

allocation of jurisdiction in matrimonial matters, in civil proceedings relating to divorce, legal separation or annulment. For the same reasons that informed and justified the implementation of Brussels II,[37] it seems that rules for the allocation of jurisdiction in cross-border disputes concerning the dissolution of *de iure* cohabiting relationships, or the cessation of *de facto* cohabiting relationships,[38] will also require to be put in place.

Pending the realisation of such rules, however, it is interesting to consider the potential ambit of operation of Council Regulation (EC) No. 44/2001.[39] Article 1 of Brussels I provides that the Regulation shall not apply, *inter alia*, to "(a) the status or legal capacity of natural persons, rights in property arising out of a matrimonial relationship, wills or succession." This bar does *not* expressly extend to rights in property arising out of an *alternative* domestic relationship, even one which may be said to be "akin to a matrimonial relationship", or (echoing the formulation employed by Scottish parliamentary draftsmen), one which is "a relationship which has the characteristics of the relationship between husband and wife, except that the persons are of the same sex."[40] Ought, therefore, the scheme of jurisdiction which was intended for civil and commercial matters, apply, by default, to the new order of domestic relationships? Taking a purposive approach to Brussels I, it is clear that the Regulation was *not* intended to apply to "personal/domestic" relationships, such as civil partnerships.[41] Similarly, it remains to be seen how the courts of Member States will operate the recognition rules contained in Brussels II when they encounter

---

Judgments in Matrimonial Matters and in Matters of Parental Responsibility, repealing Regulation (EC) No 1347/2000 and amending Regulation (EC) No 44/2001 in matters relating to maintenance (*COM* (2002) 222 final/2).

[37] Preamble to Regulation 1347/2000, paragraph (4): "Differences between certain national rules governing jurisdiction and enforcement hamper the free movement of persons and the sound operation of the internal market." Paragraph (8): "The measures laid down in this Regulation should be consistent and uniform, to enable people to move as widely as possible ..."

[38] At least insofar as the governing law of such relationships [whatever that might be] purports to impose personal, proprietary and/or financial consequences on the parties thereto. But the status issue is also important, as domestic "codes" of rules governing, *e.g.* registered partnerships, are created in an increasing number of legal systems: for is it not likely that many of these may/will require a party to cease to be a member of one partnership before he or she joins another?

[39] Council Regulation (EC) No 44/2001 on Jurisdiction and the Recognition and Enforcement of Judgments in Civil and Commercial Matters.

[40] Mortgage Rights (Scotland) Act 2001, at note 34 above.

[41] Preamble to Regulation 44/2001, paragraph 7: "The scope of this Regulation must cover all the main civil and commercial matters apart from certain well-defined matters."

judicial dissolutions of same-sex marriages from the courts of legal systems that permit such "marriage".[42]

In the absence of pan-European rules of jurisdiction such as Brussels II, it is likely that the Scottish courts would be prepared to exercise jurisdiction over a cohabiting couple, not *qua* "consistorial" forum, but rather *qua lex situs*. But the boundaries of particular bases of jurisdiction are rarely clear, and the exercise of jurisdiction *qua situs* is likely to become complicated should the issue of cohabitation emerge as an *incidental* question.[43]

For example, in terms of Article 22(1) of Brussels I (*ex*-Article 16(1) of the Brussels Convention),[44] a Scottish court will exercise exclusive jurisdiction in proceedings which have as their object rights *in rem* in immoveable property situated in Scotland. But consider the situation that would arise if the parties to such an action were registered partners according to the law of Member State X, or enjoyed rights under X law as *de facto* (rather than *de iure*) cohabitants. If one party to the proceedings were to assert that the immoveable property in Scotland is subject to the property régime applied by X law to registered partners,[45] and that ownership of the immoveable property in Scotland should, therefore, be determined in accordance with X law (which may be the personal law(s) of one or both parties), the Scottish *forum rei sitae* may find itself having to determine, *incidentally*, issues concerning the formal or essential validity of the parties' *de iure* or *de facto* cohabitation. But the question remains: can, or should, the Scottish forum (and/or any other *forum rei sitae*, whether in the alternative, or simultaneously with the Scottish forum), under the aegis of

---

[42]  See text at note 69 *et seq.* below.
[43]  CRAWFORD, E B, "*International Private Law in Scotland*" (1998), p. 53, paragraph 4.21: "An incidental or preliminary question may arise in a conflict problem if the conflict rule of the forum relating to the matter refers to a foreign law, but before the main question can be answered, it is necessary to obtain an answer to another question also containing foreign elements. The problem which then arises is whether the incidental or preliminary question is to be solved by application of the same foreign law (*i.e.* by use of *its* conflict rules) as is applied by the forum to the main question or by application of the conflict rules of the *lex fori* upon the incidental question."
[44]  Article 22: The following courts shall have exclusive jurisdiction, regardless of domicile: 1. in proceedings which have as their object rights *in rem* in immovable property or tenancies of immovable property, the courts of the Member State in which the property is situated. However, in proceedings which have as their object tenancies of immovable property concluded for temporary private use for a maximum period of six consecutive months, the courts of the Member State in which the defendant is domiciled shall also have jurisdiction, provided that the tenant is a natural person and that the landlord and the tenant are domiciled in the same Member State.
[45]  A régime imposed automatically by statute, or by private arrangement.

Article 22(1) exclusive jurisdiction, also determine the cohabitation issue, even incidentally?

Which forum, in fact, is the most appropriate to determine the personal and patrimonial consequences of cohabitation, whether *de facto* or *de iure*? As regards the allocation of jurisdiction in civil proceedings for the termination of cohabitation, and the attendant personal, proprietary and financial consequences, Brussels II provides the obvious model[46] – though, arguably, a clearer, less convoluted model would be desirable.[47]

### 2.2. A Question of Choice of Law

As well as taking the form of an incidental question, a contentious issue concerning cohabitation might arise as a *primary* question. In that context, a difficult issue is likely to be the question of capacity, namely, what law governs, or ought to govern, the capacity of an individual to enter into a personal domestic relationship other than marriage?

Even within the framework of marriage, the Scottish and English choice of law rule governing capacity (to marry) has not been without controversy or doubt. There has long been a tension between the traditional view, according to which capacity to marry is determined by the law of each party's ante-nuptial domicile[48] (and perhaps also by the *lex loci celebrationis*[49]), and the alternative view, attributed to Professor Cheshire,[50] to the effect that the capacity of both parties is to be determined by the law of the intended matrimonial domicile, being the law of the place where the parties intend to live their married life.[51] The Scottish Law Commission has recommended that, in future, the traditional view should be preferred.[52]

---

[46]   Though note the terms of the Brussels II preamble, paragraph (10): "… the Regulation does not affect issues such as … property consequences of the marriage …"

[47]   See comments in TRUEX, D, "Brussels II – It's Here" [2001] *I.F.L.* 7; EVERALL, M and NICHOLLS, M, "Brussels I and II – The Impact on Family Law" [2002] *Fam. Law* 674; and McELEAVY, P, "The Brussels II Regulation: How the EC Has Moved into Family Law" 2002 *ICLQ* 883.

[48]   *Mette v. Mette* (1859) 1 *Sw. & Tr.* 416; *Brook v. Brook* (1861) 9 *H.L.C.* 193; *Re Paine* [1940] *Ch.* 46; and *Pugh v. Pugh* [1951] P. 482. See CRAWFORD, *op.cit.*, p139, paragraph 9.17.

[49]   Marriage (Scotland) Act 1977, section 2(1).

[50]   CHESHIRE, G C H, *Private International Law* 5th ed. (1957), p. 305 *et seq.*

[51]   *In the will of Swan* [1871] 2 *V.R.* (Victoria, Australia); *De Reneville v. De Reneville* [1948] P 100; *Kenward v. Kenward* [1957] P. 124; *Radwan v. Radwan (No 2)* [1972] 3 *All E.R.* 1026; and *Lawrence v. Lawrence* [1985] 2 *All E.R.* 733. See CRAWFORD, *op.cit.*, p. 128, paragraph 9.03.

[52]   1992 Report, Recommendation 70, paragraphs 6.4.14 – 6.4.16. This has been endorsed by the Scottish Executive in *Parents and Children* (Treatment of SLC Recommendations).

Scots law has not yet had occasion to use (nor even, it seems, to develop) choice of law rules in the area of cohabitation. It is this author's submission that harmonised rules of *choice of law* probably are not necessary in this area. In the realm of marriage, there is no European and, with respect, virtually no Hague,[53] instrument which lays down uniform choice of law rules concerning capacity to marry, or the essential and formal validity of marriage. It is suggested that bespoke national choice of law rules operate well enough in the context of marriage, and that it would be difficult, therefore, to justify a different approach to choice of law in cohabitation. Naturally, bespoke rules will require to be ordered in every interested legal system.

A Scots court might require to consider the approach of Scots law to applicable law in determining whether, in its view, a Scottish domiciliary has capacity to enter into either a *de iure* or *de facto* cohabitation, and thereby (in either case) to incur personal and/or proprietary consequences. Certainly, the need for duality of any proposed rule on capacity must be acknowledged. In this regard, early attempts in England to frame (domestic) rules in respect of registered civil partnerships failed signally to address this fundamental difficulty, which may arise, of course, equally within the United Kingdom, as in cases of cohabitation with a "foreigner",[54] and indeed may be more likely to do so. Although entirely a matter of speculation, it is submitted that capacity to enter into *de iure* or *de facto* cohabitation or partnership ought to be governed by the personal law(s) of each party (which, to Scottish eyes, means the *lex domicilii*), cumulatively applied. There is an obvious comparison here with the dual domicile theory which, in Scots law, normally determines capacity to marry, and is likely, in future, always to determine such capacity. It seems inevitable, however, that any general rule of this nature would be subject to a proviso of the *lex loci contractus* (in the case of regulated cohabitation), or the proper law of the cohabitation (in the case of *de facto* cohabitation), which may require, in addition, capacity according to that law (to ensure, for example, compliance with the criminal law).[55]

---

[53]    Two Hague Conventions do exist, but the list of signatories of each is short (and, incidentally, neither includes the United Kingdom), and the impact of each has been minimal: 1902 Hague Convention relating to the Settlement of the Conflict of the Laws concerning Marriage; and 1978 Hague Convention on the Celebration and Recognition of the Validity of Marriages (Signatories – Australia, Egypt, Finland, Luxembourg, Netherlands, Portugal).

[54]    That is to say, foreign domiciliaries (to follow a traditional line), or foreign "habitual residents" (to add a further element of uncertainty), or foreign nationals (to favour Napoleon or Mancini)?

[55]    *E.g.* As to incest, or unlawful sexual intercourse.

One hopes that each corpus of cohabitation law developing across Europe and beyond has addressed, or will address, this problem; otherwise many complexities regarding property and status will arise as a result of partnerships of doubtful standing.

### 2.3. A Question of Recognition

Arguably, it is in the area of recognition and enforcement of judgments in "non-matrimonial" domestic matters that European intervention would be most welcome. Problems of recognition may arise, either in respect of a *status*, which is unknown to, or disapproved by the *lex fori*, or of the purported *incidents* of that status.[56]

In principle, status conferred by the domicile of an individual will usually be recognised by a Scots forum, subject always to a policy discretion.[57] Policy suggests that a status will be recognised, particularly if it is protective, but probably *not* if it is penal.[58] If a court is willing to recognise the status, then recognition should, in principle, extend to such incidents of the status as do not offend the forum. The question arises whether a forum will recognise not only the fact of cohabitation (*de iure* or *de facto*), and any new status purporting to derive therefrom, but also whether it will recognise a foreign dissolution or cessation order, and the proprietary/financial consequences of such an order, or foreign provision (be it mandatory or discretionary) upon the death of either cohabitant. This question assumes special significance where the foreign order or provision purports to affect property situated within the territory of, say, the Scottish forum. Will, or ought, the forum recognise the (alleged) extra-territorial effect of a foreign property régime? The question echoes that which arises in the context of matrimonial property.[59] There may even be a further problem here: how is a Scots court, for example, to prioritise the competing claims of, say, a widow, on the one hand, and a cohabitant, on the other? For it is not

---

[56] See generally CRAWFORD, *op. cit.*, Chapter 8, and GRAVESON, R H, "*Conflict of Laws: Private International Law*" 7th ed. (1974), pp. 229/230. The incidents comprise the rights, duties, powers, disabilities, capacities and incapacities which are bestowed by virtue of the status (CRAWFORD, paragraph 8.06).

[57] E.g. *Knight v. Wedderburn* (1778) M. 145; *Worms v. De Valdor* (1880) 49 *L.J.Ch.* 261; *Re Selot's Trusts* [1902] 1 *Ch.* 488; *Re Langley's Settlement Trusts* [1962] 1 *Ch.* 541; and *Re S (Hospital Patient: Foreign Curator)* [1995] 4 *All E.R.* 30.

[58] *Re Langley's Settlement* above. *Cf. Birtwhistle v. Vardill* (1826) 5 *B&C* 438, *per* Littledale, J., at p. 455: "The very rule that a personal status accompanies a man everywhere, is admitted to have this qualification, that it does not militate against the law of the country where the consequences of that status are sought to be enforced."

[59] E.g. *De Nicols v. Curlier* [1900] *A.C.* 21, and *De Nicols (No. 2)* [1900] 2 *Ch.* 410; *Callwood* [1960] *A.C.* 659; and *Chiwell v. Carlyon* (1897) 14 *S.C.* (South Africa) 61.

impossible that we should meet legal rules which impose proprietary consequences deriving from *de iure* or *de facto* cohabitation, even though the parties cohabiting were not of single marital status. The complexities in constructing a hierarchical framework would be formidable, and would involve, in a more open way than that to which we are used, conflicts between domestic and conflict law and policy.[60]

The first task for any forum would be to determine whether or not the foreign non-matrimonial domestic property régime in question purported to affect property belonging to the cohabitants and situated abroad. But, even where the purported effect is extra-territorial, the *lex situs* would nevertheless retain absolute control over property situated within the *situs*.[61] By recognised privilege, the *lex situs* will prevail over any foreign régime, statutory or private – and acceptance of the property incidents of cohabitation will depend on acquiescence by the *lex situs*.

Since, to some extent, Scots law supports private ordering,[62] one can speculate that it would be possible that a Scottish *lex situs would* recognise the purported extra-territorial effects of such a cohabitation régime, at least as regards the cohabitants *inter se*. Whilst, following an overseas divorce,[63] a Scottish court has jurisdiction to entertain an application for financial provision,[64] there is obviously not yet an equivalent jurisdiction following overseas termination, say, of a civil partnership. Therefore, at present, a Scottish forum would only be required to make a judgment about the status and incidents of cohabitation if these matters arose as an incidental question in a property dispute in respect of which, according to traditional rules, it was properly seised.[65]

Furthermore, great difficulties lie ahead in prioritising the internal law consequences of marriage (or even of cohabitation) as it may come to be regulated in Scotland and England, in a body of rules possibly significantly different from that obtaining in any given (Member) State, and of commercial law in Scotland,[66] against or in relation to the consequences of a foreign registered partnership, assuming the latter to be worthy of recognition in Scots law in general and in particular.

---

[60]    See note 67 *et seq.* below.
[61]    *E.g. Fenton v. Livingstone* (1859) 3 *Macq.* 497.
[62]    *E.g.* Family Law (Scotland) Act 1985, section 16, concerning agreements (by spouses) in respect of financial provision on divorce.
[63]    Subject always to satisfaction of strict conditions – Matrimonial and Family Proceedings Act 1984, sections 28 and 29.
[64]    Matrimonial and Family Proceedings Act 1984, Part IV.
[65]    See example in text at note 46 above.
[66]    *E.g.* Ranking in bankruptcy.

In this area, the conflict rules of Scots (or any other) law must find a new role as hand-maid to its own internal law, and the policies which the latter wishes to adopt: a new mediating, or facilitating, function for the forum. It is submitted that a Scottish court would probably, and in the author's view, rightly, be reluctant to recognise the purported extra-territorial effects of a foreign order where to do so would prejudice a claim, under Scots law, by a *third party*, such as the children or creditor (or parent or spouse) of a cohabitant. So, for example, a child's right under Scots law to receive aliment from his/her parent would probably defeat a claim under foreign law by the parent's cohabitant, to funds in the parent's Scottish bank account. Likewise, a creditor's right under Scots law to exercise diligence over assets in Scotland belonging to the debtor would probably defeat a claim under foreign law by the debtor's cohabitant. It can be seen that devising and formulating rules in this area will not be simple.

Recognition of same-sex relationships presents a slightly different problem. Since, as has been noted,[67] Scots domestic law requires that the parties be of opposite sexes to marry in Scotland whatever the domicile of the parties,[68] and since the Scottish Executive has made it clear that, for the time being, no change is proposed in this controversial area,[69] it seems likely that, as a matter of policy, a foreign same-sex relationship, even one which calls itself a marriage, will *not* be recognised as such in Scotland. If by the foreign law, there is "only one marriage",[70] capable of being entered into by different, or same-sex parties,[71] there exists a problem of characteri-sation as well as policy; and policy may manifest itself not only in the matter of recognition *per se* of the "institution" of cohabitation, but even in the foreign system's choice of law *e.g.* on capacity, of which we may possibly disapprove.[72] If the matter of a foreign same-sex "marriage" should arise in a Scots court in divorce recognition proceedings under Brussels II, the forum would entertain the question only if both parties, by their respective

---

[67] Notes 4 and 31 above.

[68] Where a marriage is celebrated in Scotland, the effect of the Marriage (Scotland) Act 1977 is to require capacity by the Scots *lex loci celebrationis* as well as by the personal law(s) of the domicile.

[69] *Parents and Children*, paragraph 6.4.2. Notes 32 – 35 above.

[70] As is believed to be the case under Dutch law.

[71] Being nationals, or domiciliaries, or merely residents, or registered inhabitants of that legal system, or of any legal system judged by it to be an appropriate one to confer capacity? And of course, there is the issue of whether the requirement would be cumulative, as regards both parties to the relationship. *Cf.* remarks above at note 55 *et seq.*

[72] Criticism of foreign choice of law rules is rare, and rarer still, direct criticism. But in a case such as *Gray v. Formosa* [1963] P. 259, the policy objection to the result upon the status of the wife and children by the Maltese annulment leads inevitably back to an inference of disapproval by the English forum of the Maltese choice of law rule in marriage.

domicile(s), had capacity to "marry". But it is probable, even then, that policy would dictate that there is "nothing to divorce", or that a so-called "divorce" granted by another member state should *not* be recognised on the ground of *ordre public*.[73] But one cannot be dogmatic about this since attitudes may well change with the passing of time – though any change in internal Scots policy ought to be expressly articulated, and only following full and open public consultation on the issue. However, in failing to define the meaning of "marriage", the drafters of Brussels II, wittingly or unwittingly, may have propagated a new "hidden homonym".[74] "Marriage" is a label that, until recently, has been uniformly interpreted across Europe; now it seems that the common label may disguise conflicting (substantive) meanings.

## 3. FACING NEW FRONTIERS

Admittedly, not much is new in these problems of jurisdiction, choice of law and recognition; the production may be modern, but the story is an old one. Over the years, it has been the task of lawmakers in each jurisdiction to develop strategies for coping with "foreign" concepts – that, of course, is the nub of the conflict of laws. Scottish and English courts, for example, have developed clear rules for dealing with polygamous,[75] proxy[76] and other types of marriage,[77] which, though not able to be celebrated or entered into in the United Kingdom, or by domiciliaries of any of the legal systems therein, nevertheless have impacted upon Scottish or English interests.

---

[73] Brussels II, Article 15(1)(a).

[74] KAHN-FREUND, O, *General Problems of Private International Law* (1976) p. 247: "The same concept may have different meanings in different systems of law, or, more correctly, the same word used in different legal systems may denote different concepts ... The hidden homonym is one of the most fruitful roots of misunderstanding in private international law. The builders of the Tower of Babel must be assumed to have realised that they did 'not understand one another's speech'. We are now dealing with situations in which people are struck by the curse of Babel and do not know it."

[75] *E.g. Sinha Peerage Case* [1946] 1 *All E.R.* 348; Matrimonial Proceedings (Polygamous Marriages) Act 1972; and Private International Law (Miscellaneous Provisions) Act 1995, section 7.

[76] *E.g. Apt v. Apt* [1948] P. 83; and *Ponticelli v. Ponticelli* [1958] P. 204.

[77] *E.g. Cheni v. Cheni* [1965] P. 85; and *Lee v. Lau* [1967] P. 14. Generally in international private law, "Novelty in itself should be no bar to the enforcement of a foreign acquired right (nor to the recognition of a foreign status unknown but unexceptionable)." (Crawford, *op.cit.*, paragraph 3.05; *Shahnaz v. Rizwan* [1965] 1 *Q.B.* 390; *Bumper Development Corporation v. Commissioner of Police for the Metropolis* [1991] 4 *All E.R.* 638) Nor need it be a bar in the matrimonial sphere (see *e.g.* speculation about Scots reception of French posthumous marriage: CRAWFORD, *op.cit.*, paragraph 9.01). But we have here something which many would consider fundamentally different from, not a mere variant upon, marriage; a contradiction in terms indeed.

But so far as concerns the new order of non-matrimonial domestic relationships, prospective legislative reform in the United Kingdom, and actual reform across Europe, has increased the likelihood of intra-U.K. and U.K./E.U. Member State (or wider) conflict. As the incidence of cohabitation has increased over the last decade, so too, over the next decade, we are likely to witness an increase in the incidence of cohabitation disputes, including those with a cross-border dimension, and an increase in rules, domestic and conflict, which seek to deal with them.

In 1866, when Lord Penzance trained his eye on domestic relationships in the realm of Christendom, he concluded that domestic relationships meant marriage, and that marriage meant the lifelong union of one man and one woman.[78] But the past, we know, is a *foreign* country.[79] In 2003, in the realm of Europe, the study of domestic relationships calls for a much wider lens. It befalls conflict and comparative lawyers to help focus the picture.

---

[78]  *Hyde v. Hyde & Woodmansee* [1866] L.R. 1 *P&D* 130, *per* Lord Penzance, at p. 133.

[79]  "... they do things differently there." HARTLEY, L P (1895 – 1972), *The Go-Between* (1953).

# CONSEQUENCES DERIVING FROM COHABITATION-RELATIONS BETWEEN PARTNERS AND BETWEEN PARENTS AND CHILDREN

Suzana Kraljić

## 1. INTRODUCTION

As well as in other states, in Slovenia there is a notable increase in cohabitation and a decrease in marriages. Since cohabitation is established in an informal way, it will never be possible to establish the exact number of such relationships. It merely concerns another form of living together that enjoys legal protection. The legal consequences are exclusively bound to the relationships between the partners. But the emergence of certain consequences is also bound to obligatory preconditions for validity, which are set by the law. All the preconditions have to be fulfilled cumulatively, in order to be able to speak of cohabitation creating legal consequences between the partners.

The reasons why the partners decide on cohabitation as opposed to marriage are different. Many young people still feel marriage to be more binding. Cohabitation seems to be more liberal and less binding, in spite of the same consequences (mainly in property law). Marriage is connected to being necessarily subordinated by the state and its norms. Another reason is that many young people decide to choose cohabitation followed by marriage. We may refer to this as a "*testing phase*". The partners wish to establish whether or not they are the proper partners for each other. Some tend to harbour their previous negative experiences regarding marriage (*e.g.* the marriage of their parents, their own previous marriage) and wish to avoid any eventual traumatic experiences. Apart from these reasons, there are also partners who fulfil all the conditions for valid cohabitation, but they conceal its existence, since they do not wish to lose certain privileges, which are enjoyed by a single person (*e.g.* maintenance by the former spouse, lower child-care payments, increased child support, etc.).

## 2. HISTORIC DEVELOPMENT OF COHABITATION

At the time of the Kingdom of SHS or the Kingdom of Yugoslavia, respectively, family law in all legal areas was strongly influenced by the patriarchal system. The oldest legal act recognising the status of cohabitation was the Yugoslav Act on Insurance of Workers from 1922.[1] After that act, the cohabitant of a deceased worker could receive material support, if she had cohabited with him for at least one year and if a child had been born during this cohabitation. Both these conditions had to be cumulatively fulfilled.[2]

Another legal act whose provisions extended into the field of cohabitation was the decree of the National Committee of Liberation of Yugoslavia from 1944 that recognised the cohabitant's right to support by the state in the same way as for a wife, if her cohabitant had been captured, was carrying out his military service or had been killed in war, subject to the condition that she had lived with him in a joint household for at least 6 months before his departure to the military and if he had maintained her mainly.[3]

The later positive provisions, and mainly the former Basic Marriage Act from 1946, did not recognise any legal consequences as a result of cohabitation. The case law of the past WW II era resulted in cohabitation being treated as something that was immoral. From the decisions it may seem that cohabitation was prohibited by the law, but such an interpretation is incorrect. Only cohabitation between minors and cohabitation between relatives was prohibited. These types of cohabitation were sanctioned by criminal law provisions.[4] But, since such cohabitation existed anyway, in practice conflicts emerged as regards property resulting from labour,[5] custody and the upbringing of children, maintenance of the cohabitant, etc. Case law took different positions on the same matters, so it was evident that such a situation could not be allowed to continue. This was also followed by the Supreme Court of Yugoslavia that provided a

---

[1]   Publ. in Službeni list Kraljevine Jugoslavije, no. 117/22.

[2]   For more on this see DRAŠKIĆ M., *Vanbračna zajednica (Cohabitation)*, Naučna knjiga, Belgrade 1988, p. 117.

[3]   See GEČ-KOROŠEC M./KRALJIĆ S., *Družinsko pravo (Family Law)*, 3. revised and completed edition, Univerza v Mariboru, Inštitut za civilno, primerjalno in mednarodno zasebno pravo, Maribor 2000, p. 121.

[4]   So DRAŠKIĆ M., p. 120-121.

[5]   Property relations emerging between cohabitants were dealt with under civil law. Thus, the cohabitants became co-owners of property resulting from. If one of the cohabitants unfairly benefited, the other had the right to redress under the rules of unjust enrichment. For more on this, see POPOVIĆ M., *Porodično pravo (Family Law)*, Savremena administracija, Belgrade 1982, p. 158.

Directive on the Way of Conflict Resolution in Connection with Cohabitation. So, at the end of the 1960s or at the beginning of the 1970s, respectively, cohabitants were recognised as having some rights, which had previously only been recognised as belonging to spouses. The use of the Directive followed the following principles:

a) *New established values* – if a cohabitant used the property of the other cohabitant in a way in which its value became significantly enhanced, he or she had a right of redress against the value of the newly created property (*e.g.* changing the use of a parcel of land from a field to a vineyard);

b) *Right of redress for consumed property* – if the property of one of the cohabitants was used to meet the needs of cohabitation and the children of the cohabitants, the partner, whose property was consumed, has the right of redress against the property's value minus the share used for his/her maintenance;

c) *Right to the property created during the cohabitation* – after the Directive, only one cohabitant could receive the right of possession (right in rem), while the other received a right in personam, i.e. the right of redress against the value of his or her share of the property resulting from labour activities, in monetary terms. The right in rem was recognised as belonging to the cohabitant whose earnings were greater. When the shares were equal, the court had a free hand also to take other factors into consideration in determining, which cohabitant would be granted the right in rem;

d) *Redress for work undertaken* – the cohabitant had a right of redress, if he or she had cared for the sick partner during the time of cohabitation or if he or she had cared for children from the former marriage or cohabitation of the cohabitant. With this regulation the cohabitant was placed in a more advantageous position in comparison to a wife who had no right of redress for work undertaken. However, this decision was supported by the reasoning that during a marriage the spouses are morally and materially obliged to support each other, while in the case of cohabitation, this obligation is not present.[6]

The family's development and its changing position in society also demanded the recognition of cohabitation by society and the law. Marriage in itself was no longer a privileged institution. Thus, the Slovenian Marriage and Family Relations Act[7] (MFRA) from 1976 also added the

---

[6]  MITIĆ M., *Porodično pravo u SFRJ (Family Law in the SFRY)*, Službeni list SFRJ, Belgrade 1980, p. 289-290.

[7]  Publ. in Ur. l. SRS, no. 15/76; 30/86; 1/89; 14/89; RS 13/94; 82/94; 29/95; 26/99; 70/2000; 64/2001, 110/2002.

recognition of cohabitation to its legal provisions. The basis for the recognition of cohabitation was derived from the Constitution of the SFRY from 1974, which determined that the family enjoys social protection (article 190 sec. 1 sentence 1). But a family can emerge within marriage as well as within cohabitation. However, after the Constitution of the SFRY, only the children born out of wedlock enjoyed protection, but not the cohabitants. Therefore, Slovenia with its MFRA was the only member within the territory of the former Yugoslavia that completely equated marriage with cohabitation in family law within the framework of personal rights and duties and in property relations. In Serbia, Kosovo, Croatia and Bosnia and Herzegovina, cohabitants were only recognised to have a right to maintenance and the right to gain and share common property.

## 3. ESTABLISHING COHABITATION

Regarding the contents of article 12 MFRA, cohabitation is a durable living community between a man and a woman, who have not entered into a marriage. For the cohabitant, such a community has the same legal consequences after the MFRA as if he or she had entered into a marriage, if no reasons, are present which would invalidate a marriage. From the wending of the legal provision it can be seen that cohabitation is established in an informal way based on the agreement between the cohabitants. Thus, the difference between marriage and cohabitation is in its establishment, since for a valid marriage, it is necessary to conclude it before the authorised state organ and in the authorised way, while cohabitation is established by the free expression of the will of both parties. In the case of divorce, there is also a formal ending of the relationship, while cohabitants may split informally, either mutually or according to the wish of one of the parties.

Thus, cohabitation is validly established subject to the following conditions:
a) *the cohabitants are of different sexes* – after the MFRA, only cohabitation between a man and a woman will be legally recognised. Cohabitation between homosexual partners does not enjoy legal protection under Slovene law. There is no conflict as regards regulating homosexual living communities, but the way in which they should be regulated has given rise to different opinions. Will they be allowed to register their relationship or will they be allowed to enter into a marriage? In spite of the fact that the Slovene public is still very reserved regarding this question, among the legal experts it is clear that such communities have to be guaranteed some legal protection, especially in the field of

property, whilst the possibility of entering into a marriage will remain reserved for heterosexual living communities;[8]

b) *existence of a living community* – exactly what is a valid living community is has not been defined by the legislator. Departing from the formulation of the MFRA, the living community of cohabitants has to have the same contents as the living community of spouses. Thus, it concerns a living community in the physical, natural, moral, spiritual, sexual and economic sense. The joint household is the most visible indicator that there is a living community between a man and a woman. Living jointly or maintaining a joint household, respectively, is a constituent element of cohabitation. The birth of children as a result of the cohabitation is not an indicator of the living community, but it may indicate some stability in the relationship between the partners.[9]

c) *existence of a durable community* – the legislator has also not precisely described the term "durable living community". The court will have to decide this issue on a case to case basis. Cohabitation has to last for a longer period of time, i.e. as long as it is necessary for a certain similarity between the community and a marriage to appear.[10] The living community in cohabitation has, besides the satisfaction of emotional, moral and economic needs, to fulfil some other conditions as well, among which are maintaining joint living and a joint household, i.e. an economic community – all this has to last for a *relatively long period of time.* Judgement by the Supreme Court of Justice of the RS no. VSO3325 from 12.11.1997. The duration of the cohabitation may be influenced by the birth of children.

d) *no existing reasons, which would invalidate an eventual marriage between them* – the persons (the man and the woman) who wish to establish a valid cohabitation, have to agree to this of their own free will. A marriage may only be concluded between adults. But the Centre for Social Work may allow a person older than 15 years to enter into a marriage, after checking all the important circumstances. The minority of one of the cohabitants, who live in a durable living community, does not in itself automatically exclude the possibility of legal consequences for the

---

[8]    This position is also held by ZUPANČIČ K., "Reforma družinskega prava (Family Law Reform)", *Pravna praksa* 31/2002, p. III and IV.

[9]    ZUPANČIČ K., "Izvenzakonska skupnost v pravu Jugoslavije (Cohabitation in the Law of Yugoslavia)", *Pravnik* 5-7/1987, p. 275.

[10]   In the former SFRY, in all family acts regulating cohabitation the "durable living community "was accepted as legal standard which was judged from case to case as condition for recognising the validity of a cohabitation. The exception was the legal system of Kosovo, where it was determined that cohabitation had to last for 15 years or a minimum of 5 years, respectively, and when common children had been born from the relationship, before the cohabitant was entitled to inherit from his or her partner.

cohabitants, which are equivalent to the consequences that a marriage would entail in their case. The consequences of the durable living community after the provision of article 12 MFRA in this case depend on the existence of well-founded reasons for neglecting the minority of (one of) the parties (article 23 MFRA).[11] For a valid cohabitation, as well as for marriage, respecting the principle of monogamy is required. This means that neither of the cohabitants may be married or cohabiting with anyone else. For the validity of cohabitation there must be no severe mental illness or incapacity. But, there is an essential difference compared to a marriage. If a marriage has been concluded when one of the spouses was suffering from incapacity, there is absolute invalidity, after the end of the injudiciousness it is voidable. In cohabitation, only incapacity lasting for a longer period of time is important, since cohabitation is established and ends in an informal way. Severe mental illness will only be relevant in the case of a durable living community. The cohabitants must not be related along direct or collateral lines up to the fourth degree. As in the case of marriage, the intention to jointly live together is also required for cohabitation, where this condition is even stricter since joint living, i.e. the living community, is an external sign of cohabitation. But, in cohabitation there is also the possibility that the partners live apart for a certain time for justified reasons (*e.g.* work abroad, medical treatment, imprisonment), but, in such a case, the other indicators of cohabitation have to be present (*e.g.* moral, spiritual, material).

## 4. THE INFLUENCE OF COHABITATION ON THE RELATIONS BETWEEN THE PARTNERS

As already stated, the MFRA determined that a validly established cohabitation has the same legal consequences for the cohabitants as if they had entered into a marriage. Regarding the fulfilment of the necessary conditions, Mladenović separates the cohabitation into:

a) *unfree* – none of the cohabitants fulfils the conditions for entering into a marriage;

b) *half free* – only one of the cohabitants fulfils such conditions, while the other partner is hindered by not fulfilling one or more conditions for entering into a marriage;

c) *free* – there is no hindrance to an eventual marriage, and only in such a case may legal consequences emerge.[12]

---

[11] Legal advice VSS adopted on 21. and 22.12.1987- publ. in Slovenski pravni register, Year IV., p. 130-131.

[12] So MLADENOVIĆ M., *Porodično pravo (Family Law)*, Book I, Porodica i brak (Family and Marriage), Privredna štampa, Belgrade 1981, p. 61.

The valid cohabitation, i.e. where all the conditions for an eventual marriage are present, results in certain legal consequences referring only to personal rights and duties and to property relations between the cohabitants. The legal consequences of marriage which refer to the personal status of the spouses (*e.g.* citizenship, business capacity, family name), do not emerge as consequences of a valid cohabitation.

After the MFRA the personal rights and duties of the spouses represent ius cogens. Since cohabitation is equated with marriage as far as personal rights and duties are concerned they represent ius cogens for the cohabitant as well. The personal rights and duties of cohabitants are:

a) the partners are obliged to *mutually respect, trust and help each other* (article 44 MFRA). The duty of mutual respect means that they recognise each other's equal rights, that they respect each other's personality, that they trust each other, that they help each other in a moral and material sense and that they are loyal to each other. The Slovene MFRA does not contain a direct provision demanding loyalty between the spouses or cohabitants, respectively. But that does not mean that it is not such a duty. Adultery means a violation of respect as well as trust in the other spouse;

b) the cohabitants *are free to decide on the birth of children.* The right to freely decide on the birth of children is already guaranteed by the Constitution of the RS (article 55 sec. 1), as an individual human right and not as a joint right of both cohabitants. The cohabitants have the same rights and duties towards the children (article 45 MFRA);

c) during the duration of the cohabitation, the cohabitants are *obliged to live together,* since cohabitation is necessarily a living community between a man and a woman (article 12 sec. 1 MFRA). The duty to live together is determined somewhat more strictly between cohabitants than in the case of marriage, since it is the only visible indicator of the cohabitation. In certain cases, in spite of living apart, the cohabitation is still valid. The reasons, for living apart, have to be justified (*e.g.* if one of the cohabitants works abroad, is complying with compulsory military service, is studying abroad, etc.). The existence of cohabitation is taken as given if the cohabitants live in mutual economic dependence in spite of living apart and, if they have an emotional and intimate relation and plan things jointly;[13]

d) the cohabitants have *the right to a free choice of profession and work* (compare article 46 MFRA), which enables them to exist (economically) independently;

---

[13]    Judgement by the Supreme Court of Justice VS02002 from 8.11.1995.

e) the place *where they jointly live is determined jointly* by the cohabitants (compare article 47 MFRA);

f) *they have a right to a joint decision on joint matters* (compare article 48 MFRA). Joint matters are those that represent the current needs of the living community. It mainly concerns the joint household;

g) the cohabitants contribute to the *maintenance of the family* in relation to their possibilities (compare article 49 MFRA). Since they are equal, they are also equally obliged to contribute to the maintenance of their family. The duty to contribute is in relation to their individual means. The cohabitant may contribute to the maintenance of the family in monetary terms or by work. If one cohabitant tries to avoid contributing to the maintenance of the family, the other may claim the payment of the missing contribution;

h) *maintenance of the cohabitant* – the cohabitant, who does not have the necessary means to provide for him/herself and is unemployed through no fault of his/her own or is incapable of work, has the right to be maintained by the other cohabitant, as far as this is within his or her ability (compare article 50 MFRA). If the personal maintenance of the maintaining cohabitant or other persons having priority (children) would be endangered, the duty to maintain is not taken into account. The amount of the maintenance is determined by the needs of the person to be maintained and the ability to pay of the maintainer (compare article 129 MFRA). Since within Slovenian law, the maintenance of the spouse, i.e. also the cohabitant, falls within personal rights and duties, they are binding provisions. Rejecting the right to maintenance during the course of the cohabitation has no legal effect (compare article 128 MFRA). In this respect the social function of maintenance is stressed and nobody may reject this right. The cohabitants may, after the termination of the cohabitation, conclude an agreement on the duty, the amount and the necessary adjustment of maintenance at the Centre for Social Work (compare article 130 MFRA). If there is no such agreement, the person entitled to maintenance may lodge a claim for maintenance at the competent court. The Court may increase, decrease or terminate the maintenance determined by an agreement or a final judgement based on an application by the person entitled to maintenance or the maintainer, if the circumstances on which it was based subsequently change (article 132 sec. 5 MFRA). The Court sends every final decision to the Centre for Social Work in the region in which the person entitled to maintenance resides (article 132 sec. 3 MFRA). The Centre for Social Work informs the maintainer and the maintained person of every adjustment and the new amount of the maintenance. The information by the

Centre for Social Work, together with the judicial decision or the eventual agreement between the cohabitants, is an executory title (compare article 132 sec. 4 MFRA). In Slovenia a marriage can be dissolved if, for any reason, it has become unbearable. That means that the MFRA does not recognise the principle of guilt in divorce, since also the "culpable"spouse is entitled to request a divorce. Thus, this principle would be unfair in certain cases of maintenance and the situation may be rectified in the sense that the Court may also take into consideration the reasons as to why the marriage became unbearable and thereby led to the dissolution of the marriage. This, by analogy, is also extended to the termination of cohabitation.

Of greater significance are the consequences that relate to property relations as most problems arise in this field (with the exception of maintenance) upon the termination of cohabitation. As already mentioned, the validly established cohabitation has the same consequences as marriage, and this is especially true in property relations in the following cases:

a) *personal property*, that was owned by the cohabitant before the cohabitation remains his/her personal property and is at his/her sole and independent disposal (compare article 51 sec. 1 MFRA). Personal property also covers property that has been obtained by the cohabitant without cost during the cohabitation (*e.g.* inherited property, gifts), but not by means of remunerated work. Any increase in the value of this personal property without any investment by the other cohabitant remains for the benefit of the original owner. But if there is any investment in such personal property and this results in increased value, the increase in the value falls within the community property of the cohabitants. In this case, there can be a claim under the law of property. But, when the investment in the personal property is not in relation to the complete value of the central object (*e.g.* new windows in a house), there can be no claim under the law of property only a claim under the law of obligations;[14]

b) *common property* is the property gained as a result of work during the period of cohabitation (compare article 51 sec. 2 MFRA). Common property is owned jointly by the cohabitants. The cohabitant may not dispose of his or her undefined share inter vivos, and he or she is especially not allowed to sell or burden it (compare article 54 MFRA).

---

[14]    Fore more on personal property see KRALJIĆ S., "Nekateri vidiki prave ureditve premoženjskih razmerij med zakoncema (Some aspects of legal regulation of property relations between spouses)", *Pravnik* 11-12/2001, p. 771 ff.

The rights to real property being common property are registered in the land register in the names of both cohabitants as their community property with undefined shares (compare article 55 MFRA). The cohabitants can only dispose of their common property together. But they can agree that only one of them will manage the whole or part of their common property, while respecting the benefit of the other In the case of such an agreement, each cohabitant may withdraw from the agreement at any time (compare article 52 MFRA). Common property is divided at the end of the cohabitation, upon the demand of a creditor[15] and during the cohabitation based either on an agreement to do so or upon the demand of one cohabitant. At the end of cohabitation, the common property is divided according to the legal presumption (equal shares). If one of the cohabitants is not satisfied with this legal presumption, he/she may prove that he/she has contributed disproportionably to the common property (compare article 59 sec. 1 MFRA). In the dispute regarding the share of the common property, the court of justice takes into account not only the income of each cohabitant, but also other circumstances, such as, for instance, assistance by one partner to the other, custody and upbringing of the children, the carrying out of domestic duties, the upkeep of property and any other form of work and co-operation in the management and preservation of the common property (article 59 sec. 2 MFRA). Before establishing the share of each cohabitant in the common property, the debts and demands against this property are established (article 61 sec. 1 MFRA). Upon the division of common property, the cohabitant may demand mainly those things that belong to his or her share and which are meant for carrying out his or her profession and that enable him or her to obtain an income. In the same way, he or she may demand those things that are exclusively meant for his or her personal use (article 61 sec. 2 MFRA). The method for dividing the property may be agreed upon by the cohabitants and such an agreement must be certified by a notary (compare article 47 sec. 1 Notaries Act (NA)).[16] Primarily, the common property shall be physically divided. When a physical division is not possible, because by its very nature the property cannot be divided or if, as a result of the physical division, the property's value would fall or its functionality would be impaired, then *a civil*

---

[15] The creditor may claim based on a final verdict when the court determines the share of the cohabitant – the debtor – and then demands the execution on this share. If in the execution procedure the sale of the cohabitant's share in the common property is allowed, the other cohabitant has the right of pre-emption, i.e. he/she is entitled to his/her share of the purchase price (compare article 57 MFRA).

[16] Publ. in Ur. l. RS, no. 13/94, 48/94, 92/94.

*division takes place. With a civil division the property is sold.* At civil division, the thing is sold and the cohabitants share the price obtained. One cohabitant may as well compensate the other in monetary terms. But when the cohabitants are not able to agree upon the division of the common property, the division will be carried out by the court in non-contentius civil proceedings (article 70 sec. 2 Law of Property Code).[17] An essential difference between establishing common property in marriage and in cohabitation concerns the moment from when common property comes into existence. Common property in marriage starts to exist when the marriage is entered into, whilst in cohabitation it is necessary that it lasts for a longer period of time. If the cohabitants have lived in a living community that, after the MFRA, does not fulfil the conditions for a valid cohabitation, during the time of this community no common property can start to exist. In such a case the cohabitants only have claims under the law of property.[18]

c) *liability for the obligations* – for the obligations of the cohabitant before cohabitation has commenced, as well as the obligations that he or she takes over after the termination of the cohabitation, he or she is solely liable. For obligations burdening both cohabitants and emerging out of the common property,[19] both cohabitants are liable in terms of their personal as well as their common property in solidum. If, when repaying a debt burdening both partners, one of them pays more than his or her debt, he or she is entitled to recourse (compare article 56 MFRA). The creditor of one of the cohabitants may demand a judicial determination of the share of his or her debtor in the common property and thereby demand the execution of this share so as to reimburse his or her claim from the common property of the cohabitants (article 57 sec. 1 MFRA);

d) *legal transactions between cohabitants* – the cohabitants may conclude with each other all the legal transactions that they would be able to conclude with other persons, and in this way they create between each other property relations with rights and obligations. For the validity of these

---

[17]   Publ. in Ur. l. RS, no. 87/2002.

[18]   VSH, no. Rev 1498/91 from 10.10.1991- case taken from LJUJIĆ B., *Zbirka sodnih odločb, Zakonska zveza in družinska razmerja (Collection of Judicial Decisions, Marriage and Family Relations)*, Bonex Založba, Ljubljana 1998, p. 2.

[19]   "Credits and loans taken over by spouses separately are considered in the determination of the share of the jointly gained property, in spite of the fact that on the one side there are more credits and loans than on the other, since the repayment of credits and loans means a burden for the family purse. Subsequently emerging repayments of credits and loans may be the basis for mutual claims, in order to adjust these burdens to the shares in the common property."- VS SRS, Pž 1381/72, from 2.3.1973- Report by VS SRS 1/63- taken from GEČ-KOROŠEC M., *Pravna ureditev življenja v dvoje (Legal regulation of living together)*, ČGP Delo, Ljubljana 1987, p. 63.

legal transactions it is necessary to obtain certification by a notary (article 47 sec. 1 NA). Certification by a notary is not necessary if it merely concerns ordinary and smaller gifts. Slovenian law does not allow spouses to conclude marriage settlements in order to change the legal property regime. Thus, the provisions on the property regime are binding and this also applies to cohabitants.[20]

## 5.  COHABITATION AND ITS INFLUENCE ON CHILDREN

The family enjoys special protection for the benefit of the children, which is derived from numerous international conventions as well as from the Slovenian Constitution and acts. Regarding the wording of the MFRA, a validly established cohabitation has legal consequences in relation to the cohabitants only, but not between them and their common children. For the children born or conceived during the period of cohabitation the legal presumption of paternity is not applicable. Therefore, the institution of recognition or even the judicial establishment of paternity is appropriate.

For the valid recognition of paternity, the following preconditions have to be fulfilled:
a) *discernment of the male who recognises paternity;*
b) *the man recognising paternity has to be at least 15 years of age;*
c) *the recognition of paternity may be made at the Centre for Social Work, at the registrar, in a public document or by last will;*
d) *the child's mother has to agree to the recognition* – if the mother does not agree or if she does not make any pronouncement within 1 month, the man recognising the child may file a claim at the court in order to establish paternity. In such a case, he will be subject to the subjective limitation period (1 year from the reception of information that the mother does not agree to the recognition or that she makes no pronouncement) as well as the objective limitation period (5 years from the child's birth).

After receiving information on the birth of a child out of wedlock, the registrar will contact the mother in order to discover the father of the child.

---

[20]  Regarding common property, a problem arises when a cohabitant is not yet divorced from a previous spouse. Since community property starts to exist in the marriage as long as the living community of the spouses exists, when the living community in a marriage comes to an end, community property ceases. In cohabitation with the cohabitant who is still married, there is no community property since the condition for the consequences of cohabitation, its validity, is the non-existence of conditions which would invalidate an eventual marriage. And in such a case we have actual polygamy (formal polygamy is legally forbidden).

If the mother provides the name of the father, the Centre for Social Work will contact him concerning his recognition. If he is not forthcoming concerning his recognition, the mother may sue him to establish paternity on behalf of the child (article 91 MFRA). When the child reaches the age of majority (18 years), it can sue for the establishment of paternity but only within five years.

When both the father and the mother agree as to paternity, there are few problems. The recognition of paternity and the mother's agreement may be given at the same time. But if there is no agreement between the mother and the man (he wishes to recognise paternity, but the mother does not agree to the recognition), the possibility of a judicial scenario becomes open. There is no establishment of paternity ex officio. The establishment of paternity (recognition or by means of a judicial decision) is a very important step, since only at this moment do the equal rights and duties of the parents towards the children born out of wedlock start to be the same as those of parents of children born within wedlock. The father of a child born out of wedlock is obliged to contribute to the costs of the pregnancy and the birth and to the costs of maintaining the mother before and after the birth in accordance with his financial means, and as long as the mother is unable to find employment (article 94 MFRA).

If cohabitation comes to an end either mutually or unilaterally, it is also necessary to reach an agreement concerning the common children. The cohabitants may agree on custody, the upbringing and maintenance of the children and on visitation rights. As there is no formal requirement for commencing cohabitation, there is also none for its termination. This means that, provided there is agreement between the cohabitants as to custody, the upbringing and the maintenance of the children, their agreement is not subject to any control. Only if the cohabitants are unable to agree the Court will intervene. The Court will only approve their agreement if it benefits the children. The agreement is to be controlled ex officio. If the Court establishes that there is no proper provision for the children, it will urge the parents to amend the agreement accordingly. If they do not do so, the Court may reach a decision of its own volition. So, the Court may decide that all children will remain in the custody of one of the parents or that certain children remain with one parent while the others will be in the custody of the other parent or that they are assigned to some third person or institution. Before the Court decides it will obtain the expert opinion of the Centre for Social Work (article 78 sec. 2 MFRA).

The Centre for Social Work has to establish who is in a better position to care for the children in a physical, moral and intellectual sense.[21]

The court determines the amount of the financial contribution to the maintenance of the children. This is determined in relation to the means of each parent and the needs of the child. Each parent or child may respectively apply for the determined contribution to be adjusted to changed circumstances (article 79 MFRA).

The cohabitant who does not have custody of the children retains the right of personal contact with them. The right to personal contact also encapsulates, among other things, the right to visit the child, the right to contribute to its upbringing, the right to decide upon events that might essentially influence the child's life, and the right to take the child on holiday. The right to personal contact is granted to the parent even when the child has been assigned to a third person or institution. Thus, the foster parent is obliged to allow the parents to visit the child and to enable and enhance contacts between the foster child and the parents, except when the parents have been prohibited from having contact (article 169 MFRA). If the parent has the right to personal contact and insists upon this right, but the child does not desire to have such personal contact, then contact will be discontinued in order to protect the child's interests. Having said that, however, the merits of each case are looked at.[22]

## 6. PROCEDURAL DIFFICULTIES CONNECTED WITH COHABITATION

By regulating cohabitation in the MFRA, the legislator wished to equate cohabitation with marriage as far as possible. As already mentioned, valid cohabitation after the MFRA results in the same property consequences as well as the personal rights and duties pertaining to cohabitants as a marriage does for the spouses. But the existence of a marriage is easier to prove due to its obligatory formality. The concluded marriage is entered

---

[21] *"In deciding to which parent the child shall be assigned, among other things, it is important with whom the child is currently living and that it is not displaced from is surroundings, whereit attends school and has friends. "*- judgement by VS Koper, case no. Cp 97/93.

[22] More on personal contacts KRALJIĆ S., "Dodeljevanje otrok v varstvo in vzgojo ter urejanje osebnih stikov po ZZZDR in pravu držav bivše SFRJ (Children's custody and the regulation of personal contact after the MFRA and the law of the states of the former SFRY)", in: *Novejše tendence razvoja otroškega prava v evropskih državah- prilagajanje otroškega prava v Republiki Sloveniji* (New tendencies in the development of children's law in the European states – harmonisation of child law in the republic of Slovenia), Collection of articles, Inštitut za civilno, primerjalno in mednarodno zasebno pravo, Maribor 1997, p. 91.

in the register of marriages and its existence is proved by the excerpt from the register that can be obtained by anyone who proves that he/she has a legal interest (compare article 30 sec. 1 Registers Act (RA)).[23] Cohabitation starts to exist according to the will of the cohabitants, in an informal way. When a conflict arises between the cohabitants, it is necessary to determine in each individual case whether there is in fact cohabitation and at what moment in time did it first commence. The determination of the moment when cohabitation starts or the moment when all the conditions for the validity of the cohabitation have been fulfilled (*e.g.* the cohabitants lived in a living community in spite of the fact that one of them was not yet divorced) is especially important when the establishment of the rights and obligations of the cohabitants are determined. The decision on the existence of a valid cohabitation only has effect in the particular matter in which this question is resolved (article 12 sec. 2 MFRA).

In the proceedings to prove the existence of cohabitation, it is primarily necessary to prove that two persons of different sexes have cohabited in a living community on a permanent basis. When these facts are established beyond doubt, the court will determine whether this community is in accordance with article 12 MFRA.[24] And after establishing its accordance with article 12 MFRA, the court can decide whether in the concrete case cohabitation in fact exists. The existence of cohabitation is therefore resolved as a preliminary issue in the concrete matter. If the contentious matter is heard before the civil court (*e.g.* a maintenance claim after the ending of cohabitation), the civil court will resolve the question of its own accord. But, since the establishment of cohabitation only has effect in the concrete issue, and since the court is not bound by any prior establishment of the contentious matter (the existence of cohabitation) as a preliminary issue, this same question may be resolved differently in different proceedings.[25] However, if the contentious matter is heard before a non-contentius civil court and if the question of the existence of cohabitation emerges and if the facts relating to the cohabitation are disputed by the parties (if there is no conflict between the parties, the non-contentius civil court may resolve this question of its own accord), the non-contentius civil court will halt the proceedings and refer the parties to contentious proceedings.

---

[23] Publ. in Ur. l. SRS, no. 2/87; RS 28/95; 29/95; 84/00.
[24] So WEDAM-LUKIĆ D., "Procesni problemi ugotavljanja obstoja izvenzakonske skupnosti (Procedural problems in establishing of the existence of cohabitation)", *Pravnik*, no. 8-10/1987, p. 405.
[25] WEDAM-LUKIĆ D., p. 406.

## 7. COHABITATION OUTSIDE THE MFRA

The MFRA recognises the legal validity of cohabitation only for its own purposes, while in other fields it is up to every individual Act to regulate whether cohabitation will be legally recognised, under which conditions it will be recognised and which legal consequences will result from it. How some singular acts have regulated cohabitation may be illustrated as follows:

a) *The Succession Act* (SA)[26] determines that, as is the case with spouses, also the man and woman who live in a long-lasting living community and who have not entered into a marriage inherit from each other, but only where there are no reasons which would invalidate a marriage between them (article 10 sec. 2 SA). That means that the cohabitant inherits by law, in the first and second order of succession. If he or she inherits in the first order of succession, he or she will inherit together with the deceased's children (natural or adopted), in equal shares (compare article 11 SA). If he or she inherits in the second order of succession (if the deceased did not have children), as a rule he or she receives half of the estate while the other half goes to the parents of the deceased cohabitant or their children based on the principle of representation (compare articles 14 and 15 SA);

b) *The Social Security Act* (SSA)[27] determines in article 26 that a family member is also a person living with the person relying on the right to financial support if they have cohabited for at least one year in a living community that can be equated with marriage as regards its legal consequences, along the lines of the MFRA;

c) *The Amnesty Act* (AA)[28] states that a petition for amnesty may be filed by a person with whom the convicted person cohabits (article 6);

d) *The Parental Security and Family Income Act* (PCFIA)[29] recognises a person as a cohabitant if he or she cohabits with another person and this may be equated with a marriage as regards its legal consequences, along the lines of the MFRA (article 11 point 3). Such cohabitation must have lasted for at least one year;

e) *The Pension and Invalidity Insurance Act (PIIA)*[30] determines that a person who has cohabited with the deceases for the last three years before his/her death in a living community which may be equated with a marriage, or has cohabited with the deceased in the last year before his

---

[26]   Publ. in Ur. l. SRS, no. 15/76; 23/78; RS 17/91; 13/94; 67/2001.
[27]   Publ. in Ur. l. RS, no. 54/92; 42/94; 26/2001.
[28]   Publ. in Ur. l. RS, no. 45/95.
[29]   Publ. in Ur. l. RS, no. 97/2001.
[30]   Publ. in Ur. l. Rs, no.106/99; 72/2000; 124/2000; 109/2001.

or her death and they together have a child, has the right to receive a widow's/widower's pension (article 114);

f) *The Code of Obligations* (CO)[31] *determines that* in the case of the death or severe mental illness of the partner, the cohabitant has the right to financial reparation for the mental pain suffered, if there is a steady living community between him or her and the deceased/mentally ill (article 180 CO).

g) *The Criminal Proceedings Act* (CPA)[32] determines that the person with whom the suspect lives in cohabitation is exempt from having to testify against his/her partner (article 236 sec. 1 point 1);

h) *The Income Tax Act*[33] considers the person who has no own means of subsistence or means that are lower than the amount of the special provision for a maintained family member, as a maintained family member, if he or she has cohabited with the insured in a living community which may be equated with marriage in its legal consequences, along the lines of the MFRA, during, the full year for which the tax is being assessed (article 11 para. 2);

i) The *Civil Procedure Act*[34] determines in article 233 sec. 1 that a witness may refuse to answer any questions, if he or she has sound reasons, especially if answering such questions would be prejudicial to him or her, his or her relatives, his or her spouse or the person with whom he/she cohabits in a long-lasting living community as determined by the act regulating marriage. "Prejudicial" in this sense means being detrimental to one's reputation or resulting in material loss or criminal prosecution;

j) *The Private International Law and Procedure Act* (IPLPA)[35] determines that in the case of cohabiting persons their lex nationalis and secondarily their joint lex domicilii is primarily applicable. For the contractual relations between cohabiting persons, the law that was applicable to their property relations at the time of concluding the contract will be applicable (article 41).

k) *The Property Code* (PC)[36] states that the prohibition on selling or burdening property may only be registered in the land register if it is determined between the cohabitants, and in this case it is also effective against third persons (article 38 sec. 4);

---

[31]    Publ. in Ur. l. RS, no. 83/2001.
[32]    Publ. in Ur. l. RS, no. 63/94; 70794; 72/98; 6/99; 66/2000; 111/2001.
[33]    Publ. in Ur. l. RS, no. 71/93; 71/93; 2/94; 7/95; 44/96.
[34]    Publ. in Ur. l. RS, no. 26/99, 96/2002.
[35]    Publ. in Ur. l. RS, no. 56/99.
[36]    Publ. in Ur. l. RS, no. 87/2002.

l) *The Penal Execution Act* (PEA)[37] determines that a close family member is a person living in cohabitation with the person against whom the penalty is being executed (sec. 10 para 3);

m) *The Labour Relations Act* (LRA)[38] states that upon a persons death, the partner who has lived with him or her in a living community for the last two years, and this living community may be equated with marriage, along the lines of the MFRA, has a right to paid leave from work for at least one working day (article 167).

## 8. A COMPARATIVE OVERVIEW OF THE REGULATIONS PERTAINING TO COHABITATION

### 8.1. Croatia

During the existence of the SFRY, the Republic of Croatia in its *Zakon o braku i porodičnim odnosima* (MFRA)[39] from 1978 also regulated cohabitation, in spite of the fact that the constitution of that time did not require such a regulation, since it only required special protection for children, regardless of their birth. In 1998 Croatia adopted a new Family Law Act (*Obiteljski zakon- OZ*),[40] article 1 of which determines that in the act also the consequences of cohabitation between a man and a woman are regulated. The basis therefore is provided in the Constitution itself under article 61 sec. 2, which states that a marriage and the legal relations within a marriage, cohabitation and the family are regulated by the law. By this constitutional provision, the grounds for regulating the consequences of cohabitation, not only in family law, but also in other legal fields, are given.[41]

Article 3 of the FA gives article 1 a more concrete form by stating that the provisions of the FA on the effects the cohabitation are applicable to the living community of an unmarried woman (*neudana žena*) and an unmarried man (*neoženjen muškarac*). So, it is clear that Croatian law also does not recognise the living communities of homosexual partners. Therefore, for the validity of cohabitation, it is only necessary that the condition of not being married has to be fulfilled, which is less difficult than under Slovenian law. At the end of long-lasting cohabitation, the cohabitant who

---

[37]   Publ. in Ur. l. RS, no. 22/2000.
[38]   Publ. in Ur. l. Rs, no. 42/2002
[39]   Publ. in Narodne novine, no. 11/78; 45/89; 59/90.
[40]   Publ. in Narodne novine, no. 162/98.
[41]   ALINČIĆ M.; V: ALINČIĆ M./ BAKARIĆ-ABRAMOVIĆ A./ HLAČA N./ HRABAR D., *Obiteljsko pravo (Family Law)*, Birotehnika, Zagreb 1994, p. 136.

does not have sufficient means for subsistence or who is not able to provide such means from his or her own property and is incapable of work or is unable to find employment, has the right to maintenance (compare articles 210, 221 and 226 sec. 1 FA). Croatian law also leaves it to the courts to interpret "long lasting living community". The cohabitant may file a claim for maintenance within 6 months (The MFRA determined a one-year period) of the end of cohabitation. In deciding upon the grounds for maintenance, the court may reject the claim if it would be obviously unfair to the other cohabitant (article 227 FA). The court may determine that the maintenance will last for up to one year if there are circumstances that indicate that the plaintiff will be able to provide for him/herself within an appropriate period of time (article 228 sec. 1 FA). In certain cases this one-year period may be prolonged, but a claim for such an extension has to be filed before the maintenance expires (article 228 sec. 2 and 3 FA). The cohabitant's right to maintenance will end when he or she enters into a marriage or when the court establishes that he or she is cohabiting with another person or is deemed not to be worthy of maintenance or, finally, if a certain condition no longer exists or that he or she became unworthy of this right or if any condition does not exist any more (*e.g.* the cohabitant now has the opportunity to seek gainful employment).

The father of a child born out of wedlock is obliged to maintain the mother of the child for one year after the birth, if the mother cares for the child, but has insufficient means (article 230 FA).

For cohabitation, the same property regime is applicable as for spouses. Everything gained by the cohabitants during their cohabitation as a result of their working endeavours is *conjugal property (bračna imovina)*, of which the cohabitants are co-owners with equal shares. That which they have gained not as a result of their working endeavours, *e.g.* by inheritance, remains their personal property (*vlastita imovina*). The cohabitants for whom the legal property regime is not appropriate may regulate their own property by means of a contract.(compare article 253 sec. 2 FA and article 262). The contract may be concluded in written form, and the signatures of the cohabitants have to be certified by a notary.

### 8.2. Macedonia

Macedonia adopted a new family act immediately after its separation from the SFRY (*Zakon za semejstvoto (ZS-RM)*.[42] This act regulates cohabitation

---

[42]    Publ. in Službeni vesnik na Republika Makedonija, no. 80/92.

for the first time, since the former republic act from 1973 (*Zakon za brakot*)[43] did not regulate this aspect. However, in its article 12 sec. 2, it is determined that the court, in proceedings for establishing paternity, has to take into consideration the living community of the child's mother with the defendant before the child's birth.[44]

During cohabitation, a community of property arises, for the division of which the provisions on the division of common property relating to marriage are valid. The ZS-RM enables spouses to choose between the legal property system of divided property (*Gütertrennung*) and the community of property gained from working endeavours (*Errungenschaftsgemeinschaft*).[45] Cohabitants do not have both possibilities, for them the property regime of common property gained from working endeavours is applicable.[46] Thus, the cohabitants each have their personal property, as well as common property. Common property is the property gained by the cohabitants by means of their working endeavours during the period of cohabitation (article 205 in connection with article 213 sec. 2 ZS-RM). From the common property the following is excluded:
– property that the cohabitant possessed before the cohabitation;
– property gained by means of an inheritance, legacy, or donation;
– things gained during the period of cohabitation and exclusively meant for the satisfaction of personal needs, as far as they are not of greater value in relation to the remainder of the common property (article 204 sec. 2 ZS-RM).

Upon the division of common property, there is a legal presumption that the shares of the cohabitants are equal. The court may, however, at the request of one of the cohabitants, determine a different share, but only if the circumstances of the case so require. At the request of one of the cohabitants property exclusively for personal use will be excluded from the division of property (article 204 sec. 2 ZS-RM). The value of the excluded property is not taken into account in determining a cohabitant's share. However, when the value of the excluded properties is high in comparison with the value of the community property in its entirely, it will

---

[43]   Publ. in Službeni vesnik SRM, no. 35/73.

[44]   ZUPANČIĆ K., "Izvenzakonska skupnost v pravu Jugoslavije (Cohabitation in the law of Yugoslavia)", *Pravnik* 5-7/1987, p. 289.

[45]   GEČ-KOROŠEC M/KRALJIĆ S./KRALJIĆ M., "Mazedonien", in: *Internationales Ehe- und Kindschaftsrecht*, 132. edition, Verlag für Standesamtswesen GmbH, Frankfurt am Main 1998, p. 28.

[46]   KRALJIĆ, "Nekateri vidiki pravne ureditve premoženjskih razmerij med zakoncema" (Some Aspects of the Legal Regulation of Property Relations between Spouses), p. 781.

be taken into account. (article 213 sec. 3 ZS-RM). The cohabitant who will have custody of the common children after the end of cohabitation, will also be assigned the property of the children, in addition to his or her share (article 214 sec. 1 ZS-RM).

### 8.3. Serbia

The SR of Serbia first regulated cohabitation under the *Marriage and Family Relations Act* (MFRA)[47] from 1980. The living community of a man and a woman, who have not entered into a marriage, is equated with a marriage in respect of the mutual living and other property relations, subject to the conditions provided by the MFRA (article 16 sec. 1). The mentioned consequences do not arise when there are legal impediments thereto: the existence of a marriage, when the parties are related by blood, full adoption, when one of the parties suffers from a mental illness or there is a case of impropriety (article 16 sec. 2 MFRA). It is important that these impediments are not present when the claim for judicial protection is instigated.[48]

The cohabitant has the right to maintenance after the end of the cohabitation, if it has been of long duration. If, however there are children from the relationship, then the cohabitation does not have to have been of long duration (article 293 in connection with article 287 sec. 1). The claim for maintenance may be filed within one year from the end of cohabitation, but subject to the proviso that the conditions for maintenance were present at the end of the cohabitation and still existed at the time of the maintenance claim (article 293 sec. 2 MFRA). The court may reject the claim for maintenance if the cohabitant requiring maintenance has behaved improperly towards the other cohabitant during the cohabitation, if he or she has wilfully ended the cohabitation without any sound reason or if the claim for maintenance is obviously unfair for the other cohabitant (article 293 sec. 4 MFRA). The court may determine the maintenance for a certain period of time, if it believes that the cohabitant requesting maintenance will be able to gain paid employment within a shorter period of time. If the cohabitation has only lasted for a short time, but children have resulted from the relationship, the court may determine the maintenance for a certain period of time or it may even reject maintenance claim, if the children are assigned to the cohabitant who is supposed to pay maintenance (article 294 sec. 2 MFRA). An agreement between the cohabitants

---

[47]   Publ. in Službeni glasnik SRJ, no. 22/80.
[48]   CVEJIĆ-JANČIĆ O., *Porodično pravo (Family Law)*, Novi Sad 2001, p. 209.

dispensing with the right to maintenance is invalid (article 296 MFRA). If a child has been born out of wedlock, the father is obliged to maintain the mother of the child for 3 months before the birth and for one year subsequent thereto, irrespective of whether or not they had in fact cohabited article 297 sec. 1 MFRA). The property acquired by the cohabitants as a result of their working endeavours during the period of cohabitation is their common property.

## 9. CONCLUSIONS

Cohabitation presents an alternative form of lifestyle for of a man and a woman . The basic difference between both cohabitation and a marriage relates to formality – for establishing a marriage, the fulfilment of all legally provided conditions is required, while establishing cohabitation depends on the free will of the cohabitants. That means that in establishing cohabitation no co-operation by any state organ is necessary. A divorce may also only be granted by the courts while cohabitation can come to an end with the will of one or both cohabitants. The legal consequences of valid cohabitation extend to the field of maintenance and other property relations between the cohabitants. However, before the court decides upon maintenance between the cohabitants it has to establish for instance, whether the living community really existed and whether all the required preconditions have been fulfilled. Here we can speak of a *probatio diabolica*, as the cohabitants may each adduce circumstances that will tend to strengthen their case (*e.g.* one of the cohabitants claims that the cohabitation only lasted for a short period of time, while the other claims that it was a longer duration).

In Slovenia, there are plans to reform family law. Currently, spouses are not able to regulate their property regime, although the proposed reform will change this. But will this influence property relations between cohabitants? Will the legislator enable them to conclude contracts as well (as in Croatia), or will it follow the Macedonian regulation where this "privilege" is reserved for spouses?

Since cohabitation is widespread in Slovenia, it is very important how the legislator intends to deal with it in certain legal provisions. The purpose of legal provisions is to fortify the protection of the cohabitant in certain situations (*e.g.* in case of death/inheritance, maintenance and the division of community property; tax relief, etc.). However, it is necessary to differentiate between a marriage and cohabitation, although the influence of the state should be limited, where the cohabitants have consciously decided that they do not wish such an influence to be exented upon them (*e.g.* the eventual registration of cohabitation).

**Table 1 –Disti nguishing features of Marriage and Cohabitation under Slovenian Law**

|  | MARRIAGE | COHABITATION |
|---|---|---|
| **BEGINNING** | Formal (state organ, prescri-bed procedure...) | Informal (free will of the coha-bitants and no state coopera-tion) |
| **TERMINATION** | Formal (divorce granted by the courts) | Informal (by one or both part-ners) |
| **CONDITIONS** | Determined by the MFRA | Marriage + living community + longer duration |
| **CONSEQUENCES** | – Personal rights and duties<br>– Property relations<br>– Personal status (family name, business capacity) | – Personal rights and duties<br>– Property relations |
| **CHILDREN** | Legal presumption on the part of the father (during marriage and 300 days after) | – Recognition of paternity<br>– Judicial establishment of paternity |
| **CUSTODY OF CHILDREN** | – Decided by the courts | – Decided by the courts (be-fore 2001 the Centre for Social Work) |
| **REGULATION** | MFRA (1976, 1989) | – Individually regulated |

**Table 2 –Cohabitation outside the MFRA**

| | |
|---|---|
| **Succession Act (1976)** | A man and a woman cohabiting in a long-lasting living community who have not entered into a marriage will inherit from each other, but only where that there are no reasons which would invalidate a marriage. |
| **Social Security Act (1992)** | A family member is also a person living with the person who applies for financial support. This cohabitation has been for at least one year and may be equated with a marriage as regards its legal consequences, along the lines of the MFRA. |
| **Parental Security and Family Income Act (2001)** | Considers a person to be as cohabitant if he or she lives in cohabitation and this may be equated with a marriage as regards its legal consequences, along the lines of the MFRA, The cohabitation must have lasted for at least one year. |
| **Pension and Invalidity Insurance Act (1999)** | Determines that a person which may be equated with a marriage as regards with the decedent in a living community which may be equated with a marriage as regards the legal consequences for the last three years before death, or has lived with the deceived during the last year before death and they together have a child, has a right to the widow's/widower's pension. |
| **Criminal Proceedings Act (1994)** | Determines that the person with whom the suspect cohabits is not obliged to testify against him/her. |
| **Code of Obligations (2001)** | In the case of the death or severe mental illness of the partner, the cohabitant has the right to financial reparation for the mental anguish suffered. |
| **Private International Law and Procedure Act (1999)** | For persons living in cohabitation their lex nationalis and secondarily their joint lex domicilii will primarily be applicable. For the contractual relations between cohabitants, the law that was applicable to their property at the time when the contract was concluded will be applicable. |
| **Labour Relations Act (2002)** | Upon a person's death, the cohabitant who has lived with him/her for the last two years, and this living community may be equated with a marriage along the lines of the MFRA, has a right to leave absence from work for at least one working day (article 167). |

**Table 3 –Comparative overview**

|  | SLOVENIA | CROATIA | SERBIA |
|---|---|---|---|
| ACT | Marriage and Family Relations Act (1976/1989) | Family Law Act (1998) | Marriage and Family Relations Act (1980) |
| CONDITIONS | – a man and a woman<br>– living community<br>– of longer duration<br>– no reasons to invalidate a eventual marriage | – a man and a woman<br>– living community | – a man and a woman (none of the following: a marriage, blood relationship, full adoption, mental illness, injudiciousness<br>– living community |
| HOMOSEXUALS | – no regulation | – no regulation | – no regulation |
| CONSEQUENCES | – personal rights and duties (maintenance)<br>– property relations | – property relations and maintenance | – property relations and maintenance |
| PROPERTY REGIME | – common property (gained from working endeavours + no marital agreements)<br>– cohabitants are joint tenants | – common property<br>– partners are co-owners<br>– marital agreements also for cohabitants | – common property (gained from working endeavours + no marital agreements)<br>– cohabitants are joint tenants |
| MOTHER'S MAINTENANCE AFTER BIRTH | – duty to contribute to the expenses of pregnancy and the birth<br>– duty to maintain before and after birth, until she is in a position to find gainful employment herself | – 1 year (insufficient means) | – 3 months before and 1 year after birth |
| MAINTENANCE AFTER TERMINATION OF THE COHABITATION | – insufficient means for subsistence and unemployed or incapable of work;<br>– end of: marriage, cohabitation, conditions for maintenance no longer in existence | – insufficient means for subsistence and not able to provide them from property and incapable of work or not able to find employment<br>– rejection- if unfair<br>– end of: marriage, new cohabitation, unworthiness, conditions for maintenance no longer in existence | – cohabitation of longer duration (children)<br>– rejection – if behaviour is wilfully reprehensible, or there are no sound reasons for ending the cohabitation<br>– end of: marriage, cohabitation, work, conditions for maintenance no longer in existence |

# 2. NEW TRENDS IN THE FIELD OF PARENTAGE AND PARENTAL RESPONSIBILITES

# PARENTAL RESPONSIBILITIES *VERSUS* THE PROGRESSIVE AUTONOMY OF THE CHILD AND THE ADOLESCENT

Rosa Martins

## 1. INTRODUCTION

This study will analyse the legal nature, concept and aims of parental responsibilities regarding the progressive autonomy of the child and the adolescent. The theme of this study came about as a result of the need to match the legal framework of parent-child relationships, in particular those of parental responsibilities, with the new challenges that we are facing today. The progressive autonomy of the child and adolescent is one of these challenges. The acceptance of this autonomy for children has gained importance ever since they were given the status of individuals with rights and since the principle of the general incapacity of minors to exercise their rights started to be questioned. It is important to know what the effects of this progressive autonomy are on the concept of parental care and on the legal regulation of parent – children relationships and, in particular, on the new configuration of parental responsibilities.

Firstly, I will describe parental care, as it has been understood by most legal authors. Secondly, I will try to outline the form in which Society, the State and the Law have shifted perspective with regards to the child and the adolescent. In this new perspective children and adolescents are considered as persons who acquire progressive autonomy as they grow in maturity. Thirdly, I will examine the effects of the acceptance of the progressive autonomy of children on the law of some European countries (Portugal, Spain, Italy, France, Germany, England and Wales) by checking to see whether the solution to this problem is a satisfactory one. Fourthly, I will pose some questions and try to answer them, which I hope will help us to go in a new direction regarding this subject. Some of these questions include the following: What is the traditional understanding of the legal nature, content and purposes of parental care? Will the progressive acceptance of the autonomy of the child and the adolescent imply a subsequent progressive reduction in the content of parental responsibilities? Will this mean a readjustment of its aims? Is the legal representative the technical-legal instrument that best fits this reality? Should the mechanism of "assistance" also be used here? Is this latter mechanism more appropriate for the right to freely develop one's personality? Finally, I will examine whether it is possible to state that unification or harmonisation of this area of Family Law is feasible.

I will try to answer these and other questions, whilst bearing in mind that the reality of parent-child relationships is one of constant change.

## 2. CONCEPT, LEGAL NATURE, CONTENT AND AIMS OF PARENTAL RESPONSIBILITIES

### 2.1. Concept

Parental responsibilities can be defined as the group of "functional powers" attributed by the Law to both parents on an equal basis so that they can care for their child and his/her property.[1] Therefore, these powers must not be exercised in an authoritarian way but in such a way as to grant children gradual autonomy in the way that they lead their lives: according to their age, capabilities and maturity.

### 2.2. Legal Nature

The legal nature of parental care is no longer a controversial question. Most authors consider it as the group of all the duties and all the rights given to both parents by the Law in order to defend and promote the interests of their minor children, whenever these duties and rights are carried out.[2] Parental care has stopped being seen as an absolute right of the parents, which they were able to exercise in a totally free way and in

---

[1]   Cf. FRANCISCO PEREIRA COELHO & GUILHERME DE OLIVEIRA, *Curso de Direito da Família*, vol. I, 2nd ed., Centro de Direito da Família da Universidade de Coimbra, Coimbra, Coimbra Editora, 2001, p. 42; JOSÉ LUIS LACRUZ BERDEJO, FRANCISCO DE ASÍS SANCHO REBULLIDA & AGUSTÍN LUNA SERRANO *et al.*, *Elementos de Derecho Civil*, IV, cuarta edición, Barcelona, Bosch Editor, 1997, p. 569, LUIS DÍEZ-PICAZO & ANTONIO GULLÓN, *Instituciones de Derecho Civil*, vol. II/2, segunda edición, Madrid, Editorial Tecnos, 1998, p. 191; TOMMASO AULETTA, *Il Diritto di Famiglia*, quarta edizione, Torino, G. Giappichelli Editore, 1997, p. 334; MICHELE SESTA, "La filiazione", estratto da "Il Diritto di Famiglia" del *Trattato di Diritto Civile* diretto da MARIO BESSONE, vol. VI, tomo III, Torino, G. Giappichelli Editore, 1999, p. 198; JACQUELINE RUBELLIN-DEVICHI, *Droit de la famille 2001/ 2002*, Paris, Éditions Dalloz, 2001, p. 679.

[2]   Cf. TOMMASO AULETTA, *op. cit.*, p. 334; JEAN CARBONNIER, *Droit Civil*, tome 2, *La Famille, l'enfant, le couple*, 21éme édition refondue, Paris, Presses Universitaires de France, 2002, p. 111; DIETER SCHWAB, *Familienrecht*, 11., neubearbeitete Auflage, Munich, C. H. Beck, 2001, p. 245.

their own interests.[3] Therefore, parental care is irrevocable, intransmissible (*inter vivos* and *mortis causa*) and controlled in an objective manner.[4]

In fact, the guiding principle for parents exercising parental care is the child's best interests.[5]

### 2.3. Content

The "powers – duties" which are included in parental responsibilities are the following: to ensure the child's security; to maintain the child; to care for the child's health; to determine and direct the child's upbringing; to represent the child; and to administer the child's property.

We can say that parental responsibilities can be exercised in two main areas: the personal care of the child (security, maintaining, health, education, and representation of the child) and caring for the child's property (administering the child's property).[6]

### 2.4. Aims

### 2.4.1. Protection

From what was previously said about the legal nature and content of parental responsibilities, one can say that their first aim is to protect the child and his/her property.

The aim of protection comes about as a result of the incapacity of minor children to exercise their rights. In fact, minor children, because of their vulnerability, are considered incapable of running their own lives and patrimony by most legal systems.

The traditional basis given for this incapacity of minor children to exercise their own rights is the need to protect the child and adolescent because

---

[3]   Cf. TOMMASO AULETTA, *op. cit.*, p. 334; JEAN CARBONNIER, *Droit Civil*, tome 2, *La Famille, l'enfant, le couple*, 21éme édition refondue, Paris, Presses Universitaires de France, 2002, p. 111; DIETER SCHWAB, *Familienrecht*, 11., neubearbeitete Auflage, Munich, C. H. Beck, 2001, p. 245.

[4]   FRANCISCO PEREIRA COELHO & GUILHERME DE OLIVEIRA, *op. cit.*, p. 172-173; LACRUZ BERDEJO *et al.*, *op. cit.*, p. 569; LUIS DÍEZ-PICAZO & ANTONIO GULLÓN, *op. cit.*, p. 191.

[5]   Cf. JACQUELINE RUBELLIN-DEVICHI, *op. cit.*, p. 680; MICHELE SESTA, *op. cit.*, p. 199.

[6]   Cf. LUIS PICAZO & ANTONIO GULLÓN, *op. cit.*, p. 193; TOMMASO AULETTA, *op. cit.*, p. 334; JACQUELINE RUBELLIN-DEVICHI, *op. cit.*, p. 679; DIETER SCHWAB, *op. cit.*, p. 204.

of their inability to make wise decisions.[7] The child must be protected because he/she has not yet developed all the intellectual, moral and emotional faculties needed to act on his/her own behalf; the adolescent also needs protection, because although he/she might have developed the required faculties, he/she does not have enough experience of using those faculties to lead his/her life and administer his/her assets.[8]

This aim of protection requires that the exercise of all the duties and rights, which the Law gives to both parents, must be carried out while the child is not considered sufficiently mature by the Law. In fact, the Law only grants the child full legal capacity to run his/her life and his/her property when he/she attains the age of majority or becomes emancipated.[9]

### 2.4.2. Promotion of the child's autonomy and independence

Nevertheless, this aim of protection is not the only one. Considering children as human beings who go through a process of development has added another aim to parental care: the promotion of the child's autonomy and independence. Parents shall promote the child's autonomy and independence through the development of his/her physical, intellectual, moral and emotional abilities, so that the child should be able to exercise his/her full legal capacity when he/she reaches the age of majority.[10]

## 3. A NEW PERSPECTIVE ON THE CHILD AND THE ADOLESCENT

### 3.1. The child and the adolescent as individuals with rights

This idea of parental responsibilities reflects a new perspective concerning children and adolescents. Indeed, the child and the adolescent are nowadays seen as individuals with rights. That is to say that they are no

---

[7] Cf. CARLOS MARTINEZ DE AGUIRRE, "La protección jurídico-civil de la persona por razón de menor edad", *Anuario de Derecho Civil*, 1992, tomo XLV, fasciculo IV, p. 1399; JEAN CARBONNIER, *Droit Civil*, tome 1, *Personnalité, incapacités, personnes morales*, 17éme édition refondue, Paris, Presses Universitaires de France, 2000, p. 199.

[8] Cf. CARLOS MARTINEZ DE AGUIRRE, *op. cit.*, p. 1414.

[9] Cf. JEAN CARBONNIER, *Droit Civil*, tome 2, *La famille, l'enfant, le couple*, 21éme édition refondue, Paris, Presses Universitaires de France, 2002, p. 101; JACQUELINE RUBEL-LIN-DEVICHI, *op. cit.*, p. 680; WHITE, CARR & LOWE, *The Children Act in Practice*, third edition, London, Lexis Nexis Butterworths, 2002, p. 56.

[10] Cf. DIETER SCHWAB, *op. cit.*, p. 204, 245; GERNHUBER & COESTER-WALTJEN, *Lehrbuch des Familienrechts*, 4. Auflage, München, C. H. Beck, 1994, p. 881.

longer seen as "objects of rights", with no ability to influence their lives, but as individuals with rights, who achieve a gradual autonomy in exercising them, according to their age, maturity and the state of development of their capabilities.

One can state that the child and the adolescent have already achieved a status of "social citizenship".[11]

### 3.2. Legal effects of this new perspective on the child and adolescent in the Law of some European countries

This new view has changed the parent-child relationship and its legal regulation. One can state that today's Family Law, in particular the section on parental care, is truly influenced by a "Theory of the Rights of the Child".[12]

The consideration of children and adolescents as individuals with rights who have a progressive ability in exercising them has led to the conclusion that the protective function of the parents should be inversely proportional to the physical, intellectual, moral and emotional development of the child. Indeed, while the children are growing up and maturing, the parents' protective role diminishes.[13] However, the other role assigned to parental care, that of promoting the child's autonomy and independence, is strengthened.

The configuration of parental care in Portuguese, Spanish, Italian, French, German and English Law reflects these ideas.

So, the Portuguese Civil Code states in Article 1878, no. 2 that the parents have the duty "of taking into account the [children's] opinion in important family matters and recognising [their] autonomy in the way they lead their own lives."

In a similar way, the Spanish Civil Code declares in Article 154 that "non-emancipated children are under the parental care of both parents. Parental care will always be exercised for the benefit of the child according to

---

[11]    Cf. STEPHEN M. CRETNEY, JUDITH M. MASSON, REBECCA BAILEY-HARRIS, *Principles of Family Law,* seventh edition, London, Sweet & Maxwell, 2002, p. 491.

[12]    Cf. DIETER SCHWAB, *op. cit.,* p. 202.

[13]    Cf. TOMMASO AULETTA, *Il Diritto di Famiglia,* quarta edizione, Turin, G. Giappichelli Editore, 1997, p. 334; STEPHEN M. CRETNEY, JUDITH M. MASSON, REBECCA BAILEY-HARRIS, *op. cit.,* p. 490; WHITE, CARR & LOWE, *op. cit.,* p. 58; DIETER SCHWAB, *op. cit.,* p. 272.

his/her personality (...). If the children have sufficient discretion, they should always be heard before any decisions that will affect them are taken (...)". However, the Spanish Civil Code goes further in recognising the progressive autonomy of children in the legal regulation of the parent-child relationship. Article 162 states that "parents are the legal representatives of their minor children". The establishment of this rule is, however, followed by a statement containing several exceptions. "Excluded [from this rule] are: 1. Acts related to exercising the rights of personality or others that, according to the Law and their [the children] maturity, they can carry out by themselves; 2. Acts in which there is a conflict of interests between the parents and the child. (...) To conclude contracts which oblige the child to make personal actions the Law requires his/her personal consent if he/she has the necessary discretion (...)".

The Civil Code in Article 147, no. 3, imposes on the parents "the obligation to maintain, to bring up and to educate their child taking into account their abilities, natural inclinations and natural aspirations".

The French Code Civil establishes in Article 371, no 1 (according to the amendment by Law No. 2002- 205, of 4 March) that "parents should make their children participate in the decisions which are directly related to him/her, according to their age and degree of maturity."

The German Bürgerliche Gesetzbuch has a similar norm. In fact, § 1626 II imposes on both parents the duty "of taking into consideration the growing ability and the growing need to act independently and with a sense of responsibility. Parents must discuss all the questions about parental care with the child according to his/her intellectual, moral and emotional development and endeavour to act in agreement".

In England and Wales, The Children Act 1989, s. 3 (1) states that: "In this Act parental responsibility means all the rights, duties, powers, responsibilities and authority which by Law a parent of a child has in relation to the child and his property."

We should emphasise that the Law Commission considered that it was not possible to draw up a list of all the rights and duties of the parents because they would need to be changed as the child matured.[14]

---

[14]  Cf. STEPHEN M. CRETNEY, JUDITH M. MASSON, REBECCA BAILEY-HARRIS, *op. cit.*, p. 533; WHITE, CARR & LOWE, *op. cit.*, p. 57; NIGEL LOWE, GILLIAN DOUGLAS, *Bromley's Family Law*, ninth edition, London – Edinburgh – Dublin, Butterworths, 1998, p. 348.

### 3.3. The progressive autonomy of the minor children has not been ignored by the Law

After a quick analysis of the law of the above-mentioned countries, one can conclude that the reality of the progressive autonomy of minor children has not been ignored by the law, in spite of the differences between the legal regimes. We should equally point out that there is no systematic laying down of certain exceptions to the principle of the general legal incapacity of minors through the establishment of "anticipated majorities" in all the legal systems.

## 4. SOME SUGGESTIONS IN ORDER TO ASSIST US TO MOVE IN A NEW DIRECTION IN THE AREA OF PARENT-CHILD RELATIONSHIPS

We should ask ourselves if this recognition of the child's and the adolescent's progressive autonomy is nothing more than a declaration of principle with practically no value in the daily relations between parents and their children.

One can say that the law has a long way to go before it will offer an adequate answer to that reality – namely providing a more tailored regulation of parental care.

### 4.1. Progressive reduction in the content of parental care

Firstly, it seems to me that the progressive recognition of the child's and the adolescent's autonomy should be reflected in a corresponding progressive reduction in the content of parental care.

As the child grows in maturity the circle of powers and duties that makes up parental care should be reduced. And this progressive reduction ought to be established in the various norms which governs the relationships between children and their parents, namely through the setting up of "anticipated majorities".[15] This would be in perfect harmony with the second aim of parental care.

### 4.2. Legal Representation or "Assistance"

Secondly, one needs to ask whether legal representation is the legal-technical instrument that best fits this situation. Would it not be better to

---

[15] For this idea see GERNHUBER & COESTER-WALTJEN, *op. cit.*, p. 882.

use the mechanism of "assistance"? Is this not the most appropriate way to fulfil the right to a free development of the personality?

In fact, parents, as the guardians of parental responsibilities, are also the legal representatives of their children. Therefore, they carry out the power/duty to represent their minor children, because of the latter's legal inability to exercise their own rights.

### 4.2.1. Legal Representation

The mechanism of legal representation consists of another person acting in the name of the person who lacks legal capacity. In other words, the legal representative stands in his/her place in legal transactions. Thus, it is not the minor who manages his/her own affairs but his/her parents.

This mechanism does not fit very well with the idea of ensuring that children develop a progressive autonomy in running their lives,[16] and with the idea of respecting the right to freely develop one's personality.[17]

The recognition of this progressive autonomy will be best suited to the legal instrument of "assistance".

### 4.2.2. "Assistance"

As opposed to legal representation, the legal mechanism of "assistance" does not mean that the person who lacks legal capacity will not enter into legal transactions. He/she is the one who acts. His/her "assistant" will only give prior consent or later approval to his acts. The "assistant" acts side by side with the person who is legally incompetent.

### 4.3. "Assistance" as the mechanism that best fits the progressive autonomy of the child and of the adolescent

Indeed, the mechanism of "assistance" is more appropriate because that permits the minor to enter into legal transactions. This is very important for those ages when the minor already has the necessary discretion to act on his/her own behalf, although he/she lacks the necessary experience to do so.

---

[16] For this idea see JEAN-JACQUES LEMOULAND, L'assistance du mineur, une voie possible entre l'autonomie et la réprésentation, *Revue Trimestrielle de Droit Civil*, Dalloz, 1997, p. 17.

[17] Cf. CARLOS MARTINEZ DE AGUIRRE, *op. cit.*, p. 1436.

Therefore, "assistance" seems to be the legal instrument that best corresponds, on the one hand, to the progressive autonomy of the child and to the right to freely develop his/her personality and, on the other, to the need to protect the child, which still remains.[18]

### 4.4. Both aims of parental care recommend co-operation between legal representation and "assistance"

It would not be appropriate to use "assistance" for all minors. A good example of co-operation between legal representation, "assistance" and the progressive autonomy of the child and the adolescent is the German legal mechanism of overriding minors' lack of legal capacity (§§ 104 and 113 BGB). According to this system children are absolutely incapable of exercising their rights up to the age of seven years old.[19] The reason for this rule is that children do not yet have all the intellectual, moral and emotional faculties to enter into legal transactions. This legal incapacity is overridden by the parents as the legal representatives of their child.

From seven years old until the age of eighteen, minors are limited in their capacity to negotiate. The validity of their acts is dependent on the prior consent *(Einwilligung)* or latter approval *(Genehmigung)* of their parents who now act as their child's "assistant".[20]

It is worth directing the following criticism towards this system: at seven years old minors are still not in possession of the necessary intellectual, moral and emotional faculties that enable them to act on their own behalf.

Modern psychology nowadays seems to place this age somewhere between twelve and thirteen years old. Thus a system of "assistance" for children above fourteen years old seems preferable.[21]

## 5. UNIFICATION OR HARMONISATION OF THIS AREA OF FAMILY LAW

From all that I have said so far one can conclude that it is possible to promote the unification or, at least, the harmonisation of this field of

---

[18]   Cf. JEAN-JACQUES LEMOULAND, *op. cit.*, p. 3, CARLOS MARTINEZ DE AGUIRRE, *op. cit.*, p. 1448-1449.

[19]   Cf. PETER GOTTWALD, DIETER SCHWAB & EVA BÜTTNER, *Family and Succession Law in Germany*, The Hague-London-Boston, Kluwer Law International, 2001, p. 31.

[20]   Cf. PETER GOTTWALD, DIETER SCHWAB & EVA BÜTTNER, *op. cit.*, p. 31.

[21]   In a similar way *see* CARLOS MARTINEZ DE AGUIRRE, *op. cit.*, p. 1448. This author proposes to substitute "the actual system of legal representation of minor children, until they reach majority (or emancipation) by a system of assistance above fourteen years old".

Family Law.[22] In fact, as Boele-Woelki[23] and De Oliveira[24] have already pointed out, the current standards regarding the influence of the progressive autonomy of the child and the adolescent in the regulation of the legal regime of parental responsibilities are more or less the same. In all the above-mentioned legal systems one can see the same trend of recognising children's progressive autonomy.

Indeed, the reflections of this trend are quite visible in the limits imposed on the parents' authority and on the strength of the notion that exercising parental responsibilities ought to respect the child's autonomy. These reflections are also visible in the emphasis that is placed on taking into consideration the inclinations and the aspirations of the child according to his/her age and maturity.

## REFERENCES

AULETTA, T., *Il Diritto di Famiglia,* quarta edizione, Torino, G. Giappichelli Editore, 1997

BOELE-WOELKI, K., "Comparative research-based drafting of principles of European Family Law", in: *Towards a European Ius Commune in Legal Education and Research,* Antwerpen, Intersentia, 2002.

BOELE-WOELKI, K., "The road towards a European Family Law", vol.1.1, *Electronic Journal of Comparative Law,* November 1997, http://www.ejcl.org/ejcl/11/art11-1.htm

CARBONNIER, J., *Droit Civil,* tome 1, *Personnalité, incapacités, personnes morales,* 17éme édition refondue, Paris, Presses Universitaires de France, 2000.

CARBONNIER, J., *Droit Civil,* tome 2, *La famille, l'enfant, le couple,* 21éme édition refondue, Paris, Presses Universitaires de France, 2002.

CRETNEY, S. M., MASSON, J. M., BAILEY-HARRIS, R., *Principles of Family Law,* seventh edition, London, Sweet & Maxwell, 2002.

DE OLIVEIRA, G., "A European Family Law? [Play it again, and again...Europe]", in: *"A Civil Code for Europe"- Studia Juridica 64,* Coimbra, Coimbra Editora, 2002.

---

[22] On the question of the practicability of unification or harmonisation of Family Law, see DIETER MARTINY, "Is Unification of Family Law Feasible or even desirable?" in : *Towards a European Civil Code,* second edition, The Hague-London-Boston, Kluwer Law International, 1998, p. 151 ff.. and KATHARINA BOELE-WOELKI, "Comparative research-based drafting of principles of European Family Law", in *Towards a European Ius Commune in Legal Education and Research,* Antwerpen, Intersentia, 2002, p. 171 et seq.

[23] Cf. KATHARINA BOELE-WOELKI, "The road towards a European Family Law", vol.1.1, *Electronic Journal of Comparative Law,* November 1997, http://www.ejcl.org/ejcl/11/art11-1.htm, p. 13.

[24] Cf. GUILHERME DE OLIVEIRA, "A European Family Law? [Play it again, and again... Europe]", in *"A Civil Code for Europe"- Studia Juridica 64,* Coimbra, Coimbra Editora, 2002, p. 134.

DÍEZ-PICAZO, L. & GULLÓN, A., *Instituciones de Derecho Civil,* vol. II/2, segunda edición, Madrid, Editorial Tecnos, 1998.

GERNHUBER & COESTER-WALTJEN, *Lehrbuch des Familienrechts,* 4. Auflage, München, C. H. Beck, 1994.

GOTTWALD, P., SCHWAB, D. & BÜTTNER, E., *Family and Succession Law in Germany,* The Hague-London-Boston, Kluwer Law International, 2001.

LACRUZ BERDEJO, J. L., Francisco de Asís SANCHO REBULLIDA, Agustín LUNA SERRANO, Francisco RIVERRO HERNÁNDEZ y Joaquín RAMS ALBESA, *Elementos de Derecho Civil,* IV, cuarta edición, Barcelona, Bosch Editor, 1997.

LEMOULAND, J.-J., L'assistance du mineur, une voie possible entre l'autonomie et la répresentation, *Revue Trimestrielle de Droit Civil,* Dalloz, 1997.

LOWE, N., DOUGLAS, G., *Bromley's Family Law,* ninth edition, London, Edinburgh, Dublin, Butterworths, 1998.

MARTINEZ DE AGUIRRE, C., "La protección jurídico-civil de la persona por razón de menor edad", *Anuario de Derecho Civil,* 1992, tomo XLV, fasciculo IV.

MARTINY, D., "Is Unification of Family Law Feasible or even desirable?", in: *Towards a European Civil Code,* second edition, The Hague-London-Boston, Kluwer Law International, 1998.

PEREIRA COELHO, F. & DE OLIVEIRA, G., *Curso de Direito da Família,* vol. I, 2nd ed., Centro de Direito da Família da Universidade de Coimbra, Coimbra, Coimbra Editora, 2001.

RUBELLIN-DEVICHI, J., *Droit de la famille 2001/ 2002,* Paris, Éditions Dalloz, 2001.

SCHWAB, D., *Familienrecht,* 11., neubearbeitete Auflage, München, C. H. Beck, 2001.

SESTA, M., "La filiazione", estratto da "Il Diritto di Famiglia" del *Trattato di Diritto Civile* diretto da Mario BESSONE, vol. VI, tomo III, Torino, G. Giappichelli Editore, 1999.

WHITE, CARR & LOWE, *The Children Act in Practice,* third edition, London, Lexis Nexis Butterworths, 2002.

# A COMPARATIVE ANALYSIS OF CONTACT ARRANGEMENTS IN THE NETHERLANDS AND DENMARK

CHRISTINA GYLDENLØVE JEPPESEN DE BOER

## 1. INTRODUCTION

At present there is immense interest focused on the onset of and/or continuance of contact between a child and the non-resident parent. Associated rights such as those of the extended family to contact with the child, independent of or dependent on the non-resident parent, are also often contested.

Conflicts regarding parental authority are most often resolved alongside divorce proceedings or at the breakdown of a relationship, with limited scope for modification unless the factual circumstances have changed dramatically. Indeed the move towards automatic joint parental authority after divorce,[1] as well as for unmarried parents,[2] reinforces joint authority as the norm, thus giving parents limited scope for contesting cases concerning parental authority. In view of these facts, it is foreseeable that conflicts in the future will centre around issues concerning, on the one hand, a child's primary residence, and on the other hand, contact between a child and the non-resident parent. The fact that contact is coming more to the forefront of the debate is evident in the Netherlands and also in Denmark. At EU level contact has also been placed centre-stage. A French initiative aimed at abolishing exequatur for the part of the decision concerning parental responsibility[3] that concerns the right of access[4] was

---

[1]    25% of marriages in the Netherlands end in divorce affecting 33,000 children, which over time means that an estimated one in six children experience their parents' divorce. In Denmark 40% of marriages end in divorce. In Denmark an estimated one in three children experience their parents either divorcing or breaking up (2000). Source; Dutch Central Statistical Office (CBS) on www.cbs.nl and Statistics Denmark on www.dst.dk.

[2]    In 2001 27% (Netherlands) and 46% (Denmark) of children were born to unmarried mothers. Source; CBS and Statistics Denmark.

[3]    The concept parental *responsibilities/responsibility* is used by the Council of Europe as well as the EU to describe the collection of duties and powers, which normally belongs to the parents. The Netherlands and Denmark still have concepts that are best translated as parental authority. In the Netherlands the concept is *ouderlijk gezag* and in Denmark *forældremyndighed*.

[4]    In the following the term contact is used.

announced in 2000. This initiative, amongst others, has provided the background for a proposed Council Regulation,[5] which was announced in may this year. The proposal incorporates these issues and further extends the scope of the regulation beyond divorce, guarantying equality of treatment for all children.

The aim of this paper is to compare the system of contact in the Netherlands and Denmark and to examine these systems within the framework of international conventions and jurisprudence. Two recent instruments of the European Council, namely the Convention on Contact Concerning Children[6] and the White Paper on Principles Concerning the Establishment and Legal Consequences of Parentage[7] will be used as the basis for the comparison. Section 3 deals with contact between parents and children and more specifically with the right to have contact (3.1), the content of contact (3.2.), procedures (3.3.) and remedies (3.4.). In section 4 contact between children and the extended family is discussed. First a brief account is given of the basic rules on parental authority in section 2.

The focus of this article is joint parental authority as it applies to parents of opposite sexes that have been married or has lived together (non-formalized relationship). The Dutch rules on parental authority, can be described like a labyrinth, since they contain separate sets of rules for both opposite-sex and same-sex partners according to whether they are married, unmarried or registered. Automatic joint parental authority may also come into play where a child is born into a same sex marriage or a registered partnership. The specific issues that may arise concerning children born in same-sex registered partnerships or marriages will not be dealt with in this article.[8]

## 2. PARENTAL AUTHORITY

The focus here is joint parental authority outside of marriage i.e. for unmarried parents and after divorce. The rules on joint parental authority will be analysed on the basis of three criteria. The first criterion is whether joint parental authority is the preferred solution. Joint parental authority is described as the preferred solution where it is not left to the parents as

---

[5]   COM (2002) 222.
[6]   Open for ratification on 14 October 2002.
[7]   CJ-FA (2001), 15.01.2002 the White Paper may result in a recommendation.
[8]   See an up-to-date account of the possibilities and differences: WENDY SCHRAMA,"Reforms in Dutch Family Law during the Course of 2001: Increased Pluriformity and Complexity", *The International Survey of Family Law*, 2002, (ed. A. BAINHAM).

a choice *e.g.* where joint parental authority continues automatically after divorce. Furthermore it is described as preferred when steps have been taken to ensure that an increased number of parents are awarded joint parental authority, as is the case when unmarried parents are encouraged to opt for joint parental authority. The second criterion is whether joint parental authority is consensus based. By consensus based, it is inferred that joint parental authority is and remains based on the parents' wishes. Joint parental authority is non-consensus based where it may be imposed against their will or against one parents' will. The third criterion is whether judicial conflict solving exists for parents who have joint parental authority i.e. if conflicts between them concerning (for example the contact arrangement, residence, school choices etc.) can be decided by a judicial authority.[9]

In January 2002 a White Paper on the "Principles Concerning the Establishment and Legal Consequences of Parentage" prepared by a working party of the Committee of experts of family law (CJ-FA) of the Council of Europe was published. Part B of the white paper deals with "Principles Relating to Legal Consequences of Parentage" i.e. the principles relating amongst other to parental responsibilities or in this article named parental authority. Part B contains seven principles (Principles 18-25) on parental responsibilities. At present, focus is directed towards the content of the principles contained in Articles 19, 20 and 22 all dealing with the division of duties and powers between the parents. The general principle is that parental responsibilities should belong to the parents jointly (Principle 19). No distinction should be made between children born in- or outside of marriage. Divorce or termination of cohabitation should not affect this position (Principle 22). Only where joint parental responsibilities are against the best interests of the child, or the parents agree on the issue, could joint parental responsibilities be exercised by one parent or divided between the parents (Principle 20(2)). The proposed principles go much further on the issue of promoting joint parental responsibility, making sole exercise of these rights the exception, than the Recommendation No R(84)4[10] on parental responsibilities presently in force. This recommendation has as its main principle that parental responsibilities should belong to parents for a child of their marriage (Principle 5). Outside of marriage or after divorce joint parental responsibilities should be based on agreement between the parents and not be

---

[9] Judicial conflict solving implies that a decision is or can be made for the parents. Measures such as mediation or counselling are not considered.

[10] Adopted by the Committee of Ministers on 28.02.1984.

enforced (principles 6 and 7[11]). The principles would, if implemented, provide us with a system in which joint parental authority is the preferred solution and in which consensus no longer forms the base of joint parental authority outside of marriage.

In the Netherlands married parents have automatic joint parental authority and since January 1st 1998 the parents continue to have joint parental authority after divorce.[12] If one of the parents wants to have sole parental authority, this may only be granted where it is deemed to be in the best interests of the child. The Dutch Supreme Court has interpreted this to mean that only where the communication problem is of such a nature that it brings about an unacceptable risk that the child is torn between the parents, and where the improvement in the communication between the parents is not foreseeable in the near future,[13] is it possible to deviate from joint parental authority and award one parent sole parental authority. The decision has since been confirmed and further elaborated on by the Supreme Court.[14]

If the parents are not married the mother will have sole parental authority unless registration of an application for joint parental authority has taken place at the Guardianship Register.[15] If the parents end their relationship joint parental authority automatically continues. If one of the parents wants to have sole parental authority this may be granted where circumstances have changed.[16] The breakdown of the relationship may constitute changed circumstances.[17]

If the parents who have joint parental authority cannot agree where the child should live it is possible to obtain a decision on the child's place of residence. Conflicts concerning contact[18] and other conflicts between the parents may also be brought before the court.[19]

The number of parents who have joint parental authority in the Netherlands has greatly increased since the reform in 1998. Statistics from the

---

[11]   Principle 7 concerning children born outside of marriage actually lays down several options for the member states.
[12]   Article 251(2), Book 1, Dutch Civil Code (D.C.C.).
[13]   Dutch Supreme Court, HR 10 September 1999, NJ 2000, 20.
[14]   Dutch Supreme Court, HR 19 April 2002, NJ 458.
[15]   Article 253b(1) and 251(1), Book 1, D.C.C.
[16]   Article 253n(1), Book 1, D.C.C.
[17]   M.J.C. KOENS, C.G.M. VAN WAMELEN: *Kind en scheiding* (Child and divorce), 2001, p. 78.
[18]   Article 377h, Book 1, D.C.C.
[19]   Article 253a, Book 1, D.C.C.

Dutch Statistical Authorities (CBS) show that joint parental authority after divorce remains in force in 96% of divorce proceedings as opposed to 34% in 1997. When the court has to decide on the issue of parental authority the mother is awarded sole parental authority in 3% of divorce procedures and joint parental authority is enforced in 1% of procedures as opposed to 1997 where the courts awarded the mother sole parental authority in 59% of the cases, the father in 3% of cases and enforced joint parental authority in 4% of cases.

In Denmark married parents also have joint parental authority and since January 2002, it automatically continues after divorce. If the parents or one of the parents requests to have sole parental authority, the courts must grant it. It is not possible to enforce joint parental authority.[20]

Unmarried parents who choose to register paternity according to a new paternity registration procedure[21] automatically acquires joint parental authority and their position is equal to that of married parents.[22] It is possible to avoid joint parental authority by choosing another paternity registration procedure. The new procedure is primarily expected to be used by cohabitating couples but cohabitation is not a requirement for the use of the procedure.

It is worth noting that the unmarried father who has cohabitated with the mother for a considerable time, but not shared parental authority, has an equal right to parental authority. This is if he applies for parental authority immediately after the relationship has ended.[23] This provision operates primarily in cases where the parents have lived together since the child was born and where the child is no longer a baby at the time of the break-up.

Joint parental authority in Denmark requires a high degree of consensus between the parents. The parents must agree where the child should live and agree on all other essential issues concerning the child. It is not possible to obtain a residence order or bring other conflicts before a court.

---

[20] Article 8, *Forældremyndighedsloven*, (Danish Act on Parental Authority), No 387 of 14.06.1995 with later changes.

[21] Article 2 (care and responsibility statement procedure), *Børneloven*, (Danish Children Act), No 406 of 07.06.2001.

[22] It is estimated that more than 90% of unmarried parents prior to the enactment of the new procedure concerning paternity registration, resulting in joint parental authority, chose this solution, Commission Report on the Legal Position of Children 1350/1998.

[23] Article 12(1), Danish Act on Parental Authority.

The only issue the parents need not agree on is how much contact the child should have with the parent with whom the child does not live.[24]

In the Netherlands and Denmark married parents have joint parental authority and it continues automatically after divorce. Joint parental authority may be described as the preferred solution for parents after divorce. With respect to unmarried parents the situation differs in the two countries. While joint parental authority for unmarried parents was introduced in Denmark as an option in legislation in 1984, it was only introduced in legislation in the Netherlands in 1995. Since its introduction in Denmark steps have been taken to promote its application amongst unmarried parents, i.e. to increase the number of parents who choose to have joint parental authority or obtain it automatically pursuant to a new paternity registration procedure and to strengthen the legal position of the unmarried father. A main goal of Danish family law legislation has been to equalise the position of children born inside and outside of marriage. In the Netherlands joint parental authority remains an option for unmarried parents and it requires positive steps to be taken to achieve this. Neither Denmark nor the Netherlands practise a system in which all parents married/unmarried, in principle, share parental authority as mentioned above in the Council of Europe White Paper.[25]

A Danish court must award one parent sole parental authority, if one of the parents seeks to have joint parental authority dissolved (for whatever reason). Joint parental authority cannot be imposed upon the parents against one parent's wish. The system may be described as consensus based. In the Netherlands sole parental authority is not necessarily granted upon one parent's wish. The Dutch system is not consensus based. The Dutch system does, however, provide conflicting parents with the possibility to go to Court and have conflicts concerning residence, contact and other issues decided by the Court. The system provides judicial conflict solving for parents with joint parental authority. In Denmark judicial conflict solving only exists for matters concerning contact.[26]

---

[24] Consensus on this issue was required until 1996 where the possibility to get a contact order for the non-resident parent who had joint parental authority was introduced. The measure was introduced to increase the amount of parents who could exercise parental authority jointly. In 2001 32% of contact cases were related to parents who had joint parental authority, Statistical report from *Civilretsdirektoratet, Samvær og børnesagkyndig rådgivning*, (Contact and child expert counselling), June 2002, p.14.

[25] Article 19.

[26] While it may appear logical that a system enforcing joint parental authority upon parents also provides judicial conflict solving, this connection is not always present. In Sweden joint parental authority may be enforced, but judicial remedies are limited to residence and →

Christina Gyldenløve Jeppesen de Boer

## 3. CONTACT PARENT –CHILD

### 3.1. The right to have contact

The Convention on Contact Concerning Children from the Council of Europe[27] states, "a child and his or her parents shall have the right to obtain and maintain regular contact with each other".[28] The right to contact is stated as a mutual right for the child[29] and the parent.[30] The right is stated broadly to include all parents irrespective of whether the parent has parental authority and/or a residence order. Contact may only be restricted or excluded where necessary in the best interests of the child.[31]

In the Netherlands it is also stated as a mutual right between the child[32] and the parent[33] who does not have parental authority.[34] The right of a parent who has parental authority is not stated in the Dutch Civil Code but is deemed to be inherent to having parental authority. Contact may be excluded temporarily or permanently; where contact would critically disadvantage the psychological or physical development of the child, where the parent clearly is unsuited or clearly not capable of having contact, where a child of 12 or older has serious objections against contact or where contact otherwise is in conflict with important interests of the child.[35]

In Denmark "the child's connection with both parents[36] is sought to be maintained by allowing the parent with whom the child does not reside, a right to contact".[37] All parents have the right of contact except the resident parent and the parent who has sole parental authority.[38] In 32% of cases concerning contact the parents have joint parental authority, in

---

[27]   contact. EVA RYRSTEDT: "Consensus in joint custody – from a comparative perspective", June 2001 on http://qsilver.queensu.ca/law/ISFLJune2001/paperryrstedt.htm

[27]   See note 7.

[28]   Article 4(1).

[29]   A child means a person less than 18 years of age in respect of whom a contact order may be made or enforced in a State Party (Article 2c).

[30]   I.e. those who by law are recognised as parents, Explanatory report CDCJ (2001)33 p. 23.

[31]   Article 4(2).

[32]   A child means a minor i.e. a person less than 18 years of age.

[33]   Parent means the person(s) who by way of law, recognition or judgment is deemed to be the legal parent.

[34]   Art. 377a(1), Book 1, D.C.C.

[35]   Article 377a(2), Book 1, D.C.C.

[36]   Parent means the person(s) who by way of law, recognition, registration based on a care and responsibility statement or judgment is deemed to be the legal parent.

[37]   Article 16, Danish Act on Parental Authority.

[38]   This is not clear from the wording of the article but follows from the preparatory works Commission report 1279/1994, p. 192.

384

60% of cases the mother has sole parental authority and in 7% of cases the father has sole parental authority.[39] Contact may be excluded where this is deemed to be necessary in the interests of the child.[40] The Act does not further specify the criteria for exclusion. The preparatory legislative work[41] contained an overview of administrative case law listing different reasons for exclusion. These are further described and elaborated in two Guides on the treatment of contact cases.[42] Out of 1289 cases from the first half of 2001 concerning contact (regarding first application for contact) a contact order was issued in 94% of cases and rejected in 6% of cases.[43] Exclusions in the first half of 2001 contained reference to the following main groups[44]:

| Exclusion of contact | % |
|---|---|
| Child's own opinion | 36% |
| Child's age | 28% |
| Special circumstances child | 28% |
| Lack of contact | 25% |
| Special circumstances parent | 23% |
| Expert report/evidence | 17% |
| Contact ceased according to agreement | 9% |
| Violence/Incest | 2% |
| Other reasons | 32% |

Some of these reasons for excluding contact will be further elaborated. The opinion of older children concerning contact is of major importance. If a child of 12[45] or older clearly states that he or she is against a contact order, no contact order will normally be made. The same applies when an older child does not want to be bound by strict time schedules but want to be in charge of when and where contact should take place him-

---

39 Statistical report from *Civilretsdirektoratet,* June 2002, p. 14.
40 Article 17(3), Danish Act on Parental Authority.
41 *Fælles forældremyndighed samværsvanskeligheder børnesagkyndig rådgivning,* (Joint parental authority contact disputes child expert counselling), Commission Report 1279/94 p.131-132
42 *Civilretsdirektoratets vejledning om behandling af samværssager, Civilretsdirektoratets* guidance notes on the treatment of contact cases, November 1999 and *Civilretsdirektoraterts vejledning om forældremyndighed og samvær, Civilretsdirektoratets* guidance notes No 214 of 20.12.1995 on parental authority and contact.
43 Statistical report from *Civilretsdirektoratet,* June 2002, p. 10.
44 Statistical report from *Civilretsdirektoratet,* June 2002, p. 13.
45 See when a child must be heard, section 3.3.

self/herself. Only 6% of contact cases concern children of 13 or older.[46] The child's age is really only an issue when the child is very young. If the person applying for contact has not lived with the child, no contact order will normally be issued before the child is four months old.[47] If the relationship between the parents is scarred by conflict, the contact order may be delayed until the child is one year old.[48] Special circumstances concerning the child's health such as diseases, handicaps or special vulnerability may also play a role. Lack of contact for a substantial period (around 5 years) as well as the reason for the lack of contact play an important role in determining whether contact should be excluded.[49]

### 3.2. The content of contact

For the purpose of the Convention on Contact Concerning Children, Contact is defined to mean (Art. 1):
i.   the child staying for a limited period of time with or meeting a person mentioned in Art. 4 (parent) or 5 (person other than parent) with whom he or she is not usually living;
ii.  any form of communication between the child and such person;
iii. the provision of information to such a person about the child or to the child about such a person.

In the Explanatory Report[50] the three forms of contact are described as three levels of contact. The first level of contact is personal (face-to-face) contact and is described as the most appropriate way to maintain contact. The second level covers other forms of contact *e.g.* telephone, letters, faxes, e-mail etc. This type of contact may be additional to direct personal contact or instead of direct contact in specific circumstances where direct contact is not possible. The third level of contact covers the provision of information about the child to persons seeking contact (parents and persons other than parents) or the provision of information about such persons to the child. The provision of information may be additional to direct or indirect contact or replace these in specific circumstances.

---

[46] Statistical report from *Civilretsdirektoratet*, June 2002, p. 10. In the Netherlands approximately 9% of cases concern children of 13 or older, source statistical material received by The Child Care and Protection Board.
[47] *Civilretsdirektoratets* guidance notes on the treatment of contact cases, November 1999, p. 3.
[48] *Ibid.*
[49] *Ibid.*
[50] *CDCJ* (2001) 33 p. 19

In the Netherlands as well as in Denmark direct and other contact correspond well with the definition given above. In the Netherlands, the general article on contact[51] is considered to include other contact.[52] There are no criteria to indicate when other forms of contact may be included in a contact order. In Denmark a special provision was introduced in 1996[53] to cover other forms of contact. Before this time it was not possible to obtain a contact order with such content. Other forms of contact may be additional to direct contact or instead of direct contact, but in any case, it is only possible in special cases.[54]

The Convention on Contact Concerning Children or the Explanatory Report[55] does not mention upon whom the duty to provide information, as provided for in Article 1(iii) should rest. From the sort of information mentioned in the Explanatory Report[56] such as recent photographs, school reports and medical reports, a duty to provide information could be laid upon the parent living with the child or a public/private institution such as a school or medical institution. In the Netherlands the duty to provide important information concerning the child to the parent[57] who has no parental authority, rests upon the parent who has (sole) parental authority.[58] In fact, the parent who has (sole) parental authority has the duty to consult the other parent on these issues.[59] Information or consultation may be excluded where the best interests of the child so require.[60] Furthermore the parent[61] who does not have parental authority may require information from third parties such as teachers, social workers and doctors[62] who has information with regard to important facts and circumstances concerning the child or its care and upbringing.[63] In Denmark the

---

[51]  Article 377a, Book 1, D.C.C.
[52]  *Tekst en Commentaar Personen- en Familierecht,* (Commentary to the Dutch Civil Code), 2002, p. 421.
[53]  Article 18, Danish Act on Parental Authority.
[54]  Hereby indicating that it should not become part of a contact order as a routine matter, Commission Report 1279/94, p. 119.
[55]  *CDCJ* (2001) 33, p. 19.
[56]  *Ibid.*
[57]  Parent means the person(s) who by way of law, recognition or judgement is deemed to be the legal parent. On the basis of ECHR Art. 8, the father who has not recognized the child but whose connection to the child amounts to family life in the sense of Art. 8 May base a claim for information on this article, Supreme Court, HR 17 December 1993, *NJ* 1994, 360.
[58]  Article 377b(1), Book 1, D.C.C.
[59]  Article 377b(1), Book 1, D.C.C.
[60]  Article 377b(2), Book 1, D.C.C.
[61]  *Ibid.*
[62]  Commentary to the Dutch Civil Code, p. 430.
[63]  Article 377c(1), Book 1, D.C.C.

duty to provide information to the parent who does not have parental authority rests solely on third parties such as schools, nurseries, social authorities and medical institutions,[64] the parent who has (sole) parental authority is under no such duty. No confidential information concerning the other parent must be revealed. This may be a problem in situations where the parent who has (sole) parental authority, has problems, which affect the child. The institutions may refuse to give the requested information if giving such information may be damaging to the child.[65]

### 3.3. Procedures

The Convention on Contact Concerning Children contains only a few provisions concerning procedures that are not related to transfrontier contact (Chapter III of the Convention) or to hearing the child, which will be dealt with at the end of this section. Three measures are named. The first is that judicial authorities must ensure that parents are informed of the importance of contact (Art. 7, a), and secondly to encourage reaching amicable agreements, in particular through the use of family mediation and other processes for resolving disputes (Art. 7, b) and finally to ensure that there is sufficient information in a case concerning contact before a decision is made (Art. 7, c).

In the Netherlands the district courts have competence in matters of contact[66] as well as in matters of parental authority. In case of divorce these issues are dealt with simultaneously. The courts also decide if measures enforcing contact should be taken. The issue of remedies will be further elaborated in the following section. Judgments and decisions of the court may be appealed to the Court of Appeal with further appeal to the Supreme Court.[67] The judge may rely on the Child Care and Protection Board[68] for advice.[69] The Board has advisory functions in matters concerning minors. In some jurisdictions an employee[70] of the Board is always present in cases where there are conflicts concerning parental authority or contact. If the conflict cannot be settled and/or the judge feels that

---

[64]    Article 19, Danish Act on Parental Authority.
[65]    Article 19(1), Danish Act on Parental Authority.
[66]    Articles 377a-377h, Book 1, D.C.C.
[67]    Before the Supreme Court only the application of the law and not the facts of the case may be tried.
[68]    *Raad voor de Kinderbescherming* has it main seat in Utrecht and local seats in the districts.
[69]    Article 810, Book 3, Dutch Civil Procedural Code.
[70]    The employees of the Council usually have a university or higher technical background in areas as psychology, social work or similar and receive further education arranged by the Council.

more information is necessary he may order the Board to make an investigation into the relationship between the parents and the child.[71] The investigation results in a report, which contains advice for the judge. An investigation by the Board begins with an interview with both parents and the child which is twelve or older.[72] The Board adopts a mediation approach. The main goal is to ensure that the parents make an agreement on contact themselves which in case of success is reported to the Court. The mediation procedure is not separated from the advisory function of the Board in other words the employees leading the mediation function may be the same ones who in case the mediation is unsuccessful writes the advice to the Court.

In Denmark the administrative authority, *Statsamt,* has sole competence in matters of contact.[73] The *Statsamt* may make use of expert evaluations and opinions concerning the parent child relationship.[74] Decisions of the *Statsamt* may be appealed to another administrative authority *Civilretsdirekto-ratet.* Competence in the field of parental authority is split between the ordinary courts and the *Statsamt.* The general principle is that non-conflict cases are dealt with by the *Statsamt* and conflict cases by the courts. When joint parental authority must end and the parents do not agree on which of them should have parental authority, the decision is always made by the court.[75] An enforcement court decides whether measures enforcing contact should be taken. The Enforcement Court may deny enforcement where the child's mental or physical health is subject to serious danger and it may require an expert opinion and postpone enforcement where in doubt[76] (Civil Procedural Act Art. 536,1). The Enforcement Court's function in

---

[71] The judge may find that that an extended psychological investigation is necessary. Such investigation is carried out by an external bureau such as the *FORA.* The result of such investigation is incorporated into the Council report. The judge may on request of a parent request contra-expertise (Article 810a, Book 3, Civil Procedural Code).

[72] A child younger than 12 may also be heard with respect of its maturity.

[73] Article 17, Danish Act on Parental Authority. A distinctive mark of Danish family law is that exclusively administrative authorities deal with a number of matters. The fact that the administrative authorities have exclusive powers means that their decisions are only subject to limited court review, i.e. a review limited to ascertain whether the decision is against the relevant act or against fundamental administrative principles. In the field of contact only few cases have been tried and none have been found to be contrary to an act or administrati-ve principle, SVEND DANIELSEN, *Lov om forældremyndighed og samvær med kommentarer* (Commentary to the Danish Act on Parental Authority), 1997, p. 325-329. Exclusive powers for the administrative authorities within the family law area are held in the following fields, adoption, child maintenance, maintenance and contact.

[74] The experts may have a background as psychologists, psychiatrists, social workers or similar and may be employees of the *Statsamt* or external.

[75] Article 19(2), Danish Act on Parental Authority.

[76] Article 536(1), *Retsplejeloven,* Danish Civil Procedural Act.

cases concerning contact and parental authority may provide a second review of the case and is often seen as providing a "backstop" in difficult cases. It is not uncommon in Denmark for a conflict concerning parental authority and contact to be played out in three different fora at the same time; the issue of parental responsibility in court, the issue of contact at the *Statsamt* and enforcement of (earlier or preliminary) decisions concerning contact and of earlier or preliminary decisions concerning parental authority in the Enforcement Court. Each forum has its own set of procedural rules and its own experts.

The court based integrated system concerning parental authority and contact is most common in Europe. The administrative solution forms the exception. While the split in competencies in Danish law might in some instances provide an "overkill" of legal action and it would seem common sense to suggest that the court should be able to make a contact order, if so requested, where it was making a decision on parental authority anyway,[77] the Danish administrative system also provides some advantages. The parent who wishes to have contact with his/her child need only write a letter requesting such contact. There are no legal fees or costs to pay and a lawyer is not required.[78] In 2001 there were approximately 3,320 contact cases in Denmark concerning 4,546 children.[79] There are to my knowledge no official estimates of how many contact cases the courts treat per year in the Netherlands. Based on figures from the Child Care and Protection Board there are approximately 3,400 cases per year involving on average 4,200 children.[80] It would seem that Denmark, though its population is approximately one third of the size of the Dutch population, has the same amount of contact cases. This result is not that surprising. Research has previously shown Denmark to have a significantly higher amount of contact cases than Sweden and Norway.[81] Considering the fact that Denmark has substantially more contact cases than other Scandinavian countries, the explanation is not likely to be that of a cultural difference, i.e. that it

---

[77] SVEND DANIELSEN, *Skilsmissesagen, Skandinaviske synspunkter,* (The Divorce Case, Scandinavian Points of View), 1989, p. 415.

[78] It is also not possible to obtain public legal aid in this situation.

[79] Statistical report from *Civilretsdirektoratet,* June 2002, p. 9.

[80] The estimation is based on material received from the Child Care and Protection Board and concern 2001, which show that they carried out 2,110 investigations concerning 2,580 children in contact cases. Further they carried out 1,254 investigations concerning 1,620 children in cases regarding parental authority. As the cases regarding parental authority may (and often does) contain a contact order I have added these figures. The figures remain an uncertain estimate as they tell us the involvement of the Board and not the amount of cases before the Court.

[81] SVEND DANIELSEN, *The Divorce Case, Scandinavian Points of View* 1989, p. 413.

reflects on a larger participation of fathers in the upbringing of children. The answer must lie in the easy procedural access to contact. It may also reflect the fact that parents more often request a minor change of an existing contact arrangement, when procedures are simpler, although the fact that only 22% of the aforementioned cases regard changes means that this explanation does not provide a complete answer.[82]

The Convention on Contact Concerning Children states (Art. 6,1) that "a child considered by internal law as having sufficient understanding shall have the right, unless this would be manifestly contrary to his or her best interests:
i    to receive all relevant information,
ii   to be consulted,
iii  to express his or her views."

Furthermore "due weight shall be given to those views and to the ascertainable wishes and feelings of the child" (Art. 6,2). The rights conferred upon the child in this article of the Convention go further than a right to be heard.[83] They do not, however, infer that the child has actual procedural capacity. Information may be held back where the information is harmful to the child's welfare and the information must be adapted to the child's age and understanding.[84] That due weight must be given to the child's views and ascertainable wishes, does not grant the child an absolute right to consent or to veto a planned decision.[85] The Convention leaves it to the Member States to determine the criteria, enabling them to evaluate whether or not children are capable and are free to make age one of these criteria.[86] The question is whether States are actually as free to decide these criteria as the Convention states. In the case of Sahin[87] the European Court of Human Rights found that the national court ought to have heard the child who at the beginning of the procedures was 3 later 5, even though a child psychologist had advised against it. Germany was found to be in breach of article 8 of the European Convention of Human Rights. What we may derive from this case which concerned an unmarried father's right to have contact with his child is in the first case that it may be an obligation of the State to ensure that very young children are heard especially when

---

[82]   Statistical report from *Civilretsdirektoratet,* June 2002, p. 10.
[83]   The rights as formulated are based on the European Convention of the Rights of the Child, ETS No 160.
[84]   Explanatory Report, p. 28.
[85]   Explanatory report, p. 29.
[86]   *Ibid.*
[87]   Sahin v. Germany, ECHR 11. October 2001.

contact is excluded. Furthermore, that the hearing of children is as much a right of the parent as of the child.

In the Netherlands and Denmark a child of 12 or older must be given an opportunity to express his or her opinion in proceedings concerning a contact order.[88] Children younger than 12 may be given that opportunity in both countries and this often happens indirectly through the use of experts. A child is not considered to have procedural capacity in the Netherlands or Denmark.[89] In the Netherlands a child is given the opportunity to contact the judge who *ex officio* can make a contact order.[90] Neither in the Netherlands nor in Denmark does the child have the right to receive all relevant information.

### 3.4. Remedies

Remedies are here considered to consist of measures such as counselling and mediation as well as enforcement measures such as fines or the physical collection of the child.

The Convention on Contact Concerning Children states "State Parties shall take all appropriate measures to ensure that contact orders are carried into effect" (Art. 9). In the Explanatory Report it is considered on the basis of the case law of the European Court of Human Rights to mean that measures must be adequate and sufficient to ensure enforcement.[91] The Convention and case law of the European Court of Human Rights allow States the scope to choose between different remedies, but these must be effective. This implies that it is not enough to have sufficient remedies if the application of these is not successful in enforcing the contact order.[92] As mentioned in Section 3.3., the Convention encourages reaching amicable agreements, in particular through the use of family mediation.

---

[88] Article 809, Book 3, Dutch Civil Procedural Code, Article 29(1), Danish Act on Parental Authority.

[89] The Netherlands M.J.C. KOENS, C.G.M. VAN WAMELEN: *Kind en scheiding* (Child and divorce), 2001, p. 48. Denmark, *Civilretsdirektoratet, Skarrildhus 1998,* (yearly message from the administrative appeal authority) actually states that children are part in administrative family law proceedings, but goes on to conclude that such rights are practised by the holder of parental authority, effectively minimising the impact of such a status. The rights inherent to such status could only be exercised by the child independently when the child is 18. At this point "the child" would for example be able to receive a copy of the case files.

[90] Article 377g, Book 1, D.C.C.

[91] *CDCJ* (2001) 33, p. 32.

[92] *Ibid.*

The State may include the following particular enforcement measures as articulated in Article 10(2)a of the Convention.

i  supervision of contact,
ii  the obligation for a person to provide for the travel and accommodation expenses of the child and, as may be appropriate, of any other person accompanying the child,
iii  a security to be deposited by the person with whom the child is usually living to ensure that the person seeking contact with the child is not prevented from having such contact,
iv  a fine to be imposed on the person with whom the child is usually living, should this person refuse to comply with the contact order.[93]

In the Netherlands mediation or counselling, as a means to solve conflicts concerning contact, is not regulated by law. The Child Care and Protection Board does, however, offer a mediation approach, within their advisory function to the Court, as described above in Section 3.3.. In 1999 the Dutch Ministry of Justice started two mediation experiments, one for divorce, which could include a conflict concerning contact and one for contact. The experiments were evaluated[94] and were generally found to be a success with the divorce mediation experiment resulting in 75% reaching an agreement and the contact experiment resulting in 50% reaching an agreement. Mediation was voluntary albeit that in contact cases mediation occurred normally upon referral of the Court where the Court used its authority to convince the parents of the usefulness of mediation. It remains to be seen if and to what extent the use of mediation in divorce and contact proceedings will be incorporated into the law.

In Denmark experiments on counselling[95] in relation to contact and parental authority started in the beginning of the 1980s. Since 1986 the *Statsamt* must offer counselling in cases concerning contact and parental authority.[96] The offer is directed towards parents and children. It is not a condition that both parents and / or the child participate. Counselling may take place with one parent and/or the child alone. Counselling takes place at the *Statsamt*.[97] The offer can be made during divorce proceedings if the divorce is administrative or in the course of a contact case. Counselling

---

[93]  The Convention also contains remedies to ensure the return of the child (Art. 10,2b. These measures will not be discussed in this article.
[94]  B.E.S. CHIN-A-FAT, M.J. STEKETE: *Bemiddeling in uitvoering*, (Mediation in Progress), July 2001.
[95]  *Børnesagkyndig rådgivning* (Children expert counselling).
[96]  Article 28(1), Danish Act on Parental Authority.
[97]  The counsellors will have special expertise regarding children. Counsellors are most often psychologists or social workers.

runs independent of the decision making of the *Statsamt*; only the result of the counselling is reported to the case officer unless the parents agree otherwise or the case officer has participated in the counselling upon request of the parents.[98] Counselling has been a success in Denmark. In approximately 57% of cases a positive outcome was reported.[99] From 2001 mediation has been offered as an alternative to counselling. Both parents must participate and it is a condition that a case concerning contact is closed before mediation may take place.[100] In 67% of the mediations a complete solution was found and in 18% of the cases the conflict was partly solved.[101]

Supervision of contact has no legislative basis in the Netherlands. The Child Care and Protection Board may in its advisory function to the Court start up a contact arrangement, which may be supervised in order to monitor the contact parent's interaction with the child. The Court cannot, however, request the Board to supervise contact following a contact order.[102]

In Denmark the *Statsamt* has a duty to provide supervised contact whenever this is deemed necessary.[103] Supervised contact may only be ordered where unsupervised contact is not possible and should only be used where it is necessary for the child.[104] Supervised contact is typically used in the following instances: to help parents who have difficulty initiating a contact arrangement, where the contact parent has had little or no contact with the child, where there is concern about the contact parent's ability to take care of the child, when information is needed for the case regarding the contact parent's interaction with the child and as a measure of protection of the child in case of the contact parent's alcohol or drug abuse. Furthermore it may be used in cases where there is risk of child abduction.[105] Supervised contact may take place in private homes under supervision of

---

[98] ANNETTE KRONBORG: "Forvaltning af familieretligt samvær (The administration of family contact)", *Juristen* No 9, 2000, p. 325-333 points out that the fact that the counselling takes place at the *Statsamt* means that parents do not experience a separation between counselling and their case in which a judicial decision must be made. The counsellors and the case officers are colleagues and the case may contain a memo indicating whether the parents have accepted an offer of counselling.

[99] Statistical report from *Civilretsdirektoratet*, June 2002, p. 35.

[100] *Konfliktmægling* (Mediation) on the website of the *Statsamt* www.statsamt.dk.

[101] Statistical Report from *Civilretsdirektoratet*, June 2002, p. 36.

[102] Dutch Supreme Court HR 29 of June 2001, *NJ* 2001, 598.

[103] Departmental order, Art. 19a.

[104] Guide on the treatment of contact cases, November 1999, p. 24.

[105] *Ibid.*

a family member, in a public institution such as a kindergarten or in a neutral place. In case information is needed for the case, an expert must be present and the rules on expert evidence must be followed.[106]

The Dutch Civil Code does not provide for specific measures that may be used to enforce a contact order. The measures that can be used are derived from the general measures available under the Dutch Civil Procedural Code and the Dutch Civil Code and encompass; a penalty, detention, a supervision order and the use of force. Furthermore it may influence decisions concerning parental authority and the primary residence of the child. The Danish Civil Procedural Act prescribes that penalties and the use of force may be used to enforce a contact order.[107] As in the Netherlands it may influence a decision concerning parental authority and is even mentioned in the Act on Parental Authority as a criteria for the transfer of parental authority. The measures will be further elaborated below.

In the Netherlands and Denmark a fine may be used in the enforcement of a contact order. The penalty is imposed on the parent who obstructs contact and with whom the child resides. In the Netherlands a penalty may be imposed for each violation of the contact order and may in fact be settled prior to the violation.[108] In Denmark a lump sum penalty, or daily or weekly penalties may be imposed until the child is handed over for contact.[109] Given the fact that the contact order and the enforcement procedures are decided separately,[110] it is not possible to settle a penalty prior to violation of the contact order. In the Netherlands the penalty imposed belongs to the wronged parent, if the other parent has no means it may in fact be futile to impose it. The sum may, however, be set off against debts such as a property claim deriving from the divorce settlement, but not against child maintenance.[111] In Denmark the imposed penalty is the property of the state. If not paid, it may be converted to detention, i.e. that the parent is detained for a day or an amount of days corresponding to the non-paid penalties.

Detaining the parent who obstructs contact is, in principle, possible in the Netherlands,[112] but not in Denmark apart from the possibility of conversion

---

[106]   *Ibid.*, p. 25.
[107]   Article 536(1), Danish Civil Procedural Act.
[108]   M.J.C. KOENS, C.G.M. VAN WAMELEN: *Kind en scheiding* (Child and divorce), 2001, p. 105.
[109]   Article 536(3), Danish Civil Procedural Act.
[110]   See section 3.3.
[111]   *Ibid.*, footnote 78.
[112]   Article 585, Dutch Civil Procedural Code.

of a penalty as mentioned above. Detaining the parent who has the main care for the child is obviously a controversial measure and it is to my knowledge not very frequently used in the Netherlands.[113]

When one talks of the use of force one refers to the physical fetching of the child from one parent in order to let the other parent exercise his or her contact rights. The measure is administered by the police in the Netherlands and by the Enforcement Court with the possibility of police assistance in Denmark.[114] It is obvious that such a measure is of a controversial nature and that contact under these circumstances may not actually benefit the child. However, in both the Netherlands and in Denmark, the criteria for issuing / excluding a contact order instead of being centred on the best interests of the child focus on whether such an order would be harmful to the child. In the Danish Civil Procedural Act,[115] it is stated that enforcement of a contact order is excluded where the child's mental or physical health is seriously threatened, indicating that some harm may be inflicted. The fact that reference to the use of force is seldom made in Dutch case law could be an indication that this is rarely used in the Netherlands.[116] While fetching the child is not the first option in Denmark it does, in my view, happen more frequently than in the Netherlands.[117]

A measure available in the Netherlands but not in Denmark is the placement of the child under supervision[118] of the youth authorities. Placing a child under supervision is considered a mild child protection measure[119] and entails a duty for the resident parent to consult with and seek support from the appointed guardian concerning the contact arrangement. The child remains living at home. A child may only be placed under supervision where the lack of contact forms a threat to the moral

---

[113] In the Dutch Supreme Court decision: HR 24 of March 2000, NJ 2000,356 it was not applied as it was considered to be against the best interests of the children.
[114] The Court may in Denmark appoint someone, usually a representative of the Social Services, to safeguard the child's interests (Civil procedural Act Art. 536,2).
[115] Article 536(1).
[116] See note to the Dutch Supreme Court case HR 3 June 1994, NJ 1995,74 in which a system of fetching the child resembling the Finnish solution which is not very different from the Danish solution is pledged for.
[117] In a recent Danish newspaper article: "Skilsmissebørn hentes af politiet" (Children of divorce fetched by the police), *Berlingske Tidende* 10 of December 2002 an estimate of 25 times per year was made.
[118] Article 254(2), Book 1, D.C.C.
[119] M.J.C. KOENS, C.G.M. VAN WAMELEN, *Kind en scheiding* (Child and divorce), 2001, p. 107.

or spiritual needs of the child and where other means of providing this contact have failed or is expected to fail.[120]

The question is to what extent a parent's "unjustified" obstruction of a contact order may influence his or her position with regards to parental authority or in the Netherlands in case of joint parental authority with respect to the child's place of residence. In the Netherlands the Supreme Court has considered that obstruction only qualifies for a change in parental authority/place of residence where the parent who has a right of contact de facto has more to offer the child .[121] In Denmark it was introduced in 1996 as a consideration (the only one mentioned) in the provisions concerning the transfer of parental authority.[122] The general criterion of the provisions is what is best for the child. The consideration was not contained in the first draft of the Act[123] but it was added in the course of the parliamentary treatment of the Act. A number of cases concerning the transfer of parental authority have since 1996 dealt with obstruction of contact, but in none of the cases has parental authority been transferred on the basis of obstruction alone.[124]

## 4. CONTACT –EXTENDED FAMILY

The Convention on Contact Concerning Children states (Art. 5,1) that "subject to his or her best interests, contact may be established between the child and persons other than his or her parents having family ties with the child". Furthermore pursuant to (Art. 5,2) "States Parties are free to extend this provision to persons other than those mentioned in paragraph 1, and where so extended, states may freely decide what aspects of contact, as defined in Art. 2 letter a shall apply".

In the Netherlands there is a provision on contact between a child and non-parents.[125] According to this provision, empowering the court to make a contact order for a non-parent, a contact order may be issued to a person

---

[120]  The Dutch Supreme Court found in HR 13 of April 2001, NJ 2002,4 that the chance that lack of contact is harmful or detrimental to the child, or brings the risk of the child being placed in a conflict of loyalty between the parents, is insufficient motivation for placing the child under supervision.
[121]  Dutch Supreme Court, HR 15 of December 2000, NJ 2001,123.
[122]  Articles 12 and 13, Danish Act on Parental Authority.
[123]  Although it was mentioned amongst other considerations in the comments, Commission report 1279/94, p. 145. The consideration (obstruction of contact) is popularly known to be the mark of the fathers' rights movement.
[124]  The Danish Supreme Court dealt with the issue in U2001.153H.
[125]  Article 377f, Book 1, D.C.C.

with a close relationship to the child. A person with a close relationship to the child does not have a "right" to contact similar to that of a parent. The issue of a contact order may be rejected if this is against the best interests of the child or a child aged 12 or older is against the measure. The rights of non-parents were recognized in the Netherlands prior to its introduction in the Dutch Civil Code in 1995. The Supreme Court found that this right existed on the basis of Article 8 of the European Convention of Human Rights, when he or she has a close personal relationship with the child[126] or in other words when there is "family life". A biological relationship is not sufficient for the creation of "family life", for example the role of a sperm donor.[127]

In Denmark only parents have the right of contact with their children. No provisions provide for the possibility of contact with other family members irrespective of the role they may have played in the child's life. Grandparents, aunts, uncles, stepparents or siblings, who may have played an active role in the child's life or even have raised the child for a considerable time, have no right to contact. Recently a stepparent made a request for contact. The *Statsamt* as well as the administrative appeal authority *Civilretsdirektorat* denied the request with the following reasoning: "The administration is not entitled to make a decision, which is not founded on Danish law, referring to an international convention [European Convention of Human Rights]. This not least when the decision will be a burden to a private person. It is of no relevance that the convention has been incorporated in Danish law by an act, when this act does not contain a provision empowering the administration to make a decision on contact".[128] The issue of contact rights to those other than parents have been considered by various Danish Commissions preparing legislation in the field of parental authority and contact legislation and have been rejected, not because it was not seen as important for a child to have contact with close relatives, but because contact was only seen to be in the best interests of the child, when it was arranged in accordance with the parent who has parental authority. Further it was stressed that more controlled contact arrangements may give hesitations as it may be difficult for the child to have normal leisure time when it has to use many weekends on meeting the requirements of several contact arrangements.[129]

---

[126] Dutch Supreme Court, HR 22 of February 1985, *NJ* 1986,3.
[127] Dutch Supreme Court, HR 26 of January 1990, *NJ* 1990, nr. 630.
[128] *TFA* (Journal of Family Law), 2001, p. 501.
[129] Commission report 1279/94 p.125-127.

In the case of Scozzari and Giunta[130] concerning inter alia contact between a grandmother and her grandchildren, it was stated that ""family life" within the meaning of Article 8 European Convention of Human Rights includes at least the ties between near relatives, for instance those between grandparents and grandchildren, since such relatives may play a considerable part in family life. "Respect" for a family life so understood implies an obligation for the State to act in a manner calculated to allow these ties to develop normally".

While the Danish arguments against contact for non-parents would seem bona fide, the fact that no contact order can be issued in any case including cases in which the child's parents have died or the child has no contact with its parents and also include near relatives who for example have taken care of the child earlier, the strength of the arguments fade. The complete lack of a possibility to issue a contact order probably infringes Article 8 of the European Convention of Human Rights. The State has not acted "in a manner calculated to allow these ties to develop normally".

## 5. IN THE LIGHT OF HARMONISATION –CONCLUDING REMARKS

The question is, to what extent there exists a common core in the legal systems of Denmark and the Netherlands concerning parental authority and contact.

With respect to parental authority it is clear that joint parental authority increasingly is applied outside of marriage in both countries. In the Netherlands the emphasis has been on enforcing joint parental authority after divorce and in Denmark the emphasis has been to equalise the position of unmarried parents with married parents, thus increasing the number of unmarried parents who have joint parental authority. Furthermore on the basis of the three construed criteria listed in section 2 (whether joint parental authority was the preferred solution, whether it was consensus based and to what extent judicial conflict solving existed) there was little congruence to be found between the two countries.

With respect to contact between parent and child seen from a practical perspective there is more congruence to be found. In both countries contact is the right of a parent i.e. the person who is deemed to be the legal parent. The primary form of contact is in both countries personal (face-to-

---

[130]  Scozzari and Giunta v. Italy, *ECHR* 13 July 2000.

face) contact with the possibility of "other" contact and the right to information. It must be remarked that Denmark does not give any rights to the child except from the right to be heard. A child has for example no right of contact. The reasoning is based on a "common sense" approach, i.e. lets not grant a right that we cannot enforce

Procedures concerning contact vary in the two countries. In the Netherlands the ordinary courts decide contact cases while in Denmark they are decided by an administrative authority. Two distinctive differences emerge from these different systems, the first is that Denmark has a much higher number of contact cases than the Netherlands, and the second is the large production of secondary regulation and statistical material in Denmark, which lays down the interpretation of the act in a much more detailed way as seen in the Netherlands and further provides us with much statistical information. In the Netherlands direct rights in the field of family law can be based on human rights such as the European Convention of Human Rights. This has not been seen in Denmark.

When it comes to contact between the extended family and the child only the Netherlands has a provision providing for the possibility. In Denmark no such right exists. The fact is, however, that Denmark's position on this point probably already infringes Article 8 of the European Convention of Human Rights.

The answer to the question posed in the beginning of this section is ambiguous, not really common core, some common core, no common core. The question is, does it matter? It would seem that the Commission on European Family Law has chosen to base its principles not only on a common core but on the "better law" approach, i.e. upon "the highest standard of modernity".[131] The unmarried father's position with respect to parental authority and the enforcement of joint parental authority after divorce, remain politically sensitive areas in which arguments for and against can be made. It is, however, quite clear that "the highest standard of modernity" at present is the system proposed by the Council of Europe in which joint parental authority is the main rule for married, divorced and unmarried parents. With respect to contact there is also little question that the new Convention on Contact Concerning Children, which emphasizes the rights as mutual rights i.e. also a right of the child and extend contact rights to persons having family ties with the child, represents modernity

---

[131]   MASHA ANTOKOLSKAIA, "The 'better law' approach and the harmonisation of family law", in this book, p. 157.

today. In my view it would be difficult to ignore the content of these international instruments when drafting principles based on the "better law" approach for the harmonization of family law in Europe.

# THE CONCEPT OF PARENTAL RESPONSIBILITY IN BULGARIAN AND ENGLISH LAW

MIGLENA BALDJIEVA

## 1. INTRODUCTION

The subject of this contribution is the private legal relationships between parents and children, on the one hand, whereas, on the other, it focuses on the public legal relations and the relevant intervention of the state. The research is of a comparative legal nature and is based on the primary legislation of Bulgaria and England and Wales. The major aspects of comparison are two concepts, which have been regulated within the two legal systems – the concept of parental rights and obligations, respectively parental responsibility, and the possibility of public intervention in parent-children relationships.

## 2. THE LEGAL FRAMEWORK OF PARENT-CHILDREN RELATIONSHIPS

By their nature, the relations between parents and children are biological and social. Most of these relations are not subject to any regulations and are mainly governed by the ethical principles established in each society. Some of the relations between parents and children, however, are subject to legislative regulations, whereby they are transformed into legal relations. In terms of Bulgarian law, the greatest importance is assigned to parental rights and obligations towards the personality and the property of the child, whereas, in terms of English law, the focus is very much on parental responsibility.

Under Bulgarian law parental rights and obligations are subject to the provisions of the Constitution (1991) and the Family Code (1985), whereas in England and Wales, parental responsibility is regulated by the Children Act (1989). At a first glance, the two pieces of legislation do not exhibit great differences and seem to settle parent-children relations in a similar way. Upon closer inspection, however, it becomes clear that their underlying philosophy is somewhat different.

The Constitution of the Republic of Bulgaria, being the main and primary law, regulates the key principles and provides the legal framework for private legal relations between parents and children. According to the Constitution,[1] the rearing and the upbringing of children until they reach the age of majority, is a right and an obligation of their parents and the state assists in this. The Family Code[2] settles the rights and the obligations of parents towards their children, who, due to their age, are placed under parental care.[3] This regulation provides the content of one of the most important institutions of family law, more specifically, the institution of parental rights and obligations regarding the children who have not attained the age of majority. Of the regulations quoted, it becomes clear that Bulgarian legislation has adopted the "parental rights and obligations" concept. The law empowers parents to care for their children. Meanwhile, parents are not merely empowered, but also obliged to exercise their rights, *i.e.*, one and the same function demonstrates the quality of both their right and their obligation.

This concept is founded upon the basic principles of the Bulgarian legal system, where relations between the subjects of civil law and, specifically, family law, are determined through legal provisions by the mutual recognition of rights and obligations. Each private legal relationship is established based on a legal norm and exists only by virtue of the latter. It is always a specific and strictly defined relationship between two legal subjects and it has a precisely defined content, which consists of legally established conduct or interaction, which is attained through either the recognition of rights or the establishment of obligations.[4]

The Children Act 1989 is comparatively new and it introduces the concept of parental responsibility. It assumes that the primary responsibility for deciding what should happen to their children should rest with the parents themselves. To emphasize the practical reality that the upbringing of children is a serious responsibility, rather than a matter of legal rights, the conceptual building block used throughout the Act is "parental responsibility". Thus, the Act covers the whole diversity of duties, powers and authority of the parents over the child.[5] Although the change in terminology from rights and duties to responsibility was neither intended nor expected to bring about any changes to the substance of the law, in itself

---

[1]    Constitution of the Republic of Bulgaria, 1991, Art. 47 (1).
[2]    Family Code, 1985, Chapter VII, Parent-Children Relationships.
[3]    See NENOVA, L., *Family Law*, 1990, p. 185.
[4]    See TADGER, V., *Civil Law of the PRB*, Common Part, Section I, 1972.
[5]    See WHITE, CARR, LOWE, *The Children Act in Practice, Second Edition*, 1995, p. 5.

it conveys quite a different message in stating that a parent has responsibilities rather than rights and duties.

Irrespective of the various concepts on which the two laws are founded, their common feature is the lack of any definition and content of the terms parental rights and obligations and parental responsibility.

In addition to the terms parental rights and obligations, the Bulgarian Family Code uses different wording to denote them, such as parental rights, parental functions or parental care. In order to regulate parental rights and obligations, the Family Code[6] stipulates that parents are obliged to care for their children and to prepare them to act for the public good. Based on this provision and on some other legal norms within the Code,[7] parental rights and obligations can be grouped in the following way: rights and obligations of the parents regarding the personality of children (determination of the proper name, rearing, upbringing and ensuring the child's education), the obligation for the common habitation of parents and children and the representative and custodial functions of parents in carrying out legal actions on behalf of the children.[8] Therefore, multiple and diverse parental functions are covered in a global sense by the texts of the Family Code, from which the main and the typical parental obligations can be derived regarding children who have not attained the age of majority.

The Children Act[9] states that parental responsibility means all the rights, duties, powers, responsibility and authority, which by law a parent of a child has in relation to the child and his property. Obviously, unlike the Family Code, the Children Act does not include what parental responsibility comprises. The Act implements the strategy recommended by the Law Commission that such a list would have to change from time to time in order to meet differing needs and circumstances and would have to vary with the age and maturity of the child and the circumstances of the case. The key elements of parental responsibility, however, may be deduced from different sources of the law, such as Common Law, Criminal Law, the Child Abduction Act, the Children Act, the Children and Young Persons Act, the Education Act etc. They namely concentrate on housing, looking after the

---

[6]    Family Code, 1985, Art. 68(1).
[7]    Family Code, 1985, Arts. 71 and 73.
[8]    See STANEVA, A., *Legal Nature of the Parental Rights and Duties, Pravna missal,* 1984/6, p. 97.
[9]    Children Act, 1989, Section 3, part I.

child, contact issues, consenting to the child's medical treatment and education issues.[10]

## 3. POSSESSORS OF PARENTAL RIGHTS

The major distinction resulting from the different philosophic backgrounds of the two acts is related to the possessors of parental rights and obligations, respectively parental responsibility and the possibility of sharing in the parental rights and obligations or, respectively, parental responsibility, by the parents or any third parties.

Under Bulgarian family law, parental rights and obligations only arise under the law. The Family Code empowers and obliges merely and only the parents to care for their children.[11] Therefore, only the parents, or the adoptive parents, respectively, can be the possessors of parental rights and obligations.[12] In those cases where no one possesses parental rights, such as where both parents are unknown, deceased or have been deprived of parental rights, then care, similar to parental care, is provided by a guardian or a trustee, but these persons do not become parents under family law. Thus the Code promotes the biological ties between children and adults rather than the social ones.

In contrast, the Children Act 1989 states that more than one person may have parental responsibility for the same child at the same time.[13] In addition, the Act regulates the acquisition of parental responsibility by a third party – individuals and local authorities. Individuals who are not the parents of the child can acquire parental responsibility by becoming that child's guardian,[14] by being granted a residence order or an emergency protection order in respect of the child. Local authorities can acquire parental responsibility namely by means of a care order[15] or an emergency protection order.[16] In cases where a third party acquires parental responsibility the main effect is that the parents do not lose this responsibility solely because someone else has acquired it through a court order.[17] This means

---

[10]  See WHITE, CARR, LOWE, *The Children Act in Practice*, Second edition, 1995, p. 38.
[11]  Family Code, 1985, Art. 68.
[12]  Family Code, 1985, Arts. 61 and 62.
[13]  Children Act, 1989, Section 2(5).
[14]  Children Act, 1989, Section 5.
[15]  Children Act, 1989, Section 33.
[16]  Children Act, 1989, Section 44.
[17]  Children Act, 1989, Section 2(6).

that each party is able to exercise its responsibilities independently of the others.[18]

From the comparison drawn so far between the Family Code and the Children Act 1989, it becomes clear that, though similar at first glance, the two legislative acts considerably differ. The Children Act 1989 introduces new aspects in determining the relations between parents and children. To the highest possible degree, the legislative regulations focus on the rights and interests of the child. Conversely, Bulgarian case law, but not the legal theory, has long been occupied with the question of the degree to which the rights and interests of children are protected under the effective legislation. The Family Code incorporates parent-children relationships in the general civil legislative framework of the classical legal relationship, which is emphasised by a number of authors.[19] On the one hand, the existence of specifically defined rights and obligations requires that the subjects in the legal relationship would obey and fulfil them. Thus, the emphasis in parent-children relationships is laid on the obligations of the parents and not so much on the protection of children's rights and obligations. On the other hand, however, these relationships have their specific aspects and regulation is required for each particular case, bearing in mind the individual aspects, the age, maturity, and the specific needs of the child. In this sense, it is necessary, in order to harmonise Bulgarian legislation with contemporary approaches and decisions in view of the best interests of the child, to reconsider the concept of parental rights and obligations as developed by the Family Code.

## 4.  STATE INTERVENTION –GROUNDS AND LIMITS

The second part of my survey relates to the possibility of the state to intervene in the private legal relations between parents and children and the consequences of such an intervention, which are related to the exercise of parental rights and obligations and parental responsibility.

According to the Bulgarian Constitution,[20] those children left without care are placed under the special protection of the state and society, whereas the conditions and the procedure for restricting or depriving parental rights are determined by the law. These constitutional principles form the

---

[18]   See WHITE, CARR, LOWE, *The Children Act in Practice*, Second Edition, 1995, p. 57.

[19]   See TODOROVA, V., "The Grounds for and the Nature of Compulsory State Intervention in Parent-Child Relationships based on Articles 74 and 75 of the Family Code", *Pravna missal*, 1996/3, p. 47.

[20]   Constitution of the Republic of Bulgaria, 1991, Arts. 47(4) and (5).

foundation of the Child Protection Act (2000) and the Family Code. The former provides for child protection measures (placement outside the family), whereas the latter provides for the restriction and/or deprivation of parental rights.

The Family Code provides for a court order to restrict or to deprive the parental rights of one parent upon the request of the other parent or the prosecutor.[21] In cases where parental rights are restricted, the court takes the respective measures in the interest of the child, placing that child (where necessary) in an "appropriate place" – in the majority of cases in a residential home. In all cases, the measures undertaken mean only a quantitative decrease of parental powers. In general, a parent continues to be the possessor of parental rights and obligations, and is obliged and empowered to exercise them.[22] In cases where parental rights have been deprived, the consequences are related to the revocation of the parent's rights and obligations as regards the child: rearing, upbringing, education, common habitation, representative and custodial functions. In this respect, the other parent remains the sole possessor of parental rights and obligations. When both parents have been deprived of their parental rights, the Family Code provides for the appointment of a guardian or a trustee,[23] who is then responsible for the rearing, the upbringing and the education of the child, to manage his/her property and to represent him/her before third parties. Trustees and guardians, however, can only exercise functions that are similar to those of parents. They are not the parents of the child and, in this sense, they do not become the possessors of parental rights and obligations. As a result of this legislation, the "measures" undertaken by the court actually have the effect of removing, in one extent or another, the culpable parent from the child and caring for that child. Intervention thereby requires a different approach and should take the form of "complementary" care where parental rights are restricted or "substitute" care, in those cases where parental rights have been deprived.[24]

To a great extent, the Child Protection Act[25] corresponds to the needs of legal regulation in this respect. The Act provides for a protective measure: placing a child outside the family. The grounds for such a court order are

---

[21]  Family Code, 1985, Arts. 74 and 75.
[22]  See NENOVA, L., *Family Law*, 1990, p. 202.
[23]  Family Code, 1985, Art.109.
[24]  See TODOROVA, V., "The Grounds for and the Nature of Compulsory State Intervention in Parent-Child Relationships based on Articles 74 and 75 of the Family Code", *Pravna missal*, p. 49, 1996/3.
[25]  Child Protection Act, 2000, Articles 25-28.

exhaustively enumerated in the Act. The request for the court order, which enforces the protective measure of placing the child outside the family, is filed either by the municipal social assistance service, the prosecutor, or the parent. The new provisions introduced by the law are related to the opportunities that it provides for substitute or complementary childcare by close friends and relatives, by foster parents or specialised institutions. They are defined as protection measures and actually identify those persons who are to take responsibility for the rearing and the upbringing of the child. Thus, the right of the child to be cared for is satisfied by substituting the parent, to one extent or another, by another person.

Similar to the Bulgarian legislation, the Children Act provides for the placement of a child in the care of a local authority. The Children Act[26] provides for a care order or a supervision order as regards a child which has not attained the age of 17 if the court is satisfied that the child concerned is suffering, or is likely to suffer, significant harm; and that the harm, or likelihood of harm, is attributable to the care given to the child, or likely to be given to him if the order were not made, not being what it would be reasonable to expect a parent to give to him or the child's being beyond parental control.

The request for such an order may only be filed by a local authority, the National Service for the Prevention of Cruelty against Children or by a person authorised by the Secretary of State. The child, as well as any person having parental responsibility, automatically becomes a party to the court proceedings. While the child is in care, the parent and the local authority exercise parental responsibility. However, this responsibility is limited, as the local authority is not entitled to intervene in some spheres such as changing the religious beliefs or the family name of the child, or to consent to the adoption of the child.[27] In this respect, parents preserve their parental responsibility.

In the case of a supervision order, the local authority is granted broad powers as regards the child, by observing, for instance, whether the child lives according to the court's instructions. Supervision orders, however, do not transfer parental responsibility, i.e. the parents preserve in full their rights, functions, powers and responsibilities regarding the child.

Several generalisations follow from the analysis presented:

---

[26] Children Act 1989, Section 31.
[27] See WHITE, CARR, LOWE, *The Children Act in Practice*, Second Edition, 1995, p. 205.

The Children Act regulates state intervention and creates a single statutory route for placing a child in care. Conversely, the Bulgarian legislation lacks a consistent definition regulating state intervention in parent-child relationships. State intervention is subject to the regulatory provisions of two pieces of legislation: the Family Code and the Child Protection Act, which use different terminology: restriction, respectively, deprivation of parental rights and enforcement of protection measures.

The existing dual regulation raises a number of important questions. Bearing in mind the similar grounds for issuing the court order, which cases will require the restriction or, respectively, the deprivation of parental rights and which will call for the enforcement of a protection measure? To what degree do the two acts correspond to one another and is there an opportunity to deliver two different court decisions concerning the same child? In this sense, on the one hand the lack of consistency in the relevant legislation contradicts the principles of civil law, on the other, it raises the question of the legitimacy and the correctness of the decisions issued by the law enforcement authorities in view of protecting of the best interests of the child. *De lege ferenda*, the Bulgarian legislators need to reconsider the existing legislative situation and to unify and harmonise the mechanisms of state intervention in the relations between parents and children as regards the determination of parental rights and obligations.

Furthermore, the Children Act foresees a statutory threshold and once this threshold has been transcended the court can make a care or supervision order. The threshold criteria are not in themselves grounds or reasons for making a care or supervision order. Those conditions are the minimum circumstances, which should always be found to exist before it can ever be justified for a court even to begin to contemplate whether the State should be given the possibility to intervene in family life. The integrity and privacy of the family is the basic principle of a free and democratic society and the need to defend such principles should be clearly perceivable in the law. Accordingly, unless there is evidence that a child is being or is likely to be harmed because of a failure within the family, the state, whether in the guise of a local authority or a court, should not interfere.[28]

Conversely, the Family Code and the Child Protection Act regulate the grounds for the court's intervention. In legal theory, these grounds are identified as circumstances which may be of two kinds: the culpable behaviour of the parent or his/her non-culpable intent, i.e. the parent's

---

[28]     See WHITE, CARR, LOWE, *The Children Act in Practice*, Second Edition, 1995, p. 6..

subjective attitude to the infringement of the child's rights is immaterial for the public legal intervention. In this sense, the intervention of the state in the relations between parents and children appears to be a sanction against the parents rather than a means for the protection of the rights and interests of the child. In restriction/deprivation of parental rights proceedings or in proceedings to enforce a protection measure, the law enforcement authority will check for the existence of one of these circumstances and, only where there are such circumstances, the court will deliver a decision which is governed by the interests of the child in each particular case.

However, in terms of the mechanisms of state intervention in private legal relations between parents and children, the greatest drawback of Bulgarian legislation is the lack of a legal subject temporarily authorised with parental powers in cases of restriction/deprivation of parental rights or the enforcement of a protection measure: placement outside the family. In this sense, the intervention of the state needs to be realised in the form of specific legally bound entities, which would be responsible for that part of the care that parent(s) are unable to provide.[29] Unlike the Bulgarian legislation, the Children Act provides for the sharing of parental responsibility by several persons and, more specifically, by the local authority. In reaching a decision on the sharing of parental responsibility, the major issue to be addressed by the court is the welfare of the child. Where third parties acquire parental responsibility, each of the possessors of this responsibility can exercise their powers individually, except for those cases where the law requires the consent of all concerned.

## 5. CONCLUSIONS

My initial idea to draw a parallel between the English and the Bulgarian legal systems has remained partly unfulfilled, as the difference between the two seems to be rather material. The Bulgarian legal system belongs to the continental legal system, the hierarchy of which incorporates respectively: the branch of law, sections, institutions and legal norms regulating the respective legal relationships, which constitute a particular relation between specific legal entities expressed in terms of rights and obligations. The legal relationship, however, is not typical of the Anglo-American legal system to which English law belongs, where the major

---

[29] See TODOROVA, V., "The Grounds for and the Nature of Compulsory State Intervention in Parent-Child Relationships based on Articles 74 and 75 of the Family Code", *Pravna Missal*, 1996/3, p. 50.

distinctions in the legislative regulations between parents and children derive.

The concepts that govern the relations between parents and children are different. Irrespective of the specific nature of these relations, the Bulgarian legislation puts emphasis on parental rights and obligations, unlike English law, where the building block is parental responsibility.

Hence, there is a difference as regards the consequences concerning the child. Bulgarian law sanctions the parents if they fail to perform their parental rights and obligations, by restricting or depriving their rights towards their children. This results in negative consequences for the children, whereas English law pays attention to the welfare of children and develops mechanisms that, as far as possible, aim to protect children's rights and interests.

# "JUST THE OVEN": A LAW & ECONOMICS APPROACH TO GESTATIONAL SURROGACY CONTRACTS

### ARISTIDES N. HATZIS*

> *"They want me to be the surrogate.*
> *It's her egg and his sperm.*
> *I'm just the oven.*
> *It's totally their bun."*
> Phoebe Buffay[1]

In late 1995, a 36-year-old woman who had had 24 consecutive unexplained miscarriages over eleven years presented herself to a University hospital in Tel-Aviv. After a series of tests, her doctors were unable to come up with a definitive diagnosis. She was referred for assisted reproduction. Four good-quality embryos were transferred to her uterus, but unfortunately pregnancy was not achieved.[2] At that stage, surrogacy became legally possible in Israel, and this option was offered to the couple. Two embryos were then transferred to a 28-year-old surrogate mother. Her pregnancy was uneventful until term, when a caesarean section was performed and a healthy male neonate was delivered (Raziel *et al.* 2000).

At about that time, in a teaching hospital in Montpellier, a 29-year-old woman was treated for bulky squamous cell carcinoma of the uterine cervix. She received primary chemotherapy and underwent total pelvic irradiation

---

\* Earlier drafts of this paper were presented at the Erasmus Workshop on Law and Economics (Hamburg, February 14, 2003) and at the Workshop on Political Sociology at Panteion University (Athens, February 21, 2003). It is based on my related work in a major project that deals with the ethical, legal and economic ramifications of surrogacy and gestational agreements. I am particularly thankful for their comments, suggestions and help to Brian Bix, Olga Dyuzheva, Pierre Garello, Theresa Glennon, Denise Lascarides, Hugh McLachlan, Nigel Lowe, Rosa Martins, Yvette Tan, Epaminontas Triantafilou and Aspasia Tsaoussis. The usual disclaimer applies. Comments are welcome at: ahatzis@phs.uoa.gr.

[1] PHOEBE BUFFAY (Lisa Kudrow) from the episode "The One with Phoebe's Uterus" of the hit American TV sitcom *Friends*. Original transmission date: January 8, 1998. Written by SETH KURLAND.

[2] According to her doctors, "another pregnancy would have probably had the same outcome as all her previous pregnancies" (RAZIEL *et al.* 2000: 105).

before a total abdominal hysterectomy. Two years after surgery, the patient had no clinical or biological signs of ovarian failure. She and her partner still desired a pregnancy. So they decided to recruit a surrogate mother in San Francisco and were completely responsible for all the details of this arrangement. The woman's French doctors began ovarian stimulation in their IVF centre in December 1998 in cooperation with the United States fertility unit. Two embryos were obtained and transferred to the surrogate mother. After nine months, the surrogate mother underwent a caesarean section, which resulted in two live and normal infants (Giacalone *et al.* 2001).

I. Surrogacy is a form of assisted reproduction through artificial insemination. A woman, who is designated as a "surrogate", bears a baby on behalf of a couple with the intention of relinquishing her rights as the legal mother of the child after birth.

In this paper, I will concentrate on the so-called gestational (full) surrogacy, *i.e.* the form of artificial insemination that applies the method of *In Vitro Fertilization* (IVF),[3] whereby a doctor implants the fertilized (by her partner's sperm) eggs of a woman into the surrogate's uterus. The surrogate[4] is not the genetic mother of the child, since there is no genetic link. The reason that surrogacy is needed is that the female partner is unable to carry a pregnancy to term because of hysterectomy, congenital defects, vaginal agenesis,[5] unexplained habitual abortions, etc.[6] Surrogate gestational pregnancies after IVF have been reported since 1985 (Goldfarb *et al.* 2000).

---

[3]   IVF has also been used as an assisted reproduction method in normal (not surrogacy) pregnancies, when there is a need to enhance fertilization in the laboratory, since 1978. The fertilized eggs are implanted into the female partner's uterus.

[4]   A more scientifically correct word would be "gestational carrier": A woman in whom a pregnancy resulted from fertilization with third-party sperm and oocytes and carries the pregnancy with the intention or agreement that the offspring will be parented by one or both of the persons that produced the gametes (Vayena *et al.* 2002: xx).

[5]   In vaginal agenesis, the cervix is either absent or hypoplastic. The most frequent form of vaginal agenesis is known as the Mayer-Rokitansky-Kustner-Hauser syndrome (the uterus is congenitally absent with normal fallopian tubes and ovaries). In this case, surrogacy is the only opportunity a woman has of becoming a mother (see *e.g.* VAN WAART & KRUGER 2000).

[6]   POSNER (1992: 420, n. 23) defines infertility in the broad sense, as the incapacity to produce a healthy child. According to this definition, the possession of recessive genes that would create a serious danger of producing a deformed child is a fertility problem (*id.*).

I am not going to discuss the oldest known form of surrogacy, i.e., the traditional/partial "Abraham-Sarah-Hagar"[7] type of surrogacy agreement, where the surrogate mother is also a genetic mother (who contributes both the ovum and the womb) and the male partner of the couple that is unable to procreate (intentional parents) offers his sperm.[8] I am also not going to examine the case of social surrogacy, when a woman decides to have another woman bear her child by choice (for cosmetic or career reasons), even though she is able to carry the child herself at no significant risk. I am also assuming that the couple entering a surrogacy contract is hetero-sexual and married. I am not going to defend (at least not in this paper) the right of unmarried women and homosexuals[9] to become parents using this technology.

There are two reasons why I am not going to discuss the above cases. Firstly, because the opposition to the enforcement of these controversial arran-gements is more adamant that the one to the "traditional family-oriented" gestational form.[10] Secondly, because there are a number of ethical and legal issues associated with these marginal cases which justify separate treatment – the most important one being that the best interests of children should be taken into consideration.[11]

---

[7]   *Genesis* 16: 2 ("*And Sarai said unto Abram, Behold now, the LORD hath restrained me from bearing: I pray thee, go in unto my maid; it may be that I may obtain children by her.*"). Traditional surrogacy was widely practised before gestational surrogacy became available. For the mid-1970s California, when surrogacy was a crime, see ERICKSON (1978) (despite the prohibitions, the practice was increasing). A more complicated (and rare) form can be egg donation: the intentional mother can carry a baby, but cannot ovulate. See COHEN (1996).

[8]   In the most extreme case of surrogacy, both intentional parents are not genetic parents (the eggs and the sperm are provided by donors). These parents, who are not biologically related to the child, become nurturing parents directly. This form is the most akin to adoption (Garrison 2000: 898). See *In re Marriage of Buzzanca*, 61 Cal. App. 4th 1410, 72 Cal. Rptr., 2d 280 (1998) (although the two women to the surrogacy contract could both prove their maternity, the legal mother is the woman who was intended to be the mother as expressed in the surrogacy or egg donation contract). Thus, it is possible that a child can have three mothers (social, surrogate, egg donor) and two fathers (social, sperm donor)!

[9]   Mostly gay men, for whom surrogacy is the only way of becoming the genetic parents of a child (GOLOMBOK & TASKER 1994).

[10]  See especially LASCARIDES (1997).

[11]  In the case of gestational surrogacy, the role of children is, as we will see below, less complicated. The main problem relating to the children in marginal cases is the emotional pain which the child would undergo upon the discovery that his/her social mother is not the genetic one (traditional surrogacy) or that his/her genetic mother opted to avoid the experience of carrying him/her (social surrogacy). In addition, traditional surrogacy is a rather peculiar method of adoption and it might be more appropriate for it to be treated as such. For a powerful defence of traditional surrogacy agreements, see POSNER (1989). The same goes for the unmarried woman who uses sperm from a bank or a friend and wishes to have a child destined to grow up in a single-parent family (for problems faced by single-

Gestational surrogacy (as well as any other type of surrogacy) can also be categorized into altruistic surrogacy (the surrogate receives no payment) and commercial surrogacy (where the surrogate receives a fee for her services). I am not going to consider altruistic surrogacy, since the arguments in defence of commercial surrogacy overlap those in support of the former.

Gestational surrogacy (via the IVF method) is a quite expensive operation; in case of failure it has a rebound time of months and it involves a complicated medical procedure:[12] The eggs of the intended mother (ova) are fertilized with the sperm of the intended father, they are allowed to grow and they are transferred into the surrogate's uterus. The appropriate preparation of the surrogate mother and the period after the insemination involves several injections of hormones, estrogen and progesterone, the taking of pills and a significant change in her way of life. Every new IVF attempt costs thousands of dollars, there is a significant miscarriage rate and the compensation to the surrogate mother in the United States where surrogacy is more widespread, begins at $15,000 for a novice surrogate mother and can go up to $25,000 for an experienced surrogate.[13] Therefore, the total cost to the intentional parents can be quite high (ranging from $20,000 to $120,000).

In most jurisdictions worldwide, gestational surrogacy is prohibited by law and even when it is permitted, in most cases the contracts between the genetic parents and the surrogate mother are not enforceable. In these cases, only altruistic surrogacy is permitted, but with many restrictions and requirements.[14] This situation is creating a major problem in federal

---

parent households, see MCLANAHAN & SANDEFUR 1994). Surrogacy on behalf of a homosexual couple is an even more complicated issue, which is closely linked to the question of allowing adoption by homosexuals. However, see the recent survey by MOONEY-SOMERS & GOLOMBOK (2000) (a mother's sexual orientation matters less for children's psychological adjustment than the quality of relationships in the family home; parents have little influence on the gender development of their children).

[12] On the other hand, traditional surrogacy is much less costly, it has a shorter rebound time in case of failure and it is a lot easier as a procedure (the surrogate can even perform a cervical insemination with sperm at her own home). However, the emotional cost to the surrogate can be intolerable. Of course, traditional surrogacy can also be achieved through intercourse (the most cost-saving method); this was actually the only available form of surrogacy before the introduction of artificial insemination techniques.

[13] My basic source are the advertisements of American fertility clinics. According to SAINT-PAUL (2002: 26), the surrogate fee is about $20,000-$30,000 ("which is above median U.S. annual income"). In 1988, the common price was $10,000 (FIELD 1988: 25-26).

[14] See MCEWEN (1999: 281-286). The most liberal regimes are those of the United Kingdom, Israel and recently Greece (see KOUNOUGERI-MANOLEDAKI 2002).

countries like the United States, where some states permit and some others restrict surrogacy contracts. The same holds true for the European Union, where most countries do not enforce surrogacy contracts.

II. In this paper, I will support the thesis that gestational surrogate contracts should be enforceable under the law. My approach is informed by the economic analysis of contract law, which is one of the most sophisticated areas of law & economics theory both in the United States and Europe. Some clarifications are necessary in order to prevent some common misconceptions. Economic analysis of law is not an attempt to monetarize human relationships and to establish economic efficiency as the law's primary goal. It is rather an approach which assumes that people are basically rational utility-maximizers who respond to incentives, and purports to use law as a system of social control, a weapon for more effective social action having as its most important goal the achievement of social welfare. According to this view, "legal policy should be evaluated using the framework of welfare economics, under which assessments of policies depend exclusively on their effects on individuals' well-being" (Kaplow & Shavell 2002: 465).[15] In the case of surrogacy, under the lens of law & economics, infertile married couples will try to maximize their utility by exploring all options in an effort to have a baby. If the law prohibits them from doing so, so much the worse for the law![16]

Economic analysis of contract law in particular has offered a theory on which promises should be enforced.[17] Under this approach, a contract should be enforced when it makes two people better off, without making anyone else worse off. Who should decide when and if the parties are better off? The parties themselves, who are the best judges of their own welfare. Their preferences and their desires should dominate any kind of paternalistic intervention by the legal system, except in some rare circumstances where the parties are demonstrably not acting rationally or when their actions have negative effects on third parties.[18]

---

[15] "[S]ocial welfare is postulated to be an increasing function of individuals' well-being and to depend on no other factors" (KAPLOW & SHAVELL 2002: 24).

[16] See especially the research by VAN DEN AKKER (2000 and 2001) for the importance of the genetic link to prospective parents. See also CHLIAOUTAKIS et al. (2002).

[17] For more on the economic theory of the enforcement of contracts, see the excellent treatment by COOTER & ULEN (2000: 184-189).

[18] Only the interests of third parties which are already protected under the law. Thus, the negative externalities to children awaiting adoption (RADIN 1987: 1931; POSNER 1989: 24) should not be considered to be a valid argument for the prohibition of surrogacy. See BLOCK (1999: 47) and more generally EPSTEIN (1995: 2320-2325) and HATZIS (2000: 209-210).

When the parties to a surrogacy contract reach agreement on the terms of the contract, apparently all of them wish the contract to be enforceable; otherwise they would not have entered into it in the first place. The parents wish to have children and they view surrogacy as their only opportunity to do so[19] and the surrogate mother wishes to obtain a sum of money, which she apparently needs for herself or for her own family. After the deal, they all feel better off, since they have acquired what they needed more in exchange for money or services, which they valued less. For example, a surrogate mother can use the money to offer a better education to her children or a better standard of living to her family. At the same time, she can derive utility from her own altruism.

The interests of the child do not represent a significant factor in the case of gestational surrogacy, since there is no confusion as to the parental rights or the genetic link,[20] not forgetting that the child owes its very existence to this contract (Harris 2000).[21] In addition, according to a recent major study, "a gestational carrier would provide potential environmental benefits for the infant" (Serafini 2001).[22] However, I am not arguing that the child will remain unaffected by the way in which he/she was born. Even in the less complicated case of gestational surrogacy, there are dangers lurking for the children, which can only be avoided by strengthening the norms of parental responsibility (see especially Shiffrin 1999). The only way to ensure children's welfare (which is more important than contracting parties' welfare in the gestational surrogacy nexus) is to limit the power of contracting parties and especially to prohibit opportunistic attempts to modify or rescind the contract.

---

[19] According to a research study of a small group of infertile women by VAN DEN AKKER (2001), half of them were devastated by their inability to have a child, and nearly two-thirds could not foresee a future without a family.

[20] See especially the discussion in the seminal California case *Johnson v. Calvert*, 851 P.2d 776 (Cal. 1993) (the woman who intended to bring about the birth of a child that she intended to raise as her own is the natural mother under California law). For this landmark decision, see Gordon (1993).

[21] For the experiences of the child born under the second gestational surrogacy, which became publicized (in Australia), see KIRKMAN & KIRKMAN (2002). The article was written by MAGGIE KIRKMAN (the mother) and includes an appendix with answers to a set of questions by ALICE KIRKMAN (the 13-year-old daughter). According to Alice: "[S]ome people are born because a man and a woman get very drunk; or when a man and a woman love each other; or when a man and a woman hire a scientist. There are different ways of being conceived. Mine was just one of them." (*id.* 144).

[22] See also DILL (2002: 259): "there is no evidence in the literature to suggest that in the vast majority of such arrangements there is any detrimental effect on the child or the other parties involved".

III. This is an idealized picture, which is increasingly being challenged by many. A major objection is that these contracts are immoral, and therefore should not be enforced on that basis alone. Most churches are against surrogacy for this reason. According to a survey for the U.S. Congress (1988), all religious groups represented in the United States were against surrogate motherhood.[23] The approach of the "Congregation for the Doctrine of the Faith" of the Catholic Church is typical:[24]

> [Surrogate motherhood] is contrary to the unity of marriage and to the dignity of the procreation of the human person. Surrogate motherhood represents an objective failure to meet the obligations of maternal love, of conjugal fidelity and of responsible motherhood; it offends the dignity and the right of the child to be conceived, carried in the womb, brought into the world and brought up by his own parents; it sets up, to the detriment of families, a division between the physical, psychological and moral elements which constitute those families.

The legislator should "prohibit, by virtue of the support which is due to the family [...] surrogate motherhood" since "[i]t is part of the duty of the public authority to ensure that the civil law is regulated according to the fundamental norms of the moral law in matters concerning human rights, human life and the institution of the family."

Despite the plain advice of the Catholic Church to the legislator, the depiction of surrogacy as an immoral practice cannot justify its prohibition. The argument that law should punish immorality is ancient, but discredited. According to the widely accepted principle of liberal neutrality, the state must remain neutral towards competing moral standards (Kymlicka 1991: 95-96; Charlesworth 1993: 16). The view that law should regulate conduct having morality as its guide was successfully rebutted more than 150 years ago by John Stuart Mill, who introduced the harm principle, an invaluable guidepost for any liberal, pluralistic society:

> The only purpose for which power can be rightfully exercised over any member of a civilized community, against his will, is to prevent harm to others. His own good, either physical or moral, is not a sufficient warrant. He cannot rightfully be compelled to do or forbear because it will be better for him to do so, because it will make him happier, because, in the opinions of others, to do so would be wise, or even right. [...] Over himself, over his own body and mind, the individual is sovereign. (Mill 1859: 13).

---

[23] With the exception of some marginal groups (Christian Scientists, Reform Jews and Mennonites). See U.S. Congress (1988: 364-368).
[24] See *Donum Vitae* (Respect for Human Life): "Instruction on Respect for Human Life in its Origin and on the Dignity of Procreation (Replies to Certain Questions of the Day)", issued on February 22, 1987.

I believe that the "harm principle" is one of the cornerstones of our legal civilization, especially after the Hart/Devlin debate.[25] Thus, I am not going to elaborate more on why conventional morality should not limit the liberty of people to engage in consensual activities[26] when these cannot harm others.[27] In this case, it is also questionable whether conventional morality contrasts with surrogacy, since there is no indication of a popular opposition or generalized hostility to surrogacy.[28] It is also worth noting that traditional surrogacy has not been controversial since Biblical times.[29] The recent attack on surrogacy on moral grounds is rather a result of the distrust of certain groups for reproductive technologies in general (Kirkman & Kirkman 2002: 136) and of an image of "unnaturalness" attributed to the surrogate mother (Burr 2000).[30]

IV. The most important moral (deontological) argument against commercial surrogacy is the commodification argument.[31] According to this argument, such an economic agreement is unacceptable, since it commodifies a woman's body and permits the surrogate mother to exchange an inalienable right (i.e. her *quasi*-parental right)[32] for money. This is morally unacceptable, since it eliminates the human dignity of this woman by reducing her body to a commodity (Radin 1987: 1928-1936; Anderson

---

[25]   For the debate, see DEVLIN (1965) and HART (1963).
[26]   See especially McLACHLAN (1997).
[27]   Of course, one could say that an issue here is the enforcement of the surrogacy agreement against the surrogate mother who has second thoughts. In such a case, a surrogate can invoke the "harm principle" (I owe this point to Brian Bix). However, the surrogate has already relinquished her rights to the child by her promise. In contract law, any promise- or reliance-based theory would call for the enforcement of the contract. Economic theories would be even more emphatic, since the opposite conclusion would create disincentives for contracting and it would harm both future intentional parents and surrogate mothers. In the case of gestational surrogacy, the issue is less complicated than in traditional surrogacy.
[28]   A utilitarian-like approach, like the one I have espoused in this paper, does not preclude any effect of morality on law (as a pure libertarian approach would do). According to a leading proponent of law & economics, STEVEN SHAVELL (2002: 255), "the existence of moral beliefs should itself influence the design of the law, given that moral beliefs constitute tastes the satisfaction of which raises individuals' welfare".
[29]   See also Genesis 30, when Isaac's servant Bilbah bore his child because Rachel was barren.
[30]   For SILBAUGH (1997: 106), "it may have as much to do with notions of femininity and a desire to elevate a romantic essentialism about femininity as it does with a desire to protect women's integrity."
[31]   For a comprehensive treatment of commodification, see RADIN (1996, especially ch. 10) (commodification describes in monetary terms all things of value to the person including personal attributes and relationships; they are considered fungible and commensurable; their only value is their exchange value).
[32]   See especially n.10 of *Johnson v. Calvert, op. cit.*

1993: 168-189).[33] According to Anderson (1993: 189), "when market norms are applied to the ways we allocate and understand parental rights and responsibilities over children, children are reduced from subjects of love to objects of use. When market norms are applied to the ways we treat and understand women's reproductive labor, women are reduced from subjects of respect and consideration to objects of use". Women's personal attributes and reproductive capacity will be commodified and monetized, which is harmful to "the identity aspect of their personhood" (Radin 1987: 1932).

We should first determine what is being bought and sold here. Is it the child? In the context of the gestational agreement, the embryo belongs to its parents. We cannot speak of "baby selling" (as we might in traditional surrogacy), since the surrogate cannot sell something that she does not have: i.e., parental rights to the newborn.[34] The surrogate is essentially selling her labour, her gestational services. These services are similar to other services offered by women who transfer to another person a limited use of their bodies in employment contracts: nannies, wet-nurses, models, athletes, actresses, manual labourers, maids, career soldiers, etc. Further-more, one cannot equate surrogacy with slavery, since there is no indication of the "alienation of the will" that is characteristic in slavery contracts (McElroy 2002: 276).[35] According to Wertheimer (1997: 1220), even if we consider surrogacy as commodification, "it does not follow that surrogacy should be prohibited or that surrogacy contracts should not be enforcea-ble."

However, the commodification argument essentially says that a woman should not have the right to contract, i.e. to transfer even a limited use of her body, because in doing so she would be treating it as a commodity. The proponents of the commodification argument perhaps fail to see that the

---

[33]    Both Radin and Anderson argue against traditional surrogacy, which they equate with baby-selling and prostitution. Their attack on commodification covers gestational surrogacy ("a lesser level of commodification" according to RADIN 1987: 1929). However, there is an inconspicuous qualitative difference between Radin's and Anderson's approach (see *e.g.* RADIN 1987: 1934, 1936 and ANDERSON 2000). See also BRAZIER (1999).

[34]    ANDERSON (1993: 174) agrees that the child does not belong to the surrogate mother, thus she cannot sell it. But even the forms of surrogacy that look like "sale of children" cannot necessarily lead people to think of children in monetary terms, since the desperate need for children will also create the incentive to think of children as persons (ALTMAN 1991: 333-334). See also EPSTEIN (1995: 2330-2334) and LASCARIDES (1997: 1240-1245).

[35]    There is almost no reference in the literature to the role of the father in such arrangements, especially the phenomenon of the "increasing marginalization" of the modern father (MANDER 2001).

woman is not treating her body as a commodity for the simple fact that she is not selling a piece of herself. She is making a trade-off, offering a service by using a part of her body (her uterus; but she could use her hand or her brain as well) to obtain something that is more valuable to her. The emotional cost of the attachment to the child and the psychic and physical costs of labouring are valued less (by the surrogate) than the goals she is going to achieve with the compensation. The surrogate is not a saleswoman selling commodities in a market; she is rather someone who has ranked her priorities in life in such a way as to achieve her most important goal in the most efficient way. The fact that only a few women will seriously consider surrogacy as a way of achieving other goals in life is an indication that this is a matter of subjectively ranking values and goals. For many women, the cost of surrogacy can be enormous and simply not worthwhile. For other women, this cost can be minimal in comparison with choices they prefer to have and which they value more. Any government intervention in this ultra-subjective calculus will lead women to suboptimal decisions about themselves and will thus harm them.

Moreover, the commodification argument deprives women of the right to privacy and self-determination (Andrews 1986) and treats them unfairly, since it accepts payments to be made to adoption agencies and fertility clinics, but not to women who are prepared to change their lives for nine months and bring a child into the world. The issue here is not that the intentional parents will pay for their child, but that the surrogate mother will give up her parental rights in return for money.[36] It might be no coincidence that anti-commodification arguments arise "when women receive money for something, not when women are paying money for something" (Silbaugh 1997: 104).[37]

The indeterminacy of the commodification argument is not only illustrated by the differentiated treatment of sperm donors and surrogate mothers, but also by the problem of the compensation for pregnancy: even the staunchest opponents of commodification would accept that surrogates should be compensated for medical, hospital and travelling expenses.[38] But what about loss of wages, maternity clothes, nutritional food? At what point does commercialization begin? If we include opportunity cost (and we should if we do not want to punish a surrogate economically for being

---

[36] BRIAN BIX's comments were instrumental in clarifying this point.
[37] For similar arguments, see EPSTEIN (1995: 2328) and MCLACHLAN & SWALES (2000: 17, n.3).
[38] In the U.K., surrogacy agreements are not enforceable, but as between individuals they are not illegal (Surrogacy Arrangements Act 1985, s 1A). Commercial surrogacy is illegal (s 2), as well as advertising for surrogates (s 3). However, the payment of expenses is allowed.

altruistic),[39] the actual difference with the market value of surrogacy could be minimal or zero.

According to Burr (2000: 112), the commodification argument has essentially reinforced the public/private divide: private is the feminine sphere, predicated upon nurturing and loving; public is the world of masculinity, characterized by commercialism and the sale of labour power (see also Shalev 1989: 17).[40] The differentiated treatment of sperm donors and surrogate mothers is more than characteristic.[41]

V. Let me now discuss the economic exploitation argument, which can be illuminated by adopting an economic perspective. As the argument goes, surrogate mothers, who are usually poor and unsophisticated, will have unequal bargaining power compared to the infertile couple who will be at least well-off, if not rich. This imbalance will lead to contracts that are unconscionable for poor women.[42] Not only will the exchange price be low, but the surrogate will have to make promises of undertaking responsibilities of such magnitude that she will turn into the couple's slave for nine months.[43]

In the most extreme case, some women are on the verge of destitution, and they choose to enter into such an agreement to ensure their bare necessities, i.e. food and shelter.[44] They engage in an activity that they deem as immoral, exploitive and inhuman, because it is their only option. They are so desperate that they will agree to do anything for money. According to this "degradation" argument (which applies to many kinds of contracts in

---

[39]  For example, RADIN (1987: 1932) believes that only "reasonable out-of-pocket expenses" should be allowed without discussing the unfairness of the undercompensation (see also *id.* 1933). See also TREBILCOCK *et al.* (1994: 696-697) (the payment should not induce women to become surrogate mothers).

[40]  But see RADIN (1987: 1930-1931) (acting in ways that current gender ideology characterizes as empowering might actually be disempowering), as well as ANDERSON (1993: 182-185).

[41]  For a powerful attack on the commodification argument, see MCLACHLAN & SWALES (2000) (treating women as child incubators does not preclude treating them respectfully).

[42]  According to ANDREWS (1995: 2362-2363), there is no evidence of the exploitation of surrogate mothers. See also LASCARIDES (1997: 1235-1236).

[43]  A related argument has been voiced by many feminist writers, emphasizing that women will be converted into breeding stock against their will. But see ANDREWS (1988: 78) (the anti-surrogacy arguments can potentially turn all women into reproductive vessels without their consent by providing government oversight for women's decisions). This view of women is greatly derogatory for their capacity to enter into a contract (MCELROY 2002: 275-278). For a fair and useful discussion of all kinds of criticism based on the exploitation argument, see WERTHEIMER (1997).

[44]  It is rather unlikely that these women will be chosen for surrogacy in the first place. If they are so poor and desperate, their health will also be problematic. See ANDERSON (1993: 185).

both the commercial and the non-commercial sphere), some people, when finding themselves in extreme circumstances, are ready to fall into deep levels of degradation as long as they are paid (Radin 1987: 1930). Thus, says the argument, we should not let them do what they would not assent to do if they were not so desperate.[45]

First, I fail to see why we should not accept and enforce a "desperation" agreement. Perhaps the only conceivable solution for people in financial despair is for the government to provide a safety net. If there is a safety net, then prospective surrogate mothers will not fall into such desperate situations in the first place. If there is no government safety net and the law prohibits their "degradation", it is essentially depriving them of the "market safety net", which might appear to some as "dirty" and "repulsive", but is nevertheless the only one available to them. Besides, by what moral authority will the legislators deprive them of food and shelter just so that they can enforce their moral standards?

Second, any argument against the exploitation of women should take into consideration the problem of personal autonomy. If the state cannot offer an alternative to these women and the market for surrogate mothers is not monopolistic,[46] then any restriction on personal autonomy is paternalistic,[47] harmful to women and inconsistent. More specifically, it is logically incompatible with the right to reproductive autonomy, which is principally exemplified in the right to abortion (Charlesworth 1993: 8). This is more so in cases where women make informed, unrestrained decisions believing that they will be better off.

Third, such situations of economic deprivation are most likely marginal. In the majority of cases when the contract seems one-sided, this can be the result of one of two factors: either there is a considerable supply of surrogate mothers and the price of their services is thus devalued in the market for surrogacy or there is a contract failure which reflects a market failure. Let us rephrase this argument using economic terminology: The fact that the parties decide for themselves what will be the benefit and what

---

[45]  See RADIN (1987: 1930, especially n. 278) for the rather indeterminate "potential double bind" argument.

[46]  This means that the woman who decides to offer her gestational services has many alternative contracting partners (fertility clinics, couples, etc.) so she can choose the best offer. In a monopolistic situation, a woman can appeal to the doctrine of "private necessity".

[47]  However, according to ANDERSON (1993: 170), "commercial surrogate contracts establish relations of domination over surrogate mothers that are inconsistent with their autonomy and with treating women with respect and consideration". But see WERTHEIMER (1997: 1225-1227).

will be the cost of their future actions does not imply that they will always and necessarily make the right decision. Even though it is widely accepted that the parties know better than anyone else where their interests lie, it is also true that the parties can make mistakes, due to imperfect information and/or uncertainty about the future. There is a chance that at least one of them will make a miscalculation of the cost or the benefit, based on inaccurate information. Another potential and more common problem is the likelihood of a change in circumstances that will overturn the previous calculation of costs and benefits and will create a new situation which is often completely different from the one the parties took as given when constructing their relationship.

All these problems are basically the result of the passage of time, that is a *sine qua non* element in any contract, and of the unavoidable lack of perfect information among market participants. The scarcity of time and money make it virtually impossible for the parties to allocate responsibility for every possible contingency due to uncertainty in a deferred exchange.

Yet another problem, added to those of imperfect information and "unforeseen contingencies", is the opportunistic behaviour of one of the parties, that is also a result of the sequential character of the performance and is pertinent to the problem of unforeseen contingencies due to asymmetric information. Even a contractual relationship that begins as a relation of parties with roughly equal bargaining power can turn into (after performance by one party) an extremely unequal relationship, a bilateral monopoly situation, with one party falling prey to the other. Even in a long-term relationship between two parties, one party's threat of a unilateral violation of the initial contract may induce a renegotiation of the contract.

What does all this mean for the surrogacy nexus? The surrogate mother might be ignorant as to what this procedure entails. It is also possible that she makes a frivolous decision enticed by the generous compensation. She might also change her mind while pregnant if she experiences emotional distress that she could not predict. Some have argued that a woman cannot really know what it is like to give up a child that she has carried for nine months.[48] Even a woman who has already had children is not able to even begin to imagine the pain of separation. According to this view, there is

---

[48]    However, "the evidence simply does not support the assertion that women uniformly identify motherhood with pregnancy" (GARRISON 2000: 914).

no way for the surrogate to give her informed consent (Anderson 1993: 178).[49]

This rather stereotypical (one could even say derogatory against women) argument is repudiated by Posner (1989: 30) and McElroy (2002: 276-277) as sexist and aprioristic. It is also unsubstantiated, since the proponents of the view that women are overwhelmed by their feelings have failed to present supporting research.[50] However, it crudely presents a real issue, that of regretted decisions of contracting parties in general and of gestational carriers in particular.[51] On the other hand, this problem is of heightened importance in traditional surrogacy, where a right to contract rescission could be offered to the surrogate. In the case of gestational services, any such right can lead to an overprotection of the surrogate in comparison with the genetic mother. As Garrison (2000: 915) aptly puts it: "without her ovum, there would be no fetus to gestate".

The parents-to-be could also have second thoughts about the original contract. Since they are initially unaware of the effects that the whole endeavour will have on their personal relationship and their financial situation, it is possible that they might consider rescinding. They could also be experiencing problems in their marriage, which will ultimately lead to a divorce during the surrogate's pregnancy. Most importantly, there is a chance that they will change their mind after learning that their future child will have some kind of disability.

All these are problems that are not unknown to the contracts concluded in an economic market. The existence of market failures does not constitute a reason for abolishing freedom of contract. The same holds true for surrogacy contracts. Any problems in the surrogacy relationship do not justify the prohibition of these kinds of arrangements (McLachlan & Swales 2001).[52]

---

[49]  "[The surrogate mother] never makes a totally voluntary, informed decision, for quite clearly any decision prior to the baby's birth is, in the most important sense, uninformed, and any decision after that, compelled by a pre-existing contractual commitment." (*In re Baby M*, 109 N.J. 396, 437).

[50]  See ANDREWS (1988: 79) citing testimony by Joan Einwohner, a psychologist who works with a surrogate mother programme.

[51]  See generally BRINIG (2000: 73-74) on imperfect information in surrogacy contracts.

[52]  See also LASCARIDES (1997: 1257-1258) (unconscionability must be determined on a case-by-case basis).

VI. Family law can simulate contract law, which has successfully regulated economic activity for thousands of years.[53] The main difference with family law is that the basic goal of contract law is to justify the wishes of the parties. This is also a legitimate goal for the law of surrogacy contracts. However, the primary goal of the regulation of surrogacy agreements should be the protection of the best interests of the child. For the above reasons, I believe that:

–  gestational surrogacy contracts should be enforced by the courts with the exception of cases where the standard formation of contracts excuses apply (incompetence, coercion, duress, failure to disclose, etc.).

–  the parents should not have the right to rescind the contract under any circumstances; regardless of the health of their baby or the status of their marital relationship, the child is theirs (see generally Shiffrin 1999: 145-148);[54] the only exception could be in the case where the gestational mother wishes to keep the child, either altruistically or because the intentional parents are willing to help her economically.[55]

–  the surrogate should have the right to obtain an abortion and the duty to demonstrate reasonable care; of course, in the case of an abortion or of miscarriage due to irresponsible, reckless behaviour, she should be liable for restitution damages;

–  after the successful delivery of a healthy baby, the surrogate who has had second thoughts about the contract, should not have the choice of damages; the contract should be "enforced" by specific performance. Even though compensation *in natura* is rather the exception in Common and Civil contract law, in the case of surrogacy any other form of compensation would be unrealistic.[56] There is no way for a

---

[53]  For a similar argument, see BUSH (1999) (law & economics can be a useful tool to guide feminist policy so as to avoid outcomes that ultimately harm the people feminists are trying to empower). For a more critical approach to law & economics (from a feminist perspective), see BELCHER (2000) (identifying masculine traits but also feminizing developments).

[54]  But see also RADIN (1987: 1934-1935) (if the parents change their mind, they should not be forced to keep and raise a child they do not want; but they bear the responsibility of providing for its future).

[55]  This certainly looks ugly for the child. However, in this unfortunate situation when the intentional parents do not want the baby, it is better for it to stay with the gestational mother for as long as she is willing to keep it. But this is likely to be an extreme case. See BLOCK (1999: 48).

[56]  See especially SHALEV (1989: 139-140) and her sculptor simile in particular. Even RADIN (1987: 1934, n.292) believes that there is essentially a binary choice concerning commercial surrogacy: either banning it or granting specific performance. See also EPSTEIN (1995: 2336-2338) (damages are not an adequate remedy; specific performance is needed). LASCARIDES (1997: 1252-1253) believes that reliance damages are preferable since they can be easily calculated.

surrogate mother to be able to pay expectation damages to the intentional parents.[57] In this case, one should also take the interests of the child into consideration.[58] I fail to see why a child would prefer a (most probably) poor surrogate mother to his/her genetic parents who, in the great majority of cases, are well off!

- the parties can also be allowed to agree that the surrogate will follow a more healthy way of life than necessary in exchange for a premium.[59]
- since the surrogate is not the genetic mother, she quite clearly waives any and all rights to the newborn (Garrison 2000: 913-917) and of course should not be entitled to visitation with the child.[60]

These principles are not as harsh as they seem (Anderson 1993: 175-176), since they discourage frivolous decisions by women and ensure that parents will not be the victims of opportunism and extortion. Additionally, if there is no compensation in case of breach, the surrogate fee will be greatly discounted in order to incorporate the risk of opportunistic or irresponsible behaviour.[61] The surrogates will not be able to signal their credibility and the couples will resort to the services of women who have already successfully rendered their services. Thus, a barrier to entry will be created for younger first-timers.

Safeguarding the best interests of the child is the basic reason why a rescission of the contract or an opportunistic or altruistic attempt to modify the contract should be avoided. Starting from the moment of insemination, a new entity is created: a child with autonomous rights and interests. Any decision by the parties that has potential negative effects (externalities) on the child should not be tolerated by the law.

Finally, for a transitory period, one can allow some regulation in contract terms such as:

---

[57] The only case I can imagine is that of an altruistic surrogacy where a rich woman offers to carry her sister's baby and then has second thoughts. However, even in this highly unlikely situation, the specific performance rule will be superseded by the dynamics of the Coase theorem (Coase 1960) (when transaction costs are low, resources are allocated efficiently regardless of the legal assignment of property rights).

[58] See *e.g.* SHIFFRIN (1999: 147) (gestational mothers are unlikely to be adequately prepared to assume primary custody or support obligations).

[59] For the fine line between such extra-care agreement and a slave contract, see the useful distinction by MCELROY (2002: 276) (a slave contract transfers all moral and legal jurisdiction over one's own body). See also ARNESON (1992: 161-162) and TREBILCOCK (1995: 366).

[60] See, however, TREBILCOCK *et al.* (1994: 692-697) (the birth mother should have an absolute right to opt-out), as well as FIELD (1988).

[61] According to POSNER (1992: 423), in the long run surrogate mothers will lose from a rule which allows them to repudiate their contracts.

- setting a minimum age for the surrogate mother (to avoid frivolous decisions),
- requiring the surrogate to already have children (thus having the necessary information for an informed decision and at the same time minimizing the cost of losing the child she is carrying),
- monitoring of surrogacy agencies (to avoid unconscionable contracts due to asymmetric information and monopoly),
- establishing a speedy court procedure and requiring counselling (to validate the contract and help the contracting parties to fully realize the consequences of their decisions), etc.

All these regulations will of course drive the price of the surrogate fee up, since they will essentially lead to a drastic decrease in supply. After the transitory period, which should be no longer than five years, the accumulated experience (in which I include the institutional experience) will help the contracting parties to acquire all the necessary information before entering into such high-risk contracts.

In concluding, I should warn about the dangers of the prohibition of surrogacy or of the non-enforcement of surrogacy contracts in the European Union. In the case of non-enforcement of contracts, the law would arbitrarily discriminate in favour of couples whose friends or relatives are willing to undergo the procedure. The prohibition is essentially applicable only to middle-class couples who wish to have a child through surrogacy. Rich couples can always go to the United States or elsewhere and poor couples do not lose an option they have not had in the first place (even though one could argue that social insurance agencies should offer this option to poor couples). Middle-class couples will have two options: either to travel to one of the countries which offer these services at lower prices and most probably under sub-optimal conditions – or to turn to the black market (McEwen 1999).[62]

VII. I have attempted to make a case for the enforcement of gestational surrogacy agreements, using mainly arguments originating from the economic analysis of contract law, whose basic goal is to enforce the wishes

---

[62] It is absolutely certain that a black market will be created almost instantaneously and the parties (especially the surrogate mothers who are supposed to be protected) will fall prey to opportunism, mafias, etc. (BRINIG 2000: 76). According to ANDERSON (1993: 176-179), the state cannot regulate surrogacy efficiently since the surrogacy lobby will influence legislation. However, the absolute prohibition she advocates will, by definition, limit a surrogate's alternatives and lead to black markets where surrogates are even more underprotected!

of the parties. According to Jennifer Burr (2000: 116), "the fact that surrogacy practices continue irrespective of the social stigma and legal and ethical discourse that operates to further stigmatize and pathologize the surrogate mother, is in itself of political significance." There is no way and there is no legitimate reason to prohibit an exchange, which makes both parties better off. This is not only inefficient, but also authoritarian. The parties will find a way to circumvent the law which will be discredited as inapplicable, not to mention the fact that this inapplicability most of the time harms the parties with less bargaining power.

It is interesting to note that the economic approach can be fully compatible with a Rawlsian perspective (Rawls 1971). There is no doubt that a woman behind a veil of ignorance would decide that surrogacy should be available to her, either as a genetic mother (because there is always the possibility that she will be infertile) or as a gestational carrier (because there is always the case that she will be financially deprived or altruistic).

My approach was also informed by the primacy of the child's best interests. In surrogacy, it is obvious that if there is no contract, there is no child (Posner 1989: 29). The protection of a child's rights presupposes the child's existence[63] and this is only possible if we permit and enforce surrogacy contracts.

## BIBLIOGRAPHY

ALTMAN, SCOTT (1991), "(Com)modifying Experience", *Southern California Law Review* 65: 293-340.

ANDERSON, ELIZABETH S. (1993), *Value in Ethics and Economics* (Cambridge, MA: Harvard University Press).

ANDERSON, ELIZABETH S. (2000), "Why Commercial Surrogate Motherhood Unethically Commodifies Women and Children: Reply to McLachlan and Swales", *Health Care Analysis* 8: 19-26.

ANDREWS, LORI B. (1986), "My Body, My Property", *Hastings Center Report* 16 (5): 28-38.

ANDREWS, LORI B. (1988), "Surrogate Motherhood: The Challenge for Feminists", *Law, Medicine & Health Care* 16: 72-80.

ANDREWS, LORI B. (1995), "Beyond Doctrinal Boundaries: A Legal Framework for Surrogate Motherhood", *Virginia Law Review* 81: 2343-2371.

---

[63] See, however, ANDERSON (1993: 174-175) advocating a rather hazy principle for the "respect of genetic ties". I find it very difficult to accommodate this principle with the statement that "[t]he most fundamental obligation of parents to their children is to love them" (*id.* 170).

ARNESON, RICHARD (1992), "Commodification and Commercial Surrogacy", *Philosophy & Public Affairs* 21: 132-164.

BELCHER, ALICE (2000), "A Feminist Perspective on Contract Theories from Law and Economics", *Feminist Legal Studies* 8: 29-46.

BLOCK, WALTER (1999), "Market-Inalienability Once Again: Reply to Radin", Working paper (Ludwig von Mises Institute).

BLOCK, WALTER (2001), "Alienability, Inalienability, Paternalism and the Law: A Reply to Kronman", *American Journal of Criminal Law* 28: 351-371.

BRAZIER, MARGARET (1999), "Can You Buy Children?", *Child & Family Law Quarterly* 11: 345-354.

BRINIG, MARGARET F. (2000), *From Contract to Covenant: Beyond the Law and Economics of the Family* (Cambridge, MA: Harvard University Press).

BURR, JENNIFER (2000), ""Repellent to Proper Ideas About the Procreation of Children": Procreation and Motherhood in the Legal and Ethical Treatment of the Surrogate Mother", *Psychology, Evolution & Gender* 2: 105-117.

BUSH, DARREN (1999), "Caught Between Scylla and Charybdis: Law & Economics as a Useful Tool for Feminist Legal Theorists", *American University Journal of Gender, Social Policy & the Law* 7: 395-430.

CHARLESWORTH, MAX (1993), *Bioethics in a Liberal Society* (Cambridge: Cambridge University Press).

CHLIAOUTAKIS, JOANNES E., SOPHIA KOUKOULI & MARIA PAPADAKAKI (2002), "Using Attitudinal Indicators to Explain the Public's Intention to Have Recourse to Gamete Donation and Surrogacy", *Human Reproduction* 17: 2995-3002.

COASE, RONALD H. (1960), "The Problem of Social Cost", *Journal of Law & Economics* 3: 1-44.

COHEN, CYNTHIA, ed. (1996), *New Ways of Making Babies: The Case of Egg Donation* (Bloomington: Indiana University Press).

COOTER, ROBERT & THOMAS ULEN (2000), *Law and Economics* (Reading, MA: Addison-Wesley, 3rd ed.).

DEVLIN, PATRICK (1965), *The Enforcement of Morals* (Oxford: Oxford University Press).

DILL, SANDRA (2002), "Consumer Perspectives" in Vayena et al. (2002: 255-271).

EPSTEIN, RICHARD A. (1995), "Surrogacy: The Case for Full Contractual Enforcement", *Virginia Law Review* 81: 2305-2341.

ERICKSON, ELIZABETH A. (1978), "Contracts to Bear a Child", *California Law Review* 66: 611-622.

FIELD, MARTHA A. (1988), *Surrogate Motherhood* (Cambridge, MA: Harvard University Press).

GARRISON, MARSHA (2000), "Law Making for Baby Making: An Interpretive Approach to the Determination of Legal Parentage", *Harvard Law Review* 113: 835-923.

GIACALONE, PIERRE-LUDOVIC, FRANÇOIS LAFFARGUE, PAUL BÉNOS, HERVÉ DECHAUD & BERNARD HÉDON (2001), "Successful In Vitro Fertilization-Surrogate Pregnancy in a Patient with Ovarian Transposition Who Had Undergone Chemotherapy and Pelvic Irradiation", *Fertility & Sterility* 76: 388-389.

GOLDFARB, JAMES M., CYNTHIA AUSTIN, BARRY PESKIN, HANNAH LISBONA, NINA DESAI & J. RICARDO LORET DE MOLA (2000), "Fifteen Years Experience with an In-Vitro Fertilization Gestational Pregnancy Programme", *Human Reproduction* 15: 1075-1078.

GOLOMBOK, SUSAN & FIONA TASKER (1994), "Children in Lesbian and Gay Families: Theories and Evidence", *Annual Review of Sex Research* 5: 73-100.

GORDON, ERIC A. (1993), "The Aftermath of Johnson v. Calvert: Surrogacy Law Reflects a More Liberal View of Reproductive Technology", *St. Thomas Law Review* 6: 191-211.

HARRIS, JOHN (2000), "The Welfare of the Child", *Health Care Analysis* 8: 27-34.

HART, H.L.A. (1963), *Law, Liberty and Morality* (Oxford: Oxford University Press).

HATZIS, ARISTIDES N. (2000), "Rights and Obligations of Third Parties" in *Encyclopedia of Law and Economics. Volume III. The Regulation of Contracts*, Boudewijn Bouckaert & Gerrit De Geest, *eds.* (Cheltenham, UK: Edward Elgar), pp. 200-222.

KAPLOW, LOUIS & STEVEN SHAVELL (2002), *Fairness versus Welfare* (Cambridge, MA: Harvard University Press).

KIRKMAN, MAGGIE & ALICE KIRKMAN (2002), "Sister-to-Sister Gestational "Surrogacy" 13 Years On: A Narrative of Parenthood", *Journal of Reproductive & Infant Psychology* 20: 135-147.

KOUNOUGERI-MANOLEDAKI, EFIE (2002), "Assisted Reproduction and Human Rights in Greece: The Proposed New Law on Assisted Reproduction," paper presented at the 11th World Conference of the International Society of Family Law (Copenhagen, Aug. 2-7, 2002).

KYMLICKA, WILL (1991), "Rethinking the Family", *Philosophy & Public Affairs* 20: 77-97.

LASCARIDES, DENISE E. (1997), "A Plea for the Enforceability of Gestational Surrogacy Contracts", *Hofstra Law Review* 25: 1222-1259.

MANDER, GERTRUD (2001), "Fathers Today: Variations on a Theme", *Psychodynamic Counselling* 7: 141-158.

McELROY, WENDY (2002), "Breeder Reactionaries: The "Feminist" War on New Reproductive Technologies", in *Liberty for Women: Freedom and Feminism in the Twenty-First Century*, Wendy McElroy, ed. (Chicago: Ivan R. Dee / Independent Institute) pp. 267-278.

McEWEN, ANGIE GODWIN (1999), "So You're Having Another Woman's Baby: Economics and Exploitation in Gestational Surrogacy", *Vanderbilt Journal of Transnational Law* 32: 271-304.

McLACHLAN, HUGH V. (1997), "Defending Commercial Surrogate Motherhood Against Van Niekerk and Van Zyl", *Journal of Medical Ethics* 23: 344-348.

McLACHLAN, HUGH V. & J.K. SWALES (2000), "Babies, Child Bearers and Commodification: Anderson, Brazier et al., and the Political Economy of Commercial Surrogate Motherhood", *Health Care Analysis* 8: 1-18.

McLACHLAN, HUGH V. & J.K. SWALES (2001), "Exploitation and Commercial Surrogate Motherhood", *Human Reproduction & Genetic Ethics* 7: 8-14.

McLANAHAN, SARA AND GARY SANDEFUR (1994). *Growing Up with a Single Parent: What Hurts? What Helps?* (Cambridge, MA: Harvard University Press).

MILL, J.S. (1859), *On Liberty* (London: J.W. Parker and Son).

MOONEY-SOMERS, JULIE & SUSAN GOLOMBOK (2000), "Children of Lesbian Mothers: From the 1970s to the New Millennium", *Sexual & Relationship Therapy* 15: 121-126.

POSNER, RICHARD A. (1989), "The Ethics and Economics of Enforcing Contracts of Surrogate Motherhood", *Journal of Contemporary Health Law & Policy* 5: 21-31.

POSNER, RICHARD A. (1992), *Sex and Reason* (Cambridge, MA: Harvard University Press).

RADIN, MARGARET JANE (1987), "Market-Inalienability", *Harvard Law Review* 100: 1849-1937.

RADIN, MARGARET JANE (1996), *Contested Commodities: The Trouble with Trade in Sex, Children, Body Parts, and Other Things* (Cambridge, MA: Harvard University Press).

RAWLS, JOHN (1971), *A Theory of Justice* (Cambridge, MA: Harvard University Press).

RAZIEL, ARIEH, SHEVACH FRIEDLER, MOREY SCHACHTER, DEBORAH STRASSBURGER & RAPHAEL RON-EL (2000), "Successful Pregnancy after 24 Consecutive Fetal Losses: Lessons Learned from Surrogacy", *Fertility & Sterility* 74: 104-106.

SERAFINI, PAULO (2001), "Outcome and Follow-Up of Children Born after IVF-Surrogacy", *Human Reproduction Update* 7 (1): 23-27.

SAINT-PAUL, GILLES (2002), "Economic Aspects of Human Cloning and Reprogenetics", *Economic Policy*, forthcoming.

SHALEV, CARMEL (1989), *Birth Power: The Case for Surrogacy* (New Haven: Yale University Press).

SHAVELL, STEVEN (2002), "Law versus Morality as Regulators of Conduct", *American Law & Economics Review* 4: 227-257.

SHIFFRIN, SEANA VALENTINE (1999), "Wrongful Life, Procreative Responsibility, and the Significance of Harm", *Legal Theory* 5: 117-148.

SILBAUGH, KATHARINE (1997), "Commodification and Women's Household Labor", *Yale Journal of Law & Feminism* 9: 81-121.

TREBILCOCK, MICHAEL J. (1993), *The Limits of Freedom of Contract* (Cambridge, MA: Harvard University Press).

TREBILCOCK, MICHAEL J. (1995), "Critiques of *The Limits of Freedom of Contract*: A Rejoinder: A Rejoinder", *Osgoode Hall Law Journal* 33: 353-377.

TREBILCOCK, MICHAEL J., MELODY MARTIN, ANNE LAWSON & PENNEY LEWIS (1994), "Testing the Limits of Freedom of Contract: The Commercialization of Reproductive Materials and Services", *Osgoode Hall Law Journal* 32: 613-702.

U.S. CONGRESS, OFFICE OF TECHNOLOGY ASSESSMENT (1988), *Infertility: Medical and Social Choices* (Washington, DC: U.S. Government Printing Office).

VAN DEN AKKER, OLGA (2000), "The Importance of a Genetic Link in Mothers Commissioning a Surrogate Baby in the UK", *Human Reproduction* 15: 1849-1855.

VAN DEN AKKER, OLGA (2001), "The Acceptable Face of Parenthood: The Relative Status of Biological and Cultural Interpretations of Offspring in Fertility Treatment", *Psychology, Evolution & Gender* 3: 137-153.

VAN WAART, J. & T.F. KRUGER (2000), "Surrogate Pregnancies in Patients with Mayer-Rokitansky-Kustner-Hauser Syndrome and Severe Teratozoospermia", *Archives of Andrology* 45: 95-97.

VAYENA, EFFY, PATRICK J. ROWE & P. DAVID GRIFFIN (2002), *Current Practices and Controversies in Assisted Reproduction* (Geneva: World Health Organization).

WERTHEIMER, ALAN (1997), "Exploitation and Commercial Surrogacy", *Denver University Law Review* 74: 1215-1229.

# 3. PRIVATE INTERNATIONAL LAW ASPECTS OF COHABITATION AND PARENTAL RESPONSIBILITIES

# NEW FORMS OF COHABITATION IN EUROPE; CHALLENGES FOR ENGLISH PRIVATE INTERNATIONAL LAW

YVETTE TAN[*]

*"In all nations it is observed that there are some families*
*fatal to the ruin of the Commonwealth"*
*(William Drummond of Hawthorne, 1585 – 1649)*[1]

## 1.    INTRODUCTION

The classic definition of marriage in English law comes from the case of *Hyde v Hyde* when Lord Penzance stated: "I conceive that marriage, as understood in Christendom may be defined as the voluntary union for life of one man and one woman to the exclusion of all others."[2] This definition denied recognition to any relationship falling short of a conventional marriage. However, in the last one hundred and thirty – seven years, the English courts have sought to evolve the rules of private international law and develop a much more liberal and tolerant policy in relation to foreign marriage recognition.

English law has already demonstrated a strong commitment to ethnic and cultural pluralism by recognising foreign marriages that differ greatly in form and substance. The best example is the gradual acceptance of valid foreign polygamous marriages under English law. Since *Hyde v Hyde*, it has taken a number of cases[3] and legislation[4] over the span of one hundred

---

[*]    I am grateful to Margaret Brazier, Caroline Bridge, Neil Duxbury, Charles Erin, Tom Gibbons, Anthony Ogus and Herman M Tan for their invaluable comments given on an earlier draft.
[1]    As quoted by R. BAILEY HARRIS, "New Families for a New Society?", in S. CRETNEY (ed.) *Family Law; Essays for the New Millennium* (Bristol, Jordan, 2000), p. 67.
[2]    (1866) LR 1 *P & D* 130 at 133.
[3]    Sinha Peerage Claim [1946] 1 *All ER* 348n, Baindail v Baindail [1946] *P* 122 at 127-128, Bamgbose v Daniel [1955] *AC* 107, [1954 ] *All ER* 263; Nabi v Heaton [1983] 1 *WLR* 626.
[4]    Matrimonial Proceedings (Polygamous Marriages) Act 1972 which abolished the old rule that polygamous marriages were not entitled to matrimonial relief; and claims under the Inheiritance (Provision for Family and Dependants) Act 1975, s 1A which was introduced by the Law Reform (Succession) Act 1975; see also Social Security and Family Allowances (Polygamous Marriages) Regulations 1975, SI 1975/561, reg 2(1); and for child benefit SI 1976/965, reg 12.

years to establish that valid foreign polygamous marriages are to be treated similarly to heterosexual marriages for most purposes.

However, at the beginning of the millennium, social evolution and the emergence of new family forms present challenges for English private international law.[5] The traditional concept of marriage,[6] and therefore, Lord Penzance's dictum no longer holds true. The requirement that the parties to a marriage should respectively be "a man and a woman" has changed due to medical and societal advances. Transsexualism is rapidly becoming more acceptable in societies worldwide.[7] In the United Kingdom, transsexuals are not allowed to marry in their new gender. However, many other jurisdictions allow transsexuals to do so. If such a marriage comes forth to the English court, would it be recognised? Or would the doctrine of public policy be used to refuse recognition?

Yet another challenge to Lord Penzance's dictum stems from an immense movement worldwide to equalise homosexuals with heterosexuals.[8] The fact that individuals of the same sex may be having private, consensual sexual acts is now considered to be socially acceptable by many jurisdictions. Homosexuality is no longer regarded as deviant behaviour.[9] It has been widely recognised that same-sex partners are capable of having the same type of emotional and sexual relationships as their heterosexual counterparts.[10] The need for same-sex couples to be treated equally to their heterosexual counterparts in relation to private and state benefits, has been a contentious issue in many Western jurisdictions. Therefore, the question of whether same-sex couples should be permitted to marry has been grappled with by many national laws. Consequently, many legislatures are in the process of, or have already enacted, a status which is similar to marriage for same-sex couples.

---

[5] ADRIAN BRIGGS, *Private International Law* (Oxford University Press, 2002), p. 46.

[6] For an incisive essay on trends in English marriage and divorce, refer to S. BRIDGE's essay in J. HERRING (ed.), *Family Law; Issues, Debates and Policy* (Collompton, United Kingdom, Willan Publishing Co, 2001).

[7] See www.ukia.co.uk (UK Intersex Association) see also www.medhelp.org/www/ais (website for those suffering from Androgen Insensitivity Syndrome) and also www.klinefelter.org.uk for those suffering from Klinefelter's syndrome. For an in depth discussion on the problems relating to intersex people, P.-L. CHAU and JONATHAN HERRING, "Defining, Assigning and Designing Sex", in *International Journal of Law, Policy and the Family* 16, (2002), 327-367.

[8] CARLA DUFF, "The Outing of Europe ", *Newsweek* November 23, 1998, pp. 33-37.

[9] M. BOWLEY, "Gay Rights – The second front", *New Law Journal* (May 26, 2000), pp. 803-804.

[10] NICHOLAS BAMFORTH, "Same-Sex Partnerships and Arguments of Justice", in ROBERT WINTEMUTE and MADS ANDENAES (ed.), *Legal Recognition of Same-Sex Partnerships; A Study of National, European and International Law* (Oxford and Portland Oregon, Hart Publishing, 2001), p. 41.

Similarly, there has been a rise in heterosexual cohabitation in many Western countries. Therefore, many jurisdictions have also enacted comprehensive legislation for cohabitees. This "status" often exists alongside marriage under the respective national laws. As this paper will show, there has been a shift away from traditional concept of marriage and a restructuring of the traditional family form. The landscape of family law has changed.

With the proliferation of new forms of partnerships, marriage is no longer the sole trigger of legal rights and obligations[11] The conundrum for English private international law is thus; if the parties to one of these new partnership forms were to travel within Europe, or internationally, would their domestic rights and obligations be recognised? Similarly to a "married" couple, the parties to one of these new partnership forms will need to have their relationship recognised for the purposes of the following; succession, maintenance rights or obligations, parental orders with respect to children, an incapacity, social security benefits or public benefits and pension rights. Thus, how would the English court recognise one of these new partnerships? Will the concept of universality of status[12] still apply? Or, would the court resort to the exclusionary doctrine of public policy? So far, English private international law still adheres to the rules of marriage recognition that depends upon the fulfillment of the place of celebration and the law of the domicile. What this paper proposes to do is to analyse the main forms of partnerships that are prevalent today and then, assess the chances of recognition of each one under English law. There has yet to be a test case, but with the emergence of so many new partnership forms, it will only be a matter of time before one comes forth.

## 2. RECOGNITION OF FOREIGN TRANSSEXUAL MARRIAGES

Transsexualism, otherwise known as *gender dysphoria* syndrome, is different from homosexuality. Although some transsexuals can also be homosexual, the two states still differ. While homosexuals are content with their sexuality, transsexuals want to change their birth sex surgically[13] and often seek psychiatric treatment. Therefore, they are normally classified as either

---

[11]  BARLOW and PROBERT, "Displacing marriage – diversification and harmonisation within Europe", *Child and Family Law Quarterly*, Vol 12, No 2, 2000, p. 154.

[12]  P.E. NYGH, "Foreign Status, Public Policy and Discretion" *International and Comparative Law Quarterly*, Vol 13, 1964, p. 39-52 in which NYGH discussed public policy in relation to polygamy, divorce decrees and nullity decrees. NYGH, however, did not predict the possibility that the fundamental nature of marriage might change.

[13]  This is known as a sex reassignment.

pre-operative or post-operative transsexuals. Surgery to change one's sex is not prohibited in English law. However, English law prohibits transsexuals from marrying in their post-operative sex. If X, a man, underwent surgery to have the appearance of a woman, and wanted to marry Y, a man, such a marriage would be prohibited. The case of *Corbett v Corbett*[14] established the determination of sex for marriage. The individual had been born a man, but had undergone a sex change operation later in his life to become a woman. Since the operation, the person had lived as a woman and had psychologically, philosophically and sociologically[15] assimilated into society as a woman. The petitioner in the case filed for a declaration that the marriage to the transsexual was null or void.

Alternatively, the petitioner wanted a decree of nullity. Although the respondent was living as a woman, the respondent was born male. In turn, the respondent contested and prayed for a decree of nullity. If the respondent was not female, then the marriage would be void according to section 11(c) of the Matrimonial Causes Act 1973. On the other hand, if the respondent was female, then incapacity or unwillingness to consummate could render the marriage voidable.[16] Ormrod J stated:[17] "Since marriage is essentially a relationship between a man and a woman, the validity of the marriage in this case, depends, in my judgement, upon whether or not the respondent is or is not a woman." Furthermore, Ormrod J was of the opinion[18] that the test the law should adopt to determine someone's sex should be "...the first three of the doctor's criteria... i.e. the chromosomal, the gonadal, and the genital tests, and if all three are congruent, determine the sex for the purpose of marriage accordingly, and ignore any specific intervention."[19] It was accepted that psychological factors can also be used to determine which gender a person belongs to, particularly in intersex cases. But the three characteristics, if congruent, determine the nature of a person's sex, and therefore, the test of sex for marriage.

Gender[20] on the other hand, is a concept that is different from sex. It has been described as a positive mental state as to which sex the individual feels comfortable in. The need for transsexuals to marry in their new gender

---

[14]   [1970] 2 *All ER* 33; [1971] *P* 33.
[15]   R v Tan and Others [1983] *QB* 1053.
[16]   sections 12 (a) and (b) of the Matrimonial Causes Act 1973.
[17]   At (106 B-D).
[18]   At (106 D).
[19]   At (106 D).
[20]   MASON and MCCALL SMITH, *Law and Medical Ethics*, 5th ed. (London, Butterworths, 1999), p. 39.

in the United Kingdom has long been debated.[21] More recently, the Government's *Interdepartmental Working Group on Transsexual People*[22] discussed the plight[23] of the transsexual at length. A leading campaigning group stated:

"In many cases, transsexual people have already been economically disadvantaged due to lengthy periods of time which career aspirations had to be put on hold, as medical treatment was sought and undergone. For many of us, social pressures will have meant that our education has suffered. Job insecurity, or failure to get a job due to prejudice, will mean that we will have spent time being unemployed. Finally, as we achieve some sort of social acceptance, we then discover that without the right to contract a marriage, [we are denied] many of the financial benefits that accrue on marriage [such as survivor's pensions]...[B]ecause only spouses and legally related children can benefit...[w]e find ourselves having to buy extra financial security for our families, and yet we are invariably already financially worse off than our peers for all the other reasons, such as entering a career late, or having missed out on formal education."[24]

England's historical refusal to allow transsexuals to marry in their new gender differs radically from other member states in the European Community.[25] Therefore, would the English court recognise a valid foreign transsexual marriage? Or would the doctrine of public policy be used? Due to recent decisions in domestic case law, such a marriage is likely to be recognised. After many years, the "grip" of Corbett[26] has finally been broken, and English law seems to be in favour of gender over sex.

---

[21] Change, FTM Network, G & SA, The Gender Trust, GIRES, Liberty, Press For Change, Meeting the Needs of Transsexual People: A Presentation to the Interdepartmental Working Group on Transsexual Issues, 19 Jan. 2000. http://www.pfc.org.uk/workgrp/jan2000.htm. See also S. WHITTLE, "An association for as Noble a Purpose as Any", *New Law Journal*, March 15, 1996.

[22] Home Office published on 26 July 2000 Report of the Interdepartmental Working Group on Transsexual People; http://www.homeoffice.gov.uk/ccpd/wgtrans.pdf. It should be noted that the Working Group did not make any recommendations, but identified three options for public consultation: "to leave the current situation unchanged, to issue birth certificates showing the new name and possibly, gender; and to grant full legal recognition of the new gender subject to certain criteria and procedures." (para 5.5) .

[23] It has been quoted by one academic that transsexuals in England have been sent into legal exile; see chapter 2 of S. M. EDWARDS, *Sex and Gender in the Legal Process* (Blackstone Press Limited, London, 1996).

[24] *Ibid.* n. 19.

[25] At least 22 of the 43 Council of Europe countries allow transsexuals to marry in their new gender.

[26] The Rees Case [1987] 2 *FLR* 111; Cossey v UK (A/184) [1991] 13 *EHRR* 622; Sheffield and Horsham v UK [1998] 2 *FLR* 928; and S-T (Formerly J) v J [1997] 3 *WLR* 1287.

## 2.1. W v W facts

The respondent was born of an indeterminate sex and was registered at birth as a boy because her father wanted a boy. The determination of her sex was due to her father's wishes as opposed to conclusive physical evidence. From a young age, she was raised by relatives who treated her as a boy, but she displayed girlish behaviour. By age 15, she had developed noticeable breasts, but was given hormone treatment by her doctor to stop her breasts from growing. In 1987, she underwent gender reassignment surgery. She then married a man in 1990. The marriage failed in 1992, and was terminated by a decree of nullity on the grounds that the parties were not respectively male and female. In 1993, she married Mr. W, but in 1996 issued a divorce petition and an application for an injunction under the Domestic and Matrimonial Proceedings Act 1976. In 1998 when the respondent issued ancillary relief proceedings, Mr. W argued that the respondent was not female, and therefore not eligible for relief under the 1976 Act.

The case of W v W[27] gave the court a chance to reconsider the position taken by *Corbett*,[28] and the determination of sex at the time of birth according to chromosomal, genital and gonadal characteristics, without regard to psychological factors. Since Mrs. W. was a case of physical inter-sex, evidence was taken by the surgeon who did the gender re-assignment surgery and a medical expert witness.[29] The medical expert witness referred the court to Professor Gooren's opinion that brain patterns in transsexuals were indicative of their chosen sex, as opposed to their birth sex. Professor Gooren, in his paper stated:

> "The decision of sex assignment is in modern medicine primarily guided by the nature of the external genitalia...The demonstrable sex differences in the brain become only manifest by the age of 3-4 years post-natally...Upon examination of a very limited number of male to female transsexuals post-mortem, their brains showed morphological differences in comparison with non-transsexual con-trols...The implication of the above scientific insight that sexual differentiation of the brain occurs after birth is that assignment of a child to the male or female sex by the criterion of the external genitalia is an act of faith." [30]

---

[27] W v W (Nullity: Gender) [2001] 1 *FLR* 324.
[28] Corbett had determined two factors; the test of sex for marriage and also whether the marriage had been consummated.
[29] *Ibid.* 331-334.
[30] *Ibid.* at p. 333 which was taken from a paper given at the XXIIIrd Colloquy on European Law in April 1993 and also approved by the European Committee on Legal Co-operation at the Council of Europe, from the judgement of W ard J in *S-T(Formerly J) v J*[1997] 3 *WLR* 1287, at p. 1306.

Charles J did not feel restricted by the *Corbett* test to classify Mrs. W. as male, although her chromosomal and gonadal indicators were both male and the genital criteria was inconclusive.[31] He was of the opinion that the *Corbett* test only applied to transsexuals, and not intersex cases. Furthermore, Charles J also considered the question of how people who cannot fulfil the biological test (such as a hermaphrodite) in *Corbett* should be classified for section 11 of the Matrimonial Causes Act 1973, which requires that a person should be either male or female.[32] One solution would be to not classify the hermaphrodite, as the hermaphrodite is neither male nor female. Charles J concluded that this approach would not work out, as it would run counter to Parliament's intention that a person should be classifiable. Furthermore, Charles J was of the opinion that upon the "true construction" of the Matrimonial Causes Act, there should be a greater emphasis upon gender rather than sex. In particular, he thought that there should be a greater emphasis upon the financial, civil, contractual and general living arrangements of marriage, rather than the "old" Corbett test that marriage is a relationship dependent upon sex.[33]

## 2.2. B v B – A lost opportunity to deviate from Corbett?

In B v B ( *Validity of Marriage – Transsexual*)[34] it was decided that *W v W* had no bearing upon *B v B* because *W v W* was a case of physical inter-sex, and *B v B* was a case of clear gender dysphoria – the three biological factors were congruent. Mrs. B was a post-operative male to female transsexual. Mrs. B wanted a declaration that she was married to the respondent, a man, at the time of the marriage. When deciding the case, Johnson J was aware of the European Court's recommendation to "keep the need for the appropriate legal measures in this area under review, having regard in particular to scientific and social developments."[35]

Again, medical evidence was brought forth to the court that supported the argument that the test for sex (and therefore, sexual differentiation) should not be determined solely by chromosomal, genital or gonadal configuration but brain patterns. Furthermore, expert witness Professor Green stated that the "criteria for designating a person as male or female is complex and very probably not simply an outcome of chromosomal, genital or gonadal configuration."[36] While Johnson J acknowledged that

---

[31]  *Ibid.*, at 350.
[32]  *Ibid.*, at 324 and at p. 361 G.
[33]  *Ibid.*, at 362 B.
[34]  [2001] 2 *FLR.*
[35]  [1998] 2 *FLR* 928, at p 942.
[36]  *Ibid.* see note 13 at p. 394 B.

medical science has come a long way from Corbett, he did not feel the pressure to grasp the opportunity to deviate from *Corbett*. Johnson J still felt that however far medical science has progressed, the criteria in *Corbett* should still hold today. Although *B v B* is regarded as a missed opportunity[37] to reconsider *Corbett*, the new medical evidence upon brain patterns in determining the gender of an individual should give impetus for the English court to recognise a foreign transsexual marriage.

### 2.3. Yet another missed opportunity at the Court of Appeal?

The case has since been taken to the Court of Appeal and was considered at length by Dame Elizabeth Butler-Sloss P, Walker LJ and Thorpe LJ. Dame Elizabeth Butler- Sloss and Walker LJ considered previous case law and the evidence of medical witnesses.[38] Butler-Sloss stated: "We are however concerned with the legal recognition of marriage, which, like divorce, is a matter of status and is not for the spouses alone to decide. It affects society and is a question of public policy. For that reason, marriage is in a special position and is different from the change of gender on a driving licence, social security payments book and so on."[39]

Butler Sloss acknowledged that the point at which a change of gender should be recognised is not easily ascertainable. She finally concluded that, while the recognition of a transsexual's gender is a pressing problem, the legal recognition of a change of birth sex for marriage is a matter for Parliament.[40] Thorpe LJ, on the other hand, dissented. He felt that there were no compelling reasons to not allow the appeal. Thorpe LJ was of the opinion that the range of rights of transsexuals falls across the family justice system, and the system should be flexible to accommodate social change through statutory construction.[41]

### 2.4. Recent Developments for Transsexuals

Although the majority did not allow the appeal, the incorporation of the European Convention of Human Rights has finally provided impetus for the right for transsexuals to marry. In July 2002, the European Court of

---

[37]   A. BARLOW, "W v W (Nullity: Gender) and B v B (Validity of Marriage: Transsexual) – A new approach to transsexualism and a missed opportunity?" *Child and Family Law Quarterly*, Vol 13, No 2, 2001.

[38]   (CA) 1055 – 1064; evidence given by Professor Gooren, Professor Green and Mr Terry, all eminent consultants and also evidence given by Miss Cox.

[39]   *Ibid.* at 1073.

[40]   *Ibid.* 1074-1075.

[41]   *Ibid.* 1092.

Human Rights ruled in the historic conjoined cases of *I. v. the United Kingdom*[42] and *Christine Goodwin v the United Kingdom*[43] that there had been a violation of Article 8 (the right for respect of family life) and Article 12 (the right to marry and found a family). This ruling has forced English law to reconsider its position. In response, the Lord Chancellor announced on December 13, 2002, that transsexuals are to be granted the right to change their birth certificates and marry in their adopted sex. However, it is unlikely that these changes would become law until 2004.

In the meantime, it is submitted that English private international law should be bolder than domestic law. There are several arguments in favour of recognition in private international law. First, by all outward appearances, a transsexual marriage is "a man" and "a woman". Unlike a homosexual marriage, a transsexual marriage is still within Lord Penzance's definition. A second argument is that a transsexual marriage should be viewed as another new form of "status", which should be recognised without resort to the doctrine of public policy by the English court. Although the recognition of a foreign transsexual marriage has been discussed occasionally by academics over the last decade,[44] the likelihood of recognition is certain now[45] because of the many changes in medical opinion and *forced change* from the European Court of Human Rights. There is, in fact, absolutely no reason to deny recognition to foreign transsexual marriages under English private international law.

## 3. COHABITATION LEGISLATION ON A PIECEMEAL BASIS

Unlike other jurisdictions, England does not have comprehensive legislation protecting the breakdown of non-marital cohabitation. Therefore, it has been argued that under English law, "cohabitees ignore the law so the law will ignore cohabitees."[46] It is well known that English

---

[42]  [2002] 2 *FLR* 518.

[43]  [2002] *FLR* 487.

[44]  Recognition argued by B.E. GRAHAM-SIEGENTHALER, "Marriage Recognition in Switzerland and Europe", Vol 32, No 1, *Creighton Law Review*, October 1998 at 125 in which she quotes M.D.A. FREEMAN, *Marriage and Divorce in England*, in *THE MARRIAGE* 214 (Rotondi: Inchieste Di Diritto Comparato, Guilo Levi ed, Dott A. Guifre; Milano 1998) at 214-215 and also the arguments of K. MCNORRIE, "Reproductive Technology, Transsexualism and Homosexuality; New Problems for Private International Law", 43 *International and Comparative Law Quarterly* 757 at 772-774.

[45]  C. ARCHBOLD, "Family Law-making and Human Rights in the UK", in M. MACLEAN (ed.), *Making Law for Families*, (Oxford, Portland Hart, 2001).

[46]  Thus, the contentious debate upon whether legal rights should be extending to cohabiting couples at the Law Society on 23 October 2000, and conference notes discussed at January [2001] *Fam Law* pp. 68-71.

law traditionally supports heterosexual marriage[47] over other family forms. This has been reinforced by the Government's recent consultation document *Supporting Families*,[48] which called for the institution of marriage to be strengthened and ignored other family forms.

It has been argued by Barlow and Probert[49] that the current legislation that does protect cohabitees only grudgingly acknowledges extra-marital cohabitation. They cite section 62(1)(a) of the Family Law Act 1996, and argue that the wording " a man and a woman, although not married to each other are living together as husband and wife" implies that a couple should be married to each other. Likewise, the Law Reform (Succession) Act 1995 requires that a cohabitant "needs to have lived with the deceased as their spouse for at least two years before making the claim for reasonable financial provision." Barlow and Probert assert that the constant reference to the "married state" by the statute regards extra-marital cohabitation as an inferior family form.[50] While cohabitation has been on the rise domestically, many other jurisdictions have taken a much more progressive approach in recognising this family pattern. In particular, many European countries have recently enacted legislation or a full status (that is separate from marriage) for cohabitees. Thus, private international law problems are bound to exist. Because of the proximity to the United Kingdom, the best example is the French PACS legislation, which will be considered later on in this section. On the other hand, countries may not have a "status" but have enacted piecemeal legislation protecting cohabitees in certain situations. How would the English court recognise either a "status" or piecemeal legislation? The next two sections will examine possible approaches taken by private international law.

### 3.1. Recognition Problems for Piecemeal Legislation

The problem with such legislation is that each is a different "bundle" of rights. A few examples shall be cited. For example, one of the earliest European statutes protecting cohabitees is Article 12 of the Slovenian Law on Marital and Other Family Relations.[51] This has been in force since the early 1970's and sought to equalise the rights of cohabitees with married

---

[47] As supported by the Lord Chancellor in his speech to the Inner Temple in June 25, 1999.

[48] Government Consultation Paper *Supporting Families* (The Stationery Office, November 1998).

[49] See generally http://webjcli.ncl.ac.uk/1999/issue3/barlow3.html (*Web Journal of Current Legal Issues*) Blackstone Press, 1999).

[50] For current trends in European cohabitation see Special Issue: Unmarried Cohabitation on Europe, Vol 15, Issue 1, *International Journal of Law, Policy and the Family*, April 2001.

[51] Published in the *Official Gazette* of the Socialist Republic of Slovenia, No 15/1976.

couples. An extract states "A man and a woman who are not married but have been cohabiting for a long period of time are subject to the same legal effects provided that there are no grounds that would render a marriage between them invalid." Such a liberal interpretation may be surprising of the former Yugoslavia, but it has been acknowledged that it does have its roots in Yugoslavian Constitutional law. P. Sarcevic[52] is of the opinion that when the Yugoslav Federal Constitution of 1974 gave protection to the family, it did not specify what kind of families were entitled to protection. Therefore, Sarcevic reasons that interpretation should be given to "all families without distinction."

Similarly, the Norwegian Joint Household Act[53] provides limited relief to cohabitees in the event of a breakdown of a household. It gives the right to occupy the joint household in some circumstances, and also provides for joint household goods upon relationship breakdown or death. It also applies to everyone who lives together for a period of two years. Yet another example of legislation comes from the Catalan Mutual Assistance Act which provides for maintenance and inheritance rights if the people living together have cohabited for the purposes of mutual assistance. This Act also provides for people who are not necessarily in a sexual relationship, but have resided with each other, and give each other financial assistance.

It is not possible to give an extensive account in this paper of the numerous European jurisdictions that provide for cohabitees.[54] However, the examples given above show that cohabitation legislation differs from country to country. Each country's protection stems from a different social purpose and has different effects. Therefore, if protection is given is just one area of law (such a succession) would it be appropriate for the English court to confer the status of marriage on the couple? On the other hand, the foreign couple may not be in favour of the English court regarding them as being "married" when they have chosen to avoid that very institution in their own country. Furthermore, if the foreign country conferred a "right" for cohabitees would it be possible for England to enforce it even if English cohabitees are not entitled to the same protection domestically? Without resorting to the exclusionary doctrine of public

---

[52] "Private International Law Aspects of Legally Regulated Forms of Non-Marital Cohabitation and Registered Partnerships", *Yearbook of Private International Law* (Kluwer Law International, 1999), p. 40.

[53] For an account of piecemeal protection given to cohabitees in Europe see C. Forder, assisted by S.H. LOMBARDO, *Civil Aspects of the Emerging Forms of Registered Partnerships*, Ministry of Justice of the Netherlands, The Hague, Fifth European Conference on Family Law, 1999.

[54] *Ibid.*

policy, it is predicted that recognition might be possible if only if there is a convention regulating recognition and enforcement. Short of this method, classification for the English court is difficult, as it does not "fit" the traditional marriage form. Recognition can be attained in this instance only by being a signatory to a convention.

## 4. COHABITATION CONTRACTS

Although marriage is often considered to be both a status and a contract[55] the institution of marriage is separate from contract law in England. However, in many foreign jurisdictions, there is a move towards the private ordering of personal relationships. Therefore, contract law has been utilised in family or marriage-like relationships in Belgium, France and in the United States. Thus, problems for English private international law are inevitable, and will come forth sometime in the near future. The following section will describe the French legislation in relation to cohabitation contracts and then analyse the possibility of recognition.

### 4.1. French PACS

Before 1999, there were two forms of legally recognised cohabitation – civil marriage and concubinage. Civil marriage requires formal expression of will of the parties through a marriage ceremony. On the other hand, concubinage involves the legal recognition of the fact that two persons are living together as spouses.[56] The third partnership form came in 1999[57] when the French legislature taken on the responsibility of protection for non-marital family forms by passing comprehensive legislation.

Since November 17, 1999, cohabiting homosexual couples have had the opportunity to get their relationship registered under French law. The new Civil Solidarity Pact[58] (PACS) is defined as a contract entered into by two persons, of the same or the opposite sex, to organise their common life

---

[55] As acknowledged by R.H. GRAVESON in chapter 8 in *Private International Law* (Sweet & Maxwell, London, 7th Ed.) and also discussed by HOGGETT, PEARL, COOKE, BATES (eds.) *The Family, Law and Society* (Butterworths, London, 1996), pp. 43-50.

[56] Discussion by D. RICHARDS, "Legal Recognition of Same-Sex Relationships – The French Perspective", *International and Comparative Law Quarterly* Vol 51, Issue 2, April 2002.

[57] http://www.legifrance.gouv.fr/html/frame_jo/html.

[58] See general discussion by D. BORILLO, "Pacte Civil de Solidarite in France; Midway Between Marriage and Cohabitation" in R. WINTEMUTE and MADS ANDENAS (eds.), *Legal Recognition of Same Sex Partnerships; A Study of National, European and International Law* (Oxford, Portland, 2001).

together[59] The parties cannot be married or bound by another contract. Similarly to a marriage, there are restrictions as to who has capacity (there are limitations of consanguinity and affinity[60] as well as detailed instructions as to how a *pacte* is to be registered. The circumstances under which a *pacte* may be terminated is also set out. Unlike the termination of a marriage, the procedure for ending a *pacte* is simpler. Immediate unilateral termination of a *pacte* is not permitted unless one of the partners marries a third party, which brings the *pacte* to an end. Otherwise the pacte will still be in existence for three months after notification of the *pacte* to the required official.[61] Domestically, the *pacte* has important consequences for the couple in public law. There are many fiscal and social security rights that are conferred on *pacte* couples. Additionally, a partner may succeed to a tenancy in the name of the other and rely upon the other's health insurance.[62] Also, on the third anniversary of the *pacte*, the couple will be taxed as if they are married. However, this is only an advantage when there is a significant disparity between the incomes of the partners. The French government does not provide pensions for these couples. But, there exists a tax relief on gifts. The first FF 300,000 is not taxed; the next FF 100,000 is taxed at 40 per cent and the rest at 50 per cent.[63]

Therefore, would a French PACS registered couple be recognised by an English court? There are several arguments against recognition. Specifically, there are several public policy related grounds upon which a marriage or a marriage – related contract could be invalidated in English law. The first ground renders a marriage contract void by reason of sexual immorality.[64] While there is a large body of contract case law that supports this ground, it could be argued that the most of the cases date between 1679 and 1938, and emphasise the nature of extra-marital cohabitation. Many of the judgements are in fact "Bible-thumping" and could be considered to be puritanical outbursts. For example, in The Lady Cox's Case,[65] the couple had been living together for over five years when the man arranged for the woman to have £1000 after his death. By today's standards of morality, this would not seem offensive at all. However, at the time, it was thought to be given in return for wicked consideration. Further evidence

---

59  Code civil, Art. 515-1.
60  Code civil. Art. 515-2.
61  Code civil, Art. 515-7.
62  Code de law securite sociale, Art. L 161-14.
63  Code general des impots, Art. 6 (1) and Arts. 885 A, 1723 ter-00 B and Art. 779 (III).
64  C. BARTON, *Cohabitation Contracts; Extra Marital Partnerships and Law Reform* (Gower, Aldershot, 1985) at pp. 37-38
65  (1734) 3 *P.Wms.* 339.

of the court's attitude can be found in the case of Upfill v. Wright, when the court stated that "fornification is sinful and immoral is clear ... the Litany speaks of fornification and all other deadly sins and the Litany is contained in the Book of Common Prayer which is in use in the Church of England under the authority of an Act of Parliament."[66]

Suprisingly, the emphasis on sexual immorality outside the institution of marriage can still be found in cases at the beginning of the 20th century. Take, for example, Omerod J[67] when he stated "such joint venture must depend on a contract express or implied between the parties which being founded on an immoral consideration would not be enforceable." While it can be asserted that English contract law does not support sexual relations to be regulated along with the law of contract, there is a body of opinion that morality, and therefore policy in general, has changed. Professor Atiyah argues[68] that in recent times, there has been a silent but crucial turnabout as to what is to be considered sexually immoral behaviour. Furthermore, it has been acknowledged that the parties will be enjoying sexual intercourse anyway outside of marriage, irrespective of the court's attitude to their contract.

The second ground of non-recognition states that a cohabitation contract may be void and prejudicial to the marital state. First of all, it detracts from the time-honoured institution of marriage. Secondly, Barton is of the opinion[69] that two "single" people who are bound by a cohabitation contract are hampered by the contract to enter into marriage, or are restrained from marrying third parties. Although this argument might be valid, it ignores the fact that many cohabitees have are intentionally avoiding the institution of marriage. For whatever reason, the parties have conscientiously decided to avoid marriage. For instance, France has a greater proportion[70] of cohabiting couples than any other country in Europe, with one in six heterosexual couples living together. Therefore, the cohabitation contract has been enacted in order to accommodate changing family structures and needs.

The third head of public policy[71] states that in cohabitation contracts there is a "lack of intention to create legal relations." Barton provides that

---

[66]   [1911] 1. *K.B.* 506.
[67]   [1959] 2. *All E.R.* 379, 384.
[68]   ATIYAH, *An Introduction to the Law of Contract*, 3rd edn, 1981 p. 257.
[69]   *Ibid.* n. 64 at p. 43.
[70]   *Ibid.* n. 56.
[71]   *Ibid.* n. 64 at p. 43.

uninformed cohabitees may not provide expressly for the necessary intention and therefore, may fall foul of the rebuttable presumption that parties to an agreement do not intend to be bound.[72] However, in relation to the PACS agreement, this argument can be rebutted because of the strict registration procedure that cohabitees have to follow. It cannot be argued that parties to a *pacte* did not intend to enter into legal relations. The fourth head of public policy[73] postulates there is room for undue influence on the weaker party, or inequality in bargaining power. If this is found, the court must decide if the will of one party has been overborne by the other party. It is, however, unclear as to what categories of "relationship" that undue influence can be applied to. Barton is of the opinion[74] that undue influence must be proven between "spouses" but can be presumed between fiance and fiancee (at least where the transaction is prima facie far more favourable to one party over another). While there is a body of academic opinion that undue influence is normally argued by the female party, it is possible that it can be applied to a man as well.[75] Furthermore, this argument ignores same-sex couples. Barton concludes[76] that if the parties take care to show an intention to create legal relations; avoid the appearance of undue influence; eschew references to sexual matters and attempts to tamper with existing rights then agreements between heterosexual couples are binding under the law.

### 4.2. Heterosexual PACS recognition favoured over homosexual PACS?

If Barton's reasoning is to be followed, this would allow recognition of a heterosexual PACS over a homosexual PACS under English private international law recognition rules. Arguably, this also leads to unwarranted discrimination at European level, as well. French law provides for both homosexual and heterosexual couples to enter into a *pacte*. There is no discrimination. Therefore, both homosexual and heterosexual couples should be entitled to recognition of this status in foreign jurisdictions. It is highlighted, however, that the real problem lies in the recognition of the marriage – contract hybrid rather than the sexual orientation of the parties. Although the French *pacte* might be refused recognition on one of the grounds of public policy described earlier, the English court should consider whether there is a completely different concept of public policy

---

72    *Ibid.* n. 64 at 44.
73    *Ibid.* n. 64 at 46.
74    *Ibid.* n. 64 at 46-47.
75    Zamet v. Hyman and Another [1961] 3 *All E.R.* 933 per Sir R. Evershed M.R. at p. 938.
76    *Ibid.* n. 64 at 48-49.

in private international law in relation to foreign marriage-contract hybrids as opposed to the public policy notion that invalidates domestic marriage contracts.[77] Which classification would the English court use? A test case has yet to come forth, so it is hoped that the English court will take a lenient approach and allow recognition without resort to the exclusionary doctrine of public policy.

### 4.3. New private international law legislation needed?

Barring the exclusionary discretion of public policy, the bigger problem, then, lies in characterisation of the *pacte*. Since English law has no equivalent marriage-contract hybrid, would the pacte be classified as a marriage? If so, will the court look to the *lex loci celebrationis* and the *lex loci domicilii*? This is a possible solution, because both can be easily ascertained.

Another recommendation would be to use the current contract rules in private international law. Finding the "applicable" law of the contract would be simple, as French law would govern the *pacte*.[78] However, since all contracts are subject to the Rome Convention,[79] the notion of applying the Convention to marriage contracts or any obligation that arises out of a family relationship[80] is not within its scope. Therefore, the use of contract in English private international law is not possible.

There are no initiatives in domestic family law to develop an equivalent status to the *pacte*; neither are there any changes being made in English private international law to accommodate recognition of a *pacte*. It is submitted, that perhaps, recognition will only come if the United Kingdom is signatory to a European Convention. Until that time, the parties to a French *pacte* (or for that matter, any other jurisdiction that has a quasi-marital contract) will be in limbo as to whether their status recognised outside the jurisdiction in which it was contracted.

---

[77]  According to KAHN-FREUND, *General Problems of Private International Law*, (A.W. Sijthoff, Leyden 1976), pp. 281-282 there should be no distinction between domestic policy and international policy. It is submitted that Kahn-Freund did not consider contract-marriage hybrids or new forms of partnerships.

[78]  This would involve finding the law of the contract, as discussed in Cheshire and North, *Private International Law*, (London, Butterworths, 13th ed.) chapter 18.

[79]  Rome Convention, The Contracts (Applicable Law) Act 1990.

[80]  *Ibid.* n. 78 in Art 1(2)(b).

## 5. REGISTERED PARTNERSHIPS

In several European countries and in the United States, a special status has been implemented for same-sex couples that is akin to, but separate from, the institution of marriage. This is known as a "registered partnership". The implementation of a registered partnership is normally the culmination of many years of lobbying and litigation. For instance, in the United States, the fight for equality for homosexuals and the fight for the right to marry has been raging for a number of years. Rights in the United States are subject to state and federal levels, but where marriage is concerned, the fifty states are the gatekeepers. Therefore, the federal government normally recognises that the states are in charge of issuing marriage licenses. To date, most claimants have preferred to invoke state constitutions over federal protection laws. It is now appropriate to discuss the developments in two jurisdictions that have enacted a registered partnership.

### 5.1. Baker v. Vermont

In *Baker v. Vermont*,[81] three same-sex couples filed suit after being denied marriage licences by their town clerks. The three couples[82] all wanted their respective partnerships to be officially recognised by the states. Their claims were centred upon the Vermont Constitution's Common Benefits Clause, which states:

> "That government is, or ought to be, instituted for the common benefit, protection, and security of the people, nation or community, and not for the particular emolument or advantage of any single person, family, or set of persons who are a part only of that community; ... "[83]

The Vermont Supreme Court focused upon whether the exclusion of statutory benefits, protections and security was, in fact, a denial of constitutionally protected rights."[84] The parties put forth three arguments in favour of recognition. First, the couples argued that they enjoy a

---

[81]   *Baker v. the State of Vermont*, No. 510009-97 CnC, slip opinion (Chittenden Superior Ct, 19 Dec. 1997), and also at http://vtfreetomarry.org/opinion121997.html; Baker v. State of Vermont, 744 A.2d 864 (Vermont Supreme Court 1999) abd http://www.legstate.vt.us./baker/baker.cfm.

[82]   Litigation discussed by A. S. LEONARD, "The Freedom to Marry for Same-Sex Couples in the US", in R. WINTEMUTE and MADS ANDENAS (eds.), *Legal Recognition of Same – Sex Partnerships; A Study of National, European and International Law* (Oxford and Portland Oregon, 2001).

[83]   (Chapter I, Article 7) of the original 1777 Vermont Constitution.

[84]   *Ibid.*

fundamental right to marry a person of their choice. They pointed out that there is no reason to exclude them from the fundamental right to marry as described by the U.S. Supreme Court in *Loving v. Virginia*[85] in 1967 which deemed marriage to be "essential to the orderly pursuit of happiness by free men." Secondly, they argued that the withholding of marriage licences amounts to sexual orientation discrimination, which is unjustifiable by the state. Finally, the claimants argued there was no legitimate reason to exclude same-sex couples from marriage. When the trial court dismissed the case, the couples appealed to the Vermont Supreme Court. The Vermont Supreme Court did not consider the issue of whether or not same-sex couples should be entitled to marriage licenses on a constitutional basis. Instead, the Vermont Supreme Court focused upon whether the exclusion of statutory benefits, protections and security was, in fact, a denial of constitutionally protected rights.

Upon much analysis and construction, the conclusion of the Supreme Court of Vermont was that "the extension of the [Constitution] to acknowledge plaintiffs as Vermonters who seek nothing more, nor less, than legal protection and security for their avowed commitment to an intimate and lasting human relationship is simply, when all is said and done, a recognition of our common humanity."[86] The solution was to allow the state legislature the opportunity to remedy the Constitutional violation. After proceedings in the Vermont Senate, the Civil Unions Law became effective on 1 July 2000.[87] Same-sex couples may apply to town clerks for a civil union licence, and will be treated as spouses under Vermont law. Hundreds of rights and responsibilities are then conferred upon the couple.

### 5.2. Danish Registered Partnership Act

The implementation of a status for same-sex couples[88] in Denmark[89] stems from having a strong tradition of interest groups and a welfare state which is based on social democratic ideas. In 1989, Denmark became the first country in the world to enact a Registered Partnership Act for same-sex couples. The registration of a registered partnership is similar to that of marriage. There exist only two differences. The parties to a Registered

---

[85]   388 *U.S.* 1 at 12 (1967).
[86]   *Ibid.* n. 81 at 889.
[87]   "An Act Relating to Civil Unions", Act 91 of 2000.
[88]   Registered Partnership Act, Law No. 372 of 7 June 1989.
[89]   L. NIELSEN, "Family Rights and the Registered Partnership in Denmark", (1990) 4 *International Journal of Law Policy and the Family*.

Partnership cannot receive a blessing in a church ceremony[90] and, also cannot adopt a child as a couple.[91] Otherwise, the rights and obligations are similar to heterosexual marriage in Denmark.

### 5.2.1. Recognition Problems for Registered Partnerships in English Private International Law

Since there are a number of registered partnerships that have been enacted around the world, private international law problems are bound to persist for England. Would the registered partnership be recognised by England or would the doctrine of public policy exclude recognition? Or would it be considered "offensive" or "repugnant" by English law? On a general "offensiveness" scale, the balance would seem to be in favour of recognition, given the legal developments in the United Kingdom over the last several years. Currently, Parliament is considering the Civil Partnerships Bill to allow recognition for same-sex couples in England. In the meantime, there already exists an unofficial marriage register (not legally recognised yet) in the London area for same-sex couples.[92]

Since England is currently considering a registered partnership of its own,[93] it *should* recognise those registered partnerships of other countries without resort to public policy.[94] While this is an unchartered area for English private international law, there has been much written in American law about the recognition of the Vermont Same-Sex Civil Unions by other states.[95] Accordingly, English private international law could take its cue

---

[90]  Report on "Registered Partnership, Cohabitation and Blessing", 1997, chap. 2. http://www.folkekirken.dk/udvalg/partnerskab.

[91]  Section 4 of the Danish Registered Partnerships Act 1989 states the provisions of the Adoption Act does not apply to same-sex spouses. However, Law No. 360 of 2 June, 1999 s.2 has amended this by allowing a registered partner to adopt the other partner's child, unless the child is adopted from a foreign country.

[92]  This was backed by Mayor of London, Ken Livingstone, and first proposed in summer 2000. The first ever ceremony was held on September 5, 2001. The ceremonies will be held at Greater London Authority's headquarters. There is no legal standing as of yet, but costs £85.00 and is also open to heterosexual couples.

[93]  Lord Lester of Herne Hill introduced a bill in January 2002 that was eventually tabled. It was expected that the bill would be re-submitted in the next session of Parliament. Moreover, on December 6, 2002, Social Exclusion Minister Barbara Roche announced that plans for a civil partnership scheme for same-sex couples would be out in the summer of 2003. http://www.labour.org.uk.

[94]  JORGE MARTIN, "English Polygamy Law and the Danish Registered Partnership Act: A Case for the Consistent Treatment of Foreign Polygamous Marriages in England ", (1994) 27 *Cornell International Law Journal* 419.

[95]  See also A. SULLIVAN, *Same-Sex Marriage – Pro and Con – A Reader* (Vintage Books, Random House, New York, 1997).

from several legal academics and practitioners who have written about this problem in the United States.[96] In particular, Mary Bonauto, Civil Rights Director of the Gay and Lesbian Advocates and Defenders, puts forth several arguments that stem from private international law and constitutional law in favour of recognition.[97] From the perspective of private international law, Bonauto acknowledges that several states have become signatory to the Uniform Marriage and Divorce Act (UMDA)[98] which has specific wording for recognising out-of-state legislation. Non-recognition of a registered partnership conflicts with UMDA's policy of marriage recognition. Thereby, the registered partnership is likely to be recognised outside it was contracted. Short of being a signatory to UMDA, Bonauto reasons that if the court looks to basic choice-of-law conflicts principles, there is authority for the recognition of the registered partnership.[99] She discusses that if the court looks to the better law of the marriage, or if the court gives predominance to the *lex loci celebrationis*, or looks to the law of the most significant relationship of the parties, the same-sex partnership should be recognised. Moreover, she states that non-recognition would throw people's lives into chaos and disarray in relation to many legal rights and obligations.

Following Bonauto's reasoning, the equivalent arguments for recognition can also be found in English private international law. English private international law could recognise a partnership by giving predominance to the present marriage recognition rules by relying upon the law of the place of the celebration and the law of the domicile. While this method is a simple way of recognition, it is submitted that Bonauto (and the other academics who have written upon this topic) is, in fact, ignoring a more complex question – what is in a name?

---

[96]   L. KRAMER, "How About a Nice Hawaiian Punch? Same-Sex Marriage, Conflict of Laws, and the Unconstitutional Public Policy Exception", *Yale Law Journal* Vol 106, No 7 (1997) KRAMER argues that non-recognition is nonsensical. Also, S. KREIMER, "Territoriality and Moral Dissensus: Thoughts on Abortion, Slavery, Gay Marriage and Family Values", *Quinnipac Law Review*, Vol. 16 (1997) Kreimer argues that the court should have regard for family values and recognise a loving relationship if contracted validly in the state of the domicile.

[97]   MARY L. BONAUTO, "The Freedom to Marry for Same-Sex Couples in the United States of America" in R. WINTEMUTE and M. ANDENAS (eds.), *Legal Recognition of Same-Sex Partnerships; A Study of National, European and International Law* (Oxford, Portland, Oregon, 2001), pp. 177-207.

[98]   UMDA, s. 210, 9 Uniform Laws Annotated 176 (1987).

[99]   *Ibid.* n. 96 at 204-205 when BONAUTO finds support for recognition in basic choice of laws principles in the *Restatement (Second) of the Conflict of Laws*, s.283(1) (1971) and in B. CURRIE, *Selected Essays in the Conflict of Laws.* (Durham, NC, Duke University Press, 1963) at p. 90 and also in R.A. LEFLAR, "Choice-Influencing Considerations in Conflicts Law", (1966) *New York University Law Review* 267.

## 5.2.2.  What is in a name?

Should a Civil Union or a Registered Partnership even be considered a marriage, and thereby, allowed recognition in English law? Again, the problem is one of classification rather than exclusion. Is the "name" even relevant when considering recognition? For example, if one country has a registered partnership, does this automatically allow recognition of registered partnerships from other countries? Or, if a country does not have a registered partnership, but has the institution of marriage, should it allow a foreign registered partnership in as equivalent to a marriage? There are now two cases for England to consider if recognition of a registered partnership should come forth.

## 5.2.3.  Burns v. Freer –A Lesson from the United States?

Darian and Susan Burns were divorced in December 1995 after seven years of marriage, during which they had three children. Susan then met Debra Jean Freer, moved to Atlanta, and then entered into a civil union ceremony in Vermont. Susan had her name legally changed to Freer. When Darian had custody of the children in 1998, he cut off visitation rights for Susan. The basis for his decision referred to a custody agreement that prohibited visitation and residence "by the children with either party during any time where such party cohabits with or has overnight stays with any adult to whom party is not married to or to whom party is not related."[100] On January 30, 2001, Floyd County Superior Court Judge Larry Salmon held that an out-of-state civil union could not be deemed the equivalent of a marriage and ruled against Debra. The American Civil Liberties Union argued that the Vermont civil union should be recognised as a marriage because it was a relationship under the second degree. Georgia law provides for relationships by blood (first degree) and relationships that are non-blood (second degree). The ACLU called for a legal definition of the what "related" means, and furthermore, pronounced that Freer's constitutional rights are being violated. However, on January 23, 2002, a Georgia appeals court[101] ruled that a civil union is not equal to a marriage.

The experts are divided in their opinion as to what would be the legal ramifications of this case. It has been argued that the ruling was only by a state court and therefore, does not apply to any other court outside Georgia. Whether the decision will impact decisions within Georgia is also

---

[100]   *Ibid.* n. 99.
[101]   Georgia State Court of Appeals at http://www.lambdalegal.org/cgi-bin/iowa/cases/record?record=166.

questionable. Professor Barbara Cox stated, "We are going down a path of accepting a status that changes drastically from location to location in a way that no one in a heterosexual marriage would say is acceptable at all."[102] Understandably, since this the first case that has arisen, the ramifications of the decision have yet to unfold. While the decision is not binding upon English law, it should be of importance if England has a test case in the near future.

### 5.2.4.  D. & Sweden v. Council –A  Lesson from the European Court of Justice?

Another example regarding the classification of a registered partnership originates closer to home. In *D. & Sweden v. Council*,[103] the Council refused to treat a Swedish same-sex registered partnership of a Council employee as equivalent to a marriage in relation to an employment benefit. While the Court of First Instance dismissed D.'s action for an annulment, the case was taken to the European Court of Justice. The ECJ dismissed the appeal. The Court's reasons for dismissal were are follows. First, the court decided that the European Community Staff Regulations, which provided for payment of a household allowance to a married official did not apply to a registered partnership. Secondly, it was also established that an unregistered same-sex cohabitation (two same-sex couples living together without the protection of a official status) was not necessarily equivalent to marriage. Furthermore, the court emphasised that a "marriage means a union of two people of the opposite sex" and, that the many European statutory arrangements protecting same-sex couples are, in fact, distinct from marriage.

### 5.3.  *Recommendations for English Recognition of a Foreign Registered Partnership*

If a registered partnership comes forth to be recognised by an English court, it is hoped that the court will deliver a reasoned judgement before simply trumping the status as offensive to public policy. If the English follows the recent judgements in *D. & Sweden v. Council* and *Burns v. Burns*, the registered partnership or civil union is *not* equivalent to a marriage. However, these decisions are in no way binding upon the English court. Therefore, the English court is free to utilise the existing marriage recognition rules and allow full recognition for a foreign registered partnership. Furthermore, it should be queried as to whether the refusal

---

[102]   *The Advocate*, March 5, 2002 at http://www.advocate.com/html/stories/858/858_freer.asp.
[103]   Joined Cases C-122/99 P, and C-125/99 P [2001] ECR I – 4319 also at http://europa.eu.int.

of the European Court of Justice and the Georgia court is merely another way of using public policy? If so, the English court should refrain from judicial ambiguity and be courageous enough to give a lenient interpretation and allow recognition to a valid foreign-registered partnership. Otherwise, recognition will only come about in a forced manner when new legislation from Europe is implemented.

## 6. SAME-SEX MARRIAGE

In the Netherlands, a registered partnerships bill was introduced in Parliament in 1997.[104] The bill was approved and entered into operation on January 1, 1998. Hundreds of rights and obligations were made available to same-sex couples that were previously open to only heterosexual couples. However, there were still some differences from marriage in relation to parenting, immigration and pensions. Given the country's political climate, the time was right for the push for full equality and therefore, full marriage. Between 1999 and 2000, several bills went through Parliament, which sought to "equalise" registered partnerships in relation to parenting, immigration and pensions with marriage. In July 1999, a bill was finally introduced which proposed opening up marriage to partners of the same sex. Finally, on April 1, 2001, the Netherlands became the first country in the world to allow same-sex partners to wed.[105]

### 6.1. Recognition of a Foreign Same-Sex Marriage in English Law

In this author"s opinion, a foreign same-sex marriage will not be recognised by the English court at this moment in time. Full marriage for same-sex couples is not as common as a registered partnership. The Netherlands was the first country in the world to have opened marriage up to homosexuals. As examined earlier, recognition of a full marriage is theoretically possible under the current marriage recognition rules, but "public policy" would deem a full marriage as still offensive as opposed to the registered partnership.

Moreover, it is unlikely that English law will open up full marriage to same-sex couples domestically. Even if Parliament is successful in passing

---

[104] Presently, only the Netherlands has full marriage for same-sex partners. However, in December 2002, other countries such as Belgium and Switzerland have proposed laws that would give homosexual partners the same rights as their heterosexual counterparts.

[105] See M. ANTOKOLSKAIA and K. BOELE-WOELKI, "Dutch Family Law in the 21st Century: Trend-Setting and Straggling Behind at the Same Time", *Netherlands Reports to the Sixteenth International Congress of Comparative Law* (December 2002); Vol 6.4 *Electronic Journal of Comparative Law*. at website http://www.ejcl.org.

the Civil Partnerships Bill, the status would still be "second class" to heterosexual marriage. Judging from the time frame in which the first registered partnership was enacted in 1989, to the proliferation of partnerships today, it is predicted that recognition by the English court of a foreign same-sex marriage will take several more years.

## 6.2. Which partnership from Europe is most likely to be recognised?

Of all the new partnership forms examined in this paper, it is this author's assertion that the same-sex marriage is the *least likely* to be recognised in English private international law. On the other hand, the time is ready for recognition of a foreign registered partnership simply because of the number of jurisdictions worldwide that have enacted this status. However, as discussed earlier, the debate still rages as to whether it should be equivalent to a marriage. Furthermore, the recognition of cohabitation contracts and cohabitation legislation is far too problematic for English law because of the difficulties that lie in classification, and association with the law of contract.

In today's climate, the English court cannot use sexual orientation *solely* as a ground of non-recognition, and declare homosexuality as repugnant and offensive when considering a valid foreign status. Societal mores and public opinion towards homosexuality and different family forms have changed drastically, particularly within the last several years. What may have been considered repugnant twenty years ago may not be considered repugnant today. Although England was progressive enough to be the first country in the world to decriminalise homosexuality,[106] the acceptance of the homosexual family form has been slow in English law.[107]

Throughout the years, pressure for recognition has been gradually growing internally through case law, debates on the "interpretation" of existing statutory legislation and political pressure. On the other hand, pressure for recognition, and therefore, restraint of the use of the doctrine of public policy, also stems from developments at European level and through the use of international law. In this manner, English law has been literally forced to change its notion of what is repugnant.

---

[106] Decriminalisation of most sex of men over the age of 21 took place in England and Wales in 1967, in Scotland in 1980 and in Northern Ireland in 1982.

[107] R. BAILEY-HARRIS, "New Families for a New Society?" in S. CRETNEY (ed.), *Family Law; Essays for the new Millennium* (Bristol, Jordan, 2000) in which she argues that there is a hierarchy of family forms in England with the homosexual family form being the lowest ranking.

## 7. CONCLUSIONS

This paper set out to analyse the main forms of partnerships prevalent in Europe, and assess the chances of recognition in England for each one. Since the nature of marriage has changed, and Lord Penzance's dictum no longer holds, English law should re-examine the institution of marriage. While the Civil Partnerships Bill is welcomed[108] for the protection of same-sex partners, this author recommends that a completely new definition of marriage should be considered for English family law. The restructuring of the family should emphasise a union or commitment based on two people, regardless of sex.

Given the many policy changes under national, European and international law, the time seems ripe to allow recognition of, *at the very least* a foreign transsexual marriage and a foreign same-sex partnership. As examined earlier in this paper, other forms of partnerships (other than a foreign same-sex marriage) are likely to be refused due to the lack of appropriate mechanisms in English private international law, and not upon the grounds of public policy.

Undoubtedly, the possibility of a European family law[109] with a community of shared values, may completely eliminate the need for the exclusionary discretion of public policy under the respective national laws. Until that time, it is imperative that English private international law takes the initiative to re-formulate the existing marriage recognition rules. If a test case were to come forth in the near future, the English judiciary should endeavour to deliver a fully reasoned judgement before blindly resorting to the escape route of public policy. It is hoped that the English court will not view the first case as an exercise in social engineering to promote the traditional, heterosexual notion of marriage, but seize the opportunity to explore possible solutions to a problem, which is going to be commonly experienced by many countries. By developing new marriage recognition rules and delivering fully reasoned judgements, English law will not only uphold the legitimate expectations of individuals worldwide, but propel English private international law into the millennium.

---

[108] See n. 93.
[109] See K. BOELE-WOELKI, "The Road Towards a European Family Law", vol. 1.1 *Electronic Journal of Comparative Law* (November 1997) http://www.ejcl.org/ejcl.11/art11-1.html.

# NEW FORMS OF COHABITATION: PRIVATE INTERNATIONAL LAW ASPECTS OF REGISTERED PARTNERSHIPS

SANDRINE HENNERON

This article focuses on the lack of international rules available to address legal issues raised by registered partnerships in International Family law. The following thoughts are largely based on French law and, in particular, on the French "Pacte Civil de Solidarité" (hereafter referred to as "PACS"), which literally translated means "Civil Pact of Solidarity". My research has led me to two proposals. The first proposal concerns the appropriate international law category for registered partnerships. The second proposal concerns the applicable law with respect to registered partnerships. Hence, this paper may have as its subtitle: Private International Law aspects of registered partnerships. Inasmuch as the registered partnership is a legal concept shared by more and more countries, these proposals may not only concern French family law, but may also be a step toward the unification of family law in Europe.

The emergence of registered partnerships throughout Europe is one of the most striking features of the current means of cohabitation. Indeed, many European legislators have enacted laws to provide rights to unmarried couples.[1] Nevertheless, it does not appear to be a uniform trend in Europe because of the diversity of opinions. Unlike France, Belgium, Spain and the Netherlands, northern countries have restricted registered partnerships to homosexual couples. Moreover, all countries, except the Netherlands,[2] reject same-sex marriages. Hence, the idea of giving rights to unmarried couples is increasing in Europe, but in a pattern without any recognizable order.

However, within this apparent disorder, some order does exist. Within the variable forms of registered partnerships in Europe, some common aspects

---

[1]    For example: Denmark – Bill of June 7th, 1989; Norway – Bill of April 30th, 1993; Sweden – Bill of June 23rd, 1994; Iceland – Bill of June 4th, 1996; France – Loi relative au pacte civil de solidarité du 15 November 1999; Belgium – Loi relative à la cohabitation légale du 29 octobre 1998.
[2]    Bill of December 21st, 2001.

allow this issue to be considered as a common issue among European countries.

European legislators, under social pressure, first provided rights to couples whose unions were still not legally recognized. This trend continues to evolve as in Italy where homosexual associations are requesting a "civil union".[3] In addition, such couples have to be distinguished from *de facto* couples that choose to remain unmarried. Indeed, not only are the registered partnerships legally recognized, but they are also bound through a ceremony establishing rights and obligations. They are commonly called "registered partnerships" due to the legal recognition, which results from their registration.

European legislations creating a new status for couples have two basic common features:
- Couples that were not legally recognized now exist both from a social and a legal point of view.
- These couples are distinct from previously existing forms of unions.

Today, adoption by same-sex partners still involves debated questions that could interfere with an international family law outlook. Indeed, international family law issues have for the most part arisen due to the mobility of registered partners in Europe. However, this article will concentrate on the relations between the couple, i.e. between the partners. Accordingly, parenthood and especially adoption will not be included.

Despite the above-mentioned common features, European legislators have enacted laws from a purely national point of view without any concern for a common European view. Indeed, it is a legislative habit that no consideration is ever given to potentially conflicting national laws. For instance, the ramifications are unknown if a couple registered under the provisions of the French Civil Pact of Solidarity move to a foreign country. A registered partnership can also be entered into between a French person and a foreign national. French law does not lay down any prohibitions for a case of this kind. In fact, in France, the PACS constitutes one of the legal criteria for a personal relationship in support of an application for legal residence.[4] Once again, no rules are provided concerning international aspects beyond France, i.e. whether the national law of the foreign partner recognizes the

---

[3]     *Revue Juridique Personnes & Famille (RJPF)*, novembre 2002, n° 11, p. 5.

[4]     Article 12 *bis*–4° ordonnance du 2 novembre 1945; "Obtention d'un titre de séjour portant mention "vie privée et familiale" pour la personne étrangère d'un couple homosexuel", *JCP*, éd. N, 2000, p. 621.

registered partnership, or whether the national law of the foreign partner ignores such a partnership.

Due to the mobility of people in Europe, potential conflicts between laws may also be on the increase. Does the fact that France recognizes a form of registered partnership mean that the French legal system recognizes other foreign registered partnerships? According to the variable forms of registered partnerships in Europe, the main issue under discussion deals with their reciprocal recognition in every country. The paradox is that it appears to be easier to legally recognize foreign marriages, even polyga-mous marriages[5] or marriages under Muslim law that stem from totally different cultures, than to provide automatic rights to foreign registered partnerships.

In Private International Law, we are faced with the issue of the legal definition of these partnerships. Some partnerships (Scandinavian) seem to be akin to marriage, while others (France, Belgium and Spain) are akin to a contract even though they influence personal status. In a classical way, these two similarities could lead to two possible legal classifications: either marriage or contract.

The application of the same law could be attained if the institutions had the same nature as a marriage or contract, which does not appear to be the case. Hence, it is necessary to classify these unions in a new autono-mous Private International Law category, based upon some minimum shared standards. Then, legal ties could be proposed to resolve conflict of laws concerning registered partnerships.

## 1.  THE PRIVATE INTERNATIONAL LAW CATEGORY

In searching for an international law category, two options can be identified: registered partnerships could be linked to an existing category or they could emerge as a new autonomous category. According to the legal definition of the Civil Pact of Solidarity (and the other registered partners-hips), the first option seems to be inappropriate, which will naturally lead us to the second.

---

[5]    Cass. Civ. 1ère, 28 janvier 1958, *D*, 1958, p. 265, LENOAN; *JCP*, 1958, II, 10 488, LOUIS-LUCAS: the French Cour de Cassation ruled that the second spouse of a Tunisian man, whose marriage was lawfully celebrated in Tunisia, could claim her status as a legitimate spouse in order to obtain maintenance from her husband.

## 1.1. The lack of opportunity for a link to an existing Private International Law category

There are two reasons that justify this notion.

### 1.1.1. Registered partnerships are not marriages

Throughout the last three decades in French law, the notion of a couple has evolved in accordance with a general trend of diversification inherent in ways of living together. Cohabitation, as a *de facto* marriage, has been given legal effect by the courts and by laws on welfare and leasehold property. In addition, cohabitation, or "concubinage" in French, was defined in the French Civil Code by the law of November 15th 1999 (Civil Code, article 515-8). Even if there is no legal effect attached to the concubinage's legal definition, it shows a clear diversification of sexual unions legally recognized by the French system. Now, there are three competing kinds of couples: marriage, concubinage and PACS. These three forms of unions represent different degrees of commitments: *de facto* marriages do not imply the same level or type of recognition by society as marriage or even PACS do.

This trend appears to be similar throughout Europe, where different kinds of couples coexist. However, in every country, each method of living together means something specific and cannot be considered equivalent to another type of couple. If Scandinavian registered partnerships have the same legal consequences as entering into a marriage, it only means that they are closer to marriage than the PACS or Belgian cohabitation. Indeed, the main provisions dealing with marriage and spouses are to be applied correspondingly to registered partnerships and registered partners. For example, under Scandinavian law, the provisions governing the division of property between spouses, the legislation on social security and income tax, and also the provisions on divorce also apply to registered partnerships.[6] Nevertheless, some other provisions dealing with marriage cannot be applied correspondingly to registered partnerships. For instance, the Danish regulations governing church marriage ceremonies cannot apply to registered partnerships.[7] Likewise, according to the Norwegian Ministry of Children and Family Affairs, "Registration is not equivalent to marriage".[8]

---

[6] See PINTENS, "Europeanisation of Family Law", in this book, p. 3.

[7] DINESEN, "L'initiative scandinave: le partenariat enregistré", in *Des concubinages. Droit interne. Droit international. Droit comparé*, Litec, 2002, p. 419.

[8] The Norwegian Act on Registered Partnerships for homosexual couples. Bill submitted by the government to the Storting in December 1992, article 6.1.

In conclusion, registered partnerships are not equivalent to marriages. Technical and pragmatic practices applying provisions dealing with marriage to registered partnerships are only practices. Institutions remain different depending upon the type of commitment involved and upon some specific conditions relating to celebration and some specific effects.[9]

The parallels between a registered partnership and a marriage deal with the consequences of two people living together in a permanent relationship. These common provisions can be considered as a fundamental law relating to any couple, regardless of the legal form. Indeed, living together entails the same problems for spouses, as it does for cohabitants or registered partners. Therefore, the need for regulations arises in the same way, which logically leads to the application of the same provisions. Accordingly, the Scandinavian way of thinking does not appear to be far removed from the French one. Under French law, beyond different technical regulations relating to couples, there appears a common basic status dealing with the notion of "communauté de vie" or community life.[10] As far as a provision concerning this legal notion is concerned, regulations are equivalent to each other, no matter what form the couple takes: marriage, concubinage or PACS. That is why economic and social rights, as well as duties, apply to every couple.

However, some differences remain, based on the commitment's intensity and nature. The Dutch legislator has taken these differences into account by admitting registered partnerships, on the one hand, and same-sex marriages on the other. More generally, when people say that registered partnerships are "*like* marriage", it is clear that it *does not mean* that it *is* a marriage. Rather, it resembles a confession: registered partnerships are not marriages.

Consequently, the category of marriage is not appropriate, even if Scandinavian partnerships are very close to that union. Indeed, the legal approach differentiates between types of couples, providing different legal statuses to various kinds of unions.

This first idea shows the lack of opportunity to link registered partnerships to the Private International Law category of marriage. The lack of opportunity for a link to an existing international law category is also evidenced by a second idea: registered partnerships are not contracts.

---

[9] The main one is to consider the question of children independently from the question of the couple.

[10] HENNERON, *La notion de famille en droit positif français*, Thesis – University of Lille II, 2002, n° 227.

### 1.1.2. Registered partnerships are not contracts

We will start with the legal definition of the PACS. Article 515-1 of the French Civil Code provides that: "A civil pact of solidarity is a **contract** [....]". Some aspects of this particular form of registered partnership take after general contractual obligations, such as, for example, the termination of the Civil Pact of Solidarity. Indeed, a unilateral dissolution of the Civil Pact of Solidarity is possible on the basis of a contract law principle. Under article 1780 of the Civil Code perpetual commitments are forbidden: nobody can commit oneself for an undefined time without being able to terminate the contract at will. The French legislator has just applied this old contract law principle to the PACS by allowing unilateral dissolution.[11]

However, beyond the letter of the text, the legal definition of the PACS does not square exactly with the contract category. Indeed, the PACS status deals with the couple's organisation of personal relations amongst themselves. The French constitutional council called it a "specific contract" and stressed that the subject matter of this contract is "une vie de couple": "a life as a couple".[12] And by "life as a couple", the constitutional council merely stated that the Civil Pact of Solidarity means more than living together as a community of interests. The PACS involves more than material/proprietary aspects. Even if the PACS does not deal with the notion of the family,[13] it does involve consequences for each partner's personal status. By this analysis, the PACS is more than a contract.

Moreover, we should keep in mind that marriage is also partly akin to a contract.[14] Nevertheless, this assertion does not mean that marriage could be considered to be a contract in Private International Law issues. Along the same lines, saying that southern European registered partnerships involve contract law aspects should not automatically lead to classifying such partnerships as being in the Private International Law contract category.

Finally, both northern and southern kinds of registered partnerships deal with personal status, even if the southern ones are more akin to contract. The common point is the couple's organization of personal relations amongst themselves.

---

[11] DEKEUWER-DEFOSSEZ, "PACS et famille. Retour sur l'analyse juridique d'un contrat controversé", *RTD civ.*, 2001, p. 529.

[12] Décision n° 99-419 DC, *JO*, 16 novembre 1999, p. 16962.

[13] HENNERON, *La notion de famille en droit positif français, op. cit.*

[14] MEULDERS-KLEIN, "L'évolution du mariage: de l'institution au contrat", in *La personne, la famille, le droit. Trois décennies de mutation en Occident*, Bruylant, 1999, p. 35.

As a consequence, registered partnerships have to be distinguished from both marriage and contract. This observation leads us to the idea that the different registered partnerships have to be treated in the same way.[15] Even if some are akin to marriage and others are akin to contract, none of them is really a marriage or a contract. Hence, the lack of opportunity for a link to an existing private international law category.

The category of registered partnerships also has to be found elsewhere. We shall now consider what this category might be.

### 1.2. The opportunity for the creation of an autonomous Private International Law category

Creating a new legal category each time a relationship does not appear to be clearly defined could seem to be a solution that is somewhat too loose. However, when this relationship cannot be exactly linked with an existing category, it may be the only solution. Private International Law has to consider this. Thus, registered partnerships appear as an autonomous category within the general category of personal status.[16]

This autonomous category would respect the new concept by giving it its own rules, as far as it is a concept that is independent of marriage and contract. The area of personal status is also appropriate due to the purpose of the partnership. As a type of couple, it refers to the personal situation of the partners. As we have previously indicated, beyond the various kinds of unions (partnerships, marriage, concubinage), the background always deals with the personal status of the partners, even if it is not clearly expressed by the law. Indeed, it constitutes a legal framework for patrimonial and personal relations between two adults. These two aspects are shared by every registered partnership with different degrees of consideration.

The determination of the category to which registered partnerships pertain, leads us to propose nexuses for the determination of the applicable law in a conflict of laws context.

---

[15] Contra: KHAIRALLAH, "Les "partenariats organisés" en droit international privé (Propos autour de la loi du 15 novembre 1999 sur le pacte civil de solidarité)", *Rev. Crit. Dr. Internat. Privé*, 2000, p. 317; MIGNOT, "Le partenariat enregistré en droit international privé", *RIDC*, 2001, p. 601: the authors make distinctions between partnerships with a direct influence on personal status and PACS-type partnerships.
[16] FULCHIRON, "Réflexions sur les unions hors mariage en droit international privé", *JDI*, 4, 2000, p. 889.

## 2. THE APPLICABLE LAW

If registered partnerships are an autonomous category, the possible ties have to be considered independently from rules governing marriage or contract.

### 2.1. Ties to be rejected

Some links should be rejected because of their consequences. For instance, the link to the personal law of the parties would raise problems instead of solving them. On the one hand, this link is sufficiently permanent to take permanent relationships into account. But, on the other hand, the personal law of the partner may not correspond to the law governing the registration of the partnership. That means that certain effects, which would be given to the registered partnership, could be very different from those expected by the partners at the time of registration.

To link registered partnerships to the *lex fori* (the law of the State in whose courts a case is pending) presents the same criticisms. In addition, this link to the *lex fori* could be artificial whenever there is no other connection, such as the citizenship of one partner, or the State law under which the partnership was registered.

### 2.2. Tie to be proposed

Due to the variability in the effects of registered partnerships in Europe, the solution might be found in a link to institutional law,[17] meaning the law of the country where the partnership is registered. Since there are various forms of registered partnerships, the best solution remains to link them to the registration law, being the law of the country under which the partners choose to enter into a registered partnership. French partners in a PACS would have no personal obligations, unlike Scandinavian partners. This link to the registration law would allow the recognition of each type of partnership all over Europe under the best circumstances. Indeed, differences between registered partnerships imply that a particular status should not be applied instead of another.[18]

The nexus of the registration law would address the partner's need for a foreseeable applicable law. Once the partners make their final choice to

---

[17]    FULCHIRON, *op. cit.*
[18]    *Idem.*

have their partnership registered, they would have certainty as to which law applies to their specific relationship, regardless of their mobility in Europe. Moreover, the stability of this connection is well suited to long-term relationships as in the case of couples.

This solution certainly presents some drawbacks. The first deals with the acknowledgement of foreign laws. One should not emphasize this limit insofar as it represents a general limit concerning any Private International Law issue. A second drawback concerns the risk of polygamous registered partnerships. Since this issue arises in the same way as polygamous marriages arise, a parallel solution could be found. For instance, each national law could easily provide that the second registration grants no legal effect since it is unlawful to enter into two registered partnerships at the same time.

Yet this proposal is aimed at discerning a coherent framework with respect to international legal issues. This framework allows one to legally distinguish registered partnerships from other couples within an evolving social pattern. The classification of competing types of couples also leads to a coherent link: the registration law. The diversity of the contents of registered partnerships would be respected, while there would be less uncertainty in determining the applicable law.

As of today, the keyword in the field of personal relationships is "diversity". Private International Law could embrace this diversity, taking advantage of such diversity rather than ignoring it. What could characterize such a shift in International family law would be less the harmonization of national rules and more the unification of State provisions concerning conflicts of laws.

# BRUSSELS II AND BEYOND: A BETTER DEAL FOR CHILDREN IN THE EUROPEAN UNION?

HELEN STALFORD[*]

## 1. INTRODUCTION

The ongoing debate over the legitimacy and appropriateness of EU intervention in the family law arena has raised a number of complex issues. Certain scholars have pointed to the need to safeguard the cultural, ideological, political and economic heritage underpinning domestic systems of family law.[1] Others have highlighted the superfluous nature of EU intervention in an area already regulated by a comprehensive range of private international law measures.[2] Despite these well voiced and, in many cases, well-founded objections, the past three years in particular, have witnessed the rapid crystallisation of a European family law. Moreover, the emphasis has steadily shifted from more pragmatic concerns to co-ordinate mutual recognition and enforcement of decisions between Member States towards a more ideological consideration of the possibilities of harmonising substantive family law measures.

A less commonly articulated concern, however, is the extent to which EU family instruments take into account the interests of children involved in cross-national family proceedings.[3] Unfortunately, the CEFL conference in December failed to fully-exploit the opportunity to generate critical discussion as to the children's rights implications of the EU family agenda.[4]

---

[*]  The author is grateful to Eric Donnelly for his invaluable research assistance in the preparation of this contribution.

[1]  For a pre-Amsterdam Treaty discussion of the perceived implications of EU regulation of family law, see BEAUMONT and MOIR (1995) "Brussels Convention II: A New Private International Law Instrument in Family Matters for the European Union or the European Community?" 20 *E.L. Rev* 268; LOWE, N. (2001) "New International Conventions Affecting the Law Relating to Children – A Cause for Concern?", *International Family Law,* 171.

[2]  See for example, MCELEAVEY, P. (2002) "The Brussels II Regulation: How the European Community has moved into Family Law", *International and Comparative Law Quarterly,* Volume 51, Issue 4, pp. 883-908.

[3]  The short piece by Michael Nicholls represents one of the few analyses of the impact of recent EU family measures on children although this is confined to a largely descriptive outline of the provisions of Brussels II. NICHOLLS, M. "Children and Brussels II" *Family Law* Vol. 31, p. 368.

[4]  In fact, only three papers throughout the three-day conference directly addressed this issue.

This oversight largely reflects the absence of any significant child-focused provision within the "Brussels I"[5] and "II"[6] Regulations and the traditional reluctance to engage in children's rights debates within an EU context. Indeed, most discussion as to the status of the child under EU law has traditionally been subsumed by more general debates as to the entitlement afforded to family members under the free movement provisions.

More recently, NGO campaigns,[7] complemented by a modest, yet growing body of academic research[8] have achieved much in drawing attention to the children's rights deficit in EU law and policy-making and separating out the needs of the child from those of the wider migrant family. The status of children both as independent rights-bearers under Community law, however, remains decidedly underdeveloped. It is with some optimism, therefore, that the Title IV (Articles 61-69) EC measures should be received, as representing a fertile and long overdue opportunity to directly address children's rights concerns within the EU.

This paper critiques the extent to which the EU institutions have embraced this opportunity. It discusses first of all how and why Title IV provides a more legitimate basis for Community intervention in the children's rights arena through a more detailed examination of the nature and scope of existing and proposed child-focused measures. Acknowledging a more explicit children's rights component within this legislation, the discussion will then consider precisely what conception of children's rights underpins it and the extent to which this is consistent with and reinforces internatio-nal obligations and domestic provision in this regard. Drawing on available

---

[5]   Regulation 44/2001 of 22nd December 2000, on jurisdiction and the recognition of judgments in civil and commercial matters *OJ* L012, 16/01/2001, p. 0001-0023, Implemen-ted on 1st March 2002.

[6]   EC Regulation 1347/2000 of May 29, 2000 on jurisdiction and the recognition and enforcement of judgments in matrimonial matters and in matters of parental responsibility for the children of both spouses. *OJ* L 160, 30/06/2000, p. 0019-0029.

[7]   Such as that of the European Children's Network (EURONET) and the European Forum for Child Welfare (EFCW), See RUXTON, S. (1999) "A Children's Policy for the 21st Century: First Steps" The European Children's Network (EURONET); LANSDOWN, G. (2000) *Challenging Discrimination Against Children in the EU: A Policy Proposal by EURONET*, Brussels: DGV European Commission; and EFCW (2002) *Child Justice: Equal Justice? – The right to be heard and the issue of discrimination against children* Brussels: EFCW.

[8]   See RUXTON, S. (1997) *Children in Europe*, London: NCH Action for Children; STALFORD, H. (2000) "The citizenship status of children in the European Union" *International Journal of Children's Rights*, Vol. 8, No. 2, pp. 101-131; ACKERS, L. and STALFORD, H. (forthcoming) *A Community for Children?: Children, Citizenship and Migration in the European Community*, London: Ashgate; and CULLEN, H. (forthcoming) "Children's Rights and the Charter" in WARD, A. CARROZA, P. and S. PEERS, S. (eds.), *The European Union Charter of Fundamental Rights: Context and Possibilities* (OUP).

empirical research, the article will then move on to consider the practical application of EU family measures and whether sufficient mechanisms are in place to sufficiently safeguard the best interests, needs and wishes of the child.

## 2. THE RIGHTS OF THE CHILD UNDER THE 'BRUSSELS" REGULATIONS

Title IV EC has yielded two important instruments which seek to regulate issues of jurisdiction, recognition and enforcement in "internal", cross-national family disputes: EC Regulation 44/2001 on jurisdiction and the recognition of judgments in civil and commercial matters ("Brussels I") and EC Regulation 1347/2000 ("Brussels II"). The former ensures the mutual recognition and enforceability of judgments in civil and commercial matters, including cross-national recognition and enforcement of child maintenance payments. The latter, on the other hand, governs matrimonial matters and matters of parental responsibility for the children of both spouses following divorce, marital separation or annulment.[9]

Both instruments were introduced with a view to removing any obstacles to cross-border mobility posed by unenforceable and ineffective divorce and parental responsibility orders, an inevitable consequence of which was to place family law issues, inasmuch as they impact upon the fluid application of free movement policy, firmly on the European agenda.

There is insufficient scope within this paper to rehearse the merits or otherwise of this development.[10] Suffice to day that many of the arguments up to now have concentrated more on the thorny issue of subsidiarity or private international law "ownership" of cross-national family regulation.

---

[9]     For a detailed account of the history behind these instruments and the content and scope of the provisions generally (aside from other papers included in this collection) see the Borrás Explanatory Report on the Brussels II Convention on jurisdiction and the recognition and enforcement of judgements in matrimonial matters, 1998 *OJ* C221/27; LOWE, N. (2001) "New International Conventions Affecting the Law Relating to Children – A Cause for Concern?", *International Family Law*, November Issue, pp. 171-181; MCELEAVEY, P. (2002) "The Brussels II Regulation: How the European Community has moved into Family Law", *International and Comparative Law Quarterly*, Volume 51, Issue 4, pp. 883-908; and STALFORD, H. (2003) "Regulating family Life in Post-Amsterdam Europe" 28(1) *European Law Review*, pp. 39-52.

[10]    Useful commentaries in this respect are provided in the edited collection of FAURE, M., SMITS, J., and SCHNEIDER, H. (2002) *Towards a European Ius Commune in Legal Education and Research*, Antwerp: Intersentia. See in particular the contribution of DIETER MARTINY, "The Harmonization of Family Law in the European Community: Pro and Contra", pp. 191-201. See also BOELE-WOELKI, K. (1997) "The Road Towards a European Family Law", Vol.1.1. *Electronic Journal of Comparative Law*, available at: http://www.ejcl.org/11/abs11-1.html.

Certainly, the practical impact of EU measures on the day-to-day experiences of children have been of largely tangential interest.

This is something of a surprise considering the emphasis that national systems and ideologies of family law now place on the welfare and rights of children. The substance and procedures espoused by English family law in particular have long since moved beyond the view that divorce is merely about renegotiating the relationship between two adults towards a prioritised concern to facilitate the ongoing relationship between parents and their children.[11] In that sense, children's rights have become integral to the application and success of domestic family law, as evidenced in the plethora of research units[12] and NGOs[13] that have emerged over the last decade and the burgeoning body of empirical research dedicated specifically to investigating and enhancing children's status in this regard.

The importance of this development has been reinforced and, indeed, triggered by activities in the international arena, notably by the introduction of the UN Convention on the Rights of the Child 1989. Indeed, it is difficult to imagine a system of private international law which would not regard as paramount the interests and needs of the child in cross-national contact, residence and maintenance disputes.[14]

Disappointingly, the EU has fallen far short of parallel international models in the formulation of Title IV measures. First of all, specific provision accommodating the rights or interests of the child remain conspicuously absent from the Brussels I Regulation – a predictable legacy perhaps of the

---

[11]  A brief history of children's rights within family law is provided by MAVIS MACLEAN in her paper, "Divorcing Families: The Economic Realities", contribution to the Care, Values and the Future of Welfare (CAVA) Seminar, University of Leeds, 21-22nd September 2001. See also, GOLLOP, M., SMITH, A.B., and TAYLOR, N.J. (2000) "Children's Involvement in custody and access arrangements" *Child and Family Law Quarterly*, 12(4) pp. 396-399; TRINDER, L. (1997) "Competing Constructions of childhood: children's rights and children's wishes in divorce" *Journal of Social Welfare and Family Law*, 19(3), pp. 291-305; and LYON, C. and PARTON, N. (1995) "Children's Rights and the Children Act 1989" in FRANKLIN, B. (ed.) *The Handbook of Children's Rights*, London: Routledge.

[12]  The Centre for Research on Family, Kinship and Childhood based at the University of Leeds, the Centre for the Social Study of Childhood at the University of Hull, the Centre for the Study of the Child, the Family and the Law at the University of Liverpool, the Centre for Family Research, University of Cambridge, to name but a few.

[13]  Such as One-Plus-One, Families Need Fathers, The Family Policy Studies Centre, National Council for One Parent Families and the National Family and Parenting Institute.

[14]  See for instance, Article 13(b) of the Hague Convention on the Civil Aspects of International Child Abduction 1980; and Articles 8, 9, 10, 22, 23, 28 and 33 of the Convention On Jurisdiction, Applicable Law, Recognition, Enforcement And Co-Operation In Respect Of Parental Responsibility And Measures For The Protection Of Children 1996.

1968 Convention on which it is based – although its personal scope remains as broad as it was under the 1968 Convention. The personal scope of the Brussels II Regulation, on the other hand, is limited to the biological or adopted children of a married couple seeking divorce, annulment or legal separation, thereby denying protection to step-children or children born to unmarried parents. Moreover, Brussels II makes only cursory reference to the rights or interests of the child. Article 3(2)(b), for instance, provides that the child's best interests will be taken into consideration in determining which jurisdiction is competent to decide on matters of parental responsibility. The second and final reference to the child is found in Article 15(2) which sets out the grounds for non-recognition of a parental responsibility order between Member States. These include cases where "(a) ...such recognition is manifestly contrary to the public policy of the Member State in which recognition is sought taking into account the best interests of the child";[15] and (b)...except in case of emergency, without the child having been given an opportunity to be heard, in violation of fundamental principles of procedure of the Member State in which recognition is sought."[16]

The lack of primacy afforded to the child under Brussels I and II confirms that the "European Family Law" to have emerged in the twenty-first Century is firmly entrenched in the traditional notion that divorce is primarily concerned with regulating the lives of adults and of only incidental importance to the child.

This stance is somewhat characteristic of the European Union's general approach to the child in other aspects of law and policy-making. Most notably, the free movement of persons provisions are notorious for their limited personal scope in that they apply only to the legally married, heterosexual migrant model.[17] The marginalised and highly vulnerable status of the children of migrant cohabitants, divorcees, and same-sex couples, particularly where one parent is of third country nationality, has been particularly heavily criticised.[18] Moreover, where children *are* in a

---

[15]   This provision corresponds with Article 23(2)(d) of the Hague Convention on Jurisdiction, Applicable Law, Recognition, Enforcement and Co-operation in respect of Parental Responsibility and Measures for the Protection of Children, 1996.

[16]   This corresponds with Article 23(2)(b) and (c) of the Hague Convention 1996.

[17]   Article 10, Regulation 1612/68 *OJ* Sp. *ed.* 1968, No. L257/2, p. 475.

[18]   See for examples, ACKERS, L. and STALFORD, H. (1999) "Children, Migration and Family Policy in the European Union: Intra-Community mobility and the status of children in EC law" in *Children and Youth Services Review* Vol. 21. Nos. 11/12 pp. 987-1010; and STYCHIN, C. "Consumption, Capitalism and the Citizen: Sexuality and Equality Rights Discourse in the European Union" in SHAW, J. (ed.) (2000) *Social Law and Policy in an Evolving European Union*, Oxford: Hart.

position to benefit from free movement entitlement, they can only do so as the indirect beneficiaries of rights that are attributed first and foremost to their parents or carers as economically active migrants.[19] Even more recent case law, whereby the ECJ has ostensibly afforded children more directly justiciable rights in respect of their education[20] or claims to social welfare,[21] are ultimately concerned with securing their parents' ongoing free movement and residence rights rather that enhancing children's status as Community citizens in their own right.[22]

The conflation of children's status with that of the family under the free movement provisions is mirrored in the Brussels I and II Regulations. This practice is based on an inherent presumption that the interests and needs of the child are coterminous with those of the parents and that parents will consistently and incontrovertibly act in the best interest of the child. It disregards not only the symbolic importance of acknowledging that children do indeed represent a distinct category of citizens with an independent voice and differing needs, but more disturbingly, ignores the very real personal dangers inherent in dispensing with children's views when making vital, life-changing decisions about custody and access.

## 3. THE PROPOSED BRUSSELS II AMENDMENTS AND THE RIGHTS OF THE CHILD

A more positive endorsement of children's rights at EU level is, however, on the horizon following a series of initiatives to incorporate more explicit reference to the interests and welfare of the child within the Brussels II Regulation.[23] These proposals have since been amalgamated into a revised

---

[19] See further, MOEBIUS, I. and SZYSZCZAK. E. (1998) "Of Raising Pigs and Children" *YEL*, Vol. 18, pp. 125-156; and STALFORD, H. (2000) "The citizenship status of children in the European Union" *International Journal of Children's Rights*, Vol. 8, No. 2, pp. 101-131.

[20] Case C-413/99, *Baumbast and "R"*, Judgment of the Court of 17th September 2002, 2002/C274/03.

[21] *Anna Humer* Case C-255/99, Reported 5th February 2002; and Case C-85/99, *Esther Offermanns and Vincent Offermanns* [2001] ECR I-02261.

[22] A similar observation is made by Holly Cullen, above note 8.

[23] See the European Commission Working Document on "Mutual Recognition of decisions on parental responsibility", Brussels 27th March 2001, *COM* (2001) 166 final; the French proposal to abolish *exequatur* as a means of facilitating the mutual enforcement of orders granting parents' international access to their under-16 children following divorce or separation *OJ* C234, 15.8.2000, p.7; and the Commission proposal to extend the existing Brussels II Regulation to *all* decisions on parental responsibility, including unmarried parents, Proposal for a Council Regulation on jurisdiction and the recognition and enforcement of judgments in matters of parental responsibility, *OJ* No C 332 of 27.11.2001, p. 269.

version of Brussels II, commonly referred to as "Brussels II *bis*".[24] The main amendments in respect of children's rights can be summarised as follows:

Firstly, the material scope of the revised Regulation is extended to the children of unmarried parents as well as stepchildren (Article 2(6)), mirroring similar amendments underway in the context of more general free movement provision.[25] The material scope of Brussels II has also altered, however, to incorporate a child's right to "maintain on a regular basis a personal relationship and direct contact with both parents, unless this is contrary to his or her interests." (Article 3). This measure echoes parallel International children's rights and family law provisions such as Article 9 of the 1989 UN Convention on the Rights of the Child.

Significantly, a new Article 4 provides a more concrete affirmation of the child's right to be heard: "A child shall have the right to be heard on matters relating to parental responsibility over him or her in accordance with his or her age and maturity".[26] This again, consolidates parallel supranational and domestic obligations in this regard.[27]

---

[24] For the full text of the proposed amendments, see Proposal for a Council Regulation concerning jurisdiction and the recognition and enforcement of judgments in matrimonial matters and in matters of parental responsibility repealing Regulation (EC) No 1347/2000 and amending Regulation (EC) 44/2001 in matters relating to maintenance, *COM* (2002) 222 final/2, 2002/0110 (CNS). The main amendments are described in STALFORD, H. and DONNELLY, E. (2002) "Brussels II revisited: an overview of proposed amendments", 32 *Family Law*, pp. 904-907.

[25] A proposed directive on free movement will radically overhaul and streamline the current cluster of free movement legislation and broaden the definition of family to grant third country nationals, divorcees and cohabitants a more secure status. Proposal for a European Parliament and Council Directive on the Right of Citizens of the Union and their Family Members to Move and Reside Freely within the Territory of the Member States, *COM* (2001) 257 final.

[26] The Commission has recommended that children be given an opportunity to be heard in a manner that is consistent with the procedure laid down in Council Regulation 1206/2001 of May 28 2001, *OJ* No L.174 of 27.6.2001, p.1. This Regulation is aimed at enhancing co-operation between the courts of the Member States in the taking of evidence in civil or commercial matters. It is important to note, however, that this instrument was not drafted specifically with children or other potentially "vulnerable witnesses" in mind and does not contain a single reference to children in family or other civil proceedings.

[27] See Article 12 of the UN Convention on the Rights of the Child; Article 13 of the Hague Convention on the Civil Aspects of International Child Abduction 1980; Article 24(1) of the Charter of Fundamental Rights in the European Union; Article 1(2)) of the European Convention on the Exercise of Children's Rights 1996, ETS No. 160; and Article 23 of the Hague Convention on the Protection of Children 1996. For an analysis of how this right has been operationalised at domestic level, see further, STALFORD, H. (forthcoming) "The voice of the child in international family proceedings: An EU perspective" *International Family Law.*

Perhaps the most apparent children's rights norm to be espoused by the amended Regulation, however, is in relation to the "best interests" principle, enshrined in Article 3 UNCRC. Articles 10-15, which determine the competent jurisdiction to regulate matters of parental responsibility, are anchored in a concern to protect and promote the best interests of the child. A similar ethic underpins other private international law measures.[28] The Member State in which the child is habitually resident, therefore, shall, as a general rule, have jurisdiction to rule on issues of parental responsibility (Article 10). Article 12(1) further provides that the Member State with jurisdiction to rule on matrimonial matters under Article 5 (divorce, legal separation or annulment) can also assume jurisdiction in matters of parental responsibility if it is agreed that this is in the best interests of the child (Article 12(1)(a)). Alternatively, in access and custody cases that are not linked to divorce or legal separation proceedings, those with parental responsibility can agree on a jurisdiction with which the child has a *"substantial connection"*. Evidence of "substantial connection" is supported by the habitual residence of the parents or the nationality of the child but, again, the paramount consideration is whether it is in the best interests of the child for a particular court to assume jurisdiction (Article 12(2)(c)). Finally, an amended Article 15 allows those with parental responsibility to request that jurisdiction to hear the case be transferred to another Member State on the basis that this is in the best interests of the child. Factors taken into consideration (by both the court transferring jurisdiction and the court receiving jurisdiction) in assessing whether a transfer of jurisdiction is in the child's best interests, relate to whether the child was previously habitually resident in the Member State in question; whether the child is a national of that Member State; whether the holders of parental responsibility are habitually resident there; or whether the child has property there.

These amendments to Brussels II suggest a much more genuine endeavour to engage with children's rights issues in the regulation of trans-national family life and to forge greater consistency with parallel and previously applicable international measures. Before heralding a new era in European children's rights, however, we need to look a little more closely at what precisely we mean by "children's rights" and what conception of children's rights underpins these new Brussels II measures.

---

[28] See for instance Article 5 of the Hague Convention on the protection of children 1996.

## 4. WHAT INTERPRETATION OF CHILDREN'S RIGHTS UNDERPINS THE BRUSSELS II AMENDMENTS?

Two fundamental principles are now universally acknowledged as underpinning children's rights: the "welfare" principle and the "agency" principle. The former is more firmly ingrained in traditional thinking about children's best interests which has been concerned more with protecting children against harm, poverty and exploitation. The latter represents a later development in the children's rights movement, particularly since the 1970s, acknowledging the need to empower children to make decisions for themselves or at least to enable then to participate more directly in decisions that affect them in accordance with their age and capacity. In that sense, it engages more with notions of children as active participants in decision-making rather than as passive recipients of provision.[29]

This paper has already referred to the fact that these two tenets received universal recognition and codification in the 1989 UN Convention on the Rights of the Child (Article 3 and 12 respectively) and continue to inform domestic, European and international law accordingly.[30] Both, of course, are equally instrumental to upholding the welfare and rights of the child in the context of family law, requiring legislatures and practitioners alike to conduct a fine balancing act between the two. Andrew Bainham[31] highlights the tensions inherent in this process, emphasising that the two notions are not synonymous; attention to children's *best interests* does not necessarily equate with promoting children's *rights* since it inevitably presumes a value-laden, adult assessment of what is best for the child in the given circumstances. English family law, for instance, has endeavoured to take these twin notions on board, at least formally, by virtue of instruments such as the Children Act 1989. Commentators have noted, however, that despite the rhetoric of children's rights and the reformulation of domestic family law to accommodate the agency principle alongside the welfare principle, empirical evidence suggests a lack of commitment to applying this in any meaningful way in post-divorce custody and access

---

[29]   For two different disciplinary perspectives on this evolution, see JAMES, A and PROUT, A. (eds.) (1990) *Constructing and Reconstructing Childhood: Contemporary Issues in the Sociological Study of Childhood*, London: Falmer Press; and BAINHAM, A. (1990) "The Privatisation of the Public Interest in Children", *The Modern Law Review*, Vol 53(2), pp. 206-221.

[30]   Article 24 of the Charter of Fundamental Rights in the European Union provides a recent illustration in this regard, as discussed by Cullen, above note 8.

[31]   BAINHAM, A. (2002) "Can we protect children and protect their rights", *Family Law*, (Vol. 32) April Issue, pp. 279-289.

negotiations.[32] Bainham illustrates this point by reference to the common practise in England to allow a custodial mother to take her child abroad following divorce or separation from the father, provided that it is reasonable and practical and not deliberately aimed at rupturing contact between the child and the father.[33] The tendency to favour the mother's application is often rationalised on the basis that to refuse leave to a mother would adversely affect her material and emotional well-being and inevitably impact detrimentally on the welfare of the child. Such unwavering commitment to the child's welfare in this instance, however, is clearly conflated with the welfare of the mother and neglects to take into account the child's *right* to maintain regular and direct contact with the father.[34]

This leads us to consider whether the EU institutions have embraced this more challenging and modern children's rights norm within their family law project. The changes to Brussels II outlined in the previous section emphasise the importance of safeguarding the child's best interests. Indeed, five out of the six provisions detailed above defer to the more protectionist best interests principle while only one provision affirms the child's independent right to be heard. While any explicit reference to the child within EU family law should be welcomed as a positive and novel development, the Brussels II amendments clearly articulate and endorse the "welfare" principle over and above the "agency" principle.

This apparent reluctance to endorse children's active and direct rights within cross-national family law carries with it some important consequences. First of all, it reinforces the paternalistic model of dependency that underpins traditional EU family legislation, suggesting that the institutions have failed to advance children's rights significantly beyond the 1960s free movement provisions. Secondly, it does little to advance national family law practises in this regard. Bainham highlights, for instance, the international legal community's obligation to sustain pressure on Member States and to provide a positive template for domestic action in respect of children's rights.[35] Although Bainham probably did not regard the EU as

---

[32]   PIPER, C. (2000) "Assumptions about children's best interests" *Journal of Social Welfare and Family Law,* Vol. 22(3), pp. 261-276. For an empirically-grounded illustration of this, see the work of SMART, C. and NEALE, B. (2000) "It's my life too – Children's perspectives on post-divorce parenting" *Family Law,* March Issue, pp. 163-169; See also ACKERS, L. (2000) "From Best Interests to Participatory Rights – children's involvement in family migration decisions" *Child and Family Law Quarterly,* Vol. 12, No. 2, pp. 167-184.

[33]   Above note 31, at p. 285. BAINHAM refers to the cases of *Payne v. Payne* [2001] 1 *FLR* 1052; *Poel v. Poel* [1970] 1 WLR 1469; and *Tyler v. Tyler* [1989] 2 *FLR* 158 by way of illustration.

[34]   Above note 31, at p. 284.

[35]   Above note 31, at p. 289.

part of this "international community" when he made this point, by imposing binding family law obligations on Member States under Brussels I and II, the EU has clearly assumed a responsibility to ensure optimum safeguards for children implicated in this process.

That is not to suggest that the EU will directly impact upon children's rights at domestic level. Indeed, the child-focused provisions enshrined in Brussels I and II clearly do not, of themselves, place any additional legal obligations on Member States. The EU should take every step to ensure, however, that it sanctions existing obligations. Certainly, a more synchronised effort at international, EU and domestic level in promoting children's rights alongside their welfare rights might well mobilise Member States to amend and improve national legal procedures accordingly.

Having considered the ideological debate around the "brand" of children's rights adopted by the European Union in its evolving family law, it is worth considering some more pragmatic issues regarding the practical application of these measures. This demands some consideration of whether or not current mechanisms tailored to cross-national family disputes meet the needs of children in an appropriate and sufficiently sensitive way.

## 5.   PUTTING BRUSSELS I AND II INTO PRACTISE IN THE INTERESTS OF THE CHILD

This paper has briefly alluded to the fact that in England the formal legal position regarding children's status in family law proceedings is often very different to the practical reality, with often harmful consequences for children. The Lord Chancellors Department, for instance, recently commissioned research into post-divorce contact between non-custodial fathers and their children where there has been a history of domestic violence.[36] This research revealed that there is a distinct presumption in English family law in favour of granting contact despite cogent evidence to suggest the prevalence of domestic violence following parental separation, with periods of child contact often used as an opportunity to inflict further abuse. While this represents the extreme end of a broad spectrum of post divorce experiences, it provides a poignant illustration of the importance of engaging children more meaningfully in potentially life-changing decisions.

---

[36]   ARIS, R., HARRISON, C. and HUMPHREYS, C. (2002) Safety And Child Contact: An Analysis Of The Role Of Child Contact Centres In The Context Of Domestic Violence And Child Welfare Concerns, project ref 10/2002.

The international element no doubt adds a variety of new complexities to children's experiences and vulnerabilities in the negotiation and application of custody and access arrangements. Research charting the incidence of parental child abduction is extremely pertinent in this regard.[37] This, again, only reveals the more sinister part of the picture, however, and further research is clearly needed on the less dramatic and more common experiences of cross-national child custody and access to complement the wealth of national "internal" studies in this regard. Put simply, in order to ensure sufficiently rigorous and effective regulation of such a critical aspect of children's lives, the law needs to be tested and supported by sound empirical research, which actively engages with individuals as policy evaluators and "professionals by experience".[38]

There is, nonetheless, very little empirical basis for the current EU law aside from a straight-forward comparison between nation states' systems of laws,[39] leading one commentator to suggest that Brussels I and II have been formulated within an "empirical and theoretical vacuum".[40] Moreover, if we are to ensure that the law reflects and accommodates the empirical reality, the methodology adopted for this type of research needs to be consistent with the objective of the law itself. In other words, it needs to empower children and young people to give their views on particular legal issues based on their own experience. This demands a departure from methodologies which engage only with adult "proxy" assessments of children's needs and experiences towards more direct dialogue with children and young people, in a manner consistent with Article 12 of the UNCRC.

That is not to say that an empirical, child-focussed approach does not carry with it certain challenges and limitations. Indeed, conducting cross-national empirical work on this scale demands considerable resources in time and money and a "transferable" methodology that will produce

---

[37] See LOWE, N. and PERRY, A. (1999) "International Child Abduction – The English Experience", *International and Comparative Law Quarterly*, Vol. 48, pp. 127-155.

[38] This phrase was coined by HAGUE, G., MULLANDER, A. and ARIS, R. in their empirical work on domestic violence, (2002) *Professionals by Experience: A Guide to Service User Participation and Consultation for Domestic Violence Services,* Women's Aid Federation of England.

[39] The Brussels I and II measures were informed very much by this model of comparative research, much of which has been carried out by national experts under the auspices of the CEFL. See further BOELE-WOELKI, K. (2002) "Comparative research-based drafting of principles of European Family Law", in FAURE, M., SMITS, J. and SCHNEIDER, H. (eds.) *Towards a European Ius Commune in Legal Education and Research,* Antwerpen-Groningen: Intersentia, pp. 170-185.

[40] MCGLYNN, C. (2001) "The Europeanisation of Family Law" 13(1) *CFLQ* p. 35.

comparable results. This usually necessitates close collaboration with research partners indigenous to the other Member States in question, an ability to negotiate and compromise culturally and ideologically-sensitive approaches in favour of a more universal, heterogeneous model, and close attention to the ethical implications of involving children.[41]

## 6. ADDRESSING A RESEARCH VACUUM

The European Commission has demonstrated some willingness to fund this type of research from the mid 1990s. Between 1997 and 2000, the author was engaged in a cross-national study funded under the former DGXXII "Youth for Europe" Programme to examine the impact of the free movement of persons provisions on children's legal status and social experiences.[42] The project, entitled "Children, Citizenship and internal Migration in the European Union", was of a qualitative, socio-legal nature involving a team of researchers in Sweden, Greece, Portugal and the UK. It involved a combination of in-depth legal and statistical analysis and interviews with 180 children, parents and some "key informants" (such as teachers) to assess the impact of migration on children's their education, health, social integration, language, identity and family relationships.[43] While this research is still very relevant to children's experiences of intra-Community mobility today and includes detailed examination of the impact of cross-national family breakdown on children, it was conducted prior to the significant developments that have taken place in the post-Amsterdam era under Title IV EC. There is still a need, therefore, for further investigation as to whether Brussels I and II serve to expedite negotiation, recognition and enforcement of parental responsibility orders in comparison to less formal or alternative private international law routes of dispute resolution.

## 7. ASSESSING LEGAL PRACTITIONERS AWARENESS AND APPLICATION OF EU FAMILY PROVISIONS

In a modest attempt to address, or at least draw attention to an identifiable empirical vacuum, the University of Liverpool funded a one-year pilot study

---

[41]   See Chapter two, "The Challenges of Working with Children in a Cross-National Context", of ACKERS, L. and STALFORD, H. (forthcoming) above note 8 for more detailed discussion of how this has been achieved.

[42]   Directed by Professor Louise Ackers, Centre for the Study of Law and Policy in Europe, Department of Law, University of Leeds and co-funded by the Nuffield Foundation.

[43]   These findings and more updated legal analysis of the free movement provisions and Title IV measures are reported in ACKERS, L. and STALFORD, H. (forthcoming), above note 8.

in 2001-2002 to explore practitioners' awareness of the Brussels II Regulation and further investigate their interplay with existing international, European and English family law.[44] The methodology involved in-depth analysis of the legal framework underpinning Brussels II followed by the distribution of a postal questionnaire to approximately 280 solicitors and barristers practising in family law across England. The typically poor response rate (approximately 20 per cent) was anticipated but did provide a useful snapshot of both awareness and application of the law shortly after implementation of the Brussels II Regulation. This was then supplemented by a small sample of five exploratory interviews with barristers, solicitors and one High Court judge.

The questionnaire involved a combination of tick-box and more open-ended questions exploring the incidence of cross-national family procee-dings, the nature and duration of cases, practitioners" views on and awareness of EU regulation of this area of the law and the extent to which children are involved in proceedings.

Of those surveyed, the majority (74 per cent) dealt with between 1 and 10 cross-national family disputes, 11 per cent were involved in between 11 and 20 cases and 4 per cent were involved in more than 21 cases per year.[45] These cases were concerned primarily with the determination of child contact (78 per cent), child residence (52 per cent) or enforcement of child contact orders (52 per cent).[46] Over half of the cases reported lasted between 1 and 2 years (52 per cent) and 22 per cent of cases were resolved within 1 year. The reported cost of cross-national proceedings varied considerably, according to the nature and length of the dispute and the complexity of the legal issues in question. Thirty per cent of respondents estimated the average cost of proceedings at between £5,000 and £10,000, 11 per cent estimated average costs at less than £5,000 while a further 11 per cent had been involved in cases running to between £20,000 and £30,000. It is interesting to speculate, therefore, on the extent to which the new European provisions which seek to harmonise recognition and enforcement (particularly with the abolition of exequatur) will serve to reduce these costs both in time and money with ultimate and inevitable benefits for any children concerned.[47]

---

[44]   STALFORD, H. "The impact of EC Regulation 1347/2000 (Brussels II) on families involved in cross-national family disputes with the EU: An English Law Perspective", RDF, University of Liverpool 2001-2.

[45]   11 per cent did not respond to this question.

[46]   Note that in many cases, respondents addressed more than one issue in a single case.

[47]   See the proposed amendments referred to above note 24.

An important aspect of the pilot project was to assess practitioners' awareness of international and EU provision in this area. When asked for their views on existing private international law, 33 per cent reported that they found it "inadequate" and 59 per cent stated that it was "confusing". Only 18 per cent identified it as "adequate" and 4 per cent felt that it was "effective". Commenting on practitioners' awareness of more recent EU legal measures, one barrister commented:

> "My guess is that 95 per cent of solicitors in this country who are dealing with family law are not aware of it."

The findings of the survey revealed a higher rate of awareness but a widespread confusion over the nature and content of the Brussels II provisions. 33 per cent of respondents were unfamiliar with Brussels II. Of those that did claim some awareness, 37 per cent admitted to finding it "confusing", 18 per cent felt that it was "inadequate" and only 4 per cent were of the opinion that it was "effective". Practitioners generally recognised the need to enhance their knowledge and understanding of this aspect of EU law. The following solicitor commented for instance:

> "I have trained only in the law of England and Wales. The EU and the ease of travel between countries is bound to make these sorts of problems crop up more and more – we need to be better educated, or better still, the systems need to be unified".

Most practitioners recognised that family law practise is no longer confined to a single nation-based legal context but demands closer attention to the interplay between domestic, European and international measures. There was almost unanimous acknowledgement, therefore, of the need for further training on the content and scope of EU family measures.

## 8. ENHANCING THE INVOLVEMENT OF CHILDREN IN CROSS-NATIONAL FAMILY PROCEEDINGS

Respondents involved in the pilot study were asked to comment in particular on the extent to which children had directly participated in decisions relating to cross-national contact and residence in their experience. 33 per cent reported "never", 44 per cent reported "sometimes" and 15 per cent asserted that this "usually" happened. There was a more even distribution of responses when practitioners were asked if they felt the child's voice was sufficiently recognised at European and International level in both law and practice. 48 per cent felt that the legal mechanisms in this regard were sufficient while 33 per cent felt that the law did not afford due recognition to the rights of the child in this regard. Views on the practical application of these measures, however, painted a different picture and, consistent with the research described above, identified a disparity between the formal legal position and the practical reality. 30 per cent of respondents were of the view that, in practice, children were adequately and appropriately involved in custody and access decisions whereas 41 per cent felt that children were disenfranchised in this respect.

A High Court judge interviewed in the course of the pilot study further expressed the view that children, particularly in the context of international family disputes, should receive separate representation in view of the added implications of decisions of this nature. He also identified the need also to ensure uniformity in different Member States' approach to representing and consulting with children:

> "I think the child needs to be represented. It's going to be an issue in England of course because representation of the child is deemed to be very expensive and only in some very special cases. I'm increasingly of the view that we are going to have to agree on a structure of cases and categories of cases which we think are important for children to be represented...particularly if we are going to have an international dispute over a child. I think it is very important for the child's voice to be heard loud and clear...The decisions are crucial: if the child is going to speak in language X or language Y...are they going to go into a foreign education system or will they have to put up with the English type of education. So all those crucial decisions to make..."

These findings, again, reveal a distinct disparity between children's formal legal right to be consulted in accordance with their age and capacity and common practice and a genuine desire amongst practitioners to implement and promote more child-friendly procedures both nationally and internationally.

## 9. THE IMPACT OF THE FIRST-SEISED RULE ON CHILDREN

The in-depth interviews with practitioners invited comments on the actual substance of the Brussels II Regulation. This revealed some dissatisfaction with the provisions over and above issues of EU competence and national sovereignty that have dogged academic debate. One particular concern identified relates to the impact of the first-seised rule (established in Article 2) on more vulnerable parties to proceedings. Most felt that such a crude mechanism for determining jurisdiction was distinctly antipathetic to children's needs in that it encourages a "race" to establish the more favourable jurisdiction to the detriment of mediation and other less litigious and antagonistic forms of negotiation. The following barrister commented:

*"The…real problem with Brussels II is that for the last 15 years we have been trying to encourage people to mediate and conciliate their problems and when we get people in, we try and sort it out. We don't want to dash straight off to court but Brussels II forces you to if you don't want to be negligent…the first thing you do is phone up the other country and say, what would this lady be entitled to in Germany or Italy…You then have to advise her literally within a matter of a couple of hours on which is the more appropriate venue and once you've decided which one it is, you must go and get your petition in 5 minutes later because otherwise he will do it in the other venue and apart from the fact that you could be negligent, you could lose your client lots and lots of money – which is not conducive to mediation and conciliation in sorting it all out sensibly in the interests of children."*

While such effects have yet to be empirically verified, such a rigid application of *lis pendens* potentially denies practitioners, parents and children alike the modicum of flexibility which is so crucial to reassessing child custody and access arrangements on an ongoing basis. This scope for re-evaluation is particularly important for children whose personal circumstances may be in constant flux as they mature, as they reach new stages in their education, or as their parents establish new relationships or move to another Member State (with added cultural or linguistic barriers for the child to overcome). It is for this very reason that more explicit recognition of children's rights, and particularly their right to be heard, is so critical to the effective application of Brussels II. In that sense, it is interesting to speculate on whether the proposed Article 4 provision (detailed above) will be widely and wisely utilised to ensure the best outcome for the child at various stages in the post divorce or parental separation process, notwithstanding the operation of lis pendens.

## 10. CONCLUSION

Prior to the Treaty of Amsterdam, the EU was merely tipping its toe into issues of family and children's rights as a necessary corollary of free movement practice. By becoming more fully immersed in family law issues under Title IV EC, it has assumed specific responsibilities in respect of the rights of the child. This paper has considered how, by dwelling on well-rehearsed debates concerning the legitimacy of EU action in the family arena, we are obscuring more crucial considerations as to the nature and quality of children's rights endorsed by the EU. The time has perhaps now come, therefore, to move beyond issues of who "owns" family law, whether it be domestic legislatures, or private international law, and turn our attention to more pragmatic concerns as to whether there are sufficient mechanisms in place to promote and safeguard the interests of children involved in cross-national custody and access disputes.

Although Brussels II, in particular, does not currently impose additional obligations on Member States to involve children where appropriate in family proceedings, it can articulate and reinforce a universal right of the child to be heard and to maintain direct contact with both parents in accordance with international human rights obligations. This task is not and should not be assigned to a single institution or legal order, but requires a co-ordinated effort by international, European and domestic authorities alike. As Freeman notes: "Law...must send out consistent messages. It must work in conjunction with other strategies and policies. We must invest in it, both ideologically and with resources."[48]

This process needs to be complemented, however, by further empirical research at a specifically cross-national level in a way that engages more directly with children and young people as policy evaluators in their own right. Only then can we reveal and address the true impact of the law on children's welfare and rights and invoke more progressive change which will empower children in the negotiation of their family relationships. In any case, the EU can no longer hide behind the European economic imperative to evade its international responsibilities in this regard but must, instead, wholeheartedly embrace children's rights issues if it is to regulate family life legitimately and convincingly.

---

[48]  FREEMAN, M. "The End of the Century of the Child?" *Current legal problems*, Vol. 53, pp. 505-558, at p. 512.

# REGULATING PARENTAL RESPONSIBILITY IN THE EUROPEAN UNION

Elena Rodríguez Pineau

## 1. PRECEDENTS

### 1.1. *EC legislative action in order to deal with the side-effects of integration*

It used to be argued that national family laws had not been much affected by Community law. This was usually explained by reference to the fact that this was an area with no obvious implications for the original goal of the Communities, namely, the well-known aim of establishing a common market among Member States.

However, the *indirect impact* that economic freedoms were bound to have on family structures and problems was already being felt some twenty years ago. In 1983, the Parliament required the Commission to pay particular attention to the different legal provisions in force in the Member States, and asked it to consider whether Community action might be necessary as regards several specific issues, such as the custody of children from separated or divorced parents, and the right of access to the non-custodial parent.[1] The realisation of the effects that a space without physical borders and controls could have in familial relationships has steadily grown since then. It was ascertained that the free movement of persons could entail an unlawful use of this freedom as far as children were concerned. The European Parliament has been especially active in this regard. Its proposals have taken stock of the existence of (rather) successful international conventions, but the European Parliament still pointed to the correlation between the removal of physical boundaries and the increasing number of abductions within the EC as the rationale for specific Community legislation in this matter.[2] Community action was thus felt to be required

---

[1]   European Parliament Resolution of 9 June 1983 on family policy within the EC, *OJ* C 184, 11.7.1983, pp. 116 ff, at p. 119.

[2]   European Parliament Resolutions on the abduction of children of 26 May 1989 (*OJ* C 158, 26.6.1989, p. 391) and 9 March 1993 (*OJ* C 115, 26.4.1993, p. 33); European Parliament Resolution on abduction of children of bi-national marriages in the Member States of 18 July 1996 (*OJ* C 261, 9.9.1996, p. 157).

in order to deal with the *side effects* that the integration process *itself* has in particular issues.

### 1.2. The U-Turn: Towards family law harmonisation

The discourse on the relationships between family law and Community law has changed considerably since the late 1990s. A strong case has been made for the harmonisation of national family laws. Such a case is closely linked to the argument that European integration is no longer to be regarded as an exclusive matter of market making. It has become a more mature political project, which must address non-economic issues affecting the daily lives of European citizens.[3] But a similar drive towards harmonisation has also been advocated from a more classical standpoint, according to which a common private law in the EC was needed in order to guarantee effective European integration. To put it differently, it has been claimed that diversity in family law constitutes a serious obstacle to the free movement of persons within the EC and, therefore, the harmonisation of national rules is needed in order to render such a basic Community freedom effective. This second rationale does not mark a substantive break with the original discourse referred in Section 1.1; however, it presupposes a different perception of the challenge ahead. More specifically, the divergence of family laws is now perceived to be akin to the divergence of laws affecting the free movement of goods or services. If individuals can move freely, they should be able to expect that their legal status will also travel freely with them.

This leaves unanswered the question of the means by which this common system is to be established. Ideally, two choices seem to be possible, namely (i) the harmonisation of substantive law (civil code) or (ii) the harmonisation of conflict rules (private international law, hereafter PIL). Certainly, the existence of a common system of family law rules would ensure that the personal status (as divorced, parent, and so on) is recognised through the whole territory of the Union.[4] However, serious doubts can be raised concerning the convenience of such a choice. Firstly, it is not clear that family matters (issues relating to personal status) have an immediate impact upon the internal market or upon some of the fundamental

---

[3]   See the references and historical development in P. McELEAVY, "The Brussels II Regulation: How the European Community Has Moved into Family Law", *I.C.L.Q.*, 2002, vol. 51, pp. 883 ff at pp. 888 ff.

[4]   Some of the arguments in favour of harmonisation may be found in K. BOELE-WOELKI, "The Road towards a European Family Law", *EJCL*, 1997, vol. 1.1., available at http://www.ejcl.org/11/art11-1.html.

economic freedoms, such as the free movement of persons.[5] Secondly, and related thereto, it is open to discussion whether there are good economic arguments favouring the harmonisation of family law; to put it differently, it is far from clear that the arguments that can be made regarding patrimonial law apply equally to family law.[6] But even if this was so, we should not forget that the achievement of certain EC aims (such as the enjoyment of certain citizenship rights) cannot be given unconditional priority; attention should be paid to other principles such as subsidiarity and respect for a Member State's identity.[7] Indeed, the substantive contents of family law provisions seem to be extensively influenced by legitimate diversity in cultural preferences.[8] Thirdly, the competence basis on which the Community could ground its harmonising rules is far from obvious[9]; moreover, it does not seem that Community institutions assume that they have a clear competence in the matter.[10]

As is very well known, conflict rules allow one to bridge the differences between legal systems and thus facilitate continuity of status, while assuming the persistence of (legal) boundaries. Certainly the problem of discontinuity will not be solved if Member States articulate their own PIL rules without taking into account what other Member States do. *Thus, harmonisation of PIL rules may be required.* Hindrances to free movement do not necessarily emanate from the different substantive legal systems; they

---

[5]   D. MARTINY, "Europäisches Familienrecht: Utopie oder Notwendigkeit?", *RabelsZ*, 1995, vol. 59, pp. 419 ff, at p. 430.

[6]   For a critical approach, stressing the weaknesses of economic arguments in favour of a European civil code, in particular as far as family law is concerned, cf. B. FAUVARQUE-COSSON, "Faut-il un code civil européen?", *R.T.D.Civ.*, 2002, pp. 463 ff, at pp. 470 ff. Sharing these doubts from a private international law point of view, see H.-P. MANSEL, "Zum Systemwechsel im europäischen Kollisionsrecht nach Amsterdam und Nizza", in *Systemwechsel im europäischen Kollisionsrecht*, 2002, Beck, Munich, pp. 1 ff, at p. 4.

[7]   Cf. CH. KOHLER, "L'article 220 du traité CCE et les conflits de juridictions en matière de relations familiales: Premières réflexions", *R.C.D.I.P.*, 1992, pp. 221 ff, at p. 236.

[8]   The influence of cultural factors upon legal norms is more accentuated in family law than in patrimonial law. See G. BETLEM/E. HONDIOUS, "European Private Law after the Treaty of Amsterdam", *E.R.P.L*, 2001, pp. 3 ff, p. 18; cf. also B. FAUVARQUE-COSSON, *op. cit.* p. 473. It should be noted that not only substantive law, but also PIL norms reflect cultural preferences. Connecting points, adjustment techniques and criteria of competence, among other things, are permeated by cultural factors. For a more detailed analysis of these features, see E. JAYME, "Identité culturelle et integration. Le Droit international privé postmoderne", *Rec. des Cours*, vol. 251, 1995, pp. 9 ff, at pp. 167 ff.

[9]   Very helpful is the analysis by B. FAUVARQUE-COSSON, *op. cit.* p. 466.

[10]   See the position established in the (A5-0133/2002) European Parliament Resolution of 15 May 2002 on the division of competences between the European Union and the Member States (P5_TAPROV(2002)0247 (doc. 2001/2024(INI)).

necessarily stem from the diversity of PIL rules.[11] On such a basis, we can venture to say that, in the absence of countervailing arguments, the approximation of family laws should be framed as a matter of approximation of conflict rules, not of substantive provisions. This would allow for proper respect for the principles of subsidiarity and cultural identity, since it would respect the diversity of national substantive legislation, while ensuring a common core of "recognition rules" (understood in a broad sense, encompassing both procedural and conflict law rules). It might be added that, since those rules would be tailored according to the needs of the integrated area, this would be a more adequate instrument by which to achieve its aims. Thus, a Community PIL will satisfy both aims, on the one hand Community purposes, and, on the other, purely PIL aims, namely ensuring individuals that their legal relationships are not hindered because of the existence of different legal systems.

Recent changes in primary Community law provide good evidence that such is the choice of the European legislator. The Amsterdam Treaty has strengthened the role to be played by the Union in the field of justice and internal affairs. This has been done by means of the partial "communitarisation" of the so-called third pillar of the European Union. Even if one would wonder whether "communitarisation" can be properly justified in the name of the "proper functioning of the internal market" (cf. Article 65),[12] the fact remains that the Union now aims to provide its citizens with a common judicial area, with proper access to justice, and with a common normative framework allocating jurisdiction among Community courts, and regulating the recognition of judgments across borders. High aspirations have been partially spelled out in concrete aims contained in the 1999 Action Plan, a blueprint for forthcoming legislative action.[13] It establishes that the purpose of the area of justice in civil matters is to "make life simpler for European citizens by improving and simplifying the rules and procedures on co-operation and communication between authorities

---

[11] For an analysis of the shift in the perception of conflicts of laws from an instrument of integration to an obstacle to trade, see J. ISRAEL, "Conflicts of Law and the EC after Amsterdam: A Change for Worse?", *MJ*, 2000, vol. 7, pp. 81 ff, at p. 91, particularly footnote 48 and the references cited therein.

[12] Rather critical in this sense, Ch. KOHLER, "Auf dem Weg zu einem europäischen Justizraum für das Familien- und Erbrecht", *FamRZ*, 2002, pp.709 ff, p. 712; A. BORRÁS, "La proyección externa de la comunitarización del Derecho internacional privado: los datos del problema", *La Ley*, 2002, núm. 5611, p. 2; W.A. KENNETT, *The Enforcement of Judgments in Europe*, Oxford University Press, 2000, p. 12.

[13] Cf. the Action Plan of the Council and the Commission on how best to implement the provisions of the Treaty of Amsterdam on an area of freedom, security and justice, JHA Council of 3 December 1998 (*OJ* C 19, 23.1.1999, p. 1).

and on enforcing decisions, by promoting the compatibility of conflict of law rules and on jurisdiction and by eliminating obstacles to the good functioning of civil proceedings in a European judicial area".[14] When the objectives of the Treaty of the European Union will be fulfilled, and the Union will be turned into an "area of freedom, security and justice", one could venture that we will have attained legal certainty, and thus have dispensed with a considerable number of obstacles to the free movement of citizens.

The basic claim made in this article is that the Community has succeeded in setting its ambitions high, while it has failed to establish a normative framework in which such ambitions will be fulfilled. In the specific area of parental responsibility, the ambitious goal of establishing an area of justice where free movement of decisions is granted, and therefore, free movement of persons is enhanced, is far from having been accomplished. Moreover, the PIL aims that legislative measures were supposed to achieve have not been forthcoming. As a consequence, the Community risks losing sight of the private law aspects that should be underlying the harmonisation of norms.

In the coming sections, I will consider the debate on parental responsibility. I will look first at the allocation of parental responsibility when a matrimonial crisis occurs; then I will consider further legislative developments within this area in a broader perspective.

## 2. EC REGULATION 1347/2000 ('BRUSSELS II')

### 2.1. The rationale behind the Regulation

We can take as a starting point the claim that the divergent Member States' PIL systems (as far as jurisdiction and recognition or enforcement of decisions is concerned) may hinder the free movement of EU residents, as well as the proper functioning of the internal market. This is at least what is stated in Recital 4 of the Regulation.[15]

Brussels II seems to assume that the free movement of spouses will be made more effective once their "personal status" is recognised through the EC. Even if it is difficult to contest that claim as far as matrimonial causes are

---

14 Cf. point 39 of the Action Plan. Further developments are contemplated in the Council programme of measures for the implementation of the principle of mutual recognition of decisions in civil and commercial matters (*OJ* C 12, 15.1.2001, p. 1).

15 Rather sceptical about these justifications is P. McELEAVY, *op. cit.*, p. 898.

concerned, it is rather doubtful whether it is equally correct when parental responsibility is at stake. It might be convenient to keep in mind that the question was simply not considered as raising a "European problem"; perceptions only changed when the French and Spanish governments inserted this question on the agenda of the Brussels II Convention, upon which the Regulation is based.[16] More substantially, we can wonder whether parents are deterred from making use of their freedom of movement because the legal status of the child after the matrimonial crisis might not be acknowledged in other Member States. Even if this would be so, it could be the case that the Regulation would render effective the freedom of movement of the parents, but only at the price of undermining the rights of the child (not only to move, but also to keep in contact with both parents). Thus, Brussels II might provide undue weight for the rights of the parents over those of the child.

## 2.2. Problems raised by the Regulation's scope of application

Without entering into a discussion on the small print of the provisions of Brussels II, it is necessary to point out that several problematic questions stem from the way in which the Regulation's scope of application is defined. If we accept that the main problem to be addressed is spelling out the parental responsibility related to matrimonial crises, the answers provided by the Community norm might be accepted as being unproblematic. But there are very good reasons to contest whether the definition of the main problem is correct. Let me illustrate these with some examples:

(a) *the personal scope of application is limited to children born within wedlock.* Children born within wedlock are unavoidably concerned when parental responsibility is considered in relation to a matrimonial crisis. However, one could wonder whether there might not be other children affected by a marital or quasi-marital crisis. For example, children born out of wedlock are exposed to similar problems when their parents bring their cohabitation to an end. We should keep in mind that the tendency is to eliminate the difference in legal treatment between such cases in all Member States. To put it differently, one can wonder what reason justifies the fact that a "beneficial" recognition system is only granted to matrimonial children.
(b) *the material scope of application is restricted to procedures related to a matrimonial crisis.* As a result, only certain legal measures are considered,

---

[16]    See p. 4 of the Commission Working document on parental responsibility (JHA A3 EK-787, 5-12 March 2001). More details on the development of and the political insights within the drafting procedure in P. McELEAVY, *op. cit.*, pp. 893 ff. It is equally interesting to note that no specific reference to parental responsibility is made in the 1999 Action Plan.

such as custody and visitation rights. But one can wonder whether it is not also important to establish means to decide in particular (non-crisis) situations when agreement between the parents is lacking. An obvious example could be the decision as to whether to give the child a religious education (and quite obviously, which one).

(c) *the temporal scope of the Regulation's application is limited to the period during which the matrimonial cause is pending.* National rules should apply once the latter is finally decided. But one could wonder whether it would not also be important that these "favourable" rules apply beyond such a period. After all, if there is a context where legal relationships are naturally evolving, then it is that of the protection of children.

All these restrictions on the scope of the Regulation are hardly justifiable from a genuine Community point of view. Moreover, they are in complete contrast with the overall goal of fostering the development of an area of security, freedom and justice.

### 2.3. Problems stemming from jurisdictional connecting factors

The previous considerations cast some doubts on the reasonability of Brussels II. Moreover, the practical effects of the Regulation reinforce concerns about the achievement of its (procedural) aims. This can be illustrated by reference to "forum shopping".

Brussels II establishes a double forum for questions of parental responsibility linked to matrimonial causes. Either jurisdiction is granted to the courts of the State where the child resides (where the matrimonial cause is being disputed) or, to the courts of the State where the matrimonial cause has been commenced, provided that the parents agree and that the competence is in the best interest of the child, and even if this is not the State of habitual residence of the child. Decisions on parental responsibility emanating from a Member State (disregarding the jurisdiction grounds according to which the court was seized) are recognised and enforced according to the Brussels II rules. Enforcement can only be denied by reference to a limited set of grounds, specifically determined by the Regulation: public policy, infringement of procedural rights (due notification and the right to be heard both for the child and persons claiming to have parental responsibility) and incompatibility with *later* judgments relating to parental responsibility granted in the forum or another (Member or non-Member) State.

A first problem concerns the ensuing wide margin of manoeuvre granted to parents in order to decide where they want to litigate, and therefore what is the law that will apply to the issue of parental responsibility. One must keep in mind that since the parental responsibility jurisdiction is linked to the matrimonial one, a decision on the latter implies a decision on the former. Given that substantive law is not uniform or harmonised across the Union, we cannot rule out that plaintiffs look for the most convenient forum in which to litigate (both from a procedural and a substantive point of view). Choosing the court means choosing the law.[17] This is slightly problematic when the parents agree to seize a court; but it is very troubling when one of the parents moves to another jurisdiction with the child, and without the agreement of the other spouse, and proceeds to file a claim before the courts which (s)he finds more beneficial to her/his case. There must be a strong presumption against these tactics furthering the best interests of the child, as this is hardly compatible with the strategic manoeuvres of one parent.

A second difficulty is related to the fact that the recognition of the decision might be blocked due to the fact that there is another *later* decision (from the forum or from another State) after the one for which recognition is required. The peculiar nature of the parental relationship is based on the development of the child and his/her relationship with his/her parents. As the parental relationship evolves, a new judicial decision might be called for. This implies that it is not possible to sustain a rigid approach to the recognition of decisions. Therefore, there is a need to introduce the correcting factor of the *later* decisions.[18] This provision is reasonable since the "interest of the child" demands a continuous revision of its status. However, as a consequence of the wide choice given to the parties, plaintiffs find no incentive in refraining from seizing the courts of other Member States. It would have been more reasonable to restrict the phrasing of the provision, so that recognition could be blocked *only* by decisions coming from a closely connected court (*i.e.* from the forum corresponding to the habitual residence of the child).[19] Without this

---

[17]  Ch. KOHLER, "Auf dem Weg...", *op. cit.*, p. 713; TH. DE BOER, "Prospects for European Conflicts Law in the XXIst Century", in *International Conflicts of Laws for the Third Millenium. Essays in Honour of F. K. Juenger*, 2001, pp. 193 ff, at p. 205.

[18]  Cf. R. WAGNER, "Die Anerkennung und Vollstreckung von Entscheidungen nach der Brüssel II-Verordnung", *IPRax*, vol. 21, 2001, pp. 73 ff, at p. 78.

[19]  The EC legislator is aware of the reasonableness of what we could call a PIL requirement: a close connection between the court and the child is called for when the decision is rendered in a non-Member State. The choice made with respect to Member State decisions (*i.e.*, disregarding the connection to the habitual residence of the child) clearly shows that *integration aims* take precedence over PIL requirements within the Community.

restriction, and in the absence of a mechanism such as *lis pendens*,[20] the present provision leaves a door which is too open to strategic behaviour, dignified by the reference to the "best interests" of the child.

## 2.4. Problems as far as applicable law is concerned

Mutual trust among legal systems is a pre-condition for the recognition of judgments and decisions. The 1968 Brussels Convention (now transformed into the Brussels I Regulation) grounded such trust in a common set of procedural rules shared by all legal systems. This renders the substantive grounds of the decision irrelevant in order to have it recognised. Having said that, it might also be said that the satisfactory functioning of the Convention was rather favoured by the existence of common applicable law rules (the Rome and Vienna Conventions), which reinforced the premise of the *conflict law indifference*. As it has been said many times, but it is worth repeating, legal security, uniformity of decisions and better protection of the legitimate expectations of the parties will only be achieved when a common application of the same rules takes place.[21] The same premise underpins Brussels II. Which substantive law is applicable is irrelevant, provided that the basis of jurisdiction and enforcement are shared among legal systems. However, the latter is a fiction: Brussels II applies *as if* there were common rules, but this is not yet the case.[22] As was said in the previous section, the final outcome of the case might vary depending on which court is seized.

However, one could still ironically regard this as a minor problem, given the difficulties that parties (practitioners, judges) might have in ascertaining the applicable law. In fact, Brussels II jurisdiction rules have altered

---

[20]   *Lis pendens* will hardly work in matters of parental responsibility when both parents each try to seize a court on the premise of the matrimonial cause. In that case, only the court of the State of the habitual residence of the child may validly assume jurisdiction; any other court needs the consensus of both parents to be validly seized. On the contrary, *lis pendens* would prove useful in those situations where one of the courts has been seized on grounds other than those foreseen in Brussels II. This could be possible if this provision was interpreted in the same sense as in Brussels I: *lis pendens* could be resorted to if both courts had been seized on matters that fall under the realm of Brussels II. But since the Member State court seized on non-EC grounds will be dealing with matters outside the scope of application of Brussels II -*i.e.* a question of parental responsibility not linked to a matrimonial cause-, resorting to *lis pendens* is precluded.

[21]   J. BASEDOW, "The Communitarisation of the Conflict of Laws under the Treaty of Amsterdam", *CMLR*, 2000, vol. 37, p. 687 ff, p. 703.

[22]   Several critical voices have been heard claiming that all EC proposals seem to be based on this very fiction, which is not devoid of rather upsetting effects. Cf., for example, Ch. KOHLER, "Auf dem Weg...", *op. cit.*, at p. 711.

the normal functioning of (partially harmonised) conflict rules in matters of parental responsibility in Member States. This can be easily proved by taking a look at the disruptive effect that Brussels II has had as regards the 1961 Hague Convention.

The Regulation foresees that its provisions supersede those encompassed in the 1961 Convention. Even if the Regulation's scope of application does not extend to conflict rules, the superseding provision casts some doubts on the extent to which the Convention keeps on being relevant to the ascertainment of conflict rules. This is so to the extent that it is not clear whether the conflict rules of the Convention have autonomous normative standing, *i.e.*, whether they can be applied without regard to the jurisdictional grounds. On the one hand, one might contend that the applicability of the conflict rules of the Convention is conditional upon the jurisdictional ground having being established by reference to the Convention itself. On the other hand, the phrasing of the Convention allows one to claim that the applicability of conflict rules does not depend on jurisdiction having been assumed on Convention grounds. More specifically, it could be said that Convention conflict rules apply *as far as* the jurisdictional grounds coincide. To put it differently, if the court has been seized on grounds that are similar to those foreseen in the Hague Convention (habitual residence or nationality), its conflict rules would also apply. Thus, where the court is that of the *habitual residence*, it can apply the law of the habitual residence. If the court has assumed jurisdiction on the grounds of being the divorce court, and it is also the *nationality* court of the child, we can assume that it will apply the "national" law of the child. In contrast, if the court cannot be said to be either that of the habitual residence or the nationality court, no solution is provided by the Convention, and then the court should resort to its own conflict rules.[23]

Having established the applicability of the 1961 Convention, we can consider the following example: a child (born to a Franco-Italian couple) lives in France but the matrimonial cause lies before a Spanish court (where the matrimonial home was located). Brussels II also makes it

---

[23] Authoritative voices have favoured another interpretation, according to which one should apply the law of the habitual residence of the child *whatever* the jurisdictional ground. See E. JAYME/CH. KOHLER, "Europäisches Kollisionsrecht 2000: Interlokales Privatrecht oder universelles Gemeinschaftsrecht ?", *IPRax*, 2000, pp. 454 ff, at p. 458; K. BOELE-WOELKI, "Brüssel II: Die Verordnung über die Zuständigkeit und die Anerkennung von Entscheidungen in Ehesachen", *ZfRV*, 2001, pp. 121 ff, at p. 124. This interpretation is certainly the most attuned to the fulfilment of the *best interest* of the child in PIL, even if at the cost of shattering the 1961 Convention's system. The latter collateral consequence prompts me to advocate the different solution proposed in the main text.

possible that a Spanish court is seized in relation to the child. However, in this hypothesis there would be no conventional rule on the applicable law because, in accordance with the Convention, the Spanish court could not have had jurisdiction. The court should then consider its internal law (Article 9.4 of the Civil code refers to the child's nationality law, and subsidiarily to the habitual residence law). Had the child been Spanish, then the court could have resorted to the 1961 Convention.

The latter example highlights several points:
(1)    the normal application of the Hague Convention can be disruptively affected; this was clearly a case falling within its scope of application (*i.e.* habitual residence of the child in a contracting State);
(2)    the national courts are also forced to resort to different conflict rules even where the basis of jurisdiction is the same EC rule;
(3)    children might be treated differently due to their nationality; there is no reasonable explanation for such different (discriminatory?) treatment within the EC.

One cannot but wonder whether this is the best way to facilitate access to justice in Europe and to foster a common judicial area. Legal certainty as to the applicable law is a necessary precondition for the smooth functioning of the recognition system. An area of security, freedom and justice demands certainty as to the applicable law and it must be seen as a necessary consequence of the respect for the right to family life as enshrined in Article 8 ECHR. Otherwise, European citizens might have the impression that the claim of the Union to be building an area of freedom, security and justice is not redeemed by the Union's actions, and more specifically by its legislation.[24]

## 3.   THE PROPOSAL FOR A NEW REGULATION ('BRUSSELS II *BIS*')

On the basis of what has been highlighted, the reader will not be surprised by the fact that proposals to amend Regulation 1347/2000 have circulated since its very entry into force (*i.e.*, March 2001). In September of that year, the Commission presented a "Proposal for a Council Regulation on jurisdiction and the recognition and enforcement of judgments in matters

---

[24]    O. REMIEN, "European Private International Law, the European Community and its Emerging Area of Freedom, Security and Justice", *CMLR*, 2001, vol. 38, pp. 53 ff, at p. 71.

of parental responsibility".[25] This was later filed and replaced by a new proposal made public by the Council on May 2002,[26] which is partially the result of the initiative of the French government. The latter had favoured the adoption of a Council Regulation on the mutual enforcement of judgments on *rights of access* to children.[27] In the so-called Brussels II *bis* Regulation, the focus has shifted away from matrimonial crises and, as a result, it should apply to *all* children in *any* situation.

### 3.1. Justification

In the explanatory memorandum to Brussels II *bis*, it is argued that the new legal text is required in order to satisfy the right of the child to have regular contact with both parents (and this is recognised in Article 3 of Brussels II *bis*).[28] This appears to be required by the child's best interests, which is also said to underpin jurisdictional criteria (cf. point 10 of the preamble). Even if this is an ambitious goal in itself, the preamble also considers as an objective of Brussels II *bis* the fostering of a common judicial area of freedom, security and justice where the free movement of persons is accomplished (see point 1 of the preamble).

Comparing the preamble with what was argued in the French initiative for a Regulation on the mutual recognition of the right of access, one notices that the emphasis on the free movement of children of separated couples has been superseded, which is something to be welcomed.[29] However, one can still wonder whether the present text fulfils the aims proclaimed in the preamble. Or, to put it differently, do EC inroads in regulating parental responsibility truly enhance free movement of children or their parents? Is it true that jurisdiction grounds are shaped in the light of the best

---

[25]   *OJ* C 332, 27.11.2001, p. 269. This document was preceded by the Commission "Working document on parental responsibility" – COM(2001) 166 final (27.3.2001). The Opinion of the Economic and Social Committee on the Proposal has also been published (*OJ* C 80, 3.4.2002, p. 41).

[26]   COM(2002) 222 final/2, 17.5.2002.

[27]   *OJ* C 234, 15.8.2000, p. 7.

[28]   This right has already been enshrined in the EU Charter (Article 24). Brussels II *bis* also proclaims the right of the child to be heard (Article 4). The latter was implicit in Brussels II in a negative sense; that is, in the absence of a proper hearing, no decision could be recognised.

[29]   According to recital 5 of the French proposal's preamble, "children of separated couples will not be able to move more freely within the Union until judgments relating to them are able to move more freely, which will be brought about by mutual recognition of the enforceability of these judgments and a strengthening of co-operation mechanisms" (*OJ* C 234, 15.8.2000, p. 7).

interests of the child? I might point to the reader some reasons as to why one should be rather sceptical in that regard.

True, the Regulation's scope of application is supposed to be closely linked to Community (internal) situations; however, it is also evident that it goes beyond this so-called intra-Community connection, insofar as it has effects as regards external (non-EC) situations. This fact might be regarded as natural from an EC perspective; it *naturally* entails the need to redefine the scope of international conventions that may clash with the Regulation, as well as the Member States' competence to ratify the said conventions. This does not seem to pose any problems from the EC's point of view:[30]

(a) On the one hand, by means of a Council decision, Member States will be authorised to ratify the 1996 Hague Convention "in the interest of the EC".[31] According to the explanatory memorandum to the decision, the Convention will make a valuable contribution to the protection of children in situations that transcend the boundaries of the Community. As a result, it will complement existing and future Community rules in the same area. But if all that is so, one cannot but wonder whether this would not be *the* instrument according to which to regulate intra-Community cases.

(b) On the other hand, it is recommended that Member States make a declaration, at the time of signing the Convention, aimed at clarifying the limits placed on Community action when Articles 23, 26 and 52 of the Convention are applied in the Community context. Therefore, the final scope of application of the 1996 Convention in relation to Member States remains as follows: (i) if the habitual residence of the child is in a Member State, then the EC rules apply; (ii) if the habitual residence of the child is in a contracting State (*i.e.* non-EC Member States), then the Convention applies; (iii) decisions rendered in a Member State should be granted recognition and enforcement in other Member States through EC rules.

---

[30] As A. BORRÁS (*op. cit.*, p. 7) vividly describes, this "steamroller effect" of Community action seems to ignore not only the Member States' sphere of competence but also the activities of other international instances.

[31] The proposal authorising Member States to sign the 1996 Hague Convention in the interest of the EU had been advanced in November 2001 as document COM (2001) 680 final. The Council adopted the Decision on 19.12.2002 (*OJ* L48, 21.2.2003, p. 1). The Council affirms the shared competence of Member States and the EC, as far as parental responsibility is concerned. Since the EC has already adopted measures on parental responsibility (in the application of the *AETR* doctrine), there is no possibility that the States will sign the Convention on their own.

This might unfortunately indicate that EC interests in order to assume legislative competence are privileged over the interests of the children and their parents to have their status recognised.[32]

### 3.2. Questions regarding jurisdiction grounds

#### 3.2.1. Stimulating 'forum shopping'?

The premises of Brussels II *bis* are the same as those that underlie Brussels II, namely, there are common grounds of jurisdiction that may apply in the conditions which the text establishes; when there is no Community jurisdiction ground, resort can be had to the so-called "residual competences". In both cases, decisions on parental responsibility rendered by Member State courts should be recognised in other Member States according to the Community rules, without any further control as to entitlement to the jurisdiction of the granting court. The grounds for non-recognition are limited and correspond to those enumerated in Brussels II.

The *fora* referred to by the Brussels II *bis* Regulation are more numerous than those contemplated in Brussels II. This is so because any case relating to parental responsibility falls under the scope of application of those rules. Setting aside the competence to grant provisional measures, with regard to the main dispute as to parental responsibility, Brussels II *bis* lays down: (a) a "general" forum, which would consist of the habitual residence of the child, that is also (b) a "continuity" forum when the court has delivered a judgment and the child has resided in a new State (not necessarily a Member State) for a period of less than six months at the time when the court is seized. Certainly these *fora* do not exclude the possibility to prorogue the competence of either (c) the courts of the Member State where the matrimonial cause is being litigated (under the same conditions in which the rule in Brussels II is applied) or (d) the courts which the parents have chosen, subject to a close link to that jurisdiction, which can be the nationality of the child, or the habitual residence of one of the parents (and which should be in the interest of the child). These rules are further completed by two subsidiary rules: (e) the presence of the child when his/her habitual residence cannot be established (in a Member State?), and there is no other Member State whose courts may be seized

---

[32] This warning has already been made by E. JAYME, "Europa: auf dem Weg zu einem interlokalen Kollisionsrecht?", *Vergemeinschaftung des Europäischen Kollisionsrechts*, MANSEL (Hrsg), 2001, pp. 31 ff, at p. 38.

according to the previous rules;[33] and (f) the residual competence; when no EC court may be seized according to the previous rules, each Member State may resort to its internal rules of jurisdiction.

With such a number of potential jurisdictional grounds, it will be rather odd that a court in a Member State will be seized on grounds other than "Community" ones. This logically entails that there is not a major risk that parallel proceedings will take place before other Community courts seized on jurisdictional grounds other than those foreseen in the Regulation. Even if Brussels II *bis* foresees the blocking effect of a later decision pertaining to the child, the incentive to forum shopping in order to obtain such a decision has thus been almost completely precluded.

Unfortunately, this does not mean that forum shopping has disappeared within Brussels II *bis*. The alleged preference granted to the courts of the habitual residence of the child is subject to several exceptions. For instance, an agreement between the possessors of parental responsibility might entail the competence of another court.[34] This opens the door to the strategic allocation of jurisdiction by the parents under the cover of acting in the best interests of the child. Moreover, such jurisdictional strategic behaviour also has its consequences on the terms of the substantive law applicable to the case, as has already been argued. Not only the matrimonial forum allows parents to do so, but also the prorogation forum multiplies the chances of this occurring to a non-negligible extent.[35] In other words, strategic resort to forum shopping has been by no means completely prevented within the EU. Consequently, one may wonder whether the solution enshrined in Brussels II *bis* is the most convenient in terms of fostering a judicial area and protecting the best interests of the child.

### 3.2.2. Is communitarisation of jurisdictional fora excessive?

Leaving aside the problem of forum shopping, the immediate effect of the proliferation of *fora* in Brussels II *bis* is a reduction of the possibilities to

---

[33]   Article 13 seems to transpose Article 6 of the 1996 Convention, but following a reverse order. According to the Convention, the relevant forum for displaced children also applies when it is not possible to establish where the habitual residence of the child actually is; Brussels II stipulates just the reverse. This has a double perverse effect. First, it (wrongly) reverses the condition of a primary and subsidiary connection; second, it may become an escape clause whenever the habitual residence of the child is outside the EC, given that the territorial scope of the provision is not specified.

[34]   Cf. point 10 of the explanatory memorandum to the Brussels II *bis* proposal.

[35]   Cf. TH. DE BOER, "Jurisdiction and Enforcement in International Family Law: a Labyrinth of European and International Legislation", *N.I.L.R.*, 2002, pp. 307 ff, at p. 329.

"internationalise" the case. This can be seen as a positive development concerning the "internal harmony" of jurisdiction within the EC. But if we consider the consequences that this has for the parties, the assessment might be less positive.

Two hypothetical examples might illustrate the risks embedded in the proliferation of jurisdictional *fora*. In both cases, we assume that the plaintiff will request a modification of measures already taken by a given court, while grounding the jurisdiction of the said court on his or her habitual residence (the Regulation assigns competence to the court of the effective habitual residence, but also to the courts of what used to be the habitual residence in the immediate six months after relocation).

(a) The child is moved to a non-Hague Convention State. The courts of the State of origin will still have jurisdiction over the child during the next six months, provided that one of the parents still resides there, and provided that an initial judgment relating to the child had been rendered. However, a twofold problem arises: First, we can wonder whether this assumption of competence really fosters the free circulation of persons within Europe, given that *the child has already left the territory*. Secondly, we can doubt whether such attribution of competence really favours the best interests of the child. After all, the plaintiff will want the decision to be recognised where the child actually *is*, something that might be far from easy, given that it is not unlikely that recognition will be denied on the ground that the granting court assumed excessive jurisdiction.

(b) The child is moved to a 1996 Hague Convention Contracting State (we assume that the declaration which should accompany the signature of the Convention has been made). Once the child has residence in a (non-EC) contracting State, the Convention is applicable. The same problem identified in the first example is also present here. The decision rendered by a court of a Member State seized under the Brussels II *bis* jurisdiction ground might not be recognised in a Hague Convention contracting State.[36] Moreover, there is an additional risk of parallel proceedings, since the non-EC court may decide to assume jurisdiction, and in that case, it is far from obvious how the *lis pendens* will be solved according to the Convention. Maybe it will not be resolved, as the prerequisite for Article 13 of the Convention to apply is that *both* courts have assumed jurisdiction on a conventional basis.

---

[36] Article 23.2 of the 1996 Hague Convention foresees the refusal of recognition if the measure was taken by an authority whose jurisdiction was not based on one of the grounds provided by chapter II of the Convention.

If that is so, we could openly question whether the Regulation actually *simplifies* matters. Moreover, one might be bold enough to question whether this communitarisation of the jurisdictional *fora* is not excessive, and whether it is justified in Community terms. The granting of jurisdiction on the basis of no matter whether strong or weak links to the EC may increase certainty within Europe, but this might not necessarily foster integration objectives. It could also be doubted whether these rules favour the recognition of the status of the child and, therefore, that they are in the best interests of children.

### 3.3. Questions regarding applicable law

It is to be doubted that the entry into force of Brussels II *bis* would improve matters concerning the determination of the applicable law. In fact, we would be confronted with the very same problems that have been referred to in the previous sections of this article. This would certainly be so if the new rules would have to be applied simultaneously with the 1961 Hague Convention. Moreover, the problems would be further aggravated due to the multiplication of jurisdictional criteria. For instance, we could wonder which law the *continuity* forum should apply.

One can only hope that the signature of the 1996 Hague Convention may contribute to making things easier. Certainly its basic and main rule (*lex fori in foro proprio*) may reduce complexity, although it does not really help in avoiding forum shopping. However, it is not obvious that the conflict norms of the 1996 Convention are applicable autonomously, that is, when a national court bases its jurisdiction on grounds other than the Convention itself. Article 15 states that "in exercising their jurisdiction *under the provisions of chapter II*, the authorities of the contracting states shall apply their own law" (emphasis added). Such a provision leaves even less room for the autonomous application of conflict rules than was the case under the equivalent norm of the 1961 Convention. The latter merely stated that the court which has been seized on the ground of the habitual residence of the child will apply its own law. As a result, we will be constrained in considering different possible interpretations of the 1996 Convention in this regard. There are there main possibilities:

(a) the Convention is deemed not to be applicable at all; this is on the basis that its conflict rules are only relevant when jurisdiction is established according to Convention rules; therefore, State conflict rules apply;

(b) the provisions of the Convention are construed similarly to those of the 1961 Convention, or, to put it another way, as far as the jurisdiction ground is similar to one of those enumerated in the Convention, its conflict rules apply; otherwise, national conflict rules are applicable;[37]

(c) the Convention is said to enshrine an implicit rule, according to which each court (whatever the basis for its jurisdiction) has to apply its own law. This would be a certain rule that would entail a limited choice of law, given the available number of *fora*. This might well be accepted within the Union on the basis of the principle of "mutual trust" between Member States, but it might encounter certain reticence in "truly" international cases.

One may wonder whether these interpretative options do not amount to a "square peg in a round hole" and, moreover, result in disturbing the Hague Convention mechanisms. If this is so, we might regret that the only solution left might be to draft EC rules which would allow for the same conflict rule indifference which underpins Brussels I.

## 4. CONCLUDING CONSIDERATIONS

In this article, I have considered the Brussels II and II *bis* (proposal) Regulations in some depth. Attention has been paid both to the *justification of Community action*, and to the concrete interpretative problems stemming from the provisions of the Regulations.

The claim that Community legislation on PIL is necessary has to be redeemed by means of making a proper argument in its favour. Such arguments were unfortunately not forthcoming with the Community legislative measures. In the absence of authoritative evidence, we can speculate as to whether the final ratio of the legislation is not the achievement of a judicial area. Even if that is the case, the effects of Community legislation are far from satisfactory on other relevant fronts. There are serious doubts as to whether this line of Community action complies with the principle of subsidiarity.[38] This reinforces the argument that *reverse subsidiarity* was probably applicable in this case. As it is well known, subsidiarity does not only constrain Community action with regard to Member States, regions and local authorities, but it can also require "the

---

[37] As argued by R. HAUSMANN, "Neues internationales Eheverfahren in der EU", *ELF*, 2000/01, 2001, pp. 271 ff and pp. 345 ff, at p. 353.

[38] Ch. KOHLER, "Europäisches Kollisionsrecht zwischen Amsterdam und Nizza", *ZeuS*, 2001, vol. 4, pp. 575 ff, at p. 592.

Union to consider whether action could be better taken at an international level".[39] This would point directly to The Hague Conference on PIL.

I have highlighted some of the interpretative challenges posed by the Brussels II Regulations. It should be stressed that they not only give rise to punctual dogmatic and practical problems; when considered systematically, they challenge the logic of the Member States' PIL system. To put it differently, they can be said to touch upon the very essence of PIL justice. One can wonder why a "regional" connection should imply that States apply different rules and therefore different private law standards.[40] The answer comes naturally if (and only if) emphasis is placed on the *integration* aims that those rules satisfy. Consider the case of controlling the jurisdiction of the rendering court at the stage of enforcing a decision: whereas it is present in the 1996 Hague Convention, it is simply non-existent in Brussels II. The principle of mutual recognition, which fosters EC aims, explains such a choice. However, in other cases, this permeating logic of integration is far from present, and one may then wonder what is the *rationale* for a different PIL solution. Take for instance the above-mentioned example of any *later* decision delivered in a Member State that is likely to block the enforcement of previous decisions relating to the child. What is the EC reason that explains this choice which runs counter to the PIL perception that *only* connected courts may deliver those decisions? It is a natural PIL requirement to ask for a connection between the non-Member State court rendering the decision *and* the child, in order to repeal the recognition of a Member State judgment (the courts of the non-Member State are presumed to be those in a favourable position to satisfy the so-called best interests of the child). But is there an EC reason that justifies granting recognition to a decision emanating from *whatever* Member State if the child is outside the EU? In other words, the idea of justice underlying PIL systems might be undermined because of the *regional* bias of EC PIL. This once again raises the question whether EC harmonising solutions are worth their cost.

In order to improve the situation in the short term, certain alternative measures might be referred, three of which might be worth highlighting: (a) the less acceptable solution in terms of fostering a judicial area and a mutual recognition system would be to reintroduce controlling the jurisdiction of the court that rendered the decision. Since this possibility

---

[39]  P. BEAUMONT/G. MOIR, "Brussels Convention II: A New Private International Law Instrument in Family Matters for the European Union or the European Community?", *E.L.R.*, 1995, pp. 268 ff, at p. 284.

[40]  Cf. E. JAYME, *op. cit.*, at p. 38.

is to be ruled out, it seems necessary to balance the approach to jurisdiction and conflict rules: either (b) we disregard the question of applicable law; this might be done on the basis that there exists an underlying Community rule (which is the real consequence that the absence of any control over the applicable law entails): *lex propria in foro proprio*; then the problems have to be dealt with at the jurisdictional level, that is reducing the number of *fora*, in order not to stimulate forum shopping; or (c) we make an inroad into the applicable law problem, in terms of materialising the idea of *conflicts law indifference*, so that, despite the growing number of competent jurisdictions, forum shopping becomes a fruitless exercise.

Solutions in the long-term require bolder proposals. If we discard reverse subsidiarity, on account of the developments that will likely follow (*i.e.*, the progressive communitarisation of PIL and the increasing concern for family law), we can suggest that the EC should abandon the piecemeal approach and tackle the whole issue of PIL on family and child matters. A "global" or "systematic" EC approach that pays attention to worldwide achievements in this area is needed. Only an all-encompassing Community PIL (with harmonised jurisdiction rules and conflict law indifference) will ensure that the Community area of justice is not achieved to the detriment of the best interests of the child.

# FIRST STEPS IN THE COMMUNITARISATION OF FAMILY LAW: TOO MUCH HASTE, TOO LITTLE REFLECTION?

PETER MCELEAVY

## 1. INTRODUCTION

In many respects it is still startling to talk of the *communitarisation* of family law. A mere ten years ago it would have been inconceivable to have contemplated significant European Community involvement in this area.[1] Today however family related issues represent an important policy objective within the Justice and Home Affairs' portfolio; one Council Regulation has entered into force[2] another is awaiting completion[3] whilst plans exist for additional instruments.[4] That this should have come to pass, without fanfare or protest, was a matter of concern for many who delivered papers or intervened at the Commission on European Family Law conference in Utrecht. Community competence in respect of family matters has simply emerged, almost imperceptibly, to become an established reality.[5]

At present that competence is limited in nature, since under the terms of Article 65 of the EC Treaty it is premised on facilitating the free movement of persons. This means that the new initiatives are centred on unifying conflict of laws rules, notably bringing about the free movement of family

---

[1]  The EC has throughout its existence addressed certain discrete family related issues where these have been inter-related with traditional Community concerns, see C. MCGLYNN "The Europeanisation of Family Law" [2001] *Child and Family Law Quarterly* 35.

[2]  Council Regulation (EC) No 1347/2000 of 29 May 2000 on Jurisdiction and the Recognition and Enforcement of Judgments in Matrimonial Matters and in Matters of Parental Responsibility for Children of both Spouses, (Brussels II), *O.J.* 2000 L160, 19–29.

[3]  Proposal for a Council Regulation concerning jurisdiction and the recognition and enforcement of judgments in matrimonial matters and in matters of parental responsibility repealing Regulation (EC) No 1347/2000 and amending Regulation (EC) No 44/2001 in matters relating to maintenance, (Brussels II *bis*), see: *O.J.* 2002 C203, 155–178. At the time of writing the only publicly available text remains that from the late Spring of 2002, although this has been substantially amended, particularly with regard to child abduction matters.

[4]  See the Action Plan adopted at the European Council meeting in Vienna on 3 December 1998, *O.J.* 1999 C 19/01.

[5]  See P. MCELEAVY "The Brussels II Regulation: How the European Community has Moved into Family Law" [2002] *I.C.L.Q.* 883-908, [hereinafter: McEleavy].

law judgments within Europe. It remains to be seen whether the unification of substantive family law rules will be targeted for Community action in the future; in this the work of the Commission on European Family Law could undoubtedly be exploited as a platform.[6] However, it would appear safe to say that any such steps could not be taken in the absence of a specific transfer of competence to the Community by Member States. This paper will seek to evaluate the manner in which the communitarisation of family law has been taken forward and consider whether it is a step too far in the European project, or, whether critics, coming from a traditional international family law perspective, are simply being too negative and conservative when faced with the realities of Community politics and law making for the first time.

## 2. A EUROPEAN COMMUNITY FAMILY LAW

An analysis of the Community's family law agenda presents particular challenges, in that it may justifiably be regarded as creating a new and distinct area of law. Self evident it may be, it is nevertheless worth reiterating that the nascent "Community family law" requires an appreciation and awareness of European as well as private international law if one is to understand fully the context in which this new project is being taken forward and the various dynamics influencing it.

Until very recently family law within the European Union was marked by certainty and predictability. Outside a core of shared principles and values[7] each Member State developed and retained its own independent family law rules. Harmonisation, where it has come, has been achieved gradually. In large measure it has been centred on specific conflict of law rules and has not necessarily been limited to the fifteen Member States. This is because the focus for these developments has not been centred on Brussels, but on Strasbourg and more particularly The Hague, through the work of the Council of Europe and the Hague Conference on Private International Law. Under the auspices of these organisations a range of instruments have been elaborated, addressing various problematic questions of

---

[6]    Cf. M. ANTOKOLSKAIA "The Harmonisation of Family Law: Old and New Dilemmas" *European Review of Private Law*, 2003, 28 at 48.

[7]    At a regional level reference can be made in particular to the influence of the European Convention on Human Rights and the resultant jurisprudence of the Court of Human Rights, see: R. REED & J. MURDOCH *A Guide to Human Rights Law in Scotland*, Butterworths, London, 2001. As regards global instruments the United Nations' Convention on the Rights of the Child has influenced the development of and respect for children's rights within Europe, see J. FORTIN *Children's Rights and the Developing Law*, Butterworths, London, 1998.

international family law.[8] These in turn have impacted on the development of substantive family law, in this reference may be made to the role of the 1980 Hague Convention in promoting the child's State of habitual residence as the primary jurisdiction for adjudication of matters relating to parental responsibility.

The approach adopted by the Hague Conference and the Council of Europe has been by the classic means of inter-governmental negotiation leading to the conclusion of a convention which is then open for signature and subsequent ratification or accession. Whether Hague and Council of Europe Conventions will continue to represent a core element of the family law of the Member States remains to be seen. The entry of the European Community into this domain has shattered the status quo as an increasing number of Council Regulations are completed and enter into effect. In many instances the latter will assume precedence over existing instruments. The received wisdom, certainly in Brussels and Paris, is that Community solutions represent progress and bring added value for the European citizen. This no doubt explains, at least in part, why European family law is now characterized by frenzied law making. Whether this is the best background for a strategic family law policy must be questioned, particularly since the Member States are often hopelessly divided as to the direction initiatives should take.[9]

The source of this family law revolution may be traced to the Treaty of Amsterdam. This instrument introduced many significant changes, but in terms of private international law it totally altered the landscape by according the Community competence for the area.[10] The uncertainty as

---

[8]  See for example: the 1980 Hague Convention on the Civil Aspects of International Child Abduction, the 1993 Hague Convention on Protection of Children and Co-operation in respect of Intercountry Adoption, the 1996 Hague Convention on Jurisdiction, Applicable Law, Recognition, Enforcement and Co-operation in respect of Parental Responsibility and Measures for the Protection of Children, the 2000 Hague Convention on the International Protection of Adults, The 1980 European Convention on Recognition and Enforcement of Decisions Concerning Custody of Children and on Restoration of Custody of Children, the 1996 European Convention on the Exercise of Children's Rights and the 2003 European Convention on Contact Concerning Children.

[9]  See infra p. 519.

[10]  J. BASEDOW "The Communitarisation of the Conflict of laws under the Treaty of Amsterdam" (2000) *C.M.L.R.* 687; G. BETLEM & E. HONDIUS "European Private Law After the Treaty of Amsterdam" (2001) *European Review of Private Law,* 3; U. DROBNIG, "European Private International Law After the Treaty of Amsterdam: Perspectives for the Next Decade" (2000) *King's College Law Journal,* 190; J. ISRAËL "Conflicts of Law and the EC after Amsterdam A Change for the Worse?" (2000) *Maastricht Journal of European and Comparative Law* 81; W. A. KENNETT, *Enforcement of Judgments In Europe,* Oxford University Press, Oxford, 2000, p.

to whether Article 65 could be interpreted as extending this competence to family law issues was resolved, somewhat unsatisfactorily, with the decision to transform the Brussels II Convention into a Council Regulation.[11] Greater legitimacy has come through the Treaty of Nice, where actual reference, albeit indirect, has been made to family matters for the first time.[12] This has been taken a step further in the current draft of the proposed European Convention where Article 14(3) of Part II refers explicitly to the adoption of "*laws and framework laws concerning family law*" and also to the adoption of "*laws and framework laws concerning parental responsibility.*"[13]

It could be said that the interpretation allowing Title IV of the EC Treaty to extend into the realm of family law is no more than an example of politico-legal expediency designed to ensure that a completed instrument, the Brussels II Convention, could be brought into operation quickly and with the minimum of fuss. Equally it is also possible that Community and certain Member State officials viewed the Treaty of Amsterdam as affording, whether by accident or design, an unmissable opportunity to let the organisation move into an area of law hitherto within the exclusive competence of the Member States. Whatever the reason, the step has been taken and Brussels is now in a position to take the lead in respect of family law matters, as it already does in so many other areas which affect contemporary European life. Advocates of a Community family law policy would undoubtedly argue that we should now simply look forward and work within the Community framework, in accordance with established procedures, to facilitate the free movement of as many different types of family law judgment as possible.

It is clear that much benefit can be brought to the field of family law through greater co-operation and the increased harmonisation of rules at the Community level, but, family law is not just another area of compe-

---

12; C. KOHLER "Interrogations sur les sources du droit international privé européen après le traité d'Amsterdam" *Rev. crit. DIP* (1999) 1; McELEAVY, *op. cit.*, p. 897; H.U. JESSURUN D'OLIVEIRA "The EU and a Metamorphosis of Private International Law in J. FAWCETT (ed.) *Reform and Development of Private International Law: Essays in Honour of Sir Peter North*, 2002, OUP, p. 111; and O. REMIEN "European private International law, the European Community and its Emerging Area of Freedom, Security and Justice" (2001) *C.M.L.R.* 53.

[11]  McELEAVY, *op cit*, p. 895 *et seq.*

[12]  Article 2(4) states that qualified majority voting will be introduced in respect of measures provided for in Article 65 of the EC Treaty, with the exception of aspects regarding family law; *OJ* 2001 C80/01.

[13]  Area of Freedom, Security and Justice, The European Convention, 14 March 2003, CONV 614/03, http://european-convention.eu.int/docs/Treaty/cv00614.en03.pdf.

tence which can be plundered and automatically absorbed into the Community empire. It was not an untilled field where inter-State agreement had been unforthcoming, on the contrary, as previously noted, Member States had an established history of working together in respect of family law issues. Experience has been gathered over decades of negotiation and law making, leaving a profound impact on policy makers. Moreover, many of the pre-existing instruments have worked well, while their scope has often extended beyond the current frontiers of the European Union and in the case of the Hague Conventions to every corner of the world. Given that issues of abduction, custody and adoption have been exposed to the phenomenon of globalisation it may even be questioned whether it is desirable at this time to seek competing regionalized solutions.[14]

For whatever reason the international family law *acquis* has not been fully recognised or appreciated.[15] Moreover the error has been compounded by the failure to acclimatize the legal community at large to the practical realities of Community competence. In the place of a smooth transition it would appear that the intention has been to make a clean break with the past. This must also be viewed in the light of the re-alignment of the international institutional balance in the aftermath of the Treaty of Amsterdam.[16] It is not an exaggeration to state that a new order has been imposed in respect of the evolution and harmonization of private international law in general and international family law in particular.

One is left to wonder why the acquisition of competence for family law, a very significant development for the Community as a whole, has been managed in this way. The lack of transparency, the reluctance to consult, and the apparent unwillingness to build on and profit from past experiences and achievements have merely served to encourage criticism and disenchantment; but, will the Community be proved right, and the new order be found to be more successful than the old in harmonizing European family conflict of laws rules.

---

[14]    Indeed one might question whether this does in fact accord with the Community's own over arching policy of subsidiarity, Article 5 EC Treaty.
[15]    MCELEAVY, *op cit.*, p. 901 *et seq.*
[16]    H.U. JESSURUN D'OLIVEIRA, *op cit.*, p. 134.

## 3. NEW ORDER V. OLD ORDER

The essence of the distinction which may be drawn in respect of private international law pre- and post- the Amsterdam Treaty lies in the manner in which steps towards harmonization are being initiated and managed, as well as the fundamental character of negotiations. It is not possible to transpose the norms and methodology of the intergovernmental framework against which family law conventions have traditionally been elaborated to an intra-Community context. The rules within Europe, both written and unwritten are very different, whilst the inherent power of the institutions, the strong collective identity they have engendered, and the underlying current of politicisation is such that a high level of control and extreme pressures are exerted on any policy initiative as well as upon those involved in the negotiation process.[17] This *modus operandi* has been built up, refined and exploited over many years, so it is understandable, if not self-evident, that it might be applied to the field of family law without further thought. To evaluate the consequences of such an approach it is essential to make a comparison with the old order.

An assessment of intergovernmental convention making and the instruments that have flowed from it, is of course a most difficult exercise and one which is inherently subjective, even if the research were to be exhaustive and all the relevant statistical data collated. That this should be so is clear, for how is one to evaluate objectively a treaty and the process by which it was elaborated. Does it come down to efficiency, the length of time spent, the ease with which agreement was reached, the satisfaction of the negotiating parties and their constituencies with the outcome, or merely through the end product? If it is simply the final text which counts, how should the latter be assessed; in terms of the instrument's legal finesse, scope, potential effect, or can judgment only be reached after several years of operation when the practical effect can be gauged and the number of ratifications identified? The variables are numerous, particularly since the viability of an instrument may depend not simply on its terms and provisions, but on external factors such as the resources devoted to making it operational and the legal framework in which it functions. With the passage of time the only assessment which undoubtedly matters for the legal world comes down to whether the instrument provides a comprehensive, workable and effective solution. Where the answer is affirmative all the other criteria, together with the drafting process as a whole, then fade

---

[17]    See generally H. KASSIM *et al.* (eds.) *The National Co-ordination of EU Policy: The European Level*, OUP, Oxford, 2001.

from view, whatever the contribution they will have made. The reality however is that success or failure, whether of the negotiating process or the final instrument, will most often be qualified rather than absolute. Uncertainty will therefore often exist and the risk of subjectivity in any analysis increases.

Against this background it is not proposed to give a definitive evaluation of the intergovernmental approach but merely to identify and evaluate its main strengths and weaknesses to in turn permit a more informed analysis of the Community model. The focus here will be the Hague Conference on Private International Law which without doubt most clearly embodies the working methods and general ethos of the old order and the 1980 Convention on the Civil Aspects of International Child Abduction, its most widely ratified family law instrument.[18] Three central themes will be considered: topic selection and preparatory work, negotiation and project management, as well as general efficiency and effectiveness.

### 3.1. Topic Selection & Preparatory Work

Many different justifications can be advanced for the selection of a topic, for example: the existence of an identifiable and pressing need, the lobbying of a powerful State or grouping of States for intervention, the issue in question being ripe for treatment or it being of a type which the organisation in question has experience in dealing with. There will be situations where all of the aforementioned criteria are clearly present, such as with international child abduction in the 1970s,[19] but not all cases will be so easy. How should an organisation respond in determining whether or not to add a specific issue to its agenda where the various factors are finely balanced. This will surely be influenced by what topic selection actually means for the organisation in question, in particular the consequences of a choice proving to be misguided.

The Hague Conference has very limited resources, both financially and in terms of personnel. This has certainly influenced its long established and very methodical pattern of law making, which is characterised by research, reflection and consultation.[20] The necessary corollary of this

---

[18]    There are currently 73 Contracting States, see: www.hcch.net/e/status/stat28e.html
[19]    P. BEAUMONT & P. MCELEAVY, *The Hague Convention on International Child Abduction*, OUP, Oxford, 1999, p. 16 *et seq.*
[20]    H. VAN HOOGSTRATEN "The United Kingdom Joins an Uncommon Market: The Hague Conference on Private International Law" [1963] *I.C.L.Q.* 148; T. BRADBROOKE Smith "Achieving Results at International Meetings: Why the Hague Conference Succeeds", in A.
→

approach is that instruments are not produced at a rapid rate. Indeed a total of four significant family law conventions in the last 25 years[21] might be criticized as being rather paltry, but it must also be recognised that this small, very specialised international organization has not focused exclusively on one particular area.[22] Quite simply the Hague Conference cannot afford, either financially or in terms of its reputation, to embark upon an initiative without having carefully considered the implications and having assessed the likelihood of success. Consequently considerable effort is placed into the selection of topics that merit and are capable of treatment.

Possible subjects are put forward and discussed by representatives of the Member States at an informal preparatory meeting of the Conference dealing with "general affairs," known as a Special Commission. Participants can then report back to their governments and informal discussions and consultations can take place domestically and internationally. In addition preliminary research may be carried out by a member of the secretariat of the Conference (Permanent Bureau) which will be circulated to Member States.[23] In the light of such work and of the various views gathered, a picture will emerge as to where, if at all, a proposal should figure on the agenda. It may be that a subject is ready for immediate action, or merely merits continuing monitoring or should not figure on the agenda at all. Whatever the position, the decision will be made at a formal meeting of the Conference in Diplomatic Session,[24] the minutes of which are published and open to public scrutiny.[25]

Once the selection is made a member of the Permanent Bureau, who will have considerable private international law experience, will assume responsibility for the project and a detailed analysis of the topic will commence. This will culminate in a report identifying the most contentious

---

BORRÁS et al. (eds.), E Pluribus Unum, Kluwer, The Netherlands, 1996, 415–444; BEAUMONT & McELEAVY, op. cit., p. 16 et seq.

[21] In addition to the Child Abduction Convention this includes the 1993 Intercountry Adoption, the 1996 Protection of Children Convention and the 2000 Adults' Convention, see supra fn. 9.

[22] During this time 5 other conventions have been completed, see: www.hcch.net/e/conventions/index.html.

[23] See for example: A. DYER Report on International Child Abduction By One Parent ("Legal Kidnapping"), Preliminary Document No. 1 of August 1978, Actes et Documents of the XIVth Session, Volume III, 1982, at p. 12.

[24] Formally the agenda of the organisation is set by the Conference's supervisory body, the Netherlands Standing Government Committee, see Article 3 of the Statute of the Hague Conference on Private International Law.

[25] The minutes of the diplomatic session, together with the Working Documents used, are published with the text of the Convention, Explanatory Report and other preparatory material in the Actes et Documents of the Session.

issues and evaluating potential solutions. The report and an accompanying questionnaire are then circulated to Member States allowing the Secretariat to acquire up to date information on the legal position in the States which will ultimately participate in the negotiations and to identify what is and is not likely to be feasible. However, the formula does not always work; even where the initial portents are good it may subsequently become apparent that an area is still not yet ripe for intervention, as the Worldwide Judgments project has most recently shown.[26] In the latter case whilst States were fully consulted and engaged, the breakdown occurred when it became apparent that key participants were not prepared to compromise on issues they considered to be fundamental to their national interests.

In such an intergovernmental forum the stature of the sponsoring organisation will also be of great relevance. The Hague Conference has little inherent power, therefore a project can only be taken forward if the support of a number of key Member States has been established and can be marshalled. The organisation itself is not in a position to ignore the views of major players or impose its own will; if anything it is at the mercy of its members, as the Worldwide Judgments project clearly shows. In this, as in respect to all the other factors influencing topic selection, the Hague Conference finds itself in a very different position to the European Community. The EC is an extremely powerful supra-national organisation rich in resources and influence, and is not subject to the constraints which so limit the Hague Conference's scope of action. This is reflected in all of its actions, including the approach to topic selection. The Commission and Member States will of course be influenced by the same criteria in selecting topics, but to this list a further important factor must be added: the pursuit of wider policy objectives deemed essential to the continuing success and progress of the Community. In the context of family law one can validly draw attention to the overarching policy of the promotion of the mutual recognition of judgments, which was identified and presented at the Tampere European Council meeting in 1999,[27] as well as the aspiration to create an area of freedom, security and justice in the European Union.[28]

---

[26]     See D. MCCLEAN "The Hague Conference's Judgments Project" in J. FAWCETT (ed.) *Reform and Development of Private International Law: Essays in Honour of Sir Peter North*, 2002, OUP, p. 255.

[27]     Tampere European Council Conclusions (VI), 16 October 1999: http://ue.eu.int/Newsroom/loadDoc.asp?max=1&bid=76&did=59122&grp=2017&lang=1

[28]     Article 2 TEU, P. BOELES "Freedom, Security and Justice for All" in E. GUILD & C. HARLOW (eds.) *Implementing Amsterdam: Immigration and Asylum Rights in EC Law*, Hart, Oxford, 2001, p. 1. and more specifically in this context, The Vienna Action Plan, O.J. 1999 C 19/01 and Biannual Update of the Scoreboard to Review Progress on the Creation of an Area of "Freedom, Security and Justice" in the European Union, (second half of 2002), *COM* (2002) 738.

The right of initiative in respect of any family related projects is currently
shared by the Commission and the Member States, although in accordance
with the terms of Article 67 of the EC Treaty, Member States will lose this
power from 1 May 2004, leaving them only with the possibility of making
a proposal to the Commission.[29] The legal basis for policy initiation may
be clear, but the manner in which these powers are exercised and the
justification for their use are certainly not. The introduction of the various
strands of the Brussels II *bis* initiative are notable for having been shrouded
in a high degree of secrecy, and unlike the Hague Conference, there are
no minutes to facilitate any degree of understanding. A working document
was issued in March 2001[30] which was followed up by a public meeting on
27 June, but even here there was little active attempt to promote awareness
and encourage dialogue with interested parties. A possible explanation is
the sensitivity of the subject matter, the legitimacy of any family related
proposal being at best questionable, but, it should be noted however that
with regard to other elements of the Justice and Home Affairs portfolio,
where firmer foundations exist, more substantive preliminary consultation
has taken place, most recently with the issue of a Green Paper on the
question of whether the 1980 Rome Convention should be converted into
a Community instrument.[31]

The absence of transparency in Community proposal initiation gives rise
to particular concern because once a proposal is adopted it is very likely
to remain in substantially the same form. One official has suggested that
around 80% of an original proposal will usually survive by the time it is
finally adopted by the Council.[32] Consequently if national officials or
permanent representative members are not in a position to intervene and
lobby Commission officials at the policy initiation stage Member States may
find themselves fighting a very difficult rear-guard action thereafter.
Conversely Member States are all too aware that if they give their support
to the Commission they will be able to advance a project to which they
attach particular importance, even in the face of strong opposition from
other Member States. This is precisely the situation which has been played
out in Brussels over the last few years with regard to the issue of international child abduction. A specific Community solution to deal with cases of
wrongful removal and wrongful retention was included in a proposal

---

[29] The shared right of initiative was established for 5 years following the entry into force of the Treaty of Amsterdam on 1 May 1999.
[30] COM (2001) 166 final.
[31] 14 January 2003, http://europa.eu.int/comm/off/green/index_en.htm.
[32] R. HULL "Lobbying Brussels: A View From Within" in S. MAZEY & J. RICHARDSON (eds.) *Lobbying in the European Community*, OUP, Oxford, 1993, 82 at 83.

adopted by the Commission in September 2001.[33] This was supported in principle by a grouping of mainly "Southern" Member States, whilst seven "Northern" Member States[34] were totally opposed to Community intervention, given that a successful global solution to this problem existed in the form of the 1980 Hague Convention. Notwithstanding this sustained opposition the core proposal remained on the table[35] until a political compromise was brokered at the Justice and Home Affairs (JHA) Council meeting on 29 November 2002.[36] While the latter guaranteed the position of the 1980 Convention, in abduction cases within the Member States the instrument will in the future have to operate in conjunction with additional rules contained in the forthcoming Brussels II *bis* Regulation. Henceforth, if the court seised of a return application under the Convention finds one of the Article 13 exceptions to have been established and exercises its discretion not to make a return order, the courts in the Member State in which the child was habitually resident immediately before the wrongful removal or retention shall be notified within a month, and if a court in the latter jurisdiction subsequently makes an order which requires the return of the child that order shall be capable of automatic recognition and enforcement in the other Member State without the need for a declaration of enforceability.[37] Consequently it can be understood that even though the Southern States and the Commission were faced down when confronted with what was quite an exceptional level of opposition, they were still able to secure some of their initial aims, namely a Community dimension to the treatment of child abduction cases together with an even more strict return regime.

This recent example shows the crucial importance of the policy initiation stage with regard to Justice and Home Affairs matters. It is also the case that some Member States have taken their role in lobbying and influencing

---

[33]    O.J. C 332 of 27.11.2001.

[34]    Austria, Finland, Germany, Ireland, The Netherlands, Sweden, and the United Kingdom.

[35]    The original Commission proposal was replaced by an alternative in Spring 2002: Proposal for a Council Regulation concerning jurisdiction and the recognition and enforcement of judgments in matrimonial matters and in matters of parental responsibility repealing Regulation (EC) No 1347/2000 and amending Regulation (EC) No 44/2001 in matters relating to maintenance, *O.J.* 2002 C203, 155–178.

[36]    J.-P. STROOBANTS, "Les Quinze adoptent une unification du droit familial pour les enfants binationaux," *Le Monde*, 1 December 2002.

[37]    Automatic recognition of the subsequent decision will depend on the court in the State of origin issuing a certificate that in the proceedings which led to the judgment: the child was given an opportunity to be heard, unless this was inappropriate given the child's age / maturity; and the parties were given an opportunity to be heard. Furthermore the court must have taken into account the reasons for and evidence underpinning the non return order made in the 1980 Convention proceedings.

topic selection more seriously than others, France for example, endeavours to have a judge from the international division of the Ministry of Justice seconded to DG JHA at all times.[38] This will clearly provide 13 Place Vendôme not only with eyes and ears at the heart of the decision making process, but also a continuous and direct link to the Brussels policy makers.[39] Notwithstanding this, France is the only Member State to date to take advantage of the shared right of policy initiative under Article 67(1). Immediately after it assumed the Council Presidency on 1 July 2000 France submitted what was in effect a completed draft Regulation on the mutual enforcement of judgments on rights of access to children.[40] Again the reasons for this are not clear; the proposal built on a policy objective identified in the Tampere Conclusions, so was clearly in keeping with Commission aspirations. Of course as it held the Presidency and would therefore have control of the agenda, the French administration may have envisaged this as a prime opportunity to advance the proposal quickly. The essence of the proposal will ultimately come to fruition as part of Brussels II *bis*, but any hope that it would do so quickly were misplaced.

The French access proposal, as with the Commission's proposals on parental responsibility, reflects a further divergence in the working methods employed within the EC and the Hague Conference. The approach used in the former is to present and indeed adopt a proposal already in the form of a text. A structure and substance is therefore set and Member States have to respond accordingly. Within the Hague Conference the approach has traditionally been for the representatives of all, or at least some, of the participating States to work together to construct a text. In this way common goals are established and there is a greater chance of a sense of shared involvement in the initiative. Of course such an approach has the drawback of being time consuming, but equally it avoids any sense of a solution being imposed, which in an intergovernmental forum could sound the death knell for an initiative.

## 3.2. Negotiation & Project Management

The fundamental differences which distinguish the Hague Conference and the European Community are reflected as clearly in their respective management of the negotiation process as in respect of their approaches

---

[38] For an explanation of the role of a *magistrat de liaison*, see the French Ministry of Justice website: www.justice.gouv.fr/publicat/note17.htm#15.
[39] See generally: A. MENON "The French Administration in Brussels" in H. KASSIM *et al.* (eds.) *The National Co-ordination of EU Policy: The European Level*, OUP, Oxford, 2001, p. 75 at 86.
[40] *O.J.* 2000 C 234/07.

to topic selection. However, this divide is accentuated yet further by a significant number of minor technical and procedural modalities related to the organisation of negotiation sessions.

In essence it might be said that while meetings of the Hague Conference involve actual negotiation and work towards the collective construction of an instrument, preparatory meetings within the European Council consist of Member States simply making comments, often determined in advance, on an existing text. In the aftermath of such meetings it is the Presidency, which in the light of the views expressed, amends the text until agreement can be reached on the initiative as a whole.[41] The entire organisation of the negotiation process within the two organisations reflects this difference.

Special Commissions of the Hague Conference are organized to facilitate fast moving, detailed law making. In having only two official languages, English and French, the potential for linguistic confusion and delay is limited. Delegations are often composed not only of civil servants but of judges, practitioners and academics, thereby ensuring a wide range of views and perspectives may be expressed and taken into account.[42] The presence of leading experts ensures that potential pitfalls may be identified and complicated problems solved. Meetings are chaired by a representative of one of the Member States, but he or she is under an obligation to act independently. In most instances the chair is often able to move the debate along and overcome delicate problems because of a deep personal knowledge of the issues being addressed. In addition, the negotiators are able to benefit from the presence of a *Rapporteur* who is able to give expert and independent advice on technical matters. He or she is also responsible for preparing draft and final explanatory reports which serve as invaluable tools in facilitating understanding of the text and the intention behind provisions. On a day to day basis the participants are able to benefit from having an independent record of the negotiations noted in the *procès-verbaux* of the proceedings. Delegates are equally at liberty to submit working documents in response to issues raised during the debates. It may also be noted that Hague Conference negotiations take place within 1, 2 or 3 weeks blocks, spread over a 2 or 3 year period. Not only is such an

---

41    In contrast to the Hague Conference, within the Community framework there is no committee, made of a selection of participants to draft the text of the instrument in the light of the decisions taken by the meeting as a whole.

42    Participation is not restricted to the 62 Member States of the Hague Conference, non-Member States may attend as observers, and while they may not vote they are entitled to participate in the discussions. Representatives of non-governmental and inter-governmental organisations are also invited to attend and participate as observers, ensuring that a very broad spectrum of expertise and views is represented.

arrangement conducive to real progress being made, facilitating detailed, probing discussions, but it ensures that there are adequate possibilities for reflection and consultation outside of the negotiations, nationally, bilaterally and multilaterally. Moreover, since the framework is planned in advance there is no sense of uncertainty or fear over what is going to happen.

The Hague format is a world removed from negotiations within the Council in Brussels. There delegations are very small, between 1 to 3 persons, and almost invariably made up of civil servants from national justice ministries or members of the Member State's permanent representation in Brussels. While many of the former have significant experience and an excellent knowledge of international family law issues, others are relative novices with only a limited grasp of private international law. However, it is not merely the breadth and depth of knowledge which might be absent, participants are put in a position where they are forced to respond and react to an agenda which is set by the Member State occupying the rotating Presidency. This Member State may wish to push a particular *dossier* at a fast pace, or, it may wish to use its influence to see a proposal wither; each new presidency is awaited with a sense of anticipation as to what will happen. Furthermore, there is no impartial and independent guidance of the negotiations; the body which might be thought to fill this role, the Commission, is driven by the pursuit of its own objectives and policy goals.

Even at a practical level meetings are organized in such a manner that one might think the intention is to prevent the negotiating committee from independently making progress; meetings take place over one or two days and there is often an absence of continuity in personnel and in the subject matter of the discussion, participants use their own language which is then interpreted into all the other Community languages, which often results in misunderstandings, particularly where complex legal concepts which may have no direct translation are being discussed.

It could be said that a sense of control pervades the negotiations. At any given time some of the Member States may not agree with the proposal on the table, but they are nevertheless obliged to participate and for reasons or overall Community politics are restricted in what action they might take. It is also the case that unlike at the Hague, the negotiations are not one dimensional. Within the Community the inherent pressure to "play the game" means that States will often acquiesce in initiatives they are not positive about; albeit prior to the Treaty of Amsterdam reforms, the United Kingdom's participation in the Brussels II Convention project is very much a case in point.[43] Where States view an issue to be of sufficient importance to take a stand, a compromise will often be brokered on the basis of concessions being made in respect of an other area of Community policy, possibly even in a different field entirely. Experienced representatives are fully aware of the behind the scenes politics which are at play and it would be facile to imagine that this does not affect their perception of the negotiations. One could view negotiations within the Council as a multi-layered game of chess which can be played out simultaneously at up to three levels, i.e. expert, permanent representative and ministerial level, depending on the status of the discussions and the level of difficulty which has arisen.[44] In moving up the levels it might be said that the legal focus decreases in direct proportion to the political dimension increasing.

### 3.3. Efficiency & Effectiveness

*Prima facie* there is no comparison to be made between the Hague and Community models with regard to "efficiency." The latter certainly appears to hold all of the aces given the inherent power of the organisation and the control that can be exercised over the negotiation process and even the Member States involved. It is a fundamental characteristic of inter-governmental law making, one exhibited not only by the Hague Conference or Council of Europe, but in different contexts by the United Nations, that a significant period of time will elapse between the initiation of a proposal and the concluded instrument ultimately operating in a significant number of States. The time differential can in certain instances be decades long, a significant inconvenience if the problem at issue requires urgent action. In the case of the Child Abduction Convention almost 8 years elapsed between the initiation of the project and the entry into force of the instrument in 1983, while a further 8 years passed before there were 25 States party. An inter-governmental organisation is totally dependent

---

[43]  Lord Chancellor's Department, "Memorandum to the House of Lords' Select Committee," Report of the House of Lords Select Committee on the European Communities "Brussels II: The Draft Convention on Jurisdiction, Recognition and Enforcement of Judgments in Matrimonial Matters" H.L. Paper 19, Session 1997-98, p. 36 at 37, para 5.

[44]  An example of this is provided by the treatment of the child abduction impasse reached in the autumn of 2002, which was only overcome when the dossier was passed the full length of the chain from the civil law committee to the permanent representatives and finally to the justice ministers at the JHA Council Meeting of 29 November. On the decision making process within the Community see H. KASSIM "Introduction: Co-ordinating National Action in Brussels" in H. KASSIM *et al.* (eds.) *The National Co-ordination of EU Policy: The European Level,* OUP, Oxford, 2001, p. 17 *et seq.* Kassim estimates that 70% of Council business is agreed at working group level, 15-20% in COREPER and the remainder at ministerial level.

on the support and goodwill of States because each one is free to decide independently when it will sign and ratify an instrument; there is no central power coordinating, or rule controlling, such matters. Moreover even if the requisite political support exists, time will often still be lost as in many dualist States steps have to be taken to prepare implementing legislation. Where political support has waned, or a State is not content with the outcome of a convention, it will not ratify or accede, regardless of the resources that may have been devoted to participating in the negotiation process. This course of action is not available under Title IV, and while the United Kingdom and Ireland do have the apparent security of the selective opt-in mechanism,[45] the primarily pro-European stance of the governments in both countries in effect renders this meaningless, since for the time being both are always likely to participate.

Whilst the power inherent in the Community model means that initiatives can be pushed through in the face of indifference, or even opposition, to become directly applicable in all the Member States within a relatively short period of time, it may still be questioned if this approach is truly efficient. In this consideration may be given to whether the Community is making the best use of its great powers, indeed employing them effectively.

In relation to specific procedures or methodology one can draw attention to topic selection and the initiation of projects, here a traditional Community formula is being used and so it might be unrealistic to expect officials or Member States to have countenanced any change of approach, but, the newness of this area of competence combined with the absence of a firm Treaty foundation are such that much greater openness and transparency should have been forthcoming. In clouding matters in secrecy and avoiding dialogue proponents of this policy have in fact damaged their cause. Across Europe judges, practitioners and academics have been astounded and often appalled at the sudden apparition of EC instruments in the family law domain. Were the legal community to be consulted in a meaningful way and engaged in the legislative process not only would this new development be regarded with less mistrust, but there is every likelihood that instruments would improve in quality.[46]

---

[45]    Under the Protocol to the Amsterdam Treaty on the Position of the United Kingdom and Ireland, *O.J.* 1997 C340/99, both States have opted out of Title IV, but can selectively opt into initiatives on a case by case basis provided notice is given within 3 months of a proposal being presented to the Council. Alternatively it is possible for either State to opt in after an initiative has been adopted.

[46]    For criticism of the drafting of the Brussels II Regulation see: P. MCELEAVY "The Communitarisation of Divorce Rules: What Impact for English and Scottish Law?" (forthcoming).

In terms of the negotiation regime it would appear that the supra-national structure which gives the Community model such power serves equally to constrain the drafting process. Put simply there is often a lack of technical expertise, no independent guidance and an atmosphere of excessive control and politicisation; consequently there is no freedom to construct coherent, thought through instruments which will provide clear, workable and practical solutions to what are real problems.[47]

Turning to the wider picture it is clear, as previously identified, that there are policy goals behind the family law project, but, there does not appear to be a developed strategic plan. If anything the piecemeal approach to family law employed to date suggests that national and Community officials in favour of Europeanisation are unable or unwilling to take a global view of what they are doing, or indeed to appreciate the wider impact of each legislative innovation. Where was the benefit in bringing matters of parental responsibility within the scope of the Brussels II Convention. France and Spain fought tooth and nail to have such matters included,[48] but it has caused nothing but confusion and unnecessary complexity since so many potential parental responsibility actions are excluded. It was a decision devoid of logic and reflection, unless of course one were to adopt the cynical view that it was purely to expand the boundaries of Community competence yet further. Recognition of the unsatisfactory nature of parental responsibility coverage in Brussels II has led to the Community family law project facing even greater ridicule, with the Commission proposing in the draft Brussels II *bis* Regulation that Brussels II be replaced, little more than 1 year after it entered into force, a decision which will cause the Member States enormous inconvenience and expense.[49] This is clearly not an organisation making an efficient and effective use of its vast powers.

## 4. CONCLUSION

This short review of the inter-governmental and Community models of law making shows how both are influenced by and reflect the contexts in which

---

[47] See generally: E.L.H. DE WILDE "Deficient European Legislation is in Nobody's Interest" (2000) *European Journal of Law Reform* 293.

[48] McELEAVY, "The Brussels II Regulation: How the European Community has moved into Family Law", *op.cit.*, fn. 5, p. 893.

[49] Proposal for a Council Regulation concerning jurisdiction and the recognition and enforcement of judgments in matrimonial matters and in matters of parental responsibility repealing Regulation (EC) No 1347/2000 and amending Regulation (EC) No 44/2001 in matters relating to maintenance, *O.J.* 2002 C203, 155–178.

they operate. One a regional grouping of States, tightly bound politically and economically, which is moving into a new area of competence, the other involving a loose grouping of States acting independently, which may be galvanised on an ad hoc basis to work towards a common objective. Law making within the Community benefits from the highly developed institutional structure which has emerged and, most importantly, the drive and impetus which can propel a *dossier* towards completion. Huge steps can be taken to address problematic issues of family law which affect the lives of EU citizens. Nevertheless present experiences make clear that the vast power which exists is not being used as best it should. The EU citizens who stand to benefit from family law initiatives, as well as the professionals who will apply them, are being excluded from this exciting new project which is being organised and conducted almost entirely in secret in Brussels. The inter-governmental and Community models may have fundamental differences but there would appear to be much that could be learnt by Community law and policy makers from the practices of other organisations. Family law is not necessarily a step too far for the EC, but there is currently far too much haste and too little reflection in the manner in which the project is being advanced.

# DRAWING TO A CLOSE

# DIVORCE AND MAINTENANCE BETWEEN FORMER SPOUSES –INIT IAL RESULTS OF THE COMMISSION ON EUROPEAN FAMILY LAW

DIETER MARTINY[*]

## 1. INTRODUCTION

### 1.1. Formulating a questionnaire

In January 2002 the Organising Committee of the Commission on European Family Law formulated a detailed questionnaire with more than one hundred questions on the grounds of divorce and maintenance after divorce. In the meantime, national reports have arrived from all the EU countries, with the exception of Luxembourg. Included are also reports from the Member States of the European Economic Area such as Norway, candidates for EU Membership such as Bulgaria, the Czech Republic, Hungary, Poland, Slovenia, and other European countries like Switzerland and Russia. The national reporters are mainly law professors, but also to some extent certain others, like judges. All the national reports are accessible on the Internet.[2] An additional integrated and printed version laid out according to the numbers of the questions will follow.[3] This will provide a relatively quick overview of the solutions chosen within the national systems.

Collecting all of these national solutions is only the first step in the project. The final goal is to establish some European principles. The necessary analysis and, it is to be hoped, the formulation of an end result, still lies ahead. Therefore in order to avoid any misunderstanding: When preparing

---

[*]  Unchanged version of the oral lecture, only the footnotes have been added. – This paper is dedicated to the memory of Dr. Peter Dopffel, former research associate at the Max-Planck-Institute for Foreign and Private International Law (Hamburg), who died on 2 July 2002. I will always remember his knowledge and experience, but also his thoroughness, independence of judgment, his willingness to help and – last but not least – his humour.

[2]  See the Country Reports concerning the CEFL Questionnaire on Grounds for Divorce and Maintenance Between Former Spouses. http://www2.law.uu.nl/priv/cefl.

[3]  See BOELE-WOELKI/BRAAT/SUMNER (eds.), *European Family Law in Action*, Vol. I: *Grounds for Divorce*, Vol. II: *Maintenance Between Former Spouses*, EFL-Series Nos. 2 and 3, (Antwerp – Oxford – New York 2003).

my paper I had not already had the opportunity to read all of the reports since some of them were still undergoing linguistic revision. Other papers were only available for a relatively short time. But apart from that, my task is not to provide a comprehensive general report but rather to give some first impressions and examples. As we all know first impressions are not always correct. A thorough evaluation will of course take more time.

However, the formulation of the questionnaire and the collection of the reports are themselves already a success because these reports will permit more comparison in a field that is generally not so readily accessible. The national reports stand in a line with earlier collections of divorce law within the framework of the Council of Europe,[4] scholarly projects such as the International Encyclopaedia of Family and Succession Law,[5] the International Encyclopedia of Comparative Law,[6] the earlier French project on the "obligation alimentaire",[7] national reports collected within the framework of several Regensburg symposia[8] and many other scholarly bilateral and multilateral studies[9] which not only collected materials but also developed useful categories for describing and analysing various types of divorce laws.

## 1.2. The choice of the subject

The Commission on European Family Law decided to start with the subject of divorce and one main consequence resulting there from, namely,

---

[4]  See DUTOIT, *Grounds for and Consequences of Divorce, European Conference on Family Law* (Strasbourg 1977); HAMILTON (ed.), *Family Law in Europe* (London 1995); SUBREMON, The Grounds for and Consequences of Divorce in Socialist Law in the USSR and Countries of Eastern Europe, European Conference on Family Law (Strasbourg 1977).

[5]  BLANPAIN (gen. ed.), PINTENS (ed.), *International Encyclopaedia of Laws – Family and Succession Law* I – IV (The Hague, London, New York; Loose-leaf 2002). Cf. also BERGMANN/FERID/HENRICH (ed.), *Internationales Ehe- und Kindschaftsrecht* I – XVIII (Frankfurt am Main 6th ed. 1983 ff. Loose-leaf).

[6]  Cf. MLADENOVIĆ/JANJIĆ-KOMAR/JESSEL-HOLST, *The Family in Post-Socialist Countries, International Encyclopedia of Comparative Law* IV ch. 10 (Tübingen, Dordrecht 1998).

[7]  *L'obligation alimentaire: étude de droit interne comparé* I – IV (Paris 1983-1988).

[8]  Especially the 6th "Symposium für Europäisches Familienrecht" (10-12 October 2002) dealt with divorce law.

[9]  Cf. RHEINSTEIN, "Trends in Marriage and Divorce Law of Western Countries", *Law & Contemp. Problems* 18 (1953) 3 ff.; LESER (ed.), *Collected Works* II (Tübingen 1979) 193 ff.; KRAUSE (ed.), *Family Law* I (International Library of Essays in Law & Legal Theory), Aldershot 1992; MEULDERS-KLEIN, "La problématique du divorce dans les législations d'Europe occidentale", *Rev. int. dr. comp.* 41 (1989) 7 ff.; ID., *La personne, la famille et le droit 1968-1998* (Brussels 1999); DUTOIT/ARN/SFONDYLIA/TAMINELLI/BISCHOF, *Le divorce en droit comparé* I (Genève 2000); GLENDON, *Abortion and Divorce in Western Law* (Cambridge Mass. 1987); ID., *The Transformation of Family Law* (Chicago 1989); RHEINSTEIN, *Marriage Stability, Divorce and the Law* (1972); Cf. also ARCHBOLD/XANTHAKI, "Family and Personal Relations Law – Fault or Failure? Divorce in Other Jurisdictions", *Irish L. T.* 1995, 275 ff.

alimony or maintenance after divorce. The number of divorces is rising in all countries of the EU or remains at least at a high level. Today in many jurisdictions, divorce as such is no longer a bone of contention among different social, political and religious groups. However, struggling with the consequences of divorce seems to be a problem nearly everywhere. It is true that also today there have been some reforms in divorce law. However, the basic principles of divorce law are generally well established so that a comparison and an account in this field can be made. It seems that the classical formulation of the English Law Commission of 1966 is now widely accepted that when a marriage has irretrievably broken down the task of divorce law is "to enable the empty shell to be destroyed with the maximum fairness and the minimum bitterness, distress and humiliation".[10] However, today's principles also have to take into account the fact that more than in the past, marriage is only one form of family relationship and that successive relationships have become widespread.

It is obvious that divorce and its consequences affect only small sections of family law and that it is not easy to isolate them from other areas of the law. Nevertheless the questionnaire concentrates on divorce law as such. Questions of constitutional law, matrimonial property law and social security law could not be expanded upon. Also the consequences for children of the marriage have been largely omitted. Therefore it is inevitable that the expected principles can only cover a relatively small area and there may be some details, which could be viewed differently in a broader context.

## 1.3. The purpose of the national reports

The purpose of collecting the national reports is to obtain an overview of the different national solutions as well as material for the development of some kind of European Principles in this field. It must also be borne in mind that this project concentrates on domestic substantive law only. Within the European context today there is, especially in the field of international civil procedure with the Brussels II Regulation on jurisdiction and recognition in divorce cases,[11] a strong tendency for more uniformity. However, Community legislation mainly covers questions of jurisdiction and recognition of foreign judgements. The assumption of the Commission on European Family Law is that, at least in the long run, there is also a

---

[10]   Cf. The Field of Choice, 1966 *Law Comm.* 6. Cf. also LOWE England No. 2.
[11]   Council Regulation (EC) No. 1347/2000 of 29 May 2000 on jurisdiction and the recognition and enforcement of judgments in matrimonial matters and in matters of parental responsibility for children of both spouses, *OJ* 2000 L 160/19.

need for harmonisation in the field of substantive family law.[12] However, the fact that there are no international conventions unifying substantive divorce law and that there are also very few Council of Europe recommendations[13] is a clear indication that uniformity will not be easy to achieve, if indeed it will ever be possible.

## 1.4. Methodology

A few methodological points concerning the formulation of the questionnaire will be briefly mentioned. The Organising Committee discussed the establishment of the questionnaire, which had to cover legal systems not only of different jurisdictions and with different divorce laws but also adhering to different legal families, *i.e.* the so-called Romanic law family, the Germanic, Common law and Scandinavian systems. Therefore the questions were formulated as independently of national legal systems as possible. The questionnaire also asked as far as possible what "law in action" actually is and was not only interested in "law in the books". It is clear that increasing divorce rates, the growing acceptance of divorce and more flexibility influence the practice in all countries. Nevertheless, the National Reports are in general not based on extensive socio-legal research. Therefore they may not reflect the actual practice in every aspect. It is obvious that the use of socio-legal studies and cross-societal comparisons would improve the accuracy of statements on the existing practice and trends in reform.[14] The Commission would be very grateful if its work could stimulate more research of this kind.

The structure of the questionnaire is relatively simple. It starts with a few general questions with respect to history and legal sources. The second part of the questionnaire deals with the different grounds for divorce and the third part with spousal support after divorce. One major difficulty not only for the development of common principles but also for the drafting of a questionnaire of this kind is that there are different national systems of divorce law. Therefore it is important not to be misled by conceptional and dogmatic differences but instead to look for functional equivalents between the national solutions.

---

[12]   Cf. MARTINY, "The Harmonization of Family Law in the European Community. Pro and Contra", in: FAURE/SMITS/SCHNEIDER (eds.), *Towards a European Ius Commune in Legal Education and Research* (Antwerp/Groningen 2002) 191 ff.

[13]   Cf. Recommendation No. R (89) 1 of the Committee of Ministers to Member States on Contributions Following Divorce (adopted by the Committee of Ministers on 18 January 1989).

[14]   Cf. GOODE, *World Changes in Divorce Patterns* (Ann Arbor 1993).

## 2. DIVORCE

### 2.1. The existence of divorce

The first principle of European divorce law will probably deal with the question whether domestic law should permit divorce. However, since after the introduction of divorce in the Republic of Ireland in 1997,[15] all countries of the European Community now recognise divorce, permitting a divorce does not seem to be a real issue.[16] Also a common definition of divorce seems to be conceivable. Divorce can generally be defined as an ex nunc dissolution of a valid marriage during the lives of the spouses by a decision of a competent authority for reasons laid down by statute and by a procedure prescribed by law.[17]

### 2.2. Grounds for divorce

A question not so simply answered is on what basis a divorce should be granted. The grounds for divorce – beginning with adultery, misconduct, intolerable behaviour, desertion, separation, but also consent etc. – seem to be innumerable also under contemporary law. Therefore the first task before a reasonable dialogue can start seems to be a systematisation of these grounds.[18]

If one looks closer at the grounds for divorce it is obvious that there are several fundamental approaches. According to an older approach *fault (faute, Verschulden)* is the sole ground for divorce, whereas according to newer approaches there are other or even multiple grounds for divorce. The original idea behind the fault principle was that a matrimonial offence was the justification for divorce[19] ("divorce sanction").[20] Therefore the purpose of divorce was to provide a remedy to the innocent spouse for a matrimonial wrong that had been committed. This not only had consequences for the dissolution of marriage. If divorce was based on fault it also seemed nearly inevitable that the guilty party would not obtain maintenance.

---

[15] See in more detail SHANNON Republic of Ireland No. 1.
[16] The only exception in Europe seems to be Malta; cf. DUTOIT/ARN/SFONDYLIA/BISCHOF 294 ff.
[17] Cf. NEUHAUS, "Ehescheidungsgründe in rechtsvergleichender Sicht", *RabelsZ* 32 (1968) 24 f.; MLADENOVIĆ/JANJIĆ-KOMAR/JESSEL-HOLST sec. 179.
[18] NEUHAUS *RabelsZ* 32 (1968) 24 – 62.
[19] NEUHAUS *RabelsZ* 32 (1968) 36 ff.
[20] DUTOIT/ARN/SFONDYLIA/BISCHOF 11 ff.

## 2.3. 'Mixed grounds" jurisdictions

Divorce laws exclusively based on the fault principle seemingly no longer exist in Europe. Today, there is a tendency for the fault approach either to have been totally abandoned or that fault is now only one ground for divorce among many others. The next question is whether there is only a *sole ground for divorce* or if *multiple grounds* for divorce exist. Today, there are jurisdictions like Germany and England and Wales, which follow such a monistic system and – despite all the differences between them – recognise only a sole ground for divorce.[21]

**Fig. 1 Divorce grounds**

|  DIVORCE GROUNDS |
| --- |

| SOLE GROUND FOR DIVORCE | MULTIPLE GROUNDS FOR DIVORCE |
| --- | --- |
| Czech Republic, Denmark, England and Wales, Hungary, Ireland, Italy, the Netherlands, Poland, Russia, Scotland, Spain, (Finland, Sweden) | Austria, Belgium, Bulgaria, Denmark, France, Greece, Luxembourg, Norway, Portugal, Spain, Switzerland |

Many legal systems, however, still cling to a multiplicity of grounds, for example Austria, Denmark, France, and Belgium.[22] Generally, in these so-called "mixed grounds" or "pluralistic" jurisdictions[23] several forms of divorce exist. One form is often a divorce based on fault; other forms of divorce are based on mutual consent, irretrievable breakdown, an extended separation period and so on. For example, in Belgium there is divorce by consent, divorce on the basis of fault, on the basis of separation, a transformation of a decree of judicial separation into a divorce and a divorce on the grounds of separation due to a mental illness of one spouse.[24]

---

[21]   See § 24 Czech Family Code; s. 1 (1) English Matrimonial Causes Act 1973; § 1565 German Civil Code; § 18 Hungarian Family Act; s. 5 (1) Irish Family Law (Divorce) Act; Art. 1 Italian Divorce Law; Art. 1:151 Dutch New Civil Code; Art. 56 § 1 Polish Family and Guardianship Code; Art. 22 para. 1 Russian Family Code; s. 1 (1) Divorce (Scotland) Act 1976.

[22]   Cf. §§ 49 ff. Austrian Marriage Act; Art. 229 ff. Belgian Civil Code; Art. 99, 100 Bulgarian Family Code; §§ 31 ff. Danish Marriage Act; Art. 229 ff. French Civil Code; Art. 1439 ff. Greek Civil Code; Art. 239 ff. Luxembourg Civil Code; §§ 20 ff. Norwegian Marriage Act; Art. 1773 ff. Portuguese Civil Code; Art. 111 ff. Swiss Civil Code.

[23]   Cf. GLENDON, *Abortion and Divorce* 69 ff. – On „systèmes pluralistes ou mixtes" see also MEULDERS-KLEIN *Rev.int.dr.comp.* 41 (1989) 12 ff.; DUTOIT/ARN/SFONDYLIA/BISCHOF 14 f.

[24]   Art. 229 ff. Belgian Civil Code.

Under the *system of fault divorce* certain grounds are recognised as fault, often adultery, desertion and/or cruelty. For instance, in Belgium there are four fault grounds: adultery, acts of violence against the other spouse, abuse of the other spouse and grave offences towards the other spouse.[25] With respect to the European principles a decision for or against a fault approach seems to be inevitable. As will be shown there is a tendency to lean towards the principle of irretrievable breakdown. From the point of view of legal policy, it is also interesting that there are reform proposals in Belgium[26] and France[27] in order to attain only one sole ground for divorce.

## 2.4. Divorce by agreement

Another form of marriage dissolution is divorce by agreement. The French Civil Code of 1804 already recognised *mutual consent* as a ground for divorce. Nevertheless, even today there is a fear of the fraudulent abuse of this ground for the dissolution of marriage. Some jurisdictions following the principle of irretrievable breakdown do not allow divorce by agreement as such, *e.g.* Poland.[28]

**Fig. 2 Divorce by consent**

| DIVORCE BY CONSENT |
|---|

| SEPARATE GROUND | FORM OF IRRETRIEVABLE BREAKDOWN |
|---|---|
| Austria, Belgium, Bulgaria, France, Greece, Luxembourg, Portugal, Switzerland | Denmark, Germany, Hungary, Italy, the Netherlands, Russia, Spain, (England and Wales, Ireland, Scotland) |

However, this kind of divorce is expressly recognised by several jurisdictions, *e.g.* Austria and France. There are many variations of this principle.[29] In some legal systems, such as in Belgium, divorce by consent is recognised as an autonomous ground for divorce and in the vast majority of cases a divorce is granted on the ground of consent.[30] However, in many systems

---

25 Art. 229 ff. Belgian Civil Code. – Cf. PINTENS/TORFS Belgium No. 36.
26 PINTENS/TORFS Belgium No. 3.
27 FERRAND France No. 3.
28 Art. 56 Polish Family and Guardianship Code
29 Cf. VERSCHRAEGEN, *Die einverständliche Scheidung in rechtsvergleichender Sicht* (Berlin 1991); DETHLOFF, *Die einverständliche Scheidung* (Munich 1994).
30 PINTENS/TORFS Belgium No. 8.

divorce by consent is only admissible as one case of irretrievable breakdown (*e.g.*, Germany, the Netherlands). It should also be borne in mind that a non-contested divorce – although not strictly a divorce by consent – comes close to such a dissolution of marriage.

There is also a great variety concerning the additional conditions of consent.

**Fig. 3 Divorce by consent –Additional elements**

| DIVORCE BY CONSENT –ADDITIONAL ELEMENTS | | | |
|---|---|---|---|
| AGREEMENTS ON CONSEQUENCES | SEPARATION | MINIMUM AGE | LENGTH OF MARRIAGE |
| Austria, Belgium, Bulgaria, Denmark, France, Greece, Hungary, Spain, Switzerland, (Germany, Portugal) | Austria, Czech Republic, Hungary, Italy, Spain, (Denmark, Germany, Finland, Norway) | Belgium, Luxembourg | Belgium, Bulgaria, Czech Republic, France, Greece, Hungary, Italy, Luxembourg, Russia, (Denmark, Norway) |

Consent seems to be a dangerous kind of marriage dissolution. So divorce law often tries to prevent an inconsiderate decision. Often there must be a *previous separation* or non-cohabitation. This period of time differs from six months in Austria[31] to four years in the Republic of Ireland.[32]

Often, as is the case in Belgium, France and Greece, there are preconditions as to the *length of the marriage*.[33] In some jurisdictions even a minimum age of the spouses is required. In Belgium, in order to initiate divorce proceedings by consent both spouses need to be at least twenty years old.[34] Divorce by consent can also be to the detriment of the *interests of the children* of a marriage. So some jurisdictions allow such a divorce only where a couple have no children.[35]

---

[31]  See § 55a Austrian Marriage Act; cf. ROTH Austria No. 27.

[32]  S. 5 (1) (a) Irish Family Law (Divorce) Act. – Cf. SHANNON Republic of Ireland No. 7, 16.

[33]  See § 55a Austrian Marriage Act; Art. 276 Belgian Civil Code; Art. 100 § 2 Bulgarian Family Code; Art. 230 French Civil Code; Art. 1441 Greek Civil Code. Cf. DU-TOIT/ARN/SFONDYLIA/TAMINELLI 13.

[34]  Art. 275 Belgian Civil Code.- Cf. PINTENS/TORFS Belgium 29.

[35]  Cf. DUTOIT/ARN/SFONDYLIA/TAMINELLI 13.

It is quite common that the parties have to present an *agreement* dealing with the consequences of the divorce. Often it is expected that the parties reach such an agreement on almost all aspects of the divorce as in Austria.[36] However, under certain circumstances this requirement can be mitigated.[37] With respect to common European principles it seems to be imaginable that consent will play a major role. Especially in view of the fact that divorce law today is not a definitive bar to a divorce, an agreement between the parties is preferable. Costly proceedings can thus be avoided and if there is an agreement in respect of the consequences this will also solve many problems. An important question of legal policy, however, is whether and, if so, what kinds of control mechanisms are necessary to prevent an abuse of private autonomy.

### 2.5. Unilateral divorce

Whereas many legal systems are more or less reluctant to grant a divorce upon the request of only one of the spouses, there are also others who basically grant a *unilateral divorce*. For this so-called "divorce on demand"[38] it is sufficient that one of the spouses no longer clings on to the marriage. In Finland[39] and Sweden[40] even the concept of irretrievable breakdown has been abandoned. This raises the question whether there should be an absolute right to divorce in the sense that it can always be enforced against the will of the other spouse. It has to be decided whether such a unilateral decision by only one of the spouses, which comes close to repudiation, can be a basis for divorce.

### 2.6. Non-fault divorce and irretrievable breakdown

Today, irretrievable breakdown is the most accepted basis for a non-fault divorce. However, when viewed somewhat closer it becomes apparent that under this heading and its French equivalent of "divorce-faillite" (or "divorce-échec")[41] several approaches are revealed.[42]

---

[36]  ROTH Austria 32.
[37]  For instance, when the parties have lived separately for at least three years they only have to prove that they have dealt with and considered all questions relating to the care and support of the children in keeping with the latter's interests, § 18 para. 2 (b) Hungarian Family law; WEISS/SZEIBERT Hungary No. 19.
[38]  Cf. GLENDON, *Abortion and Divorce* 75 ff.
[39]  See §§ 25 ff. Finnish Marriage Act.- Cf. SAVOLAINEN Finland No. 3.
[40]  See ch. 5 §§ 1 ff. Swedish Marriage Act. – Cf. JÄNTERÄ-JAREBORG Sweden No. 2.
[41]  DUTOIT/ARN/SFONDYLIA/BISCHOF 11 ff.
[42]  Cf. BOULANGER, "Au sujet de la réforme française du divorce: la notion de rupture dans les droits européens et la survie des éléments subjectifs", *Dalloz* 2002 *Chron.* 590 ff.

**Fig. 4 Divorce grounds –Forms**

| DIVORCE GROUNDS –FORMS | | | | | | |
|---|---|---|---|---|---|---|

| FAULT | NON-FAULT, BASED ON: | | | | | |
|---|---|---|---|---|---|---|
| Belgium, Denmark, France, Luxembourg, Norway | **Divorce by consent**<br><br>Austria, Belgium, Bulgaria, Czech Republic, France, Greece, Luxembourg, Portugal, Switzerland, (Germany, the Netherlands) | **Separation** | | **Irretrievable breakdown** | | |
| | | **Separation**<br><br>Belgium, Denmark, Finland, Norway, Sweden, Switzerland | **Separation & additional element**<br><br>France, Ireland, Spain | **Irretrievable breakdown**<br><br>Bulgaria, Czech Republic, Hungary, the Netherlands, Russia | **Irretrievable breakdown & additional element**<br><br>Austria, England and Wales, Germany, Greece, Italy, Poland, Portugal, Scotland, Spain |

Irretrievable breakdown (Zerrüttung) can be the single requirement for a divorce.[43] However, an objective element and an additional subjective element are often required. The objective element means that there is no longer a community between the spouses. The subjective element, especially in Eastern Europe, is formulated in the sense that the existence of the marriage has become intolerable for the couple.[44]

Another question is which role irretrievable breakdown has to play. According to one approach, sometimes named a "système uniciste"[45] or a "pure system of divorce as a legal remedy",[46] a marriage can always be dissolved after it has come to an irretrievable breakdown of marital relations or if life together has become intolerable for the couple.

As a basis for divorce irretrievable breakdown is for example accepted in the Netherlands. Also in other countries there is a tendency to the

---

[43] "Formelles Zerrüttungsprinzip" according to NEUHAUS RabelsZ 32 (1968) 42 ff.

[44] Cf. MLADENOVIĆ/JANJIĆ-KOMAR/JESSEL-HOLST sec. 190.

[45] On „systèmes unicistes" see MEULDERS-KLEIN Rev.int.dr.comp. 41 (1989) 14 ff.; DU-TOIT/ARN/SFONDYLIA/BISCHOF 14.

[46] MLADENOVIĆ/JANJIĆ-KOMAR/JESSEL-HOLST sec. 190.

distinction between the guilty and the innocent party. Irretrievable breakdown can occur in the form of a general clause. Some systems, like the Dutch, are content with such an approach and a broad general clause.[47] A distinct, more moderate system also grants divorce as a legal remedy when there is an irretrievable breakdown in the marital relations or the intolerability of life together. However, in this system there are, on the one hand some absolute grounds, which can lead to a divorce and, on the other, grounds such as the fault of the petitioner, which may hinder or even exclude a divorce.[48] There are also legal systems, like the Norwegian,[49] which do not recognise irretrievable breakdown as such but only consider separation or non-cohabitation as a ground for divorce.

It is possible, however, to specify irretrievable breakdown in the form of *enumerated grounds* for divorce. Using these grounds as an indicator for the irretrievable breakdown is conceivable. It is also possible that irretrievable breakdown must be accompanied by one of these grounds. However, even with this approach there is generally not a detailed list of all possible grounds, but only a list with relatively few groups of grounds.

### 2.7. Additional elements

The prevailing notion is that there should be additional elements restricting divorces based on irretrievable breakdown.

**Fig. 5 Irretrievable breakdown –Additional elements**

| IRRETRIEVABLE BREAKDOWN –ADDITIONAL ELEMENTS | | |
|---|---|---|
| **SEPARATION**<br><br>Germany, England and Wales (judicial separation), Nordic countries | **LENGTH OF MARRIAGE**<br><br>Belgium, England and Wales | **AGREEMENT/JUDGMENT ON CONSEQUENCES** |

One of these elements is separation. The general approach is that the longer the period of separation the easier it should be to obtain a divorce because the ties between the parties have been weakened by the course of time. Some systems, *e.g.* the Nordic countries, require a formal separation preceding divorce. Many others, however, do not require such a formal

---

[47]  Cf. BOELE-WOELKI/CHEREDNYCHENKO/COENRAAD Netherlands No. 14.
[48]  Cf. MLADENOVIĆ/JANJIĆ-KOMAR/JESSEL-HOLST sec. 191.
[49]  See §§ 19 ff. Norwegian Marriage Act.- Cf. SVERDRUP Norway Nos. 44, 46.

separation but are content with non-cohabitation. According to some legal systems there is a general requirement of separation before filing for a divorce (*e.g.* Germany). Other systems do not require such a general period of separation. However, a period of separation is necessary for specific grounds for divorce as in England and Wales.[50]

**Fig. 6 De facto separation period**

| DE FACTO SEPARATION PERIOD | | | |
|---|---|---|---|
| **GENERAL RE-QUIREMENT** | **AGREEMENT/WITH-OUT OPPOSITION** | **DISAGREEMENT** | **RECONSIDER-ATION PERIOD** |
| **4 years** Ireland | **no period** Switzerland | **2 years** Denmark | **6 months** Sweden |
| | **6 months** Austria, Czech Republic, Denmark, Finland | **3 years** Germany, Portugal | |
| | **1 year** Germany, Norway, Portugal, Spain | **4 years** Switzerland | |
| | **3 years** Hungary, Italy | | |

The length of the *period of separation* often differs according to the consent of the parties. If the parties agree, for example, six months suffice in Denmark,[51] while one year is necessary in Germany.[52] If the parties do not agree, a divorce is possible after one year of separation in Denmark.[53] In any case, the European principles will also have to take a stance with respect to the period of separation.

Should there also be a *time-limit for a divorce*? To obtain a divorce, it is necessary in some legal systems that the marriage was of a certain duration. For example, in England and Wales there is an absolute bar to petitioning

---

[50] Cf. s. 1 (1) (d) (e) English Matrimonial Causes Act 1973.
[51] See § 31 para. 2 Danish Marriage Act. – Cf. LUND-ANDERSEN/KRABBE Denmark No. 10.
[52] § 1566 para. 1 German Civil Code.
[53] Cf. § 31 para. 1 Danish Marriage Act; LUND-ANDERSEN/KRABBE Denmark No. 23.

for a divorce before the expiration of one year from the date of the marriage. Also in some other systems it is necessary that the marriage is of a *certain duration*. Under Belgian law the marriage must have lasted for at least two years before depositing the initiating petition.[54] Other divorce laws do not prescribe such a period of time. One has to take into account, however, that these legal systems often require a certain period of separation, which can only be fulfilled by a certain period of time.

That there can be an *agreement* between the parties in respect of the consequences of their divorce is widely accepted. However, the role of agreements differs. As has been shown especially in the case of divorce by consent, such an agreement is expected. In some systems, for example Germany, a judgement dealing with the consequences of the divorce has to be rendered in the case of a disputed divorce as well.

## 2.8. Obstacles to divorce

Another problem to be resolved by European principles are any obstacles to divorce. Under many legal systems, *e.g.* in England and Wales and Germany, an application for a divorce can be rejected or postponed due to the fact that the dissolution of the marriage would result in grave hardship for one of the spouses.[55] Objections based on such a hardship clause are, however, seldom raised and are only rarely successful. This is because mental harm already occurs with the separation of the spouses. Financial hardship, on the other hand, only concerns the consequences of the divorce. When the petitioner offers a minimum of financial resources the hardship clause does not generally apply. Sometimes a divorce is not permitted if it would harm the interests of the minor children.[56] To such an extent similar problems can arise.

## 2.9. The possible approach of the principles

What do all these puzzling details of divorce law mean for the development of European principles? At first, one has to decide whether, out of the known fragments, a completely new structure could be rebuilt. But if one prefers a more traditional approach, one has to recognise that also in respect of irretrievable breakdown there are several options. One solution

---

[54]  Art. 276 Belgian Civil Code. – Cf. PINTENS/TORFS Belgium No. 28.

[55]  S. 5 English Matrimonial Causes Act 1973; § 1586 German Civil Code. – On „clauses de dureté" see MEULDERS-KLEIN *Rev.int.dr.comp.* 41 (1989) 21 ff.

[56]  Art. 56 § 2 Polish Family and Guardianship Code.- Cf. MACZYNSKI/SOKOLOWSKI Poland No. 24.

could be simply to state the principle with or without a general definition. Such an approach would respect the existing diversity within Europe. On the other hand, this would be a rather meagre result because behind such a broad general clause different concepts would also co-exist in the future. To be more precise, however, could be burdensome. This comparative overview shows that the varied national legislation combines several factors with each other like the actuality and the length of separation, consent, marital misconduct and even fault in order to find a solution for the different case groups. One solution for the principles could be the establishment of a list of such different elements without more precision. Such a list would cover different combinations but also remain relatively vague. Only a closer analysis will demonstrate whether it is possible to define more precise solutions.

### 2.10. Procedure

A fundamental procedural question is who has jurisdiction in divorce proceedings. A divorce obtained by means of judicial proceedings is still the rule (*e.g.*, England and Wales, France, the Netherlands etc.). In most countries a divorce court or a family court has jurisdiction. Only in some countries like Denmark[57] and Norway[58] do administrative bodies play a role.[59] An exception is also Russia where a consensual divorce between couples without children can be obtained at the registry office.[60]

Concerning the divorce procedure there are considerable differences. Many seem to result from the problem of whether the *spouses themselves* can decide with respect to their marriage. Where the answer is yes the admissibility of a common application for divorce is the logical answer. Where the legislator is interested in more control or even in an investigation into the situation of the spouses or has even made fault a decisive element, unilateral applications and an ex officio investigation are the consequences. However, today there seems to be a tendency to simplify procedures and to favour more co-operation between the spouses in the divorce process. A joint application is permitted in many systems. And especially the regulation of the consequences of the divorce by the parties themselves is appreciated.

---

[57] Cf. LUND-ANDERSEN/KRABBE Denmark No. 7.
[58] In Norway most divorces are granted administratively, see SVERDRUP Norway Nos. 7, 8.
[59] Cf. also MEULDERS-KLEIN *Rev.int.dr.comp.* 41 (1989) 29 ff.
[60] Cf. MLADENOVIĆ/JANJIĆ-KOMAR/JESSEL-HOLST sec. 187.

The idea of judicially controlling the dissolution of the marriage seems to lose its persuasiveness. In many countries the judge will not enquire as to whether an irretrievable breakdown of the marriage has really taken place.[61] The law departs from the general assumption that if two adults declare that their marriage has irretrievably broken down, this will be accepted as being true. The idea that the privacy of the parties should be respected is also gaining ground.

According to modern tendencies the question arises whether there should be some kind of *mediation*[62] in the forthcoming European principles. There are different tendencies. On the one hand, the hope that a kind of reconciliation procedure could save the marriage seems to have been increasingly abandoned. Therefore mediation in this sense is often not required. Instead emphasis shifts to the consequences of the divorce. Especially in this respect the parties are encouraged to use techniques of mediation in order to reach an agreement concerning parental responsibility, access and other questions.[63]

## 3. MAINTENANCE

### 3.1. Granting maintenance

Divorce is often only one step in the final dissolution of a marriage. A settlement concerning the consequences of divorce and especially maintenance is also a major issue. There seems to be a basic consensus that maintenance after divorce concerns periodical financial contributions but also lump sum payments. However, if one looks for common principles in the field of maintenance one encounters several difficulties.[64] This is not surprising. If one looks at maintenance from the angle of sources of income it is only one possible source. Other sources are gainful employment, old-age pensions and other social security benefits. So, according to *the national legal and social background,* maintenance after divorce plays a different role. In legal systems where the employment of divorced parents is encouraged, where there are efficient forms of child benefit, income support or social assistance, maintenance after divorce is of lesser importan-

---

[61]    Cf. BOELE-WOELKI/CHEREDNYCHENKO/COENRAAD Netherlands No. 14.
[62]    *Cf. Recommendation No. R (98)1 of the Committee of Ministers to Member States on Family Mediation (Adopted by the Committee of Ministers on 21 January 1998).*
[63]    Cf. for Norway SVERDRUP No. 50.
[64]    Cf. LÜDERITZ, "Der Ehegattenunterhalt bei Trennung und Scheidung – Ein rechtsver-gleichender Blick über die Grenzen", in: Deutscher Familiengerichtstag (ed.), *Fünfter Familiengerichtstag* (Bielefeld 1984) 67 ff.

ce. For example, in Sweden where it is assumed that a divorced parent has access to sources of support other than maintenance the emphasis is on spousal self-sufficiency.[65] On the other hand, in other countries maintenance is still seen as a major source of income (*e.g.* Germany). In many legal systems there are constant controversies surrounding the question of who in the end pays the bill for the dissolution of the marriage.

An important distinction is whether maintenance is conceived as a more or less *isolated system* of financial contributions. This is the case in many civil law countries. For example, in Belgium maintenance after divorce has a specific and independent ground. There is a link with matrimonial property law only insofar as income obtained within the scope of a distribution of matrimonial property can reduce need and thus maintenance claims.[66] On the other hand, especially in England and Wales,[67] but also in Ireland,[68] there is an overall assessment of property. Maintenance is only a part of a comprehensive distribution. Typical for this solution is also that this assessment is open to the judge. It is true that to a certain extent the devices are interchangeable.[69] It is hardly conceivable, however, that such a system of equitable distribution could be acceptable for civil law countries. On the other hand, the French "prestation compensatoire" is a good example of a mixture of elements of maintenance and matrimonial property also in a civil law country.[70]

### 3.2. *Maintenance as a consequence of divorce*

To a certain extent, maintenance after divorce reflects the *type of divorce* and depends upon it.

---

[65]   Cf. GLENDON *Transformation* 236.
[66]   PINTENS/TORFS Belgium No. 60.
[67]   LOWE England No. 59.
[68]   See SHANNON Republic of Ireland No. 59, 60.
[69]   Cf. GLENDON *Transformation* 197 ff.
[70]   Cf. FERRAND France No. 56 ff. – Cf. also MARTÍN-CASALS/RIBOT/SOLÉ Spain No. 58 ff. for the "pensión compensatoria".

**Fig. 7 Maintenance after divorce –Systems**

| MAINTENANCE AFTER DIVORCE – SYSTEMS | |
|---|---|
| **ONE TYPE** | **SEVERAL CLAIMS ACCORDING TO THE TYPE OF DIVORCE** |
| Czech Republic, Denmark, England and Wales, Germany, Hungary, Italy, the Netherlands, Norway, Russia, Scotland, Sweden, Switzerland | Austria, Belgium, France, Luxembourg |
| Greece, Portugal, Spain | Poland |

Therefore it is not surprising that there are systems where there is basically only one regime governing financial relief after divorce such as *e.g.* in England and Wales and Germany. In other countries maintenance differs according to the type of divorce (Belgium, France). The multiplicity of the grounds for divorce is reflected by a multitude of different consequences. From the point of view of a possible unification these often very complex regimes at first glance do not look very promising. One has to concede, however, that also systems starting with only one type of maintenance eventually have to make many subtle distinctions, which can produce complex results.

Under the principle of fault maintenance after divorce is basically a sanction for the shortcomings in the marital duties and compensation for the innocent party.[71] The guilty party generally cannot expect to receive maintenance or will only obtain a minimum amount based on equity. With the introduction of *non-fault divorce* viz. the doctrine of irretrievable breakdown, it has become more difficult to find a convincing justification for post-divorce maintenance.[72] One line of argumentation is that there exists a kind of post-divorce solidarity between the spouses. This is an argument, for example, that the German Constitutional Court used when confirming the constitutionality of the German maintenance provisions.[73] More common, however, is the idea that maintenance after divorce should primarily be support for a transitional period.[74] Another justification with much support in North America is the idea that maintenance should amount to compensation for the detriments of

---

[71] Cf. PINTENS/TORFS Belgium No. 61.
[72] Cf. DUTOIT/ARN/SFONDYLIA/BISCHOF 19.
[73] See MARTINY/SCHWAB Germany No. 58.
[74] Cf. BOELE-WOELKI/CHEREDNYCHENKO/COENRAAD Netherlands No. 68; HAUSHEER/WOLF Switzerland No. 68.

the marriage.[75] These approaches are often combined or mixed with each other. For legislative purposes, at least two different alternatives exist. One, which is used, for example in Switzerland, is to establish a list of factors which can justify the granting of maintenance, for instance the length of the marriage, the age and health of the spouses.[76] The other, more complicated, alternative is to develop a system of different maintenance claims reflecting various situations.[77]

From the point of view of the principles of non-fault divorce and irretrievable breakdown the existence of *fault* should be irrelevant. This is in fact the position in the Nordic countries and in the Netherlands.[78] One also has to take into account, however, that even in the systems which in general follow the principle of irretrievable breakdown, an element of fault still exists. The fault of the debtor can be a condition for a maintenance claim. Fault on the part of the claimant is sometimes recognised as a defence against a claim for maintenance and can lead to the loss of or a reduction in the maintenance.[79] Especially the German list of seven cases of "gross unfairness" where spousal maintenance can be denied or reduced is a good (or a bad) example of this tendency.[80]

### 3.3. Calculation of maintenance

*Lack of means on the part of the claimant and an ability to pay* as far as the debtor is concerned are general conditions for the existence and the amount of a maintenance claim.[81] However, there are practical differences concerning how strictly the principle that each spouse shall support

---

[75] See SCHWENZER, "Die Scheidung – clean break auch für die nacheheliche Versorgung?", *Bitburger Gespräche Jahrbuch* 2001, 53 ff.

[76] Art. 125 Swiss Civil Code. – Cf. HAUSHEER/WOLF Switzerland No. 61.

[77] §§ 1569 ff. German Civil Code.- Cf. MARTINY/SCHWAB Germany No. 64.

[78] See BOELE-WOELKI/CHEREDNYCHENKO/COENRAAD Netherlands No. 65; JÄNTERÄ-JAREBORG Sweden No 65.

[79] Cf. HAUSHEER/WOLF Switzerland No. 65.

[80] See § 1579 German Civil Code.- Cf. MARTINY/SCHWAB Germany No. 98, 100.

[81] Cf. §§66, 69, 69a (but see § 68a) Austrian Marriage Act; Art. 301 Belgian Civil Code; Art. 84 Bulgarian Family Code; § 96 para. 1 Czech Family Code; § 50 Danish Marriage Act; §48 para. 1 Finnish Marriage Act; Art. 271French Civil Code (prestation compensatoire); §§ 1577, 1581 German Civil Code; Art. 1442 Greek Civil Code; § 21 para. 1 Hungarian Family Act; s. 20 (2).Irish Family Law (Divorce) Act; Art. 5 No. 6 Italian Divorce Law; Art. 300 para. 2 Luxembourg Civil Code; Art. 1:157 para. 1 Dutch New Civil Code; § 79 para. 2 Norwegian Marriage Act; Art. 60 Polish Family and Guardianship Code; Art. 2016 Portuguese Civil Code; Art. 125 Swiss Civil Code. Cf. also s. 25 (2) English Matrimonial Causes Act 1973; Art. 97 para. 1 Spanish Civil Code.

him/herself after divorce and that maintenance shall only be granted in exceptional cases is adhered to.[82]

The method for *calculating maintenance* is of decisive importance. So far, there has only been little comparative analysis of national systems for making such a calculation.[83] In some legal systems, a judge has wide discretion with respect to the claims of the divorced spouse (*e.g.* England and Wales), whereas in others a sophisticated system of different claims exists (*e.g.* Germany). The practice of the courts is very different. In some systems, especially in England and Wales,[84] but also in countries like France,[85] there is only an individual assessment of maintenance based on the discretion of the court. In other legal systems there are tendencies for a more or less standardised calculation. Some have developed percentage systems like Austria;[86] others use quotas as Germany does.[87] There is a tendency in some systems to place an upper limit on maintenance contributions, *e.g.* one third of the income of the debtor.[88] Amounts of this kind are, however, difficult to compare and it is doubtful whether European principles could add more than a few truisms.

### 3.4. The length and the termination of maintenance obligations

In many jurisdictions there is a tendency to encourage *lump-sum payments*. However, often the necessary capital is simply not available. The experience with the French "prestation compensatoire" shows that a substitution by periodic payments often occurs.[89]

In some legal systems, such as in Germany, the traditional idea of a lifelong maintenance obligation is still recognised, at least in theory,[90] whereas others prefer a limitation and prescribe the *length of the maintenance obligation*. In the Netherlands there is an absolute limitation of 12 years,[91]

---

[82]    For Norway cf. SVERDRUP No. 56, 58.
[83]    Cf. MARTINY, *Unterhaltsrang und -rückgriff* I (Tübingen 2000) 131 ff.
[84]    LOWE England No. 63.
[85]    Cf. FERRAND France No. 70.
[86]    See ROTH Austria No. 70.
[87]    MARTINY/SCHWAB Germany No. 70.
[88]    Cf. PINTENS/TORFS Belgium No. 72. A maximum amount also exists in Denmark, see LUND-ANDERSEN/KRABBE No. 72. There is no prescribed maximum limit for maintenance *e.g.* in Bulgaria, England and Wales, Germany and the Republic of Ireland.
[89]    See FERRAND France No. 62.
[90]    Cf. MARTINY/SCHWAB Germany No. 68.
[91]    Art. 1:157 para. 3 Dutch New Civil Code.

in Norway[92] and in Greece partially three years,[93] in Sweden one to four years.[94] One reason for the different approaches seems to be the availability of work for women. It seems unlikely that a uniform limitation for Europe will be found.

Of practical importance is the question of the *cohabitation of the claimant*. Often an approach with several stages exists. The fact that the maintenance creditor receives some support from a third party diminishes his or her needs and this can reduce his or her maintenance claim. Where the new relationship becomes more intensive the question arises when the maintenance claim should be suspended. However, at least if there is a new stable relationship the question arises whether the maintenance claim should extinguish.[95] In this respect several principles seem to play a role. It is widely accepted that a second marriage extinguishes a maintenance claim against the former spouse.[96] Therefore it seems to be just that the creditor should not profit from avoiding a formal marriage. The new financial situation of the creditor cannot be ignored. On the other hand, the ex-spouses are no longer married and are free to regulate their personal relationships.

### 3.5. Priority of claims

The relationship of post-divorce claims to maintenance claims between relatives is not equally important for all countries. In the Common Law countries[97] and Scandinavia *no such claims by adults* exist.[98] Only the relationship between child support and maintenance after divorce has to be defined.[99] So it is doubtful to what extent European principles could harmonise this subject.

---

[92] Cf. SVERDRUP Norway No. 56.
[93] Art. 1442 Greek Civil Code.
[94] JÄNTERÄ-JAREBORG Sweden No. 68.
[95] Cf. FERRAND France No. 97, 98; MARTINY/SCHWAB Germany No. 98; HAUSHEER/WOLF Switzerland No. 98.
[96] See § 75 Austrian Marriage Act; § 94 para. 1 Czech Family Code; § 51 Danish Marriage Act; s. 28 (1) (a) English Matrimonial Causes Act 1973; Art. 283 French Civil Code; § 1586 para. 1 German Civil Code; Art. 1442 § 2 Greek Civil Code; Art. 1:160 Dutch New Civil Code; § 82 Norwegian Marriage Act; Art. 60 § 3 Polish Family and Guardianship Code; Art. 2019 Portuguese Civil Code; Art. 120 § 2 Russian Family Code; Art. 101 Spanish Civil Code; Art. 130 § 2 Swiss Civil Code. In some legal systems it is only a change of circumstances, cf. JÄNTERÄ-JAREBORG Sweden No. 97.
[97] Cf. LOWE England No. 91.
[98] See LUND-ANDERSEN/KRABBE Denmark No. 91; SVERDRUP Norway No. 91; JÄNTERÄ-JAREBORG Sweden No. 91.
[99] Cf. MARTINY, *Unterhaltsrang und -rückgriff* I 476 ff.

However, in all systems the relationship between *the claims of the ex-spouse and a new* spouse must be defined.[100] It is obvious, however, that under systems that favour an early final solution, especially by means of a lump-sum payment after divorce, conflicts will be minimised. Especially in the case of long-term obligations, conflicts will arise. In some systems, as in Sweden, there is a clear preference for the new spouse[101] whereas in others, such as in Germany, there is a preference for the former spouse.[102]

## 4. METHODOLOGICAL POINTS

In establishing European principles *many methodological problems* arise. One important question is whether it will be possible to develop principles that are acceptable to Civil Law countries and to Common Law countries alike. Despite all the differences there is no absolute barrier between the systems; also in Common Law countries statutes regulate the subject. However, there are major differences in the approach to financial support after divorce. The attitude towards claims and in respect of the role of the court is also different. The divorce law of the former socialist countries is still in transition. However, the structure of their divorce law does not seemingly pose insurmountable obstacles.[103]

It is obvious that a simple description of the European situation alone cannot provide a solution. An *assessment* is necessary. However, within the framework of a comparison certain patterns become apparent. Law reforms within the national systems are an important indicator because they show what kind of solution is accepted or called into question and where there is still a need for reform. Reforms in non-European countries should also be taken into account.

It is always difficult, however, to estimate the process of societal change. In their chapter on interspousal relations in the International Encyclopedia of Comparative Law, Rheinstein and Glendon mentioned a general report on matrimonial property based on eleven national reports, which all stated that their national systems worked quite satisfactory. Forty years later in each of these systems major reforms have taken place.[104]

---

[100]    Cf. MARTINY, *Unterhaltsrang und -rückgriff* I 506 ff.
[101]    Cf. JÄNTERÄ-JAREBORG Sweden No. 92.
[102]    See § 1582 German Civil Code. – Cf. SCHWAB/MARTINY Germany No. 92.
[103]    Cf. MLADENOVIĆ/JANJIĆ-KOMAR/JESSEL-HOLST sec. 178 ff.
[104]    RHEINSTEIN/GLENDON, Interspousal relations, *Int. Encyclopedia comparative law* IV ch. 4 sec. 223 (1980).

In establishing general principles, the problem of what is the best solution cannot be omitted. However, who can answer this question? Shall there be options in the principles or shall there be only one solution? To merely impose one solution because it represents the majority of the legal systems cannot be a proper way of dealing with the diversity of law and legal culture. The real or apparent trend can only provide an indication; opportunism as such is not a good recommendation in the long run.

Divorce and the consequences of divorce always occur in the context of a certain legal system, a certain judiciary, the activities of public institutions. It can be difficult to find a level of abstraction that is appropriate. It has to be decided how detailed common principles will be formulated. It is quite obvious that principles are not as detailed as statutory provisions. On the other hand, statements without any specific content do not make much sense. Also the use of too many general clauses and terms like "appropriate" or "reasonable" is not a satisfactory solution.

## 5.  CONCLUSION

The idea of Common European principles of divorce law has already stimulated research. The collected national reports provide an unique insight into various European divorce laws and modern trends. It is now time to analyse and to categorise the findings and then, on the basis of a realistic and future-orientated approach, to try to develop a new, practicable and convincing framework of rules.

# A FAMILY LAW FOR EUROPE:
# NECESSARY, FEASIBLE, DESIRABLE?

Esin Örücü

## 1. INTRODUCTION

### 1.1. Overture

These closing remarks of this the first Conference on Perspectives for the Unification and Harmonisation of Family Law in Europe organised by the Commission on European Family Law which has allowed a most fruitful exchange of ideas, are inspired by a question posed by Professor Katharina Boele-Woelki in her opening speech. This is a quotation from Dieter Martiny: "Is unification of family law feasible or even desirable?" What better place to end than by looking at whether harmonisation and unification of the field of Family Law is indeed necessary, feasible or desirable. The three crucial words "necessary", "feasible" and "desirable" can each form the gist of a separate question.

It might have been wise at the start to separate the issues of harmonisation and unification, as those who might say "yes" to harmonisation in answer to all the three questions might feel inclined either to say "no" to all if they are related to unification, or might regard such a venture, although necessary, as being neither desirable nor feasible. However, since the title of the Conference, by putting "unification" even before "harmonisation", seems to have reached the foregone conclusion that harmonisation is not in doubt, and that what should be discussed is the next and ultimate step of unification, this paper does not differentiate between the two at this stage.

Keeping the papers delivered at the Conference in mind and relying on this writer's intuition on the possible perspectives, it is possible that there will be quite a number of options in answering these questions.

## 1.2. Possible positions

The possible positions that can be taken as regards these three questions can be summarised as: "Yes" to all, "no" to all or a qualified choice, a choice between altogether six further options. The following table may help.

| NECESSARY | FEASIBLE | DESIRABLE |
|-----------|----------|-----------|
| Yes | Yes | Yes |
| No | No | No |
| Yes | Yes | No |
| Yes | No | No |
| Yes | No | Yes |
| No | No | Yes |
| No | Yes | No |
| No | Yes | Yes |

Some of the options may look improbable as it is difficult to imagine someone who thinks that although the activity is not necessary, it is both feasible and desirable; or necessary but neither feasible nor desirable; or not necessary, not desirable but still feasible. Thus some of the options seem to be there for the sake of mathematical accuracy.

I am sure we could have found at least one representative for most of these positions among those of us who attended the Conference. When we look into these positions, however, certain secrets may be revealed.

## 1.3. Who might opt for which position?

One might have a political agenda for European integration with a final aim of a Federal Europe, that is, one might be an integrationalist in which case answers to all the questions would be "yes". This is quite an open secret. The "yeses" here would be even firmer as we move from harmonisation to unification. This position may also be regarded as utopic.

One might have a political agenda of "keeping apart" or "living apart together" at best, in which case answers to all the questions would be "no". This position would be that of the realist and the sceptic, which can also be regarded as an open secret. However, it may also hide a number of other secrets, such as conservatism, strong religious bias, nationalism, fear of the different, feelings of superiority, and a fear of the superior. These covert secrets will not be analysed here.

One might be a dedicated Private International lawyer and feel that once Family Law is unified, then there will be no need for conflict lawyers; and might instead advocate the harmonisation and possibly the unification of some conflict rules.

One might be a comparatist who belongs to the integrationalists camp or new *ius commune* seekers and would therefore prefer to stress similarities, to work for harmonisation in as many fields as possible, to pave the way to unification and in the long run be prepared to lose his/her job.

One might, however, be the so-called "post-modern" comparatist and feel that context and culture is the name of the game and therefore would like to stress differences or even claim that there can be no convergence and surely no unification in this or any other area of law, that harmonisation, let alone unification, will ruin diversity and identity.

However, middle of the road comparatists might also feel that their services would no longer be required when harmonisation or unification takes place and for that reason alone, they would oppose such a move as an end result, although they would support working towards it. In this category we see young comparatists who are not necessarily post-modernist but need to stress difference in order to be in current demand.

I am a comparatist and not very young and have no fears on this count since, this being a long process at the very best, by the time we have a European Family Law, my job will have come to an end long ago. Thus an old comparatist such as myself may answer "yes" to all the questions whether related to harmonisation or unification but advise painstaking scholarly research and kid gloves to be worn for converting the "others" dedicated to causes dear to their hearts, for whatever reason.

There may be some further hidden secrets or agenda, but perhaps these should be best left well alone!

## 2. A VIEW FROM THE COMPARATIVE LAW VANTAGE POINT

### 2.1. Comparative lawyers today

As a comparative lawyer, I should say first that today we are questioning our subject matter, methodology, theoretical basis and the topics we have hitherto covered. In addition, we are questioning the theory of legal families, the regions we work in and apologise for being Eurocentric. We are discussing convergence and divergence, legal borrowings and transpositions, and harmonisation as well as harmony in diversity. For us, this is a time of upheaval.[1]

Comparatists are also being challenged by others who would like to rely on their work or use their services, but find the material provided to be wanting. So comparatists are criticised for weakness and a lack of orientation and for having lost sight of their target audience.[2] And yet, we have become more important than ever before, to the extent that we are regarded as powerful political players and even dangerous.[3] In spite of all this, we are in demand both by societies whose legal systems need change to adapt to the requirements of globalisation and those who want to understand and do business in these societies.

### 2.2. Areas hitherto neglected

Until quite recently, comparative lawyers worked in a rather limited field. They were mostly private lawyers concerned particularly with the law of obligations and contracts, but also working in other related fields of private law. This was so extensively the case that many Comparative Law Chairs went together with Private International Law ones, especially in the civil law tradition.

Public Law, for example, was not an area that comparatists wanted to touch, as it was regarded as part of political science rather than law. Today, we are talking of a *"ius commune* in human rights" and comparative constitutionalism is in vogue.[4] Shared values form the fundamental basis, and the belief that universalism trumps exceptionalism is at the essence of these developments. There is a growing market for the exchange of ideas between constitution-makers and the judiciary who deal with the review

---

[1] See E. ÖRÜCÜ, "Unde Venit, Quo Tendit Comparative Law?", in A. HARDING & E. ÖRÜCÜ (eds.), *Comparative Law in the 21ˢᵗ Century* (London, Kluwer Law International, 2002) pp. 1-17.

[2] See B. MARKESINIS, "Comparative Law – A Subject in Search of an Audience", (1990) *Modern Law Review*, 1.

[3] See I. WARD, "The Limits of Comparativism: Lessons from UK – EC Integration", (1995) 2 *Maastricht Journal of European and Comparative Law*, 23; and G.P. FLETCHER, "Comparative Law as a Subversive Discipline" (1998) 46 *American Journal of Comparative Law*, 683.

[4] See A. HARDING, "Comparative Case Law in Human Rights Cases in the Commonwealth: Common Law of Human Rights", Chapter 9 in E. ÖRÜCÜ (ed.) *Judicial Comparativism in Human Rights Cases,* (London, BIICL, UKNCCL Comparative Law Series, 2003), forthcoming.

of constitutionality. Reception and transposition in these areas, unthinkable two decades ago, are now common and successful.[5]

Family Law also was regarded as being so culturally defined that it was not seen as appropriate for much meaningful comparison to take place in this field. Now we offer courses called Comparative Family Law. A pragmatic approach to Family Law has meant that not only should the area be approached comparatively but that most aspects of it should be harmonised.[6] Changing social, religious and economic conditions give rise to principles in this area that apply to divergent societies.[7] Many developments transcend the so-called "common law – civil law divide" and "cultural identity". Certain principles that exist in a number of societies have historically violated interests by relying on adverse traditions with social legitimacy. The fact that we live in an era of "equality" and "freedom" overrides these established values. This development must now be reflected in the law. Comparatists are needed to assist in creating the suitable receptive environment for a modern Family Law.[8] Many of the principles of our age have universality and therefore transferability. A cosmopolitan pragmatism trumps culturalism.

### 2.3. Differences or similarities?

It is a truism of comparison, that between any two things compared there are always both differences and similarities unless they are identical. Though objectivity demands that we talk of both difference and similarity, when policy decisions are made, our choices may be restricted by these decisions. We may stress one rather than the other depending on our purpose, even as comparative lawyers. Therefore those who uphold

---

[5]  See A. HARDING, "Comparative Public Law: Some Lessons from the South East Asia", in A. HARDING & E. ÖRÜCÜ (eds.), *Comparative Law in the 21ˢᵗ Century* (London, Kluwer Law International, 2002) pp. 249-267; and also J. BELL, "Comparing Public Law", in *ibid.*, pp. 235-248.

[6]  See for such work, K. BOELE-WOELKI, "The Road Towards a European Family Law", (1997) 1:1 *EJCL* http://law.kub.nl/ejcl/11/art11-1.html, and also K. BOELE-WOELKI, "Comparative Reasearch-Based Drafting of Principles of European Family Law" in M. FAURE, J. SMITS, H. SCHNEIDER (eds.) *Towards a European Ius Commune in Legal Education and Research* (Intersentia, Antwerp – Groningen, 2002) pp. 171-201. Also see, D. MARTINY, "The Harmonization of Family Law in the European Community: Pro and Contra", in *ibid*, pp. 191-201.

[7]  See P. DE CRUZ, "Legal Transplants: Principles and Pragmatism in Comparative Family Law", Chapter 6 in A. HARDING & E. ÖRÜCÜ (eds.), *Comparative Law in the 21ˢᵗ Century* (London, Kluwer Law International, 2002), pp. 101-121.

[8]  See, for example, M.V. ANTOKOLSKAIA, "The Process of Modernisation of Family Law in Eastern and Western Europe: Differences in Timing, Resemblance in Substance", (2000) 4:2 *EJCL* http://kub.nl/ejcl/42/art42-1.html.

integrationalism and claim that legal systems are converging, especially when referring to Europe alone, will stress the similarities they find between the legal systems compared. To find similarity where difference was expected is indeed exciting and opens the vista for explanations, which is the main concern of comparatists. Those who value cultural exceptionalism, who see the diversity of legal systems as an asset, and claim that no real convergence is taking place, will highlight differences. Diversity is valuable, and especially diversity between systems which are otherwise similar and this is the food of comparatists, but, even those who hold the firm view that diversity is the essence of valuable comparative law work do concede to, and opt for, harmony in diversity rather than discord. There is also the fact that to be controversial brings recognition.

## 3. A FAMILY LAW FOR EUROPE: A TASTE OF THE CONFERENCE ON PERSPECTIVES FOR THE UNIFICATION AND HARMONISATION OF FAMILY LAW IN EUROPE

### 3.1. General overview

The Conference dealt with the Europeanisation of Family Law, arguments for and against the unification and harmonisation of Family Law, the methodological aspects of such a harmonisation, the "better law" approach, the unification of Private International Law, and divorce and maintenance. The related topics of human rights, the expansion of Europe, and the American experience were also covered. The workshops looked at a number of papers under the general subjects of aspects of parental responsibility, new forms of cohabitation and new problems of parentage.

These topics were discussed at a time of increasing Europeanisation in all fields of law within the framework of European integration and flourishing new *ius commune* studies, a time of seeking European rather than international solutions to vital problems. The topics on the whole were approached with the belief that the goal of the European Union is now to create an "area of freedom, security and justice", and the least to be achieved is action in the field of judicial co-operation in civil matters, especially in those civil matters that have cross-border implications which are necessary for the proper functioning of an internal market.

In this context it could be argued that since the quest is for certainty at a European level, this by definition advances, among other things, a general Family Law agenda. If it is assumed that a single Family Law policy is needed in Europe, should not issues of Family Law such as marriage, the matrimonial regime, divorce, legal separation and annulment, maintenance claims, filiation, succession, custody, parental responsibility and access rights be resolved at the European level and be directly applicable in all member states? Feelings of fairness, justice and security, equality, and somewhat more pressing, convenience and expediency, demand this.

### 3.2. Options

When we look through the papers delivered at the Conference and published in this volume, certain points stand out.

The first one to consider is the call for spontaneous approximation and common principles to be gleaned and placed into a Restatement. "Common core research" was put forward accompanied by functional equivalence; so was the "better law" approach. "Better law" need not be the most permissive law, but the one that provides the most choice. These positions could be regarded as being placed on a continuum. We can thereby draw a spectrum extending from the status quo to a replacement, thus:

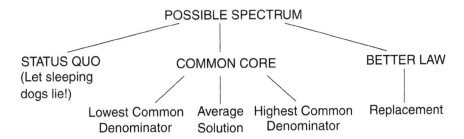

The European Community approach, which was to take averages, has now moved to the lowest common denominator approach, and with the expansion of Europe this may change and shift further still. Thus, if we as academics want to advocate a Family Law for Europe we must move now. There is a lot at stake, from protecting the vulnerable such as the child and the elderly, to combating discrimination and achieving financial balance between partners.

### 3.3. Questions

Diverse approaches emerged at the Conference related to the necessity, feasibility and the desirability of a harmonised or unified Family Law for Europe. These views may be analysed through the following questions:

Should freedom of movement be the vehicle for protecting family life?
Should Family Law be regarded as part of economic law?
Who says there is a need to harmonise Family Law in Europe?
Who says there is a need to unify rather than harmonise Family Law?
Why should conflict rules not be sufficient?

Should harmonisation extend to substantive law or stay at the level of procedure?

Who has the task of harmonisation: researchers and academics, legislators, judges?

Who is competent to harmonise or to unify Family Law in Europe?

How should harmonisation and unification be achieved? Through general principles, a Restatement, competition of rules, directives, regulations, a Code, top-down, bottom-up?

What about legitimacy? Obviously, if this work remains at the level of an academic activity, the question of legitimation does not arise, although arrogance might!

Should any such development be applicable to cross-border family ties only?

Is this a deliberate step towards a European political union? If so, is there anything to be learnt from the United States of America? What lessons can be drawn from the Scandinavian experience?

Is there respect for diverse family forms in the present Family Laws? Are human rights concerns adequately voiced? What is "respect" and which rights will be protected and respected?

If there is European consensus on European standards in Family Law, should these standards be in place before the enlargement of Europe or should other experiences emanating from the Central and Eastern Europe be amalgamated into the European vision?

Is there anything the so-called "progressive North" and the "conservative South" can learn from the emerging value statements of Central and Eastern Europe?

Should the basis of family rights be EU citizenship and human rights rather than the free movement of persons?

Should the basis of harmonisation be traditional values or value pluralism?

Whichever view is taken and whatever the answer, the family should not be instrumentalised in the name of any value preferences, neither should the individual be commodified.

Should the principle of subsidiarity be respected where global European solutions may be more appropriate for issues concerning principles such as "equality", "freedom", "interest of the child", "free movement of persons" and property rights?

Then, there is an important group of questions: What is our aim, what do we want to achieve and is it politically and socially advisable? What is the justification for keeping things as they are and what is the justification for change? It is imperative that we should ask ourselves these questions. These most fundamental questions could be both the first bundle and the last bundle in the above set of questions.

### 3.4. Answers

The task now is to consider how these questions were dealt with in various papers submitted at the Conference. As indicated earlier the above questions themselves have been extracted from the views expressed in these papers.

Europeanisation of Family Law as a general issue is considered by Walter Pintens, who says that a common European Private Law will not be achieved through legislation but through a didactic elaboration of a new *ius commune* based on common principles, using the technique employed by American Restatements, these principles serving as the basis of a European Private law. As law is not a purpose in itself but an instrument by which to regulate human relationships, cherishing law as a symbol of culture can only lead to intellectual rigidity and isolation.

Looking at the harmonisation of matrimonial regimes, Pintens asks whether this is a technical subject. The divergences here related to property law could be overcome by a European legal regime offering a regime of community of property and a regime with deferred community. Looking at the harmonisation of registered partnerships and the adoption of children by same-sex partners, one cannot detect a common core but can detect a mainstream in registered partnerships, and in matrimonial property, neither a common core nor a mainstream.

Pintens points out that harmonisation is materialising in Europe through the Council of Europe and more so through the European Court of Human Rights. However, only some subjects are covered, and only minimum standards are maintained. Within the European Union, the European Court of Justice treats aspects of Family Law under "freedom of movement", but it cannot make groundbreaking rules. In addition, the EU has no competence regarding the unification of family and succession laws. Combating discrimination is there, but the other issues can only be dealt with when they are imperative for the functioning of the common market.

Even if judicial co-operation in civil matters is transferred from the 3rd pillar (co-operation in judicial and legal matters) to the 1st pillar (Community law), this does not push Family Law unification any further. Nevertheless, the Charter of Fundamental Rights acknowledges the importance of the family. Thus existing rules can be interpreted in a wider sense.

In conclusion, Pintens considers the institutional unification of substantive Family Law as difficult and currently not advisable, a prior spontaneous approximation as being necessary, and harmonisation as a task for research and education. Legal doctrine is needed to stimulate Comparative Family Law. Here we see how vital the activities of the present Commission are.

Arguing for the unification and harmonisation of Family Law in Europe, Nina Dethloff points to difficulties that exist as a result of cross-border Family Law in a world where spouses and children have dual or even multiple citizenship; in fact, in the EU 5% of the population do not possess the citizenship of the state in which they live. The problems are a lack of legal certainty and the cost of determining the applicable law; a loss of or a change in the legal position; a lack of internationally uniform decision making and therefore limping partnerships, marriages, divorces and fatherhood (recognition can solve this but is only relevant in areas covered by the Brussels I); and a change in the applicable law by changing one's residence. The loss of status or legal position due to changing one's place of residence can harm rightful expectations.

Dethloff suggests that "free movement of decisions" can be a solution. The unification of the "Family Law of conflicts" in Europe has been envisaged for marriage, property and inheritance through Rome III and IV. This would patently not solve the whole problem. Harmonisation of substantive law is needed. However, should this be only for binational couples?

History tells us that there are already common historical and religious roots in the area of Family Law. It is only after secularisation that diversity occurred; yet secularisation is also a shared value. European cultural identity is expressed in the ECHR. Social realities in Europe are also similar. It seems that all legal systems are moving in the same direction but at different speeds. In view of all this, Dethloff advocates starting from common fundamental values and discovering the most appropriate solutions through a process of cross-fertilisation. In the EU, the free movement of people should not be restricted and separate Family Law provisions can act as a restriction. European families need harmonised European Family Law.

Assuming that we all agree on harmonisation and that it is feasible, Ingeborg Schwenzer considers the methodological aspects of harmonisation of Family Law and offers a practical analysis, considering the appropriate method to be the comparative one. She regards the functional approach as the starting point because she believes that many surrounding issues have to be considered in determining the answers to any one of the questions. She sees converging tendencies in European Family Law such as in the rise in divorce rates, the increase in the age of first marriage, the increase in cohabitation, the decline in fertility rates, the substantive law of divorce, and formal equality between spouses. Her recipe is "uniform law through evolution" as legal changes reflect socio-demographic developments in familial behaviour. However, large differences remain, such as in codification techniques and the amount of discretion given to the courts. She believes that blanket formulae take us away from harmonisation, and she asks, "can one build a uniform law on the convergence tendencies alone?" There are also divergences due to different structures of administration of justice and the law of procedure; different family policies and family realities; and different value systems. Searching for a "working family law", Schwenzer advocates looking at labour law, social security law, tax law etc.; as well as the sociology of law, and interdisciplinary research. She believes that differences arise in values on three points: the importance of marriage as the basis of family law, gender issues and the conceptual dualism of private and public spheres. "Examples demonstrate that deinstitutionalisation of family relationships and growing awareness of gender issues in Family Law go hand in hand with the family moving more and more into the public sphere." The call is for not hindering people in the quest for individually satisfactory family structures and for protecting the interests of the vulnerable. Drafting will only be possible after using the comparative method, undertaking interdisciplinary discussion and resolving important value issues.

According to Masha Antokolskaia who promotes the "better law" approach to harmonisation of Family Law, although there is no broad consensus there is some agreement on harmonisation; yet, there is also resistance. She queries the methods to be used when drafting harmonised Family Law. Principles can be either "common core" based with a low level of modernity and innovation, or based upon the highest standard of modernity provided by the "better law" approach. Obviously the drafters can also formulate new rules themselves. Antokolskaia admits that the "common core" is the easiest to use as it makes justification simpler by restating what represents the majority. This method needs to be supplemented by the functional equivalence approach, thereby gathering rules that achieve the same end.

The problem is that similar legal concepts may hide functionally different results. Thus American Restatements could not be successfully used in Europe. So the drafters have to select either the "better law" or engineer one. It is crucial to justify the choice made, however.

Antokolskaia then discusses the ideological dimension of family law. For example, in England the goal is to save marriages, while in Sweden it is to make getting out of a marriage as easy as possible. In answer to the often-used "cultural constraints" argument she looks at the origins of diversity in Europe and asks whether differences are the unique products of national cultures. Does the whole population of a single European country share the same family culture or does this culture change from family to family along the conservative-progressive divide?

The justification of "better law" lies in the shared notions of human rights in Europe. However, the European Courts are also looking for justification and legitimation, by referring to European "consensus" and "common European standards". The concern is that this can sometimes result in a low level of protection, even in a minimalist approach, and in the lowest common denominator. "My conclusion is that the level of modernity of human rights based Principles would be unsatisfactorily low. The drafters of the Principles should of course invoke the shared notion of human rights in every case when Community law or the case law of the ECHR reaches a sufficient level, but this might not often be the case." Therefore the drafters of the Principles of Family Law should go beyond the level of the shared European notion of human rights, prefer permissive law over restrictive law and must opt for the "better law" approach, and either choose the best rule or create one. Discussing divorce alone, she proposes a move towards a more modern Family Law. Starting with a rather loosely construed "common core" in divorce, which would define the lowest level of protection, the member states and the courts can try to raise this level. This model would be no threat to national cultures or national sovereignty but would be "libertarian".

Maarit Jänterä-Jareborg, on the other hand, argues against the unification of Family Law even at the level of Private International Law. She claims that topics such as jurisdiction, the choice of the applicable law, recognition and enforcement of foreign judgments and international judicial assistance cannot all be treated in the same way. For her, rules on recognition are the cornerstone of cross-border co-operation, with unified rules on jurisdiction next in importance. Unifying choice of law rules is not a prerequisite for a genuine judicial area in Europe, as claimed. The application of foreign law may greatly differ from forum law, thus there would be a need for a new law on public policy throughout Europe. For her, harmonisation of domestic law is the most suitable alternative, and unified rules of Private International Law with a harmonisation of domestic law are what are needed.

The EU lacks competence in respect of substantive Family Law. A special European Family Law for cross-border situations may be necessary and there is a legal basis for this in the Amsterdam Treaty. Jänterä-Jareborg is not happy with developments to create an international Family Law within the EU. There is no need for special EU rules as there are enough international instruments dealing with, for example, the rights of the child and parental responsibility. The EU instruments (Brussels) should not be used to solve inter-member state problems. According to her, what these instruments are introducing now is not progressive or innovative but traditional in approach, mostly duplicating what is already there, and the working method is costly and ineffective.

Lessons to be learnt are the following: moderation (areas ripe for EU regulation for her are only marital property law, succession law and the law of unmarried cohabitation); the improvement and supplementation of existing instruments (used when other measures have failed); the identification of key-issues after careful study with the aim of introducing progressive rules; and mutual trust (exequatur is a sign of mistrust). It is further suggested that the Scandinavian experience might be a lesson for the EU.

Maire-Thérèse Meulders-Klein investigates the idea of a European Civil Code on Family Law. She approves of a qualified harmonisation but strongly opposes unification. Looking at the aims pursued and the means used, she questions the technical feasibility, political desirability or advisability of any attempt at unification. She sees harmonisation as a gentler approach avoiding conflict and clashes, since she considers reconciliation to be the greatest concern. Advocating goodwill and dialogue, she says "no" to voluntary or imposed uniformisation and sees a Code as the most radical means, a centralising authoritarianism.

Pointing out that European countries do not have a common legal tradition of shared values, she identified the motives of unification as utilitarian, political, philosophical and ideological. Family Law is not merely private law but also public policy; and diversity is deeply rooted in history, culture, mentality and values. Despite converging trends towards equality and freedom, national differences are important and there is no common core. For her the means are interstate dialogue on the basis of comparative studies and Restatements, Council of Europe treaties and the ECHR.

The judicial review of the conventionality of domestic law including Constitutions – *Res interpretato* and relative *res judicata* authority – is already an unpredictable and piecemeal development. Now EC law and the ECJ also enter the field. Furthermore, Family Law is not within the jurisdiction of the Community and unanimity cannot be reached so as to legislate in this area by means of a Code.

Meulders-Klein is also critical of the "better law" approach and is concerned about which would indeed be the best law, the model. She states that there is an urgent need to clarify the debate, and the best democratic path towards an approximation of domestic legislation is the reasonable, pluralistic and flexible path of open dialogue and voluntary acceptance of solutions, possibly on the basis of Restatements respectful of the values and cultures of all European citizens.

For David Bradley the search for a Family Law for Europe is a hopeless quest with innumerable problems related to legitimation, political economy and sovereignty. It is not only a practical impossibility but is not necessary for the functioning of an economic community. He looks at Family Law as an aspect of national sovereignty and discusses what is at stake for individual jurisdictions and the barriers to be overcome if they are to adopt this Commission's proposals. He also considers the problem of legitimation, justifying the selection of particular legal models for harmonisation. Bradley surveys the Nordic countries in an attempt to assess the success of harmonisation movements. According to him, tradition, ideology and culture are not the insurmountable obstacles to the construction of a European Family Law, but it is policies on political economy that are in the way of convergence. Family Law complements social and labour market policies, and it has implications for income and class equality, social welfare and the provision of social security.

In Bradley's view, in times of transition there is scope for change in Family Law and this was the case in the 1960-70 period with changes in rules on divorce, illegitimate children, maintenance and marital property. So what has changed since then to justify new harmonisation?

"One interpretation of the convergence thesis is that Family Law in each jurisdiction can be located at a point on a continuum," from canon law at one extreme and Enlightenment values at the other, with the "common core" representing a basic threshold or mid-point; and better law representing modernity. Bradley believes that the convergence thesis is an oversimplification. The three general trends in Europe in Family Law are liberty, equality and secularism; but these strike at traditional legal policy and have to be responded to by each jurisdiction, and the nature of these responses varies significantly.

There then follows an analysis of Family Law as a component of political economy by looking at Sweden and Finland and their diverging laws. Bradley further observes that there is divergence in legal policy especially in areas such as the status of same-sex couples and adoption. Registered partnership laws are now being discussed Europe-wide. Economic considerations underpin disputes over extra-marital relationships, homosexuality, divorce and abortion. Child support, the cost of informal cohabitation and property entitlements upon divorce will be future areas for discussion. Pension division will also become very important and child custody is yet another pressing issue. "Variations in legal policy between jurisdictions will not be eliminated so long as there are independent nation states with distinct fiscal policies and welfare models." Family laws form a part of an integrated political design. Bradley claims that to detect a "common core" or to come up with a "best law" is therefore a technical and legal exercise. However, there is direct intervention from European institutions on central issues of legal policy in Family Law. This is certainly a top-down pressure, but with cautious accommodation of sovereignty. Bradley's conclusion is that "time will tell"!

To enhance discussion, the perspective is widened with Ewoud Hondius considering developments and the current situation in other fields of private law such as contract, tort, trust and civil procedure, where the "Principles", "Codification", and "casebook" approaches have been used in a number of projects to bring about harmonisation or unification in their respective areas. He points to advantages, and disadvantages, and the problems encountered by various Commissions set up for these purposes. Again to facilitate possible action in Europe in the field of harmonisation of Family Law, the shortfalls of the "American Experience", where substantive Family Law is a subject matter reserved for the individual states, and the role Restatements can play, are demonstrated by Nancy Maxwell. She portrays the tensions and inconsistencies in this field.

In this group of papers bringing a wider perspective, there is also a general introduction to the unification of Private International Law in Europe and the influence of European Family Law on the Family Law of countries acceding to the European Union, such as Poland.

The relationship between human rights and family law is the topic of discussion by Clare McGlynn. The EU Charter of Fundamental Rights is specifically examined and criticised. McGlynn shows how the EU has not fully embraced the human rights aspect of Family Law. When it has been considered, this has been on traditional grounds. As the Charter impacts this area, the hope is that a more progressive and rights-based approach to Family Law issues will emerge. McGlynn advocates a future EU Family Law based on respect for human rights rather than freedom of movement, with transparency as to which human rights are to be protected and what is meant by "respect".

The initial results gathered from the 22 jurisdictional reports to the questionnaire sent out by the Commission on divorce and maintenance between former spouses are introduced by Dieter Martiny. At present the research is restricted to divorce and maintenance. Some preliminary analysis of similarities and differences between the systems is presented and an integrated version identifies a measure of "common core". In areas where a "common core" is lacking, then the "better law" approach is to be employed in the drawing up of principles in these two fields. The great variety of national concepts is immediately obvious, but, there are also certain shared assumptions, such as the existence of divorce and a preference for divorce due to irretrievable breakdown. This paper makes fascinating reading enabling comparatists to trace the similarities and differences and shows the invaluable work carried out by the Commission. Some tentative proposals as to what should be contained in the European Principles are also presented here.

Within the above survey of the papers on the main theme, we can find answers to the questions posed earlier. Now we can look at the papers presented at the workshops. These cover topics of the future collected under three headings: the new problems of cohabitation, new trends in the field of parentage and parental responsibility, and the Private International Law aspects of these two topics. This writer could not attend all the workshops as they were taking place simultaneously, and can only mention a few of the papers.

Elena Rodriguez Pineau, for example, looks at regulating parental responsibility in the EU. She claims that diversity in Family Law constitutes a serious obstacle to the free movement of people within the EU. The alternative must be Private International Law, conflict rules bridging differences, respecting principles of subsidiarity and cultural identity, with a common core of recognition rules. Parental responsibility was only raised in the Brussels II Regulations. The Regulations could help the free movement of parents but is detrimental to the child, both for movement and for contact with parents. Jurisdictional grounds can lead to forum shopping. Therefore, the recognition of judgments is needed. The Brussels II A still has flaws, and it creates further jurisdictional problems. There is an absence of a proper legislative policy design in the EU on parental responsibility, and Community PIL legislation is unsatisfactory. Problems of applicable law must be resolved. She suggests that the whole issue should be re-enacted from a global rather than an EC angle.

Rosa Martins also looks at parental responsibility but versus the progressive autonomy of the child. She notes that children have the status of individuals with rights and this has an impact on "parental care". The progressive autonomy of the child has implications for existing law. She asks whether there is a shared solution in Europe, and whether progressive autonomy reduces parental responsibility. The guiding principles in the parental exercise of care of the child and the child's property, due to the incapacity of the child, is the child's welfare principle. "Children as individuals" has added another purpose to parental care: to develop their capacity (progressive autonomy), with possible conflict between the two purposes. This progressive autonomy of the child as a restriction on the scope of parental care was considered by most legal systems in Europe even before the Convention on the Rights of the Child. The relationship should "anticipate majority". The concept of "assistance" could be substituted for "legal representation". Her conclusion is that it is possible to promote unification in this area.

Aristides Hatzis takes a law and economics approach to gestational surrogacy agreements. In most jurisdictions worldwide gestational surrogacy (IVF treatment) is prohibited by law and, even when it is permitted, the contract is not enforceable. Only altruistic surrogacy is permitted with certain restrictions. This paper argues for the enforceability of such contracts, the view being based on an economic analysis of contract law. The maxim is "a contract should be enforced when it makes two people better off, without making anyone else worse off". The major criticism has been that these contracts are immoral. Then there is the commodification argument. According to Hatzis, this line of argument deprives women of self-determination and privacy. Surrogate mothers should be compensated for medical, hospital and other expenses, lost wages, material wear and nutrition. Such contracts should be treated as any other contract. If there is no such contract, there is no child, so an enforceable contract is in the best interest of the child. "Europe needs this", is his conclusion.

Aspasia Tsaoussis-Hatzis aspires to a child-centred European divorce law. She says that at the end of the 1960s there were sweeping reforms in the area of divorce law, but despite the good intentions of the reformers, no-fault divorce often led to the impoverishment of women and children and sent the wrong message, weakening spousal commitment. Today, commitment norms are not enforceable. Tsaoussis-Hatzis proposes the introduction of covenant marriage statutes in the context of a unified European marriage law, so adding another contractual freedom. The assumption is that services are needed to prevent family breakdown since an intact two-parent family is preferable. Some empirical research is provided to support this stance. The parents' decision to divorce represents a classical case of conflicting interests between the parents and the child. A good base for argument is reference to children's interests. In the USA a number of states have introduced "covenant marriage" with a "child first" approach whereby, with a contractual relationship, the spouses opt out of the no-fault system. This is an option for a stricter marriage. The solutions suggested by Tsaoussis-Hatzis are that this should be one of the options in the harmonised or unified European Family Law to strengthen couples' commitment to their children; the joint custody regimes adopted in Sweden and Germany should be borrowed by all European states and become the preferred regime for Europe; improved child support policies are also needed.

Yvette Tan writes on the recognition of new forms of partnership in the English Private International Law showing that a liberal and tolerant policy has developed in the English courts in relation to the recognition of foreign marriages with strong commitment to ethnic and cultural pluralism in the form of acceptance of polygamous marriages. But social evolution and the emergence of new family forms present challenges; transsexualism has become a problem with medical and societal advances, and equating the status of homosexuals with heterosexuals is another. Heterosexuals now also want to cohabit without marriage. There is a general shift away from the traditional concept of marriage and a restructuring of family forms. How does the law, especially Private International Law cope? The new relationships have to be recognised for the purposes of succession, maintenance, parental orders, social security and pension rights. What will happen to public policy? English law looks at *lex loci celebrationis* and *lex domicilli*. The paper then considers the kind of answers which English law might provide in the recognition of transsexual marriages, cohabitation contracts, registered partnerships and same-sex marriages by looking at cases. It is submitted that English Private International Law should be bolder than domestic law. The paper also looks at piecemeal legislation in the European Community and the USA. The question is then asked: Is a new Private International Law legislation needed? For example, how should a French "*pacte*" be classified? Can current contract law rules be used? This is not possible under English law. A European Convention is needed and the United Kingdom should sign this. English law is soon to allow registered partnerships, so it should recognise such partnerships from foreign jurisdictions. The EU does not have competence in relation to family law or civil status. But the EU, being a continuation of member states, mirrors member states' trends. Employment law may be covered by the freedom of movement principle, but can a common ground be found for a European Family Law? Tan notes a few discernible trends. She suggests that if there is automatic recognition within the EU then some of the above problems will not occur. Also via the ECHR and Convention case law, with rights interpreted in their present-day meanings, things will change. The English courts will soon not be able to use the public policy exclusion. What was in the past offensive and repugnant has changed and is changing. The family is an evolving concept. There can be a minimum or a maximum degree of recognition. A quasi-marital contract must be devised in order to accommodate recognition.

Again on the theme of new forms of cohabitation, Sandrine Henneron states that some aspects of registered partnerships cannot be covered by present Private International Law and gives the French "*pacte*" as an example. Pointing out that "living together" is currently more and more outside marriage, and by some form of registered partnership, she sees the landscape to be in disorder. The mobility of people in Europe may lead to conflict. Nevertheless she shows that there are some common aspects. Some partnerships resemble marriage, and some resemble contract. It is proposed here that the new forms of partnership should be regarded as a new autonomous Private International Law category within the general category of personal status, and there should be a link to institutional law recognised in the whole of Europe. The solution would be through the unification of regulations concerning conflicts of laws rather than harmonisation of legal content.

Looking at consequences of cohabitation and especially at relations between partners and parents and children, Suzana Kraljic takes the example of Slovenia. There, cohabitation, as a form of living together, is on the increase and enjoys legal protection. The legal consequences of cohabitation, though informally established by agreement, are defined in the Marriage and Family Relations Act, and are similar to those of marriage. However, cohabitation has no effect on the common children. There has to be a judicial establishment of paternity or recognition of paternity. Some other consequences are determined by other laws such as the Succession, Social Security, Parental Security and Family Income Acts and the Property Code. There are no regulations concerning homosexuals. The paper further looks at Croatia, Macedonia and Serbia. In all these jurisdictions *lex nationalis* and then joint *lex domicilli* apply.

Matteo Bonini-Baraldi makes suggestions on the themes of status, contract and the sexuality of same-sex couples. He states that private autonomy and public interest can be seen as contract and status (common law and continental law), and that in Family Law this distinction is blurred. He queries the complex interconnection and consequence of this interaction at the European level. Looking at legal systems Bonini-Baraldi sees three models related to same-sex families: interpretive, institutional and hybrid (quasi, pseudo and matrimonial). He is concerned that EC legislation remains traditional, that the laws of the member states, following a slow process, are minimal and yet the recognition of same-sex couples "is a human rights issue that calls into action the constitutional values of equality and freedom to marry, as well as legal personhood and capacity." According to Bonini-Baraldi the promotion of these issues cannot be seen as an academic exercise but as a legal duty. European citizenship will have major implications for Family Law.

Other workshop papers deal with topics such as domestic and conflict difficulties inherent in regulating the new order from a Scottish perspective (Janeen Carruthers), parental responsibility in Bulgaria and the United Kingdom (Miglena Baldjieva), contact agreements in the Netherlands and Denmark (Christina Jeppesen-de Boer), children's participation in cross-national family disputes (Helen Stalford), and the communitarisation of family law in too much haste and with too little reflection (Peter McEleavy).

## 4. CONCLUDING REMARKS

If nothing else, now more than ever, the increasing migration of peoples in Europe necessitates European integration rather than fragmentation.

Forging a European identity encompasses common values, and where better to forge this than in Family Law. The European citizen will seek European solutions. Diversity of culture and moral views using such arguments as "harmonisation destroys national identity", should not hamper the search for Europe-wide solutions as member states face new problems such as same-sex marriage, adoption by cohabiting couples, cross-border adoption, and acquisition and loss of nationality of minors. What is at stake here is the rights of spouses, partners and children. European norms and the European Convention on Human Rights and the European Courts have already had an impact on national family law. The next step should be the creation of Europe-wide standards to run at least parallel with, if not to replace, national legislation. A workable starting point would be to keep culturally specific aspects aside at first, to harmonise the rest and then incrementally try to cover the field.

The initial results of the questionnaire formulated by the Commission on European Family Law has findings on divorce and maintenance which are yet to be fully analysed, but one can already see the differences and the similarities. This questionnaire and the setting up of this Conference are the first steps taken by the Commission towards the creation of a European Family Law. At the Conference various views were aired with vigour, and lively and fruitful discussion took place. We are awaiting the next steps and wish the Commission well. Even if little is achieved in the short term, the Conference has been a most valuable contribution to raising consciousness and awareness as to what lies ahead. In the long term pragmatism and cosmopolitanism will prevail.

The totality of instruments related to various aspects of Family Law, such as the 1961 Hague Convention, the 1968 Brussels Convention, the 1970 Hague Convention, the 1980 Council of Europe Convention, the 1980 Hague Convention, the 1996 Hague Convention and even the 2001 Council Regulation (Brussels II), a new departure for the European Community, may need to be amalgamated into a single instrument for the peoples of the European Union.[9] A Family Law for Europe will inevitably reduce the necessity for further developing the rules of Private International Law in this field.

---

[9] See for an analysis of these instruments, P. McELEAVY, "The Brussels II Regulation: How the European Community has moved into Family Law" (2002) 51 *International & Comparative Law Quarterly*, 883.

There is no question as to whether Family Law in Europe should be going through a harmonisation process. In fact, harmonisation has been taking place for the last two decades through the efforts of the Council of Europe. As stated by Katharina Boele-Woelki, "the train has left the station".[10] So the question is, can a European Family Law be created to reach beyond the harmonised rules in various areas of Family Law? If the answer is "yes" then the related question becomes, should this aim be achieved through a Regulation, a Restatement, General Principles of European Family Law or a Family Law Code?

At this stage the work is academic. An academic exercise is bound to remain at the level of finding the rules, analysing and comparing them and then formulating and presenting General Principles of Family Law. This, however, is the starting point. Europeans need a European Family Law. The hope must be that the outcome of these activities will be taken seriously as has been the case with the European Principles of Contract Law. This Conference should be a building block in the creation of a European "*acquis communautaire*" in family values.

Two things must always be remembered, however. One is that uniform legal standards at the level of Europe will not by themselves build effective legal systems. A high level of voluntary compliance with the legal rules is vital. The other point is that in the field of Family Law there is a strong interdependency between rules; all aspects of Family Law add together and make up a whole. It will not be enough to remain at the level of divorce and maintenance for harmonisation and unification purposes. Eventually what will be needed is standardisation of the whole of Family Law for Europe.

A final word should be said on the workshops. A fascinating array of topics was covered in the workshops by young, energetic and capable experts. The fields covered are the issues of the future; and those who covered them, are our future.

---

[10]  K. BOELE-WOELKI, "Comparative Reasearch-Based Drafting of Principles of European Family Law" in M. FAURE, J. SMITS, H. SCHNEIDER (eds.), *Towards a European Ius Commune in Legal Education and Research* (Intersentia, Antwerp – Groningen, 2002), p. 183.

EUROPEAN FAMILY LAW SERIES

1. *Legal Recognition of Same-Sex Couples in Europe*, K. Boele-Woelki and A. Fuchs (eds.)
2. *European Family Law in Action Volume I: Grounds for divorce*, K. Boele-Woelki, B. Braat and I. Sumner (eds.)
3. *European Family Law in Action Volume II: Maintenance Between Former Spouses*, K. Boele-Woelki, B. Braat and I. Sumner (eds.)
4. *Perspectives for the Unification and Harmonisation of Family Law in Europe*, K. Boele-Woelki (ed.)